POLITICS IN THE MIDDLE EAST

POLITICS IN THE MIDDLE EAST

FIFTH EDITION

James A. Bill
College of William and Mary

Robert Springborg
MacQuarie University

An imprint of Addison Wesley Longman, Inc.

New York • Reading, Massachusetts • Menlo Park, California • Harlow, England
Don Mills, Ontario • Sydney • Mexico City • Madrid • Amsterdam

Editor-in-Chief: Priscilla McGeehon
Acquisitions Editor: Eric Stano
Associate Editor: Jennie Errickson
Marketing Manager: Megan Galvin
Full Service Production Manager: Patti Brecht
Project Coordination, Text Design, and
Electronic Page Makeup: Pre-Press Company, Inc.
Cover Designer/Manager: Nancy Danahy
Senior Print Buyer: Hugh Crawford
Printer and Binder: The Maple-Vail Book Manufacturing Group
Cover Printer: Coral Graphic Services, Inc.

Library of Congress Cataloging-in-Publication Data

Bill, James A.
    Politics in the Middle East / James A. Bill, Robert Springborg. — 5th ed.
       p. cm.
    Includes bibliographical references (p.) and index.
    ISBN 0-321-00537-6 (alk. paper)
    1. Middle East—Politics and government—1945–   I. Springborg,
    Robert.   II. Title.
  DS63.1.B54   1999
  320.956—dc21   99-29689
                                                   CIP

Please visit our website at http://www.awlonline.com

ISBN 0-321-00537-6

2345678910—MA—0201

To
Ann Marie and Anne-Marie
for their beautiful love, great patience, and unwavering support

Contents

Chapter 9

Petroleum, Politics, and Development 305

Preface

The Middle East enters the twenty-first century torn by political uncertainty, economic inequity, social turbulence, and psychological incoherence. The two Persian Gulf wars of the late 1980s and the early 1990s had not yet run their course by late 1999. Indeed in the late 1990s, the United States found itself increasingly entangled in the complexities of Gulf politics as Iraqi leader Saddam Hussein presented an exasperating and defiant challenge to U.S. interests in the region. In neighboring Iran, where a new democratically elected president came to power in 1997 on a platform stressing individual freedom, judicial reform, and civil society, the United States found itself trapped in a diplomatic cage built on a self-defeating, outdated foundation of confrontation and condemnation. Meanwhile, ugly signs of political instability bubbled to the surface in Bahrain and Saudi Arabia, while Qatar witnessed a coup that brought to power the Crown Prince. Signs of political unrest also marked events in Oman and Kuwait.

Elsewhere in the region, vicious, anarchic violence continued to prevail in the countries that bracketed the Middle East. Both Algeria on the west and Afghanistan on the east were the scenes of tragic and uncommonly bloody civil wars. In Algeria in particular, the world watched uneasily as hideous massacres became the order of the day. By 1999, nearly 100,000 Algerians, most of them innocent citizens, had lost their lives in the mayhem. Sporadic violence and periodic instability were also in evidence in Turkey, Egypt, Jordan, Israel, Pakistan, and Sudan.

With the collapse of the Soviet Union, political instability in Central Asia broke out, and conflict surfaced in places like Tajikistan, Armenia-Azerbaijan, and Chechnia. Increasingly, the Central Asian republics became political and economic appendages to the Middle East region proper. Many of the same problems that plagued the Arab world, Iran, Pakistan, and Turkey also confronted the republics of Central Asia.

Unresolved questions of identity, authenticity, and legitimacy continue to confront the peoples of the Middle East. As democratization takes root in much of the world, most Middle Eastern governments continue to resist transforming their political systems and cling to power through alternating policies of coercion and cooptation, repression, and reform. In this delicate equation, political strategies tilted in the direction of coercive control as subregional tensions in the Gulf and Eastern Mediterranean increased.

Genuine political development defined in terms of institutionalized participation remains a distant goal in the Middle East. Because the winds of democratization have been blowing across the world and because the world's sole superpower is associated with these winds, various Middle Eastern political elites have felt it prudent to develop policies more in line with the times. There has been, therefore, a flurry of activity whereby government leaders include in their vocabularies terms such as "civil society" and cautiously announce constitutional reform, electoral plans, and the establishment of consultative and legislative bodies of one kind or another. These policies of political self-defense have appeared as the gathering force of resurgent populist Islam challenges the contemporary status quo across the region.

Existing along with these internal forces of incoherence is the thorny Arab-Israeli imbroglio where hopes and aspirations have repeatedly been dashed on the shoals of stubborn intransigence, insensitive leadership, limited imagination, and blind and narrow self-interest. The promising accords signed in Madrid in 1991 and in Oslo in 1993 ground to an ignominious halt in 1997 and 1998. On the Arab side, the Palestinian Authority has lost much credibility among its own people due to its personalistic, unaccountable exercise of power. On the Israeli side, the assassination of Yitzhak Rabin in November 1995 brought to power an inflexible Likud leadership that has gone out of its way to stifle the peace process. Narrow-minded, hardline fundamentalists in Israel hold the peace process for ransom. Their counterparts on the Palestinian side vent their twisted frustrations through extremist tactics that include suicide bombings. Just as the Palestinian-Israeli conflict defies easy solutions, it also defies effective analysis. Middle East politics involve a situation where settlements settle nothing, where containment doesn't contain, where religion breeds irreligion, and where peace comes to pieces.

In the Middle East, political events across the region are intertwined with each other. A political ailment that develops in one part of the region quickly metastasizes throughout the other countries of the region. Trouble travels. Conflict is contagious. In brief, the Middle East resembles a huge, multistranded spiderweb. Pressure, conflict, and movement at one part of the web are immediately transmitted to other sections of that web. When violence breaks out in Afghanistan or Algeria, it affects politics in places like Egypt, Saudi Arabia, Libya, and Pakistan. When revolutionary upheaval bursts forth in Iran, it directly influences the behavior of Saudi Arabia, Iraq, Turkey, and the Persian Gulf shaikhdoms. When Israeli planes bomb Lebanon, the actions change the thinking and the policy of countries like Syria, Jordan, and Iraq. Conflict in one part of the system tends to promote, catalyze, or intensify violence in other parts of the system.

It is often argued—and with some justification—that if the Palestinian-Israeli issue were resolved tomorrow, instability and violence would persist in the Middle East. Such unresolved issues as ethnic, religious, national, and class conflict would continue to plague the region. On the other hand, given the centrality and intensity of the Palestinian-Israeli conflict and the entangled nature of the Middle East web system, the resolution of this issue would inevitably have a salutary effect on other conflicts endemic to the region. A solution to the Palestinian problem, for example, would have six constructive results.

First, at least a portion of the vast resources expended on military and security forces would be available to help meet the economic needs of the underclasses that still exist in all Middle Eastern countries. Second, Israeli-Arab cooperation in business and trade would accelerate badly needed economic development throughout the region. Third, traditional authoritarian regimes in the region, which have survived partly by deflecting attention to the Palestinian-Israeli conflict, would have to focus their energies increasingly upon their domestic problems or face collapse. Fourth, an end to the Israeli-Palestinian conflict would alleviate the security concerns of both peoples, concerns that have colored virtually all areas of public policy. Fifth, extremist elements that inhabit both camps would lose much of their raison d'etre, and their negative influence would begin to fade. Finally, a successful resolution to the Palestinian-Israeli issue would weaken the credibility of dictatorial leaders such as Saddam Hussein who use the conflict as a means to prop up their own brutal regimes.

Despite the social turbulence and political upheaval that prevail in the Middle East, this fifth edition of *Politics in the Middle East* is similar to earlier editions because it analyzes problems, issues, and processes that transcend particular events and that chronologically and geographically cut across the region. This latest edition, nevertheless, contains a number of significant changes.

Chapter 1, Political Development and the Challenge of Modernization, is rewritten to take into account the more recent theoretical work focusing on such concepts as civil society, democratization, and participation. The authors also present a new typology of Middle Eastern political systems based on their developmental characteristics. Chapter 7, The Arab-Israeli Conflict, and Chapter 9, Petroleum, Politics, and Development, have been thoroughly updated and extensively revised. All the other chapters have undergone some revision and have been updated. We have paid special attention in this edition to important new international developments that have occurred in Central Asia and the continuing culture of war in the Persian Gulf. In terms of internal political dynamics, we have revised the book with special sensitivity to the much-debated issues of democratization and civil society. In this context, we have also examined closely the deepening and broadening challenge of resurgent Islam.

This fifth edition owes much to the numerous suggestions offered by colleagues across the country who have used the book in the classroom. Their judgments and, most importantly, the comments and recommendations of their students lie behind many of the revisions. By responding seriously to these critiques, we hope we have produced a better book.

The system of transliteration in this study generally follows the format used by the *International Journal of Middle East Studies*. We have decided to delete all diacritical marks with the exception of the ayn (') and the hamza (') when they appear in the middle of a word. This decision may upset a number of careful scholars of Middle Eastern history and linguistics. It is done, however, to assist students and non-area specialists who have expressed their reluctance to plow through numerous dots and dashes sprinkled throughout the text. Arabic, Persian, or Turkish words commonly used in English are spelled as they appear in *Webster's Third International Dictionary* or in *Webster's Geographical Dictionary*. Well-known proper names are presented as they generally appear in English or as they have been transliterated by the individuals themselves—for example, Gamal Abdel Nasser, Anwar Sadat, Kemal Ataturk, Ayatollah Ruhollah Khomeini, and Saddam Hussein. This approach leads to inconsistencies, but we quote T. E. Lawrence in response: "Arabic names won't go into English exactly, for their consonants are not the same as ours and their vowels, like ours, vary from district to district. There are some 'scientific systems' of transliteration, helpful to people who know enough Arabic not to need helping, but a wash-out for the world."

The wisdom and support of many individuals have been indispensable to the creation of this book. Over the years, distinguished scholars such as Gabriel Almond, Manfred Halpern, and George Lenczowski have had a great impact on our thinking. We have also benefited from the work of Ervand Abrahamian, Momtaz Ahmad, Fouad Ajami, Shahrough Akhavi, Abbas Amanat, Hooshang Amirahmadi, Lisa Anderson, John Duke Anthony, Ahmad Ashraf, Ali Banuazizi, Peter Bechtold, Joel Beinin, Leonard Binder, Michael Bonine, Ralph Braibanti, Daniel Brumberg, Laurie Brand, Louis Cantori, Sheila Carpico, William Cleveland, Juan Cole, Jill Crystal, Hamid Dabashi, Dale Eickelman, Herman Eilts, Kail Ellis, John Esposito, Tawfic Farah, Robert Freedman, Mark Gasiorowski, Gregory Gause, Shafeeq Ghabra, Cyrus Ghani, Grace Goodell, Yvonne Haddad, Jo-Ann Hart, Farhad Kazemi, Victor LeVine, Manuchehr Khowsrowshahi, John Limbert, David Long, Ian Lustick, Hafeez Malik, David Menashri, Mark Miller, Roy Mottahedeh, Monte Palmer, John Peterson, James Piscatori, William Quandt, Abdul Karim Rafeq, Farhang Rajaee, R. K. Ramazani, Bernard Reich, Alan Richards, Thomas Ricks, Sara Roy, Curtis Ryan, Eliz Sanasarian, Mowahid Shah, Diane Singerman, Oles Smolansky, Robert Snyder, Michael Suleiman, Antony Sullivan, Joseph Szliowicz, Mark Tessler, Robert Vitalis, John Voll, John Washburn, John Waterbury, Marvin Weinbaum, John Williams, and Marvin Zonis.

Scholars and teachers such as Bahman Baktiari, Bruce Borthwick, John Damis, Manochehr Dorraj, Gene Garthwaite, Arthur Goldschmidt, Eric Hooglund, Paul Hoyt, Tareq Ismail, Ersin Kalaycioglu, Mehran Kamrava, Yasumassa Kuroda, Victor LeVine, John Lorentz, Abbas Manafy, Phebe Marr, Mohsen Milani, Robert Noel, Gwen Okruhlik, Robert Porier, Hossein Razi, Eliz Sanasarian, and Farzin Sarabi have used the book in the classroom or have offered suggestions that have been extremely useful. Published reviews of early editions by Amir Ferdows, Michael Hudson, Don Peretz, and Frank Tachau were especially constructive. Special expertise and assistance have also been provided by Abdul-Reda Assiri, Marguerite Bouraad-Nash, Laurie Brand, Sheila Carpico, Houchang Chehabi, Steven Dorr, Bruce Drury, Irene Gendzier, Clement Henry, Metin Heper, Michael Humphrey, George Irani, Mark Katz, Jacob Landau, Ira Lapidus, Fred Lawson, Ann Lesch, Emile Nakhleh, Mehdi Noorbaksh, Richard Norton, Othman Rawwaf, Glenn Robinson, William Royce, Hisham Sharabi, Denis Sullivan, and Andrew Vincent.

Finally, we thank our editors, Jennie Errickson, Jessica Bayne, and Pamela Gordon of Addison Wesley Longman for their unwavering support throughout the production of this latest edition.

James A. Bill
Robert Springborg

The Middle East

COMMONWEALTH OF INDEPENDENT STATES

BLACK SEA

CASPIAN SEA

●Ankara

TURKEY

Tabriz

Meshed ●

●Aleppo

PRUS

SYRIA

Tehran ●

Kabul ●

Beirut
LEBANON

Tigris R.

IRAQ ●Baghdad

IRAN

AFGHANISTAN

●Damascus

Tel Aviv

Isfahan ●

ISRAEL

●Amman

Jerusalem

Euphrates R.

Basra

Alexandria

iro

JORDAN

Kirman ●

PAKISTAN

YPT

KUWAIT

Kuwait

SAUDI
ARABIA

BAHRAIN

PERSIAN GULF

Karachi

QATAR

Aswan ●

●Medina

Riyadh ●

Dubai

INDIA

UNITED ARAB
EMIRATES

Muscat

●Mecca

OMAN

RED SEA

ARABIAN SEA

DAN

Sanaa ●

rtoum ●

ERITREA

YEMEN

Nile R.

DJIBOUTI

Aden

GULF OF ADEN

SOCOTRA

INDIAN OCEAN

SOMALIA

ETHIOPIA

| 0 | | | | 500 miles |
| 0 | | | | 800 kilometers |

Chapter 1

Political Development and the Challenge of Modernization

In our world caught in the midst of rapid transformation, the Middle East is marked by political turbulence, economic uncertainty, and social upheaval. The dialectical clash between the challenging forces of modernity and the persistence of tradition is a fundamental reality in the region. Old human relationships crumble while new patterns are not yet born. In the midst of such incoherence, many citizens hold a vision of an unknown but promising future; others refuse to let go of a more familiar past. From Morocco and Algeria on the west to Afghanistan and Pakistan on the east, the peoples of the Middle East find themselves confronted by the challenges of unprecedented change.

Politically, traditional rulers, elected leaders, military juntas, and religious elites live side by side. No form of government seems immune from threats of political violence. Domestic disaffection sparked by social and political grievances and regional warfare dominated by the persisting Arab-Israeli conflict and the fragile situation in the Persian Gulf have become integral parts of the political tableau.

The effects of the developmental challenge in the Middle East extend far beyond the confines of the area itself. The international impact of the 1973 oil embargo, the Lebanese civil war begun in 1975, the Iranian revolution of 1978–1979, the Soviet invasion of Afghanistan in 1979, the 1982 Israeli military attacks on Lebanon, the Persian Gulf wars of the 1980s and 1990s, the collapse of the Soviet Union in the early 1990s, the unsettled nature of Central Asia in the late 1990s, and the bloody civil strife in Algeria and Afghanistan during this same period are among the cases in point. Meanwhile, the continuing impact of the message of revolutionary Iran and the broad appeal of the Islamic revival will have a deep influence across the world in the twenty-first century.

At the level of everyday living, change is highly evident. Ancient customs and ways of life are under siege. This is particularly true in the related areas of occupation, communication, transportation, recreation, education, and technology. Stenographers and typists working with the latest computers are rapidly replacing calligraphers and scribes; machines have transformed the textile and metal industries; and factories and assembly lines are replacing village workshops and cottage industries. In the realm of transportation, donkeys and camels have lost their centuries-long dominance to automobiles, trucks, and airplanes. Throughout the Middle East, herdsmen and shepherds listen to transistor radios, and television sets now adorn village teahouses. The urban young flock to movie houses, dance halls, bowling alleys, pool halls, and ski resorts.

Countering this drive to modernity has been a growing trend to recapture important practices of the past. Throughout the region, large numbers of young women of all social classes have returned to the veil. Middle Easterners are preoccupied with questions of identity and authenticity. The appeal of resurgent Islam must be viewed in this context. Social change in the Middle East, therefore, is marked by a bizarre blend of tradition and modernity. The jagged course of change has left in its wake a number of inconsistencies, inequalities, and enigmas: discotheques and mosques, luxury hotels and mud huts, nuclear energy programs and the fuel of animal droppings, F-18s and old rifles, huge libraries and continuing illiteracy, computers and abacus boards.

Central to the entire problem of change as it is manifested in the Middle East are the related issues of modernization and political development. Modernization and the politics of development are two of the most critical problems confronting Middle Eastern peoples. The peoples of the region are caught in a grim struggle for equal opportunity, genuine participation, and justice. The importance of these demands is matched only by the difficulty in coming to grips intellectually with them. The following section will present the definitions and distinctions essential to our analysis of the processes of modernization and political development in the Middle East.

The Challenge of Modernization

Modernization is herein defined as the process whereby men and women increasingly gain control over their physical environments. The most dramatic dimensions of modernization involve the technological revolution, which carries with it impressive advances in the areas of industrialization, economic development, and communication. Throughout the developing world, the physical transformations are graphic evidence of technological development. The world has entered the age of the computer. Skyscrapers, highway grids, subterranean metro systems, elaborate airports, huge dams, state of the art petrochemical plants, and steel mills sprout forth everywhere.

Closely related to technological advancement are the strides that have been taken in education. The numbers of schools and universities continue to increase at a rapid rate. The result has been a heightened consciousness and an expanded scientific and technical knowledge. Acting as a catalyst to all this, of course, are technological forces such as advances in communications and the mass media that provide the means by which information can be transmitted quickly, effectively, and universally.

Technological and educational changes have a number of organizational and psychological implications. Organization is becoming more elaborate and specialized, and formal institutions are beginning to replace informal, personalistic administration. As values and expectations become more secular, important shifts in attitudes are occurring. The traditional emphasis on the spiritual and the magical waxes and wanes.

The patterns that constitute the modernization syndrome are mutually reinforcing. This reinforcement accelerates modernization even in societies where resources are scarce and the population continues to pursue traditional lifestyles. Technological progress promotes educational advancement that, in turn, influences attitudes and values that define organizational settings. Moreover, value systems and organizational styles that are in a state of transformation are highly supportive of effective technological and educational change. It is easy to understand why modernization is a major global obsession.

Modernization is inevitable. It has always existed in society. In the past, the wide variety of responses to environmental challenges produced some very disparate results; this legacy is evident today in much of the developing world. In the twentieth century, rapid communication not only facilitates the discovery that stages of modernization other than one's own are possible, but it also enables the experiences of certain cultures to be transmitted to other contexts in the process termed *globalization.*

At the dawn of the twenty-first century, the societies that have been relatively more modernized have tended to be in the West. Hence, the process has sometimes been misleadingly referred to as *Westernization.* The inevitability and universality of modernization are products of the increasingly interdependent world in which we live. Although the societies in the Middle East will all struggle in one way or another to modernize, not all will succeed to the same degree. The unevenness of the success of modernization in the various Middle Eastern societies is itself a source of tension and conflict.

Modernization is an unsettling and disruptive process. The comforts of traditional life are lost as old habits are uprooted. In modernizing societies, new processes and institutions seem always to be trapped in a state of becoming, and, as a result, the expected uncertainties of the past have given way to the more frightening insecurities of the present. In the Middle East, where all societies have begun to modernize, any slowing or reversal of the process causes great stress. Yet the uneven supply of national resources, the lack of many technical skills, and the weakness of political leadership are all impediments to continuing modernization. In most developing societies, the gap between increased aspirations and their attainment threatens to become a chasm. The consequent frustrations promote social upheaval and political unrest.

There are few regions in the world where the forces of modernization are moving more rapidly than in the Middle East. Technological growth, industrial development, and the expansion of transportation, communication, and housing facilities are everywhere evident in the region. Military expenditures are extremely high; countries such as Saudi Arabia and Israel are among the world leaders in this category. A number of the world's most sophisticated weapons systems have migrated to the Persian Gulf, where the availability of huge wealth exists alongside of political insecurity, especially in countries with small populations directed by fragile family rule. Six of the ten countries that lead the world in military expenditures as percent of GDP are Middle Eastern and include, in descending percentage of expenditure, Oman, Iraq, Kuwait, Saudi Arabia, Israel, and Pakistan.[1]

Gigantic advances have also been made in the fields of health and education. School buildings, clinics, and hospitals sprout everywhere in the Middle East. The numbers of students enrolled in primary, secondary, and higher education in the Middle East have increased more than twelvefold since 1950. In the twenty years between the late 1970s and the late 1990s, literacy rates doubled in Egypt, Tunisia, Libya, Jordan, Morocco, and Iran. In Saudi Arabia, the United Arab Emirates, and Qatar, the number of literate citizens tripled. In recent years, the education explosion has been especially evident at the college and university levels.

The modernization boom has accelerated sharply since 1974, when a four-fold increase in the price of oil provided a huge pool of financial resources that became available to promote modernizing ventures. In 1970, the petroleum revenues of the eight major Middle Eastern oil-producing countries were less than $6 billion. By 1974, the figure had ballooned to more than $82 billion. By 1980, Saudi Arabia alone was receiving over $100 billion in petroleum revenues annually. Although falling oil prices throughout the 1980s and 1990s reduced the size of these revenues, they remain huge.

The Middle East is rich in resources other than petroleum. Iran, for example, has the second-largest natural gas reserves in the world. Only Russia has more. Algeria and Saudi Arabia also possess generous amounts of this important hydrocarbon. One of the world's richest deposits of copper has been discovered in Iran. Turkey is the international leader in wolfram production and the third-largest producer of chromium. Both Turkey and Iraq have very large deposits of lignite and iron ore. Morocco accounts for more than 90 percent of the exports of phosphates in the world and is the fourth-largest producer of cobalt. Tunisia, Jordan, and Egypt also have substantial phosphate reserves. Afghanistan has one of the largest iron deposits in the world and is also rich in copper and chromium. As the oil revenues pour into these nations, the money is used for the exploration and extraction of other valuable natural resources. Continuing modernization will be one of the persisting effects of this wealth.

Aggregate data and statistical indices such as annual per capita gross national product (GNP) figures illustrate the advances in modernization. The United Arab Emirates, for example, has a per capita GNP larger than that of the United Kingdom. The per capita GNP of Kuwait is larger than that of any of the thirty-six Latin American countries. In the early 1950s, Libya's per capita GNP was about $40; today it is over $5,000. Iran's per capita GNP rose from less than $300 in

[1]United Nations Development Programme, *Human Development Report 1997* (New York: Oxford University Press, 1998), p. 103.

1960 to over $2,000 in 1980. Despite the ravages of war and revolution, Iran's per capita GNP is approaching $2,500 at the end of the twentieth century.

Although modernization data are impressive to many observers, they avoid the critical political questions. Quantitative measurements in fact explain very little about the qualitative effects of economic wealth. In brief, they do not address political scientist Harold Lasswell's fundamental question: Who gets what, when, and how? Surely, in any study of the modernization of society and politics, it is necessary to get some sense of how these benefits affect society at large. How are the goods and priorities distributed? This question is in essence a political question.

Over the past several years, observers have developed various indices and statistical mechanisms to measure the actual distribution of power and wealth in societies. These devices have included indices such as the physical quality of life index of the Overseas Development Council, the human development index of the United Nations Development Programme, and the social indicators of development prepared by the World Bank. Regardless of the instrument utilized, the Middle East ranks as that region of the world where the gap between modernization on the one hand and political/human/social dimensions of development on the other has been consistently the largest. Data indicate, for example, that although the Middle East generally has a higher GNP per capita than Latin America, the Latin American countries boast a much higher human development index.[2] This situation is exacerbated by the pronounced gap between the haves and the have-nots within particular Middle Eastern societies. The reason for this spiraling cluster of imbalances in the Middle East is to be found largely within the complex experience of political development in the region.

The direction and depth of the drive for modernization are determined largely within the political system. The political elites of the various Middle Eastern societies make the decisions that shape the strategies of modernization. Modernization in turn affects the capacity of the political system to respond to political challenges. For reasons such as these, the important issue of political development is closely interwoven with the problem of modernization.

The Concept of Political Development

Political development involves the capacity of a government to generate and absorb persistent transformation. The political system is not only a responsive, reactive mechanism that passively absorbs and digests challenges. It is preeminently a system with a primacy and autonomy that directs the generation of change. It is the political system that leads, guides, and decides. The political

---

[2] The United Nations Development Programme's statistics reveal that although the per capita GNP of a Middle Eastern country was generally twice that of countries of Latin America, the human development index of Latin American societies was over 20 percent higher than was the case in the Middle East. The GNP per capita is one measure of overall national wealth, while the human development index sheds insights into the distribution of that wealth. The human development index is the collapsed score of three indices, life expectancy, adult literacy, and educational enrollment. The data of these conclusions are available in United Nations Development Programme, *Human Development Report 1997* (New York: Oxford University Press, 1998), pp. 146–148.

leadership both fosters and satisfies demands that focus on such public goods as security, freedom, participation, and justice. The satisfaction of these demands is much more difficult to achieve than demands that derive directly from the material and technological facets of life.

Political development includes the capacity to provide more and more individuals with the means to improve their own positions in society on the basis of talent and merit rather than on ascriptive criteria. New groups and classes continually appear in society and must be brought effectively into the political process. Finally, individuals of different ethnic, religious, and regional backgrounds must have equality of opportunity and must enjoy the protection of a rule of law. In the words of T. M. Sallah: "And, tell me, what use is the ship-of-state if all are not on board?"[3]

By defining political development in terms of a capacity to stimulate and meet demands, one is able to avoid a number of ethnocentric problems that have long haunted developmental studies. The tendency to define political development in terms of a Western-oriented view of democracy is one example of this ethnocentricity. Many "democratic" systems may not succeed in political development because of their lack of effective institutions at the center of the system. In the Middle East, Lebanon has been a tragic case in point.

It is possible that an authoritarian system that is able to provide a serious experience of participation may be relatively successful in the developmental game. This definition of political development enables us to account for the developmental process as it existed in many ancient and traditional systems. Indeed, traditional Islamic societies were at times more highly "developed" than some contemporary societies. This need not be surprising because these traditional systems had more limited demands placed upon them. To speak of political development as if it were something unique to our modern era hinders our ability to understand the dynamics of change because such an approach distorts important historical realities.

The contemporary age, however, is fundamentally different from any earlier time. Scientific advances and technological revolution have wrought unprecedented changes in all systems by which men and women organize their lives. Revolutionary changes and challenges metastasize across the globe. Modernization, or humanity's growing control over the environment, races onward at a breakneck pace. The impact of this modernization on the patterns of political development has been profound. Modernization and political development must be analyzed together.

The Dialectics of Modernization and Political Development

Political elites often seek to promote the processes of modernization within their societies, in part to maximize their own power and authority. Political decision-

---

[3]As quoted in World Bank, *World Development Report 1997* (New York: Oxford University Press, 1997), p. 110.

makers naturally attempt to improve technological skills, medical care, educational quality, and military capacities in their particular societies. They have a vested interest in improving the standing of their countries in the community of nations. The unleashed forces of modernization, in turn, influence the behavior and policies of the elites. Modernization and political development are mutually interactive. Political elites forge modernization policies that strongly affect their own decision-making capacities and abilities to rule.

Once modernization has begun, it becomes a pervasive process. The political leadership that has encouraged the modernizing movement often loses its ability to control the process. Demands increase and may outstrip any capacity to cope with them. Thus, modernization is a highly problematic process. The existence of modernization does not signal the presence of political development. Modernization tends to run out ahead of political development. This gap, in turn, promotes instability and fragility in society.

Modernizing change usually occurs in the physical environment and is most evident in the areas of technology and economics. Such change, however, does not necessarily signal basic alterations in the political system. Traditional patterns of power and authority tend to resist fundamental change. Issues of personal equality, political participation, and social justice are usually the last problems confronted by political elites. These elites have vested interests in preserving ongoing political patterns. Yet, if political development is to take place, it must involve a capacity for continuous change, especially with respect to these social and political issues. No matter how much technological and economic growth may occur, there can be no political development without accompanying change in the power and authority structures.

Political development is a process driven by a dialectical dynamic that marks the relationship between demands and capacity. In more conventional terms, the struggle is one for both liberty and security. Figure 1.1 provides a diagrammatic view of this process. Scholars of development have identified liberty and security as two basic political goods that societies must provide their populations. Gabriel A. Almond and G. Bingham Powell, Jr., for example, argue that the provision of both of these goods has long been the classic dilemma of politics. In their words: "At the logical extremes, at least, there seem to be negative trade-offs between liberty and security, and no ready ethical answer dictates the most appropriate balance between them. . . . At some point, liberty for some individuals threatens the security of others. . . . Part of the problem of liberty concerns the use that citizens wish to make of it, and part of the problem of security concerns who shall enforce it."[4]

The increasing demands for liberty and related values such as equality of opportunity, participation, and justice must be confronted in today's world. Political leaders have the capacity either to satisfy these demands or to repress them. Demands are satisfied by distributing the available rewards equitably throughout the system. In the Middle East, this response is accompanied by the

---

[4]Gabriel A. Almond and G. Bingham Powell, Jr. *Comparative Politics: System, Process, and Policy,* second ed. (Boston: Little, Brown and Co., 1978), pp. 411–412.

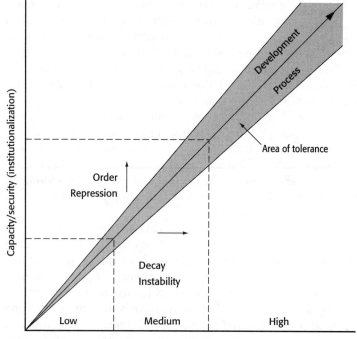

Figure 1.1 The developmental process

centralization and concentration of authority as ongoing relations must be uprooted and new ones created.

By providing political elites with more sophisticated techniques of control,
the proponents of modernization can enhance their capacity either to satisfy or
to stifle demands. Calls for liberty, participation, and justice can be smothered
by "security" forces superbly equipped with the latest technology. When this occurs, demands are not satisfied. Security through repression is often a harbinger
of violence and conflict. At the other extreme are political systems that lack authority and those where power is severely fragmented. The central core of government is weak, and anarchy and chaos reign supreme. In the absence of effective political institutions and a strong, guiding central authority, these kinds of
societies shatter and unravel.

A Typology of Political Development

In analyzing the dialectic of the developmental process, one can proceed by presenting a typology that evaluates political systems on the basis of their policies
that affect the security-liberty balance. Inspired by the formulations of Almond
and Powell, we have formulated a six-part typology of societies based on

their place on the security-liberty continuum.[5] The six political categories are: Democratic-Participatory, Clerical-Populist, Decentralized-Anarchic, Traditional-Monarchical, Technocratic-Moderate, and Technocratic-Repressive.

Democratic-Participatory societies are those in which the citizens enjoy substantial degrees of both liberty and security. In these systems, patterns of democratization and participation are relatively important. Here, the judicial system effectively checks executive power. Meaningful electoral politics and institutions such as political parties and parliaments play a significant role in government in Democratic-Participatory societies, and tolerance and toleration mark political debate and dissent. Although these societies are characterized by relatively low levels of conflict, they do witness short pendulum-like movements between an emphasis on liberty and an emphasis on security. Oftentimes, depending on the political and economic crises of the day, the pendulum freezes in a prolonged position of repressiveness. Democratic-Participatory societies are rare in the Middle East. They include Israel and, to an increasingly lesser extent, Turkey. Other examples of countries where participatory politics are seen from time to time include Yemen and Kuwait. At the beginning of the twenty-first century, however, the trend in all of these Democratic-Participatory examples is away from liberty and toward a preoccupation with security.

Iran stands as the major example of a Clerical-Populist society, a category that may also include Sudan. This political type shares many of the mechanisms of political participation with the Democratic-Participatory model. These religious-guided societies can boast lively electoral politics, robust parliamentary debate, and a limited freedom of speech, press, and assembly. On the other hand, this system reflects strong fundamentalist tendencies and authoritarian proclivities. Self-righteous clerics often promote religious orthodoxy in Clerical-Populist societies.

The case of the Islamic Republic of Iran reveals that the political situation is constantly changing and that the liberty-security pendulum swings back and forth. During the first decade of the revolution (1978–1988), for example, Iran was governed harshly, and the developmental dialectic was heavily skewed in the direction of repression. With the death of Ayatollah Khomeini and the end of the Iraq-Iran war, the Islamic Republic began a long, slow movement toward participatory politics. This shift culminated in the election of a moderate cleric, Mohammad Khatami, in the national elections of 1997. President Khatami began immediately to preach the politics of participation, and terms such as "freedom

---

[5]Over the years, Gabriel A. Almond and G. Bingham Powell, Jr. have presented various useful typologies of political systems based on developmental strategies. Their most recent formulation describes six types of "authoritarian regimes" in "pre-industrial nations." The categories are: "Neotraditional Political Systems," "Personal Rule," "Clerico-Mobilizational Regimes," "Technocratic Repressive," "Technocratic-Distributive," and "Technocratic-Mobilizational." There is a seventh category termed "Democratic." We have revised the Almond and Powell formulation in order to increase its relevance to the Middle Eastern experience. We have altered the terminology as well. See Gabriel A. Almond and G. Bingham Powell, Jr., *Comparative Politics Today: A Worldview* (New York: HarperCollins, 1996), pp. 148–150.

of speech," "civil society," and "the rule of law" became part of his vocabulary. As Iran approached the twentieth anniversary of its revolution in 1999, it provided a Clerical-Populist model of politics that could stand as an alternative to the militant fundamentalism often associated with Islamic governments. In surveying thirty-nine Muslim countries in 1994, the *Economist* counted only seven that could in any way be called democracies. In a world in which Islam has a "democratic deficit," the *Economist* wrote that "surprised respect is due to the Islamic revolutionaries of Iran for holding freeish elections that have produced a parliament happy to argue with the government."[6]

Decentralized-Anarchic cases are represented by those countries where ethnic, class, religious, and political-ideological tensions are so deep and pervasive that violent anarchy prevails. In these cases, the developmental pendulum swings away from security, back through liberty, and ultimately into anarchy. Political incoherence and civil war prevail. The center of the system loses control. There are two paths to the Decentralized-Anarchic experience. In the first, a tenuous form of democratic participation breaks down in the face of internal ethnic and religious division. "After a substantial amount of liberty appears, the society collapses into civil war, and security vanishes completely."[7] The prototype of this iteration of Decentralized-Anarchic societies is Lebanon, a society torn both vertically and horizontally by religious and class strife. The second path to political anarchy is visible in countries like Algeria and Afghanistan. In these nations, the breakdown occurs as a result of fierce competition between parties contending for political control. Excellent examples of this anarchic society type outside of the Middle East proper are found in the grim experience of the former Yugoslavia.

The Traditional-Monarchical category is the first of three types in which security and order take precedence over liberty and justice. The political regime in power sacrifices participatory politics for central control. This category of society is best exemplified by the monarchies and mini-monarchies of the Persian Gulf. The prototype of the Traditional-Monarchic system is Saudi Arabia, but it includes the shaikhdoms as well. Over time, the harshness of control has intensified in places like Saudi Arabia and Bahrain, while in Oman, the United Arab Emirates, and Qatar there has been a recent trend in favor of more participatory politics.

Technocratic-Moderate regimes are those that provide a serious degree of political participation. Political parties, parliaments, and electoral politics exist in a situation where there is a degree of freedom of press, speech, and assembly. Nonetheless, the political leaders in these technocratic societies in the end stress order and control. Although there are similarities between Clerical-Populist regimes and Technocratic-Moderate systems, the basic difference is that the latter category is more secular and less ideological in makeup. Resurgent Islamic movements remain locked out of power, whereas the political leadership in the religious populist model is clerical by definition. The outstanding example of

---

[6]"Islam and the West: A Survey," *Economist,* August 6, 1994, p. 12.

[7]Almond and Powell, *Comparative Politics,* p. 413.

the Technocratic-Moderate system is Egypt. In the wake of the Gulf wars of the 1980s and 1990s, a handful of traditional family-run regimes have opened their systems enough to qualify for moderate status. Kuwait, Jordan, and Morocco have been experimenting with participatory politics.

The final category in this developmental typology is the Technocratic-Repressive government. In these systems, the political leaders rule by outright fear and resort to imprisonment, torture, and execution as means of maintaining their control. The best example of the Technocratic-Repressive case is Iraq, where Saddam Hussein and his security forces have systematically crushed all forms of suspected opposition. The Technocratic-Repressive regimes are police states. Although most of the types of political systems described in this typology resort to repressive tactics from time to time, the Technocratic-Repressive leadership has institutionalized rule by fear and oppression. Less severe cases of countries that have on occasion resorted to a harsher mode of repression while curtailing political participation include Syria and Libya.

An examination of this typology of political systems yields a number of conclusions. First, the major trend is in the direction of control and security over participation and liberty. Not only is it difficult to find any Democratic-Participatory examples, but those that most closely approximate the model, countries such as Israel and Turkey, are themselves moving away from participatory politics and toward repressive rule. The same is true of the Technocratic-Moderate and Traditional-Monarchical models. The weak countertrend whereby countries such as Iran and Kuwait reveal some evidence of successful political development only highlights the dominant trend of deepening political failure.

Second, the push and pull between the regime's desire for control and the populace's desire for freedom changes constantly. Societies move from one type to another. Algeria, for example, was a classic example of a Technocratic-Repressive society when central control was imposed by France. After the revolution in 1962, Algeria survived a brief period as a Decentralized-Anarchic case. Ahmad Ben Bella was at the time unable to consolidate control at the center. In the late 1980s, the Algerian political elite, led by Chadli Benjedid, sought to introduce genuine political development by balancing popular demands and central authority. This developmental effort expressed itself in the form of national elections in December 1991. Algeria seemed comfortably on the road to a Democratic-Participatory system. This was not to be the case.

When the Islamic movement scored a surprisingly strong electoral victory, the ruling elite became alarmed. Benjedid resigned, and the old leadership represented by the High Security Council and the military declared the December elections null and void. They then canceled the second round of elections scheduled for January 1992. These arbitrary acts effectively derailed Algeria's developmental train and gave birth to a bloody civil war the excesses of which have horrified the world. Algeria, therefore, has moved from centralized control to the anarchy of civil war to a short period of participatory politics to repressive government and back to political anarchy. In other words, history has witnessed Algeria move from Technocratic-Repressive to Decentralized-Anarchic to Democratic-Participatory to Technocratic-Repressive and back to Decentralized-Anarchic.

Third, the Algerian case demonstrates the delicate dialectic that rests at the core of the process of political development. The outcome of political development is shaped, however, within the larger field of modernization. Modernization can retard or promote political development. Economic and technological growth heighten demands. They can also strengthen the capacity of the political elite to exert control. In order to muster the strength necessary to exploit scarce resources and to weld together countries divided deeply by sectarianism, Middle Eastern leaders have often relied on authoritarian political methods. These methods, in turn, expose them to the serious risks of sliding into repression, which weakens their capacities for political development.

On the other hand, if political elites govern loosely and weakly, they may also forfeit their developmental capacities as society breaks down into conflicting ethnic, regional, and class-based cliques. As Figure 1.1 indicates, the developmental process is a wobbly path between repressive rule and anarchical instability. The process is a delicate balance of capacity and demands. Development involves a constant push and pull between the two sides of this dialectic. Meanwhile, the fires of modernization continue to crackle, complicating the developmental process by constantly altering balances, demands, responses, and capacities.

Political Development in the Middle East

Processes of modernization run far ahead of political development in the Middle East. Moreover, the capacity to generate and absorb persistent transformation varies widely from society to society. In all cases, however, the ability to transform fundamentally the basic power configurations has been the rarest form of change. Even when governments have occasionally sought to alter their systems, they have tended to lack the capacity in the face of a resistant and resilient tradition. Transformations in the economic system have come easiest, followed by alterations in the social system. Political development lags conspicuously.

Spurred by economic growth that rides the waves of black gold and by social modernization that accompanies technological change, many Middle Eastern societies possess an increasing capacity to generate change in the political realm. By sponsoring advancements in education, Middle Eastern political elites have been indirectly responsible for the development of burgeoning professional middle classes. The members of these middle classes are among those demanding political reform. In failing to address these demands, the leaders exhibit their unwillingness to absorb and institutionalize political transformation. This resistance begets a situation in which expanding gaps, like bubbles, burst into one another. The gap between modernization and political development is widened by the capacity to generate transformation and the failure to absorb it. More specifically, these overall systemic gaps increase the imbalances within particular Middle Eastern countries.

Change dominates the history of Middle Eastern political systems, yet radical alteration of the underlying power and authority structure has been extremely rare. The legitimating authority structure and the fundamental power patterns have consistently weathered changes of rulers, elites, and dynasties. The traditional political patterns of the Islamic Middle East survived by being in a state of constant movement. Continual modification and piecemeal revision have deterred system transformation. Political elites in the Middle East have shrewdly implemented policies both of co-optation and coercion. Selective mobility and sporadic repression have ensured the preservation of ongoing political patterns by introducing carefully apportioned doses of modifying change.

The most critical dimension of political development is participation, which requires that the demands of the population for an effective voice in matters that affect their lives be satisfied. The literature on political development and "democratization" generally argues that participation involves electoral politics buttressed by the existence of formal institutions such as political parties and parliaments. The Middle East experience provides some differing insights into this issue.

In general terms, elections are not always evidence of political development. Oftentimes, polls exist as political window-dressing and serve as devices cleverly controlled by political elites that are busily building counterfeit democracy. Second, electoral politics can produce what one observer calls "illiberal democracy."[8] Democratic practices may exist, but constitutional limitations on government are absent. The rule of law and basic human rights such as freedom of speech, assembly, and religion are sacrificed on the altar of pseudo-participation. In the Middle East, elections have failed to promote genuine participation in countries like Tunisia, Egypt, Jordan, and Kuwait. In Algeria, when elections did not produce the result desired by the ruling junta, the results were simply dismissed, giving rise to a bloody and bitter civil war.

On the other hand, in much of the Middle East where Traditional-Monarchical and Technocratic-Repressive regimes are in control, even electoral window dressing is absent. From Saudi Arabia and Bahrain to Iraq and Syria, competitive electoral politics are unknown. In this situation, any sign of serious electoral procedures would represent a step forward. The experience of Iran since the revolution of 1978–1979 is an important case where elections are a strong sign of growing participatory politics. Yet, in the Middle East, genuine political development has been lacking not because of the absence of participatory mechanisms but rather because of the existence of strong traditional forms of these mechanisms. Ironically, the existence of traditional developmental modes has stunted and stifled the appearance of effective political development in the region today.

Informal institutions have always existed in the Middle East. Masses and elites were bound together by a number of linkage structures that included elaborate networks of intermediaries composed of messengers, adjutants, clerics, secretaries, advisors, bureaucrats, cousins, and confidantes. The existence of an informal assembly (the *majlis*) in the traditional Arab world enabled individuals from all walks of life to approach their leaders directly for assistance

---

[8]See the provocative article by Fareed Zakaria entitled "The Rise of Illiberal Democracy," 76 *Foreign Affairs* (November–December, 1997): 22–43.

and aid. This kind of personalized institutionalization resulted in numerous channels of communication through which demands and grievances moved upward to the political elite while orders and policies poured downward to the middle and lower classes. In this system, grievances could be aired and demands could be heard. The political elite, however, enjoyed the prerogative of action and redress. The petitioners lacked the power to guarantee the satisfaction of their demands.

The appearance of political parties and parliaments has not significantly changed this form of participation. Parties have often existed as loose collections of personal cliques that have penetrated little beyond the upper crust of society. Here, political parties have served largely as the instruments of the ruling elites. Middle Eastern legislatures, like political parties, tend to exist as Western-style institutions grafted to Middle Eastern political systems. Nonetheless, the history of the Middle East has been the history of a thriving civil society. Guilds, brotherhoods, professional organizations, religious networks, regional associations, and a rich variety of majlises have been the traditional instruments of political development. This form of organizational dynamics has deflected and deterred the appearance of effective modern modes of participation. Once again, the Middle East has avoided fundamental political change by promoting a culture of piecemeal modification. In other words, the culture and experience of the Middle East have combatted the fires of political development through the use of traditional developmental crossfires.

The burgeoning literature on civil society in the Middle East has constructively called attention to the intermediate groups that have buffered state power while providing examples of participatory politics. On the other hand, this literature has sometimes overlooked the fact that the instruments of civil society have often impeded rather than promoted political development. In the first place, the units of civil society have existed for centuries in the Middle East, where political development has been conspicuously absent. Second, ruling elites in the Middle East have consciously encouraged the existence of regional political activity as a kind of participatory catharsis. By involving themselves in local micropolitics, many politically conscious Middle Easterners have lacked the time and energy to participate in national decision making. Political elites have sought to keep the people preoccupied with family feuds, religious debate, and local politicking. When this activity occasionally generated demands for participation at the national level, the authoritarian political leadership has stood ready to smother such activity.[9]

Not all the formulations of scholars of civil society are open to the criticism discussed above. One school of thought, represented in the work of Richard

---

[9]There has been a great flurry of discussion and debate about the role and development of "civil society" in Middle East contexts. For the major statement concerning this issue, see Augustus Richard Norton (ed.), *Civil Society in the Middle East* (Leiden: E. J. Brill, 1995). See also the Spring 1995 special issue of the *Middle East Journal* devoted to the subject of civil society. For a brief but excellent presentation of the civil society thesis applied across the Middle East, see Jillian Schwedler (ed.), *Toward Civil Society in the Middle East? A Primer* (Boulder and London: Lynn Rienner Publishers, 1995).

Norton and Muhammad Muslih, for example, moves beyond the identification of intermediate groups to stress the need for these traditional units of participation to give way to nationwide political participation. This participation is institutionalized through inclusive organizations such as meaningful political parties and truly representative parliaments with serious decisional power. The parochial and particularistic institutions of the past fail to meet the demands of the masses of people today.

The traditional networks of personalistic groups and cliques often reflected an inbuilt rivalry and institutionalized conflict that belied true political development. If there is to be a balance between authority and liberty, then the leadership must help promote an atmosphere of tolerance and toleration. Political development involves a certain state of mind, and civil society can help promote this mindset. In the words of Richard Norton: "Civil society is more than an admixture of various forms of association; it also refers to a quality—civility—without which the milieu consists of feuding factions, cliques, and cabals. Civility implies tolerance, the willingness of individuals to accept disparate political views and social attitudes; sometimes to accept the profoundly important idea that there is no right answer."[10] For this reason, militant religious fundamentalist groups—whether Muslim, Christian, or Jewish—stand as major impediments to the processes of political development. Reformist religious collectivities, however, can play a positive developmental role.

The Dynamics of Political Participation in the Middle East

Political participation is a process whereby individuals engage in activity that directly affects the national power and authority structure of society. This activity can be system-challenging or system-supportive. System-supportive participation exists when large numbers of individuals come to support an authority structure to which they have meaningful access and that represents their interests. As the process of participation develops and matures, the masses of people are continually brought into the decision-making process. Increasing social and political demands emanating from the lower and middle classes accompany this movement. The political elite will both encourage and attempt to meet these demands for expanding representation. Genuine political participation, therefore, can no longer be provided by traditional clientalistic politics of the majlis and the family.

In the Middle East, the first important break with the past signaling the serious advance of political participation was the overthrow of a number of monarchical regimes. Turkey and Egypt are the two most dramatic early examples

---

[10]A. R. Norton, "The Future of Civil Society in the Middle East," 47 *Middle East Journal* (Spring, 1993): 214.

of this kind of revolution. The Iranian revolution of 1978–1979 represented a multiclass movement that overthrew the ruling Pahlavi dynasty. Even in these three cases, however, the destruction of corrupt autocracies did not guarantee the appearance of political development. Although the Ataturks, Nassers, and Khomeinis may have performed impressively in many facets of their leadership, their authoritarianism limited severely their capacity to build successful patterns of participatory politics.

Traditional patterns of power and authority in the Middle East resist change. The trauma of political upheaval promotes destruction over construction. Capacity is weakened by an uneven distribution of resources. Often the crucial resources that do exist are drained away in emotion-charged international adventures. The festering Arab-Israeli conflict has stunted the growth of political development among the Palestinians, Egyptians, Israelis, and in the region as a whole. The Iran-Iraq war of the 1980s had the same effect on the political systems of these two countries. Saddam Hussein's invasion of Kuwait in 1990 further compromised any chance for effective political development in Iraq. The existence of an attacking outside foe enables regimes to tighten arbitrary and authoritarian rule. Meanwhile, human casualties, physical destruction, shattered morale, national insecurity, and political disillusionment—the inevitable byproducts of such conflict—all combine to weaken developmental capacities.

The delicate dialectic between demands and capacity, between anarchy and repression, between participation and institutionalization, between liberty and security is a critical issue in the Middle East. Demands increase dramatically as more people seek political participation. Harried elites threatened by serious domestic and international problems struggle to maintain their own authority while at the same time striving to modernize their societies. Moderate authoritarianism begins to slip into the mode of harsh repression as ruling elites gradually stifle demands in the name of "national security." In the footrace between modernization and political development in the Middle East, modernization always runs out ahead. Manfred Halpern's "authoritarian road to democracy" is in fact a narrow path fraught with hidden danger and false exits.[11]

The challenge of political development is complicated by five general factors. First, the existence of a fragmented, personalistic, and particularistic form of participation has a long history in the Middle East. The priority of informal politics has long been a reality in the region. The power of clientelism and the strength of majlis politics have slowed the appearance of larger, more inclusive institutions such as powerful legislatures and autonomous judiciaries. The traditional units of civil society have stunted the growth of effective and efficient institutions that are necessary as societies grow and modernize. The remnants of tradition often cripple participatory democracy.

Second, no Middle Eastern society has yet found that it could relax in its quest for development. There are no plateaus and no end points in this journey. Both monarchs and their military-oriented successors have learned this lesson

---

[11]Manfred Halpern, *The Politics of Social Change in the Middle East and North Africa* (Princeton, N.J.: Princeton University Press, 1963), pp. 223–226.

the difficult way. Witness the fate of the shah of Iran and Anwar Sadat of Egypt. The clerics who have succeeded the shah and the political descendants of Sadat have all learned that they too must face this reality.

Third, there is no particular political or ideological path that ensures developmental success. Clerical-Populist, Traditional-Monarchical, Technocratic-Moderate, and Technocratic-Repressive systems all have failed at one time or another. Even the Democratic-Participatory model so much admired in the West has an inconsistent record. By the end of the millenium, the former Democratic-Participatory system in Lebanon was struggling to put back the pieces. The promising systems in Israel and Turkey were closing into increased repressiveness. Middle Eastern political leaders must write their own prescriptions for development. Thus far, such prescriptions have been singularly unsuccessful.

The fourth developmental complication concerns the historical and cultural backdrop against which development must occur. Specifically, the complex relationship between religion and politics influences the developmental dynamic. In a world of incoherence, Islam—a religion, civilization, and way of life—claims it has the answer to the questions of identity, legitimacy, and participation that confront all believers. As a universalistic force and one that pervades all facets of human behavior, Islam is in a critically important position to influence the related challenges of modernization and political development. The Islamic experience with politics in Pakistan, Iran, and Sudan reveals that thus far Islam has been more effective as an ideology of political opposition than as an ideology of political rule. In this context, the Iranian model looms very large.

Finally, the issue of political development in the Middle East is complicated by interregional and international considerations. The Arab-Israeli conflict has already been mentioned. Both the collapse of the Soviet Union and the international energy issue have also had profound effects on developmental politics in the Middle East. The massive infusions of military aid into the region have complicated rather than alleviated the problem of political development. These activities have not only deflected attention and resources away from the central issue of development but have also tended to strengthen the forces of security at the expense of liberty and participation.

In the Islamic Middle East, Turkey and Egypt have over the years been considered to be among the leaders in political development. Although both countries have witnessed many instances of social unrest and political instability, they both have middle-class regimes that have been relatively supportive of political participation and the rule of law. In the 1990s, however, both Turkey and Egypt slipped into authoritarianism. In Turkey, the secular leadership backed by the military has increased their repressive treatment of the Kurds while outlawing by fiat the popular Refah Islamic party. In Egypt, Husni Mubarak's government, threatened by an Islamist insurrection and growing poverty and corruption, has become more autocratic over time, and human rights have been sacrificed to central control.

The Technocratic-Repressive regimes in Iraq, Syria, and Libya have an even less distinguished record of political development. Iraq and Syria labor under the severe handicap of deep sectarian, ethnic, and ideological divisions. Iraq, under Saddam Hussein's leadership, is best described as an oppressive tyranny.

Although sensitive to the need for popular participation and economic equality of opportunity, the Libyan regime is dominated by the personality of Mu'ammar Qaddafi, who clutches all power in his own hands.

The families that rule the Persian Gulf shaikhdoms have generally avoided the business of political development. Because of their exceptional wealth and tiny populations, they have taken strides in the areas of health, education, and housing. This cushion of wealth has muffled the cries for political participation. Nonetheless, political control remains firmly in the hands of a few members of ruling families. The Iraqi invasion of Kuwait in 1990, however, has forced the leaders of these ministates to rethink their political strategies and to consider seriously broadening political participation. Kuwait has been the leader in this reassessment.

Particularly serious developmental problems in the Islamic Middle East exist in the major monarchies such as Saudi Arabia. In these societies, traditional power and authority relations exist alongside growing middle classes and deeply religious lower-middle and lower classes whose members remain locked out of the corridors of power. These Traditional-Monarchical countries lack the will to alleviate the tensions arising from the increasing gap between economic modernization and political development. Furthermore, the traditional mechanisms of civil society are drying up and withering in countries like Saudi Arabia and Morocco. The vitality of the majlis system and the lively politics of informal primordial groups have begun to lose their dynamism. Jordan, Morocco, and Oman lack resources and revenues. The situation is aggravated by conspicuous corruption. For these countries, the stubborn refusal to promote political development can only have violent and costly consequences.

Traditionally, the Middle East was the scene of a bustling, thriving form of personalistic civil society, a civil society that provided limited but reasonably effective forms of political participation. Participation prevailed over democratization. Personalistic networks stretched within, across, and throughout these societies, providing the population with access to those with power. Rather than "bringing the state closer to the people," as the World Bank prescribes, it was a case of bringing the people closer to the state.[12] Few areas of the world witnessed this degree of traditional, participatory dynamics. Those regions heavily under Western influence, areas such as Latin America, for example, experienced a tradition that was more formal-legal in character. These Western-oriented states, therefore, were better positioned to implement institutionalized democratization and the rule of law.

In the late 1990s, scholars of democracy were busily counting and comparing countries on the basis of their democratic demeanor. In this exercise, Middle Eastern societies have not fared well. In brief, Middle Eastern traditional modes of participation are failing in the face of expanding populations and rapid modernization. Clientelism, kinship support systems, majlis mechanisms, and religious guilds and brotherhoods can no longer meet the demands and satisfy the needs of the general populations. In addressing this situation, Middle

---

[12]World Bank, *World Development Report 1997*, pp. 110–130.

Eastern political leaders have swung away from policies that stress liberty and participation and have moved toward more centralized control and authority.

The Middle Eastern experience reflects the complex delicacy of the developmental process. In a constantly changing situation, there are few obvious success stories and no easy developmental strategies. On the other hand, the present state of incoherence that exists in the Middle East provides an opportunity for the developmental pendulum to swing back in the direction of equality of opportunity, nationwide and effective participation, and justice protected and promoted by the rule of law. The seeds of political development, after all, have germinated in the cultural soil of the Middle East for many years. When they will bloom and blossom remains to be seen.

Many of the major problems that now confront the peoples of the Middle East are directly related to these defining issues of modernization and political development. These challenges will be analyzed in the following chapters.

SELECTED BIBLIOGRAPHY

Ajami, Fouad. *The Arab Predicament.* New ed. Cambridge: Cambridge University Press, 1992.

Almond, Gabriel A., and G. Bingham Powell, Jr. *Comparative Politics Today: A World View.* Sixth ed. New York: HarperCollins, 1996.

Antoun, Richard, and Iliya Harik, eds. *Rural Politics and Social Change in the Middle East.* Bloomington: Indiana University Press, 1972.

Ayubi, Nazih N. *Over-stating the Arab State: Politics and Society in the Middle East.* London: I. B. Tauris, 1995.

Bill, James A., and Robert Hardgrave, Jr. *Comparative Politics: The Quest for Theory.* Washington, D.C.: University Press of America, 1982.

Brynen, Rex, Bahgat Korany, and Paul Noble, eds. *Political Liberalization and Democratization in the Arab World.* Vol. 1. Boulder, Colorado: Lynne Rienner Publishers, 1995.

Cleveland, William L. *A History of the Modern Middle East.* Boulder, Colorado: Westview Press, 1994.

Garnham, David, and Mark Tessler, eds. *Democracy, War, and Peace in the Middle East.* Bloomington: Indiana University Press, 1995.

Ghadbian, Najib. *Democratization and the Islamist Challenge in the Arab World.* Boulder, Colorado: Westview Press, 1997.

Goldschmidt, Arthur, Jr. *A Concise History of the Middle East,* fifth ed. Boulder, Colorado: Westview Press, 1995.

Halpern, Manfred. *The Politics of Social Change in the Middle East and North Africa.* Princeton, N.J.: Princeton University Press, 1963.

Hudson, Michael C. *Arab Politics: The Search for Legitimacy.* New Haven: Yale University Press, 1978.

Kamrava, Mehran. *Democracy in the Balance: Culture and Society in the Middle East.* New York and London: Chatham House, 1998.

Long, David E., and Bernard Reich, eds. *The Government and Politics of the Middle East and North Africa,* third ed. Boulder, Colorado: Westview Press, 1995.

Moore, Clement Henry. *Politics in North Africa: Algeria, Morocco, and Tunisia.* Boston: Little, Brown and Co., 1970.

Muslih, Muhammad, and Augustus Richard Norton. *Political Tides in the Arab World.* New York: Foreign Policy Association, 1991.

Norton, Augustus Richard, ed. *Civil Society in the Middle East.* Leiden: E. J. Brill, 1995.

Palmer, Monte. *Dilemmas of Political Development,* fourth ed. Itasca, Ill.: F. E. Peacock Publishers, 1988.

Peretz, Don. *The Middle East Today.* fifth ed. New York: Praeger Publishers, 1988.

Perry, Glenn E. *The Middle East.* Second ed. Englewood Cliffs, N.J.: Prentice-Hall, 1992.

Richards, Alan, and John Waterbury. *A Political Economy of the Middle East,* second ed. Boulder, Colorado: Westview Press, 1996.

Sharabi, Hisham. *Neopatriarchy: A Theory of Distorted Change in Arab Society.* New York: Oxford University Press, 1988.

Chapter 2

States, Beliefs, and Ideologies

Political discourse in the modern Arab world, according to a prominent scholar of the region, "has been awash in ideology."[1] The same could be said of politics in the non-Arab Middle Eastern states of Iran, Turkey, and Israel. Middle Eastern political leaders typically pepper their speeches with ideological terms, nationalist and religious imagery, and attacks on domestic opponents and foreign enemies. By comparison, political discourse in the emerging industrial states of Asia tends to focus more explicitly on economic issues, suggesting that political legitimacy there is measured more in terms of national economic growth than it is in the Middle East. Partly because the pace of industrialization in the Middle East has lagged behind East Asia's and Latin America's, Middle Eastern governments seek to legitimate themselves less through references to financial statements than through manipulating nationalist, religious, and other symbols. In the Middle East the primary purposes of ideology, which consists of beliefs and assertions that rationalize behavior, are not to define concrete objectives or identify strategies through which they might be achieved. Instead, ideologies are intended "to reassure both articulator and audience, to engender solidarity, and to resolve problems of personal or group identity." They are, in the words of Clement Henry Moore, "expressive" rather than "practical."[2]

Ideologies are both formal dogma and personal guidelines by which individuals define themselves in relation to society. In both of these manifestations

---

[1]Michael C. Hudson, *Arab Politics: The Search for Legitimacy* (New Haven: Yale University Press, 1977), p. 20.

[2]Clement Henry Moore, "On Theory and Practice Among the Arabs," *World Politics* 19 (October 1971): 106–126.

Middle Eastern ideologies tend toward instability and fragmentation. They are unstable in that they are prone to rapid change, and they are fragmented because they do not inspire the wholehearted commitment of all those for whom the message is intended. Many countries in the region have ethnic, linguistic, and/or religious minorities that subscribe only partially, if at all, to the ideologies sanctioned by their respective states. Kurds, for example, an ethnolinguistic minority group who are overwhelmingly Sunni Muslim, reside in Iraq, Iran, Turkey, and Syria. In the latter they number a few hundred thousand, constitute less than 2 percent of the population, and are scattered among Muslim and Christian Arabs in Damascus and in the north. Having no hope of achieving independence or even autonomy from the government in Damascus, Syrian Kurds, although strongly aware of their own ethnicity, do not publicly articulate demands. They nevertheless covet the right to use the Kurdish language in schools and in the media and to be permitted other legal forms of ethnic expression. Fellow Kurds across the borders with Turkey and Iraq, however, do constitute large minorities whose powers are enhanced by their geographical concentration. Kurdish demands there, and to a somewhat lesser extent in Iran, have been far more expansive than in Syria, extending to claims for autonomy and even independence. Kurdish insurrections in Turkey and Iraq are paralleled at the ideological level by rejections of Turkish and Iraqi nationalisms and their claims to sovereignty in favor of a well-articulated Kurdish nationalism and its implied claim to the same territories.

Throughout the region, Christians' sense of their own national identities likewise varies in accordance with their possibilities of achieving autonomy or independence. In Lebanon, the collapse of the government in the wake of the 1975–1976 civil war made it possible for the large Christian minority, which constitutes about one-third of the population, to carve out an autonomous region that had many of the attributes of a sovereign state until Syria asserted control from late 1989. The ideology of the Lebanese Forces, the most powerful of the Christian militias and political movements at that time, was a strident form of Christian nationalism. It accentuated Lebanon's "distinctive" identity, which it traced to the ancient Phoenicians, thereby devaluing Muslim contributions to Lebanese accomplishments.

Christians in the Middle East as a whole, however, constitute only some 3 percent of the total population. Outside Lebanon they have virtually no chance of attaining political autonomy. Accordingly, they typically seek to express themselves politically within a majoritarian rather than minoritarian framework. Christian Palestinian Arabs have played leading roles in formulating Palestinian nationalism and organizing its various political expressions. In the mid-nineteenth century, Syrian Christian intellectuals laid the foundations for Arab nationalism. In Egypt, Coptic Christians played prominent roles in the interwar nationalist movement and continue to play important public roles.

As the cases of Kurdish and Christian minorities suggest, political behavior and beliefs are strongly conditioned by immediate demographic and political circumstances and are, therefore, subject to change according to those circumstances. This plasticity at the communal level is mirrored by the multiplicity and flexibility of personal identities. Different components of those complex identities are evoked by varying circumstances. Samir Wahhabi, for example, is a notable from the village of Bait Jann in the Galilee in northern Israel and one-time member of the Knesset (Israeli parliament) for the right-wing Likud Party. He identifies himself as follows: "I belong to the Druze sect, which is part of the Arab minority in Israel. It is part of the Arab nation, and personally my state is the State of Israel. In the past this land was called Palestine, so I could say I belong in that historical sense."[3] To many other Druze from that village, however, Wahhabi's identification with Israel is inappropriate and opportunistic. In their minds the proper Druze identity is Arab and Palestinian but not Israeli.[4] Variability of identities of non-Jewish Israelis is not limited to Druze. A sample of Palestinian Arab citizens of Israel were asked in 1966 whether they identified themselves as Israeli, Arab, or Palestinian. The majority replied that they preferred to call themselves Israelis. A year later, following the June 1967 war, a comparable sample ranked Arab identity first, followed by Palestinian and then Israeli. Seven years later a third survey revealed that only 14 percent of respondents believed the term *Israeli* described them, while 63 percent thought of themselves as Palestinian.[5] This shift in the self-identifications of Palestinian Arabs in Israel reflects the traumatic events of the 1967 war and, more generally, the politicization of that community and its increasing hostility toward Israeli Jews.

Survey research conducted among young citizens from virtually all Arab countries carried out since 1967 for the purpose of gauging preferred identifications of respondents has revealed not only that such identities are multiple but also that they tend to respond to political events and trends. The identities mentioned have included those of family, tribe, ethnic group (Arab, Kurd, Armenian, etc.), religion, citizenship, political party, movement, and ideology. The percentage of respondents identifying themselves as Arab has declined over the past decade, while preferences for Islamic or specific national identities have increased. These changes parallel what many observers believe to be a declining importance of pan-Arabism and its gradual replacement by state-based nationalisms or political Islam.[6]

Multiplicity and plasticity of identity are a reflection of political reality, not personal capriciousness. In this century, the Middle East has been forced to endure upheavals that have repeatedly altered the structural conditions upon which politically relevant beliefs and identities rest. A Lebanese in his or her late eighties, for example, would have entered the world as a subject of the Ottoman Empire and would then, for a brief period, have been under the control of the short-lived Damascus-based Arab state of Amir Faisal. Subsequently this person

---

[3]Julia Slater, "Palestinians in Israel: Who Are They?" *Middle East International* 329 (July 8, 1988): 16.

[4]*Ibid.*, p. 16.

[5]Lewis W. Snider, "Minorities and Political Power in the Middle East," in *The Political Role of Minority Groups in the Middle East*, ed. by R. D. McLaurin (New York: Praeger, 1979), pp. 247–248.

[6]For a review of this survey data, see Tawfic E. Farah, "Introduction," in *Pan-Arabism and Arab Nationalism: The Continuing Debate*, ed. by Tawfic E. Farah (Boulder, Colorado: Westview Press, 1987), pp. 1–18.

would have become a citizen of French-ruled Lebanon and, after World War II, a citizen of independent Lebanon. For almost a decade and a half after the onset of civil war in 1975, with the almost total collapse of that state, the life of this octogenarian would have been heavily influenced by one or more of the powerful militias that have all but displaced state authority. Since then, Syria has assumed quasi-sovereign status, rendering Lebanese nationality politically, if not psychologically, marginal.[7]

The Lebanese are not unique in having endured historical odysseys that in a lifetime have taken them through numerous national and subnational administrative arrangements and corresponding demands for political loyalties and identities. Palestinians now in their late eighties, for example, have been subjects of the Ottomans, British, and either the Israelis, Jordanians, or perhaps some other Arab state. These changes in citizenship, combined with the mosaic-like character of religious, ethnic, and linguistic groups in the region, help to account for the failure of any political ideology to be permanently established and thereby utterly transform and homogenize personal political identities.

Ideologies tend to sweep through the area gathering strength like hurricanes, then dissipate without having achieved their objectives. Personal identities modified in response to political victories, charismatic leaders, or ideological slogans can just as easily revert to their original forms when the new ideology and its champion encounter defeats. In the wake of the June 1967 Arab-Israeli war, for example, radical Palestinian nationalism tinged by Maoism swept through the Arab world. The Arab states, having promised to "liberate Palestine" but having in fact worked assiduously to contain Palestinian radical nationalism, were discredited by the crushing defeat. In the postwar climate, guerrilla war, rather than the armies of Egypt, Syria, and Jordan, held out the promise of victory over Israel. The Arab states regrouped, however, reestablished their power, and in Jordan in September 1970, which became known as Black September, the Palestine Liberation Organization was crushed. In the wake of that violent confrontation between Palestinian revolutionary mass mobilization and the power of Arab states, infatuation with Palestinian radicalism rapidly faded. Large numbers of Egyptians, Syrians, Iraqis, and other Arabs who had strongly but tem-

---

[7]These rapidly changing configurations of sovereign authority, further exacerbated by Lebanon's involvement in the wider Middle East, spawned numerous potential affiliations upon which identities and ideologies can rest. The plethora of choices confronting Lebanese Maronite Christians is instructive:

> If nationalism has rapidly "invaded" the Arab mind, it has not been met with a clear definition of where the nation is. Take the example of a Maronite Lebanese who is told by the historians of his community (and modern warlords) that the Maronite nation has existed for ages. However, those Maronites who have rallied round the 1920 French-defined "Grand Liban" tell him that if the Maronites have ever constituted a nation, this nation has now been diluted in the wider Lebanese modern one. Then the proponents of Greater (or Natural) Syria tell him that Lebanon is a purely artificial creation of colonialist France and that his loyalty should go exclusively to a Syrian nation present since Sumer and the Akkadians. Arab nationalists will insist that the Arab nation is the only "true" nation.

Ghassan Salamé, "Introduction," in *The Foundations of the Arab State*, ed. by Ghassan Salamé (London: Croom Helm, 1987), p. 4.

porarily identified with the transnationalist revolutionary message disseminated by Palestinians, witnessing the superior power of their own states, reverted to their original national identities and concerns.

In Iran, the 1978–1979 revolution stimulated a wave of enthusiasm for Khomeinism that then swept through the Sunni Muslim Arab world. Impressed by the success of radical Islamic fundamentalism in overthrowing the shah and confronting the United States, Arab Muslims in great numbers became convinced that in radical political Islam they might find solutions to their own problematic confrontations with Israel, the United States, and the authoritarian Arab governments under which they lived. However, the Khomeinist image was quickly tarnished by the war with Iraq, by excesses of the new regime, and by the Islamic Republic's inability to put the economy on a sound footing. Enthusiasm for Khomeinism waned, and although Islamic political activism has persisted, in most cases it has distinguished itself from the Iranian version.

That political ideologies are subject to bandwagon effects—rapidly gaining adherents in response to successes and then losing them as a result of setbacks—indicates that those ideologies are not reinforced by being integrated into political structures. Political leaders, unwilling to have their choices constrained, use ideologies not to institutionalize power but as political weapons to gain popular support that can be used to joust with enemies. Ideologies, in short, are seen as useful adjuncts to political power and are nurtured for that purpose. The Safavids, for example, a Turkish-speaking nomadic people who seized power in Iran at the outset of the sixteenth century, cemented ties to their Persian subjects by converting them from Sunni to Shi'i Islam. For this purpose they recruited Shi'i *ulema* (religious scholars) from what are now Bahrain, Lebanon, and Iraq and lavished them with patronage. In return, the ulema propagated a religious doctrine that emphasized subordination to established authority, thereby reinforcing the Safavid claim to rule.

Four and a half centuries later, Gamal Abdel Nasser of Egypt sought to enhance his powers by championing Arab nationalism and Arab socialism. A man of action rather than words, he delegated the important but mundane tasks of formulating ideology and reconciling it with specific political decisions to *apparatchiks* (party professionals), who previously had perfected their skills when working in radical opposition organizations, such as the Communist Party. In 1962 Saudi Arabia, entering into a military struggle with Egypt in North Yemen and into a broader ideological confrontation with radical Arab nationalism, founded the Muslim League. Its primary purpose was to stimulate Islamic consciousness and, in so doing, to undercut the appeal of radical secularist ideologies, including Nasser's versions of Arab nationalism and socialism. The Muslim League and its successors, the Islamic Pact (formed in 1966) and the Islamic Conference Organization (created in 1972) were staffed with religious functionaries who might be thought of as equivalents to Nasser's secular apparatchiks.[8]

---

[8]On these Islamic organizations see Malcolm H. Kerr, *The Arab Cold War: Gamal'Abdal-Nasir and His Rivals, 1958–1970* (London: Oxford University Press, 1971), pp. 106–114.

In the wake of the second Gulf war, Galal Amin, an Egyptian academic with a wry sense of humor, identified the qualities that Arab rulers desire in their intellectuals. Shaikh Jabir al-Ahmad al-Sabah of Kuwait requires those who can "evoke Islam, but in moderate dosage and without the least hint of any socialist or Arab nationalist shading." Intellectuals serving King Fahd of Saudi Arabia must be especially knowledgeable about the Quran, particularly "words related to the punishment on the day of atonement . . . while able to skirt any mention of foreign and domestic policy, Israel, or the situation of the mass of Muslims in Saudi Arabia itself." King Hussein of Jordan required virtually acrobatic skills of those who served him, so that the delicate balances that sustained his kingdom were not jeopardized. For this advocate "there is nothing wrong with Arab nationalism, socialism and even Israel, provided all this talk is academic in nature and remote from current affairs and any critique of a specific Arab government." In Egypt intellectual hypocrisy in support of the regime "is full of light spirit and good cheer. . . . Both the hypocrite and the subject of hypocrisy are not taken seriously. . . . They function rather like the singer at weddings who celebrates the beauty of the bride while everyone knows that she is very ugly."[9]

The considerable resources expended by the Safavids, Nasser, the Saudis, and others to disseminate religious beliefs or political ideologies (and in this context there is no real difference between the two) bespeak the comparative absence of structural legitimacy of their governments. Structural legitimacy—or what Max Weber has termed "rational-legal authority"—obtains when rules, supported by institutions to enforce them, underpin popular acceptance of government.[10] Such legitimacy is weak in the Middle East. New rulers must somehow solve the problem of how "some men come to be credited with the right to rule over others."[11] Their task is complicated by ethnic, linguistic, and religious diversity. In nine countries in the Middle East, such minorities constitute at least 25 percent of the population. In Syria, Lebanon, Bahrain, and Iraq, religious minorities control the government. In four Arab states bordering the Persian Gulf, resident aliens significantly outnumber citizens.[12] Nevertheless, the heterogeneity of Middle Eastern populations and its consequences for ideological fragmentation and instability can be overstated. Unifying roles are also played by the predominant language and religion. Arabic, despite local dialects and a sharp distinction between its written and spoken forms, is the mother tongue of the overwhelming majority of residents of Arab countries. In fact, as ranked by linguistic diversity, Arab countries "are among the most homogeneous in the

---

[9]Galal Amin, "The Arab Intellectual and the Crisis in the Gulf," *The Arabs and the Calamity of Kuwait* (Cairo: Madbuli, 1991), pp. 50–57, cited in Raymond Baker, "Imagining Egypt in the New International Order," paper delivered to the annual conference of the Middle East Studies Association of North America (Washington, D.C.: November 23–26, 1991), pp. 26–27.

[10]Max Weber, *The Theory of Social and Economic Organization* (New York: Oxford University Press, 1947), pp. 130–132.

[11]Clifford Geertz, "The Politics of Meaning," *The Interpretation of Cultures* (New York: Basic Books, 1973), p. 317.

[12]R. D. McLaurin, "Minorities and Politics in the Middle East: An Introduction," *The Political Role of Minority Groups*, pp. 1–16.

world."[13] Only Iraq, which is about one-quarter Kurdish, is more linguistically fragmented than the majority of the world's nation-states. Islam is another unifying force, being the predominant religion in all states of the region except Israel. So the linguistic and religious bonds that unite most people of the region have often been drawn upon to reinforce political ideologies. Persisting ideological instability and fragmentation must, therefore, be accounted for by causes other than those of ethnic, linguistic, and religious differences.

Ideology and State Formation

The historical development of European ideologies provides a precedent that may be useful in understanding the development of political beliefs in the Middle East. From the time of the French Revolution up to the twentieth century, numerous ideologies contended for supremacy on the European continent. Various nationalisms and versions of democracy, fascism, socialism, and communism emerged as Europe was being carved into its present configuration of nation-states. Indeed, it was the very process of state formation, including the mobilization of citizens, the creation of national economies, and the construction of legitimate political orders that both required and gave birth to those ideologies. These processes were highly conflictual. As Europe was developing its state system and accompanying ideologies, it was wracked with what amounted to almost perpetual civil war from the Napoleonic era until 1945. Since 1989 the state system established by Soviet communism in Eastern Europe has been unraveling, and competitive nationalisms have been reemerging.

The Middle East today is wrestling with the same problems of state formation that have confronted Europe. The states of the Fertile Crescent, which extends from the southeastern Mediterranean coast northward into Syria and down the Tigris and Euphrates rivers into Iraq, were created as a result of the dissolution of the Ottoman Empire and were immediately placed under British or French control. Other countries in the region, including Egypt, Iran, Turkey, and those on the Arabian Peninsula, at the very least had their borders determined through the intervention of imperial powers. In some cases they were entirely the creations of such interventions. All these countries have confronted the interlocking tasks of nation- and state-building. The former is the process whereby a sense of shared national identity, patriotism, and loyalty to homeland develops. State-building refers more specifically to the construction of governmental and political institutions.

The more artificial the country, the more difficult are the challenges of nation- and state-building. Countries of the Fertile Crescent, for example, were carved out of the Ottoman Empire in accordance with British and French desires. National aspirations and identities of residents were not coterminous with state boundaries. To some of these residents, the idea of *nation* referred to their

---

[13]Hudson, *Arab Politics*, p. 38.

specific ethnic or religious groups, many of which, as the result of new nation-states having been created, were fragmented, scattered among two or more countries of the region. The Druze were divided among Syria, Lebanon, and Palestine. Kurds, whose nationalist aspirations were frustrated despite their having been supported by President Woodrow Wilson at the Versailles Peace Conference, were left scattered as described above. To many Arabs, the division of their heartland into several small sovereign units, each under the control of Europeans, was a violation of the promise of a united Arab nation made by the British to induce Arab leaders to revolt against the Ottoman Turks during World War I. In their eyes, this fragmentation was also against the natural order of things. To these nationalists, because the region was populated primarily by Arabs it should therefore constitute a single Arab state. Given this array of subnational and transnational identities competing with the new states for the loyalties of their residents, it was inevitable that the Fertile Crescent would become an arena for ideological confrontation. This tendency was further aggravated by Zionist claims on Palestine and, after 1948, by the presence of Israel in the midst of Arab states.

New governments struggled to establish their ideological hegemony over competitive calls for loyalty and identity, a struggle that they have gradually been winning but that is not yet over. Ba'thist ideology, for example, with which the contemporary governments of Syria and Iraq seek to legitimate themselves, originally and unambiguously elevated the principles of Arab nationalism and Arab unity to primacy of place. The concept of *al-qawmiyyat al-Arabiyya,* or loyalty to the generalized Arab nation, was ideally, in Ba'thism, preeminent over *wataniyya,* which is patriotism centered on a specific state. Arab states, in Ba'thist terminology, are still referred to as *aqtar* or *iqlim* (regions.) The term *nation* remains reserved for the Arab world as a whole, but this terminology now has little practical significance. Indeed, since the mid- to late 1970s, the leaders of both Iraq and Syria have increasingly emphasized the indigenous in official historiographies. In Iraq this has meant ascribing an Arab character to all ancient Mesopotamian civilizations, which is a straight-out fabrication, while in Syria it is manifested by references to Greater Syria, a historical-geographical unit centered on today's Syria, Lebanon, Jordan, and Israel. In short, *wataniyya* is displacing *qawmiyya* in Ba'thist ideology.[14] In Lebanon, loyalty to religious sects—or what, as a result of European influence, came to be called confessions—has seriously eroded patriotism focused on the nation-state. In Jordan, the most artificial of the Fertile Crescent states and one whose very existence is challenged by the commitment of its large Palestinian population to Palestinian nationalism, loyalty to the ruling royal family is engendered as the principal element in an otherwise comparatively diffuse and weak nationalism.

For Turkey, Iran, and Egypt, the nation-building process has been easier. Their peoples have stronger national identities based on impressive historical records of accomplishment and traditions of administrative autonomy. For the

---

[14]Amatzia Baram, "Territorial Nationalism in the Arab World," *Middle Eastern Studies* 26 (October 1990): 425–448.

Turks, the dissolution of the Ottoman Empire provided the opportunity to re-define the remaining geographical core of that entity based on Anatolia as a modern nation-state. Turkish ethnicity was substituted for Islam as the means by which the nation-state was legitimated. Pan-Ottomanism, an unsuccessful nineteenth-century attempt to foster a European-style secular nationalism to in-tegrate the multiethnic, religiously diverse, and disintegrating empire, was abandoned. Iran is centered on a Persian-speaking people who have for millen-nia inhabited the central plateau area of that country and who constitute a ma-jority of the population. While constructing an identity to serve as the basis for their nation-state, Iranians drew upon both the legacy of a monarchical, imper-ial tradition that predates Islam and the distinctive Shi'i faith that has for almost five centuries set off Iran from its neighbors. Similarly Egypt, unlike the Arab states in the Fertile Crescent, has a long if intermittent history of governmental autonomy, to say nothing of a remarkable civilization of antiquity whose remains provide visible reminders of what was once achieved.

Yet even for Turkey, Iran, and Egypt, nation-building has not been without difficulties and sudden, dramatic changes of course. Turkey has not resolved the contradictions resultant from basing national identity squarely on secularism and Turkish ethnicity. This definition is unacceptable to significant numbers of committed Muslims who want Islam to be enshrined as the state's religion. Simi-larly, emphasis on Turkish language and ethnicity relegates Kurds to what is at best an ambiguous status. Thus, Islamic revivalism and Kurdish militancy both pose threats to the definition of Turkish national identity.

Reza Shah and his son, Muhammad Reza Shah, like Turkey's Mustafa Kemal (Ataturk), were ardent secularists who sought to construct an Iranian national identity on non-Islamic foundations, which included both European ideas of na-tionalism and references to ancient Persia. Ayatollah Khomeini and his support-ers challenged that conceptualization of Iranian nationalism, legitimating their revolution and the government it established solely on the basis of Shi'i Islam.

Egypt has had persisting problems reconciling national and transnational ideologies. In the first quarter of this century, an Egyptian nationalism centered on that state, and its native Arabic-speaking inhabitants, inspired the anticolo-nial movement. At the end of the 1930s, the spread of Arab nationalism in the Fertile Crescent, combined with the increasingly violent confrontation between Arabs and Jews in Palestine, stimulated in Egypt the growth of Arabism. It was that sentiment that Nasser, after 1952, enshrined as the central feature of his na-tionalist, or, more accurately, transnationalist ideology. While Anwar Sadat and, to a much lesser extent, Husni Mubarak worked to displace Arab nationalism with an Egyptian-centered patriotism, the growing trend of Islamic fundamen-talism now offers a new transnationalist ideological challenge to the Egyptian government.

In the Arab states of the Fertile Crescent, nation-building has confronted greater obstacles and suffered more setbacks than it has in Turkey, Iran, and Egypt. Subnational, national, and transnational ideologies continue to compete for the loyalties of Lebanese, Syrians, Iraqis, Palestinians, and Jordanians. Many observers believe, however, that in the struggle to establish ideological he-gemony, the Arab states are all gradually eroding minoritarian identities at the subnational level and defeating appeals by secular Arab nationalists and Islamic radicals to forge loyalties at the transnational level. Pan-Arabism, according to Fouad Ajami, "is nearing its end, if it is not already a thing of the past. . . . Now . . . *raison d'état,* once an alien and illegitimate doctrine, is gaining ground. Slowly and grimly with a great deal of anguish, a 'normal' state system is becoming a fact of life."[15] Abdul-Monem al-Mashat argues that the Arab world as a manifestation of the pan-Arab ideal is disintegrating, while William R. Brown describes the Arab nation as dying while, phoenix-like, Arab states are emerging from it.[16] Others, however, are not so sure. Walid Khalidi contends that in the doctrine of pan-Arabism *"raison d'état* is heresy," for in comparison with the "super-legitimacy" of pan-Arabism the legitimacy of individual Arab states "shrinks into irrelevance."[17] Hassan Nafaa argues that "a workable pan-Arab system of states based on the concept of *raison d'état* is hardly conceivable" because of the various conflicts between those states and because the ideology of pan-Arabism remains vibrant and motivating.[18] In a survey conducted between 1977 and 1979 of 6,000 residents of ten Arab countries, 78.5 percent of respondents said they believed in the existence of an Arab entity, and 77.9 percent agreed that this entity constitutes one nation; 53 percent believed that this nation is divided by artificial borders.[19] *Al-Mustaqbal al-Arabi,* a prominent Arabic journal, editorialized that the failure of the Arab State . . . in achieving true independence [and] . . . in liberating the occupied Arab territories in Palestine . . . will sooner or later strengthen the Arab citizen's conviction that the state has failed to achieve the major objectives it has set for itself. Consequently, this same Arab citizen will be inclined to work at a national [pan-Arab] level and transcend the local state phenomenon.[20]

There are, then, doubts as to whether the Arab world (and the Middle East more generally) is progressing toward the emergence of a regional political system founded on coherent states legitimated by nationalist ideologies, capable of sustaining productive, nonconflictual interstate relations while rejecting transnational appeals for unification. This should not be surprising. The Middle East, in comparison to Europe, is in relatively early stages of state- and nation-building. That does not mean, however, that those processes will exactly parallel

---

[15]Fouad Ajami, "The End of Pan-Arabism," *Foreign Affairs* 57 (Winter 1978–1979): 355–373.

[16]Abdul-Monem Al-Mashat, "Stress and Disintegration in the Arab World," and William R. Brown, "The Dying Arab Nation," in *Pan-Arabism and Arab Nationalism,* pp. 165–176 and 152–164, respectively.

[17]Walid Khalidi, "Thinking the Unthinkable: A Sovereign Palestinian State," *Foreign Affairs* 56 (July 1978): 695–696.

[18]Hassan Nafaa, "Arab Nationalism: A Response to Ajami's Thesis on the 'End of Pan-Arabism,'" in *Pan-Arabism and Arab Nationalism,* pp. 133–151.

[19]Saad al-Din Ibrahim, *The Trends of Arab Public Opinion Toward the Issue of Unity* (Beirut: Center for Arab Unity Studies, 1980) (in Arabic), cited in Bahgat Korany, "Alien and Besieged Yet Here to Stay: The Contradictions of the Arab Territorial State," in *The Foundations of the Arab State,* pp. 53–54.

[20]K. Hasib, "The Words of *al-Mustaqbal al-Arabi,*" in *al-Mustaqbal al-Arabi* 73 (1985): 7, cited in Ghassan Salamé, "'Strong' and 'Weak' States: A Qualified Return to the Muqaddimah," *The Foundations of the Arab State,* p. 226.

those of Europe. Middle Eastern socioeconomic and political systems prior to the rise of nation-states were fundamentally different from those of Europe. The methods that have been followed in building nation-states also differ. To understand contemporary Middle Eastern ideologies, therefore, one must look in greater detail at the nature of political beliefs prior to the establishment of the modern state system and then at the process by which those nation-states have been formed.

Premodern, Preideological Phase

According to Max Weber, a state is a "compulsory political association with continuous organization [whose] administrative staff successfully uphold a claim to the monopoly of legitimate use of force in the enforcement of its order . . . within a given territorial area."[21] Other definitions of the term typically stress powers to implement laws and extract taxes and to command the loyalty and allegiance of citizens.[22] States vary in strength according to their capacity to regulate the behavior of citizens and their ability to remain autonomous from those social forces that seek to capture the state and use it for their own purposes. These social forces can be classes, ethnic and religious groups, tribes, or other units. A state must extract enough revenue in order to pay for armies, bureaucracies, and the other structures that support it. According to Giacomo Luciani, "A state structure will tend to be stable in history if it commands sufficient resources to guarantee its own survival."[23] In the Middle East prior to the nineteenth century, the viability of states, as measured by their longevity and degree of control over what was nominally their territory, was highly variable. This was due both to the comparative scarcity of resources and to the segmented, unmobilized nature of society, which impeded the state's access to the resources that did exist. Wealth in the premodern Middle East tended to be generated more from long-distance trade than from agriculture, which itself was extensive rather than intensive except in the Nile Valley and along the eastern Mediterranean coast. By its nature, trade was an activity that governments had difficulty controlling and taxing. Extracting a surplus from agricultural production when farming was widely scattered and mainly at a subsistence level was likely to cost the state more than it would obtain in revenues. The relatively harsh climate, presence of mountains, deserts, and other significant geographical obstacles to transportation and communication, and a general absence of adequate roads further raised the cost to governments for extraction and regulation. *Bedouin*

---

[21]Weber, *The Theory of Social and Economic Organization*, p. 154.

[22]See, for example, the definition offered by Iliya Harik, "The Origins of the Arab State System," in *The Foundations of the Arab State*, p. 23. For a discussion of definition of the term *state* and the application of that concept to the Middle East, see Bahgat Korany, "Alien and Besieged Yet Here to Stay," pp. 47–74.

[23]Giacomo Luciani, "Allocation vs. Production States: A Theoretical Framework," in *The Rentier State*, ed. by Hazem Beblawi and Giacomo Luciani (London: Croom Helm, 1987), p. 64.

(tribally organized nomads), who in the premodern period constituted about one-fifth of the population of the Middle East, were particularly resistant to governmental control. Even settled urban dwellers, however, were insulated from the weak states that presided over them by a far more dense and complex network of kinship connections than was the case in premodern Europe.

Forced to extract revenues in circumstances of limited and intermittent control over populations and territories, governments developed second-best strategies of indirect taxation. One of them was to hold ethnic, religious, tribal, and other groups responsible for payment of taxes, leaving it to the communities' leaders to collect them. Another method of raising revenue was to rely on *multazims,* or tax farmers. The state would grant *iltizams* (farms) in return for payment of taxes, which the multazims would extract from peasants. These arrangements enabled governments to raise revenues when otherwise none might have been collected. They were inefficient, however, because those individuals who were placed between governments and taxpayers—whether multazims or local notables—retained as high a proportion of revenue as possible for their own use. The pecuniary interests of such middlemen demanded that they seek to weaken government.[24]

Geographical, economic, and social conditions thus limited interactions between rulers and ruled to far fewer transactions than occur in a modern nation-state. Prevailing beliefs about the proper relationship between ruler and ruled reinforced this loose relationship. That system of belief was founded in Islam.

ISLAMIC DOCTRINE AND ORGANIZATION

Like other religions, Islam is at the same time theological and sociological. It is comprised of both religious doctrine and patterns of social, including political, relationships.[25] The creed of Islam is straightforward and universalistic. The message of the Prophet Muhammad to the residents of Mecca, whose beliefs in the early seventh century were shaped by animistic and totemistic religions as well as by Christianity and Judaism, was that God had last revealed himself to humanity by issuing through Muhammad the Quran. That volume, compiled after Muhammad's death, in conjunction with the *hadith,* the teachings and sayings attributed to Muhammad, the compiled form of which is called the *sunna* (tradi-

---

[24]As late as the mid-nineteenth century the Ottoman annual land tax (*miri*) was collected primarily through middlemen. The consequences of this indirect method are described by Samir Khalaf as follows:

> Officially, the *miri* was supposed to be levied upon all sown land . . . yet neither in its assessment nor collection was the system consistent or regular. Indeed, the tribute was arbitrarily set and varied considerably with changing circumstances. Rather than being proportional to wealth, the *miri* was often a reflection of the amir's power or special standing vis-à-vis the Ottoman Pasha.

Samir Khalaf, *Lebanon's Predicament* (New York: Columbia University Press, 1987), p. 26.

[25]Suad Joseph, "Muslim-Christian Conflicts: A Theoretical Perspective," in *Muslim-Christian Conflicts: Economic, Political, and Social Origins,* ed. by Suad Joseph and Barbara L. K. Pillsbury (Boulder, Colo.: Westview Press, 1979), pp. 1–45.

tions), together constitute the sources for the *sharia* (Islamic law). Conversion to Islam, which literally means the surrender of man to God (Allah), requires only the profession of the faith *(shahada)*: "There is no god but God and Muhammad is the messenger (prophet) of God." The requirements of the faith, its "five pillars," are the shahada, *salat* (prayer), *sawm* (fasting) during the month of Ramadan, *zakat* (almsgiving), and making the *hajj* (pilgrimage) to Mecca at least once during a lifetime.

The simplicity of Islamic doctrine and the ease of conversion to the religion are essential to its universalism. It is intended not as the religion of a specific tribe, group, or nation of peoples or as a faith delineated by specific territory but as a religion appropriate anywhere to which anyone may convert. The period prior to the revelation of God's message to Muhammad in the early seventh century is known to Muslims as the *jahiliyya* (age of ignorance), in which tribal and other particularistic loyalties divided humanity. Islam is thus meant not only to rescue individuals from personal ignorance but also to serve as an antidote to sociopolitical incoherence and conflict.

This universalism in Islam has for politics been a two-edged sword. It facilitated Islam's expansion from the Arabian Peninsula to Indonesia in the east and the Iberian Peninsula in the west, from being a religion of the Arabs to being a faith that now encompasses members of virtually all of the world's major ethnolinguistic groupings and claims one billion adherents. On the other hand, unlike some other religions that are associated with a specific tribe or ethnic group, such as Judaism, or that are nonproselytizing, such as the heterodox Druze faith, Islam, once it had spread beyond the confines of Arabia, no longer benefited from reinforcing tribal, ethnic, or other solidarities. The socioreligious identity that characterizes Muslims is that they are members of the *umma al-Islamiyya,* the community of believers. Unlike adherents to the "political religions" of secular European nationalisms, who identify themselves with reference to a specific territory and state, members of the Islamic *umma* do not constitute a state, nor is their faith associated with any specific land. Islamic doctrine, therefore, is, strictly speaking, incompatible with nationalism, which refers to a specific people in a particular place.[26] Nationalism to Muslims, according to P. J. Vatikiotis, "implies a pre-Islamic kind of tribal particularism, jahiliyya."[27] The political cost of Islamic universalism has been high. "The most closely integrated states are those with a *raison d'[ê]tre* . . . a 'state idea.'" Such an idea "convinces all the people in all the regions (of the state) that they belong together."[28] Zionism, which is the nationalist ideology of Jews, has clear advantages over Islam because it is focused on territory. This is hardly surprising, for Zionism was heavily influenced by European nationalisms, which are themselves powerful state ideas defining common national identities with reference to

[26]Hamid Enayat, *Modern Islamic Political Thought* (Austin: University of Texas Press, 1982), pp. 111–159.

[27]P. J. Vatikiotis, *Islam and the State* (London: Croom Helm, 1987), p. 10.

[28]Alasdair Drysdale and Gerald H. Blake, *The Middle East and North Africa: A Political Geography* (New York: Oxford University Press, 1985), p. 178.

place of residence. In the Islamic Middle East, however, "The nation is considered in religious terms to encompass those beyond and across the territorial boundaries of the individual states. There is a constant clash between the exigencies of the modern territorial state, and the wider nation, or community of believers."[29] While James Piscatori's argument is correct that Muslim political authorities have throughout history accommodated themselves to the reality of statehood, he underemphasizes the fact that the idealized myth of the Islamic umma remains potent.[30] The unresolved paradox of Islamic universalism and a world composed of nation-states periodically assumes political importance, as exemplified by the transnational appeals of the Islamic Republic of Iran and by indictments of sovereignty and nationalism as heretical in Islam by such Islamic activists as Ayatollah Khomeini and the Egyptian Muslim Brother, Sayyid Qutb.[31] There remains, in short, a continuing disjunction between the theory of Islam and the practice of the nation-state.

The universalism of Islam complicated the task of forging a compelling state idea from its doctrine. So too has its political theory caused problems for those who seek to draw upon Islamic doctrine in creating nation-states. The implementation of God's will, which is the principal obligation of Muslims, is not exclusively an individual act. It requires the creation of a social order that operates by Islamic precepts. Accordingly, there is ideally no separation between religion and politics—Islam is both *din wa dawla* (religion and state). In historical reality, however, Christian and Islamic doctrine did not lead to sharply different forms of government. Caliphs (successors to the prophet) had, by the tenth century, become subordinate to sultans, secular leaders whose authority rested primarily on their political power and only secondarily on their religious legitimacy. Since that time and even before, theocratic government in the Middle East has been notable by its absence. Nevertheless, Islam's insistence on the unity of individuals' personal, social, and political life has meant that although outright secular government that explicitly denies Islam's relevance to politics began to take shape in the Middle East from the early nineteenth century, its reconciliation with Islamic doctrine—hence its legitimacy—has never been completely accomplished.

A second aspect of Islamic political theory that has proven difficult to accommodate to the idea of the nation-state is its treatment of the relationship between rulers and ruled. Elegantly simple and well suited to the requirements of the *umma al-mu'minin* (community of believers) when it consisted of Muhammad and his followers, Islam enjoins believers to "Obey God, obey his Prophet, and obey those in authority over you." This fifty-ninth verse from the fourth *sura* (chapter) of the Quran points to a fundamental difference between the concep-

---

[29]Vatikiotis, *Islam and the State,* p. 13.

[30]James A. Piscatori, *Islam in a World of Nation-States* (Cambridge: Cambridge University Press, 1986).

[31]Qutb denounces *al-hakmiyya* (sovereignty) in his most famous work, *Ma'alim Fi al-Tariq (Signs Along the Path)* (Cairo: Wahba Books, 1964) (in Arabic). For an analysis of Qutb's writings, see Gilles Kepel, *Muslim Extremism in Egypt: The Prophet and the Pharaoh* (Berkeley and Los Angeles: University of California Press, 1986), pp. 43–52.

tion of legitimate government in Islam and that in the contemporary Western world. In Western systems, sovereignty in theory resides with the people who are, therefore, the ultimate authority to which government is responsible. In Islam, sovereignty rests with God, to whom both rulers and ruled alike are responsible. While rulers, like their subjects, are bound by the provisions of the sharia, in the historical absence of institutions to constrain arbitrary rulers, their nominal subordination to religious law was often meaningless.

In the early days of Islam, the issue of mutual obligations between rulers and ruled was a subject of lively controversy and debate. By the twelfth century, however, the sultanate was so ascendant over the barely surviving caliphate that Islamic scholars, including the renowned al-Ghazali (died 1111), devised justifications for that reality. The community of the faithful was enjoined to obey its ruler simply because the alternative was chaos. This particular resolution of the dilemma besetting relationships between ruler and ruled was not, however, quite the end of the story. Precisely because it so tilted the balance in favor of the sultan, there subsequently arose extreme statements of the rights of the ruled. In the early fourteenth century Ahmad Ibn Taymiyya, a "religious firebrand" in Cairo and Damascus, to whom the political philosophies of numerous contemporary Islamic activists have been traced, preached that Islam justified the right to rebel against unjust rulers.[32] He was executed in 1328 by the Mamlukes then ruling Egypt. Since that time, there have been attempts to resuscitate doctrines similar to those propounded by Ibn Taymiyya, but the major thrust of Islamic political theory and practice has continued in the direction charted by al-Ghazali, who emphasized the obligation of obedience to authority. While that underpinning for government sufficed in the premodern period, appeals for obedience are inadequate bases for legitimacy for nation-states seeking to penetrate their societies to a much greater degree. Increasingly that legitimacy depends on the perceived effectiveness of political participation by citizens.

Even in religiously conservative Saudi Arabia, the issue of whether sovereignty derives from Allah or the people has become of paramount political importance. In the wake of the second Gulf war, King Fahd, seeking to reduce discontent caused by the war and his authoritarian rule, declared that a sixty-member *majlis al-shura* (consultative council) would be created. He reserved the right to appoint all members to that council to himself, however, claiming, "The democratic system prevailing in the world does not suit us in this region. . . . The system of free elections is not part of Islamic ideology." Secularized, liberal Saudis contested the king's assertion on the grounds that Islam has long recognized democratic practices and noted that even the Islamic Republic of Iran has a 270-seat elected parliament. For their part, ultrareligious Saudis argued against Fahd on the grounds that proper Islamic government requires true *shura* (consultation), which can only be ensured through elections. Muham-

---

[32]On the influence of Ibn Taymiyya on contemporary Islamic activists, see, for example, Emmanuel Sivan, *Radical Islam: Medieval Theology and Modern Politics* (New Haven: Yale University Press, 1985), pp. 94–107. The term *religious firebrand* is his.

mad Hudaibi, leader of the Egyptian Muslim Brotherhood, when asked if Saudi Arabia was a true Islamic society replied, "Of course not, because it does not have an elected government."[33]

Radical Islamic activists are divided among themselves over the issue of whether Islam does or does not require democracy of a Western sort. A spokesperson for Rashid Ghannouchi, head of *al-Nahda* (The Renaissance), the leading Tunisian Islamicist party, argues that "in Islam and in the Koran, the idea of liberty is fundamental. . . . [T]he closest political system to Islam is the democratic system of the West—especially the American Constitution." Ali Benhadj, on the other hand, a prominent figure in an equivalent Islamicist political party in Algeria, has stated that "Democracy is apostasy."[34]

The relative absence of a lexicon of democratic terminology in the major Middle Eastern languages associated with Islam, which are Arabic, Persian, and Turkish, reflects Islam's different conceptualizations of sovereignty and relations between government and the governed. These languages in their classical forms did not have a term for *citizen*. The neologism *muwatan* was coined in the nineteenth century.[35] When confronted with the task of finding a term to convey the meaning of freedom, the Arabic translators of Napoleon's famous declaration to the Egyptian people upon his arrival there in 1798 used the word *hurriyya,* which previously was a term used to distinguish free men from slaves.[36] In Turkish and Arabic, the word now used for independence, *istiqlal,* prior to the latter half of the nineteenth century was principally an Ottoman administrative term that meant "to act alone," referring to the discretionary powers of high officials.[37] In addition to coining terms to apply to concepts of government that were introduced in the eighteenth and nineteenth centuries, Muslim proponents of democracy began to "scour religious literature in search of prescriptions for the rights of the individual and checks on state power."[38] Rifa'a Tahtawi (1801–1873), for example, after a traditional education in Egypt, went to Paris as part of a mission sent by Muhammad Ali. He returned to Cairo and spent much of the remainder of his life reconciling Islam with Western notions of democracy. Tahtawi contended, for example, that the French idea of freedom had its equivalent in the Islamic concept of *adl* (justice, right, equality).[39] This exercise and others like it, however, tended to treat Quranic verses out of context and to stretch analogies, suggesting in the process that classical Islamic political doctrine and European democratic theory were quite different. The organization of Islam, like its political doctrine, has also not made the tasks of state- and nation-building any easier. There is, for example, no organizational equivalent in

---

[33]Caryle Murphy, "Saudi Arabia: A True Islamic Society?" *Washington Post* (April 28, 1992), p. 2.

[34]Cited in James Walsh, "The Sword of Islam," *Time* (June 15, 1992), pp. 30, 34.

[35]Enayat, *Modern Islamic Political Thought,* p. 126.

[36]Bernard Lewis, *The Political Language of Islam* (Chicago: University of Chicago Press, 1988), pp. 109–111.

[37]Ibid., p. 112.

[38]Enayat, *Modern Islamic Political Thought,* p. 131.

[39]Ibid., p. 131.

Sunni Islam to the Christian church. The ulema, not having an organization autonomous of government, seldom imposed their will on political authorities. "Unwilling to admit the de facto dualism of religious and political affairs to which they had accommodated themselves," the ulema had to adopt a discourse that "tended to be expressive, defending the status quo, rather than practical, instigating fundamental change."[40] While they occasionally mobilized portions of the population, as they did against the Napoleonic invasion of Egypt at the end of the eighteenth century and as they did more frequently in Shi'i Iran, the ulema generally lacked the organizational structure necessary to institutionalize their leadership and power, and so to constrain government. Moreover, while the church served as a model for secular political organization in the West, the absence of an equivalent organization in Sunni Islam meant that secular groupings had no archetype to emulate.

Islamic doctrine and the comparative weakness of the religion's formal organizational structure do not alone account for the absence in the premodern Middle East of a "prolific network of institutions . . . between the state and the individual . . . which simultaneously connects the individual to authority and protects the individual from total political control," thereby creating what has been termed "civil society."[41] Indeed, in the Middle East prior to the rise of modern nation-states, subjects were in any case protected from "total political control" by a rich array of family, tribal, communal, and other groupings. The power of government over individuals was checked by these cohesive social units as well as by the physical barriers mentioned earlier. It is true, however, that there were comparatively few linkages between those traditional organizations and government. Their role was not so much to participate in government to affect decisions but rather to avoid its reach. When governments, as a result of technological modernization, eventually did obtain the resources required to subdue farflung populations, the traditional organizations of these peoples were simultaneously being undermined through the broader processes of modernization; thus were societies deprived of at least some of the network of institutions that comprise civil society and that both protect individuals and link them to government.

The degree to which Islam contributed to the weakness of civic organization is a highly contentious issue. Some scholars believe that intermediate groups situated between individuals and rulers confronted an impossibly difficult task in limiting arbitrary authority precisely because of Islamic theory and practice. Charles E. Butterworth argues, for example, that there is an absence of democracy in the Arab world.

> There is nothing within the history of Arabic political thought comparable to the radical break with the past effected by Machiavelli and Hobbes in the sixteenth and seventeenth centuries and then refined into a doctrine of liberal democracy. . . . In

---

[40]Moore, "On Theory and Practice," p. 114.

[41]Bryan S. Turner, "Orientalism and the Problem of Civil Society in Islam," in *Orientalism, Islam, and Islamicists,* ed. by Asaf Hussain et al. (Brattleboro, Vt.: Aman Books, 1984), p. 27.

sum, then, the absence of an unquestioned, perhaps unquestionable, belief in the fundamental need for popular sovereignty is what primarily explains why political life in the Arab world differs so markedly from political life in the west."[42]

Other scholars deny that differences in religious doctrine and organization account for the presence of an established tradition of legitimate opposition to arbitrary governments in the West and the absence of such a tradition in Islam. Civil society in the West is said to have developed because of the prior existence of legal rights for vassals in feudalism and because a strong, independent middle class emerged comparatively early in Europe.[43] Their equivalents were lacking in the Middle East. Also, prior to the nineteenth century in the Middle East, government was limited and remote, hardly affecting the lives of a great number of its nominal subjects. "It is a recurring historical truth," according to Hazem Beblawi and Giacomo Luciani, "that demands for democratic participation become louder, sometimes unrestrainable, whenever the state must ask for sacrifices, be they under the form of increased revenue or reduced expenditure."[44] In the West, such demands for participation arose much earlier than in the Middle East because from the end of the feudal era in the fourteenth century, the state began to acquire significant fiscal powers. It was not until the nineteenth and even twentieth centuries, however, that the unquestioned supremacy of government over financial and other matters made it the central focus for its subjects in the Middle East. Even though Islam regulates the daily lives of most Middle Easterners and profoundly influences their beliefs and attitudes, politics is too complex a phenomenon to be determined entirely by religion, even such an all-embracing one as Islam. Socioeconomic factors have constituted a major contribution to the development of political authority structures and attitudes toward them, but precisely how and to what degree is difficult to determine. What can be said with certainty is that in the premodern Middle East, prior to the emergence of nation-states that regulate comparatively closely the affairs of their citizens, there was a functioning system of government that worked remarkably well and in which Islam played an important role. According to Ira Lapidus, this system was "composed at base of small-scale, local communities unified by an embracing religious affiliation—Islam . . . and organized and identified in lineage, tribal, and ethnic terms."[45] In the words of Albert Hourani, pre-

---

[42]Charles E. Butterworth, "State and Authority in Arabic Political Thought" in *The Foundations of the Arab State*, pp. 91–92, 111.

[43]See, for example, Turner, "Orientalism," p. 35, and Enayat, *Modern Islamic Political Thought*, pp. 131–135. According to Ira Lapidus, under feudalism, vassals had "rights to be consulted, rights to be judged by peers and guarantees as to their incomes and properties. All of these are the basis of our parliamentary notions of democracy and ideas about 'no taxation without representation.' So here is a cultural, conceptual fact which reinforces the institutional differences between the two societies and has favored the formation of European democracies." Personal communication to the authors, September 20, 1988.

[44]"Introduction," in *The Rentier State* (London: Croom Helm, 1987), p. 19.

[45]Ira Lapidus, *Contemporary Islamic Movements in Historical Perspective* (Berkeley: Institute of International Studies of the University of California, 1983), p. 50.

modern Islamic societies comprised "not so much a single community as a group of communities each of which claimed the immediate loyalty of its members. These communities were regional, religious, or functional, or, to some extent, a mixture of all three."[46] The political regimes that prevailed over these local communities but only loosely regulated their affairs were comprised of royal courts and bureaucratic as well as quasifeudal institutions, all of which were at least partially legitimated by Islam. Before the rise of the nation-state in the Middle East, Islam did provide the essential ingredients for functioning political systems. It defined sociopsychological identities and presented an explicit code for the conduct of relations between Muslims and non-Muslims. A comprehensive legal system was supplied by the sharia and those ulema, including *qadis* (Muslim judges), skilled in legal interpretation and adjudication. Finally, Islam legitimated the ruler and, to a lesser extent, the system of governance by virtue of the Islamic injunction on subjects to obey established authority. That this system worked well is attested to by the accomplishments of the great Islamic empires, the first of which came into being over 1,300 years ago, and the last of which, the Ottoman, was only finally extinguished in this century. Yet, it is also fair to say that from at least the eighteenth century, the states of the West, increasingly legitimated by nationalist ideologies and capable of mobilizing the energies of their citizens, were far more powerful than Muslim governments of the Middle East. The latter were unable to harness the energies and resources of the remarkably diverse and inward-looking groups of which Middle Eastern societies were composed. The most important of these groups were the various religious communities.

RELIGIOUS DIVERSITY

Sunni and Shi'i Islam   There are two major branches of Islam—Sunni and Shi'i, the former constituting almost 90 percent of the world's Muslims. This division originated in the seventh century as a political dispute between the Shi'a (party or faction) of Ali, the cousin and son-in-law of the prophet Muhammad, and those who opposed his ascension to the caliphate in A.D. 656. The latter became known as Sunnis because of their identification with the Sunna (precedents set by the prophet) and their veneration of the "Golden Age" of Islam under the *Rashidun*, the first four successors (caliphs) to Muhammad (Abu Bakr, Umar, Uthman, and Ali). The Sunnis rose in revolt against the succession of Ali after the murder of the third caliph, Uthman. Mu'awiya, the governor of the Syrian province of the new Arab empire, cousin of Uthman and member of the aristocratic Umayyad family, led the uprising that culminated in A.D. 661 with the defeat of Ali's forces.

Mu'awiya created the Umayyad dynasty (A.D. 661–750), and his son and successor, Yazid, finally ended the possibility that Ali's descendants might ultimately

---

[46]Albert Hourani, *Arabic Thought in the Liberal Age, 1798–1939* (London: Oxford University Press, 1962), p. 29.

regain the caliphate by having Ali's second son, Hussain, and his followers massacred at Karbala (in today's Iraq) in A.D. 680. From that time, differences between Sunnis and Shi'is, which had been confined until then to the issue of the succession to the caliphate, broadened to include ritual, legal, and theological matters. The schism ultimately took on ethnic and geographic dimensions, for over 50 percent of the world's Shi'is now reside in Iran. The other principal concentrations of them in the Middle East are in the Arab littoral countries of the Persian Gulf, including Iraq, Bahrain, Kuwait, the United Arab Emirates, and the Eastern Province of Saudi Arabia, although there are also significant Shi'i communities in Lebanon, North Yemen, and Syria.

Division of the *Dar al-Islam* (House of Islam) into Sunni and Shi'i has through history exacerbated the problems of state-building for Sunnis. With the major exceptions of Fatimid Egypt (A.D. 968–1171) and post-fifteenth-century Iran, as well as intermittently in Yemen in the twentieth century and Syria since the mid-1960s, the Sunnis have led every government in the area. The Ottomans, beset with the difficulties of ruling a far-flung, heterogeneous empire and having constantly to engage in warfare against the West, had also to contend with a condition of more or less permanent hostility with the Shi'i dynasties in Iran—first the powerful Safavids, subsequently the weaker Qajars. Ottoman-Persian relations, in the absence of religious division, may have taken a different course and one less enervating for both sides.

Of greater and more enduring importance to the issue of state formation in Sunni political systems has been the presence within them of groupings of Shi'is. The writ of government has run up to, but until recently not usually beyond, the boundaries of these communities. Their refractory nature resulted from their minority religious status and accompanying anxieties, and from the inherent weakness of premodern Islamic governments in comparison with the strength of Shi'i informal organizations.

The majority of Shi'is are known as Imamis, or Twelvers, because they trace the line of rightful descent from Ali, who is the first Imam, through twelve successors. The last, Muhammad al-Muntazar (Muhammad the Expected), vanished in about A.D. 873 and is expected to return as the *Mahdi* (savior) of humanity at a propitious time. The Twelver sect has adherents in Iran, Lebanon, Iraq, and many Arab countries of the Persian Gulf. In Iran, Twelver Shi'ism is the state religion and the faith of the great majority of the population. Another group of Shi'is, the Isma'ilis, is known as Seveners because they regard Isma'il as the rightful seventh and last Imam. They are to be found principally in Pakistan, India, and Iran, while a few descendants of the Assassins—radical Isma'ilis who opposed Mamluke rule in the twelfth and thirteenth centuries in the Fertile Crescent—are still resident in the coastal mountains of central Syria. Still another sect, the Fivers, who trace a separate line of succession from the fifth Imam, are also known as Zaydis after the founder of the sect, Zayd, a grandson of the martyred Hussain, son of Ali. The Zaydis are to be found principally in Yemen.

The Kharajites are a non-Shi'i sect who broke with Ali and his supporters because of their disapproval of his willingness to compromise with his Umayyad opponents and his desire for the caliphate to be hereditary. Kharajite survivors, known as Ibadi Muslims, established themselves both in Oman, from whence in the eighteenth century they established a sizable empire, and in southern Algeria. The Druze, who currently reside principally in Lebanon, Syria, and Israel, are an offshoot of the Fatimids, who controlled Egypt from the tenth to the twelfth centuries. The Alawis, so named by virtue of their veneration of Ali, who over the past two decades have dominated the Syrian government, are a heterodox sect whose claim to be Shi'i is disputed by some Muslims who consider their profound attachment to Ali, veneration of Jesus, and other of their beliefs to be heretical.

The proliferation of Shi'i sects, each with its own esoteric doctrine to which its supporters frequently adhere with extreme commitment, has rendered governmental control difficult and in some cases impossible. The Assassins are but an extreme case of Shi'i resistance to outside control. Holed up in their mountain redoubts, they fought off Mamluke rule for decades. Such geographical isolation has long characterized Shi'is living in Sunni-ruled lands. The mountains of South Lebanon and coastal Syria, the marshes of southern Iraq, the Jabal Akhdar (Green Mountain) of Oman, the rugged south central area of Anatolia in Turkey, and the oases of southern Algeria are among the traditional bastions of Shi'i and Ibadi preponderance.

In recent years Shi'is have poured out of these peripheral enclaves into the major cities of the Middle East in search of educational, vocational, and other opportunities. Even here, though, they have maintained cohesive communities, which in many instances are within sprawling slums. Like Shi'i societies in the remote areas they left, these new, urban ones are remarkably resistant to governmental control. The poor suburb of al-Thawra in Baghdad, for example, has since the 1960s been a center of Shi'i political activism, providing a constant test of the Iraqi government's control. What have become known in Beirut simply as "the suburbs," by which is meant the southern periphery of that once cosmopolitan Mediterranean city, are, along with the Beqa Valley and the South, the centers of Shi'i strength in Lebanon. The inability of government troops to enter those suburbs during the long-running civil war and continuing reticence to do so provide graphic evidence of how Shi'i communities have through history succeeded in thwarting governmental control. In Bahrain, Kuwait, and the United Arab Emirates, ministates too small for geography to provide a buffer between community and government, Shi'is have erected a dense network of social institutions centered on clubs, homes, mosques, *diwaniyyas* (assemblies), and *hussainiyyas* (centers for mourning). This network performs the function of sharply defining the community's identity and reinforcing its separateness from Sunnis and their government.

Doctrinal elements of Shi'ism have facilitated challenges to Sunni hegemony and frustrated state-building efforts. *Taqiyya*, the practice of disguising one's true beliefs to hide them from a potential oppressor, is a quietist Shi'i response to perceived threats. Activist political behavior is also condoned by Shi'i doctrine, which emphasizes usurpation of power by the Sunnis, the martyrdoms of Imams Ali and Hussain, and the sufferings of Shi'is everywhere. The themes of usurpation and martyrdom, for example, are portrayed vividly in annual Ashura rites, which commemorate the martyrdom of Hussain in the form of a passion play conducted in the streets. Prior to the Islamic revolution in Iran, *ta'ziyyas,* as passion plays are called there, were used as a vehicle of political protest and mobilization. The evil Yazid, the Umayyad caliph who had Hussain killed, was portrayed as being analogous to the shah.[47]

Further reinforcing the solidarity of Shi'is and delineating the border that separates them from Sunnis is the Shi'i theory and practice of *ijtihad* (interpretation). From the beginning of the tenth century, Sunnis tended to restrict further interpretation, so the "door of ijtihad," if not altogether closed, was nearly so. The possibility that theologians and jurists could apply independent, novel reasoning when interpreting the Quran and the Sunna was substantially reduced. Shi'is, on the other hand, never concurred in this conservative step. Their doctrinal tradition emphasized independence. That predisposition was structurally reinforced by the existence of *mujtahids,* which is the term given to Shi'i ulema, or mullahs as they are known in Iran, and means "those who interpret." The practice of *ijtihad* thus underscored the importance to Shi'is of their ulema, providing the need and justification for an independent clergy that Sunni Islam has always lacked. The Shi'i ulema have thus provided an organizational backbone to their religious community and in so doing further enhanced its distinctive and separate nature. This independence has clearly hampered the integrative tasks of state-building of those Sunni-dominated governments that have presided over Shi'is.[48]

But doctrinal differences between Shi'is and Sunnis can be overemphasized. Both are Muslims and as such believe in the same pillars of the faith. There are few sharp divergences in their legal systems. As Bernard Lewis observes, divisions between them are "not as rigid as the differences between Protestants and Catholics, or between the different Protestant churches in Christendom."[49] In communities with but one mosque, for example, Sunnis and Shi'is both pray in it. Among Sunnis there is widespread respect and reverence for Ali and Hussain. So there are enough similarities to facilitate amicable communal relations. Conversely, there are sufficient differences to stimulate antagonisms and conflicts. Which condition prevails is determined more by the larger environment within which Sunni-Shi'i relations are conducted than by factors inherent to the faiths themselves.

Al-Islam al-rasmi versus al-Islam al-sha'bi (Establishment versus Populist Islam) Most religions, and especially scripturalist ones that are founded on a corpus of written doctrine, such as the Quran, the Torah, or the Bible, have both established, official versions and populist, unofficial variants. Establishment religion is that which adheres closely to the ideal as described in texts and interpreted by religious scholars. In many instances it is a state religion and as

---

[47]Peter J. Chelkowski, ed., *Ta'ziyeh: Ritual and Drama in Iran* (New York: New York University Press, 1979).

[48]For an excellent discussion of Shi'i resistance, see Augustus Richard Norton, *Amal and the Shia: Struggle for the Soul of Lebanon* (Austin: University of Texas Press, 1987).

[49]Bernard Lewis, "The Shi'a in Islamic History," in *Shi'ism, Resistance, and Revolution,* ed. by Martin Kramer (Boulder, Colorado: Westview Press, 1987), p. 22.

such is formally bound up in the legitimacy of government.[50] Populist religion, on the other hand, comprises those religious beliefs and practices that prevail among the people; it emanates from the underside, the periphery of society. Residence in outlying provinces or sprawling slums, illiteracy, and other factors that impede access to religious scholars and written texts, distance populations from established religions and make possible the existence of lively populist movements.

Virtually throughout Islamic history, there have been official and populist Islams, and both have political relevance. Muslim rulers have typically sought to cloak themselves in the legitimacy provided by al-Islam al-rasmi. In return for material favors and recognition of their status, the ulema have generally facilitated that legitimation process by using their prerogatives accordingly. Preaching Friday sermons that underscore obedience to authority, issuing *fatwas* (Islamic legal opinions) supportive of governmental policies, and in general by emphasizing the inseparability of Islam and government, the establishment ulema have contributed to the close identification of al-Islam al-rasmi with the government in control.

Relations between governmental power and populist Islam have been more ambivalent. Recognizing the mobilizational capacities of an Islam that is not under the direct control of the ulema and that frequently contains highly emotive beliefs and practices, rulers have been wary of al-Islam al-sha'bi. One approach has been to outlaw various manifestations of it. In the latter half of the nineteenth and early part of the twentieth centuries in Egypt, for example, the government, under pressure from European powers, sought to suppress what it termed the "excesses of popular religion."

Many of these efforts were directed at Sufi *tariqas* (orders), which are brotherhoods of Islamic mystics. Sufism, a search for divine knowledge through the emotions rather than purely through the intellect, emerged in the ninth century as an antidote to the austere, scripturalist, rational nature of Islam. It has always met with an ambivalent response from the ulema, some of whom have opposed Sufism and others of whom have themselves joined *tariqas*. Large orders, such as the Naqshbandiyya, have swept through the Muslim world at various times in history, carrying with them the potential of widespread political mobilization and disruption. It is not surprising, therefore, that Egyptian governments, like many others, sought at early stages in their consolidation of power to bring Sufi orders under control. Initial efforts focused on ridding orders of distinctive practices that reinforced their identities and elicited strong loyalties and sacrifices from their members. Thus the practice of the *shaikh* (leader) of the order riding on horseback over the backs of prostrate members, as well as self-infliction of wounds, was outlawed in the late nineteenth century. The eventual subordination of Sufi orders to the state, however, was accomplished only years later, when a Supreme Council of Sufi Shaikhs was created, over which was

---

[50]The prominent Egyptian writer Fu'ad Zakariyya dubs establishment Islam "Petro-Islam," for it is underpinned by financial subsidies from the conservative, oil-rich Arab states. For a discussion of Zakariyya's indictment of this type of Islam, see Issa J. Boullata, *Trends and Issues in Contemporary Arab Thought* (Albany: State University of New York Press, 1990), pp. 154–157.

appointed a Shaikh of Shaikhs, who in fact is a civil servant responsible to the government in Egypt.

Governments have also enlisted the support of the ulema in condemning various popular beliefs and practices as non- or anti-Islamic. The *zar*, for example, is a public ceremony in which women, led by an exorcist and accompanied by song and dance, seek to counter the influence of *jinns* (evil spirits) and, according to some interpretations, carve out a sphere of female autonomy in a male-dominated society.[51] Zars have long been officially discouraged in Egypt, yet they still occur. Saint worship, which in strict interpretations of Islam is considered irreligious, is nevertheless widespread. One manifestation of it is pilgrimages to tombs of those venerated as saints and whose *baraka* (heavenly blessing, grace, or power) is sought to assist in resolving personal and social problems. Living persons can also be attributed with baraka, which can reinforce claims to political leadership. Muhammad Ahmad, known as the Mahdi, cultivated a popular belief in his baraka to reinforce his leadership of the anti-British uprising in the Sudan in the 1880s. Mu'ammar Qaddafi is an example of someone having more or less failed in the attempt to appear as one possessed of baraka, while former King Hassan of Morocco enjoyed somewhat greater success in a similar effort.

Fitting loosely within the category of populist Islam are those members of the ulema who have in recent years directed their messages to the masses disaffected from the state and from official Islam. Egypt has had the greatest number of such ulema, many of whose reputations have spread throughout the Arab world. Some, like Shaikhs Abd al-Hamid Kishk and Omar Abd al-Rahman, have been accused of being associated with violent underground *jama'at* (groups) of Islamic activists, while others, like Shaikh Mitwalli Sha'rawi, have with the aid of television succeeded in developing a style that appeals to Muslim masses but does not directly challenge established authority. The government of Egypt, like those of other Arab states, monitors very closely the activities of such preachers and occasionally restricts their movements, imprisons them, or closes the mosques in which they preach.

Mosques, in fact, are frequently sites of confrontation between official and organized variants of populist Islam—between government and Islamic activist opposition. Islamic activism, the roots of which are to be found partially in Islamic populism, has in recent years increasingly been centered both in some of the most venerable mosques in major Middle Eastern cities and in the newer, much more humble ones that have sprung up, especially in poorer urban areas. Frequently these new mosques are constructed or dedicated by private individuals and are nothing more than basements of apartment buildings, garages, or other empty spaces. In Egypt, between 1970 and 1981, the number of such *ahli* (private, independent) mosques increased from 20,000 to 40,000.[52]

---

[51]On zars, see Cynthia Nelson, "Self, Spirit, Possession and World View—Illustration from Egypt," *International Journal of Social Psychiatry* 17:3 (1971): 194. On popular religious festivals, see Joseph Williams McPherson, *The Moulids of Egypt* (Cairo: N. M. Press, 1941).

[52]Hamied Ansari, "The Islamic Militants in Egyptian Politics," *International Journal of Middle East Studies* 16 (March 1984): 123–144.

Governments have sought to control such religious spontaneity and underscore their own religiosity. They have attempted to control more closely the activities of imams who preach in mosques and to prevent the proliferation of private mosques. Religious faculties for the training of imams have been expanded out of the calculation that providing officially recognized training for imams and placing them on the public payroll will reinforce their political loyalties and commitment to al-Islam al-rasmi. Over the past two decades, governments have also indulged in a frenzy of mosque building and restoration. The erection of new structures and the cleaning and repair of old ones are meant to attest to governmental devoutness and to attract worshipers away from mosques less closely supervised by the representatives of official Islam. The struggle to control mosques, which can serve as symbols of either al-Islam alrasmi or al-Islam al-sha'bi, attests to the contemporary intensity of the conflict between these two Islams.

Non-Muslims About 3 percent of Middle Easterners, mainly in the southern Sudan, believe in non-Muslim tribal religions. Another 3 percent or so are Christian, less than 2 percent are Jewish, and small numbers of Baha'is, Zoroastrians, and believers in other religions are scattered throughout the area. The greatest concentration of Christians is in Egypt, where the some 5 to 8 million Coptic Orthodox and Coptic Catholics constitute more than 6 percent of the population. While Lebanese Christians, including Maronites (a Latin-rite church), Greek Orthodox, Greek Catholics, Armenian Orthodox, and various smaller sects, make up somewhat less than half of the Lebanese population, they number only around 2 million.[53] Jews, of whom there are fewer than 5 million, are now overwhelmingly concentrated in Israel, whereas prior to the creation of that state in 1948, significant communities of Sephardim, who are also termed Oriental Jews, were found in most Arab states. In Morocco, for example, 1 of every 25 citizens in 1948 was Jewish, whereas now the ratio is 1 of every 1,400, even though the 16,000 Jews still in Morocco constitute the largest community of Middle Eastern Jews outside Israel.[54] Despite the comparatively limited numbers of non-Muslims, they, in combination with Shi'is, have complicated state- and nation-building in the region. From its inception, Islam accorded a subordinate but protected status to Christians and Jews, who as "people of the book" (Bible and Torah, respectively) were respected by Islam. They were obliged to pay a special tribute known as the *jizya,* but otherwise, like other *dhimmis* (tolerated peoples), their individual and collective rights, including those of worship, property, security, and legal autonomy, were recognized and protected. This arrangement was

---

[53]Demographic statistics on the Middle East are notoriously unreliable, in part because governments are reluctant to release census figures that pertain to such sensitive questions as numbers of religious minorities. Lebanon, in fact, has not had a census since 1932 because the Christian-dominated government did not want it officially established that their confession is a minority.

[54]Dale F. Eickelman, "Changing Perceptions of State Authority: Morocco, Egypt and Oman," in *The Foundations of the Arab State,* p. 182.

ultimately regularized by the Ottomans who, having captured Istanbul in 1453, appointed patriarchs of the Greek and Armenian Orthodox and Jewish communities. These minority groups were termed *millets,* a term that by the mid-nineteenth century had been broadened to include ethnic as well as religious communities. According to Suad Joseph, "The dhimmi and millet systems further deterred the development of state institutions," for they segmented the empire, the unity of which was limited to transitory conditions of factional balance.[55] The millets were themselves only loose collectivities, serving more as tax categories than cohesive, self-aware, and self-governing communities. Segmentation of the Ottoman political community and economy was further increased by the fact that religious and ethnic minorities tended to concentrate in various crafts and occupations.

Millets provided channels through which Western influence, both economic and intellectual, began to flow as the Ottoman Empire weakened. Through the Capitulations, which had originally been granted in the sixteenth century to resident foreign communities by Ottoman rulers to facilitate trade but that were subsequently utilized by the West to extract further concessions and were broadened to include local Christians and Jews, significant economic and legal advantages were provided to those minorities. As the "sick man of Europe" decayed further, the European powers, in their scramble to secure concessions, cultivated religious minorities. They legitimated their imperial ambitions by claiming to protect the persecuted. The French cemented ties to Maronite Christians in the Levant, a move the British countered by "protecting" the chief opponents of the Maronites, the Druze.[56] The Russians sought to expand their influence, particularly in Jerusalem, through the Russian Orthodox faith. For the European nations, missionaries performed not just religious but also political roles, mobilizing Eastern Christians in support of Western ideas and specific political claims.

By the beginning of this century, the Ottoman millet system had all but broken down under pressures resultant from increasing Western influence and the expanding power of the Ottoman state. Spreading ideas of secular nationalism inspired hope among minorities who sought to escape their subordinate status. In the pre-nation-state period when political control had been weak and intermittent, religious identities had not been sources of major political conflict and had been a sufficient basis on which to organize communal affairs and relations with higher authority. However, the European secular model held out the promise to minorities in the Middle East that religion could be effectively separated from politics. In this way, the political community could be redefined so that Muslims and non-Muslims would be equal citizens. As Middle Eastern gov-

---

[55]Joseph, "Muslim-Christian Conflicts," p. 2

[56]The relationship between the French and the Maronites was so intense and wide ranging that in the wake of the Druze-Maronite conflict of 1840–1841 Viconte Onffroy, a French colonial official, saw fit to try to alleviate the situation by encouraging Maronites to migrate to Algeria where they could participate with the French in the colonization of that country. On his plan, see Daad Bou Malhab Atallah, *Le Liban, Guerre Civile ou Conflict International? A Partir du Milieu du XIXe Siecle* (Beirut: Dar al-Hurriyat, 1980), pp. 247–248.

ernments began to demand more of their subjects, so did those subjects, Muslims and non-Muslims alike, increasingly insist on new relationships with that expanding authority. Political ideologies thus developed in tandem with the process of state formation.

The Emergence of Modern States and Ideologies

COMPARISON WITH EUROPE

The emergence of European nation-states, accompanied as it was by a protracted civil war, nevertheless occurred in more favorable circumstances than those surrounding the state-building process in the Middle East. The principle of secularism had in much of Western Europe been established by the late eighteenth century.[57] From the seventeenth century, the European economy had been expanding rapidly. The bourgeoisie—that class to which secular nationalism most appealed—gained the upper hand against the aristocracy in the nineteenth century. Moreover, Europe was not at the mercy of stronger imperial powers constantly meddling in its internal affairs.

In the Middle East, none of these favorable conditions were obtained. In the nineteenth century, as the Iranians and Ottomans began to modernize their societies in order to defend themselves against Western domination, they encountered difficulties in assimilating, organizing, and mobilizing their populations. They drew upon two sources in constructing ideologies to facilitate those tasks: religion and secular nationalism. While the latter came to assume greater importance, it never succeeded in supplanting religion as a major source of politically relevant personal identity. This is because "the relationship between nationalism and religion in the Middle East is complex and curvilinear. Both value structures are to varying extents held by an overwhelming majority of the population and generate at times mutually reinforcing, and at other times conflicting, patterns of behavior."[58] Thus political ideologies in the Middle East resemble a museum of intellectual history, for they range from Marxist-Leninism, to classical liberalism, to versions of Islamic fundamentalism that look to the Golden Age of the seventh century for their inspirations.

Whereas European economies were expanding rapidly during the state-formation period, Middle Eastern economies grew unevenly and at a much

---

[57]Secularization in Europe, which began with peasant revolts and the Reformation initiated by Martin Luther in the sixteenth century and that was then facilitated by the great religious wars of the seventeenth century, finally came to fruition in conjunction with and possibly only because of the development of modern industrial society. On the travail that accompanied European secularization and its implications for the Middle East, see Bassam Tibi, *The Crisis of Modern Islam: A Preindustrial Culture in the Scientific-Technological Age* (Salt Lake City, Utah: University of Utah Press, 1988), pp. 127–148; and Tamara Sonn, *Between Qur'an and Crown: The Challenge of Political Legitimacy in the Arab World* (Boulder, Colorado: Westview Press, 1990), pp. 1–30.

[58]G. Hossein Razi, "Legitimacy, Religion and Nationalism in the Middle East," *American Political Science Review* 84 (March 1990): 82.

slower pace. Imperialism did stimulate production of some commodities in the Middle East, especially agricultural raw materials such as cotton and silk, but it undermined production of many others, particularly manufactured goods. The net result was that economies did not expand with sufficient speed or across a broad enough front to provide states with the additional revenues required to finance the necessary institutions. This failure, in turn, reduced the speed and extent to which segments of the population were integrated into the new nation-states. Because states and economies could not effectively demonstrate an ability to provide the resources necessary to ensure the livelihoods of ever-expanding numbers of citizens, the population clung to kinship, sect, and client loyalties that had traditionally provided sources of employment and security.

In Lebanon, where rapid economic growth did occur, the state—hobbled at the outset by the unwillingness of the leaders of the country's major religious sects to surrender their powers to the new government—never achieved sufficient control over the economy to wean citizens away from their dependence on confessions and kinship groups. Those primordial ties provided jobs, licenses, and other resources that the state could not deliver impartially or directly, a fact of which the Lebanese were all too aware. The Lebanese state, according to Samir Khalaf, "compared to other forms of primordial loyalties and communal allegiances, has always been an enfeebled and residual institution."[59]

In those countries where the state did achieve greater leverage over primordial groupings, faltering economies have subsequently eroded state power, thereby clearing the way for primordialism to reemerge or other challenges to the state to arise. In Egypt, for example, the Egyptian government expanded very rapidly after Nasser consolidated his power in the mid-1950s. The necessary resources were provided by the confiscated assets of foreigners and wealthy Egyptians, while foreign aid made available further revenues to underwrite Nasser's Arab socialism. A fairly comprehensive social welfare system was created, education was made free at all levels, graduates were guaranteed jobs in the civil service, and government employment mushroomed. The state's domination of the economy and its ability to provide resources to citizens underpinned the appeal of Nasserism, an ideology that combined Arab nationalism with socialist ideas and practices while being careful not to appear as anti-Islamic. By the mid-1960s, however, it was apparent that the regime had overextended, there being insufficient economic resources to support such a large state. Erosion of the appeal of Nasserism to Egyptians closely paralleled deterioration in the government's ability to provide adequate jobs, welfare payments, health and educational facilities, and the like. Under Sadat and Mubarak, as economic growth has failed to keep pace with population expansion and the government's share of national wealth has also declined, so have a network of populist Islamic *jam'iyyat* (societies) moved to fill the breach. They provide unemployment insurance, textbooks and free tutors to poor students, clinics and hospitals, and other important services. Not surprisingly, the appeal of Islam as a political doctrine has grown accordingly. To many of those provided services

---

[59]Khalaf, *Lebanon's Predicament*, p. 234.

by such societies, "Islam (and not the semisecular state) is the solution"—the slogan of Egypt's Muslim Brotherhood. That Islamic societies are becoming "a state within a state" attests to the continued deterioration of the government's ability to influence the lives of citizens.

Role of the Bourgeoisie   The comparatively slow expansion of Middle Eastern economies and, in cases like Lebanon, the state's limited control over resources, have set the Middle Eastern process of state-building apart from that of Europe. The role of independent merchants, manufacturers, and professionals (the *bourgeoisie*) was also vastly greater in Europe than it has been in the Middle East. The reasons for the relative weakness of the bourgeoisie in the Middle East are contentious. One view is that Islam is incompatible with the rise and existence of an independent entrepreneurial class. Ernest Gellner, for example, has argued that because Islam propagates the belief that "the duty of the state is to proscribe evil and enforce good," it habituates Muslims to the idea that resources "should be distributed according to moral and political requirements, and not be left to the vagaries of the market."[60] Gellner implies that the hostility toward a market-based economy creates an inhospitable environment for entrepreneurialism. On the other hand, Maxime Rodinson, a noted French scholar of the Middle East, has written a lengthy book to dispel the belief that Islamic doctrine is hostile to entrepreneurialism.[61] Fawzy Mansour attributes the weakness of the Middle Eastern bourgeoisie to the fact that judicial authority was insufficiently independent and absolute to guarantee impartial, binding adjudication of contractual disputes.[62] Alternatively, Peter Mansfield contends that "a self-confident and enterprising Islamic bourgeoisie did exist in the Middle Ages but it never succeeded in achieving political power as a class because from around the eleventh century this was in the hands of the Mamlukes and other Turkish and Caucasian military."[63] Since these rulers frequently were of tribal origin and more interested in waging war and in agriculture, "they tended to leave trade and commerce to European traders and to non-Muslim ethnic minorities (such as Greeks, Armenians, and Jews) who were, however, completely at the mercy of the despotic power of the Ottoman state."[64] The Middle Eastern bourgeoisie, lacking independence from government, could, in this view, be neither the economic nor the political equivalent of the bourgeoisie in the West that played such an important role in creating capitalism and strong nation-states.

After reasonably strong states did emerge in the Middle East in the 1950s and 1960s, elites in control of them then used those states "to inhibit the development of an independent bourgeoisie . . . which might have threatened political

---

[60]Ernest Gellner, "Foreword," in *From Nationalism to Revolutionary Islam,* ed. by Said Amir Arjomand (London: Macmillan, 1984), p. x.

[61]Maxime Rodinson, *Islam and Capitalism* (London: Allen Lane, 1974).

[62]Fawzy Mansour, *The Arab World: Nation, State and Democracy* (London: Zed Books, 1992), p. 72.

[63]Peter Mansfield, *The Arabs* (London: Penguin Books, 1985), pp. 84–85.

[64]Bassam Tibi, *Arab Nationalism: A Critical Enquiry* (New York: St. Martin's Press, 1981), p. 51.

stability" by demanding democratization of those polities and liberalization of their economies.[65] Moreover, Middle Eastern economies have been insufficiently independent and developed to provide adequate foundations upon which indigenous merchants, financiers, and manufacturers might construct internationally competitive enterprises. Hanna Batatu summarizes the comparative role of the bourgeoisie in Europe and the Arab world as follows:

> It is not an accident that the "third estate" played an important role in the emergence of such European nation-states as France or England in the dawn of the modern age, or that the process of German unification was impelled in the 1860s in part by the manufacturing classes of the Rhine region, or that the shipping, manufacturing, and commercial interests in America's thirteen colonies were an important motive force in the 1780s behind the trend toward a strong federal government. In the Arab countries the counterparts of these classes have never been strong in the modern era. International economic relationships have been so structured, the financial, organizational, and technical powers of the multinational corporations have been so overwhelming, and Arab conditions so under-developed that, with some exceptions, Arab private entrepreneurs have not been able to grow autonomously, or have been able to thrive only as appendages of either the multinational corporate system or of their own governments.[66]

Classes Created Through State Formation   Whereas in Europe the state and its ideological underpinning, which was provided by secular nationalism, were fashioned by the bourgeoisie, in the Middle East the state emerged independently of that or any other class. Created as a result of the efforts by ruling elites to defend their territories against the West, and subsequently by colonial administrators, the state in the Middle East was not the product of the bourgeoisie nor of secular nationalism. Instead, the state itself fostered the growth of certain classes and specific ideologies.[67] Seeking to expand and centralize their personal control, rulers "were logically moved to weaken the classes most identified with Islam, especially the ulema, and to establish what is often called secularism, although state control over religion would be a more accurate designation."[68] Muhammad Ali, who ruled Egypt for most of the first half of the nineteenth century, was the first major Middle Eastern ruler to adopt this strategy. Having been assisted by the ulema in his rise to power amid the chaotic conditions that prevailed after the withdrawal of the French expeditionary force in 1801, once he

---

[65]Lisa Anderson, "The State in the Middle East and North Africa," *Comparative Politics* 20 (October 1987): 11.

[66]Hanna Batatu, "The Pan-Arab Experience of Syria's Ba'th Party," in *Arab Nationalism and the Future of the Arab World,* ed. by Hani A. Faris (Belmont, Mass.: Association of Arab-American University Graduates, 1986), p. 63.

[67]For an analysis of Tunisia and Libya from this perspective, see Lisa Anderson, *The State and Social Transformation in Tunisia and Libya, 1830–1980* (Princeton, N.J.: Princeton University Press, 1986).

[68]Nikki R. Keddie, "Ideology, Society and the State in Post-Colonial Muslim Societies," in *State and Ideology in the Middle East and Pakistan,* ed. by Fred Halliday and Hamza Alavi (New York: Monthly Review Press, 1988), p. 11.

received Istanbul's formal confirmation of his status as ruler he quickly subordinated the ulema to his will. He and his successors progressively divorced religion from education by sending Egyptians to Europe for advanced training and by creating a state-sponsored educational system. Dar al-Ulum, the famous teacher's training college, along with other state educational institutions and private, European-sponsored ones, gradually marginalized al-Azhar, the thousand-year-old premier Egyptian institution of Islamic learning. Graduates of the state educational system and private European schools played a prominent role in fashioning the secular version of Egyptian nationalism that contributed to the Ahmad al-Arabi and 1919 revolutions, the first of which, in 1882, caused the British to invade Egypt and the second of which resulted in their granting Egypt nominal independence.

Subsequent state-builders elsewhere in the region similarly fostered changes that simultaneously undermined traditional Islam and its leaders, created new social groups and classes, and contributed to the growth of bureaucracies, armies, and other modern state institutions. Ataturk and Reza Shah (whose careers will be examined in greater detail in Chapter 5), for example, both encouraged women to enter the work force so that their labor power would be available to the state and the hold of traditional Islam over them would be reduced. Ataturk's assault on Islam and the Turkish ulema was relentless, including such measures as the abolition of the caliphate, banning of the *fez* (hat with Islamic connotations) and *tekkes* (Dervish groups), and substituting the roman for the Arabic alphabet. Reza Shah, confronting ulema whose independent power was reinforced by Shi'i doctrine and by the financial autonomy resulting from their access to *zakat* and *khums* (Islamic taxes) and from control over income from *waqf* (religious endowments), had to tread more warily. That neither Reza Shah nor his son, Muhammad Reza Shah, ever fully succeeded in subordinating Iranian ulema to the state was made abundantly clear by the revolution of 1978–1979. The growing influence of Islam over Turkish society and politics suggests that Ataturk's steamroller approach suppressed Islam but did not eradicate it as a root source for social and political thought and behavior.

Muhammad Ali, Ataturk, Reza Shah, and other Middle Eastern modernizing rulers greatly enhanced the size and power of the bureaucratic middle class as a by-product of their expansion of public bureaucracies, civilian and military alike. That class, whose interests were coincidental with an expanding state, became the primary bearers of nationalism, whether in the Turkish, Iranian, Egyptian, or Arab variants. Before seizing power in their own right in Turkey, in Egypt, and elsewhere in the Arab world (and briefly in Iran during the Musaddiq interlude from 1951 to 1953), this class had to overcome not only traditional rulers but also another class that had likewise risen to preeminence as a result of the state-formation process. That class comprised rural elites, usually landowners, whose support was required by modernizing governments in order to control the countryside, extract revenues from it, and provide political support against various opponents.

The importance of the landowning class varied in proportion to the strength of the central government. In Turkey, where Ottoman reforms in the nineteenth century paved the way for Ataturk's unrelenting centralization of power, the government did not have to rely heavily on rural notables to control the peasantry or extract revenues. Thus Ataturk's Turkish nationalism has always been much more closely associated with the bureaucratic middle class than with any other social force. In Iraq, by contrast, the precarious hold of the regime in Baghdad forced King Faisal's government to rely heavily on large landowners and tribal shaikhs. As David Pool has argued, government in Iraq was comprised of a tripartite coalition consisting of landowners-shaikhs, bureaucrats, and the king with his entourage.[69]

Similarly, in Egypt, governments have since the Muhammad Ali period relied on landowners for purposes of rural control and extraction. As a result, landowners, despite having been subjected to three agrarian reforms during the Nasser period, have been amazingly successful in maintaining their presence within the political elite.[70] In Iran, large landowners comprised a key element of support for the regime of Reza Shah. His son, who wanted greater political autonomy, sought to undermine some of their power through the land reforms that he promulgated in 1963. While he did succeed in reducing their political influence, the loss of the political support of landowners helped contribute to the shah's overthrow in 1979.

The landlord class brought into existence by state-building contributed some famous leaders to national movements, such as Sa'd Zaghlul in Egypt. In general, however, this class was not as stridently nationalist, nor did it exhibit as much ideological homogeneity as the bureaucratic middle class. Both Islamic reformism and secularism attracted the landowning class, further exacerbating fissiparous tendencies characteristic of most political organizations based on rural notables. Landowners tended to be classic liberals, favoring a restricted rather than an interventionist role for government, which put them at odds with forces seeking to build stronger states. The period of landowner ascendancy, which was the first half of the twentieth century, has been referred to as the liberal era.

Conflict between the two major classes that had been fostered by state-building processes came to a head after World War II. In most instances, the bureaucratic middle class was able to shoulder aside landowners and other elements of the ancien régime. The success of the bureaucratic middle class was due to its close association with the military, to the discrediting of landowners and their allies as defenders of privilege and collaborators with imperialism, and to the superior organization characteristic of middle-class politics. Members of the bureaucratic middle class were strong proponents of secular nationalist ideologies, despite the fact that the large majority of these countries' populations remained religious traditionalists. The existence of this gap, and the

---

[69]David Pool, "From Elite to Class: The Transformation of Iraqi Political Leadership," in *The Integration of Modern Iraq*, ed. by Abbas Kelidar (New York: St. Martin's Press, 1979), pp. 63–87.

[70]See Leonard Binder, *In a Moment of Enthusiasm: Political Power and the Second Stratum in Egypt* (Chicago: University of Chicago Press, 1978).

failure to bridge it, accounts in large measure for "the return of Islam" since the late 1960s.

The Contending Ideologies

ARAB NATIONALISM

While the state-based nationalisms of Turkey, Iran, and Egypt were from the outset propagated by modernizing rulers, the history of Arab nationalism was different. The earliest manifestations of the Arab Awakening, as George Antonius called it, were the writings of Syrian and Lebanese intellectuals, both Muslim and Christian.[71] In the second half of the nineteenth century, these writers began to articulate thoughts of Arab distinctiveness and identity. Theirs was a response to the increasing emphasis on Turkish ethnicity and, for the Christians at least, Islam, the two chief alternative beliefs/identities through which their proponents sought to legitimate and perpetuate the Ottoman Empire.

Another factor that stimulated the Christians' search for a new political ideology was the breakdown in Muslim-Christian relations that ensued after the withdrawal of Egyptian forces from Syria in 1839. Ibrahim Pasha, Muhammad Ali's son, had sought the support of religious minorities after occupying Syria in 1831. "In every town he occupied," observes Kamal Salibi, "Ibrahim removed the traditional restrictions imposed on Christians and Jews and placed these communities on an equal footing with Moslems."[72] Christians were even granted exemptions from impositions levied on Muslims and Druze. When Egyptian protection was withdrawn less than a decade later, Christians in particular came under threat from Syrian Muslims who resented their favorable treatment and collaboration, real or imagined.

Christian ideas of Arabism and modes of expressing it were also influenced by educational experiences in Western-supported institutions, most important of which was the Syrian Protestant College, which subsequently became the American University of Beirut. The Arabist literary *nahda* (Renaissance) was led by such Christian scholars as Nasif al-Yaziji (1800–1871), Faris al-Shidyaq (1805–1887), and Butrus al-Bustani (1819–1883). Subsequently, organizations of intellectuals began to spring up, and in 1875 the first "secret society" with a specifically political intent was organized at the Syrian Protestant College.

Christian Arabs, who shared ethnic and linguistic but not religious identities with fellow Arabs, sought to emphasize Arab history and the Arabic language while deemphasizing or altogether eliminating religion as a source of personal and national political identity. In one variant of Christian-propagated Arab nationalism, Antun Sa'ada identified common geographical origins in Greater Syria as the tie that should bind together Syrians, Iraqis, Jordanians, and Palestinians. Sa'ada founded the Syrian Social Nationalist Party in 1932. It was a

---

[71]George Antonius, *The Arab Awakening: The Story of the Arab National Movement* (Beirut: Khayyat's, 1955).

[72]Kamal S. Salibi, *The Modern History of Lebanon* (New York: Fredrik A. Praeger Publishers, 1965), p. 28.

major force in Lebanese and Syrian politics until the early 1960s and was still operating in the 1990s.[73]

Ba'thism, the most successful of the intellectual trends within Arab nationalism in that it actually came to power in two states, is most heavily indebted for its principal ideas to the Greek Orthodox thinker and activist Michel Aflaq. His way of dealing with the issue of Islam was to relegate it to the status of having been a historically formative force but one with no specific contemporary ideological or political role. By saying that Islam *was* Arab nationalism, Aflaq could then go on to spell out a romantic, vague, but essentially secular interpretation of that nationalism. Similarly, versions of Arab nationalism that have drawn most heavily on Marxist theories are also typically the products of Christians. George Habash, for example, is a Greek Orthodox doctor trained at the American University of Beirut. Prior to founding the Marxist-oriented Popular Front for the Liberation of Palestine, Habash organized the radical Arab Nationalist Movement, which established branches in numerous Arab countries.

Although Christians contributed disproportionately to the Arabist literary revival of the late nineteenth century, the emergence of the Arabist protonationalist movement shortly before and during World War I, and then its conversion into full-fledged Arab nationalism after that time, was due principally to the efforts of Muslim political activists.[74] Like Christians, they had increasingly been alienated by the Ottoman elite's growing emphasis on Turkish ethnicity and language, which, among other things, prejudiced their chances for recruitment and promotion in the Ottoman bureaucracy. Muslim Arab nationalists of this era were also influenced by Islamic modernism or reformism, which held that a revitalization of the true Islam—the Islam of their ancestors—would necessarily restore those to whom Islam was first revealed, the Arabs, to preeminence in the Muslim world. Following the collapse of the Ottoman Empire, Arab nationalism spread rapidly in the newly created Arab states, especially those in the Arab heartland stretching from the Mediterranean coast to the Iran-Iraq border. The relative paucity of wataniyya, combined with the occupation of Syria, Iraq, Palestine, and Lebanon by the British and French, underlay the attraction of al-qawmiyyat al-Arabiyya. The rapid expansion of state structures under colonial control stimulated the growth of the bureaucratic middle class, to whom Arab nationalism had a particularly strong appeal.

Sati al-Husri (1882–1968), a prominent Muslim Arab nationalist whose writings served as textbooks for Arab students of post-World War II generations, personified many of these broader trends. His father, a Syrian, was the Ottoman Qadi in Yemen. Sati al-Husri received a traditional Islamic education. Subsequently he studied in Europe before being assigned by the Ottoman govern-

---

[73]On the Syrian Social Nationalist Party, also known as the PPS, see Labib Zuwiyya Yamak, *The Syrian Social Nationalist Party: An Ideological Analysis* (Cambridge, Mass.: Harvard Middle Eastern Monograph Series, vol. 16, 1966).

[74]For an analysis of the changing historiography of the Arab nationalist movement, see Rashid Khalidi et al., *The Origins of Arab Nationalism* (New York: Columbia University Press, 1991).

ment to a number of teaching and administrative posts. During the twilight of the Ottoman Empire, he made contact with the Arab nationalist underground in Syria. When an Arab state under Amir Faisal was created in Damascus in 1920, Sati al-Husri was named minister of education. After the French thwarted that attempt at statehood some four months later, he accompanied Faisal to Iraq, where the latter was proclaimed king and al-Husri was appointed dean of the Baghdad University Law School. In 1941 he was deported to Syria, following a British-backed coup to overthrow the anti-British government of Rashid Ali al-Gailani. He later went on to Cairo, where for twenty years he worked for the Arab League, which had been founded in 1945.

Sati al-Husri's career reveals much about Arab nationalism. An Ottoman official, he rejected Ottomanism for Arabism. Educated in Islamic schools, he modified Islamic formulations to accommodate European conceptualizations of nationalism. His writings inspired innumerable students and political activists, including Michel Aflaq. His very presence in Cairo from 1947 to 1966 not only served to spread Arab nationalist ideas among Egyptians but also, from the mid-1950s, provided tangible evidence of Nasser's claim that Egypt (and by implication Nasser himself) should be leader of the Arabs.[75] Sati al-Husri, like other prominent intellectual Arab nationalists such as Aflaq, was not just a political thinker but also a symbol exploited in inter-Arab struggles for power and by governments seeking to legitimate themselves.

By the 1960s Arab nationalism appeared to have triumphed. Leading Arab states vied with one another in the claim to be the purest embodiment of that ideology. But their very audacity and grandiose claims, their inability to develop adequately their economies and, ultimately, their defeat by Israel in 1967 not only undermined those governments but eroded the appeal of Arab nationalism itself. That process was further hastened by the new balance of power in inter-Arab politics. Conservative Arab states, especially those in the Gulf, had always been skeptical of Arab nationalism, both because of its radicalism and because it had been used as a foreign policy tool against them by Egypt, Syria, Iraq, and other Arab states. These conservative states, therefore, seized the opportunity to undercut radical Arab nationalism. Their new oil wealth, especially after 1973, made it possible to offer incentives to Arab rulers to establish amicable state-to-state relations, while at the mass level those funds were used to encourage the growth of Islamic ideas, or "Petro-Islam," at the expense of secular versions of Arab nationalism.

The speed with which Arab nationalism was displaced, however, cannot be explained entirely by the defeat in 1967, by the lure of petrodollars, or by the vagaries of inter-Arab politics. Arab nationalism had never been fully secularized or firmly established as the undisputed state idea of countries such as Egypt, Iraq, and Syria. Arab nationalists had seized power through the military, and

---

[75]On Sati al-Husri, see William L. Cleveland, *The Making of an Arab Nationalist: Ottomanism and Arabism in the Life and Thought of Sati al-Husri* (Princeton, N.J.: Princeton University Press, 1971); and Tibi, *Arab Nationalism.*

their ideology remained "confined to learned elites."[76] The states over which they presided were never strong enough to relate secular nationalism systematically to political institutions and hence to instruct citizens in precisely what being an Arab nationalist meant. Under these conditions, the political elite gave way to the inevitable by blurring the distinction between Arabism and Islam, for the latter is much more readily understood and accepted at the mass level. This left nationalist elites and their states vulnerable to political appeals couched in straightforward Islamic terminology.

ISLAMIC REFORMISM

Two strains of Islamic political thought and action have attracted the support of Muslims for more than a century. That which appealed initially to the wealthy, partly Westernized elite, of whom landowners were the most important element, was a modernist, reformist Islam that took shape from the mid-nineteenth century as a result of interaction with European thought. Rifa'a Tahtawi, one of the earliest and most influential Islamic reformers, instructed his fellow Egyptians that Islam was compatible with European conceptions of state, nation, and patriotism. Jamal al-Din al-Afghani (1839–1897), a colorful Iranian thinker and political militant, advocated a "defensive modernization" of Islam, whereby it would be strengthened through a rediscovery of its heritage and by unification of Muslims under a single government. Afghani's ideas served as a point of departure for his Egyptian disciple Muhammad Abduh (1849–1905), whose Salafiyya movement emphasized that Islam could be revitalized only through Western-style rational inquiry and, unlike Afghani's message, by "cultural rather than political activity."[77] While Afghani's and Abduh's thoughts both contributed to the development of Arab nationalism through such thinkers as the Syrian Abd al-Rahman al-Kawakibi and also influenced Islamic revivalism through Abduh's disciple Rashid Rida, the main thrust of the Salafiyya movement was essentially apolitical, hence conservative. Abduh was himself a figure of the religious and social establishments, rising to the post of Qadi with the encouragement of Britain's Lord Cromer, the virtual ruler of Egypt.

Reformist Islam did not become a powerful political movement in its own right for several reasons. Its moderation and stress on accommodation cut it off from a mass base. It was appropriate for the conservative upper class, but that class itself was being challenged by the more radical bureaucratic middle class. When reformist Islam shaded in the direction of anti-imperialist political activism, it immediately encountered the opposition of the occupying power and the local government under its control. Afghani, one of whose followers assassinated Nasir al-Din Shah of Iran in 1896, elicited the fear and scorn of the British. He was eventually banished from Egypt. The more moderate Abduh, on

---

[76]Saad Eddin Ibrahim, "The Concerns and the Challenges," in *Pan-Arabism and Arab Nationalism*, p. 62.

[77]Tibi, *Arab Nationalism*, p. 66. *Salaf* means "ancestors," referring to the leaders of Islam in the Golden Age.

the other hand, was patronized by Lord Cromer out of the calculation that he posed no serious political threat.

Another factor that prevented a reformist Pan-Islam from emerging as the dominant ideology to challenge colonialism was that its legitimacy was tarnished by the last ruling Ottoman sultan, Abd al-Hamid. He terminated the Young Ottomans' experiment with liberalism in 1876, hoping to substitute Pan-Islam for the appeal of political liberty. In so doing he further discredited Islam among those bent on reform, especially the members of the rising middle classes. Finally, moderate, reformist Islam was eclipsed during the colonial and immediate postcolonial periods by Arab nationalism and by Islamic revivalism because both of those alternatives embodied more activist responses to the threat posed by Western intervention and therefore had greater popular appeal.

Contemporary Islamic reformers, like their forerunners, are in conflict with more radical Islamicists. Fu'ad Zakariyya, for example, cautions Egyptian Islamic activists against religious dogmatism and the supposition that contemporary government can be based on Islamic ideals embodied in the Quran or sharia. According to him, "Islam is what Muslims have made of it in history; it is not some ahistorical system beyond human experience."[78] To him, revivalists stress the form rather than the content of Islam, placing undue emphasis on such matters as dress codes at the expense of substantive issues such as welfare and justice. Fu'ad Zakariyya's colleague, Faraj Fuda, an even more trenchant critic of revivalists and a staunch defender of secularism, was gunned down in the streets of Cairo in June 1992 by members of the Islamic Jihad organization.

ISLAMIC REVIVALISM

Islamic revivalism, also referred to as fundamentalism, Islamic activism or populism, or simply as Islamism or Islamicism, can be traced back to rural tribesmen, such as those associated with the Mahdi in the Sudan or with Abd al-Qadir (1807–1883) in Algeria, who, like the Sudanese Mahdi, resisted foreign control with the aid of radical Islam. Gradually, Abd al-Qadir's movement and other rural uprisings were suppressed as remote areas and their populations were brought under state control. Accompanying that process was the emergence of a new social force to whom Islamic revivalism appealed. This group comprised those individuals who had been profoundly, and generally negatively, affected by the expansion of state power. Even though many had had modern educations, they remained excluded from the benefits and privileges enjoyed by those with better training and preferential access to the state.

Hassan al-Banna, for example, who founded the Muslim Brotherhood in Egypt in 1928, was a poorly paid schoolteacher in the provincial city of Isma'-iliyya. Those he recruited to his cause were predominantly of similar lower-middle-class backgrounds. They saw in revivalist Islam a means of overcoming the social injustice they believed to be perpetrated by the secularists in control of

---

[78]Fu'ad Zakariyya, *al-Haqiqa wa-l-Wahm fi al-Haraka al-Islamiyya al-Mu'asira (Reality and Delusion in the Contemporary Islamic Movement)*, cited in Boullata, *Trends and Issues*, p. 155.

the state. Since the 1920s, Islamic revivalism in Egypt and elsewhere in the region has recruited heavily from such marginal elements, including those in traditional occupations threatened by modernization as well as recently urbanized, moderately well-educated individuals who have not been able to find employment commensurate with their educations and expectations.[79]

In recent years revivalism has also been attracting even those who are comparatively well situated in their social orders and political economies. This is due to a general erosion of the quality of life in the poorer countries and the widespread belief there that incumbent governments, seen as being subservient to the West, are responsible for the deterioration of services, rising unemployment, skyrocketing inflation, and corruption. In the rich Arab oil-exporting countries of the Gulf, revivalism attracts Shi'i as well as Sunni Muslims who chafe under the control of the family-based regimes that dominate those states and which are also seen to serve the interests of the West rather than their own populations.

The ideological worldview of revivalism, according to John Esposito, includes the following beliefs: Islam encompasses all aspects of life; shortcomings in Muslim societies result from deviations from the "straight path of Islam" in the direction of Western secularism and materialism; the renewal of society depends on a return to Islam and the emulation of its earliest practices; Islamic law must replace Western-inspired legal codes; science and technology are acceptable but must be subordinated to Islam; and re-Islamization requires organizational activity. More radical Islamic revivalists believe that violent revolution is required to achieve these objectives because Muslims confront the power of the West and Zionism. They also contend that God has commanded Muslims to live under Islamic government; that governments not based exclusively on the sharia are illegitimate, as is "establishment" Islam; and that jihad against unbelievers, including Christians and Jews, is a religious duty.[80]

While in its extreme forms Islamic revivalism may well be incompatible with democracy, Islamic activists and their organizations throughout the Middle East have both called for and participated in *ta'addudiyya,* the process of political pluralization.[81] In Algeria, Egypt, Jordan, Kuwait, Lebanon, Morocco, Sudan, Tunisia, and Yemen, Islamic movements have contested parliamentary elections. Throughout the region, Islamic activists are debating the relationship between Islam and democracy. One school of thought contends that the Quranic concepts of *shura* (consultation), *ijtihad* (interpretation, independent reasoning), and *ijma* (consensus) constrain autocracy or even underpin popular sovereignty. Another view, whose most articulate spokesperson was Egypt's Sayyid Qutb, is that democratization necessarily usurps God's sovereignty and therefore is a form of *jahiliyya,* or ignorance.

---

[79]On recruitment of the former type, see Hanna Batatu, "Syria's Muslim Brethren," *Merip Reports* 110 (November-December 1982): 12–20. On recruitment of newly urbanized lower-middle-class elements, see Hamied Ansari, *Egypt: The Stalled Society* (Albany: State University of New York Press, 1986), pp. 211–230.

[80]John L. Esposito, *Islam: The Straight Path* (New York: Oxford University Press, 1991), pp. 163–164.

[81]On this process, see Michael Hudson, "After the Gulf War: Prospects for Democratization in the Arab World," *Middle East Journal* 45 (Summer 1991): 407–426.

The question arises among those fearful of Islamic revivalism as to whether representatives of that movement would continue to be democrats when and if they rose to power. As demands for ta'addudiyya spread in the region, and as governments permit more political participation, this becomes an ever more central question. In Algeria in January 1992, the military provided its own answer. When it appeared inevitable that the Islamic Salvation Front (FIS) would come to power through the ballot box, the army staged a putsch, justifying its actions on the ground that the FIS would usurp all power and abolish democratic practices. The Algerian military thus averted the first vital test of Islamic revivalists' real commitment to democracy. The issue thus remains unresolved, hanging over governments and oppositions alike.

State-Building and the Challenge of Ideology

Arab governments, most of which have rested their claim to legitimate rule on versions of Arab nationalism, have grimly persisted in the face of a growing challenge from those who would seek to mobilize the masses with an Islamicist message. Governments have sought to counter Islamic revivalism by emphasizing their commitments to Islam and by using the powers of the state to stem its growth. The powers of the state, however, are nowhere so firmly established that its preeminence is guaranteed. In the poorer Arab countries, rapid population growth, stagnating economies, and a decreasing governmental share of national income are eroding the quality of government services. As public infrastructure (roads, hospitals, schools, sanitation services, provision of utilities, and so on) deteriorates, so do questions arise, not only about the competence of political elites but also about the appropriateness of the political ideologies they have propagated. Religious organizations, both Muslim and Christian, some with strong political commitments, are pouring into these administrative and ideological vacuums.

In the wealthy Arab oil-exporting countries, which have been referred to as *rentier* states because they live off "rents"—income from oil—there are other problems.[82] These states have sought to buy the loyalties of their populations by distributing a vast array of goods and services. They too have been unwilling to permit widespread political participation. Dirk Vandewalle observes:

> The rentier nature of state revenue thus militates against the creation of a strong state or the involvement of its corresponding society. In this light the massive revenues accruing to the government in a rentier state are a double-edged sword, allowing the local governments to dole out revenues with minimum attention for representation, on the basis of the reverse principle of no representation without taxation.[83]

---

[82]On rentier states, see Beblawi and Luciani, *The Rentier State.*

[83]Dirk Vandewalle, "Political Aspects of State Building in Rentier Economies: Algeria and Libya Compared," in *The Rentier State*, p. 160.

Rentier states have sought to depoliticize their populations and to prevent the spread of political ideologies, which they perceive as potential challenges to their power and legitimacy. As substitutes for ideology they have provided "bread and circuses." Kuwait, for example, prior to its invasion by Iraq in 1990, had the world's most comprehensive welfare system, and "circuses" in the form of such diversions as ice rinks and other entertainment complexes. As a result of these policies, "Politics fades away, not merely as a subject for serious discussion, but even as a favorite topic of gossip."[84]

What typically passes as semiofficial ideology in these rentier states is a mix of Islam and loyalty to the ruling family, with a thin veneer of Arab nationalism, which governments are seeking to replace with state-based nationalisms. In sum, neither the poor nor the rich Arab countries have succeeded in creating nation-states based on widespread institutionalized political participation. These governments will, therefore, continue to confront challenges to their legitimacy as the process of state formation proceeds.

In addition to organized opposition movements the largest and most effective of which are Islamicist, there is in many countries a sprawling, unorganized, alienated, and potentially volatile mass public. Often only recently and insecurely urbanized, living in poor quarters, and generally young, those who fall into this category are not yet mobilized by organizations or ideologies. They are, however, ready participants in quasi-organized street violence, such as the bread riots that have affected various countries since the 1970s. This potential opposition force may be the most dangerous of all. It is in some countries comparatively large and strategically located in capital cities. Because its members have so little to lose, they are willing to engage in truly desperate acts. The secret police are unable to track down and arrest leadership elements precisely because of the comparative lack of organization. Finally, this sprawling urban lower class provides a vast recruitment pool for radical organizations, especially those of revivalist Islam.

In the face of the challenge mounted by these real and potential opposition forces, governments have responded with placatory policies, such as maintenance of subsidies for basic foodstuffs, and by seeking to divide and rule the opposition, balancing one against the other. They have sought to drive home to reformist and revivalist Muslims the differences that separate their two movements, and to secularists the gap between themselves and Islamicists. They have alternated policies of repression with concessions. In short, they have played for time, hoping that the current phase of oppositional strength and governmental weakness will not be a lasting one. Ultimately they could be successful in this strategy, in part because they may be forced to expand political participation in order to contain the threat to their existence. State formation, in this scenario, would be facilitated by the process of political competition. The government, in creating arenas in which contending forces struggle for power, would serve as midwife to the birth of a participatory political order.

---

[84]Afsaneh Najmabadi, "Depoliticization of a Rentier State: The Case of Pahlavi Iran," ibid., p. 213.

Alternatively, one or more of the organized opposition forces could seize power, or the unorganized opposition could simply swamp political systems by bringing about a protracted breakdown of order. That such scenarios are even possible attests to the magnitude of the problems currently confronting Middle Eastern governments and to the progressive deterioration of ideological consensus. In the absence of such consensus, governmental legitimacy is limited. Secularism is unacceptable to vast numbers of the religiously committed in Arab countries, Turkey, Iran, and Israel, while theocracy is anathema to secularists in those countries. Whether governmental weakness will facilitate a compromise between these and other conflicting forces, or whether it presages the establishment of a new order dominated by one of them, will be the major political question in this region of the world at the end of the twentieth century.

SELECTED BIBLIOGRAPHY

Antonius, George. *The Arab Awakening: The Story of the Arab National Movement.* Beirut: Khayyat's, 1955.

Beinin, Joel, and Joe Stork. *Political Islam: Essays from Middle East Report.* Berkeley: University of California Press, 1997.

Ben-Dor, Gabriel. *State and Conflict in the Middle East: Emergence of the Postcolonial State.* New York: Praeger, 1983.

Boullata, Issa J. *Trends and Issues in Contemporary Arab Thought.* Albany: State University of New York Press, 1990.

Chelkowski, Peter J., and Robert J. Pranger. *Ideology and Power in the Middle East: Studies in Honor of George Lenczowski.* Durham, N.C.: Duke University Press, 1988.

Cole, Juan R. I., and Nikki R. Keddie, eds. *Shi'ism and Social Protest.* New Haven, Conn.: Yale University Press, 1986.

Dorraj, Manochehr. *From Zarathustra to Khomeini: Populism and Dissent in Iran.* Boulder, Colo.: Lynn Rienner Publishers, 1990.

Eickelman, Dale F., and James Piscatori. *Muslim Politics.* Princeton, N.J.: Princeton University Press, 1996.

Enayat, Hamid. *Modern Islamic Political Thought.* Austin: University of Texas Press, 1982.

Esposito, John L. *Political Islam: Revolution, Radicalism, or Reform?* Boulder, Colo.: Lynne Rienner Publishers, 1997.

Esposito, John L., and John O. Voll. *Islam and Democracy.* New York: Oxford University Press, 1996.

Farah, Tawfic E. *Pan-Arabism: The Continuing Debate.* Boulder, Colo.: Westview Press, 1987.

Hourani, Albert. *Arabic Thought in the Liberal Age, 1798–1939.* London: Oxford University Press, 1962.

Kayali, Hasan. *Arabs and Young Turks: Ottomanism, Arabism, and Islamism in the Ottoman Empire, 1908–1918.* Berkeley: University of California Press, 1997.

Kepel, Gilles. *Muslim Extremism in Egypt: The Prophet and the Pharaoh.* Berkeley: University of California Press, 1986.

Khalidi, Rashid, et al., eds. *The Origins of Arab Nationalism.* New York: Columbia University Press, 1991.

Khouri, Philip S., and Joseph Kostiner. *Tribes and State Formation in the Middle East.* Berkeley: University of California Press, 1990.

Lapidus, Ira. *A History of Islamic Societies.* New York: Cambridge University Press, 1988.

Munson, Henry, Jr. *Islam and Revolution in the Middle East.* New Haven, Conn.: Yale University Press, 1988.

Piscatori, James P. *Islam in a World of Nation-States.* Cambridge: Cambridge University Press, 1986.

Salamé, Ghassan, ed. *The Foundations of the Arab State.* London: Croom Helm, 1987.

Salem, Paul. *Bitter Legacy: Ideology and Politics in the Arab World.* Syracuse: Syracuse University Press, 1994.

Sivan, Emmanuel. *Radical Islam: Medieval Theology and Modern Politics.* New Haven, Conn.: Yale University Press, 1985.

Tibi, Bassam. *Arab Nationalism: Between Islam and the Nation-State,* third ed. New York: St. Martin's Press, 1997.

Williams, John Alden, ed. *The Word of Islam.* Austin: University of Texas Press, 1994.

Chapter 3

The Genes of Politics: Groups, Classes, and Families

 In the Middle East, individuals express their social and political demands through membership in various groups. These collectivities range from family units to class aggregations, from recreational groupings to religious affiliations, from personal cliques to political associations.[1] Middle Eastern societies contain a kaleidoscopic array of overlapping and interlocking groups in constant flux. Individuals maintain membership in a large number of groups. In so doing, they build webs of personal connections that constitute the basic sinews of the social system.

Group formations dominate the vertical dimension of stratification as family, friendship, ethnic, religious, professional, recreational, and political groups exist in a state of continual interaction. The social and political systems resemble mosaics composed of a "limitless crisscross of groups."[2] This web of fluctuating groups, however, is not a seamless one. Differing levels of power, wealth, and prestige indicate a system of stratification. The lines etched into this system cut horizontally across other group configurations. In this sense, family, tribal, and religious groups, for example, are embedded within a structure of interrelated classes.

The key political dimensions of power and authority are shaped in the Middle East largely by the prevailing group and class structure. A complex prism of

---

[1]For purposes of our analysis, a *group* is defined as a collectivity of individuals who interact in varying degrees in pursuance of a common interest or goal. This definition is broad enough to include aggregations exhibiting a wide variety of organizational styles yet narrow enough to exclude collectivities of individuals who neither interact nor share similar goals.

[2]This is Arthur F. Bentley's phrase. See Bentley, *The Process of Government* (Cambridge, Mass.: Harvard University Press, 1967), p. 204.

group formations filters political demands and helps determine public policy. Although a changing political system tends to alter the social structure, political changes are often the result of a shifting social structure. The politics of development and modernization are profoundly influenced by the patterns and processes that mark group and class relationships.

In all societies, social structure strongly influences the political process. The patterns of group interaction, however, vary considerably from one area of the world to another. Distinctive characteristics mark the styles of group and class interaction in Islamic cultures and Middle Eastern societies. Some of these patterns are congruent with patterns in other societies; some of them are not. The Middle Eastern patterns are the subject of our analysis.

Group Structure: Vertical Stratification

In the East persons were more trusted than institutions.

T. E. Lawrence

SEVEN PILLARS OF WISDOM

The Middle Easterner belongs to a number of groups that vary greatly in their membership, goals, and modes of organization. These groups also differ in their capacity to further the interests of their membership. On the basis of organizational style, groups in the Middle East can be divided into two major categories, formal and informal.[3]

Formal groups are corporate collectivities that are officially organized and visibly operating. Membership is clearly defined, and the members have specific and sharply differentiated roles. In our group taxonomy, formal groups include both associational and institutional structures.[4] Associational groups are highly organized structures that are formed for the articulation of a specific interest. Examples include trade unions, business organizations, civic clubs, and ethnic, religious, professional, and political associations. Institutional groups exist primarily to perform a certain function but also act to promote their own interests. Although officially organized, like associational groups, they generally operate somewhat more loosely. Institutional groups are usually governmental bodies and include legislatures, bureaucracies, armies, and political parties. Formal

---

[3]The terms *formal* and *informal* risk exposing us to the criticism of ethnocentricity. From the viewpoint of many non-Westerners, even informal groups have form and can therefore be considered formal. We use the term *informal*, however, to refer to an unofficial, fluid, personalistic, and relatively covert type of group structure.

[4]Associational and institutional interest groups are part of an important typology of groups developed by Gabriel Almond in his comparative study of political systems. For the original presentation of this schema, see Gabriel A. Almond and James S. Coleman, eds., *The Politics of the Developing Areas* (Princeton, N.J.: Princeton University Press, 1960), pp. 33–38. For Almond's most recent formulation of interest group categories, see Almond and G. Bingham Powell, Jr., *Comparative Politics Today: A World View* (New York: HarperCollins, 1996), pp. 70–85.

groups always maintain a corporate apparatus that includes officials and functionaries with clearly defined responsibilities.

Informal groups are noncorporate, unofficially organized collectivities that articulate their interests in a relatively diffuse manner. This category includes kinship, status, and regional groups as well as anomic aggregations that tend to form spontaneously, such as rioting crowds and demonstrations. Most often, however, informal groups are cliques, factions, or coteries. They are highly personalistic in character and take shape on the basis of constantly fluctuating relations among individuals. The personalistic and amorphous nature of informal groups enables them to maintain a degree of fluidity and flexibility that is absent in the more rigid formal groups.

PATTERNS OF GROUP INTERACTION

Formal political associations have been conspicuously absent in the social history of the Islamic Middle East. Even economic associational groups have been of limited significance, despite the sporadic appearance of trade union organizations during this century. Nor does the mere existence of associational groups necessarily indicate that they play an active role in the sociopolitical life of the area. Often they exist only as empty organizational shells, while their functions are performed by other structures. This generalization is, of course, more applicable to certain Middle Eastern countries than to others. In Morocco, Algeria, Turkey, and Bahrain, labor unions have not only existed but have on occasion had an appreciable impact on political processes. In Iran and Iraq, on the other hand, the existence of modest union organization has been more a facade than a force. In still other countries, such as Saudi Arabia and Oman, there have been no trade union organizations.

Institutional groups have played more important roles in Middle Eastern political history than have associational groups. Although parliaments and political parties are recently established institutional groups, bureaucracies and armies are of more ancient vintage. Thus, while associations are generally twentieth-century phenomena in the Middle East, certain institutional groups have roots that extend back many centuries. These groups, however, have tended to be large, sprawling conglomerations composed of personal cliques, familial networks, and regional factions. Middle Eastern military systems today are often analyzed in terms of various officer cliques, while bureaucracies are best understood as systems of administrative factions.

Associational and institutional groups that have played a critical role in Western political systems have been considerably less significant in the Middle Eastern context. The dominant group structure in the Islamic world has been the informal group.[5] Group organization hardens around particular individuals and kinship structures. Small, shifting clusters of individuals form cliques that resemble one another only in their personalistic, informal, fragmented mode of

---

[5]As we will see in Chapter 4, informality is one of the major characteristics of patrimonial social and political systems.

organization. Key political decisions are made in the context of this kind of group. Formal groups exist either as extraneous facades or as general structures within which small, informal groups carry out their important activities. Informal groups penetrate and many times suffuse the more formal aggregations. Decisions attributable to the formal organization may in fact be the product of a parasitical informal group within it.

In local Moroccan politics, for example, political parties are perceived by the people "as amalgamations of individuals bound together by a multiplicity of different personal ties rather than by any all-pervasive organizational structure or ideological commitment. . . ."[6] In Lebanon, "loyalty to patrons, relatives or nonrelatives, takes precedence over loyalty to labor unions."[7] In national Iranian politics, the *majlis,* or parliament, "masks a fluctuating and fractionating network of personal cliques, and it is here where decisions are made and business is transacted."[8] The army in such countries as Iraq and Syria has been described as a "collection of factions."[9] The situation is excellently summarized by Clifford Geertz: "Structure after structure—family, village, clan, class, sect, army, party, elite, state—turns out when more narrowly looked at to be an ad hoc constellation of miniature systems of power, a cloud of unstable micropolitics, which compete, ally, gather strength, and very soon overextended, fragment again."[10]

The growth of effective formal groups in the Middle East has been stunted by a number of interrelated factors. The technical, social, economic, and political conditions of organization are often absent. The formation of a viable formal group structure requires a certain level of organizational skill, a minimal degree of trust and cooperation, a reservoir of funds for administration, and a willingness on the part of political elites to tolerate the existence of such groups. In Middle Eastern societies, these conditions of organization are seldom all present at once. Social and political demands, therefore, are formulated and presented in a much different organizational environment.

Groups in the Middle East are necessarily more limited in size in order to maximize trust and cooperative endeavor. Group members protect the private and secret nature of their proceedings in order to strengthen their position against both rival groups and the national political regime. Individuals attempt to retain the greatest possible personal freedom so that they may move in and out of groups, depending on their perception of their own best interests. This, in turn, promotes considerable fluidity and fragmentation, since group mem-

---

[6]Lawrence Rosen, "Rural Political Process and National Political Structure in Morocco," in *Rural Politics and Social Change in the Middle East,* ed. by Richard Antoun and Iliya Harik (Bloomington, Ind.: Indiana University Press, 1972), p. 299.

[7]Fuad I. Khuri, "The Changing Class Structure in Lebanon," *Middle East Journal* 23 (Winter 1969): 40.

[8]James A. Bill, "The Politics of Legislative Monarchy: The Iranian Majlis," in *Comparative Legislative Systems,* ed. by Herbert Hirsch and M. Donald Hancock (New York: The Free Press, 1971), p. 365.

[9]See P. J. Vatikiotis, *Conflict in the Middle East* (London: George Allen and Unwin, 1971), p. 108.

[10]Clifford Geertz, "In Search of North Africa," *New York Review of Books* 16 (April 22, 1971): 20, as quoted in Dale F. Eickelman. "Is There an Islamic City? The Making of a Quarter in a Moroccan Town," *International Journal of Middle East Studies* 5 (June 1974): 280.

berships continually change in a manner that defies any rigidity, officiality, or formal routinization.

Besides these negative reasons for the lack of effective formal groups in the Middle East, there are a number of positive explanations. Small, informal groups are able to attain their common goals readily enough to preclude the need for larger groups. Over the centuries in the Islamic world, small groups have simply proven to be more efficient and effective structures than larger groups. Recent research by economists and political scientists who work with "collective good" theory casts serious doubt on the assumption that it is rational for individual members of a large group to work to achieve the collective good of that group.[11] Instead, it is argued that the individual who fails to contribute to the large group will still stand to share in the reward once the group's goal is attained. In large groups, it may well be that an individual's effort will make no perceptible difference in the attainment of the group's goal. In this situation, the rational individual will not contribute to the group's effort. Such is the case in most associational and institutional groups.

In a smaller group, each individual's efforts are more likely to make a difference in attaining the group's goal. In such a group the individual will be more susceptible to the pressures of other group members, who can further cooperation through mutual personal persuasion. In Middle Eastern social history, where groups have been not only small but also highly personalistic, this has been especially true. In such societies, there is much doubt about the efficacy of membership in, or attachment to, large or mass institutional groups. Personal ties based on kinship, friendship, and religious and regional affiliation have been among the best means of ensuring effective individual effort.[12]

One further reason for the emphasis on personal ties in the Islamic Middle East has been a belief in the nobility and generosity of manner. Individuals in Islamic culture who believed in these virtues joined various brotherhoods and guilds that incorporated characteristics of both formal and informal organization. These guilds and brotherhoods have been important political aggregations throughout the history of the Islamic world. The Islamic guild, for example, has generally represented the interests of the lower- and lower-middle-class members of society. It was "a spontaneous development from below, created, not in response to a State need, but to the social requirements of the labouring masses themselves. Save for one brief period, the Islamic guilds have maintained either

---

[11]For the basic presentation of this theoretical approach, see Mancur Olson, Jr., *The Logic of Collective Action: Public Goods and the Theory of Groups* (New York: Schocken Books, 1968).

[12]Ibn Khaldun's theory of social solidarity (*asabiyya*) proposes that asabiyya is critical to successful group activity and ultimately to civilization. Asabiyya is the cement of human relations and is based first on common ancestry and eventually on common interest and life experience. Asabiyya was most easily developed in small, informal, and highly personalistic groups. As Muhsin Mahdi writes: "Solidarity comes into being as a result of common ancestry, but it is usually sustained by external factors: the feeling of relatedness is dictated by the necessity of cooperation and self-defense." (Muhsin Mahdi, *Ibn Khaldūn's Philosophy of History* [London: George Allen and Unwin, 1957], p. 197.) See Ibn Khaldun's own writings about group formation in the Islamic world in *The Muqaddimah: An Introduction to History,* trans. by Franz Rosenthal (Princeton, N.J.: Princeton University Press, 1967).

an open hostility to the State, or an attitude of sullen mistrust, which the public authorities, political and ecclesiastical, have always returned."[13]

The early craft guilds resembled Byzantine structures and were organized on the basis of a common craft or skill. With the passage of time, and particularly following the rise of the Qarmatian (Carmathian) movement during the ninth to the twelfth centuries,[14] the guilds became deeply infused with a moral and often mystical spirit. This attitude contributed greatly to organizational cohesion and inspired the members to dedicate themselves to furthering group goals. Although the various guilds and brotherhoods had differing organizational emphases, they generally blended formal and informal characteristics. On the one hand, they exhibited such formal accoutrements of organization as elaborate ceremonial activity and a rigid internal hierarchy. On the other hand, they were intensely personalistic and highly secretive. The term *tariqa* ("brotherhood" or "order") literally means a "way" or "path" and refers to a mode of conduct, not to a formal association.[15] Thus, in the Middle Eastern context, even structures as corporate as guilds have an element of informality that renders them a highly diversified composite of organizational types. Like the familial group, which we examine later in this chapter, the guild has managed to span the formal-informal dichotomy.

Since the activity of informal groups is herein considered the most dominant form of group politics in the Middle East, our discussion emphasizes this type of group rather than associational and institutional groups. This does not mean that we choose to ignore formal groups but that we will accord them an emphasis somewhat more commensurate with the political influence they wield in the area of our investigation. To state it quite baldly, a Middle Eastern legislature, for example, is much less important as a decision-making apparatus than are the informal groups that penetrate it, control it, and, most important, survive it.

THE POLITICS OF INFORMAL GROUPS

Informal groups, usually referred to as cliques or factions, are a fundamental unit of political action in many societies. In contrast to northern European and

---

[13]Bernard Lewis, "The Islamic Guilds," *Economic History Review* 8 (1937): 35–36. The research of Gabriel Baer indicates that the craft guilds were both more formally organized and more closely linked to the government than is commonly thought. Baer's arguments, however, are most applicable to guild structures after the eighteenth century. Also, the brotherhoods were always better examples than the guilds of the type of informal group that existed in opposition to governmental power. The state was better able to infiltrate and control guild structures than brotherhood organizations. For Baer's conclusions concerning Turkish guilds, see "The Administrative, Economic, and Social Functions of Turkish Guilds," *International Journal of Middle East Studies* 1 (January 1970): 28–50.

[14]This was a great liberal movement that swept through the Muslim world, advocating social reform in general and justice and equality in particular. The movement appealed to all classes, sects, and religions but found special acceptance among the artisans, skilled, and semiskilled workers. See L. Massignon, "Karmatians," *The Encyclopaedia of Islam*, 4 vols. (Leiden, The Netherlands: E. J. Brill, 1927), vol. 2: 767–772.

[15]This point is made in Fazlur Rahman, *Islam* (Garden City, N.Y.: Anchor Books, 1968), pp. 189–190; and in Morroe Berger, *Islam in Egypt Today* (Cambridge: Cambridge University Press, 1970), p. 67.

North American societies, where formal groups play a prominent role, the informal group is dominant in southern European, North African, Middle Eastern, and Latin American cultures.

It is true that wherever human beings are gathered, they will develop informal groups. Thus, in American society there are many obvious manifestations of informal-group politics. However, even within the United States, the tendency to organize informal rather than formal groups differs in strength from one area of the country to another. In the South and the Southwest, nonassociational groups are active. This once led an observer to characterize the state of Louisiana as "the westernmost of the Arab states."[16] Generally, however, the American political process places relatively less emphasis on informal groups and relatively more on such aggregates as trade unions, legislatures, and political parties. This is not the case in much of the world. Studies of Brazil, India, Burma, Taiwan, Japan, and Italy, for example, impressively demonstrate that informal and nonassociational-group polities are dominant in these societies.

The gradual recognition of the critical role that informal groups play in the less industrialized world has been recently accompanied by preliminary analysis (by a small number of scholars of contemporary Middle Eastern political systems) emphasizing this phenomenon. Amal Vinogradov and John Waterbury, for example, introduce the term *security group* to refer to a factional group that "is the maximal unit in which there is some predictability in the exercise of power and authority."[17] Clement H. Moore discusses what he terms *contingent interest groups* that cut across associational interest groups and serve as "gatekeepers" for North African political systems. According to Moore, "Examples of contingent interest groups range from sets of Algerian cousins and fellow maquisards or a Moroccan family of notables to professional veto groups or a handful of individuals out to convince Bourguiba that Ben Salah's Plan is a menace."[18]

The most crucial units of interest aggregation in the Middle East remain informal groups. In Iraq this kind of collectivity is referred to as a *shilla* or *jama'at,* and in Saudi Arabia the term most often used is *bashka.* The Egyptians also use the word *shilla* to refer to a group of approximately two to twelve members who socialize together and who work to help one another advance politically and economically. A slightly more diffuse Egyptian informal group is the *duf'a,* or old-boy network. The duf'a (literally "pushing out") is often the general structure from which the more tightly knit *shillas* are formed. In Kuwait, the *diwaniyya* is an informal gathering where men meet to discuss and determine important political questions. Other words in the Arab world that carry the idea of cliques and factions but that sometimes also indicate a higher level of formality include *kutal* and *fi'at.* In Iran, the sociopolitical system is backed by a gigantic

---

[16]For reference to this memorable quote, see T. Harry Williams, *Huey Long* (New York: Bantam Books, 1970), p. 194.

[17]Amal Vinogradov and John Waterbury, "Situations of Contested Legitimacy in Morocco: An Alternative Framework," *Comparative Studies in Society and History* 13 (January 1971): 34.

[18]Clement Henry Moore, *Politics in North Africa: Algeria, Morocco, and Tunisia* (Boston: Little, Brown and Co., 1970), pp. 201–202.

network of informal, personalistic cliques referred to as *dawrahs* ("circles"). Afghan group dynamics are dominated by loose factional aggregates referred to as either *dastahs* ("handfuls of individuals") or *girdabs* ("little whirlpools"). One of the most important of the informal groups in Turkey is the personal collectivity based on *hemşeri* ("from the same region") relations. The hemserilik is a group that forms and re-forms as fellow villagers and "hometowners" aggregate to assist one another with social, economic, occupational, and political aims. In Egypt, the same kind of group formation prevails in the *baladiyya,* which is in fact a kind of informal, extended family group.[19]

The juxtaposition of informal groups with formal political associations is seen in the case of Bahrain, an archipelago off the coast of Saudi Arabia, just west of the Qatar peninsula. An early modernizer, Bahrain is the oldest petroleum-producing state in the Persian Gulf and had already established a girls' school in 1928. Strikes and labor unrest have occurred in this small shaikhdom ever since the mid-1950s. Ruled absolutely by the al-Khalifa family, this country has nonetheless had notable experience with municipal and national consultative bodies. The actual politics of Bahrain have taken place within an extensive network of clubs (*nawadi*) and societies (*jam'iyyat*). Numbering approximately one hundred, these informal groups, "whose memberships include a majority of Bahrain's elite public, have played the essential functions performed by political parties in other political systems."[20] Ostensibly organized for social, professional, and recreational purposes, these clubs are often intensely political. The 250-member al-Arabi Club, for example, is composed of educated Bahrainis who push for nationalistic and democratic goals. The University Graduates' Club, on the other hand, is oriented more toward the elite and consists of college-educated intellectuals from both the middle and upper classes. It is the establishment's liberal conscience. These kinds of informal groups in Bahrain coexist both with formal organizations and with the ruling family, whose tentacles reach deep down into the club network.

Informal-group activity in the Middle East has manifested itself in a myriad of ways. Ranging from tiny dyads that plug in and out of one another to enormously complex coalitions based on kinship, these groups have little in common besides their personal, informal nature. Personal homes have served as locations for the meetings of the more exclusive of the groups, while mosques, coffeehouses, teahouses, common rooms, and bazaar shops have served as meeting places for the more inclusive of the groups. Informal groups operating in these kinds of settings constantly relay information through the various societies. It is largely on the basis of this information that personal and political decisions are made. In addition, it is in precisely such groups and such settings that middle-grade army officers sometimes decide to intervene in the political affairs of their countries.

---

[19]For two more recent studies of networks of informal politics in Middle Eastern urban settings, see Guilain Denoeux, *Urban Unrest in the Middle East* (Albany, N.Y.: State University of New York Press, 1993); and Diane Singerman, *Avenues of Participation* (Princeton, N.J.: Princeton University Press, 1995).

[20]Emile Nakhleh, *Bahrain: Political Development in a Modernizing Society* (Lexington, Mass.: Lexington Books, 1976), p. 41. Most of the information in this paragraph is drawn from the Nakhleh book.

One of the important characteristics of informal-group politics is an intense and pervasive spirit of personalism. The fundamental social and political ties tend to be personal in nature.[21] In moving into a wide variety of informal groups, the individual strives to broaden personal contacts in order to gain representation on as many fronts as possible. What determines the Middle Easterner's power and influence "is not the fact that he holds a certain office or even that that office affords certain opportunities for personal aggrandizement but the extent and success with which he as an individual is able to cumulate a wide range of personal ties, to display to others a number of highly valued personal characteristics, and . . . to merge them into a larger framework of political importance reaching up to the very highest government levels."[22] In this kind of environment, individuals develop great skills in personal persuasion. Decision making is determined by personal push and pull, as is interestingly indicated by the Turkish expression *torpil* and the Iranian term *parti*. While the formal group tends to deemphasize the personal element, the informal group preserves and promotes personalism.

The personal nature of group politics in the Middle East is exemplified well by the Lebanese *zu'ama* system (singular: *za'im*). In the Lebanese context, the za'im is an informal group leader whose followers support him on the basis of personal loyalty and personal rewards. The personal power of the za'im is rooted in local and regional communities and is buttressed by the fact that the leader and his followers share a common religion or sect. Among the important zu'ama families are the Frangiehs (Maronites), the Jumblatts (Druze), the Shihabs (Sunnites), and the al-As'ads (Shi'is). Leaders with names such as these have been present for years in the national political institutions of Lebanon. When the Maronite leader and Lebanese president-elect Bashir Gemayel was assassinated in 1982, he was replaced in his presidential position by his brother, Amin Gemayel. The strength of the family ties of the zu'ama system is very great indeed.

At the level of the informal group, the argument that Middle Eastern politics is basically nonideological is quite convincing. Commitments are more often to individuals and family units than to ideas. The precedence of personal ties over ideology is seen in the striking examples of family units that contain within themselves all shades of political and professional commitment. Such families are able to transcend regime changes and even revolution. The Marei family in Egypt is a case in point.

The father, Ahmad Marei, was a well-to-do supporter of the old regime, a member of the Wafd Party, and a parliamentary deputy. During the Nasserite revolution, the influence of the family remained intact. One brother (and the patriarch of the family today), Hassan Marei, was appointed minister of commerce and industry in 1954. Another brother, Sayyid Marei, the most powerful member of the family over the years, had served as a member of Parliament for six years during King Farouk's rule. Under Nasser, Sayyid was minister of agriculture for many years and an important official in the Arab Socialist Union. A

---

[21]See Chapter 4 for a detailed discussion of personalism in the Middle Eastern variant of patrimonial polities.

[22]Rosen, "Rural Political Process," p. 216.

third brother, Marei Marei, served as director of the chemical organization during the Nasser period. During these years, the Marei family had the added connection of their more radical cousin, Ali Sabry, a former member of the Free Officers, secretary-general of the Arab Socialist Union, and one of Nasser's five premiers. Despite Sabry's removal from power by President Anwar Sadat in May 1971 and his subsequent imprisonment, the Marei brothers survived well.

During the Sadat period, Hassan Marei remained influential in the industrial community, while Marei Marei held a directorship in a state holding company. In 1974, Marei Marei took charge of the very lucrative economic relationships between Egypt and Iran. In September 1971, Sadat appointed the ubiquitous Sayyid Marei deputy premier and minister of agriculture. In October 1974, Sayyid became speaker of the assembly, and four years later, he settled in as presidential advisor to President Sadat himself. The Marei-Sadat relationship was cemented by the 1975 marriage of Sayyid Marei's son, Hassan, to Sadat's daughter, Noha. Because Sayyid and Hassan were so closely associated with the Sadat era, from which Mubarak has tried to distance himself, the new president has not allowed them to reemerge in public life. Hassan has, with his brother Nasr, become a highly successful businessman. Sayyid's brother Marei, who was not a high-profile member of the Sadat entourage, has become the family's active politician. He is the chairman of the foreign relations committee of the Consultative Assembly. The first loyalty of "the Mareis and most other Egyptians is to the family itself, and political ideology is not sufficiently compelling to undermine primordial family ties."[23]

This pattern of family tenacity and ideological malleability has also prevailed in such countries as Iran, Iraq, Lebanon, and Morocco. Even the leading families of the very conservative shaikhdoms of the Persian Gulf have had members who have espoused radical causes. Shaikh Saqr bin Sultan, who ruled Sharjah between 1951 and 1965, is a notable example. Saqr, a strong Arab nationalist with Nasserist sympathies and a dislike for the British, was deposed in 1965, primarily for these reasons. In 1972, he returned from exile in Cairo and failed in an attempt to regain the throne.

An informal group "is like a cluster of bees round a queen bee. If the queen is damaged they quickly find another to cluster around."[24] The exigencies of politics require an individual to shift positions periodically in order to maintain as much manipulative leeway as possible. The informal group itself will often switch goals and alter the ideas that brought its membership together. Such changes, of course, always mean that a certain percentage of the membership will be lost, but this is one important by-product of the fluidity of this type of group. Individuals retain the capacity to circulate among a host of collectivities, depending on what they consider to be in their own interests. Coalitions are fragile and alliances fleeting in such social and political systems. Even the

---

[23]Robert Springborg, *Family, Power, and Politics in Egypt* (Philadelphia: University of Pennsylvania Press, 1982), p. 75.

[24]This statement was made concerning informal-group politics in India. See B. D. Graham, "The Succession of Factional Systems in the Uttar Pradesh Congress Party, 1937–1966," in *Local-Level Politics: Social and Cultural Perspectives,* ed. by Marc J. Swartz (Chicago: Aldine, 1968), p. 355.

strongest social cement, personal ties, can be cracked. However, the adhesive quality remains, so the relationship can be reestablished whenever the winds of fortune dictate that it be reestablished. This plasticity of informal-group politics promotes an underlying systemic stability in the Middle East.

Informal groups in the Middle East are characterized by alternating fission and fusion. "It is always possible to divide them, to prevent powerful coalitions from forming, for their solidarity, of course, is inversely proportional to their breadth. Hence political showdowns rarely occur."[25] Although tension, conflict, and competition infuse this network of "many-stranded coalitions,"[26] the overall group system persists and prevails. The tension promotes balance. "Equilibrium in conflict is not achieved by both or all sides desisting from conflict but rather in both or all sides persisting in conflict. . . . The best defense of a security group lies in keeping up steady pressure against its rivals short of attack."[27] This principle of counterbalancing in group politics is prevalent throughout the Middle East, although it manifests itself somewhat differently from one society to another. In the traditional countries of the Gulf and Morocco, it helps foster systemic fluidity and flexibility. In Lebanon, on the other hand, it froze into a more rigid pattern, in which groups directly confronted one another; there, the more common pattern of many sides balanced against one another gave way to confrontations between two sides. The fragility of this situation became all too clear in April 1975 when the society exploded into bloody civil war.

This network of floating factions could not persist without a sturdier group backing to help anchor it in the social structure. Individuals require a more reliable vehicle than factions and cliques to defend their interests and to achieve their goals. In the Middle East, this mechanism is the kinship group in general and the family in particular.

THE PRIMORDIAL GROUP NEXUS: THE FAMILY

Kinship units represent a very special kind of informal group. The family, which is the basic unit and building block of groups in the Middle East, retains characteristics that render it more rigid than most factional and nonassociational groups. Although the lines of association that mark personal cliques and political factions appear and disappear with amazing rapidity, true kinship relations are much more difficult to create and destroy. Ties of kinship remain in existence whether or not political actors choose to recognize them. Since family networks are virtually impossible to destroy, they provide the element of permanence needed to offset the impermanence of other informal groups. Family groupings are the linchpins of the system of group interaction in the Middle East. Indeed, lineage patterns are "the invisible skeleton of the community."[28]

---

[25]Moore, *Politics in North Africa*, p. 202

[26]This phrase is borrowed from Eric Wolf, *Peasants* (Englewood Cliffs, N.J.: Prentice-Hall, 1966), and is quoted in Khuri, "Changing Class Structure," p. 35.

[27]Vinogradov and Waterbury, "Situations of Contested Legitimacy," p. 35.

[28]This phrase is John Gulick's. See Gulick, *Social Structure and Culture Change in a Lebanese Village* (New York: Wenner-Gren Foundation, 1955), p. 104.

This skeleton, however, contains the moving force of the community. In the words of Dale Eickelman; "Kinship relationships should be treated as something which people make and with which they accomplish things."[29]

The traditional Middle Eastern family unit is an extended family, usually consisting of a man, his wife (or wives), his unmarried sons and daughters, and his married sons and their wives and children. In the contemporary urban Middle East, the institution of the extended family is increasingly giving way to the nuclear family, which includes only the husband, wife, and children. Family groups, whether extended or nuclear, are consciously and carefully shaped. Marriage patterns are critical, since they determine the direction in which the family group will move. The most distinctive traditional trait of Middle Eastern marriage is the preferred marriage of a man and his father's brother's daughter (*bint'amm*). This paternal first cousin marriage was designed to strengthen important blood ties and to solidify a constantly expanding family unit. Such an endogamous marriage pattern has significant political implications. In the Middle East, it enabled family heads to enlist the critical support of their brothers and their brothers' sons. In societies deeply divided, this minimal unit of coalition was a relatively effective action group. Few family clusters could afford the internecine conflict that might otherwise have occurred among brothers, nephews, and cousins.[30]

Every individual in the Middle East thus begins with membership in one important informal group—the family. This group seeks to magnify its kinship ties in at least three different ways. First, contacts are strengthened and regular communication is maintained with as many blood relatives as is practically possible. Even when there is great geographical and genealogical distance separating kinfolk, family members seldom hesitate to approach one another for needed economic and political assistance. In Egypt, for example, "While members of the descent group may not socialize regularly with one another, and may indeed be quite distant genealogically speaking, they have no compunction about asking their kin and affines for economic and political favors."[31]

The second way in which family ties are expanded in the Middle East is by a very broad and flexible definition of kinship. The Afghan concept of *qawm*, for example, defines actual kinship on the basis of deep social and political cooperation among those who live in the same area. Somewhat the same applies in Morocco, where the term *qaraba* or "closeness" is expressed as a blood tie "even when no demonstrable ties exist, because however such ties are valued in practice, they are considered permanent and cannot be broken."[32] Also, kinship ties are often fictitiously manufactured in an attempt to enhance the influence of a particular individual or group. The most common examples of fictive kinship

---

[29]Dale F, Eickelman, *The Middle East: An Anthropological Approach* (Englewood Cliffs, N.J.: Prentice-Hall, 1981), p. 134.

[30]For an excellent discussion of the marriage patterns of Middle Eastern families, see Dale F. Eickelman, *The Middle East: An Anthropological Approach*, second ed. (Englewood Cliffs, N.J.: Prentice-Hall, 1989), pp. 151–178.

[31]Springborg, *Family, Power, and Politics*, p. 54.

[32]Eickelman, *The Middle East*, second ed., p. 156.

are elaborate arguments that purport to document one's direct descent from the family of the Prophet Muhammad.

Finally, family contacts are broadened by the incorporation into the kinship group of new individuals and families through marriage. This is why in the Middle East, "Arranging marriages is a highly serious matter, like waging war or making big business deals."[33] The process by which two families are brought together through intermarriage can be described as "family nesting." "Family nesting occurs when two families, tied together through marriage, reinforce that connection through a series of social, economic, and political exchanges."[34] The branches of the family trees in the forests of Middle Eastern society and politics are filled with family nests. In Egypt, the Marei family discussed previously nests with other powerful kinship units such as the Muhy al-din, Sabri, Shamsi, Abaza, Mashur, and Elwan families. The Mareis have even nested with the Sadat family. ". . . It is by nesting with other families that the descent group of the Mareis performs the greatest services for its members. The sheer number of family members involved in these nests, and the scope of their various economic and political activities, provides a complex of opportunities for the exchange of economic and political favors."[35] From the era of Farouk to that of Mubarak, families with whom the Mareis nested were among the most influential in the country.

For the family group to remain strong, its members must maintain a continually updated knowledge of the intricate kinship structure to which they belong. In the Ottoman system, for example, "Every member of the clan kept a genealogical map in his head to orient him in his relations with others."[36] In Turkey, the situation is one "of everyone having to know very precisely to what extended family, to what kin village, to what lineage, to what clan, to what clan federation and to what principality or khanate he belongs."[37] This awareness of precisely where one stands with regard to other group members contributes greatly to group solidarity and, ultimately, to the capacity to attain group objectives. Strands of kinship serve, at the very least, as relatively permanent lines of access among group members. It is in the individual's self-interest to be familiar with as many of these connections as possible.

Like all other group formations in the Middle East, the kinship group (whether family, tribe, or clan) is internally divided and fragmented. Intrafamilial tensions, quarrels, and feuds are common. However, within the nuclear family, the divisions are not as deep or the tensions as intense as they are outside the family. More important, the kinship group presents a united front against outside competitors. Fragmented collectivities gain solidarity and cohesion through

---

[33]Hildred Geertz, "The Meanings in Family Ties," in *Meaning and Order in Moroccan Society,* ed. by C. Geertz, H. Geertz, and L. Rosen (New York: Cambridge University Press, 1979), p. 363, as quoted in Eickelman, *The Middle East,* second ed., p. 170.

[34]Springborg, *Family, Power, and Politics,* p. 73.

[35]Ibid., p. 88.

[36]Şerif Mardin, "Historical Determinants of Stratification: Social Class and Class Consciousness in Turkey." Paper prepared for the Comparative Bureaucracy Seminar, Massachusetts Institute of Technology, Spring 1966, p. 19.

[37]Ibid.

the pressure exerted by external rival forces. In this system of balancing opposition, the family unit always fares best. This is because the kinship group is the most cohesive and tenacious of the Middle Eastern group formations.

In addition to being both a biological and an economic unit, the family is very much a political aggregation. Family members support one another in their drives to improve their respective power and authority positions in the particular society. Besides providing support for its members in their efforts to attain political goals, the kinship group is politically relevant in many other ways. It serves, for example, as the staging ground from which individuals can move on to membership in other groups, both formal and informal. The family, in fact, determines much of its members' participation in other collectivities. Such informal groups as personal cliques and political factions have fathers, sons, brothers, nephews, cousins, and in-laws strategically sprinkled throughout them in patterns that tend to benefit the particular family unit. As often as not, a single family is represented in rival political factions, parties, or movements. Thus, although informal-group membership cuts across kinship lines, it is also true that the filaments of kinship cut across the boundaries of cliques and factions. A major function of distributing family members among various other groups is the construction and maintenance of channels of communication among these groups, whether they be rivals or allies.

The ligaments of kinship bind the system of groups into a working whole. They run through rival collectivities, thus softening tensions. Through membership in both formal and informal groups, blood relatives and in-laws help bind these two major organizational types together. Family members in such institutions as bureaucracies and parliaments are in close touch with relatives who are members of cliques and factions. Decisions made in one context are directly influenced by what occurs in another context.

Morocco has sometimes been referred to as the kingdom of cousins, and monarchical Iran was frequently called the country of one thousand families. Observers have labeled Farouk's Egypt as the land of two thousand families and contemporary Pakistan as the country of sixty families. The intricacies of family relationships explain a great deal about the orientations, formation, and behavior of political elites in the Middle East. The more traditional the society, the more useful kinship analysis will be in understanding it. In all the Middle Eastern countries, however, patterns of kinship and marriage are valuable in understanding the structure of power and authority. Those societies that are developing politically and modernizing rapidly may have a relatively large number of ruling families, as well as a high rate of familial mobility. A study of such family structures can explain much about national elites and the political processes of the societies under investigation. Selected examples follow.

In the three decades prior to 1958, the Iraqi political elite represented a tight cluster of families. The core of the elite included such families as the al-Saids, the al-Askaris, the Kannas, and the Kamals. The famous Nuri al-Said held the post of prime minister fourteen times and that of minister twenty-nine times! Ja'far al-Askari, who was assassinated in 1936, was prime minister twice and minister eight times. Nuri al-Said and Ja'far al-Askari married each other's sisters. Tahsin al-Askari followed in the footsteps of his assassinated brother, Ja'far, when in 1942 he assumed two ministerial positions. He was the brother-in-law of

Ibrahim Kamal, who was himself a cabinet minister twice. Another al-Askari brother, Abd al-Hadi, married his daughter to Khalil Kanna, who held ministerial posts six different times. Two of Khalil Kanna's brothers were members of the Iraqi parliament.[38]

The Iraqi revolution of 1958 did not destroy the political power of the families. The Ba'thist regime of strongman Saddam Hussein al-Takriti is dominated by Saddam and his relatives from the town of Takrit. In the early 1980s, Saddam's two leading intelligence and security chiefs were his half-brothers Barzan Ibrahim al-Takriti and Watban Ibrahim al-Takriti. Saddam himself was the foster son, nephew, and son-in-law of Khayrallah al-Tulfah, the longtime governor of Baghdad. In the words of a leading scholar of Iraqi politics, the Takritis' power is so great that "it would not be going too far to say that the Takrītīs' rule through the Ba'th party, rather than the Ba'th party through the Takrītīs."[39]

In the shah's Iran, national politics were dominated by family considerations, since the political elite that clustered around the ruling Pahlavi family came from a small number of families. Among the most influential of the elite families in Pahlavi Iran were the following: Alam, Diba, Qaragozlu, Esfandiari, Ardalan, Bayat, Sami'i, Farman-farmaian, Bushehri, Jahanbani, and Emami. The ties among key members of these families were easily as close as the ties among the families in Iraq. Longtime minister of culture Mehrdad Pahlbod was the husband of Princess Shams, a sister of Muhammad Reza Shah. Former major general Minbashian was the brother of Pahlbod (formerly Ezzatullah Minbashian). The influential Senator Bushehri was the father of the husband of powerful Princess Ashraf, the twin sister of the shah. Former air force commander Muhammad Khatami was married to the shah's sister Fatima. Ardeshir Zahedi, Iranian ambassador to the United States, was once married to the shah's daughter Shahnaz. During the last years of the shah's rule, there were forty national elite families that dominated the economic and political systems in Iran.

Despite the shattering nature of the Iranian revolution of 1978–1979, political influence in the Islamic Republic has tended to follow the primordial lines of kinship and family. The strands of kinship about which power coagulates extended outward from the person of Ayatollah Ruhollah Khomeini himself. One of Khomeini's daughters, for example, was married to the influential Ayatollah Eshraqi. More important, Khomeini's son, Ahmad, was a close advisor to his father after they returned together to Tehran in 1979.[40]

With the election of reformist president Mohammad Khatami in 1997, the system of personal and familial ties persisted. Chairman of the influential Expediency Council and two-term president of the Islamic Republic, Ali Akbar Hashemi-Rafsanjani has a brother, Mohammad Hashemi, who serves as vice

---

[38]This information is drawn from Nazar T. Al-Hasso's excellent Ph.D. dissertation. See Al-Hasso, "Administrative Politics in the Middle East: The Case of Monarchical Iraq. 1920–1958." Ph.D. diss., The University of Texas, Austin, Texas, 1976.

[39]Hanna Batatu, *The Old Social Classes and the Revolutionary Movements of Iraq* (Princeton. N.J.: Princeton University Press, 1978), p. 1088.

[40]Detailed information on the web of kinship ties that bound the early leaders of the Islamic Republic is found in an article that appeared in *Iran Times,* February 6, 1981, p. 9 (in Persian).

president for Executive Affairs for President Khatami. Khatami's brother, Hadi, is also a presidential adviser. Iranian foreign minister and longtime Iranian ambassador to the United Nations Kamal Kharrazi has an older brother who is a member of the Assembly of Experts and who maintains a close friendship with the Leader, Ali Khamenei. Khamenei's brother, Hadi, served in the Islamic Parliament until 1992 and then became editor of an influential daily newspaper.

Family connections loom even larger in the shaikhdoms of the Persian Gulf where the core of the political elite always consists of members of the ruling family. The remaining members of the elite are drawn from other wealthy, aristocratic families. Political decision making in Saudi Arabia, Kuwait, Qatar, Oman, the United Arab Emirates, and Bahrain is monopolized by the ruling families in these countries. In Bahrain, where political and economic decision making is dominated by Shaikh Isa bin Salman Al-Khalifa and his brother, Shaikh Khalifa bin Salman Al-Khalifa, the names of the leading families such as Kanu, Fakhru, Shirawi, and Mu'ayyid are well known.

The following anecdote illustrates that in Bahrain, family is more important than any formal governing body: While in the marketplace in 1973, an elderly Bahraini was told to go vote in the elections for the Constitutional Assembly. The old man looked around and asked, "Who owns that building?" "A Kanu," he was told. "And who owns this one?" "A Mu'ayyid," was the response. "And this third one?" "Shaykh Khalifa." The old man then asked, "Will the elections change any of this?"[41] The right family connections remain an important passport to the elite in much of the Middle East.

Political revolution and economic modernization have hardly lessened the role of the family group in government. It is true that the form of family organization has changed considerably and that kinship relations now crystallize in new ways. The most evident change of this sort is the transfer from the extended to the nuclear family style of household. This change, however, has not fundamentally altered the important role that kinship relations play in the political process. Fuad Khuri writes that "the change from the extended family subculture to that of the nuclear family does not imply the loss of family ties and duties. Family ties and duties, no doubt, continue, but in new forms."[42] The physical living arrangements of the family may be changing, but its sociopolitical demands and supports remain essentially the same.

THE POWER OF WOMEN: A CASE STUDY OF INFORMAL POLITICS

When one examines the informal nature of group politics in the Middle East, a number of previously overlooked and underemphasized dimensions of the political game suddenly come into sharper focus. Persons who were formerly considered peripheral to political decision making take on more central signifi-

---

[41]This story is presented in Nakhleh, *Bahrain,* p. 129 n.

[42]Khuri, "Changing Class Structure," p. 38.

cance. This is precisely the case in cultures where there is no sharp distinction between the private and the public spheres or where key community and national decisions are made in informal settings by individuals often considered peripheral to politics. An important case in point is the Middle Eastern woman. Studying the woman's role in society can provoke new insights into the kinds of actors and actresses who play out the political drama and can indicate both the importance of informal politics and the special place that family relationships have in Middle Eastern politics.

For years, Middle Eastern women have been stereotyped as an oppressed and passive group who have been hidden by veils and whose lives have been dominated by men. Western writers in particular have presented the Muslim woman as someone held captive in the kitchen or harem while her husband frolics personally and protects politically a system of polygamy that rationalizes female servitude. Quotations from the Quran and the relative absence of females on the public political stage have sometimes led outsiders to conclude that the woman in Islamic society has been little more than a personal and political cipher. This perspective has been reinforced by Middle Eastern historians and chroniclers who have traditionally downplayed the role of women in their writings. In addition, essayists and polemicists, both male and female, have distorted the historical position of women for various purposes.

In stressing the formal, public, and institutional aspects of political behavior at the expense of the private and informal dimensions, Western analysts have overlooked precisely those individuals who dominate the private realm. In the Middle East, women are important political forces because of their critical positions as personal nodes in the webs of informal relationships. In the crucial world of informal, private groups, women have been more than the homemakers. They have also been "the matchmakers and the peacemakers."[43] As anthropologist Emrys Peters puts it,

> The pivotal points in any field of power in this, a superficially dominant patrilineal, patrilocal and patriarchal society where the male ethos is vulgar in its brash prominence, are the women. What holds men together, what knots the cords of alliances are not men themselves, but the women who depart from their natal household to take up residence elsewhere with a man, and who, in this critical position, communicate one group to another.[44]

This quotation refers to only one of the ways in which Middle Eastern women shape political events at all levels of the societies in which they live.

---

[43]We are indebted to Gerald J. Obermeyer for this phrase.

[44]Emrys Peters, "Consequences of the Segregation of the Sexes Among the Arabs." Paper delivered at the Mediterranean Social Science Council Conference, Athens, 1966, p. 15. This important observation has been quoted by such scholars as Cynthia Nelson and Carla Makhlouf, whose works stress the political power of women in the Middle East. Anthropologically inclined analysts have been much more sensitive to this power than have political scientists. Two further examples are Elizabeth Warnock Fernea, who has done field work in Iraq, Egypt, and Morocco, and Lois Grant Beck, who has worked in Iran. Cynthia Nelson's field observations come from Egypt, and Carla Makhlouf's from Yemen.

In both the traditional and the modern Middle East, women have exerted political influence through the wide variety of roles that they have played. Perhaps the most important of these have been natal and marital kinship roles. Such natal roles as daughter, sister, cousin, aunt, mother, and grandmother and such marital roles as wife and mother-in-law have been politically strategic throughout Islamic history. The special relationship between mother and son is particularly relevant to our understanding of Middle Eastern political events. As we shall see in the examples here, only the role of wife has been more important in the female repertoire of political roles. One knowledgeable observer writes that "it is hardly surprising that the relationship to the mother is preferred to the paternal one, and that every patriarchal society is condemned to be matriarchal on the edges. On the edges? Not at all! It is a question here of the depths of existence."[45]

Other roles in which Muslim women have exerted influence in the political arena include such diverse traditional callings as prostitute, concubine, entertainer, servant, religious leader, soothsayer, and advisor. More modern roles, such as career woman and politician-stateswoman, are becoming more important with time. Female revolutionaries and guerrillas are also increasingly active.

Among the tools that Middle Eastern women have used to exert influence are such resources as wealth, beauty, intelligence, and information, as well as both psychological and physical coercion. They have often converted the very signs of their oppression into formidable offensive weapons that have enabled them to secure their interests. Excellent examples of such weapons are the harem and the veil that segregate the sexes. The conventional wisdom is that it is the women who are excluded from the male world, but, as one scholar has recently written: "One can venture to assert that it is in fact the men who are excluded from the female world, as much, if not more, than females are excluded from that of man."[46] This researcher goes on to give a number of examples of how much easier it is for women to penetrate men's gatherings than for males to participate in those of women.

A survey of Middle Eastern history indicates the important contributions that women have made to the political process. From the very beginnings of Islam, women have been critical political forces. Indeed, as we shall see in Chapter 4, there is little doubt that the Prophet Muhammad could not have succeeded in his mission without the indispensable support of his first wife, Khadija. Other women who helped shape the early social system of Islam were Muhammad's wife A'isha and his daughter Fatima. Fatima's sister-in-law Zaynab

---

[45]A. Bouhdiba, "The Child and the Mother in Arab-Muslim Society," in *Psychological Dimensions of Near Eastern Studies*, ed. by L. Carl Brown and Norman Itzkowitz (Princeton, N.J.: Darwin Press, 1977), p. 133. For another fine discussion of the power of the mother and mother-in-law in Muslim society, see Fatima Mernissi, *Beyond the Veil: Male-Female Dynamics in a Modern Muslim Society* (Cambridge, Mass.: Schenkman Publishing Co., 1975), pp. 69–79.

[46]Carla Makhlouf, *Changing Veils: Women and Modernisation in North Yemen* (Austin, Tex.: University of Texas Press, 1979). This study contains fascinating material showing how the veil has traditionally provided Middle Eastern women with a mobile form of security and anonymity and has even facilitated the expression of aggressiveness. More than religious fervor is involved in the return to the veil in the 1980s and 1990s by numerous liberated young women in countries such as Egypt.

was also a powerful force in early Islamic history, as were the wives of the various imams who were the direct descendants of Fatima and her husband Ali.

The political role of women in the famous Umayyad and Abbasid caliphates is little known. In both instances, it was critical. This was especially true during the golden age of the cosmopolitan Abbasid dynasty in the late eighth and early ninth centuries. At a time when Europe was plunged into its Dark Ages and when Charlemagne and his lords "were reportedly dabbling with the art of writing their names,"[47] the powerful Abbasids, ruling from Baghdad, were debating philosophic texts and making gigantic intellectual strides in medicine, astronomy, mathematics, and the arts. The glory and grandeur of this period are captured in romantically imaginative terms in *The Thousand Nights and a Night,* and such rulers of the period as Harun al-Rashid (A.D. 786–809) and his brilliant son the caliph al-Ma'mun (A.D. 813–833) are among the most renowned of Eastern rulers. Names such as Umm Salama, Khayzuran, and Zubayda, however, are considerably less known, even among scholars of the area. Umm Salama was the wife of Abu al-Abbas and thus served as a critical link between the two dynasties. A strong personality, she directed her husband's affairs, and he "took no decisive measure without Umm Salamah's advice and approval."[48]

Khayzuran was the favorite wife of the third Abbasid caliph, Muhammad al-Mahdi; she was also the mother of the fourth and fifth caliphs, Musa al-Hadi and Harun al-Rashid. A slave girl born in Yemen, she received an excellent education and caught the eye of the caliph al-Mansur, who brought her to the court, where his son al-Mahdi married her. For thirty years, during the reigns of three caliphs, Khayzuran's political power was enormous. Her agents and secretaries were spread throughout the empire; she intervened directly in the administration of justice; she influenced the rise and fall of the caliph's closest advisors; she financed the construction of public works; and she directed the succession of kings. It was Khayzuran who held the system together and ensured the smooth transition of kings both upon the death of her husband and then again when her eldest son, al-Hadi, passed away. Khayzuran was an owner of extensive property, and, next to her illustrious son Harun al-Rashid, she was the wealthiest person in the Muslim world of her day. In describing Khayzuran's role during the caliphates of her two sons, one writer succinctly summarizes her position: "The ambitious mother travels in state on the imperial highway of power."[49]

Better known in the annals of Islamic history than Khayzuran is her niece Zubayda, the wife of Harun al-Rashid. One of the greatest builders of public works in Islamic history, Zubayda is remembered particularly for sponsoring the construction of over ten miles of complex aqueducts leading into Mecca. She spent over 75 million dinars in digging the Mushshash Spring in that holy city— a spectacular feat in any age. Like Khayzuran, Zubayda was intimately involved in all the important political issues of the time. She had influence over judges, police officials, and military generals, not to mention her husband. The observation that "Zubaidah had (complete) control over Hārūn's mind and did with

---

[47]Philip K. Hitti, *The Near East in History* (Princeton, N.J.: D. Van Nostrand Co., 1961), p. 244.

[48]Nabia Abbott, *Two Queens of Baghdad* (Chicago: University of Chicago Press, 1946), p. 11.

[49]Ibid., p. 132.

him as she pleased"[50] is perhaps only a slight exaggeration. In the succession battle between her son Muhammad Amin and al-Ma'mun, she played a critical role in Amin's victory. Zubayda was a major force also in turning Harun against the powerful Persian Barmecids, who had directed the political fortunes of the Abbasid dynasty more than any other family. Indirectly, but very effectively, she helped bring about their destruction. Zubayda left her imprint deeply in the sands of Abbasid social and political history.

Moving chronologically onward and geographically southward, we come to the Sulayhid dynasty, which ruled in South Arabia from 1037 to 1138. This Shi'i dynasty made its capital in Sanaa and later in the Dhu Jibla of today's Yemen. The Sulayhi "educated their daughters to the same standards as their menfolk, instilled in them the same moral and political principles, and made them their equals in astuteness, ability, and judgement."[51] The greatest of the Sulayhid queens was Urwa bint Ahmad al-Sulayhi, who upon her husband al-Mukarram's death in 1084 took complete command and ruled for fifty-three years. A woman of great political acumen, Queen Urwa ruled the Sulayhid state by judiciously emphasizing tactics of compromise, personal maneuver, and the wise appointment of assistants and advisors. Urwa's political success is perhaps largely attributable to the training she received under the direction of another woman, Queen Asma, the wife of the founder of the Sulayhid dynasty.

The Ottoman Empire, which boasts a political history that extended from the thirteenth to the twentieth centuries, is a much more significant example of an Islamic system in which women wielded political power. The Ottoman style, however, is more similar to the Abbasid style of indirect kinship control than to the Sulayhid style of direct rule by a queen. Although one can select any particular sultan and discover in association with him a number of women active in the central decision-making process, we will cut into Ottoman history at its height of grandeur, the reign of Suleyman I the Lawgiver (1520–1566). Suleyman was known for his legal promulgations and his empire for its architectural creations, naval strength, and military expansion deep into Europe. Surrounding Suleyman were three women of particular note—his mother, Hafsa Hatun, and his wives, Hurrem Sultan and Gulbahar Hatun. Their political influence was great, especially in controlling the sultan and the grand vazir, the most important administrative official in the Ottoman system. Of these three women, the most powerful was Hurrem Sultan, a former Russian slave girl known in the West as Roxelana. It was she who convinced Suleyman to let her live with him in the seraglio, "where she obtained complete ascendancy over the Sultan and ruled supreme in the harēm until her death in 1558."[52]

---

[50]F. Wustenfeld, *Die Chroniken der Stadt Mekka*, vol. 3, p. 15, as quoted in Abbott, *Two Queens*, p. 256.

[51]Robert W. Stookey, *Yemen: The Politics of the Yemen Arab Republic* (Boulder, Colo.: Westview Press, 1978), p. 67.

[52]N. M. Penzer, *The Harēm* (Philadelphia: J. B. Lippincott, 1937), p. 186. There are many sources that describe this period of Ottoman history. For an excellent example, see Stanford Shaw, *History of the Ottoman Empire and Modern Turkey*, vol. 1 (Cambridge: Cambridge University Press, 1976), pp. 87–111.

Hafsa Hatun and Hurrem Sultan formed an alliance of convenience to expel one grand vazir and appoint another early in the reign of Suleyman. The new vazir, Ibrahim Pasha, felt indebted to Hafsa Hatun for his position and was careful to do her bidding. Meanwhile, he was independently linked to Suleyman himself, who permitted the vazir to run the empire. Ibrahim Pasha in the process became one of the most powerful of the grand vazirs in Ottoman history. An extraordinarily ambitious person politically, Hurrem Sultan came to regard the vazir as a major competitor and sought to destroy him. When her mother-in-law died in 1534, she moved quickly against the vazir. The now exposed Ibrahim Pasha found an ally in Suleyman's first wife, Gulbahar Hatun, who was anxious that her son Mustafa become the heir apparent. Hurrem Sultan, with her own sons' interests at heart, gathered other supporters (including the French ambassador) and was able to prevail in the struggle. In 1536, Ibrahim Pasha lost not only his job but also his life.

Hurrem Sultan then succeeded in getting her eldest son, Mehmet, named as heir to the throne. With his untimely death, however, Gulbahar Hatun, with the assistance of the new vazir, Hadim Suleyman Pasha, finally placed her son Mustafa in the coveted position. Hurrem Sultan's power, however, was not to be denied, and she forced this vazir into exile. She now ensured that someone more reliable got the post: Her own son-in-law, Rustem Pasha, became vazir. This new alliance resulted in the execution of Gulbahar Hatun's son Mustafa. When there was a revolt in 1555, partially against this execution, Hurrem Sultan's son Bayizat successfully put it down. When Hurrem Sultan died in 1558, she had determined that one of her sons would become the next sultan. Her son Selim succeeded Suleyman to the throne in 1566 and ruled for eight years as Sultan Selim II. Selim's wife Nurbanu Sultan in fact ruled the empire during his reign. During the rule of her own son, Sultan Murad III, she shared political power with her daughter-in-law Safriyah Sultan, and so it continued. It is small wonder that the Ottoman Empire during the sixteenth and seventeenth centuries has come to be historically known as the Sultanate of Woman (*Kadinlar Sultanati*). (For a diagrammatic representation of the women of Suleyman the Lawgiver's reign, see Figure 3.1.)

Early in this century, women played an important part in the various constitutional and revolutionary movements that swept across the Middle East. An ex-

Figure 3.1   The women of Suleyman the Lawgiver's reign. The names of the women in the system appear in boxes.

cellent case in point is Halide Edib Adivar, a leading Turkish intellectual, nationalist, and supporter of Mustafa Kemal's movement for independence. Born in 1883, she was educated at the American College for Girls and then began writing and speaking for liberal causes. Her inspired public speeches in support of the nationalist revolution earned her national and even international fame. Her statement that "governments are our enemies, peoples are our friends, and the just revolt of our hearts our strength" became the rallying cry of Turkish nationalists.[53] Halide Edib Adivar actually served in Kemal's army as a corporal, a sergeant, and a sergeant major.

Women also played a critical role in the Iranian constitutional movement from 1905 to 1911. They organized themselves into informal meeting groups (*anjumans*) and did not hesitate to take to the streets in support of their political ideals. When the newly established parliament (*majlis*) faced extinction in 1911, a large group of women marched on the building:

> Three hundred women surrounded the entrance to the *Majlis,* or Parliament, recently formed, and demanded admission. A few only were admitted. They walked in closely veiled, but when they found themselves in the assembly they tore their veils aside, and said that their intention was to kill their husbands, their sons and themselves if the liberty and dignity of Persia were not firmly upheld. They offered their money and jewels, saying: "We are women and cannot fight, but we can give to our country." They had their own places of assembly where they discussed these matters, and they used the Press, and personal influence was largely exerted.[54]

As time has passed, Muslim women have assumed a more direct and dramatic role in Middle Eastern politics. In the Algerian war of independence, women were an important part of the resistance and did everything from hiding fugitives to throwing bombs. National heroine Jamilah Buhrayd, for example, rather than becoming a seamstress, became a revolutionary and was eventually shot, after having been imprisoned and tortured by the French. Young women have been very conspicuous in the Palestine guerrilla movement. Laila Khaled, for example, gained international notoriety when she was captured as part of a four-plane hijacking operation in September 1970. In May 1972, two young Arab women, former nursing students, participated in the hijacking of a Sabena Boeing 707 to Lod Airport in Israel. There are many other examples. One observer writes: "Mostly young and often educated in the West—France, England, the United States—the Palestinian girl fedayeen have a better political understanding than their male counterparts. Indeed, they are more the material from which real revolutionaries are made. Proportionate to their numbers they have caused the Israelis more trouble than have their male comrades."[55]

---

[53]Elizabeth Warnock Fernea and Basima Qattan Bezirgan, eds., *Middle Eastern Muslim Women Speak* (Austin: The University of Texas Press, 1977), p. 189.

[54]C. Colliver Rice, *Persian Women in Their Ways* (London: Seeley, Service and Co., 1923), p. 270. For an even more dramatic description of this event, see W. Morgan Shuster, *The Strangling of Persia* (New York: Century Co., 1912), p. 198.

[55]John Laffin, *Fedayeen: The Arab-Israeli Dilemma* (New York: Free Press, 1973), p. 138.

This revolutionary role of Muslim women in influencing Middle Eastern politics is only one of many more direct and formal ways that they now exert power. As their legal rights expand and as they gain greater stature in the formal governmental arena, Middle Eastern women are acquiring political authority. Women's movements are present in the Middle East, and women are slowly taking their places in government bureaucracies. In so doing, however, they have not relinquished their traditional influence in the informal sphere of power. It is as part of the informal group or family that women continue to operate most effectively.

In Pahlavi Iran, Empress Farah Diba did not confine herself to social work and charitable causes. Although she headed nearly forty different social organizations, she was also involved in political issues. In the latter half of the 1970s, the empress was the shah's last important line to reality and was the only person left among his advisors who could take issue with his decisions. Toward the end, the shah refused to take the advice of his wife seriously. If he had, the political outcome in Iran might possibly have been different.

In Tunisia, Wassila bin Amar, the wife of former President Bourguiba, was long embroiled in national politics. Her advice and opinions often shaped the course of events in that country. In November 1977, she visited President Sadat in Cairo to indicate her country's support for his direct approach to peace in the Middle East. Jihan Sadat, the wife of the assassinated Egyptian president, was an important force in Egyptian society and politics. She had a significant power base in the presidency, the government more broadly, and within the wealthy bourgeoisie. It took President Mubarak almost five years to dismantle the foundations of her power.

With the resurgence of Islamic movements across the region, women continue to wield influence from behind the veil. The indomitable, independent women of Egypt, for example, have in many cases gone back to traditional garb while at the same time maintaining their integrity and even increasing their power. In Iran, women played a major role in the revolution, donating their jewelry and organizing demonstrations in support of the movement. Since the revolution, veiled women quietly hold influential positions in governmental organizations such as the Ministry of Foreign Affairs and in the major universities in the country. In the division of physical sciences at Beheshti University in the 1990s, women held three department headships.

Muslim women in the Middle East have never enjoyed legal equality with men and have suffered discrimination in many areas of existence. Any study of the formal scaffolding of the social and political systems clearly demonstrates their lack of authority. Such inequity, however, is not the same as the lack of power. Middle Eastern women have never been powerless. Indeed, they have played a pervasive and persistent part in shaping political decisions and determining political events ever since the time when the widow Khadija married and then materially and psychologically supported the young man Muhammad. Only by analyzing politics at the informal level does one begin to understand and appreciate the significance of women to the entire political process.

Our brief survey of Middle Eastern women in politics yields several general observations. First, women throughout Muslim history have had a more profound impact on political events than is generally thought. Second, this political power has usually been wielded indirectly through men. Natal and marital relationships have been particularly crucial here. Third, there has been a movement over the past several decades among Middle Eastern women for legal equality and social and political rights. Although this movement has been slowed in recent years by the reassertion of Islam, it is still very much alive, even in the most traditional of countries, such as Saudi Arabia.

In the Middle East, women's liberation is a drive not so much to acquire power as to add authority to power: Why must women's political influence be indirect and confined to the informal arena? Middle Eastern women are on the move. They refuse to accept second-class status and to wield influence only in informal, private settings. In fact, they are using their informal group membership as the catalytic grounding for the formation of new political rights and empowerment. In the meantime, they continue to exert power informally, personalistically, and derivatively.[56]

Class Structure: Horizontal Stratification

It is He who has made us the inheritors of the earth, who has elevated us one above the other by degrees in order to help us experience His gifts.

QURAN, CHAPTER 6, VERSE 165

Although informal groups and networks must be taken into account in any study of Middle Eastern politics, the political process is not played out in a seamless web of interacting groups. The cases presented here, for example, indicate that it is usually only women of the upper class who in fact influence the national polity. The masses of women (like the masses of men) have little if anything to say about major political decisions. By emphasizing only the group dimension, we suggest that group pluralism promotes equality. What is left out of the equation is the issue of horizontal stratification. Slashing across the web of groups are lines of stratification that profoundly affect not only the group dynamics previously discussed but also the entire political process of the Middle East. Serif Mardin cogently summarizes this point when he writes that although membership in a kinship group "raised the expectations of a less prestigious member of the group that he could rise in society, the fact that he belonged to a well-recognized stratum led to frustrations as regards the actual capacity to rise in society."[57]

G. E. von Grunebaum once wrote that "the Muslim's personal equality with his fellows in the faith which is guaranteed, so to speak, by his right to a direct relationship with his Lord does in no way preclude elaborate social stratification within

---

[56]For a fascinating and realistic symposium discussion by an articulate group of scholars and Middle Eastern women about their struggle for both power and authority, see A. Richard Norton, et al., "Gender, Politics and the State: What Do Middle Eastern Women Want?" in *Middle East Policy* 5 (September 1997): 155–189.

[57]Mardin, "Historical Determinants," p. 4.

the community of Islam."[58] The group network and communalism discussed above cloak a system of horizontal stratification in which Middle Eastern societies break down into a relatively small number of interrelated classes.[59] A class structure always involves entities in superior and subordinate positions. The overall hierarchy of classes is founded on the unequal possession of one of the fundamental values of social and political life. In the sociological literature, class is most often defined according to one of three different emphases: wealth, status, and power. An individual's place in a social class is determined by his or her position with respect to one of these characteristics. Although all three determinants are interrelated in the sense that the possession of one may strongly affect the acquisition of another, the question of which is the basic criterion remains open. In this volume on the Middle East, we define *class* in terms of power and employment position.[60]

CLASS AND POWER IN THE MIDDLE EAST

For our purposes, *power* refers to one's ability to shape and control the behavior of others.[61] This ability may rest as much upon indirect personal maneuvering and verbal persuasion as upon direct threat, coercive demand, or economic inducement. The basis of power may be located in the political, economic, social, educational, religious, or psychological systems. Because Islam is a way of life that involves all of these dimensions, power relations in Islamic societies usually involve a subtly integrated complex of factors. One Islamic scholar writes, for example, that "political influence, military power, administrative rank, wealth, birth, and schooling, in every possible combination, strengthened or counteracted one another in assigning a given individual his place in society."[62] Wealth is but one of a number of important variables that determine one's position in the class structure. Material resources have seldom been enough to enable individuals consistently to attain their goals. Personal contacts, social manipulation,

---

[58]Gustave E. von Grunebaum, *Medieval Islam: A Study in Cultural Orientation,* second ed. (Chicago: University of Chicago Press, 1961), p. 170.

[59]For an important study in which *class* is the basic tool of analysis, see Ervand Abrahamian, *Iran Between Two Revolutions* (Princeton, N.J.: Princeton University Press, 1982).

[60]For two explicit attempts to discuss class analysis as it applies to Middle Eastern society and politics, see Jacques Berque. "L'Idée des Classes dans L'Histoire Contemporaine des Arabes." *Cahiers Internationaux de Sociologie* 38 (1965): 169–184; and James A. Bill. "Class Analysis and the Dialectics of Modernization in the Middle East," *International Journal of Middle East Studies* 3 (October 1972): 417–434. The latter article provides the conceptual and theoretical underpinnings for the linkage of class and power. For a recent formulation, see Alan Richards and John Waterbury, *A Political Economy of the Middle East,* second ed. (Boulder, Colo.: Westview Press, 1996).

[61]This definition of power is slightly broader than those provided by scholars who have chosen to reword Max Weber's original definition. In our view, a power relation can involve more than getting someone to do what he or she would not otherwise do. It can be a reinforcing pattern whereby one individual encourages another to continue behaving in a certain way, or it may simply be a case of one person's causing another to translate a predisposition into action.

[62]Von Grunebaum, *Medieval Islam,* p. 212.

saintly ancestry, mystical strength, familial solidarity, higher education, political maneuvering, and an innate sense of timing are all crucial ingredients that help determine one's class standing.

Among the more common, if seldom recognized, dimensions of power that have been instrumental in shaping the formation of Middle Eastern class structure are the following:

1. Exchange transactions in which one person convinces others to accede to his or her wishes by rewarding them for so doing
2. Informational exchanges that involve dispensing and withholding information of varying degrees of value
3. Decisional situations in which one person controls the decision-making environment and thus the decisions made therein
4. Debt-inflicting relationships in which one does favors for others with the confident expectation that they will someday be returned
5. Overt deference behavior by which one person gains the trust of another and thus makes the temporarily more powerful person vulnerable
6. Bargaining interactions that occur in environments of doubt and rest upon such techniques as the bluff and the compromise
7. Kinship patterns in which family members strive to assist one another to improve their relative positions in the class structure
8. Modes of misrepresentation that distort reality in a manner designed to shift the balance of interpersonal influence

The exchange transaction is the simplest and most direct means of exerting power; it is a major pattern in all societies. It is most often expressed as financial dealings, which range all the way from salary transactions to bribery payments. In the Middle East, a disproportionately high percentage of exchange transactions occur in noneconomic terms, since the objects of exchange include personal loyalty, political service, religious approval, and reliable information. Informational exchanges are critical in societies where informality cloaks the exercise of power and where decisions are made within personalistic networks. Indeed, information is a valuable commodity in the Middle East. Political elites constantly seek information concerning the actual and potential opposition forces in their societies. Individuals and groups in the middle and lower classes both hoard and barter information in order to improve their own positions in the social structure.

Another dimension of the power syndrome is the phenomenon of "nondecision making," whereby superordinately situated individuals control the behavior of subordinates through the manipulation and control of the environment in which the latter must operate.[63] An example of this phenomenon in the Middle East is the executive control of parliaments and political parties. Decisions tend to be made in the parliaments and parties according to what the deputies believe the will of the ruler to be. It is not necessary that there be any communi-

---

[63]See Peter Bachrach and Morton S. Baratz's classic discussion of the "nondecision-making process" in "Two Faces of Power," *American Political Science Review* 56 (December 1962): 947–952.

cation between the leadership and the representative. If deputies do not correctly anticipate what the ruler wants and do not act accordingly, they may find themselves politically unemployed; or, as happened in the mid-1970s in Bahrain and Kuwait, the rulers simply dissolve the parliamentary bodies themselves. Control is thus built into the structure of the system in a less than obvious manner. Learning how to interact in this kind of system is essential to the determination of one's class standing.

One of the most distinctive facets of power relations in Middle Eastern society is debt infliction. In the Muslim community of North Africa, "Every act requires some form of reciprocation as an inherent aspect of its very nature: Every act creates an obligation or expresses a right held."[64] Those upon whom debts are inflicted are put into a disadvantageous position of dependence. It is in this sense that Fredrik Barth describes the mechanism as it manifests itself in the Swat Valley in Pakistan. The relationship to political power is unmistakable here, since even "gift-giving and hospitality are potent means of controlling others. . . ."[65] As one Lebanese citizen puts it, gifts are "the lubricants of social interaction."[66]

Deference, which is part of the somewhat extravagant patterns of courtesy and politeness that obtain in the Middle East, can be used effectively to balance highly uneven personal relationships. When properly displayed, deference can loosen the control of the more powerful actor over the less powerful individual. Deferential behavior can stimulate a false sense of security in the superior person in any relationship, thus heightening his or her vulnerability. It was in this spirit that the Ziyarid prince Kai Ka'us Ibn Iskandar wrote his son that "if you are being fattened by someone, you may expect very quickly to be slaughtered by him. . . ."[67]

Another context in which power exchange occurs in the Middle East is bargaining, in which the actors in fact agree to disagree. Each side in the encounter uses a wide variety of persuasive techniques in order to further his or her interests. The outcome of the confrontation remains in doubt until the very end of the process, when one side indicates a willingness to accept the terms of the other. An individual who is able to use an effective blend of candor and the bluff, as in bargaining, can greatly enhance his or her position in the social and political hierarchy.

The final two tactics of control and influence have to do with kinship ties and modes of misrepresentation. As we noted earlier, the family is the most cohesive unit in Middle Eastern society. As such, it is least susceptible to radical change and most reliable as a unit of personal and group support. The mobility of one family member affects the potential mobility of the whole family. Entire families often move up in the class structure. They are also downwardly mobile.

---

[64]Lawrence Rosen, "Muslim-Jewish Relations in a Moroccan City," *International Journal of Middle East Studies* 3 (October 1972): 438.

[65]Fredrik Barth, *Political Leadership among Swat Pathans* (London: Athlone Press, 1959), p. 79.

[66]Fuad I. Khuri, *From Village to Suburb: Order and Change in Greater Beirut* (Chicago: University of Chicago Press, 1975), p. 86.

[67]Kai Ka'us Ibn Iskandar, *A Mirror for Princes* (The Qābūs-nāma), trans. by Reuben Levy (London: Cresset Press, 1951), p. 191.

Because of the centrality of the family in determining one's position in the power structure, individuals constantly seek to attach themselves to prominent families. This is usually accomplished through marriage, but it is also often done through fictive kinship ties. This is only one of the forms of misrepresentation designed to help improve one's class position. To exaggerate and falsely embroider reality at propitious times is a technique more frowned upon in the West than in the Middle East, where such behavior often deflects conflict and prevents violent confrontation. It also is a dimension of influence that must be considered when explaining class membership and class conflict.

THE MIDDLE EASTERN CLASS SYSTEM

Throughout Islamic history, a person's power position has been closely intertwined with his or her occupational skill. Mode of employment to a large degree determined an individual's capacity to utilize the techniques and to operate effectively in the environment discussed above. An individual was best able to wield power using skills and talents one already possessed. The military, cleric, and bureaucratic occupations provided their practitioners with unusual opportunities to strengthen their positions in the class structure through informed use of the coercive, religious, and political dimensions of power. The intimate connection between power and employment was a direct result of the development of Islamic social history and the Prophet Muhammad's early strictures concerning the occupational bases of the community of Islam. One of the earliest foundations for stratification was the assignment of the believers "to a more or less definite hierarchy of professions."[68] For purposes of the following empirical analysis of horizontal stratification in the Middle East, we define classes as the largest aggregates of individuals united by similar modes of employment and maintaining similar power positions in society.

Classical Islamic thinkers have presented views of horizontal stratification that range from two-class to eight-class hierarchies. According to the criteria developed above, the traditional Middle Eastern Islamic social structure consisted of seven interrelated classes: the upper (ruling) class, the bureaucratic middle class, the bourgeois middle class, the cleric middle class, the traditional working class, the peasant class, and the nomadic class. This schema includes one upper, three middle, and three lower classes. This designation of upper, middle, and lower refers to the general power categories, while the more specific labels are assigned on the basis of both power and employment. The nomenclature of each class indicates its employment function.

The upper class in the traditional Islamic social structure represented a tiny percentage of the population, usually less than 2 percent. The upper class was a ruling class, because it possessed a monopoly of the instruments of power and authority in society. This class was composed of the elites that rested at the very apex of the governmental, landholding, religious, tribal, military, and business pyramids of influence. The rulers and the networks of ruling families were at the core of the upper class. Also included were the military leaders, the large native

---

[68]Von Grunebaum, *Medieval Islam*, p. 177.

landlords, the highest-level bureaucrats (the vazirs, for example), the leadership of the ulema who supported the system, the tribal chieftains and khans, and the wealthiest merchants and business entrepreneurs. This ruling class exhibited exclusive and inclusive characteristics that tended to balance out one another, ultimately stabilizing membership size. In most cases, a single member of this class had a number of power-laden functions. For example, a member of the ruling family was often at the same time a military leader and a large landlord. The tribal nobility maintained large landholdings and were often among the highest-ranking military officials. In this way, wealth, influence, and coercive power reinforced one another and strengthened one's class position. This helped to narrow upper-class membership. On the other hand, the kinship mechanism tended to expand the size of the upper class while at the same time linking this class to the various middle classes. The extended family ties of a ruler, vazir, or landlord brought new waves of individuals into ruling-class ranks. Indeed, one of the best ways even today to understand ruling classes in Middle Eastern societies is to analyze the structures of leading families.

Ruling classes in the contemporary Islamic Middle East are shaped by the lines of kinship along which power flows. Family ties and intermarriage patterns help solidify an inherently fragmented and fissured upper class. The lack of any strong class consciousness, at least among the ruling class, is partially compensated for by a kind of interfamilial and intrafamilial consciousness. Although studies show that family membership in Middle Eastern upper classes is relatively unstable, there are indications that a small number of families remain in upper-class ranks over time. The informality of family structure in many ways mirrors the character of the upper class, which is also relatively fluid. In a study of the upper class ("patriciate") of Muslim Nishapur from the tenth to the twelfth century, Richard Bulliet writes that "the reality of the patriciate consisted in individuals and families who knew each other and recognized each other as being above the ordinary run of people. There was no formal membership in the patriciate."[69] In sum, the upper class in Islamic history has been a complex of leading clerics, generals, vazirs, khans, and merchant kings familially and informally bound together around the person of the ruler and his family. By virtue of its advantageous power position, this ruling class directs the political system of society.

The bureaucratic middle class has been the most powerful of the three traditional middle classes. Its membership is composed of the mass of governmental employees who staff the administrative system. Possessing a minimum of traditional education, these individuals are the scribes, accountants, recorders, and bureaucratic functionaries of traditional Middle Eastern society. Like the ruling class, this middle class is rather loosely and informally organized. Although in many Islamic societies there were families that came to be known as bureaucratic families, kinship ties are not as important as class indicators here as they are in the upper class.

In our concentric circles of class and power, the bureaucratic middle class most closely rings the ruling class. It is an important intermediary class that

---

[69]Richard W. Bulliet, *The Patricians of Nishapur: A Study in Medieval Islamic Social History* (Cambridge, Mass.: Harvard University Press, 1972), p. 86.

translates the directives of the ruling class into action. This administering class appears to be almost an appendage to the upper class because of its many points of contact with the rulers. Owing to this proximity, the bureaucratic middle class has more often served the interests of the ruling class than those of the other middle and lower classes. While maintaining an important power of its own, this class traditionally viewed its interests as intertwined with those of the upper class. The proximity to power always held out to the bureaucratic middle class the possibility of movement into upper-class ranks.

Located approximately between the bureaucratic and cleric middle classes is the bourgeois middle class, which is a class of businessmen, merchants, and traders. The symbol and center of activity of this class is the bazaar, or *suq*. As an individual, the merchant or trader has relatively little economic power and virtually no political influence. As a class, however, this bourgeoisie has considerable political power. When ruling-class policies have seriously endangered the interests of commerce and the lifestyles of the merchant, the bazaar has often become the heart of opposition to the regime in power. It was out of the ranks of the bourgeoisie that Islam itself developed as a community and civilization. Also, throughout the history of Islam, a number of social and religious movements have sprung up from this class in opposition to the prevailing political order.

There are three reasons why the merchants and tradesmen have been able to give birth to opposition movements. First, the members of this class managed to institutionalize their traditional informal patterns of interaction in a system of guilds and brotherhoods. Second, their organizational apparatus had a semblance of ideology, which helped provide a rationalization for their activities. This ideology was composed of various folk and mystic Islamic beliefs. Finally, this kind of organizational and ideological framework linked the business middle class with important elements in both the cleric middle class and the traditional working class. The suqs and bazaars were the meeting place for merchant, cleric, and artisan.

The cleric middle class, which is composed of the lower and intermediate ranks of the ulema, is the third traditional middle class. The members of this class enjoy neither the political influence of the bureaucrats nor the wealth of the businessmen. They have, however, possessed important religio-psychological influence over those members of society who are practicing Muslims. They also have controlled the educational system through their role as teachers and directors of the traditional educational institutions (*maktabs* and *madrasas*). The constituency of the clerics has been largely concentrated within the lower classes, and because of this, the interests of the cleric middle class have been closely entwined with those below them in the social structure.

The three traditional middle classes were closely related to one another in a number of ways. The members of all these classes were the products of the same educational system—a system that was directed by the ulema and that stressed reading, writing, religious law, rhetoric, and the Quran. The educational method used was rote memorization. One result of this was that all traditional middle-class individuals had a similar value system, largely conservative. This meant that these classes rebelled only under very special circumstances, consisting of either a severe and adverse disruption of business conditions or a series of policies by the ruling class that contradicted the tenets of Islam. Usually both these conditions had to come about simultaneously in order for these middle classes to move to active opposition. Even then, the bureaucratic middle class seldom participated.

The bulk of the population of all Middle Eastern societies falls into the three lower classes, consisting of workers, peasants, and nomads. Ideally, Islam commands that the community treat the poor and least powerful with compassion. The giving of alms is one of the acts that all the faithful are expected to practice. In describing the class structure of Islamic communities, Imam Ali, son-in-law of the Prophet, said of the lower classes: "Lowest of all are the afflicted and the poor who are the unfortunate and the suffering. They are always the broken-hearted and the weary."[70] In fact, however, the situation of the lower classes has been little improved by such words of sympathy and ideals of charitable assistance. The harsher realities of class structure are reflected in another scheme of classification presented by the Abbasid courtier Yahya al-Fazl. He divides society into four classes and then writes that "the remainder are filthy refuse, a torrent of scum, base cattle, none of whom thinks of anything but his food and sleep."[71]

Most of the members of the lower class belong to the peasant class. In preponderantly agricultural societies, these are the individuals who work the land under a variety of arrangements that only alter the degree of their poverty, dependence, disease, and ignorance. The peasant class, located at the very bottom of the social structure, has very little power and is thus exposed to exploitation by all the other classes in society. For the individual peasant, this usually means abuse at the hands of landlord, merchant, and government official. Peasants have also often suffered from manipulation by the clerics and from the raids of tribesmen. The situation of the nomadic lower class is not much better than that of the peasants. The tribal masses have existed in a state of subjection to a hierarchy of khans and have had to struggle to make a living from an often inhospitable land. Because of a modicum of natural freedom and their occasional importance as military forces, the tribesmen have been a cut above the peasant in the power structure.

The traditional working class includes such groups as servants, manual laborers, craftsmen, and artisans. In the Middle East, this class has been as much a rural as an urban phenomenon. Like the members of the other lower classes, these workers have earned their livelihood through the use of their physical skills. Working with their hands, they have been scorned by the middle and upper classes. The members of this class have often joined guilds and brotherhoods; accordingly, they have enjoyed some organizational protection. This has placed the traditional working class in the best power position among the lower classes.

The traditional class structure in the Islamic Middle East remains in place to a large extent in contemporary Middle Eastern society. There have been, however, a number of obvious changes that have largely resulted from the forces of

---

[70]Imam Ali, Farman to Malik Ashtar, governor of Egypt, *Sukhanan-i Ali [The Words of Ali]*, trans. by Javad Fazil (Tehran, 1966), p. 242 (in Persian).

[71]Ibn al-Faqih, *Kitab al-Buldan*, as quoted in Reuben Levy, *The Social Structure of Islam* (Cambridge: Cambridge University Press, 1957), p. 67.

modernization discussed in Chapter 1. Land reform programs, coupled with the increasing emphasis upon industrialization, have caused a shifting of the bases of power of the ruling class. Land ownership, which was an important upper-class power credential for centuries, has given way to industrial investment in the form of contracting, banking, export-import trade, and business concessions of all kinds. The traditional middle classes have grown in size relative to the upper and lower classes, with the bourgeois middle class expanding at an especially rapid rate. Nomadic tribes are slowly being forced to settle, and as a result are grudgingly blending into the peasantry. Strong rural-to-urban migration patterns have resulted in the mushrooming growth of shantytowns and the appearance of an unemployed proletariat that continues to expand along the edges of the major cities. This last change is a dramatic one, since it represents the appearance of an important modern addition to the centuries-old class structure.

The relatively recent appearance of two new classes is a significant break with the past patterns of horizontal stratification in the area. Both an industrial working class and a professional middle class have emerged as definite formations in the second half of this century. Both classes are the products of the accelerating process of modernization, and their roots trace back to the growth of large industry and the development of modern systems of education in the Afro-Asian world.

Industrialization and urbanization have been the major catalysts for the appearance of the new urban industrial working class. Census data indicate that this class still represents a small proportion in the various Middle Eastern countries, but that it is growing at a rapid pace. The growing masses of unemployed migrants referred to above are a ready pool of unskilled and semiskilled labor for new industry. This new lower class is more powerful than the traditional lower classes because of its strategic and visible location in the large cities as well as its growing social awareness. The industrial working class, however, has barely begun to realize its potential as a social and political force. This is not the case with the second and more recent class formation.

THE PROFESSIONAL MIDDLE CLASS

The forces of modernization and the acceleration of accompanying social change have given rise to the formation of a new middle class in the Middle East.[72] This class, which we here term the professional middle class, is one whose members derive their power from skills obtained through a modern higher education. Many members of the new class seek to advance themselves through their professional skills and talents rather than through the use of wealth and personal connections, two resources that most of them lack in any case. The professional middle class is not a bourgeois middle class, since its members earn

---

[72]For the pioneering study of this class, see Manfred Halpern, *The Politics of Social Change in the Middle East and North Africa* (Princeton. N.J.: Princeton University Press, 1963). For an analysis of this class as it challenged the shah's regime in Iran, see James Alban Bill, *The Politics of Iran: Groups, Classes, and Modernization* (Columbus, Ohio: Charles E. Merrill, 1972).

their livelihoods less through ownership of property or entrepreneurship in business than through salaries, technical fees, scholarships, and professional activities. This class is composed of white-collar workers engaged in technical, professional, cultural, and administrative occupations. Its membership is drawn largely from such groups as teachers, bureaucrats, professors, students, technocrats, engineers, physicians, writers, artists, journalists, and middle-ranking army officers. Among the army officers, we must include political leaders such as Gamal Abdel Nasser, Anwar Sadat, and Husni Mubarak of Egypt; Houari Boumedienne of Algeria; Mu'ammar Qaddafi of Libya; and Hafez al-Assad of Syria. All rose to power on the wave of the aspirations of the new middle class.

Although the professional middle class is not a class of intellectuals, it may be properly termed an intelligentsia, since it composes the intellectual elite in society. Unlike the educated members of the ruling class, who enjoy the twin privileges of great wealth and political authority, the members of the professional middle class have little other than their education to fall back on. Whereas the members of the traditional middle classes rested their power on the older educational system, dominated by religion, the individuals in the new middle class draw their influence from the modern educational system. This is what makes them an increasingly indispensable segment of society. Modernization results in constantly accelerated demands for qualified physicians, engineers, technocrats, teachers, and soldiers. Economic and industrial development guarantees the growth of the new middle class.

In Turkey, Egypt, Libya, and Tunisia, members of the professional middle class have come to hold political power and have begun to implement developmental programs with varying degrees of success. In Iraq, Syria, Algeria, and Sudan, individuals from the new middle class have taken political control but have failed to solve the problem of division and discord among groups and classes. This failure has severely retarded political development and modernization. In Morocco, Saudi Arabia, Jordan, and the various Gulf shaikhdoms, the professional intelligentsia remain largely locked out of the political arena. In Morocco and Jordan, where this class is a relatively large one, a number of its members have moved into the political elite as the result of a calculated policy of co-optation on the part of the ruling class. All in all, membership in the professional middle class throughout the Islamic Middle East is rapidly approaching 15 to 20 percent of the population.

The professional middle class is a threat to the traditional sociopolitical system in the Middle East. Many of its members decry the old network of personalism, favoritism, nepotism, and influence wielding that continues in many cases to suffocate their own opportunities to move forward on the basis of professional merit. What makes this class such a serious threat to the traditional social structure is not so much that all its members are agents of modernization but that some of its members demand political development. The latter refuse to relate to the ruling class in terms of subservience and deference. Instead, they demand a share of political authority and promise to uproot the power relations upon which the authority structure rests.

The professional middle class is composed of many individuals whose goals include a transformation of power relations and the authority structure. Many of them prefer professionalism to personalism, justice to wealth, intellectual freedom to imposed stability, and effective political participation to political co-optation. Even in Saudi Arabia, a growing professional middle class chafes at the monopolizing power of one family and the social control and economic corruption that prevail in the country. In Lebanon, the new middle class is very weak economically. "But in no sense should this detract from its vital role as carrier of new skills, ideologies, and styles of life. And this is certainly more relevant to its role as an agent of modernization."[73] It was shortly after the Egyptian coup in 1952 that Ahmad Baha'eddine wrote that this new middle class was "the greatest hope we have for progress."[74]

The professional middle class has seldom borne out such hope, however, as it has not been as much a force for development as might have been expected. Besides the extraordinary strength of the traditional political system, there are other reasons why the new middle class has failed to implement much deep-seated reform.

Like every other social unit in the Middle East, this class is torn by internal cleavages and tensions. These divisions are along the lines of kinship, ethnicity, religion, occupation, social origins, geography (urban and rural), and university background. All of these divisions in turn affect the individual's orientations toward modernization and political development. The influence of those who would uproot the traditional patterns of power and authority tends to be nullified by those who seek to preserve the traditional processes in order to improve their own positions in the system. This group usually supports modernization at the expense of political development. These are the maneuverers in the new middle class who survive by manipulation while lacking the civility and courteous charm that was the hallmark of the aristocrats of the older generation. It is this segment of the professional middle class that is readily corruptible. In a stirring indictment of this group within the intelligentsia, one novelist writes: "Every country east of the Mediterranean is torn to bits by ever-competing jealous politicos coming to power by some kind of inheritance. . . . But I can envisage the day when these countries will be even worse, torn by degree-holders more self-interested and sycophantic than their predecessors, and far, far less charitable. If you think the sheikh grinds the faces of his tribesmen you should wait and see the Ph.D. grind the faces of all and sundry, without even a touch of the magnanimity we pride ourselves on."[75]

The professional middle class remains crippled in its challenge to traditional sociopolitical relations in the Middle East. The deep fissures throughout

---

[73]Samir Khalaf, "Urbanization and Urbanism in Beirut: Some Preliminary Results." Paper prepared for delivery at the Twenty-first Annual Near East Conference, Princeton, N.J., April 9–10, 1970, p. 37. This paper documents the important appearance of a new professional middle class in the Hamra district of Beirut. See also Samir Khalaf and Per Kongstad, *Hamra of Beirut: A Case of Rapid Urbanization* (Leiden, The Netherlands: E. J. Brill, 1973).

[74]Ahmad Baha'eddine, "Al-iqta'iyyun wal-ra'smaliyyun wal-muthaqqafun" ["Feudalists, capitalists, and intellectuals"], in *Rose Al-Yussif,* no. 1353 (May 17, 1954), as quoted in Anouar Abdel-Malek, *Egypt: Military Society,* trans. by Charles Lam Markmann (New York: Vintage Books, 1968), p. 178.

[75]Jabra I. Jabra, *Hunters in a Narrow Street* (London, 1960), as quoted in *A Middle East Reader,* ed. by Irene L. Gendzier (New York: Pegasus, 1969), p. 114.

the class are intentionally deepened by the ruling class in order to weaken the cohesiveness of this challenging unit. The political elite encourages those elements in the new class that are most susceptible to the blandishments of bribery and personal aggrandizement.

The new middle class carries another major weakness. It is separated from the lower class masses by an enormous social and cultural gap. Engineers or physicians with modern higher educations have separated themselves from the illiterate citizens that make up the majority of their own people. Often educated in universities of the West, multilingual in speech, fashionably chic in dress, secular in thought and belief, the professional represents the antithesis of the illiterate, suspicious, destitute, and deeply religious peasant. This division became most apparent in the Middle East in Iran after the revolution, when the masses turned to the religious leaders and tradition and away from the secular intelligentsia.

Today, the members of the professional middle class find themselves increasingly swimming against the tides of Islamic fundamentalism. Although they are still dedicated to the transformation of traditional patrimonial rule, there is no longer any guarantee that they are destined to become the leaders of the new political systems. The fact that the religious leaders, with their mass constituency, have hijacked the Iranian revolution is an indication that the professional middle class may no longer be the political force of the future in the Middle East. Increasingly, members of this class are returning to Islam as part of a general search for their dignity, roots, and personal heritage.

Despite all this, the professional middle class continues to grow. A few voices within the class continue to clamor for radical social and political change. Also, because the ruling class desperately needs the skills and talents of these individuals in order to implement its programs of modernization, these uprooters are slowly improving their power positions. On the basic issues of power and authority relations, the ruling class grudgingly gives ground while working to preserve the ongoing class structure from the challenges presented by the new class. Regardless of who ultimately takes control of future revolutions in the region, the professionals, technicians, and scientists will remain an indispensable part of society. Even the revolutionary regime in Iran has required skilled technicians in the oil fields, talented physicians in the hospitals, competent planners and managers in the bureaucracy, and capable pilots and officers in the military.

THE DYNAMICS OF GROUP-CLASS INTERACTION

The dynamics of Middle Eastern social structure develop out of an integrated system of both vertical and horizontal stratification. The overall social structure might best be viewed as an intricate web of groups that is partitioned along class lines. Group and class structures relate to each other reciprocally, and it is this reciprocity that builds coherence into the sociopolitical system. The multistranded sinews of group relations bind the class structure together by crisscrossing class cleavages. Ethnic, tribal, religious, and military groups, for example, often draw their membership from several different classes. Here class distinctions are somewhat softened by common group affiliation. At the same time, group formations are molded and shaped to a considerable degree by class. Groups are often structured along class lines, and their memberships remain confined within the boundaries of a single class. Family units, for example, tend to belong to a single class. Certainly, class divisions serve to retard individual and group mobility.

Class conflict in the Middle East is a muted phenomenon. There are three major reasons for this, and all of them relate to the impact of vertical stratification. First, the existence of a wide variety of important intraclass groups in the Middle East renders class units relatively diffuse. Fissures within classes are numerous and deep enough to weaken class cohesion and to retard class consciousness. Loyalty to primordial groups such as the family takes precedence over loyalty to class. Second, the plethora of groups with multiclass membership promotes interclass communication and draws together individuals from differing classes on the basis of shared group goals. As we have pointed out, this helps to integrate the class structure and therefore to mellow class conflict. Third, the group structure provides a system of mobility channels through which individuals can rise and fall in the class hierarchy. This constant individual movement across class lines lessens the harsh impact of class confrontation.

The pages of Middle Eastern history are dotted with dramatic examples of individual and group mobility. As one writer puts it, in the Middle East "one can be a liar in the morning, a vizir in the evening, and perhaps hanged on the following day."[76] Stretching vertically through the class structure are a number of shifting ladders of group configurations that, although unsteady and unpredictable, nonetheless can be negotiated by enterprising individuals. Many of the rungs of such ladders are difficult to discern because of the informal and concealed nature of their formation. Informal groups are, in general, the most reliable of the groups that span class divisions. Examples of groups that connect the middle and upper classes include military officer cliques, mystic orders, high administrative caucuses, and interfamilial marriage clusters. Let us examine the last example in more depth.

Nuclear families more often tend to be intraclass groups than do extended families, since the latter include a larger number of individuals, each striving to improve his own position in the social system. However, once one member of either a nuclear or an extended family is able to improve his class standing, he subsequently acts as a force that helps to propel other family members forward in the power structure. At the very minimum, the individual in the higher class will be able to protect and defend his family's interests. Always, however, when familial membership is spread among classes, it acts as a brake on class tension and conflict. A more significant aspect of family-group structure in relation to class interaction is the mechanism of interfamilial marriage. In the Middle East, the marriage of two individuals is better described as the union of two families. When the marriage partners are of different social classes, entire family clusters develop relatively tight interclass relationships. Indeed, it is very common and increasingly possible for individuals of middle-class background to search consciously for a mate who comes from a powerful upper-class family.

---

[76]Vincent Monteil, *Morocco* (New York: Viking Press, 1964), p. 141, as quoted in Rosen, "Rural Political Process," p. 223.

Many members of the middle-class intelligentsia attempt to improve their power positions by marrying into the ruling class. Some pursue this strategy in a very calculating manner. Others are torn between their commitment to merit and achievement and their desire to gain enough political leverage to enable them to implement their social and political ideas. Practically all of them are forced to rely upon familial connections at many junctures in their professional and political lives. To the more professionally competent and politically radical among them, this is unpalatable business, and many are visibly embarrassed by the fact that they either belong to the ruling class or have married into it. Middle-class professionals thus find themselves in the unenviable position of denigrating their familial ties while at the same time being forced to use these ties in order to survive and advance in society. This kind of pressured compromise is another factor reducing the effectiveness of their class as a revolutionizing force. In terms of this discussion, it represents a method whereby the challenging middle class is bound to the ruling class. Family clusters cut across class lines and then serve as bridges for the upwardly mobile members of the kinship group.

Groups, then, are much more fluid collectivities than classes in the Middle East because they have much greater ranges of mobility. A class can improve its position only by rather limited incremental movements. The ruling class will always be the upper class, and so it is down the line. By definition, classes must always remain in a power hierarchy. Individuals and groups, on the other hand, can rise dramatically or fall meteorically within the social structure. The great movement of individuals and groups increases flexibility in a class structure that would otherwise be fragile and much more susceptible to upheaval and radical change.

This social structure is a formidable obstacle to the processes of modernization and political development that are under way in the Middle East. The traditional social system refuses to be torn, and the basic power and authority relations that make up this system are extraordinarily difficult to uproot. Since class conflict, often the agent of transformation, is neutralized, change involves chipping away at pieces of the mosaic. This modifying change seldom disturbs the underlying network of power relations that is the basis for the group and class structure of Middle Eastern societies.

The situation analyzed above varies considerably from one Middle Eastern society to another. Some societies, for example, are relatively congenial to modernization and political development. In these societies, the lines of horizontal stratification are only weakly intersected by communal cleavages. As a result, the traditional social structure is more easily torn, because class configurations are more cohesive internally and more bared to conflict externally.

Much can be explained about the outbreak of the Lebanese civil war when it is recognized that the lines separating ethnic and religious groups had come to coincide more and more closely with class lines. The groups lost their crosscutting character and gradually reinforced the explosive class divisions. In other words, the vertical structure of stratification gradually collapsed until it became a reinforcing part of the system of conflicting classes. The Lebanese upper class was dominated by Christian Arabs, while the lower class was overwhelmingly Muslim. Although there was some noticeable overlap, this had become less the case with time. When the explosion came, therefore, it was fueled by both group and class conflict. The presence of the Palestinians, a highly politicized appendage to the Lebanese lower class, only exacerbated the struggle. When group and class lines begin to coincide in the Middle East, the system begins to lose its balanced stability. Violent conflict is often the result, and the consequent changes can either accelerate or retard development. In Chapters 4 and 5, we will examine those individuals who do most to determine the directions that these changes will take.

SELECTED BIBLIOGRAPHY

Ahmed, Leila. *Women and Gender in Islam: Historical Roots of a Modern Debate.* New Haven: Yale University Press, 1992.

Barth, Fredrik. *Political Leadership among Swat Pathans.* London: Athlone Press, 1959.

Bill, James A. *The Politics of Iran: Groups, Classes, and Modernization.* Columbus, Ohio: Charles E. Merrill, 1972.

Binder, Leonard. *In a Moment of Enthusiasm: Political Power and the Second Stratum.* Chicago: University of Chicago Press, 1978.

Cantori, Louis J., and Iliya Harik. *Local Politics and Development in the Middle East.* Boulder, Colo.: Westview Press, 1983.

Denoeux, Guilain. *Urban Unrest in the Middle East: A Comparative Study of Informal Networks in Egypt, Iran, and Lebanon.* Albany: State University of New York Press, 1993.

Eickelman, Dale F. *The Middle East: An Anthropological Approach,* second ed. Englewood Cliffs, N.J.: Prentice-Hall, 1989.

Gellner, Ernest, and John Waterbury, eds. *Patrons and Clients in Mediterranean Societies.* London: Duckworth, 1977.

Ghabra, Shafeeq N. *Palestinians in Kuwait: The Family and the Politics of Survival.* Boulder, Colo.: Westview Press, 1987.

Khalaf, Samir. *Lebanon's Predicament.* New York: Columbia University Press, 1987.

Levy, Reuben. *The Social Structure of Islam.* Cambridge: Cambridge University Press, 1957.

Sanasarian, Eliz. *The Women's Rights Movement in Iran.* New York: Praeger Publishers, 1982.

Singerman, Diane. *Avenues of Participation: Family, Politics, and Networks in Urban Quarters of Cairo.* Princeton, N.J.: Princeton University Press, 1995.

Springborg, Robert. *Family, Power, and Politics in Egypt.* Philadelphia: University of Pennsylvania Press, 1982.

Sullivan, Dennis J. *Private Volunteer Organizations in Egypt.* Gainesville: University Press of Florida, 1994.

Sullivan, Earl L. *Women in Egyptian Public Life.* Syracuse, N.Y.: Syracuse University Press, 1986.

Swearingen, Will D. *Moroccan Mirages: Agrarian Dreams and Deceptions, 1912–1986.* Princeton, N.J.: Princeton University Press, 1987.

Tucker, Judith E. *Women in Nineteenth-Century Egypt.* Cairo: American University in Cairo Press, 1986.

Waterbury, John. *The Commander of the Faithful: The Moroccan Political Elite: A Study in Segmented Politics.* New York: Columbia University Press, 1970.

Chapter 4

The Politics of Patrimonial Leadership

An important component of the politics of power and change in the Middle East is the issue of political leadership. Although societies are composed of an interrelated network of groups and classes, there is always one group of individuals that has a disproportionate amount of power and political influence. Sometimes referred to as the political elite, this group of leaders shapes the political style and molds the political system of a society. In this chapter, we shall analyze the social characteristics and political methodology of Muslim leadership. In the process, it is also important for us to understand how individuals are recruited into leadership positions.

Middle Eastern political leaders vary considerably from country to country. As the last stronghold of absolute monarchy in the world, the Middle East is the home of four kingdoms and four shaikhdoms that are located along the Persian Gulf. In order of ruling experience, the major monarchs include the following: King Hassan of Morocco, Sultan Qabus of Oman, King Fahd of Saudi Arabia, and King Abdullah of Jordan. The other countries are almost all governed by modern authoritarian leaders, most of whom came to power as the result of a military coup or national war of independence. In Iran, a form of Islamic authoritarianism modified by participatory parliamentary politics was born in 1979. Besides these types of authoritarian control, more representative structures exist imperfectly in Israel and Turkey.

Despite all the differences that separate Middle Eastern leaders and elites, there are in the Muslim world a number of deep-seated and persisting similarities in rule. These similarities, which are the subject of this chapter, have existed throughout Islamic history and can be traced to the days of the Prophet Muhammad, himself the model par excellence of political leadership.

The processes of leadership in the Islamic Middle East have been shaped by the life of Muhammad. Through the establishment of a new world community in the seventh century, the Prophet combined the roles of messenger of God and leader of men and women. Today, throughout the Islamic world, Muslim political leaders often imitate the leadership style promoted by the Prophet Muhammad in Arabia some 1,400 years ago.

The very success of Muhammad as a political leader is one of the reasons that he remains a shadowy, distorted, and even frightening figure to many Westerners. In the pantheon of great world leaders, the Prophet has been the one most maligned by Western writers, who have for centuries found him a difficult figure to interpret sympathetically. He has been presented in Western literature as a thug, sorcerer, sex fiend, murderer, and epileptic, and even as a defrocked Roman Catholic priest. The ridiculous extreme of this perspective is seen in Guibert de Nogent's statement that Muhammad died "through excessive drunkenness and that his corpse was eaten by pigs on a dung-hill, explaining why the flesh of this animal and wine are prohibited."[1]

Dante's and Voltaire's views on the subject were only slightly more enlightened than those of de Nogent, and Diderot stated that Muhammad was "the greatest friend of woman and the greatest enemy of sober reason who ever lived."[2] Even Edward Gibbon and Washington Irving, whose writings about Muhammad were more objective, viewed him negatively. In concluding *Mahomet and His Successors,* Irving says that Muhammad had "mental hallucinations," which "continued more or less to bewilder him with a species of monomania to the end of his career, and that he died in the delusive belief of his mission as a prophet."[3]

These views of Muhammad undoubtedly result from ignorance and from insecurity because of the threat that his mission carried for the Western world. After all, Islam has been the only major non-Western, non-Christian movement that both posed a genuine political threat and provided an attractive alternative civilization while challenging Christendom on its own soil. Today, our understanding of the genius of Muhammad's leadership as well as of the patterns of rule of the contemporary leaders of Islamic countries remains sketchy and superficial. The fact that partisan Muslim scholars have tended to view Muhammad idealistically, defensively, and uncritically has not helped to improve this situation. In this chapter, we will attempt to avoid both extremes by analyzing Muhammad primarily and objectively as a political leader. By beginning our analysis with the general patterns of rule that Muhammad generated, we hope to be better able to understand the more contemporary political leaders to be discussed in Chapter 5.

---

[1]Emile Dermenghem, *The Life of Mahomet* (London: George Routledge, and Sons, 1930), p. 119.

[2]Tor Andrae, *Mohammed: The Man and His Faith* (New York: Barnes and Noble, 1936), p. 175.

[3]Irving, *Mahomet and His Successors,* vol. 1 (New York: G. P. Putnam's Sons, 1893), p. 491.

Muhammad: The Politics of a Prophet

The Prophet Muhammad was born in Mecca in A.D. 570. Social and political life was then dominated by the interaction between clans and tribes, and desert nomads were gradually moving into a more settled world of commerce and trade. This was a time of transition marked by continual feuds among clans and by intense commercial rivalry. The Prophet's personal environment was also unstable; by the time he was six, he had lost both of his parents. Muhammad was raised first by his grandfather and then by his uncle Abu Talib, who was the head of the clan of Hashim. Although little is actually known about his early life, it is safe to assume that he worked in menial positions related to commerce and caravans. During his first twenty-five years, Muhammad gained firsthand experience and knowledge of the business, religion, and politics of the day. We know that he traveled to Syria and was in constant touch with peoples throughout that part of the world.

As an orphan and a member of one of the declining clans of the Quraysh tribe, Muhammad lacked many of the resources necessary to develop any important influence of his own. The first turning point in his life was, therefore, his marriage to the wealthy and twice-widowed Khadija. For the next two decades, Muhammad lived in the community as a prosperous businessman. During this time, he acquired contacts and influence that were to be of fundamental importance to him in his role as prophet and preacher.

In about A.D. 610, Muhammad began receiving revelations, and shortly thereafter he began preaching in Mecca and presenting himself as a prophet. Although there were Christians and Jews in Arabia at that time, most of the peoples were pagans and worshipped many gods. Muhammad preached the greatness and goodness of one God and emphasized the Judeo-Christian prophetic tradition. Few Meccans, however, chose to follow him. His earliest converts included his wife, Khadija, his cousin Ali, his adopted son Zayd Ibn Haritha, and Abu Bakr, a respected and prominent Meccan.

As Muhammad continued his preaching and teaching, opposition to him grew. The reasons were many. He threatened the established economic and political order of the day, including the handsome income of the Meccans as custodians of the pagan shrines in their city. In a climate of escalating commerce and preoccupation with profit, his teachings emphasized the illusory nature of material wealth while encouraging such virtues as generosity, charity, and compassion. His criticism of the obsession for material gain was especially provoking, since he had made his own fortune in commerce. By striking at the idea of accumulating wealth, the Prophet was delivering a frontal attack on the Meccan lifestyle.

Besides presenting an economic challenge, Muhammad posed a serious political threat to the leaders of Mecca. By questioning the economic basis of society and attacking the established order, the Prophet could only weaken the existing system. By attracting followers and building a community of his own, he offered the possibility of an alternative order. It is small wonder that the political leaders and influentials in Meccan society became his dogged enemies. Muhammad's following was dominated by the young, the poor, and the dispossessed.

Despite strong opposition, the Prophet established the core of his Muslim movement while in Mecca. He received most of his revelations and gathered his original followers there during a decade of intense missionary activity. There are two basic reasons why this was possible. First, Muhammad was discreet about his activities. His first efforts were directed toward those in whom he had most trust, such as close relatives, fellow clansmen, and intimate friends.[4] At times, important converts were brought into the community through marriage. This was the case with Uthman, a wealthy merchant who married one of Muhammad's daughters. Outside of this intimate circle of family and friends, attention was directed to those individuals who were most prone to conversion. D. S. Margoliouth writes, for example, that "Abu Bakr probably was aware that women are more amenable to conversion than men, resident foreigners than natives, slaves than freemen, persons in distress than persons in prosperity and affluence."[5] A number of slaves were among the first to embrace the teachings of Muhammad. Finally, the activities of the first Muslims were carried out very quietly and unostentatiously. They took place in informal settings and personal homes, where they would not invite direct confrontation and public condemnation. The most famous site of this kind was the home of al-Arqam, where Muhammad could usually be found during the day and where his followers came and went at their convenience. From the very earliest days of its development, therefore, Islam has been what has been described as a "secret society."[6]

The second explanation for the Prophet's ability to survive in Mecca concerns the clan politics of the time. Each clan had learned that, in the interests of self-preservation, individual clan members had to be protected from all threats emanating from outside the clan. An individual could rely deeply on the support and protection of his fellow clansmen. Muhammad's clan, headed by his uncle Abu Talib, stood by him and provided him with a protective umbrella against his powerful opponents. Unable to penetrate this front of clan unity, the opposition attempted to institute a policy of isolating and boycotting Muhammad's entire clan. In this system of seventh-century politics, however, even the boycott failed and was abandoned after two years.

The Prophet continued his activities in Mecca as long as his own clan shielded him. With the death of Abu Talib in 619 and the accession of Abu Lahab as head of the Hashim clan, Muhammad lost his clan's protective support. In the same year, his wife Khadija died, and he was gradually forced out of Mecca. After numerous hardships, he fled to Medina in 622 in what is known in

---

[4]Abu Bakr, one of the Prophet's very first converts, was an influential Meccan cloth merchant. He was an extremely valuable ally and possessed a "readiness to follow the fortunes of someone else with complete and blind devotion, never questioning nor looking back: to have believed much was with him a reason for believing more. Mohammad, a shrewd judge of man, perceived this quality and used it," D. S. Margoliouth, *Mohammed and the Rise of Islam*, 3d ed. (New York: G. P. Putnam's Sons, 1905), pp. 83–84.

[5]Ibid., p. 97.

[6]See ibid., pp. 83–117.

history as the *hijra* ("Hegira"). He was welcomed in Medina, a city deeply torn by interclan strife. It is generally argued that the Medinans saw in Muhammad a leader who could serve as an effective mediator between the warring factions in their city. At the same time, they calculated that the enemy of Mecca would serve them as a friend and that Meccan hegemony in the area would in this way be weakened.

The significance of the hijra to Islamic political development cannot be overemphasized. It marked the beginning of the end of parochial clan politics and the origination of the *umma,* or "community." Clan divisions were to lose their meaning as clans were absorbed into a new religion and a new way of life. The community now had a "religious base" and could be described as a kind of "supertribe."[7] It was during his residence in Medina that Muhammad came to practice the style of leadership that formed the great Islamic community. During these last ten years of his life, he consolidated his position in Medina, defeated and took control of Mecca, converted numerous Arabian tribes to his cause, and began a campaign of expansion that was to continue and spread long after his death.

Crucial to the success of Muhammad in Medina were his military campaigns, which escalated through time. Initially, they were confined to small *razzias,* or "raids," against Meccan commercial caravans. Although these campaigns had very limited success in terms of capture and booty, they served the important purpose of binding together individuals of different clans in a common cause. It was nearly two years before a Meccan caravan was actually captured. Through the constant camaraderie in the relatively safe enterprise of caravan raiding, the followers of Muhammad gradually developed an esprit de corps that enabled them to defeat the Meccans in the critical battles that were to follow. In this regard, it is instructive to note that the significant battle of Badr in A.D. 624 developed out of an intended caravan raid. In this battle, the Prophet's forces decisively defeated the Meccans. One year later, Muhammad's forces fought a large attacking Meccan expedition to a standstill in the battle of Uhud. In this encounter, the Prophet himself played an important part in the fighting. Finally, in A.D. 627, Muhammad and his community withstood a two-week siege of Medina. This was the last great effort by the Meccans to defeat the new community.

At Medina, the Prophet built solidarity into the community in a variety of ways. Besides the numerous military campaigns directed against a common enemy, there were other catalysts to unity. Those clans in Medina that adamantly opposed Muhammad were either expelled or destroyed. Preeminent among these opposition groups were the three Jewish clans of Qaynuqa, Nadir, and Qurayza. Scattered cases of political assassination also indicate that Muhammad condoned the use of this kind of force against particularly recalcitrant opponents.[8] This kind of civil violence was, however, used only as a last resort. The

---

[7]W. Montgomery Watt. *Muhammad: Prophet and Statesman* (London: Oxford University Press, 1961), pp. 94–95.

[8]An example was the poet Ka'b Ibn al-Ashraf, who continually and bitingly attacked Muhammad and the Muslims. He went so far as to travel from Medina to Mecca, where he attacked the Muslim community in his poetry. He was assassinated in A.D. 624.

emphasis was on conversion and reconciliation. A primary means of accomplishing reconciliation was the web of intermarriage that not only bound the Emigrants (original Muslims from Mecca) closer together but also helped bind the Emigrants to the Helpers (Medinan Muslims).

The most outstanding example of the Prophet's flair for consolidation by compromise is the Treaty of Hudaybiya, which was negotiated in A.D. 628. Muhammad decided to make a pilgrimage to Mecca and was accompanied by some 1,500 men. The Meccans, who doubted his intentions and suspected a military invasion, prepared to fight. Muhammad camped at al-Hudaybiya on the outskirts of Mecca and from there entered into negotiations with the Meccans. In the end, an agreement was reached whereby the Prophet and his men were to return to Medina. They had permission, however, to return in the following year to carry out their pilgrimage. The treaty provided for a ten-year nonaggression pact between the Muslims and the Meccans. Despite strong pressures from numerous individuals in his entourage who considered the expedition a failure, Muhammad returned to Medina. In so doing, he was implementing a brilliant policy of diplomatic tact that ensured the peaceful conquest of Mecca two years later. The treaty convinced the Meccans that the Prophet was a reasonable man who did not plan to destroy Mecca. The journey to Hudaybiya was a political foray, not a religious pilgrimage.

When the Prophet Muhammad died in A.D. 632, he left behind a community of peoples that was to expand into one of the great civilizations of history. Tribes and clans, cities and empires were drawn together and unified under the ideology of Islam. The political acumen and astute leadership of Muhammad were instrumental in making this possible. These and other qualities of the Prophet have been noted and imitated by Muslims for centuries; Muhammad is the ideal model for all Believers. The reasons are not only that he was the Seal of the Prophets, the Mirror of the Almighty, and the Founder of Islam but also that he was intensely human. Unlike Christ, Muhammad was not considered divine. One leading Islamic scholar writes that the Prophet "married, had a household, was a father and moreover he was ruler and judge and had also to fight many wars in which he had to undergo painful ordeals."[9] In the words of another analyst: "It is a likeable characteristic of Muhammad that he never claimed perfection or infallibility, but always admitted frankly that he was guilty of shortcomings and mistakes like other men."[10] He lived, in short, as a convincing and believable model after whom all Muslims could pattern their lives.

THE COURSE OF COMPROMISE

Muhammad was born into a world of interpersonal feuding, factional strife, and tribal conflict. The political system was an atomistic one in which families and clans ceaselessly battled one another. The lines of confrontation that crisscrossed the system were drawn so rigidly that there was little room for flexible

---

[9]Seyyed Hossein Nasr, *Ideals and Realities of Islam* (London: George Allen and Unwin, 1966), p. 69.
[10]Andrae, *Mohammed*, p. 179.

policies of retreat and advance. This was an era of the blood feud, punitive reprisal, and the *lex talionis* ("law of retaliation"). It was into this climate of division and distrust that the Prophet carried the strategy and spirit of compromise. The need to unite was a fundamental issue in the Middle East then, and it remains a basic issue in the Middle East today. A leader's political success rests to a great extent on an ability to integrate and unite the divided and fragmented groups that compose society. An indispensable tool to the implementation of this kind of program is a strategy of political flexibility and compromise.

Muhammad's willingness to compromise is particularly noteworthy because of the climate of feuding in which it occurred. One of the most dramatic demonstrations of this talent is, of course, the Treaty of Hudaybiya, where age-old hatreds and animosities were overcome. After twenty years of struggle with the Meccans, the Prophet returned victorious to Mecca in the year A.D. 630. "There, at a moment when the very people who had caused untold hardships and trials for the Prophet, were completely subdued by him, instead of thinking of vengeance, which was certainly his due, he forgave them."[11]

Although many Islamic scholars tend to explain this forbearance in terms of the great nobility, generosity, and compassion of the Prophet, it can also be analyzed as one in a long series of wise political policies. It is significant that the moral virtue of compassion and the political strategy of compromise were inseparably linked in the career of Muhammad.

Throughout his political career, Muhammad struggled to soften confrontation and to gain strength and unity by bargaining. Thus, he and his followers entered numerous marriage pacts with both actual and potential opposition forces. Many tribes joined the Muslim community as a result of the Prophet's long and peaceful march to Tabuk on the Gulf of Aqaba in 630. When Muhammad dispatched two missions to Yemen, he told the leaders of both missions, "Make it easy and do not make it too difficult. Be the carriers of good tidings, and do not cause disaffection."[12] Resort to violence and warfare occurred only after other avenues to agreement had been closed.

The success of tribal societies in developing a relatively respected and influential place in the world community is almost directly proportional to their ability to overcome internal dissension and to resist external encroachment. The clans or tribes in Middle Eastern history that have formed the basis for national communities have been precisely those that have been able to overlook past conflicts and to weld themselves into political units seeking common goals. The will and capacity to compromise at critical junctures is an essential element in this process of integration. The Prophet's style of political leadership included this ingredient.

---

[11]Nasr, *Ideals and Realities,* pp. 71–72.

[12]Hasan al-Karmi, "The Prophet Muhammad and the Spirit of Compromise," *Islamic Quarterly* 8 (July and December 1964): 90.

THE CHARACTER OF CHARISMA

The Prophet Muhammad viewed himself "as a man who had been given a special commission by God."[13] Although he was thoroughly human, he was not an ordinary human. He was considered to be the messenger and prophet of God, and his spiritual teachings were bound up in his social and political life. According to sociologist Max Weber, a charismatic individual is one who "is set apart from ordinary men and treated as endowed with supernatural, superhuman, or at least specifically exceptional powers or qualities."[14] A charismatic leader is one who possesses a special grace and whose followers are irresistibly drawn to that leader because of this grace. There is a sensed otherworldly quality that engenders in others trust, commitment, and a willingness to follow. In Islam, there is an important concept that is remarkably similar to the idea of charisma. This is the concept *baraka,* which is a special blessing of divine origin. "God can implant an emanation of *baraka* in the person of his prophets and saints: Muhammad and his descendants are especially endowed therewith. These sacred personages, in their turn, may communicate the effluvia of their supernatural potential to ordinary men. . . ."[15] In contemporary political analysis, the term *charismatic* has come to be applied so loosely and indiscriminately that it has lost the force of its original meaning. If one stands by the Weberian definition, however, genuinely charismatic leaders have been rare in world history. Despite the exclusiveness of this definition, the Prophet Muhammad remains an outstanding case of the charismatic leader.

All of Muhammad's personal, social, and political activities carried a deep spiritual significance. As a prophet and receptacle of revelation, he held an extraordinary position in the eyes of his followers. The teachings and tenets of Islam became the ideology of his rule, and all aspects of community life were regulated by this ideology. Muhammad's charisma was derived from his role as prophet of God and publicizer of the word of God. As a result, his position as political leader had a solid ideological foundation. Members of the Islamic community, because they were Muslims, considered Muhammad to be the temporal, social, political, and religious leader of society. Muhammad "had been marked out from his early youth, even from his birth, by supernatural signs and qualities."[16] He was a charismatic personality in the full sense of that term.

One of the basic principles of political leadership is that a leader be able to justify his special position by developing a supporting system of ideas and ideals. This kind of ideology may bear little relation to the hard realities of politics and society, but it can play a crucial role in enabling a leader to maintain power and

---

[13]Watt, *Muhammad,* p. 15.

[14]Max Weber, *The Theory of Social and Economic Organization* (New York: Oxford University Press, 1947), p. 358.

[15]G. S. Colin. "Baraka," *The Encyclopedia of Islam,* new ed. (London: Luzac and Co., 1960), vol. 1, p. 1032.

[16]Watt, *Muhammad,* p. 2.

to institute effective policies. Muhammad emerges as a model of success in this regard, since the divine and the human, and the spiritual and the material, are inextricably entwined in his message. Muslims did not think of questioning his authority in the community. Thus, he stands in contrast to numerous contemporary Muslim leaders, who assiduously attempt to build supportive ideologies only on the basis of flimsy and fabricated relationships to Islam or to the Prophet himself.

Much of the appeal of Muhammad's ideological message undoubtedly derived from the social and political content of that message. Islam called for equality, compassion, and unity in a world dominated by inequality, self-aggrandizement, and disunity. In its stress upon equality and simplicity, the message appealed to the downtrodden masses. Muhammad himself lived what he preached. Thus, Edward Gibbon could write: "The good sense of Mohammed despised the pomp of royalty; the apostle of God submitted to the menial offices of the family; he kindled the fire, swept the floor, milked the ewes, and mended with his own hands his shoes and his woollen garment."[17]

THE POLITICS OF PERSONALISM

Another pattern of politics that enabled the Prophet Muhammad to consolidate a strong leadership position in the nascent Islamic community was the pervasive pattern of personalism. In societies where clans and kinship groups were the key social and political realities of life, personal ties were the basic channels of power and influence. By analyzing and exploiting the intricate web of personal relations that existed in seventh-century Arabia, Muhammad and his associates were better able to form their new community. Abu Bakr's expertise as a genealogist, which is emphasized in many sources, is highly significant when viewed in this light. As Muhammad's chief advisor, Abu Bakr continually used his deep knowledge of the complex relations of kinship, as well as of the factions and feuding, that marked the society of the day.

One of the major means of consolidation and integration for the Prophet was the manipulation of this personal web through marriage. For Muhammad, "Many of his marriages were political ones which, in the prevalent social structure of Arabia, guaranteed the *consolidation* of the newly founded Muslim community. Multiple marriage, for him, as is true of Islam in general, was not so much enjoyment as responsibility and a means of *integration* of the newly founded society."[18] Muhammad married at least nine times, and one could argue that all of his marriages, including the union with Khadija, were political in nature. W. Montgomery Watt writes that for a "poor orphan" to make his way, "The one possibility was to find a rich woman to marry him, so that he could, as

---

[17]Gibbon, *Decline and Fall of the Roman Empire* (New York: The Modern Library, 1932), vol. 3, p. 116. No matter what their ultimate judgment concerning Muhammad might be, well-known Western interpreters of world history are united in their recognition of the simple and spartan life that he led. Besides Gibbon, Toynbee and Durant also comment specifically about this facet of Muhammad's life.

[18]Nasr, *Ideals and Realities,* p. 70. Italics ours.

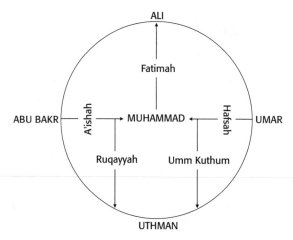

Figure 4.1 Consolidation by marriage: The core of the community.

it were, enter into a business partnership with her."[19] It was through marriage that the Prophet hardened the nucleus of his community while softening the resistance of those outside the community.

The central leadership of the Islamic community was tightly bound together through marriage. The Prophet developed family ties with those among his closest followers who were later to become the first four caliphs (see Figure 4.1). Muhammad himself married A'isha and Hafsa, who were the daughters of Abu Bakr and Umar, respectively. At the same time, he married three of his own daughters to Uthman and Ali. Ali married Fatima, and Uthman first wedded Ruqayya and then upon her death renewed this important tie by marrying her sister Umm Kulthum.[20] The concern for holding the community together can also be seen in the tendency for leading Muslims to marry the widows of those members of the community who died in battle. Four of the Prophet's wives, for example, were widows of prominent early Muslims. Three of these Muslims had been killed in the important conflicts at Badr and Uhud.

The second category of marriages involved those that were contracted with members of potential or actual opposition forces. Many personal ties were developed with tribal groups throughout Arabia by means of this mechanism. Muhammad himself married three women who were the daughters of non-

---

[19]Watt, *Muhammad,* p. 10. Watt emphatically emphasizes the importance of the political motive in the Prophet's various marriages. In this study alone, he makes the argument in eight separate places. See pp. 10–12, 79, 102–103, 131, 155–157, 195, 206, 233. In another book, Watt writes that "all Muhammad's own marriages can be seen to have a tendency to promote friendly relations in the political sphere." See Watt, *Muhammad at Medina* (Oxford: Clarendon Press, 1956), p. 287. Although, like Watt, we have stressed the political dimensions of Muhammad's marriages, we do not mean to deny the human and personal motives that were also obviously involved.

[20]Ali also married a granddaughter of Muhammad's while Umar married both a granddaughter of Muhammad's and a daughter of Ali's.

Muslim tribal notables. In each case, the marriage neutralized much political tension. The most important personal ties established through wedlock, however, were those involving the opposition in Mecca. By marrying the daughter of the influential Meccan leader Abu Sufyan and then one year later wedding the sister-in-law of the new head of the Meccan clan of Hashim, al-Abbas, Muhammad managed to establish intimate personal ties that were crucial to his tranquil conquest of Mecca.[21]

The original Muslim community functioned politically solely on the basis of personalities and personalism. In this sense, it differed very little from the pre-Islamic style of tribal and clan politics. Ruling institutions such as formal administrative organizations were unknown. The Prophet appointed specific individuals to lead military campaigns, diplomatic expeditions, and economic missions, depending on the exigencies of the moment. As we have seen in the case of the marriage mechanism, personalism had distinct political advantages. Not the least of these was the introduction of a degree of social and political flexibility, which is crucial in the construction of a new social and political system.

THE UNITY OF THE COMMUNITY

Through the interrelated patterns of compromise, charisma, and personalism, the Prophet Muhammad was able to build unity into a system prone to disintegration. Through a universal message delivered by a charismatic leader, peoples of widely differing backgrounds were attracted to a single community. This process of integration and consolidation is the main principle of Muhammad's message, for, as Seyyed Hossein Nasr has written, "Unity is the alpha and omega of Islam."[22] Muhammad's charisma was an integrating force that intertwined the spiritual with the material and combined the social, the religious, and the political. The leader himself exhibited an internal unity by combining such virtues as compassion and strength, and this in turn strengthened his charismatic appeal.[23] The ideology professed by a charismatic personality was a key ingredient in sealing the fissures in the social structure. The more practical political policies of compromise and personalism as adopted by Muhammad then enabled him to confront on a daily basis the centrifugal social tendencies. The capacity to compromise dulled old antagonisms in a way that allowed policies of personalism to acquire new meaning. Personal ties could now signal a kind of cooperation and conciliation that often led to conversion and consolidation. These three qualities of compromise, charisma, and personalism were the key elements in the Prophet Muhammad's style of leadership.

---

[21]See Watt, *Muhammad at Medina.* For an excellent discussion of the role of A'isha in the early Muslim community, see D.A. Spellberg, *Politics, Gender, and the Islamic Past: The Legacy of A'isha bint Abi Bakr* (New York: Columbia University Press, 1994).

[22]Nasr, *Ideals and Realities,* p. 29.

[23]For an interesting discussion of this point, see Frithjof Schuon. *Understanding Islam* (London: George Allen and Unwin, 1963), pp. 87–105.

Patterns of Patrimonialism in the Middle East

My good Pasha, the will of the people emanates from my will.

KING FAROUK OF EGYPT[24]

In his important typology of traditional political systems, Max Weber includes two types that he labels patriarchal and patrimonial systems.[25] The patriarchal system is the core of all traditional systems and is generally confined to household kinship groups. In patriarchy, the authority relation is one that binds master and family. The head of the household "has no administrative staff and no machinery to enforce his will. . . . The members of the household stand in an entirely personal relation to him. They obey him and he commands them in the belief that his right and their duty are part of an inviolable order that has the sanctity of immemorial tradition. Originally the efficacy of this belief depended on the fear of magical evils that would befall the innovator and the community that condoned a breach of custom."[26]

The patrimonial system, on the other hand, is one in which an identifiable administrative structure develops and spreads throughout the particular society or empire. The tasks of government become more specialized, complex, and elaborate. As a result, the ruler's relation with the ruled tends to be filtered through a huge network of bureaucrats. Owing to the introduction of a more complex and differentiated administrative apparatus, the emphasis on the mysterious and the magical is softened.

The literature that has attempted to analyze this Weberian typology has greatly overemphasized the differences between the patriarchal and patrimonial forms of rule. This has resulted in a misplaced preoccupation with such issues as specialization of roles and differentiation of structures. The key to understanding the traditional processes of leadership rests in the fundamental human relations that bind ruler and ruled. These were shaped in the patriarchal environment and were hardened and routinized in the patrimonial system. In essence, the patrimonial form of rule represents an extension and expansion of the patriarchal system. The relations that bind ruler and ruled, leader and led, master and servant, and king and subject are fundamentally the same in both Weberian categories. Reinhard Bendix defines patrimonial rule, therefore, as "an extension of the ruler's household in which the relation between the ruler and his officials remains on the basis of paternal authority and filial dependence."[27]

In most Islamic societies, patrimonial patterns of leadership have been dominant. The particular manifestation of patrimonial rule that has marked these

---

[24]As quoted in P. J. Vatikiotis, *The Egyptian Army in Politics: Pattern for New Nations?* (Bloomington, Ind.: Indiana University Press, 1961), p. 39.

[25]A third type is the feudal system, which was the dominant traditional system in Western societies. For the presentation of Weber's analysis of patriarchal and patrimonial politics, see Weber, *The Theory of Social and Economic Organization*, pp. 341–358; and Reinhard Bendix, *Max Weber: An Intellectual Portrait* (Garden City, N.Y.: Doubleday and Co., 1962), pp. 330–360.

[26]Bendix, *Max Weber*, pp. 330–331.

[27]Ibid., p. 360.

societies is referred to by Manfred Halpern as a "relationship of emanation." The politics of emanation involve an "encounter in which one treats the other solely as an extension of one's self. The other accepts the denial of his own separate identity because of the mysterious and overwhelming power of the source of this emanation—a yielding which is rewarded with total security."[28] When the Spanish Ummayad caliph Abd al-Rahman al-Nasir died at the turn of the tenth century after fifty years of rule, he was publicly eulogized in terms that capture the basic meaning of rule by emanation: "The souls of the people were absorbed in his soul: when he died they died also."[29] There is little doubt that this caliph possessed baraka in abundance.

In the Islamic world, where religion and politics have been inseparable, shahs, sultans, and shaikhs have tended to rule in a paternal, patriarchal, and patrimonial manner. Government has been personal, and both civil and military bureaucracies have been little more than extensions of the leader. In the cases of the Ottoman, Safavid, and Moghul empires, the royal household developed into a huge administrative octopus, with the leader as head and the leader's gigantic retinue of personal servants and confidants as tentacles. In patrimonial politics, "bureaucratic recruitment and advances are based on personal confidence and not on objective qualifications; they reflect the more or less precarious balance reached by the prince in his effort to create and maintain a bureaucracy completely dependent upon his power. In each case, the position of the patrimonial bureaucrat must remain what it originally was—an emanation of his relation of purely personal submission to the Lord. . . ."[30]

In the patrimonial Middle East, the sovereign is located at the center of the political system. He is surrounded by advisors, ministers, military leaders, personal secretaries, and confidants. The one thing that all members of this inner circle share is unquestioned personal loyalty to the leader. This is best indicated by their continual reflection of the will and personality of that leader. These individuals may relate submissively and passively to the leader, but they do not relate in this way to their own peers and followers. Here, they are caught up in intense manipulations and machinations. The reason for this, of course, is that a minister who relates passively to a monarch on one level is the central source of leadership on another level. Therefore, within his own ministry, he may be the emanating influence, and his subordinates survive by remaining passive before him. Although the vertical relations tend to be one-sided, the horizontal patterns are characterized by balanced rivalry. Those of relatively equal power and authority are locked in constant conflict. This conflict can occur only below the

---

[28]Halpern, "Four Contrasting Repertories of Human Relations in Islam," *Psychological Dimensions of Near Eastern Studies,* ed. by L. Carl Brown and Norman Itzkowitz (Princeton, N.J.: Darwin Press, 1977), p. 64. In this article, Halpern sensitively explores the significance of the politics of emanation to the Middle Eastern peoples and political systems. We have chosen to emphasize his conceptualization of emanation as the central pattern in patrimonialism.

[29]Lisan al-Din Ibn Khatib [Book of works by leading authors concerning those accepted as kings of Islam] (Rabat, Morocco: New Press, 1934), p. 44 (in Arabic).

[30]Magali Sarfatti, *Spanish Bureaucratic-Patrimonialism in America,* Politics of Modernization Series, no. 1 (Berkeley, Calif.: University of California Institute of International Studies, 1966), p. 8.

level of the sovereign, since the sovereign has no equal in a patrimonial context. This kind of division is constantly being sharpened by the competition among the rivals to demonstrate the greatest loyalty to the leader. The leader, in turn, encourages and manipulates this competition. The traditional politics of patrimonial leadership in the Middle East, therefore, tends to consist of chains of vertical emanation and horizontal competition that cut through the sociopolitical fabric (see Figure 4.2).

In the patrimonial style of Middle Eastern leadership, the leader becomes the fount of all important ideas and strategies. Policies and programs emanate from him. New ideas and suggestions must somehow be submitted to the leader, who may propose them as his own. Historically, the Middle Eastern political landscape is littered with individuals who attempted and failed to project themselves into the political limelight through their own ideas and ambitions. Often, they were the very closest confidants of the leader himself; by staking claim to their own political ground, they challenged the very relation of emanation and hastened their own inevitable political demise. This is precisely what happened when Abbasid caliph Harun al-Rashid in 803 disposed of his powerful Barmecid friend and advisor Ja'far ibn Yahya and imprisoned the other members of Ja'far's family. Numerous similar examples exist in both Ottoman and Persian history.

A famous example of a leader turning against an independent-minded subordinate in Persian history occurred in the mid-nineteenth century during the rule of the Qajar dynasty (1779–1925). Nasir al-Din Shah, who ruled Iran for half a century, gave the orders that led to the dismissal and death of his strongwilled and illustrious minister, Mirza Taqi Khan Amir Kabir. Mirza Taqi Khan has gone down in Persian history as that country's greatest reformer and most beloved prime minister. Because of this man's brilliance and political acumen, the young shah's light only flickered until Mirza Taqi Khan was assassinated in 1851 after having served three years in the post. As we shall see in Chapter 5, there are many contemporary examples of this pattern.

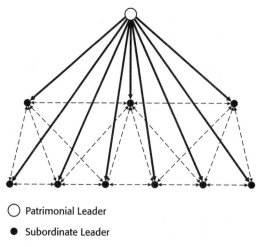

○ Patrimonial Leader

● Subordinate Leader

Figure 4.2 Patrimonial leadership.

The nearer individuals are to the patrimonial leader, the more likely they are to have their ideas accepted and implemented by the leader. In such a personal system of politics, physical nearness to the leader is an especially significant variable in explaining the distribution of power and influence. It would be wrong to assume that, in a patrimonial system, those who surround the leader have no influence at all. They always exert a subtle and passive influence, largely by having their ideas absorbed into those of the leader. In such a system, "advisors" never demand, seldom suggest, and only advise when advice is actively sought. They more often applaud than appraise. Although their influence on the leader may be sporadic, their influence on everyone else will usually be very intense. The closer an advisor is to the leader, the more influential that adviser will be both with the ruler and with the people.[31]

Middle Eastern societies have been governed by authoritarian patrimonial systems throughout most of history. Islam fostered patrimonial patterns both through its ideals and in reality. The entire philosophical framework that evolved with Islam stressed relations of emanation. The term *Islam* itself means "submission," and Islam demands that all believers perfect their acceptance of the Almighty. The Prophet Muhammad is the prototype of the leader linked in the chain of emanation, since he is the one who relates the material to the spiritual. Muhammad represents perfect passivity before God and perfect activity before man. He was the mirror who reflected the word of God, and "he saw nothing except in God and through God."[32] In his relations with man, however, the Prophet lived a vigorous social, political, and religious life, since he traded, fought, judged, and ruled. He was "that warrior on horseback who halts before the mountain of Truth, passive towards the Divine Will, active towards the world. . . ."[33] As Muhammad modeled his life after the Divine, millions of Muslims labor to model their lives after his. The Prophet's community in Medina was a patrimony infused with the charisma of a special leader.

The intermeshing of religion and politics in Islam has meant that political leaders have often had the opportunity to present themselves as linked directly to God. This has helped invest them with a mysterious and otherworldly aura that has allowed them to be exalted as models to be imitated by the people. This is one reason why political leaders in Islamic societies have historically attempted to trace their ancestry back to the family of the Prophet. The only innate aristocracy in Islamic civilization consists of those individuals in the community who are related to the family of the Prophet Muhammad.

---

[31]Because of the continual competition and wielding of influence that occur at all levels of Islamic society; the intricate but effective manner in which subordinates can have their ideas incorporated into those of the ruler; and the constant challenging of particular relations of emanation by those who wish to assert their own power, we cannot characterize Islamic leadership as either "Oriental despotism," to use Wittfogel's term, or "sultanism," to use Max Weber's term. As we shall see, the informal, bargaining, and balancing nature of Middle Eastern politics contradicts such an emphasis on absolute authority, total power, and hardened hierarchy.

[32]Nasr, *Ideals and Realities,* p. 84.

[33]Ibid., p. 9.

The personal rivalry that has always been central to patrimonial society has led to numerous schisms and divisions within the Islamic community. What has marked all of these splinter movements, however, has been their tendency to reform themselves by placing extreme emphasis on leadership by emanation. Part of the reason for this is the need for any political movement playing the role of challenger to legitimate its existence. This must be done as convincingly and dramatically as possible. All Shiʻi societies have exhibited the patrimonial rule by emanation in its most pronounced form.[34] This is seen in the significant figure of the Imam, who is the leader par excellence in the Shiʻi community.

Ali was the first Imam, and he has been succeeded by other imams, their number varying with the different sects. The Imam is not selected by the community but succeeds by virtue of divine appointment, or *nass*. The Imam is the vicegerent of God, and the line of Imams consists of a divinely fashioned chain of emanation that is unquestioned in the minds of the believers. Whereas the Sunni caliph is an ordinary mortal, the Shiʻi Imams exist in a state of permanent grace that renders them infallible, impeccable, and immaculate. The Imam is the one who rules by the will of God and in the name of God. In the Iranian version of Shiʻi Islam, the twelfth and last Imam has gone into hiding and is meanwhile represented by the important cleric leaders known as *mujtahids*. According to strict Shiʻi doctrine, as representatives of the Hidden Imam, these mujtahids are the major sources of interpretation for all social, political, and religious affairs. The shahs, however, traditionally attempted to lock themselves into the legitimizing tradition of the Imams. Historically, much of Iranian politics revolved about the relationship between the mujtahids and shahs as they competed for legitimacy by emanation. In the Iranian revolution of 1978–1979, the mujtahids finally triumphed and took control of the political system of the country.

Muhammad's early community was organized according to patrimonial principles. The Prophet stood at the head of the sociopolitical household, and personal ties and relations knit the entire community together. These relations were made particularly binding by the fact that most of the leaders and followers were brought into the Prophet's own household. The dynamics of Muhammad's leadership that have been briefly sketched highlight these patterns. Muhammad's charismatic personality and his relation to the Divine enabled individuals such as Abu Bakr to accept his leadership completely. The special charismatic nature of the Prophet's rule by emanation overcame much of the intramural dissension and conflict endemic to systems of patrimonial politics. It was when Muhammad died that all of these submerged dissensions broke to the surface and schisms became common.

The patrimonial leaders who succeeded the Prophet found relations of emanation less persuasive and effective. This became increasingly the case as dynastic heads became further removed from the days of Muhammad's rule. Islamic history, therefore, is replete with examples of leaders at all levels who made dra-

---

[34]For a fine analysis of the Fatimid caliphate, which emphasizes the theoretical aspects of patrimonial patterns of emanation, see P. J. Vatikiotis. *The Fatimid Theory of State* (Lahore, Pakistan: Orientalia Publishers, 1957).

matic efforts to strengthen the patrimonial patterns by infusing new life into unbelievable relations of emanation. This was done in two complementary ways: (1) the original charismatic leaders to which the new leaders were attached were accorded supernatural status; and (2) a proclaimed leader attempted to build a special relation between himself and the earlier prototype.

In the first case, the leaders in early Islam are glorified and purified until in some instances they appear to have possessed godly qualities. This has been particularly true in the case of Ali, the fourth caliph and son-in-law of the Prophet. In the second instance, communities develop around individuals who claim to be special representatives or messengers of either of these early patrimonial heroes or even of God. Saints and holy personages play an important role in Middle Eastern politics and society. One scholar writes, for example, that "the most characteristic social institution of North African religious life is the saint, the holy personage. As Islam does not enjoin celibacy, saints proliferate and form lineages and dynasties."[35] Mahdis, marabouts, and imams have formed political movements of great influence in the Middle East. The Moroccan marabouts were the major force shaping the social and political systems in large areas of North Africa until the end of the nineteenth century.[36] In a patrimonial political system, the basic patterns, which often shatter and disintegrate, have traditionally been reknitted through the appearance of a new leader claiming either special supernatural power or a special relation with those who are believed to have had such power.

Patterns of leadership in the Middle East have been highly congruent from institution to institution and from community to community. In the family, school, guild, and government, patrimonialism prevails. Much of the reason for this is the influence of Islam, which penetrates all aspects of a believer's life. In patriarchal or patrimonial societies, the patriarch is the main social and political reality. He is the model, the guide, the innovator, the planner, the mediator, the chastiser, and the protector. The community wraps itself around the leader, who governs through a constantly expanding web of personal relations.

Within the family, which is the basic social unit in the Middle East, the father is the unrivaled leader. The situation is best summarized as follows: "The Muslim family has remained patriarchal, and the head of it maintains his authority . . . down to the last day of his life."[37] As we have seen in Chapter 3, however, the other family members, especially the wives and the mothers, have plenty of room to maneuver in order to realize their particular goals. A patriarchy or patrimony in the Middle East does not negate the influence of family

---

[35]Ernest Gellner, "Sanctity, Puritanism, Secularisation and Nationalism in North Africa: A Case Study," mimeographed (n.p., n.d.), p. 1. See also Gellner's fine study, *Saints of the Atlas* (Chicago: University of Chicago Press, 1969).

[36]Dale Eickelman tells this story well. He defines marabouts as persons "to whom is attributed a special relation toward God which makes them particularly well placed to serve as intermediaries with the supernatural and to communicate God's grace (*baraka*) to their clients." See Eickelman, *Moroccan Islam* (Austin: The University of Texas Press, 1976), p. 6.

[37]Maurice Gaudefroy-Demombynes, *Muslim Institutions* (London: George Allen and Unwin, 1961), p. 128.

members other than the father. While the father may have authority, he has no monopoly on power. The intensity of the competition within the family is seen, for example, in sibling rivalry. Brother competes against brother, and various shifting alliances are formed as mothers, children, cousins, grandparents, aunts, and uncles are pulled into the continual competition and conflict.

In educational and occupational settings, the roles and styles of leadership are essentially the same as those that mark the family and the government. The master-apprentice, teacher-student, and shaikh-*murid* ("brotherhood disciple") relations are patterns of superordination and subordination in which the follower's existence is often an extension of the leader's being. The teacher-student relation is, in fact, somewhat closer to the father-son relation than to the patterns found in guild and brotherhood organizations. The latter have preserved much more of the otherworldly quality that serves to strengthen the bonds of emanation. This quality has been gradually lost in the educational system as the religious direction of education has given way to secular control. The basic pattern, however, can still be seen in many Middle Eastern classrooms, where the teacher's person is deferred to and the teacher's word is memorized.

In the environment of guilds and brotherhoods, deference becomes devotion, and shaikhs, who are the leaders, command a charismatic control that is generally absent in familial, governmental, and formal educational institutions. In the case of Sufi brotherhoods, "all authority and allocation of authority positions in the hierarchy lie within the purview of the Sheikh, and the subordinates derive their statuses from him."[38] Those who are closest to the shaikh's person have the greatest influence in the order. Therefore, the personal secretaries and attendants of the shaikh are extremely important figures in these organizations. They are, of course, entirely devoted to and dependent on the leader. In describing this kind of relation between a private secretary and the shaikh in a contemporary Egyptian brotherhood, one member explained that the secretary does not even go to sleep "until the Sheikh tells him to."[39]

Patrimonialism has been the dominant pattern of leadership in Middle Eastern politics for centuries. The strength of this pattern has fluctuated greatly, however, depending on the leader, dynasty, society, and era. Patrimonialism was most evident in the heyday of the shahs and sultans. Nonetheless, even though the patterns of patrimonialism may be less prominent in the Middle East today than in the past, they are still major realities in all Middle Eastern political systems. The politics of patrimonial leadership as manifested in the Middle East reflect six major characteristics: personalism, proximity, informality, balanced conflict, military prowess, and religious rationalization.

Personalism   Patrimonial society rests upon personal relationships. The community or society is essentially an enlarged household, and the personal ties that dominate in the household are the model for the ties in any other patrimonial

---

[38]Michael Gilsenan. "The Sufi Orders and the Modern World," mimeographed (n.p., September 29, 1967), pp. 7–8.

[39]Ibid., p. 45.

unit. Middle Eastern societies and political systems grew out of tribal constellations, and the personalism that prevailed in the family and the clan has had a pervasive and protracted influence. Formal organizations and institutions have seldom effectively intervened. Even when institutions such as formal bureaucracies have developed, the real business of ruling and political decision making has resided in personal networks. These networks tend to hold together groups of people, and it is through these networks that the leader has attempted to establish as wide a range of contacts as possible.

In order to rule in this kind of setting, it is essential that the leader gather and retain as much personal information about others in the network as possible. One famous eleventh-century manual on the conduct of kingship advises the prince, "never omit to inform yourself of the doings of others . . . ,"[40] and tells the king that "it is your duty not to be ignorant of conditions in your realm, of the circumstances of your people or those of your soldiers. More particularly you must be vigilant concerning the doings of your vizier. He should not be able to swallow a drink of water without your knowing it. . . ."[41] In this setting, the art of genealogy and the knowledge of friendship relations are serious political pursuits.

The prevalence of personalism is best seen in the great Islamic dynastic systems, where the rulers built gigantic households around their own persons. A more formal bureaucratic state organization also evolved in these systems in answer to the pressure to administer the large political empires. A distinguished Islamic scholar summarizes this situation as follows: "Throughout the whole system of the Eastern Muslim political organization there runs like a red thread the division of all the organs of administration into two main categories, the dargah (palace) and diwan (chancery)."[42] In the Iranian Safavid system, the royal household was referred to as the *khassah,* and the state bureaucracy was known as the *divan.* In the Turkish Ottoman system, the division was between the "imperial household" and the "central administration." In traditional Islamic polities, the royal household was the crucial arena of politics, since it consistently dominated the state bureaucracy proper. This has occurred not only because of the superior concentration of power within the royal household but also because the personalities of the palace have infiltrated the state bureaucracy. Hence, the royal household, which is organized around the person of the king, has in turn wrapped around itself the bureaucracy, which expands with the growth of the political unit itself.

The actual transition from a completely personal pattern of leadership to one with bureaucratic and institutional appendages occurred mainly during the rule of the Abbasids (749–1258). This represented, in Weber's terms, a movement from a patriarchal to a patrimonial stage. The Abbasid leaders built an elaborate administrative system that included the office of *vazir* ("prime minister")

---

[40]Kai Ka'us Ibn Iskandar, *A Mirror for Princes (The Quabus-nama),* trans. by Reuben Levy (London: Cresset Press, 1951), p. 194.

[41]Ibid., p. 235.

[42]V. V. Barthold, *Turkestan Down to the Mongol Invasion,* second ed. (London: Oxford University Press, 1928), p. 227.

and more than a dozen large organizational boards that were in turn composed of numerous departments.[43] Despite this bureaucracy, personal relations dominated the system, and the court staff remained the critical force. This dependence of the more formal state bureaucracy on the person of the king is seen in the role of the vazir himself. Although the vazir usually headed the state bureaucracy in these political systems, he did so as the personal servant of the king and as a leading member of the royal household. It was the *person* of the vazir, not the *office* of vazir, that was the important political consideration.

This traditional style of political rule has carried over into contemporary Middle Eastern politics to a surprisingly large degree. Personalism predominates in such societies as Morocco, Jordan, Saudi Arabia, and the shaikhdoms that still have traditional authoritarian leaders. In other Middle Eastern countries, the personal dimension of leadership prevails more at the subnational level, in such institutions as the family, the school, and the guild. In all of these societies, however, patrimonial personalism continues to shape leadership processes, although it is more and more submerged beneath the growing facade of formal institutions and bureaucratic machinery. Contemporary Middle Eastern political monarchs constantly describe their societies as large families and emphasize their own special positions as heads or fathers of these families. It is in this spirit that former King Hassan of Morocco spoke about "the innate nature of our family, characterized by its profound wisdom, its great nobility, and the solid communion which unites us ultimately to our people."[44]

Proximity   Patrimonial leadership attaches particular significance to physical proximity. Regardless of occupational designation or formal title, those who live closest to the leader regularly hold major political positions in the traditional Middle Eastern system. Zayd Ibn Haritha, who was a black slave adopted by Muhammad and Khadija, illustrates the power of proximity. Because he was the Prophet's adopted son, and despite his status as slave, Zayd became one of the leading figures in early Islam. Throughout Islamic history, slaves have risen to great influence. One of the most powerful Islamic political systems was built by a dynasty whose kings were once slaves. These were the Mamluks; the word *mamluk* itself means "owned" or "possessed." They were originally slaves who had served as bodyguards to the Ayyubid dynastic leaders. Proximity to leadership has meant that slaves, cooks, musicians, and stable keepers have often been able to exert political power in traditional Muslim societies.

Although proximity is a consideration relevant to any political system, it assumes special importance in those societies where leadership is built on a far-flung network of personal relations. Here, those closest to the *person* of the leader tend to be the most influential. In patrimonial politics these are often, in the first instance, such family members as brothers, wives, mothers, and uncles. Those who marry into the leader's family and become in-laws also become po-

---

[43]Vazir is most closely translated as prime minister. It is sometimes transliterated as vizir or vizier.

[44]John Waterbury, *The Commander of the Faithful: The Moroccan Political Elite—A Study in Segmented Politics* (New York: Columbia University Press, 1970), p. 150.

tential centers of influence. The special personal ties and ideal position of proximity of relatives often mean that when the pattern of emanation is broken, it is broken within this familial core. If anyone makes direct suggestions to the patrimonial leader, or criticizes him, it is almost always a member of the ruling family. Certainly, it is from this source that new ideas are most likely to be entertained and absorbed. In an extended household administration, or patrimonial system, those in the core household or nuclear family will play major roles in political decision making. Western discussions and condemnations of nepotism, ascription, and favoritism must be reevaluated in light of the realities of patrimonial politics.

Proximity counts most in systems where decision making is highly centralized, highly personal, and highly informal. In nonpatrimonial systems, decision making tends to be more equally distributed throughout the society. Such systems also have formal and associational channels that carry the ideas of those distant from the centers of political decision making to the leader. In the patrimonial Middle East, the most effective way to submit a request or present a petition is to get as close as possible to the leader. The closer an individual is to the center of the personal web of politics, the more likely that person is to share in decision making. It is for this reason that there is constant and unrelenting pressure toward the center of power in traditional patrimonial politics. The leader is always pressed in upon by individuals who attempt to be in the leader's presence as often and as long as possible. At the same time, those closest to him, such as his advisors, ministers, and confidants, attempt to resist and control the flow of others to this precious territory. In *A Mirror for Princes,* Muslim vazirs are warned, "Wherever the king goes, accompany him; do not leave him alone. . . ."[45]

It is proximity rather than professional merit or occupational position that explains why gardeners, cobblers, barbers, and physicians have moved into positions of considerable influence in Islamic politics. The patrimonial leader has more often sought the counsel of these individuals than of any others, and at times such service personnel have eventually replaced their masters and become political leaders in their own right. Even in the contemporary Middle East, political leaders rely heavily on their personal attendants for advice and information. The late Shah of Iran, for example, said that he relied on his valet and gardener when he needed information. Ayatollah Khomeini listened closely to the advice of his son Ahmad, who was one of the few who had direct access to the Ayatollah.

Those nearest to the person of the leader serve to filter demands and requests, act as information bearers and receptacles of advice, and stand as influential intermediaries between the leader and the masses. Where power is personal and politics are patrimonial, the issue of proximity is critical. The concept of the "inner circle" is particularly relevant to Middle Eastern politics.

Informality   Personal politics tend to be informal politics in the sense that the most important leaders are those who are not bound by formal contracts or limited by institutional constraints. Even those leaders who visibly combine power

---

[45]Iskandar, *A Mirror for Princes,* p. 214.

and authority have consistently operated in highly personal settings rather than in well-defined formal organizations.

In today's bedouin society, the great importance of the informal leadership structure is still in the person of the *rajal khayr,* or "good man." In the Ayshaybat tribe in western Egypt, this person is more influential than the *aqila,* in whom resides the contractual authority of the tribe. The aqila is, in other words, the formal leader. The rajal khayr is a cultural and political broker who has the loyalty and friendship of the people as well as the attention of high regional government officials, who prefer to work through him. As G. J. Obermeyer writes in an excellent case study of bedouin leadership, "The power of the āqila is limited by the very structure of the role. The role of the rajal khair, being less institutionalized and structured, is less confined with respect to the kind and amount of influence the role-player might exert."[46]

Political decision making in the Middle East has been marked by behind-the-scenes planning and negotiation. Leaders have seldom emphasized the establishment of formal political institutions such as parliaments and parties. Where such formal institutions have been constructed, they have often been rationalizing gestures more than seriously conceived political organizations. Once in existence, formal bodies have had relatively little impact on a leader's political activities.

Informal patterns of control and authority have been responsible for a great deal of uncertainty in the decision-making environment. Middle Eastern political processes reflect a high level of intrigue and counterintrigue as leaders at various levels maneuver in secret and semisecret settings. It is partially because of this emphasis on secrecy and organizational informality that rumors have always been an important political phenomenon in the Middle East. Secrecy and uncertainty breed speculation, and the ability to uncover decisions and deals is an important political resource.

The propensity for informal organization that has marked Middle Eastern social life is most evident in the numerous secret and informal groups. These include secret orders and societies, religious brotherhoods, underground minority organizations, political cliques and *anjumans,* informal coffeehouse groups, Sufi meetings, ritualistic religious gatherings, regular meetings of extended families, royal social circles and *khalvats,* and bureaucratic and parliamentary factions.[47]

Middle Eastern leaders have tended to operate as the centers of webs of personal relationships in which the lines of power and authority are indistinct and constantly changing. Spheres of political authority overlap. Hence, there is always doubt concerning who is closest to the leader and who influenced what decision. With the possible exception of the national political leader, there is even a question about *who* the leader really is. Often the most influential political actors remain in the background, where they are members of the family, the harem, or

---

[46]Obermeyer, "Leadership and Transition in Bedouin Society: A Case Study," *The Desert and the Sown,* ed. by Cynthia Nelson (Berkeley, Calif.: University of California Institute of International Studies, 1973), p. 164.

[47]*Anjumans* are usually translated as "societies." *Khalvat* was a term used in Iran to refer to a regular social gathering of the shah and his closest male advisors.

friendship circles. In Middle Eastern politics, an informal personal organization has tended to rest behind the formal institutional organization. Observers are confused because of the presence of the identifiable leader at the center of both organizations and the presence of certain advisors and confidants in both.

This environment of informality has carried several political advantages for the patrimonial leader. It has provided him with an unusually flexible system, since lines of authority and responsibility tend to be fluid and blurred. In such a system, it is difficult for opposition forces to concentrate because targets are neither stable nor well defined. At the same time, the leader enjoys a broad capacity to intervene in governmental affairs and to move subordinates around with ease. Since there are no clearly defined responsibilities, and since hard and fast assignments are nonexistent, the patrimonial leader can interpret spheres of authority in almost any way he chooses. Those individuals who are most apt to challenge the leader find themselves severely crippled in this environment. They lack institutional foundations and formal supports that they can cling to, and therefore find themselves highly dependent on the personal whim of the leader. Informal politics tend to conceal the merit of aspiring statesmen, and as a result these statesmen are seldom able to build the popularity necessary for the crystallization of opposition to the leader. Finally, informality builds distrust among those who are relatively influential in the system. Individuals report confidentially and personally to the leader, and this often involves statements about the activities and ambitions of other political figures. Such a semisecret pattern of politics enables the leader to engender a great deal of division and distrust among his subordinates. This division has been institutionalized as overlapping lines of authority by which officials exert control in one another's area of expertise.

In patrimonial leadership, visibility and formality have been subordinated to personalism and covert organization. This characteristic has provided Middle Eastern leaders with a maximum amount of maneuverability and a minimum degree of accountability. Even in the contemporary Middle East of complex and sophisticated organization charts, the business of politics is negotiated outside of and in spite of these instruments. Political blueprints such as constitutions and fundamental laws heavily mask the actual patterns and processes by which political leaders make decisions and protect their interests.

Balanced Conflict   The patrimonial leader in the Middle East has ruled on the foundation of pervasive division and personal rivalry. In the Middle Eastern context, the dictum "divide and rule" takes on special meaning. Cutting through all levels in the Islamic system is a built-in rivalry that marks interpersonal, intergroup, and interclass relations. The leader who seeks to divide and rule, therefore, has an ideal social system within which to operate. Rivalry is institutionalized in the system, and the traditional ruler had only to encourage processes that were already at work. This is why unity is the most sought-after and least achieved goal in Islamic history.

Personal rivalry has so permeated the Middle Eastern social structure that it manifests itself in institutions all the way from the family to the national bureaucracy. In Egyptian village society, for example, intense sibling rivalry is considered essential to a child's growth. Parents continually intensify rivalry among their children. This is done in numerous dramatic ways, including labeling the children with names that invite conflict. In one Egyptian family, for example, the elder brother was called "the stupid one," while the younger brother was nicknamed "the clever one."[48] In a study of Lebanese village life, it was found that fewer than half of the children sampled could name three persons they considered friends. The reasons for this reported scarcity of friendship relations were explained in terms of grudges, feuds, and rivalries.[49]

At the national political level, the same pattern is evident in the way that leaders and rulers play off their advisors and subordinates against one another. The contemporary rulers of Morocco, Jordan, and Saudi Arabia have become especially adept in this skill. In Iran after the revolution, Ayatollah Khomeini shrewdly remained above the conflicting factions. From here he played off political groups against one another, for example, the radical leftists against the extremists on the right. By splintering the potential opposition forces and at the same time standing above them as supreme arbiter, several Middle Eastern leaders have managed to maintain firm control in the political arena. Any concentration of skill, energy, or power is immediately shattered through leadership tactics of division and redivision. In the traditional Abbasid, Ottoman, Safavid, and Moghul administrative systems, the most important and influential political functions were constantly divided and redistributed among larger and larger numbers of officials. When a political figure became particularly influential, his title and function were given to a second and rival administrator, and influence was thus divided and shared. Tension was thereby instilled into the particular political sphere, and the personal power of the individual in control of this sphere was substantially lessened, if not halved.

The politics of rivalry and conflict not only served to buttress leadership positions but also reinforced systemic stability. The tension was balanced in such a way that overwhelming concentrations of power seldom developed outside the sphere of the national political ruler. Manfred Halpern analyzes the Islamic system in terms of its "ability to convert tensions into balances" and its capacity to bind society together "through conflict no less than through collaboration."[50] In contemporary Morocco, "All seek to maintain in the midst of the group that tension which is life, that variety that is solidarity."[51] The Moroccan monarch operates a system in which "no group may be permitted to become too strong, and to counter hegemonic tendencies life is breathed into rival groups."[52] In Iran, the late shah created a stable balance of tension in which ministers, courtiers, security agents, military leaders, industrialists, and clerics were systematically di-

[48]Hammed Ammar, *Growing Up in an Egyptian Village* (New York: Octagon Books, 1966), p. 110.

[49]Judith R. Williams, *The Youth of Haouch El Hariml: A Lebanese Village,* Harvard Middle East Monograph Series, vol. 20 (Cambridge, Mass.: Harvard University Press, 1968), pp. 91–92.

[50]Manfred Halpern, *The Politics of Social Change in the Middle East and North Africa* (Princeton, N.J.: Princeton University Press, 1963), pp. 10, 18.

[51]Jacques Berque, *Structures Sociales du Haut-Atlas* (Paris, 1955), p. 449, as quoted in Waterbury, *The Commander of the Faithful,* p. 61.

[52]Waterbury, *The Commander of the Faithful,* p. 148.

vided against one another at all levels. The last four kings of Saudi Arabia have promoted the distrust and animosity that mark the relationships between many of their half-brothers, while at another level the national guard stands in direct rivalry with the regular army. The Nassers, Bourguibas, Saddam Husseins, Qaddafis, and al-Assads have also promoted rivalry. In the Middle East, political leaders have traditionally expended much of their energies in manipulating personal networks of stabilizing tensions. A premium has been placed upon a leader's ability to sense the location of threatening power concentrations and then to splinter those concentrations either by deepening existing divisions or by fostering new rivalries.

Military Prowess   Max Weber writes that "with the development of a purely personal administrative staff, *especially a military force* under the control of the chief, traditional authority tends to develop into 'patrimonialism.'"[53] The key to patrimonial politics is the existence of a military force that is at the personal disposal of the leader. Within the Islamic world, this consideration has been a central one. Here, among the most highly respected qualities of leadership are personal bravery and physical courage. Islamic scholars present "combativeness" as one of the three great characteristics of the Prophet Muhammad.[54] The famous Islamic leaders are known and remembered for their bravery in battle and their victory in military campaigns. The warrior hero is a deeply admired figure in Middle Eastern history. Leaders who have been able to conduct themselves well on the field of battle have always had a marked advantage in the arena of domestic politics.[55]

This emphasis on physical courage and military prowess is to be expected in a culture that developed out of a tribal context. Throughout the Middle East today, groups still exist that follow the Shi'i path or worship Ali primarily because of his personal courage and valor, which are summed up in his titles Lion of God and Sword of Islam. This inspiration was key to the fighting commitment of the young Iranian soldiers who died in large numbers in the war with Iraq in the 1980s.

The emphasis on personal courage and valor runs deep throughout Middle Eastern society. Bravery is so highly esteemed that it carries favorable moral connotations. The Arabic word *shaja'a,* which is also commonly used in Persian, implies a personal bravery that is especially infused with virtue and uprightness. It implies a kind of chivalrous courage. Throughout Middle Eastern history, the personally brave and physically courageous have had about them an aura of knightliness. Combativeness and chivalry could not be separated. Local champions such as *pahlavans* not only had tremendous physical strength but also were exceptionally kind, generous, and noble. Islamic guilds and brotherhoods traditionally supported and promoted ideals of physical and moral courage. Military

---

[53]Weber, *The Theory of Social and Economic Organization,* p. 347. Emphasis ours.

[54]See, for example, Nasr, *Ideals and Realities,* p. 73; and Schuon, *Understanding Islam,* p. 88.

[55]The reverse is also true, since failure in combat is as much a moral as a physical blow to Islamic leaders and societies. The impact of the Arab-Israeli conflict, for example, must be interpreted in this light.

valor and success, therefore, have invested Islamic leaders with additional strength and appeal in the eyes of their followers.

Military force was a major factor in the rise to power of Middle Eastern political leaders. A strong and effective military has also been an important tool in enabling a ruler to continue to rule. A leader who has had several successful foreign military campaigns to his credit has been more effective in preserving his domestic rule. The deep patterns of division and discord described above persistently threaten to shatter the system and to destroy the ruler in the process. One scholar stresses the fact that "a patrimonial system is characterized by constant tension between centripetal and centrifugal forces."[56] The patrimonial leader's key instrument in encouraging and buttressing the centripetal forces is his military organization. While promoting tension and discord in particular areas throughout the system, the leader must at the same time guard against having balances become imbalances and rivals unite in a common front against him. It is only his military that can enable him to salvage his position and his life in such circumstances.

Despite its importance, the military organization is subject to the same patterns and pressures that characterize other institutions in patrimonial settings. The leader or ruler attempts to control the military as an emanation of his own will and personality and usually assumes the title Commander-in-Chief or Commander of the Faithful. The military forces are his "personal instrument."[57] The centrality of the leader in military matters can be seen diagrammatically in the Middle Eastern "battle order" described by Ibn Khaldun.[58] Surrounded by his closest confidants, the ruler stands at the center of his forces. The latter consist of four armies, situated at the front and rear and on the right and left flanks of the leader.

Throughout the history of the Middle East, the characteristics of personalism, proximity, informality, and balanced rivalry also pervaded the military organization. Only the most trusted relatives and confidants were appointed military leaders. Those closest to the ruler, such as bodyguards and armed retainers, were recruited among slaves, orphans, and prisoners, and as a result maintained no entangling alliances or loyalties outside of their relation to the leader. It was essential that they be completely subsumed in the shadow of the ruler, to whom they owed everything. To ensure this kind of absolute loyalty and submission, the mechanism of balanced rivalry is seen in perhaps its most critical manifestation in the arena of the armed forces. Different military leaders and different military bodies have existed in constant tension with one another and have served as watchdogs of one another. Sometimes these intramilitary divisions reflected tribal cleavages; sometimes entirely new tribes were created both to strengthen loyalty and to serve as armed checks against other military units.

---

[56]Robert H. Jackson, "Social Structure and Political Change in Ethiopia and Liberia," *Comparative Political Studies* 3 (April 1960): 38.

[57]Bendix, *Max Weber,* p. 344.

[58]Ibn Khaldun, *The Muqaddimah,* trans. by Franz Rosenthal (Princeton, N.J.: Princeton University Press, 1967), p. 225.

The modern Middle East has its authentic military heroes. For the Turks, Ataturk was the great hero of the First World War. Abdul Aziz Ibn Saud was the illustrious warrior king in Saudi Arabia. The late King Hussein of Jordan demonstrated physical courage on numerous occasions. Both Gamal Abdel Nasser and General Naguib, the titular leader of the 1952 Egyptian coup, had distinguished records in the fighting in Palestine.

There is a close connection between military upheaval and the turnover of political leaders. The proliferation of military coups that have characterized Middle Eastern politics represents the failure of leaders and rulers to establish viable patrimonial patterns with respect to the military. The challenge to leadership has come not so much from the society at large as from within the military itself. When leadership rests so heavily upon the military reed, then it must be prepared to collapse whenever that reed breaks.

Religious Rationalization   Islam provided the patrimonial leader with an ideology that buttressed the political patterns by which he ruled. Chains of emanation are more firmly fashioned when they lead to the Almighty, and Islamic leaders have traditionally endeavored to demonstrate their own linkages with God and the Prophet Muhammad. Although actual effective theocratic leadership died with the Prophet in 632, Islamic leaders ever since have sought to be theocratic leaders. As time passed, this tendency became more and more pronounced, while theocratic leadership became less and less credible. The political meaning of the word *caliph* was gradually transformed from "deputy of the emissary of God" to "God's representative on earth."[59] The Islamic political leaders, who had at one time been considered the Prophet's deputies, later became known as God's deputies. Even the concept of *sultan,* which developed a connotation of secular as opposed to religious authority, soon made the linkage with the Divine. This occurred when the actual sultan began referring to himself as the Shadow of God.[60] The concept of *Imam* has been the best example of leadership related directly to the Divine, for unlike the caliph and the sultan, the Imam has always been considered the infallible vicegerent of God. Despite the various titles and personalities involved, however, the Middle Eastern style of patrimonial leadership has usually meant the conscious establishment of some form of linkage between the leader and the Divine.

This pattern has provided political leaders with a rationalization and justification for their positions. It has been argued that "stiff religious cement" has been the strength of the patrimonial system of rule.[61] In one of the classic studies of politics, Gaetano Mosca analyzes the traditional strength of the Turkish nation in the following terms: "The Turkish peasants in Rumelia and Anatolia believed sincerely and deeply in Islam, in the Prophet, in the sultan as the

---

[59]V. V. Barthold, "Caliph and Sultan," *The Islamic Quarterly* 7 (July and December, 1963): 124–125.

[60]Ibid., p. 130.

[61]Gaetano Mosca, *The Ruling Class,* trans. by Hannah D. Kahn (New York: McGraw-Hill Book Co., 1939), p. 345.

Prophet's vicar, and the beliefs for which they were asked to make the utmost sacrifices were the beliefs that ordinarily filled their lives and made up their moral and intellectual worlds."[62] In a smoothly functioning system of leadership by emanation, to challenge the leader often meant nothing less than to challenge the rule of God. It is for this reason that political rebellion took the form of religious schisms and that the challenging political figures stressed their own special relation to the Almighty.

THE POLITICS OF PATRIMONIAL RECRUITMENT: GENERAL OBSERVATIONS

Contrary to what is often thought, the ranks of Middle Eastern political leadership are relatively permeable. Within certain patrimonial limits, vertical mobility is possible, and outsiders are often able to penetrate elite circles. In such systems, the personalistic networks of leadership can be penetrated, especially on the basis of family, kinship, and friendship relations. As Almond and Powell point out, "Perhaps the oldest and most traditional means of access to political elites is personal connection. By personal connection channels we mean the use of family, school, local, and social ties as instruments for contacting political elites."[63] In the Middle East, the determination of who is to move in or out of the elite is often still determined by these factors.

Built into and stretching throughout these webs of personal connections are three broader channels of mobility. These are the military, bureaucratic, and religious channels. It is through these channels that most individuals have made their entrance into the political elite. Although the personalistic-patrimonial factors discussed here decidedly influence who moves through these channels, the very existence of the channels has helped to institutionalize mobility.

The Middle Eastern patrimonial system of leadership remains in evidence today. There are, however, a number of strong recruitment considerations that increasingly influence leadership composition. The most important of them are professional skill, talent, and merit. Political elites have been driven, because of the forces of modernization, to recruit individuals who have technical and professional competence. Ministries of health are increasingly headed by medical doctors and health administrators; national petroleum companies are directed by better and better qualified petroleum engineers, geologists, and economists; national educational systems are guided by Middle Eastern specialists in the field of education. Even in the most traditional of patrimonial systems, such as Saudi Arabia, Kuwait, and Oman, the educated technocrats have moved into decision-making positions.

Despite the changes in some of the qualifications necessary for entry into the elites, there are indications that the traits of patrimonialism prevail.

First, recruitment processes are personally and firmly controlled from the center of the system. This is as true in more radical systems such as those in Syria

---

[62]Ibid., p. 108.

[63]Gabriel A. Almond and G. Bingham Powell, Jr., *Comparative Politics: System, Process, and Policy,* second ed. (Boston: Little, Brown and Co., 1978), p. 178.

and Iraq as it is in such traditional countries as Jordan and Morocco. In all of these systems the considerations of political loyalty, personal connections, and complete central control remain at least as important in determining entry into the elite as those of professional expertise, personal merit, and institutional position.

The second sign of patrimonial persistence in the Middle East concerns the directional flow of the recruitment patterns. In an analysis of the politics of elite recruitment, Almond and Powell stress that the political party is the most common contemporary channel of recruitment.[64] This has not been the case in Middle Eastern patrimonial politics. Although political parties exist in most of the societies, political leaders are not generally recruited from the parties. Instead, the parties (as well as the legislatures) are headed by individuals who are already national political leaders. The patrimonial head selects the party leadership from among proven confidants, advisors, or ministers. In several Middle Eastern systems, party positions (whether leadership or rank-and-file) more often reflect a move out of than a move into the national political elite. Parties and legislatures many times serve as the political dumping grounds for former members of the elite who have fallen from favor in the patrimonial establishment.

The continued strength of patrimonialism in the Middle East has meant that the personalistic networks that are directed from the center have a profound effect on both the shape of the political system and that system's capacity to confront the problems of modernization and political development. The patrimonial leaders and the political elites that surround them play a disproportionate role in determining the future of their societies. Although their policies at one level may be very similar from society to society, at another level there are striking differences. In some societies, the traditional webs of patrimonialism operate today very much as they have for centuries; in other societies, these webs have begun to be torn and are unraveling in differing ways. In Chapter 5 we will examine a number of case studies of Middle Eastern patrimonial leaders with special focus on the differing ways that they have coped with the challenge of change.

SELECTED BIBLIOGRAPHY

Andrae, Tor. *Mohammed: The Man and His Faith.* New York: Barnes and Noble, 1935.

Dekmejian, R. Hrair. *Patterns of Political Leadership: Lebanon, Israel, Egypt.* Albany: State University of New York Press, 1975.

Frey, Frederick W. *The Turkish Political Elite.* Cambridge: Massachusetts Institute of Technology Press, 1965.

Gellner, Ernest. *Saints of the Atlas.* Chicago: University of Chicago Press, 1969.

Guillaume, A. *The Life of Muhammad: A Translation of Ishaq's Sirat Rasul Allah.* London: Oxford University Press, 1955.

Hinnebusch, Raymond A. *Egyptian Politics Under Sadat: The Post-Populist Development of an Authoritarian-Modernizing State.* New York: Cambridge University Press, 1985.

Khuri, Fuad I., ed. *Leadership and Development in Arab Society.* Beirut: American University of Beirut, 1981.

---

[64]Ibid., pp. 123–126.

Lenczowski, George, ed. *Political Elites in the Middle East.* Washington, D.C.: American Enterprise Institute, 1975.

Margoliouth, D. S. *Mohammed and the Rise of Islam,* third ed. New York: G. P. Putnam's Sons, 1905.

Rustow, Dankwart A. *Philosophers and Kings: Studies in Leadership.* New York: George Braziller, 1970.

Tachau, Frank, ed. *Political Elites and Political Development in the Middle East.* Cambridge, Mass.: Schenkman, 1975.

Vatikiotis, P. J. *The Fatimid Theory of State.* Lahore, Pakistan: Orientalia Publishers, 1957.

Watt, W. Montgomery. *Muhammad at Medina.* Oxford, England: The Clarendon Press, 1956.

Watt, W. Montgomery. *Islam and the Integration of Society.* London: Routledge and Kegan Paul, 1961.

Weber, Max. *The Theory of Social and Economic Organization.* New York: Oxford University Press, 1957.

Zartman, I. William, ed. *Political Elites in Arab North Africa.* New York: Longman, 1982.

Zonis, Marvin. *The Political Elite of Iran.* Princeton, N.J.: Princeton University Press, 1971.

Zonis, Marvin. *Majestic Failure: The Fall of the Shah.* Chicago: University of Chicago Press, 1991.

Chapter 5

The Politics of Leaders and Change

Political leaders play a critical role in determining developmental policy in the Middle East. As we have seen in Chapter 4, the political processes of patrimonial systems are shaped around the patrimonial leader, who plays a disproportionate role in the decision-making process. The centrality of the national political leader assures him a key position in confronting the important related issues of modernization and political development. The leader's tactics and strategies in this regard have far-reaching consequences for the political system and for the peoples of the society concerned.

Throughout Middle Eastern history, leaders have held a wide variety of attitudes toward change. In many cases, the political leadership has chosen to resist the forces of change. In other cases, Middle Eastern leaders have taken a more flexible stance and have attempted to meet the challenge through programs of reform and revision. Their strategy has been to forestall major transformations by encouraging incremental adjustments. In still other instances, leaders have pursued revolutionary goals that involve radical social and political change. In all these cases, however, the leader has maintained a special position: He has controlled the instruments of persuasion and coercion that are essential to the formation and implementation of any of these policies.

In this chapter, our analysis will emphasize Middle Eastern political leaders who have in this century chosen to promote various programs of change. Modernization has been a goal shared by all of these leaders. Political development, however, has not always been favored. We will analyze three twentieth-century leaders from three major Middle Eastern countries. These are Mustafa Kemal Ataturk of Turkey, Muhammad Reza Shah Pahlavi of Iran, and Gamal Abdel Nasser of Egypt. Furthermore, we will discuss comparatively the individuals who succeeded the three principal leaders. These successors include Inonu of Turkey, Khomeini, Rafsanjani, and Khatami of Iran, and Sadat and Mubarak of Egypt.

Before discussing these leaders, we shall devote a few paragraphs to the more traditional Middle Eastern leader. It is against this backdrop of traditional leadership that the more contemporary and often more progressive leaders have operated. In all of these case studies, traditional patrimonial tactics have still been very much in evidence.

Twentieth-Century Traditional Leaders

Twentieth-century Middle Eastern political history has been largely dominated by a number of colorful traditional leaders who did much to shape the destinies of their nations. In most cases, they resisted change and as a result became its victims. Some were hopelessly corrupt and venal in their personal and political lives; others were models of integrity. All failed in one way or another to understand a changing world. Among the least impressive of these leaders are King Farouk of Egypt, Regent Abd al-Ilah of Iraq, Sultan Mehmet V and Sultan Mehmet VI of Turkey, Shaikh Shakhbut of Abu Dhabi, and Sultan Said bin Taymur of Oman. Traditional leaders of considerably more talent and integrity include King Idris of Libya, Zahir Shah of Afghanistan, King Abdullah of Jordan, King Muhammad V of Morocco, and King Abdul Aziz Ibn Saud of Saudi Arabia.

Sultan Said bin Taymur ruled Oman for thirty-eight years (1932–1970). Although he was educated at a British school in India, the Sultan spent nearly four decades walling in his country against the forces of change. Even after oil was discovered in Oman, he stubbornly refused to expend his resources on development programs. During his rule, no tractors were allowed in the sultanate; the occasional importation of an automobile had to be personally approved by the Sultan himself; houses could be rebuilt only from the actual material with which they were originally constructed; women were forbidden to accompany their husbands abroad; and Omanis educated overseas were not allowed to return to work in their own country.

Sultan Said was opposed to education, financial expenditure, and modernization in his country. He felt that the British lost India because they had educated the people, and, just before he was deposed in 1970, he closed the only three primary schools in Oman. He considered the schools to be hotbeds of communism. The Sultan ruled supreme and kept his people in fear and subjection. The channels of access that were such an essential part of Islamic patrimonial politics were destroyed by this traditional leader. After 1958, he kept himself in isolation in the coastal city of Salala. His officials, working in an atmosphere "made even more oppressive by his absence, one might describe it as disembodiment, in Salala,"[1] made no decisions. Sultan Said even locked up his son Qabus

---

[1]Ian Skeet, *Muscat and Oman: The End of an Era* (London: Faber and Faber, 1974), p. 168. Most of the material in this section has been drawn from Skeet's informed and entertaining book or from Fred Halliday, *Arabia Without Sultans* (New York: Vintage Books, 1974), pp. 277–315.

(the present ruler of Oman) when Qabus returned to Oman in 1966 after receiving a British education at Sandhurst.

British disappointment with the old Sultan led to his overthrow in July 1970. His demise was inevitable; his long period of reactionary rule had resulted in a guerrilla war that broke out in the province of Dhufar. By 1970, the opposition forces had taken most of Dhufar. The Sultan had been consistent in his determined opposition to any kind of change or innovation. Because of British support and his geographic position in what were then the backwaters of the Middle East, he made this policy stick for a surprisingly long time. In the end, however, he failed. As Ian Skeet presciently wrote before the Sultan's fall, his kind of policy "is just plugging the holes in the barbed wire round the country's borders; one day the barbed wire will be rolled aside, and none of the Sultan's restrictions will help him one iota."[2]

If Sultan Said is one of the least successful traditional leaders in the Middle East of this century, King Abdul Aziz Ibn Saud is one of the most successful. Ibn Saud's style of leadership very closely approximated that of the classical model analyzed in Chapter 4. Born in 1880 in Central Arabia, Ibn Saud grew up in an environment of vigorous conflict among clans. In 1901, he was a banished youth whose clan was ruled by its enemies and whose immediate family was in exile in Kuwait. By 1934, he had conquered the territories of Najd, Hasa, Hijaz, and Asir and had welded them together into one political unit known as the Kingdom of Saudi Arabia. In so doing, he had healed the rifts within his own family, defeated or co-opted the other clans, taken Hasa from the Turks, and conquered Mecca and Hijaz at the expense of the Hashemite King Hussein (the great-grandfather of the late King Hussein of Jordan).

Abdul Aziz Ibn Saud ruled personally, informally, and patriarchally. He ran his kingdom as a gigantic personal household, which it in fact very nearly was. Ibn Saud had an estimated three hundred wives in his lifetime, as well as large numbers of concubines and slave girls. In 1955, it was estimated that there was one prince for every 5,000 persons in Saudi Arabia.[3] Like the Prophet Muhammad, after whom he patterned his life, Ibn Saud used marriage as an important political tool. Through the years, he married into all the leading tribal families in Najd. His links with the Sudairi family, from which four of his wives came, were especially strong; these wives bore fifteen of his sons. Today, King Fahd is the most influential of seven full brothers who are the sons of Ibn Saud and Hussa bint Ahmad al-Sudairi.

In this setting, Ibn Saud balanced rivalries and directed the personal and political fortunes of all of the other main actors in the system. He made it his business to stay informed. "He had a deep knowledge of his people, their friendships and intermarriages, their blood feuds and causes of quarrel, so that he could play the one against the other."[4] He never allowed power to concentrate at any point in the system other than at his own feet. He once stated, "Two things I will

---

[2]Skeet, *Muscat and Oman*, p. 196.

[3]H. St. John Philby, *Sa'udi Arabia* (London: Ernest Benn, 1955), p. 298.

[4]H. C. Armstrong, *Lord of Arabia* (Beirut: Khayyat's, 1944), p. 111.

not stomach: firstly a rebel (*marij*); and secondly the feigned loyalty of two persons inwardly leagued against me."[5] Ibn Saud was also famous for his accessibility and approachability. Quite unlike Sultan Said, he spent several hours each day listening to the complaints and petitions of his people.

Finally, Ibn Saud was a great warrior. The first thirty years of his leadership were a time of constant warfare. It was during this period that he became a legend as he personally developed military strategy and led his soldiers into battle. At the end of these three decades of military struggle and political consolidation, Ibn Saud carried the marks of a dozen wounds, all attesting to the central role he played in the business of physical combat.

Although he founded a country and forged a following of disparate peoples into a nation, he stumbled when confronted with the challenges of modernization and political development. Between the time when oil was discovered at Jebel Dhahran in 1938 and when he died in 1953, Ibn Saud clung desperately to tradition. As a result, he was unable to cope effectively with the new forces and demands that burst upon him and his society. He did not think to concern himself with widening the base of political participation; he watched social and economic gaps widen among his people; he failed to stem the tide of peculation, corruption, and waste that washed through his kingdom; he did little to build health and educational facilities. These tasks were only taken up later by his successors.

Still, Abdul Aziz Ibn Saud was the greatest Middle Eastern traditional leader of this century. He combined wit and physical courage with personal charisma and deep religious beliefs to consolidate a people and build a nation.[6]

The political leaders discussed in the following sections attempted to move out ahead in their societies and to confront the forces of modernization. The one who did this earliest and most dramatically was a Turk born only a year before the great Ibn Saud. He came to be known as Ataturk.

Ataturk: The Revolutionary Father of Turkey

The modern Turkish state owes its political form and indeed its very existence to one remarkable military and political leader—Ataturk. First called Mustafa, he was given the additional name of Kemal ("perfection") by an instructor in secondary school. After his victory over the Greeks at Sakarya in 1921, the Grand National Assembly at Ankara gave him the title of Ghazi ("victor"). In 1934, the Assembly bestowed on him the surname Ataturk, or Father of the Turks. In this book, we will refer to him both as Kemal and as Ataturk.

Kemal was born in Salonika in Macedonia in 1881. His family was of the very lowest echelons of the middle class. His father, a onetime low-ranking civil servant, was a failure in both the timber business and the salt trade and died when Kemal was only eleven. An extremely independent personality, Kemal was thrown out of one school before he settled into a military education that in-

---

[5]H. St. John Philby, *Arabian Jubilee* (London: Robert Hale, 1954), p. 106.

[6]For more detailed analysis of the patrimonial politics of Abdul Aziz Ibn Saud, see J. A. Bill and C. Leiden, *The Middle East: Politics and Power* (Boston: Allyn and Bacon, 1974), pp. 125–133.

cluded military prep school in Salonika military academy at Monastir and the War College and the Staff College at Constantinople. In 1905, he graduated from the Staff College as a captain in the sultan's army. On his final examination and in his personnel file, the following assessment was reportedly written: "A brilliant student officer, difficult in temperament, precise and technically a perfectionist, politically unstable."[7] Shortly after graduation, Kemal was arrested and imprisoned for plotting against the ruling authorities.

Kemal was born into a world of transition in which ancient social and political institutions were crumbling. The once powerful Ottoman Empire was on its last legs. On all its borders, the empire was besieged by various ethnic minority groups who sought political autonomy. Meanwhile, liberal ideas from the West were breeding dissatisfaction among the empire's educated middle-class population. It is thus not accidental that the Young Turk movement was born and nurtured in the westernmost sector of the empire. Macedonians were conspicuous among the revolutionaries.

The sultanate in Constantinople was corrupt and venal, and its policies were increasingly unpopular. When pushed, Sultan Abdul Hamid had declared some reforms, only to repeal them when pressures were relaxed. In 1876, he agreed to a constitution providing for the establishment of a consultative assembly; in 1877, he dissolved the assembly; in 1896, a major coup attempt failed. Meanwhile, political opposition had spread everywhere and had become deeply rooted even within the sultan's own armed forces. Kemal was one of the most disenchanted of the young officers who saw their decrepit system crumbling around them. A fierce nationalist, he determined from the beginning that the Turkish nation had to be reformed, strengthened, and regenerated.

After a few months in jail, Kemal was posted to the Fifth Army in Damascus, where he immediately began to establish political opposition societies among his military colleagues on the Syrian front. His Vatan ("Fatherland") Society was soon swallowed up by the Young Turks' Committee of Union and Progress, which on July 23, 1908, forced the sultan to restore the constitution and to recall his consultative assembly. Between 1908 and the outbreak of World War I in 1914, Kemal floated on the fringes of the Young Turks in a relationship marked by mutual distrust. Although his military skills were used by Enver Pasha and the other leaders during this time, he was carefully locked out of the corridors of power. "He was a realist, who thought in terms not of gestures but of action, thoughtfully conceived, scientifically planned and systematically executed. Too many of those whom he saw around him, and who were pretending to govern the country, were men of words, of undigested feelings and vague ideas."[8]

---

[7]Ray Brock, *Ghost on Horseback: The Incredible Atatürk* (Boston: Little, Brown and Co., 1954), p. 21. Although this book tends toward the sensational and owes too much to the fertile imagination of the author, it makes interesting reading and succeeds in capturing the colorfully human nature of Kemal.

[8]Lord Kinross, *Atatürk: The Rebirth of a Nation* (London: Weidenfeld and Nicolson, 1964), p. 44. This remains the best biography of Ataturk. For a fine article-length study, see Dankwart A. Rustow's own analysis in his edited volume *Philosophers and Kings: Studies in Leadership* (New York: George Braziller, 1970), pp. 208–247.

Although Kemal personally opposed the Turkish alliance with Germany in World War I, he earned his place in military history for his brilliant defense in 1915 at Gallipoli, where the Turks repelled a major Allied offensive spearheaded by the finest soldiers of the British Empire. Poorly armed and outnumbered, the Turkish troops under Kemal successfully held off the seasoned Australian, New Zealand, and British troops who desperately fought to break through to the Dardanelles and to clear the way to Constantinople. During this nine-month siege and bitter fighting, Kemal proved himself to be not only a brilliant military tactician but also an inspiration to his soldiers. He moved constantly among his men in the front trenches and miraculously survived a direct hit in his chest when shrapnel shattered the watch in his breast pocket. As he told his outgunned Fifty-Seventh Regiment, "I don't order you to attack, I order you to die; others troops and commanders can come and take our places."[9] The men of the Fifty-Seventh did die for their leader and for their country. Kemal somehow survived; he had taken the first major step toward becoming the Father of the Turks.

The Allies' victory in 1918 ended the Young Turks' ascendancy and forced their leaders into exile. The British appearance in Constantinople and a subsequent Greek movement into Smyrna were shocking and unacceptable events for Turkish patriots. Kemal left for Anatolia, where he began an opposition independence movement. In 1919, he organized congresses at Erzerum and Sivas, where delegates drafted and ratified a national pact legitimizing their movement. Turkey was in upheaval. During the next four years, Kemal put the pieces of the country back together. The task was a formidable one because he had to organize a political and military force that would not only hang together but also be strong enough to defeat the tribes and brigands in Anatolia; repulse and drive a major invading Greek force from the heart of Turkey; maneuver the British and Russians out of the area; and replace the Sultan's government—still claiming legitimacy in Constantinople—with a new nationalist government resident in Ankara.

In three and a half years of brutal but brilliant military campaigns and pressure-packed political infighting, Kemal accomplished all these goals. In November 1922, he proclaimed the abolition of the sultanate; in October 1923, Turkey was declared a republic, and Kemal became its first president; and in March 1924, the caliphate was abolished. Kemal was president of Turkey until his death in 1938.

During his fifteen years as president, Ataturk did not choose to rest on his military laurels. Instead, he began a program of social, cultural, and political modernization that shook the country to its roots. His program struck at the foundation of the conservative religious culture of the day and stressed national, secular, and modern goals. In a characteristic style, he directly and publicly attacked the very symbols of the old system by outlawing the fez, condemning the veil, and reforming the alphabet.

These shattering changes in important symbols were accompanied by major reforms in the fields of administration, education, and law. One of Ataturk's

---

[9]Kinross, *Atatürk*, p. 76.

Table 5.1
Life of Ataturk: Major Events

1881	Born in Salonika
1893	Enters military secondary school in Salonika; given added name Kemal
1899	Enters War College in Constantinople
1905	Graduates from Staff College with rank of captain
1908	Young Turk revolution
1914	Beginning of World War I; Turkey signs secret alliance with Germany. Russia, Britain, and France declare war on Turkey.
1915	Kemal distinguishes himself at Gallipoli.
1919	Leaves for Anatolia; issues declaration of independence; calls nationalist congresses at Sivas and Erzerum
1921	Defeats the invading Greeks at Battle of Sakarya
1922	Proclaims abolition of the sultanate
1923	Founds the Republican People's Party; becomes president of the Turkish Republic
1924	Abolishes the caliphate
1926	Trials and suppression of opposition at Izmir and Ankara
1934	Takes name of Ataturk; women given the right to vote in parliamentary elections and to become members of parliament
1938	Dies in Istanbul

---

most important contributions was the successful establishment of an independent and effective judiciary. The programs of reform were backed by an international policy that was astutely conceived and implemented. This foreign policy was based on a premise stressing the consolidation of national power, not the expansion of national boundaries. It also emphasized the necessity of avoiding international entanglements such as the one that contributed to the disaster of World War I. It was Ataturk who established the policy that enabled Ismet Inonu to keep Turkey out of World War II. Despite tremendous pressures, Turkey did not take a formal position until February 1945, when it declared war on the Axis powers.[10]

Ataturk was not a liberal democrat. He was an authoritarian ruler who exercised power bluntly and forcefully. In his own words, "I don't act for public opinion. I act for the nation and for my own satisfaction."[11] He had climbed the ladder of power by himself and had survived everything from several serious

---

[10]For Ataturk and his successors as makers of foreign policy, see Metin Tamkoç's excellent book, *The Warrior Diplomats* (Salt Lake City: University of Utah Press, 1976).

[11]Kinross, *Atatürk*, p. xvii.

illnesses[12] and difficult military campaigns to political plots and assassination attempts. When he finally reached a position of national political power, he did not hesitate to take severe measures against those whom he considered threats to himself or to his programs. The major example of this occurred when, in 1926, Kemal used an abortive plot against his life as a rationale for imprisoning, exiling, or executing those he considered members of a serious political opposition. Among them were several of his oldest friends who had stood behind him in the difficult years in Anatolia. Many of these individuals were liberal thinkers who had begun to resist his personal, arbitrary rule. As Kazim Karabekir, a trusted military leader whose assistance was crucial to Kemal's success in Anatolia, put it, "I am in favour of the Republic, but I am against personal rule."[13]

Yet there is another side to the story. Kemal was always scrupulously careful to seek legitimation for his actions and to base them upon legal principles emanating from the people. Even as a rebel, he insisted on congresses and constitutional pacts that would provide political legitimacy for his movement. He also campaigned hard among the people and created a major political party, the Republican People's Party. He twice experimented with a two-party system but gave it up when it proved unworkable. Ataturk once admitted that he was a dictator, yet went on to point out, "But I have not had pyramids built in my honour like the Pharaohs of Egypt. I did not make people work for my sake, threatening them with whips when I wanted an idea to be accepted by the country. I first called a congress, I debated the situation with the people, I carried out my plans only after taking authority from the people."[14] His may not have always been a government by the people, but it was in many ways a government for the people.[15]

PATTERNS OF RULE

Ataturk was one of the most colorful political leaders of this century. He was a man of imposing appearance, with peculiarly striking eyes. "Wide-set beneath the broad brow and the eyebrows that curled upwards like whiskers, they gleamed with a cold steady challenging light, for ever fixing, observing, reflecting, appraising, moreover uncannily capable of swivelling two ways at once so that they seemed to see both upwards and downwards, before and behind."[16]

---

[12]Physical ailments plagued Kemal throughout his life, yet he conquered these problems just as he overcame the social and political problems that confronted him. Besides sustaining a minor battle wound and some broken ribs, he survived two major attacks of malaria, three severe cases of influenza, a debilitating ear infection, and kidney problems that tormented him for twenty-five years. As a young man, he contracted gonorrhea, the effects of which were lasting. He died of cirrhosis of the liver and complications thereof.

[13]Kinross, *Atatürk*, p. 382.

[14]Ibid., p. 438.

[15]This terminology is Kemal Karpat's, as presented in his study, *Turkey's Politics: The Transition to Multi-Party Politics* (Princeton, N.J.: Princeton University Press, 1959), pp. 50–51. It is quoted in the writings of Metin Heper.

[16]Kinross, *Atatürk*, p. 163.

Kemal's personal life was uninhibited. He drank and gambled incessantly; he enjoyed the company and entertainment provided by women and spent a good part of his life in cafes, hotels, and brothels. During the early years of his political opposition both to the sultan and to the young Turks, Kemal's personal activities led the establishment forces to underestimate the danger that he posed to them. At the same time, Kemal used these informal gatherings to discuss social and political issues and to gather information that passed through these grapevines. Just as Ismet Inonu was able to convert his physical liability of near-deafness into a political asset, Kemal's personal habits were not complete liabilities to him. A French writer wrote at the time that Turkey was governed by one drunkard, one deaf man, and three hundred deaf-mutes (the assembly deputies). When he heard this, Kemal responded, "The man is mistaken. Turkey is governed by one drunkard."[17]

Ataturk's political style in many ways sharply broke with traditional Middle Eastern patterns. Although he would on occasion use the *hocas* (clerics) to legitimize a particular political move, he refused to use Islam as any kind of overarching ideology. Quite to the contrary, he had a strong personal aversion to religion and sought to smash its influence. Much is written about his charismatic personality, and he indeed had many of the extraordinary attributes of a charismatic leader. This can be seen even today in Turkey, where the anniversaries of his death are national mourning days, and where thousands upon thousands of Turkish citizens continue to file past his mausoleum in Ankara. However, Ataturk was little impressed by his own charisma. He was often annoyed, for example, when other dignitaries would fawn over him. He once became so irritated when the mayor of a city he was visiting insisted on waiting on him in person at the dinner table that he snapped, "For God's sake, sit down! Are you a waiter or the mayor of this city?"[18] Ataturk institutionalized and routinized his charisma by building organizations, such as the Republican People's Party, that would transcend the existence of one man. In the words of one leading authority on Turkish politics, Ataturk was "an organization man thrown into a charismatic situation."[19]

Although Kemal learned to play his subordinates one against the other and on occasion to maneuver clandestinely, he was essentially very direct. In the context of Turkish politics of the day, this directness often seemed crude, brutal, and even stupid. As his major biographer writes, "He detested the shifts and evasions of the oblique approach to Oriental politics, the circumlocutions and imprecisions of its thought and speech. He liked to speak his mind directly, to call spades spades. His outspokenness indeed not only infuriated his enemies but, on occasion, embarrassed his friends."[20] Nor did Kemal play favorites with friends and relatives. One of the major reasons he divorced his wife Latife was that she continually interfered in matters of national politics. Finally, Ataturk was not interested in amassing a fortune for himself and his

[17]Ibid., p. 261.

[18]Ibid., p. 368.

[19]Rustow, *Philosophers and Kings,* p. 212.

[20]Kinross, *Atatürk,* p. 45.

family. Although he lived comfortably, he was by no means financially corrupt. His lifestyle was in fact quite modest.

Ataturk was above all a realist. He understood power and people and had an unusual ability to bridge the gap between ideal and reality. He used idealists and dreamers, but he never trusted them. He considered them much more dangerous than the small-time politicians who lacked vision. Ataturk himself was both a visionary and a hard, experienced political realist.

CHAMPION OF CHANGE OR CAMOUFLAGED CONSERVATIVE?

A number of excellent analyses of the Ataturk period make compelling arguments that Kemal's programs and policies were in essence conservative and non-revolutionary. Although this school admits that dramatic changes were initiated in the cultural and religious systems of Turkey, the question at issue is that of social structure. Ataturk's programs were initiated without basically altering the traditional class structure. Special care was taken to avoid upsetting the local landlords and aristocracy who controlled power throughout the country. Those at the bottom of the power structure witnessed very little change in their standard of living. If anything, the peasants' standard of living became worse during Kemalist rule. Land reform, for example, was almost completely ignored during Kemal's lifetime. In the words of Arnold Leder:

> From its earliest days in the Turkish War of Independence when it sought the cooperation of the local notables in the countryside, the Kemalist movement became a collaborative movement. The nationalist struggle led by the Kemalists was fought against foreign enemies and not against a particular social class. The Kemalists did not undertake radical change in Turkey's social structure. In fact, they established a tacit alliance with the traditional elites in the countryside. This alliance was reflected in Kemalist political organization where local notables dominated the lower levels of the Republican People's party.[21]

Another study by a leading Turkish political scientist concludes that "the Atatürk Revolution exploited the basic bifurcation between the educated elite and the uneducated masses, rather than deploring it or immediately attacking it."[22]

This failure to transform the national class structure has been one factor in the political problems that have plagued Turkey since Ataturk's death. Indeed, the creation of the Democrat Party in 1946 and its stunning victory over the Republican People's Party in the general election of 1950 may have been major symptoms of the depth of the social and political problems inherited from the days of Ataturk. Since Ataturk's time, there has been a broadening diffusion of

---

[21]Leder, "Collaboration Politics and the Turkish Revolution." Paper delivered at the 1976 Annual Meeting of the Middle East Studies Association, Los Angeles, 11–13 November 1976, p. 29.

[22]Ergun Özbudun, *Social Change and Political Participation in Turkey* (Princeton, N.J.: Princeton University Press, 1976), p. 43.

power into the Turkish countryside, although the real inclusion of the provincial lower classes within the national decision-making structure remains to be seen.[23]

Questions concerning the depth of Ataturk's reforms are legitimate ones. His revolution did not transform the social, political, or economic conditions of the masses of Turkish peasants. Still, this failure should not be allowed to obscure the immensity of the social and political changes that Ataturk did implement successfully. At bottom, his revolution was a middle-class movement that destroyed a number of traditional symbols and built a new political system. In this sense, it was more radical than the American Revolution and in some respects paralleled the French Revolution, also a middle-class affair. In the context of the time, it stands as a revolution of modernization and a movement of substantial political development.

Politically, a 600-year-old national ruling institution and its attendant ruling class were destroyed and replaced by a middle-class elite that introduced new political ideas and institutions, including a political party of genuine consequence. These were structural transformations of lasting impact, which set the stage for subsequent political development, such as the birth of a political opposition (the Democrat Party) that was permitted to win in elections. In this rare political event, in which an authoritarian regime voluntarily relinquished power, it was Ataturk's old lieutenant, the dedicated Kemalist Ismet Inonu, who made the decision to permit the opposition to win.[24]

In the section above, we have seen how Ataturk broke many of the traditional interpersonal patterns that had dominated Ottoman patrimonial rule. These and the broader political changes discussed above were successfully implemented despite the serious opposition of at least four groups. Of these groups, two were obvious forces of the ancien régime—the sultanate's political establishment and the omnipresent religious hierarchy. The two others, however, were groups of former liberal allies who were, ironically, more conservative than Kemal. These were the Young Turks on the one hand and the group of his earliest supporters and comrades on the other hand. In the case of the former, ". . . theirs was essentially a conservative revolution. . . . Imperialists in essence, blind to the new nationalist forces now at work in the modern world, the Young

---

[23]See Frank Tachau, "Turkish Provincial Party Politics," in *Social Change and Politics in Turkey*, Kemal H. Karpat et al. (Leiden, The Netherlands: E. J. Brill, 1973), pp. 282–314; and Karpat's own article "Political Development in Turkey, 1950–1970," *Middle Eastern Studies* 8 (October 1972): 349–375.

[24]Inonu's decision was based on a number of personal, political, and ideological factors. First, he hoped at the time to demonstrate to the West the democratic nature of his regime. See Dankwart A. Rustow, "The Development of Parties in Turkey," in *Political Parties and Political Development*, ed. by J. La Palombara and M. Weiner (Princeton, N.J.: Princeton University Press, 1966), p. 122. Second, Inonu felt that the establishment of an opposition political party would help lower the level of discontent in the country. See Leslie L. Roos, Jr., and Noraloo P. Roos, *Managers of Modernization* (Cambridge, Mass.: Harvard University Press, 1971), p. 40. Third, Inonu and his advisors believed that the Republican People's Party was strong enough in the Turkish countryside to guarantee victory in any election. See Kemal Karpat, "Society, Economics, and Politics in Contemporary Turkey," *World Politics* 17 (October 1964): 58. These positions are all drawn together and analyzed in the writings of Arnold Leder.

Turks aspired merely to conserve, if in a more liberal form, the Ottoman Empire of their forebears."[25] At the same time, old comrades such as Hussain Rauf, Ali Fuad, and Kazim Karabekir were more liberal idealists and preferred democracy over revolutionary change. "Kemal was embarking on a social revolution. Rauf and his friends, at this stage, preferred social evolution."[26] Despite this encircling and committed opposition, Ataturk rammed through as much radical political change as was possible at the time.

A comparison of Ataturk and Ismet Inonu, his longtime friend and trusted lieutenant, also helps demonstrate the nature of Ataturk's revolution. Inonu had served Kemal loyally and was the one lieutenant who survived his leader's inner-circle purges.[27] The two men complemented each other perfectly. Ataturk was direct, forceful, and mercurial, while Inonu was conservative, retiring, and unspectacular. When Ataturk died in 1938, Inonu was the natural choice to replace him as president. For the next thirty-five years, he played a prominent role in directing Turkey's political destiny. Inonu's most famous political decision was his call in 1945 for the formation of an opposition party. This remarkable move transformed Turkey into a multiparty state. In taking this action, Inonu not only broadened participatory politics in Turkey but also carved out a place for himself, independent of Ataturk, in the pantheon of Turkish political leaders.

Although many observers interpret Inonu's programs as moving far beyond the policies of Ataturk in the field of political development, there is another position that needs to be presented. The argument is that in promoting liberalization and introducing pluralist politics into Turkey, Inonu hampered the system's capacity for development. By stepping aside and opening the arena to all comers, he introduced a period of tense and competitive factional politics that have ever since slowed the Turkish drive to develop. From the days of Menderes's prime ministry, beginning in 1950, to the debilitating political struggles in 1977 and 1978 between Suleyman Demirel of the Justice Party and Bulent Ecevit of the Republican People's Party, the political process in Turkey has been weakening. The severity of the crisis is seen in the direct intervention of the military into the political arena in 1960, 1971, and 1980.

---

[25]Kinross, *Atatürk*, p. 30.

[26]Ibid., p. 392. These associates were generally of well-to-do upper-class and upper-middle-class background and were therefore more closely tied to the old system than Kemal, who was obviously their social inferior. In 1924, this group resigned from the Republican People's Party and formed their own organization, called the Progressive Republican Party. Kemal used a Kurdish rebellion as the major excuse for disbanding the Progressive Party. For an analysis of the character of Ataturk's political elite, see Joseph S. Szyliowicz's study of leadership in modern Turkey in *Political Elites and Political Development in the Middle East,* ed. by Frank Tachau, (Cambridge, Mass.: Schenkman Publishing Co., 1975), pp. 23–68. Another good source is Frederick Frey's article in *Political Elites in the Middle East,* ed. by George Lenczowski (Washington, D.C.: American Enterprise Institute, 1975), pp. 41–82

[27]Toward the end, personal tensions that had been building up for many years between Ataturk and Inonu began to break into the open. Kinross reports one such exchange that took place in 1937. The pressured and normally unflappable Inonu lost his temper and blurted to Ataturk, "How much longer is this country going to be governed from a drunkard's table?" To this Ataturk coldly responded, "You seem to forget that it was a drunkard who appointed you to your post." Kinross, *Atatürk*, p. 486.

This position is supported strongly in an excellent and provocative study by a young Turkish social scientist and diplomat, who wrote that with Inonu's "democratization of political life, the principle of revolutionism was effectively shelved. . . . The capacity of Turkish leaders to introduce orderly change from above, a capacity that was in evidence during Ataturk's time, was lost for the sake and as a result of democracy. Ataturk had started a revolution; Inonu arrested it."[28]

There is certainly truth in both sides of this debate, which focuses directly on the developmental dialectic discussed in Chapter 1. Authoritarianism at the center endangers participation in the periphery (Ataturk's case). Liberalization, however, tends to create fragmentation, which in turn weakens capacity for development (Inonu's case). The parallel processes of modernization and political development must be continuing ones. Ataturk started a revolution. It was up to his successors to continue it, widen it, and deepen it.

Muhammad Reza Shah Pahlavi: The Traditionalism of a Modernizing Monarch

In June of 1934, President Kemal Ataturk welcomed an important neighboring head of state to Turkey for a three-week official state visit. The visitor was Reza Shah, the founder of the Pahlavi dynasty of Iran. Like Ataturk, Reza Shah was a man of imposing presence. Standing well over six feet in height, he had the flashing eyes of an eagle and a personality that scorched friend and foe alike. The two leaders had much in common. Both were military men and avid nationalists who consolidated their nations and built strong central political control over their peoples. Both leaders also sought to modernize and reform their countries. Reza Shah, who was three years older than Ataturk, was greatly impressed by the latter's reform programs as well as by the level of modernity he witnessed in Turkey. Partly as a result of this visit, he lashed out at such symbols of tradition as the ulema, while at the same time sporadically modernizing the economic, educational, and military systems in his country. Yet Reza Shah's programs of reform never approached the depth or breadth of those instituted by his contemporary in Turkey.[29]

After participating in the military coup of 1921, Reza Khan crowned himself shah of Iran in 1926. In so doing, he chose to continue patrimonial monarchy, a

---

[28]Osman Faruk Logoglu, "Ismet Inonu and the Political Modernization of Turkey, 1945–1965." Ph.D. diss. (Princeton University, 1970), p. 255. With regard to Ataturk's strategy of change, Logoglu writes: "There has been no rigorous exposition of the meaning of the well-established proposition that Ataturk tried to convert only the elite or the intelligentsia and did not really try to reach the peasant masses. The meaning of the corollary proposition that Ataturk had the insight to realize he could not change the masses without first transforming the elite needs to be restated as well." See pp. 255–256.

[29]The major comparison of Ataturk and Reza Shah as modernizers is Richard H. Pfaff, "Disengagement from Traditionalism in Turkey and Iran," *Western Political Quarterly* 16 (March 1963): 79–98.

system of leadership that Ataturk had vigorously dismantled in Turkey. Patrimonial monarchism dominated Iranian politics until 1979, when Reza Shah's eldest son, Muhammad Reza, was overthrown by a massive revolutionary movement.

Although an impressive nation-builder and leader who rose to power from a lowly and illiterate background, Reza Shah in the end only shuffled the old power relations in Iran. The major political change was the existence of a new royal family at the center of the system. By the time he abdicated in 1941, Reza Shah had acquired in his own name the largest landholdings in Iran and was drawing an annual income of well over $3 million a year.[30] Although he maintained parliamentary forms and procedures, he completely controlled the political process. His rule was absolute and oppressive; he disposed of whomever he considered to be a threat to himself or to his son.

It was within this repressive political climate that Reza Shah built a railway, founded a modern educational system, developed a national army, and supported such strong symbolic measures as the unveiling of women and the condemnation of the clerics. The old social structure and the traditional patrimonialism were strongly protected, however, by the new ruling Pahlavi family. One Persian source describes the patrimonial role of Reza Shah as follows: "The Shah expected that all government employees consider themselves completely subservient to his desires and that they not show any personality of their own. . . . Those favored by the Shah did their best to carry out his desires while at the same time trying to insure that these efforts did not become too well known and thus draw fame upon themselves."[31] The last shah of Iran, Muhammad Reza, once wrote that "all over the world, the father helps shape the character of the son. In my case, my father influenced me more by far than has anyone else."[32]

Muhammad Reza Shah Pahlavi was born on October 26, 1919. At the age of thirteen, he began his studies at Le Rosey School in Rolle, Switzerland. He returned to Iran four years later, and between 1936 and 1941 he received a military and political education that was directed primarily by his father. With the Allied invasion of Iran in 1941 and his father's humiliating abdication, Muhammad Reza became shah of Iran. The next dozen years were very painful and insecure for the young shah, as is well symbolized by the attempt on his life in 1949, which, face-to-face with an armed assassin, the shah survived by "shadow-dancing and feinting."[33]

The shah managed to dodge and weave his way through the 1940s, during which time he was the target of challenges emanating from many different directions. On the left, the Communist Tudeh Party threatened to capture the entire political system, while on the right, both knowledgeable statesmen and conservative clerics sought to take power themselves. Foreign interference was intense, and the young ruler found himself sandwiched between nationalist fer-

---

[30]Great Britain, Public Record Office, F. O. 371/18992, from Mallet (Tehran), November 28, 1935.

[31]*Sharq-i Tarik* [The Dark East] (Tehran: Taban Press, 1942), pp. 69–71. In Persian.

[32]Mohammad Reza Shah Pahlavi, *Mission for My Country* (New York: McGraw-Hill, 1961), p. 45.

[33]Ibid., p. 57.

Table 5.2
Life of Muhammad Reza Shah Pahlavi: Major Events

1919	Born in Tehran
1926	Reza Khan crowned shah of Iran; Muhammad Reza declared Crown Prince
1932	Enters Le Rosey School in Switzerland
1936	Returns to Tehran; enrolls in military academy
1941	Reza Shah abdicates; Muhammad Reza takes oath as shah of Iran; Tudeh Party established in Tehran.
1946	Russian army withdraws from Azerbaijan.
1950	Shah announces intention to divide lands among peasants.
1951	Muhammad Musaddiq becomes prime minister; nationalization of Anglo-Iranian Oil Company.
1953	Fall of Musaddiq; shah reassumes power.
1957	Establishment of Security Organization (SAVAK)
1959	Shah marries Farah Diba.
1960	Birth of Crown Prince Reza
1963	Announces White Revolution; countrywide riots and demonstrations put down with force.
1967	Formal coronation of Muhammad Reza Shah and Empress Farah
1971	Celebration of 2,500 years of Iranian monarchy
1975	Establishes one-party system—the National Resurgence Party
1978	Masses of Iranian citizens riot and demonstrate against the shah's rule; shah institutes government by martial law.
1979	Shah goes into exile; Ayatollah Ruhollah Khomeini returns to Iran after fifteen years in exile.
1980	Muhammad Reza Shah dies in Egypt.

---

vor and imperialist power. It was during these early years that the shah learned the art of political maneuver and perfected the traditional techniques of divide and rule. When such basic rationalizations of rule as charisma and religion are absent, the patrimonial leader is forced to rely entirely on personal manipulative techniques. This was exactly the situation for the shah of Iran in the 1940s; besieged and surrounded by opponents and critics, he managed to survive by constantly refining those methods of patrimonial rule that were at his disposal.

In the early 1950s, the shah and the monarchy of Iran were faced with a challenge of the most serious proportions. A charismatic personality rose within Iran and, rallying the masses behind him, confronted the shah and threatened to transform social and political patterns. Muhammad Musaddiq rose to influence primarily on the basis of his attack against foreign interests in Iran and his drive to nationalize the Anglo-Iranian Oil Company. Although the apologetic (as opposed to analytic) literature concerning Pahlavi politics has attempted to portray Musaddiq as somehow being in league with the British, the British had already, in their diplomatic reports in the 1930s, tagged him as "a demagogue and a windbag."[34]

Musaddiq was known in Iran as an impeccably honest personality who refused to accede to foreign interests. The dramatic proof of this was his successful campaign to nationalize the oil company. Musaddiq was prime minister from April 1951 to August 1953. During this time, he became internationally famous as he nationalized the oil company and slowly undermined the power of the shah. He fell from office during the chaotic events of August 1953, which included the shah's returning to Iran and the throne a few days after a hurried flight out of the country. Street fighting and military activity that month involved the Tudeh forces, proshah elements, Musaddiqists, and Americans who directly intervened on behalf of the shah.[35]

Much of Musaddiq's support came from the rising professional middle class, whose members tended to be highly nationalistic and critical of the corruption that pervaded Iran. Musaddiq, who retained in his behavior vestiges of the old aristocracy from which he had come, nonetheless entertained middle-class values and was able to gain strength and support across class lines. Although he may have been a poor politician in the Iranian context, Musaddiq was a charismatic leader who challenged the very roots of Pahlavi patrimonialism.

The Musaddiq challenge represented an intolerable situation for the shah, since it directly struck at the very foundation on which all patrimonial leaders must base their power—their indisputable and central right to rule. The threat from Musaddiq was particularly serious because he donned a patrimonial mantle of his own that was heavily embroidered with charisma.[36]

Following the fall of Musaddiq, the shah began a concerted program to solidify his position as leader of all Iranians. Between 1954 and 1961, he pursued a policy of consolidation through coercion and thus adopted political tactics reminiscent of those used by his father in the 1930s. Besides building up military resources such as the army and the gendarmerie, the shah organized an extensive secret-police system (SAVAK) in 1957. SAVAK became a key element in Pahlavi politics from then on.

Beginning in 1963, the shah's style of leadership shifted to an emphasis on the introduction of reform programs. Policies of coercion were balanced with programs of co-optation as the shah initiated a campaign to foster reform from

---

[34]Great Britain, Public Record Office, F. O. 371/20837, Seymour to Eden, April 12, 1937. For the convoluted reasoning that implies Musaddiq's proximity to the British, see Ramesh Sanghvi, *Aryamehr: The Shah of Iran* (New York: Stein and Day, 1968), pp. 142–245, 213.

[35]For recent detailed analyses of these events and of the Musaddiq period in general, see James A. Bill and William Roger Louis, eds., *Musaddiq, Iranian Nationalism and Oil* (Austin: University of Texas Press, 1988).

[36]E. A. Bayne writes that "the Shah's historic image was dimmed by the burning fire of Mossadegh's charisma." Bayne, *Persian Kingship in Transition* (New York: American Universities Field Staff, 1968), p. 160.

above. In the mid-1960s, he spoke often about the need for revolutionary programs in Iran. By the end of the 1960s, he was quoting Lenin in his speeches, and many of his supporters were referring to opponents of the regime as reactionary, feudal, and right wing. The shah outlined the core of the reform program in January 1963, when he announced the six principles of the White Revolution. This "Revolution of the Shah and the People," as it was referred to in Persian, was expanded until it included nineteen different points. The most important were the first twelve:

1. Land reform
2. Nationalization of forests and pastures
3. Public sale of state-owned factories to finance land reform
4. Profit sharing in industry
5. Reform of electoral law to include women
6. Literacy corps
7. Health corps
8. Reconstruction and development corps
9. Rural courts of justice
10. Nationalization of the waterways
11. National reconstruction
12. Educational and administrative revolution

Despite these reforms, which were never effectively implemented, political opposition and violence increased in Iran during the last fifteen years of the shah's rule. By the mid-1970s, urban guerrillas dedicated to the overthrow of the shah clashed constantly with security forces. Between 1970 and 1976, the shah's longtime policy of blending programs of repression with those of reform was abandoned, and a period of stifling police rule was ushered in. People were arrested and harassed arbitrarily and often; censorship became unusually heavy-handed and indiscriminate; and for the first time during the shah's rule, torture was systematically utilized in the prisons. A 1976 study prepared by the International Commission of Jurists reported that "there can be no doubt that torture has been systematically practiced over a number of years against recalcitrant suspects under interrogation by the SAVAK."[37] When questioned about torture, the shah said, "I am not bloodthirsty. I am working for my country and the coming generations. I can't waste my time on a few young idiots. I don't believe the tortures attributed to the SAVAK are as common as people say, but I can't run everything."[38]

---

[37]William J. Butler and Georges Levasseur, *Human Rights and the Legal System in Iran* (Geneva: International Commission of Jurists, 1976), p. 22. For various sources discussing the severity of secret police tactics in Iran, see Amnesty International, *Annual Report, 1974–75* (London, 1975); U.S. Congress, House Committee on International Relations, Subcommittee on International Organizations, *Human Rights in Iran* (Washington, D.C.: Government Printing Office, 1977).

[38]Gérard de Villiers, *The Imperial Shah: An Informal Biography* (Boston: Little, Brown and Co., 1976), p. 259.

This sharp shift in the direction of repressive rule sacrificed the more subtle dimensions of patrimonial rule to harsh police control. One result was a marked rise in opposition activity, which took the form of urban violence promoted by expanding guerrilla groups. Thousands of incidents occurred throughout Iran; new, superbly organized opposition groups even managed to infiltrate the shah's highly touted security forces. The tighter the police turned the screws, the more fanatic the opposition became. Dozens of young women, along with the men, joined the guerrillas as a vicious circle of repression and reaction set in. Meanwhile, in the mosques throughout the country, religious leaders increased sharply their critical social and political commentary.

Then, at the end of 1976 and in early 1977, and coinciding partly with the appearance of the Carter administration in Washington, the shah began to cut back on the repression and tried to return to more flexible patrimonial tactics. A period of liberalization began and was accompanied by a marked decrease in guerrilla-sponsored violence. Letters, petitions, and communications of all kinds flooded the offices of the shah and his political elite. When a leading Iranian newspaper raised a question in one of its columns concerning "what is wrong in Iran," it received over 40,000 letters. This kind of overwhelming response frightened the regime, which reverted to heavy-handed police tactics resulting in a wave of violence that shook the country to its roots in 1978.

Drawing its inspiration from the charismatic, uncompromising leadership of Ayatollah Ruhollah Khomeini in exile in Iraq and then France, the popular opposition gathered strength as the year progressed. Rallying around the Shi'i religious leaders, individuals drawn from all social classes demonstrated violently against the shah's rule in the city of Qom in January, in Tabriz in February, and in Tehran and other cities in March, April, and May. Then in August, September, and December of 1978, the opposition to the shah exploded into mass marches and demonstrations involving hundreds of thousands of dissatisfied citizens.

Shaken and stunned in the face of massive national rebellion, the shah tried a number of desperate measures of both concession and repression. Concessions were half-measures that only whetted the appetite of the popular opposition; repression gave the revolution over 10,000 martyrs and strengthened the resolve and commitment of the challenging forces. When the traditional twin tactics of alternating coercion and co-optation failed to stem the revolutionary tide, the shah was left baffled and bewildered. Already somewhat weakened by a five-year struggle with cancer and psychologically unwilling to relinquish the mantle of absolute monarchy, he watched in disbelief as his people, always chanting "marg bar shah" ("death to the shah"), rose to overthrow him.

On January 3, 1979, the Iranian Majlis approved the shah's reluctant appointment of Shahpour Bakhtiar, a liberal and former National Front member, as prime minister of Iran. On January 16, Muhammad Reza Shah left Iran for a "vacation" abroad—a vacation from which he was never to return. On January 31, Ayatollah Khomeini, the implacable foe of the shah, returned to Iran in triumph after fifteen years of exile abroad. The shah spent the last eighteen months of his life seeking a permanent residence in exile. After shuffling from Egypt to Morocco to the Bahamas to Mexico to the United States to Panama, the shah returned to Egypt, where he died of cancer on July 27, 1980.

PATTERNS OF RULE

Muhammad Reza Shah Pahlavi was a political leader who practiced the techniques and tactics of patrimonial rule for nearly four decades in Iran. He was presented to his people as the source of all ideas and the fount of all good. Each of the points in the White Revolution, therefore, was attributed to the shah, and much has been written about how these ideas suddenly came to his mind.[39]

Individuals competed relentlessly with one another to have their ideas presented to the shah, who, they hoped, would include them in his personal program for national development. In his book published in 1978, the shah patrimonially discussed his role as national mentor, teacher, and creator of revolutionary ideas: "I accept most willingly this mission for teaching and advice because of the knowledge I command on the most extensive scale of my country's national and international problems and because I am, myself, the architect and founder of the social revolution of which all Iranian developments of the day are the reflection."[40] The strength of this pattern is also seen in the words of former prime minister, minister of court, tribal aristocrat, and lifelong friend and confidant of the shah, Asadollah Alam: "I cannot say that he is faultless. Everyone, as you say, has faults. . . . [H]is fault to my mind is that he is really too great for his people—his ideas are too great for we people to realize it."[41] This kind of subservience, displayed even by the most important officials, is a central ingredient in patrimonial rule.

A special effort was made in Iran to portray the Shah to his people as an unquestioned patrimonial leader. Because he had to bargain for survival during the first twelve years of his rule and because he lacked charisma, the years following the fall of Musaddiq were years in which "a sophisticated apparatus would work assiduously to create the supreme patriarchal image, and a secret police would guard it."[42]

The source of power must be visible to everyone everywhere. Pictures of the shah and his immediate family adorned government offices and public places throughout the country. Statues of the shah stood in the middle of village squares, city parks, and even on the tops of mountain peaks. Shrubbery in public gardens was cut in the form of Persian script spelling out the shah's name. His likeness was woven into Persian carpets, and over seventy-five different sets of Iranian postage stamps carried the royal portrait. Millions of colored lights were lit throughout the country on the shah's birthday, and a huge party was held annually in his presence at Amjadieh Stadium in Tehran.

The shah attempted to legitimize his rule in a number of other ways. He sought to develop systems of thought, for example, that stressed monarchical,

---

[39]See, for example, "Brilliant Idea Was Born on a Murky Day," *Kayhan International* (Tehran), November 22, 1966, p. 4. This article explains how the idea of a literacy corps suddenly popped into the shah's mind.

[40]Mohammed Reza Shah Pahlavi, *Towards the Great Civilization* (Tehran: n. p., 1978).

[41]Margaret Laing, *The Shah* (London: Sidgwick and Jackson, 1977), p. 231.

[42]Bayne, *Persian Kingship,* p. 167.

religious, and reform considerations. The ideology of reform was developed to buttress the traditional rationalizations of monarchy and religion. The elite constantly argued that the Iranians had an inherent need for monarchy. This was manifested in the continuous national celebrations that were organized for almost a decade to commemorate Iran's 2,500 years of monarchy. Nevertheless, it became increasingly difficult to reconcile philosophies of reform with philosophies of monarchy, since "the dialectic of king and modernizing polity has not been fully resolved."[43]

The use of religion as a legitimating device was also difficult for the shah, who had to compete in this regard with the mujtahids, who were the representatives of the Hidden Imam in society. The shah attempted in various ways, therefore, to reveal his special relation with the divine. He argued that the peasants often referred to him as the Shadow of God, and he apparently believed that he was guided and guarded by some superhuman force. In his autobiography, the shah credited his numerous escapes from personal and political disaster to "some unseen hand" and claimed that from childhood he "felt that perhaps there is a supreme being who is guiding me."[44] He stated that "my reign has saved the country, and it has done so because God was on my side," and that "God is my only friend."[45]

The traditional characteristics of personalism, proximity, informality, and balanced conflict permeated the rule of Muhammad Reza Shah. His was an "individual approach to kingship,"[46] and he ruled at the center of a complex web of personal relations. It was especially in the early and middle years of his rule that the shah had contact with as many officials and personalities as possible. In this kind of political setting, the issue of physical proximity assumed reciprocal significance. Individuals held influence commensurate to their nearness to the patrimonial leader, while the leader felt it important to be in personal contact with advisors, friends, officials, and confidants. Just as the family patriarch deems it essential to his position as patriarch to maintain personal communication with all of his children, so also did the patrimonial leader consider it important to his position to be in touch with as many members of his society as possible. In Pahlavi Iran, there was tremendous pressure constantly exerted by individuals everywhere to move toward the shah, who was the locus of power. At the same time, the shah stated that "one of the principal problems of government is to know the right people and in necessary numbers. Either these people must be presented to you—and you need time to become acquainted and to know them—or you must search for them."[47]

In this highly personal system of patrimonial rule, informality prevailed, and individuals were balanced against individuals. The shah operated through infor-

---

[43]Ibid., p. 97

[44]Pahlavi, *Mission for My Country,* pp. 55, 58.

[45]See "An Oriana Fallaci Interview: The Shah of Iran," *The New Republic* (December 1, 1973): 17; and de Villiers, *Imperial Shah,* p. 273.

[46]Bayne, *Persian Kingship,* p. 239.

[47]Ibid., p. 193.

mal meetings, personal cliques, and trusted groups of friends and family. Rivalry and tension were omnipresent; over the years, the shah proved himself a master at playing off key subordinates against one another. As a result, for years no one became overly powerful, and the leader remained far above any potential challenger. In the shah's Iran, the network of balanced rivalry encompassed the royal family, courtiers, personal adjutants, ministers, military officers, and all economic and political figures of any important standing. This pattern was reflected most dramatically in the case of twelve different military and security organizations, all of which stood in rivalry with one another. It was the patrimonial leader who kept these lines of tension finely adjusted.

Finally, the shah of Iran sought to maintain a special and direct control over the military. As shah and commander in chief, he handpicked the military leaders, primarily on the basis of their loyalty to him. The downfall of several important politicians of the past occurred after they challenged the shah for control of the military. The shah prided himself on his knowledge of military science and claimed that he understood the necessity of military power. His special emphasis on the military is seen in the huge expenditures that were funneled into military and security establishments. By the late 1970s, they absorbed approximately 40 percent of the Iranian budget. Between 1972 and 1977, U.S. military sales to Iran totalled $16.2 billion, while the Pahlavi defense budget increased by nearly 700 percent over this six-year period.[48] The shah of Iran once summarized his own view of his relation to the military in the peculiarly patrimonial phrase, "I am the army."[49]

THE PATRIMONIAL PATH TO REVOLUTION

As long as Muhammad Reza Shah pursued proven programs of patrimonialism seasoned with the flavor of reform, he was able to buy time and to maintain control. His land reform and literacy programs co-opted the ideas of the challenging professional middle class while proposing to improve the living standards of the masses of Iranian people. The Pahlavi game plan called for massive economic growth blended with moderate and controlled social reform all in the service of the preservation and perpetuation of the traditional patrimonial political status quo.[50]

The fact that the shah's reform program was designed to protect rather than to transform traditional political patterns can be documented by analyzing the direction and the methodology of the reforms. The core of the "White Revolution" consisted of programs that could only buttress the patrimonial position of

---

[48]U.S. Congress, Senate Committee on Foreign Relations, Subcommittee on Foreign Assistance, Staff Report, *U.S. Military Sales to Iran* (Washington, D.C.: Government Printing Office, 1976); and *The Christian Science Monitor,* January 20, 1978, p. 5.

[49]Bayne, *Persian Kingship,* p. 186.

[50]For a detailed study of the shah's strategy of patrimonialism and system preservation, see James A. Bill, *The Politics of Iran: Groups, Classes and Modernization* (Columbus, Ohio: Charles E. Merrill, 1972). See also Marvin Zonis, *Majestic Failure: The Fall of the Shah* (Chicago: University of Chicago Press, 1991).

the ruler. Viewed from this perspective, the land reform program served to weaken precisely those forces that traditionally threatened the patrimonial leader, that is, the old aristocratic, landed families and the Shi'i religious establishment. By cutting back on the economic power of the ulema, the shah hoped to improve his position relative to theirs. By replacing aristocratic officials at the national political level with workers and bureaucrats with no independent power base, the shah sought to strengthen his own position.

The actual administration of the reform program was implemented according to traditional patterns. Personalism, rivalry, insecurity, distrust, and uncoordinated ad hoc decision making prevailed. Political opportunists entered the arena and tainted and impeded the programs. The built-in rivalry that debilitated reform efforts was seen in the important task of land reform. At first, the ministries of agriculture, interior, and economy competed for control of the program. Later, a separate ministry of land reform and rural cooperatives was established, as well as a ministry of agricultural products and consumer goods and a ministry of natural resources. There was also an agricultural bank and an agricultural development fund. All of these organizations, and others (e.g., the plan organization) were bound together in an interlocking network of competition that prevented any individual or any ministry from becoming too powerful—or too effective. It also prevented successful land reform from occurring.[51]

The shah's reform programs suffered from other serious maladies. Patrimonial politics are susceptible to the abuses of corruption, favoritism, cronyism, and nepotism. In the shah's Iran, these abuses bubbled outward from the very center of the system and became both more pronounced and more visible through the decade of the 1970s. When oil revenues increased from slightly more than $2 billion in 1972 to over $20 billion in 1974, the opportunities for graft, bribery, and general corruption also increased tenfold. In the process, the gap in income distribution increased significantly and the masses of Iranian people found themselves relatively worse off after the reform program than they were prior to 1963. By using and then abusing patrimonialism, the shah in the end only alienated the very constituency whose support he was seeking to gain.

In 1970, the shah of Iran began a dramatic shift in his tactics of patrimonial rule. Coercion and repression took precedence over co-optation and reform. A major target of this new, hard-line policy was the ulema. In a system of patrimonial rule, it is extremely difficult for the leader to tolerate competing centers of leadership. It is especially difficult when these individuals carry charismatic qualities derived from the ideology of Islam. Yet over the years, the Iranian shahs had managed to live in a state of uneasy coexistence with the Shi'i clerics and had allowed them to maintain their own sphere of influence. Between 1970 and 1976, however, the shah's security apparatus attacked the religious leaders frontally; many were arrested and imprisoned, and some were executed. In the process, the Iranian government closed down religious publishing houses, disbanded re-

---

[51]For documentation, see Eric J. Hooglund, *Land and Revolution in Iran, 1960–1980* (Austin: The University of Texas Press, 1982).

ligious student groups, and infiltrated mosque and endowment (*awqaf*) organizations. This policy alienated the entire religious establishment, and the clerics rallied to the leadership of Ayatollah Ruhollah Khomeini, a leading mujtahid with unassailable opposition credentials.

The ineffectiveness of many of the reform programs and the generally sad state of the lower-class masses provided a ready constituency for the harried religious leaders. Meanwhile, the shah himself had lost his patrimonial touch and had committed the grave error of isolating himself from his people. The patrimonial leader at the center of the familial polity had cut himself off from his advisors and his people. With the deaths of shrewd old patrimonial cronies and advisors, such as Asadollah Alam and Manuchehr Eghbal, and with his own increasing megalomania, the shah lost touch. Toward the end, he even refused to listen to the advice along his last line to reality, that of Empress Farah.[52] Instead, the shah consulted seriously only with the American and British ambassadors, two outside diplomats whose own understanding of Iran was flawed.

The very fact that the Pahlavi government was so deeply involved with the West (especially the United States) also only exacerbated the situation. Not only had the patrimonial leader lost touch with his own constituency, he had shifted his attention more and more to political, economic, and military alliances with outsiders. In the view of many of his former constituents, therefore, the shah had forsaken the country, culture, and Shi'i Islam for external, alien friends. In the eyes of the Iranian people, the patrimonial leader had deserted his family.

Ayatollah Ruhollah Khomeini, the immediate successor to the shah and the hero of the revolution, led Iran according to patrimonial principles. This is symbolized by the fact that when the shah fell, Iranians immediately replaced his pictures with those of Khomeini. Revolutionary Iran was marked by mobs and masses of Iranian citizens behaving as the very embodiment of the Ayatollah. All the characteristics of patrimonial politics have prevailed during the post-Pahlavi period: personalism, proximity, informality, balanced conflict, and military activity. There has also been considerable violence and insecurity. Yet the Khomeini style of patrimonialism differed significantly from that of the last shah; it carried several important advantages.

First, Khomeini was a genuinely charismatic personality. In this sense, he was much more similar to Musaddiq than to the shah, who always had to labor under the disadvantage of an unimpressive and ordinary personality. The shah's person was deferred to largely because of the power that inhered in the office. Second, Khomeini held legitimate religious credentials. The shah always had to stretch fact and imagination to portray a special Islamic legitimacy. Third, the Ayatollah was never accused of personal corruption but rather led a simple, spartan life. This appealed to his popular constituency, which viewed him as a leader of, for, and from the people. It was also in direct contrast to the shah, whose world included the splendor and opulence of palaces, banks, American

---

[52]As the Pahlavi monarchy collapsed, the empress stated that the shah refused even to listen to her advice and counsel. Among other things, she said, "The husband does not always listen to the wife." Personal interview (Bill) with Empress Farah Diba, November 29, 1978, Niavaran Palace, Tehran.

movie stars, aircraft, modern art, and the Rockefellers. Fourth, the slogan "Neither East nor West" indicates the Khomeinian preoccupation with the destruction of all outside influence in Iran's social and political system. Since the West in general and the United States in particular were most closely associated with the former regime, they were the major targets of attacks by the revolutionary regime. The Soviet Union and communism, however, were also criticized and condemned by the Ayatollah. This strain of patrimonial independence was much more appealing than the policy practiced by the shah, who was widely viewed as a puppet and client of the United States.

These factors all combined to give Khomeini's revolutionary mode of patrimonialism its fifth and major strength: As patrimonial leader, Khomeini managed to build a mass base of support. While he turned on the old upper and middle classes, Khomeini sought to improve the life of the masses of Iranian people. By stressing the needs of those he called the *mustaza'fin* ("downtrodden," "dispossessed"), he managed to build a large and committed constituency. His government took from the haves and gave to the have-nots. He was, in essence, a patrimonial populist. The Ayatollah was able to remain a patrimonial leader with a mass constituency, unlike the shah, whose patrimonialism rested on only the tiniest and flimsiest of support bases.[53]

Ayatollah Khomeini's immediate successor, Ali Akbar Hashemi-Rafsanjani, also guided Iran patrimonially. Although he lacked Khomeini's charisma and extraordinary revolutionary credibility, Rafsanjani, who served as president of the Islamic Republic between 1988 and 1997, guided his country through a difficult period. The personalism, political rivalry, and corruption that marked Rafsanjani's presidencies were offset by the successful institutionalization of the political process and the beginning of genuine political participation. Rafsanjani, relying partially on patrimonial principles, in fact paved the way for the presidential victory of an individual whose style of rule represented a sharp break from the long tradition of patrimonialism in Iran.

Mohammad Khatami, a progressive fifty-year-old cleric, won a surprise victory in the presidential elections of May 1997. Khatami received 70 percent of the vote as the younger generation, professionals, women, and other groups, who desired fundamental change and a return to normalcy in Iran, voted in overwhelming numbers for the new president. It soon became clear that Khatami intended to move Iran in new directions. In his speeches, Khatami repeatedly emphasized the importance of rule of law, civil society, freedom of expression, and international diplomatic cooperation. Khatami's public commentary on the role of women demonstrated as much as anything else that he was a new kind of leader. In his words: "In our society women have never been treated equally with men. We must eradicate this shortcoming. I believe women must be awarded special privileges because they were oppressed in the past."

From the very beginning, Khatami threw aside many of the trappings of patrimonialism. He condemned factionalism, personalism, favoritism, and the lan-

---

[53]For an excellent study that presents Khomeini as a populist rather than a fundamentalist, see Ervand Abrahamian, *Khomeinism* (Berkeley and Los Angeles: University of California Press, 1993).

guage of false deference that often accompanies patrimonial politics. Although patrimonial practices were not completely uprooted in Khatami's Iran, there is little doubt that Mohammad Khatami represented a new man and a new leader in the Iranian social and political context.[54]

Gamal Abdel Nasser: Patrimonialism and Transformation

> The man is at once feline and massive. His square build speaks of a peasant ancestry, the long remembrance of stubborn, fleshy gestures, the recompense of a heavy, miserable diet over many generations. But this son of the Middle Valley also carries Arab descent in his blood: a Bedouin strain had pursued for several centuries in Bani Murr District the synthesis of Ishmael and Pharaoh. Perhaps this gives his physique that deliberate alertness, his face that sharp breadth, his eyes that brooding nostalgia behind their hard, almost green, gaze. The Arab has risen ponderously, one might say, from his long submergence in the soil of Egypt.[55]

Recent Middle Eastern political history is marked by the existence of a handful of leaders who have attempted to uproot many of the traditional social and political patterns that have prevailed in their societies. Besides Kemal Ataturk, the other major case in point is Gamal Abdel Nasser of Egypt. Like Ataturk, Nasser adopted tactics of transformation that left some areas largely untouched, while in other areas fundamental efforts at change were made. The life and leadership of Gamal Abdel Nasser in particular deserves to be analyzed in this light, since Nasser introduced many revolutionary programs in a society that contains nearly one-third of the world's Arab population.

Gamal Abdel Nasser was born on January 15, 1918, in Alexandria. He was raised in the village of Beni Morr in Upper Egypt, the ancestral home of his family. Nasser's father was a postal clerk; his mother died when Gamal was eight years old. Since his father had remarried and was constantly being moved about in his work, Gamal spent long periods living with various relatives. As a secondary school student, he developed a deep social and political consciousness. He harbored an early concern about the British presence in Egypt; at the same time, he grew to dislike the debility and dependence that marked the status of his country.

Nasser graduated from secondary school in Cairo in 1936 and afterwards entered the Egyptian Military Academy. Upon graduating from the academy in 1938 with the rank of second lieutenant, he was sent to serve with an infantry company in Upper Egypt. In 1943, Nasser was promoted to the rank of captain

---

[54]For Khatami's views on society and politics, see his extensive 1997 interview translated and presented by Minoo and Milton Buffington, *Meet Mr. Khatami* (Washington, D.C.: Middle East Insight, 1997).

[55]Jacques Berque, *Cultural Expression in Arab Society Today,* trans. by Robert W. Stookey (Austin: The University of Texas Press, 1978), pp. 15–16.

and was appointed an instructor at the military academy. In 1948, he distinguished himself in a losing cause in the Palestine campaign. As a patriotic officer, he was disgusted at the inefficiency and decrepitude of the Egyptian political regime. During the 1940s, moreover, Nasser began to blame imperialism and feudalism for the constantly deteriorating state of his country. He read widely and, as a history instructor, refined his social and political ideas. It was during this period that he helped form the Free Officers movement and came into contact with the group of fellow officers who were to play the vital role in changing the course of Egyptian history over the next two decades.

On July 23, 1952, the Free Officers movement carried out a coup that overthrew King Farouk and his traditional regime. A Revolutionary Command Council of twelve officers, including General Muhammad Naguib, took control of the government. At first Naguib was the titular political leader, but by the end of 1954 Gamal Abdel Nasser had ousted him and taken control. Nasser remained the internationally famous leader of Egypt until his heart attack and death on September 28, 1970. During these years, both Nasser and Egypt survived numerous vicissitudes, including crises ranging from an assassination attempt to an invasion by the combined forces of three foreign powers. During his eighteen years of leadership in Egypt, Nasser's political activities were divided into three general and overlapping categories: (1) consolidation and maintenance of political power; (2) introduction and continuation of policies of social, economic, and political change within Egypt; and (3) development of an independent foreign policy.

During the first few years of his leadership, Nasser was preoccupied with the task of protecting the ascendant position he had acquired. This meant maintaining the cohesion of the military in general and the Free Officers group in particular, while at the same time repelling opposition forces mobilized by the Communists on the left and the Wafd Party and Muslim Brotherhood on the right. Nasser had strongly suppressed the Brotherhood by 1955; in the late 1950s and early 1960s, he moved sharply and successfully against Communism within Egypt; and by 1965, he had largely managed to destroy the influence of the wealthy bourgeoisie that had formed the backbone of the Wafd Party.

Although these were the most serious organized threats to his power, Nasser's government was faced with political challenges throughout its existence because his revolutionary programs were continually threatening vested interests. As his authoritarianism hardened in order to withstand these kinds of challenges, Nasser came to alienate substantial segments of supporters within the intelligentsia, who chafed under a cloak of repression that suffocated criticism and innovation from below. Democratization was deliberately sacrificed, since the consolidation and maintenance of power were considered essential to successful modernization.

Because Nasser was able to consolidate his forces, he was in turn able to institute change from above. Although individual freedoms were often ruthlessly sacrificed, Nasser nonetheless instituted enough fundamental change to lay a new social, economic, and political foundation for Egyptian society.

Gamal Abdel Nasser once stated that he was a revolutionary and not a politician. He wrote, "Every people on earth goes through two revolutions: a political revolution by which it wrests the right to govern itself from the hand of tyranny, or from the army stationed upon its soil against its will; and a social revolution, involving the conflict of classes which settles down when justice is secured for the citizens of the united nation."[56] In analyzing the political history of post-1952 Egypt, Maxime Rodinson concludes that the two main goals of Nasserism were national independence and modernization.[57] Among the important sociopolitical achievements of Nasser's revolution are (1) the agrarian reform program, (2) the transformation and partial leveling of the class structure, (3) the elimination of conspicuous corruption in the personal household of the national leader, (4) the continuing rise of achievement at the expense of ascription in the administrative system, (5) the expulsion of foreign influence, and (6) the strengthening of the pride and dignity of the Egyptian people. In his attempt to transform the traditional power structure, Nasser came to the conclusion that the process must be a continuing one. Land reform alone could not bring about this transformation, since it was neither deep enough nor fast enough to undercut the power of the traditional ruling class. It was in this context that Nasser instituted the extensive nationalization laws of the 1960–1963 period.

The successes and failures of Nasser's domestic programs rested to a great degree degree on his ability to guide Egypt through the stormy seas of international politics. It was in this broader area that the Egyptian president expended most of his political energy, and it was here that he witnessed his greatest triumphs and his greatest defeats. His tenure as leader of Egypt was clouded by deep problems directly associated with the Arab-Israeli confrontation, the American-Soviet cold war, the general drive for Arab unity, and the differing Arab stances concerning the entire issue of social and political change. In 1955, President Nasser attended the Bandung Conference, where he rubbed shoulders with Nehru, Sukarno, and Chou En-lai and where he was considered a new leader of the Afro-Asian world. He returned home a hero for his role in a conference that condemned "neocolonialism" and supported "non-alignment." A few months later, Nasser accepted a Soviet arms offer and concluded a deal with Czechoslovakia that electrified the Arab world, since it indicated that Egypt was no longer dependent on the West and would pursue a course of positive neutralism.[58] That same year, Nasser refused to align Egypt with the Anglo-American-sponsored Baghdad Pact, and in 1956, John Foster Dulles withdrew the American offer to help Egypt finance the critically important Aswan High Dam. One

---

[56]Gamal Abdel Nasser, *Egypt's Liberation: The Philosophy of the Revolution* (Washington, D.C.: Public Affairs Press, 1955), pp. 39–40.

[57]See Maxime Rodinson, "The Political System," in *Egypt Since the Revolution,* ed. by P. J. Vatikiotis (New York: Frederick A. Praeger, 1968), pp. 87–113.

[58]The arms deal took a great deal of personal and political courage on Nasser's part, since it was signed in the face of deep United States opposition. This was a time when American intelligence forces had helped rearrange political regimes in Iran (1953) and Guatemala (1954). When Egypt's panicky ambassador to the United States urged Nasser not to defy Washington in this way, he kept repeating the phrase: "Remember Guatemala, remember Guatemala." Nasser finally said, "To hell with Guatemala" and went ahead with the arms agreement. See Leonard Mosley, *Dulles* (New York: Dial Press, James Wade, 1978), p. 388.

week later, Nasser announced the nationalization of the Suez Canal Company, which in turn brought about the abortive invasion of Egypt by Great Britain, France, and Israel. The Soviet Union then took charge of the financing and construction of the High Dam. These events brought together the masses of Egyptians behind Nasser, who had proved to them that Egypt was an independent nation whose dignity could no longer be trampled on. The significance of the Suez crisis "reached far beyond the event itself, causing a revolutionary transformation of the technocratic, reformist government."[59] It was a "charismatic situation"[60] that helped invest Nasser with extraordinary powers as a political leader.

These early successes were of sufficient magnitude to enable both Nasser and Egypt to ride out later disasters. The most serious of these was the June War of 1967, in which Israel (in an impressive and efficient military campaign) left Egypt battered and demoralized. Nasser, who must bear part of the blame for occasioning the conflict, resigned his position, to be called back only hours later by the Egyptian people, who genuinely wanted and demanded his leadership. The existence of Israel haunted Nasser's rule, and he was never able to confront this situation with the same style and success with which he addressed other thorny problems.

In the area of intra-Arab politics, the Egyptian president was only slightly more successful. The United Arab Republic, which was a political and economic union with Syria formed in 1958, was dissolved in 1961 when, among other things, the wealthy Syrian bourgeois families feared the impact of Nasser's revolutionary programs. Nasser successfully supported the Algerian rebels in Algeria, although in Yemen direct Egyptian military support failed to enable the revolutionaries to take control of the country. The latter adventure cost Egypt dearly in terms of domestic resources and international prestige. Despite this, however, President Nasser's revolutionary programs and ideas spread through the Middle East and acted as catalysts for change in the Arab world. If they did not lead to revolution from below, they inspired the traditional leaders to try to dissipate discontent by initiating reform from above. The land reform programs in Syria, Iraq, Tunisia, Iran, and Turkey, for example, all followed the Egyptian experiment in agrarian reform begun in 1952.

PATTERNS OF RULE

Gamal Abdel Nasser's leadership broke with many of the patterns of traditional patrimonial rule. Although strongly authoritarian, Nasser's techniques did not include the promotion of self-deification. It is true that his image was protected and polished by his governmental and security forces, but he resisted pressures to invest huge resources in the glorification of his person. There were no statues of Nasser, for example, dotting the Egyptian landscape. Nor did his face adorn postage stamps and currency. The Egyptian president consciously sought to tran-

---

[59]Jean Lacouture, *The Demigods: Charismatic Leadership in the Third World,* trans. by Patricia Wolf (New York: Alfred A. Knopf, 1970), p. 110.

[60]Ibid.

Table 5.3
Life of Gamal Abdel Nasser: Major Events

1918	Born in Alexandria
1936	Graduates from Al-Nahda Secondary School in Cairo
1938	Graduates from Egyptian Military Academy
1948	Participates in Palestine campaign; distinguishes himself at Faluja
1952	Free Officers carry out coup against the government of King Farouk
1954	Becomes prime minister and then president of Egypt
1955	Attends Bandung Conference; concludes Soviet arms deal
1956	Nationalization of the Suez Canal Company and invasion of Egypt by Israel, France, and Great Britain
1958	Formation of the United Arab Republic; Nasser elected president.
1961	Passage of wide-ranging nationalization laws; United Arab Republic dissolved.
1962	Arab Socialist Union organization formed.
1967	Arab-Israeli June War; Nasser resigns, but returns to power with massive popular support.
1970	Dies in Cairo

---

scend the temptation to permit and promote personal exaltation and hero worship. One keen Western observer of Egyptian affairs wrote that "nothing irritates Nasser more than being treated like a modern pharaoh."[61]

A truly charismatic personality need not build monuments to himself and myths for his people; his charisma is based on his extraordinary actions. In Nasser's case, the leader also eschewed any special connection with the divine, whether it be in terms of common ancestry or private visions. Although he never attacked the Islamic clerics in Egypt the way Ataturk did in Turkey, at the same time he did not attempt to build any particularly close political relations with them.[62] The fact that Nasser's charisma is traceable neither to manufactured mythology nor to religious connections indicates how divorced his leadership was from the traditional mold. It is precisely this kind of charisma that invested Nasser with the special strength necessary to maintain power and to promote deep change in the face of formidable problems, both internal and external.

The role of the military was crucial to Nasser's leadership. It was through a military coup that he first came to power, and it was through the support of the military that he maintained his position. In the absence of an efficient civil bureaucracy, the Egyptian president was able to call upon personnel from within the military organization to implement administrative and economic programs.

---

[61]Ibid., p. 119.

[62]For the finest investigation of Nasser's relationship to Islam, see Josef Muzikar, "Arab Nationalism and Islam," *Archiv Orientalni* 43 (1975): 193–323.

As in traditional patrimonial systems, the military was an important prop in Nasser's political structure. There is, however, one important quality that separates the Nassers and the Ataturks from the more traditional leaders. The latter continue to present themselves in military guise and garb in order constantly to display their special and intimate relation with the military. They often explicitly state that they are an embodiment of the military. Nasser, on the contrary, retired from the army in 1955 and deliberately refrained from maintaining any military rank or title.

Personalism and informality are two related characteristics of patrimonial rule that persisted in the leadership of Gamal Abdel Nasser.[63] Nasser never succeeded in moving from rule by personalism to political institutionalization, and as a result there was a lack of political participation and a surplus of political insecurity in Nasser's Egypt. In the latter days of his presidency, heavy-handed maneuverers, such as presidential advisor Sami Sharaf and interior minister Sha'rawi Gom'a, were directing an increasingly disreputable intelligence system that reached into all corners of Egyptian society.

There is evidence that Nasser was not insensitive to the need for wider political participation. He tried three times to construct a mass political party in order to insure a measure of popular participation. His last attempt, which was also his most successful, involved the formation of the Arab Socialist Union in 1962. Such structures were largely ineffectual in Egypt, since they existed as rather sterile appendages to Nasser's personal rule, which Nasser felt bound to strengthen in order to carry on the revolution. Despite the presence of personalism and informality, Nasser was able to break a number of the patterns that follow in the wake of patrimonialism.

The nepotism that stems from personalism and the corruption that often thrives in the net of informal politics were relatively absent in Nasser's style of leadership. Nasser himself was above reproach in this regard, and he led an austere life much in the style of Chou En-lai and Fidel Castro. Throughout the Middle East, Nasser was known for his personal honesty and integrity. He spoke out constantly against opportunism, corruption, and favoritism. When he died in 1970, he was still living in the modest house that he had purchased as a young officer prior to the 1952 coup. He refused to use his power to further the causes of his family and relatives. Two of his uncles remained *fellahin* (peasants) in the village of Bani Morr, and his own daughters were unable to attend Cairo University because their entrance examination scores were not high enough.

Mohamed Heikal writes that Nasser "was never interested in women or money or elaborate food. After he had come to power the cynical old politicians tried to corrupt him but they failed miserably. His family life was impeccable."[64] Heikal goes on to point out that although Nasser received millions of pounds in

---

[63]For a source that emphasizes and analyzes the informal, personalistic politics of patrimonialism in Egypt, see Robert Springborg, *Family, Power, and Politics in Egypt* (Philadelphia: University of Pennsylvania Press, 1982).

[64]Mohamed Heikal, *The Cairo Documents* (Garden City, N.Y.: Doubleday and Co., 1973), p. 20. Some of Nasser's leading officials, including what Edward Sheehan calls "the Sharaf-Goma cabal," whose members "were nearly all corrupt," were less principled. Edward R. F. Sheehan, "The Real Sadat and the Demythologized Nasser," *New York Times Magazine*, July 18, 1971, pp. 6–7, 33, 35, 38, 42.

donations, he died with only 610 Egyptian pounds in his personal account. The programmatic manifestations of this new style fostered by Nasser are evident in the Egyptian land reform policy, for, as one expert writes, "The evenhandedness with which the distribution was carried out deserves commendation; no suggestion of favoritism in either the taking of land from large owners or the distribution of it to recipients has arisen—a remarkable accomplishment in view of the inherent temptations to corruption."[65]

Although Gamal Abdel Nasser resorted to the traditional tactic of divide and rule, his colleagues and confidants generally operated as a team in leading society. Admittedly, the team was a small and exclusive one. Lenczowski has pointed out that, with only three exceptions, Nasser managed to keep his group of young officers together through more than twelve years of the revolution.[66] While he undoubtedly made the final decisions, the Egyptian president did consult seriously with his close advisors.

The patterns of patrimonial politics were partially uprooted by President Nasser as he endeavored to revolutionize his society. Although personalism continued to prevail, many of the other traditional traits were destroyed. This represents a fundamental step in moving forward with the social and political dimensions of change.

TRANSFORMING LEADERSHIP

Despite some oil discoveries, Egypt remains one of the poorest and most densely populated societies in the world. Just before the 1952 military coup, a Rockefeller Foundation team reported that the situation of the peasants in Egypt was worse than that of the peasants in any other country in which they had carried out investigations—and this included China and India. According to this report, on a scale of 106.5 for perfect health, India rated 54 and Egypt 15. In one of the villages surveyed north of Cairo, nearly 100 percent of the population had bilarzia, a debilitating parasitical disease that attacks the kidneys and liver; 89 percent had trachoma; over 20 percent were typhoid or paratyphoid carriers. In a village with a population of 4,172, there was not one healthy person. Most of the villagers had from one to four major diseases.[67]

At the time of the report, the political system was a patrimonial monarchy in which all the negative characteristics of that kind of system were magnified. King Farouk often made national political decisions on the advice of his infamous "kitchen cabinet," composed of his valet, mechanic, butler, pilot, and doctor, among others. An Italian barber became Farouk's closest advisor, and Farouk named his brother-in-law (an honorary "colonel") minister of war. Nepotism prevailed in a demoralizing environment of political vice and personal corruption. Against this background, the changes wrought under Nasser's leadership

---

[65]Kenneth B. Platt, *Land Reform in the United Arab Republic,* A.I.D. Spring Review of Land Reform, Second ed., vol. 8 (Washington, D.C.: Agency for International Development, 1970), p. 61.

[66]George Lenczowski, "The Objects and Methods of Nasserism," in *Modernization of the Arab World,* ed. by J. H. Thompson and R. D. Reischauer (Princeton, N.J.: D. Van Nostrand Co., 1966), p. 207.

[67]For a summary of the findings of the Rockefeller Foundation study from which these figures have been drawn, see Austin L. Moore, *Farewell Farouk* (Chicago: Scholars' Press, 1954), pp. 59–60.

were dramatic. Measured against the demands of the day and the progress of other non-Western societies, such as Israel, Japan, and China, Egyptian social and political change is less impressive.

Gamal Abdel Nasser was a transforming leader for three basic reasons: He consciously and determinedly sought to ensure that his revolution be radical, political, and continuing in nature. In the 1962 Charter he wrote, "The needs of our country were such that it was not enough to patch up the old and decaying building, try to keep it from falling by means of supports and give the exterior a fresh coat of paint. What was needed was a new and strong building resting on firm foundations and towering high in the sky. . . ."[68] By distinguishing between reforming and transforming change in these kinds of terms, Nasser often indicated his sensitivity to the need to support fundamental social and political transformation. Because of this radical philosophy, Nasser "refused to endorse programs which were primarily political palliatives."[69]

Whereas the reforming leader tends to support economic and material development without altering the political system, the revolutionary leader begins with and emphasizes the political dimension of change. Anouar Abdel-Malek writes that, in Nasser's case, "the principal blow was struck on the sociopolitical level"; Majid Khadduri asserts that "the Revolution's fundamental achievements were essentially political"; and Maxime Rodinson concludes that under Nasser the political structure was "completely reshaped."[70] The political change can be seen at two levels. The first level concerns the patterns of relations through which the political leader personally wields power. As is documented above, Nasser transformed these relations at several key points. The second level involves the more general and collective distribution of power, reflected primarily in the class structure. During Nasser's rule, the Egyptian class structure underwent radical change as the influence of the former ruling class, which was composed of both the landed and the industrial aristocracy, was destroyed. The gaps between the various classes were consequently greatly narrowed as a professional middle class composed of technocrats, managers, and professionals took control. It is on this basis that one observer has referred to the Egyptian revolution as "the first true revolution in the Middle East."[71]

Nasser carefully referred to the Egyptian revolution as *thawra* ("a persisting and lasting event") rather than as *inqilab* ("an overthrow"), since he recognized the need for the movement to press forward continually.[72] This forward movement, of course, was essential in order to prevent the old power structure from slowly seeping back into prominence. The modernizing head of government is

---

[68]Nasser, The Charter, as quoted in J. C. Hurewitz, *Middle East Politics: The Military Dimension* (New York: Frederick A. Praeger, 1969), p. 133.

[69]Keith Wheelock, *Nasser's New Egypt* (London: Atlantic Books, 1960), p. 38.

[70]For these quotations, see Anouar Abel-Malek, *Egypt: Military Society,* trans. by Charles Lam Markmann (New York: Vintage Books, 1968), p. 157; Majid Khadduri, *Political Trends in the Arab World* (Baltimore, Md.: Johns Hopkins University Press, 1970), p. 162; and Rodinson, "The Political System," p. 111.

[71]Harry Hopkins, *Egypt: The Crucible* (Boston: Houghton Mifflin Co., 1969), p. 181.

[72]Lacouture, *The Demigods,* p. 94.

especially exposed to this danger since "the bourgeoisie attempts to minimize its losses by puffing up the leader. It cuts off some of its own flesh and feeds it to the hero to fatten him up, blow him up, lull him to sleep. Soon enough the deified leader will proclaim the revolution fulfilled in him and the class struggle resolved in him."[73]

In Nasser's Egypt, the old forces of patrimonialism made gallant efforts to infiltrate back into power, and in the late 1950s they were backed and provisioned by the wealthy bourgeoisie. Nasser confronted this challenge and overcame it with his nationalization programs of 1960–1963. This effectively tore the web of families who were the proponents of traditionalism. They had managed to survive the land reform program, since their control spanned industry and trade as well as land.

Although he successfully uprooted the traditional power structure in Egypt, Nasser never managed to establish a new sociopolitical system. Because of the resilience of the old system and the limited resources at hand, the Egyptian president felt it necessary to maintain an authoritarian technocracy, which alienated the intelligentsia and stifled creativity in the society. He was unable to broaden political participation, and therefore the revolutionary patterns he introduced at the center did not take root in the countryside. The resources and energies fruitlessly expended in activities against Israel and in Yemen seriously weakened his capacity to carry out social change in Egypt. Despite all this, Nasser survived and, although badly scarred, continued to fight for the transformation of his country. His achievements were impressive enough to distinguish him sharply from most Middle Eastern leaders, both past and present.

Nasser's two successors, Anwar Sadat and Husni Mubarak, moved away from Nasser's style of leadership and reintroduced traditional patrimonial rule. After cleverly outmaneuvering the other contenders for Nasser's mantle, Anwar Sadat became president of Egypt in May 1971. Once president, Sadat found himself under great domestic and international pressure. Despite this, he managed to maintain himself in power for over a decade. He made up for his lack of Nasser-like charisma through a brilliant ability to make astute political moves at precisely the right times. While floating somewhere above political factions, he often darted down to center stage to announce dramatic political decisions—decisions that left the world gasping. The most noteworthy of these moves included the expulsion of Soviet advisors from Egyptian soil in July 1972, the initiation of the fourth Arab-Israeli war in October 1973, the historic trip to Israel in November 1977, and the announcement of a framework for peace with Israel at Camp David in September 1978. Whenever domestic political discontent threatened his government, President Sadat responded by announcing a major new policy with special flair and flamboyance.

Despite his dramatic foreign policy activities, Anwar Sadat was a traditional patrimonial leader par excellence. In his first book, published in 1957, Anwar Sadat penned a line that could serve as a classic lead sentence in any manual on patrimonial rule: "In Egypt, personalities have always been more important than

---

[73]Ibid., p. 293.

164 CHAPTER 5

political programs."[74] Sadat acted accordingly by drawing his family and friends into the center of the political system. Besides his wife, Jihan, and his brother-in-law Mahmud Abu Wafia, who were involved in political machinations, two of his daughters married members of the wealthiest aristocratic families in the country, the families of Sayyid Marei and Osman Ahmad Osman.

Anwar Sadat loved the pomp and circumstance so important to traditional patrimonial leaders. He had a dozen presidential villas and wore field marshal's uniforms designed by Pierre Cardin. He spent more time with the international jet set than with his own people. The enormous gap here was visible in September 1979, when Frank Sinatra performed a concert before the Sphinx for one of Jihan Sadat's favorite charities. The spectacle was attended by "over 400 partygoers from the United States and Europe who enjoyed what was probably the most extravagant social affair Egypt had seen since before the 1952 revolution that overthrew King Farouk." Before dedicating a song to Mrs. Sadat, Sinatra ventured an opinion about President Sadat: "He really is a great cat. I just adore him." Before the show, the wealthy international guests dined on cold lobster, veal, and crepes. "Outside the enclosure's flapping cloth walls, a cordon of white-uniformed policemen, some with automatic rifles, shoved away curious Egyptians from a nearby village.[75]

Between 1971 and 1981, political unrest broke periodically to the surface in Egypt. In June 1981, serious riots between Muslims and Copts flared again in the working-class districts of Cairo. By the fall of that year, Sadat was hard-pressed politically as signs of widespread disaffection and alienation bubbled ominously to the surface. Muslim associations and organizations multiplied in number and size, and an estimated 40,000 private mosques served as centers for critical discussion of the problems that plagued Egypt.

In the first week of September, President Sadat suddenly ordered a major crackdown on all sources of potential opposition. Among other things, his police arrested over 1,500 people, closed down 7 publications, and moved to place 40,000 "free" mosques under government control. Sadat angrily justified this crackdown by stating that it represented an attack against "indiscipline" that had come to dominate Egyptian society. This was the very word that the shah of Iran had often used to justify the repressive policies of his regime in the years just prior to the Iranian revolution.

On October 6, 1981, one month after he had carried out his political crackdown, President Anwar Sadat was reviewing a military parade held to commemorate Egyptian successes in the October 1973 war. At approximately 12:40 P.M., four Egyptian soldiers leaped from a truck and charged the presidential reviewing stand in a lightning grenade and automatic weapon attack. In this surprise attack, the soldiers assassinated Anwar Sadat as he stood to greet them on a public stage before the eyes of the world.

In the end, Anwar Sadat was a patrimonial leader who became a pseudomonarch and who governed Egypt according to his interpretation of modern, Western pomp and circumstance. According to one informed Egyptian scholar,

[74]Anwar el-Sadat, *Revolt on the Nile* (New York: John Day Co., 1957), p. 27.

[75]The quotations in this paragraph are taken from *The New York Times,* September 28, 1979.

"Sadat lost control of the internal situation and was, in response perhaps, turning into a neurotic despot slashing right and left."[76] He shifted from being "the paternalistic pious head of the Egyptian family to the single-minded, threatened, vindictive dictator who eliminates any criticism of him and any opposition to his programs. . . . Two processes were at work in the meantime: a Sadatization of Egypt on the one hand, and a deification of Sadat on the other—the rebirth of the Egyptian pharaoh."[77]

Sadat's successor, Husni Mubarak, took office as president of Egypt in October 1981. An air force officer for twenty-five years and the loyal vice president of Sadat for six years, Mubarak was closely associated with Sadat and his policies.

Initially, Mubarak consciously avoided the opulent and visible patrimonial style of President Sadat. He sought to attack corruption and to seek to compromise with the various opposition forces. By the mid-1990s, however, Egypt witnessed the "Sadatization" of Mubarak who took on the political style of his predecessor. Traditional patrimonialism prevails. Although President Mubarak does not have a large extended family, his nuclear family is heavily involved in politics and in business. His two sons, Gamal and Ala, for example, wield considerable influence. Gamal, the younger son, is often mentioned as a possible heir apparent. A former banker in London, he now chairs the important Egyptian-American Businessmen's Council. Ala uses his family name to great advantage in the world of business and finance. Mubarak's wife, Suzanne, is a major political force who maintains close connections with several cabinet ministers.

As Muslim opposition forces challenged the Egyptian government over issues of corruption, inequality, injustice, and political participation in the 1990s, Mubarak resorted to increasing repression to maintain control. By 1999, the harshness of this response had created an environment of confrontational politics that cast a dark cloud over the future of the Mubarak regime. Internationally, the Egyptian president aligned his country closely with the United States, adopting U.S. objectives in regional issues such as Persian Gulf policy and the Arab-Israeli conflict.

Although Husni Mubarak has exhibited surprising political resiliency and political longevity, his return to traditional patrimonialism in the face of Egypt's deepening demographic, economic, and social problems gave reason for little optimism for Egypt's political future at the dawn of the twenty-first century.

Leaders and Change: A Concluding Perspective

Our case studies of selected Middle Eastern leaders indicate the extraordinary persistence of patrimonial politics in the area. Even revolutionary and charismatic leaders such as Ataturk and Nasser retained characteristics of the patrimonial style. This is one reason why it is supremely difficult to transform national

---

[76]Fadwa El Guindi, "The Killing of Sadat and After," *Middle East Insight* 2 (January/February 1983): 23.

[77]Ibid.

power structures and to introduce political development in Middle Eastern countries: Can one build new political systems using old tools?

Kemal Ataturk and Gamal Abdel Nasser did indeed introduce significant change at various points in their social and political systems. Although it has become common to question the depths of the changes they wrought, there can be little doubt that they were in many ways revolutionaries. But they had unusual advantages. Both gathered great personal and political momentum because of their impeccable credentials as nationalists. They had successfully defied and defeated great European colonialist powers. And both men had an impressive charisma that is seldom seen in the Middle East.

In succeeding their illustrious predecessors, Ismet Inonu and Anwar Sadat were faced with the need to continue and deepen ongoing programs of revolutionary change. Both men chose initially to liberalize and to expand political participation in their societies. Lacking the charisma of Ataturk and Nasser, they sought to build a broader platform of legitimacy and support. Ironically, in the process of doing so they oversaw the gradual decline of revolutionary programs in their societies. The traditional power groups and classes that had been defeated and dismantled by Ataturk and Nasser regrouped and returned to influence. In the case of Egypt especially, the negative dimensions of patrimonial politics seeped back into the nooks and crannies of the system.

The challenges of the day are such that patrimonial modes of rule alone will not enable Middle Eastern leaders to satisfy the demands of new social groups and classes. Although this style of rule is so strong that it will perhaps always be present in the Middle East in one form or another, it must be exercised in the context of a strengthened capacity to generate and absorb transforming change. Traditional patrimonial monarchs (such as the last shah of Iran), who promote limited change, provide only a limited answer to the challenge. Modern patrimonial moderates (such as the late Anwar Sadat of Egypt), who stifle political development while promoting a certain level of modernization, are also unable to confront the mounting social problems of their societies successfully. In this context, it is not accidental that both the shah and Sadat met grim personal and political fates. Even newer and bigger versions of the Ataturks and Nassers would have a difficult time in the contemporary world of the Middle East. The problems are many; strong but sensitive leaders are few.

SELECTED BIBLIOGRAPHY

Abrahamian, Ervand. *Iran Between Two Revolutions*. Princeton, N.J.: Princeton University Press, 1982.

Ansari, Hamied. *Egypt: The Stalled Society*. Albany: State University of New York Press, 1986.

Baker, Raymond William. *Sadat and After: Struggles for Egypt's Political Soul*. Cambridge, Mass.: Harvard University Press, 1990.

Baktiari, Bahman. *Parliamentary Politics in Revolutionary Iran*. Gainesville: University Press of Florida, 1996.

Beattie, Kirk J. *Egypt During the Nasser Years: Ideology, Politics, and Civil Society*. Boulder, Colo: Westview Press, 1994.

Bill, James A., and William Roger Louis, eds. *Musaddiq, Iranian Nationalism, and Oil.* Austin: University of Texas Press, 1988.

Gasiorowski, Mark. *U.S. Foreign Policy and the Shah.* Ithaca and London: Cornell University Press, 1991.

Goldschmidt, Arthur, Jr. *Modern Egypt: The Formation of a Nation-State.* Boulder, Colo.: Westview Press, 1988.

Heikal, Mohamed. *The Cairo Documents.* Garden City, N.Y.: Doubleday and Co., 1973.

Hooglund, Eric. *Reform and Revolution in Rural Iran.* Austin: University of Texas Press, 1982.

Kinross, Lord. *Ataturk: The Rebirth of a Nation.* London: Weidenfeld and Nicolson, 1964.

Limbert, John. *Iran: At War with History.* Boulder, Colo.: Westview Press, 1987.

Mottahedeh, Roy P. *The Mantle of the Prophet.* New York: Pantheon, 1986.

Ozbudun, Ergun. *Social Change and Political Participation in Turkey.* Princeton, N.J.: Princeton University Press, 1976.

Springborg, Robert. *Mubarak's Egypt: Fragmentation of the Political Order.* Boulder, Colo.: Westview Press, 1989.

Volkan, Vamik, and Norman Itzkowitz. *The Immortal Ataturk: A Psychobiography.* Chicago: University of Chicago Press, 1984.

Waterbury, John. *The Egypt of Nasser and Sadat: The Political Economy of Two Regimes.* Princeton, N.J.: Princeton University Press, 1983.

Weinbaum, Marvin G. *Egypt and the Politics of U.S. Economic Aid.* Boulder, Colo.: Westview Press, 1986.

Chapter 6

Institutions of Government: Militaries, Bureaucracies, and Legislatures

Third World political systems are characterized by the dominance of policy-implementing institutions, including the military and the bureaucracy, over policy-making structures such as legislatures, political parties, and formal interest groups. According to a leading scholar of development administration, "The relative weakness of political organs means that the political function tends to be appropriated, in considerable measure, by bureaucrats."[1] Military officers have, if anything, exceeded bureaucrats in their zeal to appropriate political functions. However, the balance between governmental institutions of administration and coercion on the one hand and political structures on the other varies from one region of the Third World to another. In Africa and the Middle East, governmental institutions are especially predominant, or, in the words of an Arab intellectual, "The State means everything and it monopolizes almost all facilities, while the society means very little."[2] In Latin America and East Asia, political institutions have had greater success in expanding their authority. A simple measure of the balance between state administrative institutions and structures that facilitate political participation is the presence of legislative bodies. In the mid-1970s, an observer of comparative legislative development noted that "the overwhelming number of countries without legislatures are in Africa and the Middle East."[3] Constitutional government, which requires

---

[1]Fred W. Riggs, "Bureaucrats and Political Development: A Paradoxical View," in *Bureaucracy and Political Development,* ed. by Joseph La Palombara (Princeton, N.J.: Princeton University Press, 1963), p. 120.

[2]Bassam Tibi, "Political Freedom in Arab Societies," *Arab Studies Quarterly* 6: 3 (Summer 1984): 225.

[3]Joseph La Palombara, *Politics Within Nations* (Englewood Cliffs, N.J.: Prentice-Hall, 1974), p. 113.

the differentiation of separate structures of government and politics in order to perform a wide range of functions, clearly lags in the Middle East.

Effective institutions of political participation that could vigorously defend personal political freedoms have yet to take root in many countries of the region. This is due in part to factors beyond the control of the countries themselves. In much of the Third World in the nineteenth and twentieth centuries, the twin phenomena of defensive modernization militated against the institutionalized expression of political demands by the population. Local rulers such as Muhammad Ali of Egypt and Ahmad Bey of Tunisia sought through defensive modernization to develop their armies and administrative apparati to defend their territories from European encroachments, and then colonialism itself.

Defensive modernizers did not seek to expand political participation. They were instead intent on rapid military and bureaucratic development to counter foreign threats. Also, the societies they sought to modernize were dominated by traditional elements who, if permitted to engage in politics, would have challenged the authority of the defensive modernizers themselves. Similarly, colonial rulers had scant desire for expanding the political awareness of subject peoples. As Charles Issawi has observed, "No real democracy could develop in Egypt, Iraq, Jordan, Lebanon, and Syria as long as British or French armies of occupation were the determining factor in all political matters. . . . Nor was the situation of unoccupied countries, such as Iran and Turkey, very much better, for both have lived under the shadow of two powerful neighbors."[4]

Examples of colonialist intervention to contain the expansion of political participation in Middle Eastern countries are legion. The British and French stood behind the autocratic Egyptian ruler Khedive Isma'il when in 1878 he was challenged by the Assembly of Notables that sought to restrict monarchical absolutism. In 1942, British tanks surrounded King Farouk's palace in Cairo to force the dismissal of an elected, pro-Axis government. In 1924, the British even refused permission to conservative traditionalist Amir Abdullah of Transjordan to hold elections for a parliament. Instead, the British resident supported the creation of an appointed legislative council to serve as a rubber stamp for the executive. "At this particular moment in Jordan's history," according to one of the country's leading political scientists, "the British intended to retard, as they indeed continued to do later, rather than advance the cause of parliamentary government."[5] On the creation of Iraq in the wake of World War I, the British rejected demands for participatory government by nationalist leaders and instead installed Amir Abdullah's brother Faisal on the throne. Shortly thereafter they employed the Royal Air Force to bomb concentrations of tribesmen in the Middle Euphrates region in what was one of the first examples in history of an imperial power using an air force against guerrilla insurgents.

---

[4]Charles Issawi, "Economic and Social Foundations of Democracy in the Middle East," *International Affairs* 32 (1956), reprinted in *The Arab World's Legacy* (Princeton: The Darwin Press, 1981), pp. 243–244.

[5]Kamel S. Abu Jaber, "The Legislature of the Hashemite Kingdom of Jordan: A Study in Political Development," *The Muslim World*, LIX 3–4 (July–October 1969): 220–250, reprinted in Jacob M. Landau, ed., *Man, State, and Society in the Middle East* (New York: Praeger Publications, 1972), p. 93.

The French record of hostility toward democratic practices in its Middle Eastern mandated territories is also notable. They deposed the popularly endorsed King Faisal in Damascus in 1920 and replaced him with a puppet government. Like the British in Iraq, the French in Syria were then forced in 1925 to intervene militarily to put down a revolt against the government they had imposed. In both Syria and Lebanon, the French employed divide-and-rule tactics to exacerbate religious and ethnic tensions in order to frustrate the emergence of unified, mass-based nationalist movements. The last gasp of British and French imperialism in the Middle East was their invasion, along with Israel, of Egypt in 1956, a military action intended to topple the overwhelmingly popular government of Gamal Abdel Nasser. While the Middle East is by no means unique by virtue of its having had to endure foreign interventions (many of which have been intended to frustrate collective national political action), the degree of intervention is singular. "Because of its focal geographic position at the juncture of three continents and two oceans, the Middle East has been, throughout recorded history, the most frequently invaded region of the globe."[6]

The end of colonialism in the region was not accompanied by a termination of interventionism. Instead, the United States and the Soviet Union, who in the 1940s and 1950s supplanted British and French domination, perpetuated the practice, albeit in modified form. The CIA and KGB have had significant and sustained covert involvements in the domestic affairs of the region's states. The overthrow of the popular nationalist government of Muhammad Musaddiq in Iran in 1953 has been pointed to by CIA operatives as one of their greatest triumphs.[7] Less trumpeted by those same CIA agents were their bungled attempts to subvert the Syrian government in the mid-1950s and their failed efforts to topple Nasser in Egypt.[8]

The Middle East remains the most active theater of operations in the Third World for American intelligence activities. Direct military interventions by the United States against Lebanon, Syria, Iran, and Libya occurred during the Reagan administration. Operation Desert Storm, launched against Iraqi-occupied Kuwait and Iraq itself on January 17, 1991, involved the greatest concentration of U.S. military force since World War II. Since then, the U.S. has pursued a policy of "dual containment" of Iran and Iraq that has intermittently spilled over into actual combat with the latter and which in early 1998 nearly resulted in yet another major round of fighting.

The Soviet Union, prior to its collapse, also actively and directly intervened in the area. The most dramatic case of its coercive intervention occurred in Afghanistan during the decade beginning in December 1979. In January 1986,

---

[6]Dankart A. Rustow, "The Military in Middle Eastern Society and Politics," in *The Military in the Middle East: Problems in Society and Government,* ed. by Sydney Nettleton Fisher (Columbus: Ohio State University Press, 1963), p. 5.

[7]Kermit Roosevelt, *Countercoup: The Struggle for the Control of Iran* (New York: McGraw-Hill, 1979).

[8]See Miles Copeland, *Game of Nations* (New York: Simon & Schuster, 1969); William Eveland, *Ropes of Sand: America's Failure in the Middle East* (New York: Norton and Co., 1980); and Douglas Little, "Cold War and Covert Action: The United States and Syria, 1945–1958," *The Middle East Journal* 44 (Winter 1990): 51–75.

the Soviets along with East German and Cuban forces, sided with the pro-Moscow faction of the ruling Yemeni Socialist Party in a civil war that erupted in South Yemen after a failed assassination attempt on President Ali Nasir Muhammad.

The threat of violence hanging over Middle Eastern governments is due not only to the actions of outside powers. Indeed, the region has been consumed by warfare between and within states almost without cease since World War II. In the 1980s and 1990s, civil wars or violent insurgencies have occurred in Algeria, Egypt, Lebanon, Sudan, Iraq, Iran, Morocco, Syria, Turkey, Yemen, and territories occupied by Israel. One of the world's most intense and costly wars in the twentieth century in terms of casualties, destruction, expense, and duration was fought between Iran and Iraq from 1980 to 1988. Two and a half years after that war ended, Iraq was devastated by Operation Desert Storm. Between 1948 and 1992, inter- and intrastate conflicts in the region resulted in 1,825,000 casualties, displaced 13,600,000 Middle Easterners from their homes, and cost an estimated $2.3 trillion.[9] Ballistic missiles have been used for military purposes ten times in the world since 1973—all but two of those firings were in the Middle East (the other two were in Afghanistan and Bosnia).[10] "With the exception of North Korea virtually all of the world's concern about weapons proliferation focuses on countries in the greater Middle East . . . This is the region where there is most expectation that weapons of mass destruction will be used in war."[11]

Middle Eastern governments can reasonably expect to employ their militaries against neighboring states or their own populations; they therefore prepare for such eventualities. In Israel, over half the industrial labor force is employed in defense industries.[12] The military is by far the largest employer in the region. One out of every fifty people is a soldier. "If irregular forces (like the Revolutionary Guards in Iran) and militias (like those in Lebanon) are included with regular soldiers, there may be as many as 10 million people in military service in the Middle East."[13] Military spending increased 1,600 percent in real terms in the Middle East from the mid-1960s to the mid-1980s. In the 1980s, three-quarters of all Third World arms agreements involved a country in the Middle East. During that decade, the region spent $600 billion on the military. Saudi Arabia and Iraq alone accounted for 30 percent of the world's arms purchases.[14] Between 1972 and 1988, Middle Eastern countries spent more than 11

---

[9]Saad Eddin Ibrahim, "Liberalization and Democratization in the Arab World: An Overview," in Rex Brynen, Bahgat Korany, and Paul Noble, eds., *Political Liberalization and Democratization in the Arab World*, vol. 1. (Boulder, Colo.: Lynne Rienner, 1995), pp. 29–57.

[10]Aaron Karp, "The Demise of the Middle East Arms Race," *The Washington Quarterly*, 18, 4 (1995): 29–51.

[11]Geoffrey Kemp and Robert E. Harkavy, *Strategic Geography and the Changing Middle East* (Washington, D.C: Brookings Institution Press, 1997), p. xiii.

[12]Yoram Peri, *Between Battles and Ballots: Israeli Military in Politics* (Cambridge: Cambridge University Press, 1983), p. 22.

[13]"Living by the Sword—A Primer," *Middle East Report* 144 (January–February 1987): 23.

[14]Robert Bailey, "Defence," *Middle East Economic Digest Special Report* (October 31, 1987); and Alasdair Drysdale and Raymond A. Hinnebusch, *Syria and the Middle East Peace Process* (New York: Council on Foreign Relations Press, 1991), pp. 163, 218.

percent of their gross national product (GNP) on arms—compared with the 2.3 percent spent in Latin America and the 6.3 percent in Asian developing countries. By comparison, the Pentagon's budget for weapons acquisition in 1992 was 1.6 percent of the U.S. GNP.[15] Although military expenditures have declined globally and in the Middle East in the 1990s, a leading American analyst notes that "at least in the near term, Israel and its neighbors will continue to spend some 20 percent to 30 percent of their central government expenditures, as much as 10 percent of their GDP, and as much as 10 percent of their annual hard currency imports on military forces. . . ."[16] The preponderance of militaries in labor forces and in economies more generally, coupled with the effects of the generalized perception that political violence is inevitable, have perpetuated the imbalance between political institutions and the military.

According to Leon Carl Brown, for over two centuries the Middle East has been plagued not only by military confrontations but also by what he calls "the penetration of its political systems."[17] The protracted decline of the Ottoman Empire invited the European powers to become involved in its politics. Since independence, interference by states of the region in their neighbors' politics has become commonplace. Unassimilated ethnic and religious minority groups and underground political oppositions provide fifth columns through which such influence is wielded.

Governments typically try to counter penetration of their political orders by restricting political freedoms. When further extending the Emergency Decrees reimposed after almost a decade in abeyance and that enable the government to rule without reference to the constitution, President Mubarak in 1988 cited the threat of foreign subversion and the need to counter it. Similarly, one of King Hussein's advisors told an American author that restrictions on political freedoms were necessary in Jordan because there were too many foreign "lines" running through Jordan.[18] In 1986, the Kuwaiti parliament was prorogued, partly because of Saudi pressure and fear of Iranian subversion. Accompanying the dissolution of parliament was a crackdown on the comparatively freewheeling Kuwaiti press. Forty-nine journalists were arrested—all of them resident aliens. In the wake of the killings by Islamist militants of fifty-eight foreign tourists in Luxor, Egypt on November 17, 1997, President Mubarak lashed out at England for "harbouring terrorists." He was referring to England's unwillingness to extradite Islamists convicted of terrorist offenses by military courts in Egypt, an unwillingness based on the British assessment that those trials did not meet acceptable legal standards. Throughout the Middle East, rulers cite the example of Lebanon as what will happen if too much political freedom is allowed,

---

[15]Norman Kempster, "Hopes for Stopping Mideast Arms Race," *Los Angeles Times* (May 12, 1992), p. 2.

[16]Anthony H. Cordesman, *Perilous Prospects: The Peace Process and the Arab-Israeli Military Balance* (Boulder, Colo.: Westview Press, 1996), p. 2.

[17]Leon Carl Brown, *International Politics and the Middle East: Old Rules, Dangerous Game* (Princeton, N.J.: Princeton University Press, 1984).

[18]Arthur R. Day, *East Bank/West Bank: Jordan and the Prospects for Peace* (New York: Council on Foreign Relations, 1986), pp. 44–45.

the implication being that citizens will seek foreign allies against their domestic enemies and by so doing bring about a descent into anarchy. Thus the intensity of cross-border interactions in the Middle East results in a widely held belief that political freedoms are bound to be abused by foreign enemies working with fifth-column elements. The most common solution to this problem is for regimes to not permit independent political organization or expression.

The dominance of state structures over institutions of political participation can also be accounted for in the Middle East, as elsewhere in the Third World, by the absence of social and economic prerequisites. Charles Issawi's list of such requirements includes reasonable levels of economic development, industrialization, the egalitarian distribution of wealth, homogeneity of language and religion, educational attainments, and a "habit of co-operative association." Writing in the 1950s, he concluded that by these measures "in the Middle East the economic and social soil is still not deep enough to enable political democracy to strike root and flourish."[19]

Other observers emphasize development deficiencies that take the form of vacuums into which state structures have expanded, thereby stunting the growth of political institutions. For some, the vacuum is the absence of a middle class, or bourgeoisie, that spearheaded the drive for democracy in the West. In Turkey, for example, "the state or the Kemalist cadre who controlled the state apparatus was the driving force behind this scheme of modernisation. In the absence of a modernising bourgeoisie, the bureaucracy had shouldered the task of nation-building."[20] The destabilization of Turkish politics since the mid-1950s is partially the consequence of the political challenge launched by the entrepreneurial middle class against the supremacy of the bureaucracy and the military.

Absence of political institutions at the early stages of political development perpetuates administrative and military supremacy. Once they begin to perform the functions typically associated with parties, legislatures, and interest groups, bureaucracies and militaries render those political institutions irrelevant. Participatory impulses are diverted into administrative bodies, "which not only makes independent political parties functionally redundant but 'politicizes' the bureaucracy."[21] According to Manfred Halpern, "Bureaucracies in the Middle East not only administer laws, but, in the absence of parliamentary institutions, usually fashion them."[22] In Sudan, for example, "The bureaucratic sector is dominant and all powerful. There is a grave developmental imbalance between it on the one hand, and parliaments and political parties . . . on the other."[23]

[19]Issawi, "Economic and Social Foundations of Democracy," pp. 244, 258.

[20]Dofu Ergil, "Turkey" in *Electoral Politics in the Middle East: Issues, Voters and Elites*, ed. by Jacob M. Landau, Ergun Özbudun, and Frank Tachau (London: Croom Helm, 1980), p. 13.

[21]Lisa Anderson, "The State in the Middle East and North Africa," *Comparative Politics* 20: 1 (October 1987): 8.

[22]Manfred Halpern, *The Politics of Social Change in the Middle East and North Africa* (Princeton, N.J.: Princeton University Press, 1963), p. 340.

[23]Mukhtar al-Assam, "Bureaucracy and Development in the Sudan," *Journal of Asian and African Studies* 24 (1989): 47.

State hegemony over political institutions may also result from factors specific to Middle Eastern political culture. There are doctrinal underpinnings and historical antecedents for an emphasis on military action and intervention by the military into politics. Islamic theology accords legitimacy to warfare. The doctrine of *jihad,* or holy struggle, sanctions military action to expand the *Dar al-Islam* (Abode of Islam) at the expense of the *Dar al-Harb* (Abode of War). Eliezer Be'eri sees a link between the historical existence of slave soldiers (mamlukes or janissaries) and the contemporary role of the military in the Middle East:

> Although one should not overestimate the influence on contemporary political life of an historical phenomenon, which ceased to exist more than a hundred years ago, neither should one disregard the influence on recent developments of relationships which prevailed uninterruptedly for 2 thousand years. . . . In Middle-Eastern society, where there is ample and long precedence of an officer corps separate from the rest of the populace, the corporateness of the officer corps is to a great extent conditioned by its history.[24]

Other scholars dispute the claim that the slave-soldier tradition of rule has contemporary relevance and that contemporary Middle Eastern officer corps are corporate entities. Fuad Khuri, for example, emphasizes that contemporary military institutions can be traced to Western penetration and resultant state-building rather than to earlier antecedents in the classical Islamic empires. "Except for Egypt, Morocco, Turkey and Iran, which had a longer history of professional militarism (dating to the nineteenth century), armed forces, as specialized institutions, came up only after World War I when many of the countries of the Middle East were made separate states under colonial tutelage or protection. Establishing an army or a police force then was part of an effort to build state institutions."[25]

Alasdair Drysdale has demonstrated that assumptions about the legacy of military traditions even over much shorter periods may be misleading. Under the French mandate, minorities, particularly Alawis, were overrepresented in the Syrian officer corps as part of a strategy to suppress the nationalist movement. After the mid-1960s, Alawi officers again came to dominate not only the military but all other key structures of the state and the Ba'th party itself. However, Drysdale observes, there is not an unbroken connection between the colonial and contemporary periods. In the first five postindependence classes of officer training school, some 80 percent of all graduates were Sunni Arabs, compared with less than one-half prior to independence. In the 1950s and early 1960s, the Syrian military was "genuinely an agent of national integration in an otherwise fragmented society, a national symbol in a precarious republic."[26] Sub-

---

[24]Eliezer Be'eri, *Army Officers in Arab Politics and Society* (Jerusalem: Israel Universities Press, 1969), p. 298.

[25]Fuad I. Khuri, "The Study of Civil-Military Relations in Modernizing Societies in the Middle East: A Critical Assessment," in *Soldiers, Peasants, and Bureaucrats: Civil-Military Relations in Communist and Modernizing Societies,* ed. by Roman Kolkowicz and Andrzej Korbonski (London: George Allen and Unwin, 1982), p. 10.

[26]Alasdair Drysdale, "The Syrian Armed Forces in National Politics: The Role of the Geographic and Ethnic Periphery," in ibid., p. 58.

sequent deterioration of the Syrian military into a vehicle of minoritarian domination came about as a result of political conflict in the mid-1960s. The contemporary Syrian officer corps should not, therefore, according to Drysdale, be interpreted as a legacy of colonial divide-and-rule policies. It is instead the product of contemporary politics.

Evidence from other Middle Eastern countries supports the contention that the military has intervened in politics not because of its corporate, separate nature but precisely because it is insufficiently differentiated from society. Recruits into the Egyptian officer corps after nominal independence in 1936, such as Nasser and Sadat, joined not because their families had a tradition of military service but because the corps provided a channel of upward mobility. The army in Egypt, and elsewhere in the region, has until very recently not been so much a distinctive, separate institution as just another part of the state bureaucratic structure. Attitudes of Arab military officers as measured by a content analysis of their journals suggests that "the value orientations of the military do not seem to differ from the adult male behavior expectations."[27] The Prussian officer corps, which emerged in the nineteenth century as the first European force to be professional both in self-conception and by virtue of being above politics, provides a prototype yet to be adopted in its entirety in the Middle East.

Military institutions created in the nineteenth and twentieth centuries as part of the formation of modern states in the Middle East were departures from previous practices, but they may nevertheless have been affected by indigenous traditions. Contemporary political institutions, essentially Western in origin, have probably also been influenced by local traditions that govern relations between rulers and ruled.

In the Arab polities of the Gulf, for example, explanations given by rulers when creating consultative assemblies have been couched in Islamic and tribal terms. The Quran enjoins rulers to consult prominent persons on issues of public concern, while "Arab tribal tradition also requires the chief (shaykh) of each tribe to consult notables and senior members of the tribe about their affairs. . . . Without consultation, no allegiance is owed to a chief who does not 'sit in majlis' with the notables and senior members of the tribe to exchange views on all matters of public concern."[28]

However, the Islamic and tribal injunctions to consult have not, through history, served to buttress institutions of effective widespread political participation, nor are they presently doing so. The tradition of consultation restricted that privilege to prominent personages; it did not make provision for an organized, loyal opposition, nor did it provide for representation as opposed to consultation. According to Michael Hudson, "Tribal democracy may be as remote from contemporary forms of government in the Arab world as the New England town meeting is to modern government in America."[29]

---

[27]Khuri, "The Study of Civil-Military Relations," p. 13.

[28]Majid Khadduri, "Foreword," in J. E. Peterson, *The Arab Gulf States: Steps Toward Political Participation* (New York: Praeger, 1988), pp. ix–x.

[29]Michael Hudson, *Arab Politics: The Search for Legitimacy* (New Haven, Conn.: Yale University Press, 1977), p. 91.

The comparative lack of vigor of participatory political organizations may reflect not only the continuing impact of the tradition of consultation rather than representation but also the influence of nondemocratic authority structures that obtain in a wide variety of social settings, including families, religious organizations, professional associations, voluntary political organizations, neighborhood groups, and so on. "Social scientists," according to the Egyptian sociologist Saad Eddin Ibrahim, "have increasingly come to the realization that other societal institutions must provide a 'democratic infrastructure' for the political system if democracy is to succeed. The family, in particular, is cited as pivotal in this regard. Individuals socialized in an authoritarian type of family are not expected to enhance democratic practices in the political sphere of society at large."[30] Andrea Rugh argues that "the character of social institutions like the family in Egypt tends to promote an authoritarian rather than a democratic style of leadership, with a policy that acquiesces to rather than challenges that leadership. The leaders as father-figures in any case tend to take it as a personal offense when their 'children' become unruly and unwilling to submit to the authority of their elders."[31] While it would be incorrect to assume that behavioral patterns characteristic of small social units are reproduced unchanged in much larger ones, President Sadat's behavior suggests that some connection may exist. He referred to himself as "Father of the Egyptian Family" and chastised his critics as errant children. When that admonition failed of its objective, he dissolved parliament, banned opposition parties, and then, just prior to his assassination, threw some 1,600 opposition political activists in jail.

Throughout the Middle East, autonomous, formally organized political activity is rare. Voluntary associations are closely monitored by governments that require "individuals desiring to form an association [to] submit a formal request to the government, usually the Ministry of the Interior." However, Kevin Dwyer adds, "Either with the authorization or without it, the association is likely to be under constant observation . . . and control or harassment from above become more onerous the more controversial are the group's aims."[32] Local government in the area with power to tax and spend is notable by its absence. Cairo, for example, did not have its own municipal government until the mid-twentieth century. In most countries, administrative subdivisions are run by officials appointed from the capital. Where local elections do occur, they tend to be dominated by governmental organizations or by traditional social units, such as tribes, on which government relies when its power is insufficient to govern districts or towns directly. There are, in sum, few arenas in which those aspiring to play public political roles could engage in open, participatory politics.

It is important to note, however, that while democratic practices in formal political institutions are restricted, there is not a complete absence of pluralism

---

[30]Saad Eddin Ibrahim, "The Socio-Economic Requisites of Democracy," in *Democracy in Egypt. Cairo Papers in Social Science* 1, 2, ed. by Ali Dessouki (1978), p. 59.

[31]Andrea Rugh, *Family in Contemporary Egypt* (Cairo: American University in Cairo Press, 1985), p. 45.

[32]Kevin Dwyer, *Arab Voices: The Human Rights Debate in the Middle East* (New York: Routledge, 1991), pp. 146–147.

in the political system, nor is the state able to interfere in all aspects of people's lives. The private sphere is populated by innumerable kin and communal groupings, and the public sphere—that which is dominated by the state—is, by Western standards, relatively constricted. As Suad Joseph observes:

> The organization of society is much more contested in the Middle East than in the West. Middle Eastern states and their rulers have not succeeded as have their Western counterparts in imposing their hegemony. Kinship and communal power flourish: rulers rely on them as a mainstay of their power, while citizens turn to them to protect themselves from state repression or to compensate for inefficient administration. The domestic sphere is a lively arena of social, political and economic action in the Middle East—far more so than in the West.[33]

The division between the private, domestic sphere and the public, governmental one means that even if democratic, egalitarian relations are obtained within the former, which they certainly are in many instances, they are often peripheral to formal politics, which is the government's domain.

Transformational Versus Adaptive Modernization

During the process of state formation, administrative and political institutions based on Western models have been superimposed on local structures and traditional practices. Results have been uneven. The tradition of military exploits may have facilitated the growth of newly created military organizations, but the long history of unified military and political leadership may also have impeded the professionalization of the officer corps and its subordination to civilian political leadership. Tribal and Islamic traditions of consultation have served as inspirations and justifications for the establishment of legislative and quasi-legislative bodies, but the consultative tradition has not yet been translated into truly representative parliaments.

Such uneven development is typical in the Third World. "The process of modernization in the developing countries is marked by the progressive creation of formally distinct social structures, adapted from Western models, to which differentiated political and administrative tasks are assigned. But in this process the older institutional base of a traditional society lingers on. Although eroded and embattled, it struggles to remain alive, to retain positions of influence."[34] Scholars of development disagree about the preferred outcome of this battle between Western-inspired, formal organizations on the one hand, and traditional institutions and practices on the other. The view held by many general theorists of development, such as Gabriel Almond and Bingham Powell, is that for stable governments capable of managing social and technical change to emerge, rational,

---

[33]Suad Joseph, "Women and Politics in the Middle East," *Merip Middle East Report* 138 (January–February 1986): 4.

[34]Riggs, "Bureaucrats and Political Development," p. 411.

secular organizations capable of harnessing the energies of large and expanding numbers of people must prevail. According to this position, traditional institutions are too small, too dependent on face-to-face interactions to cope adequately with the loads imposed by population growth, social mobilization, and technological advancements.[35] Modernization, in sum, requires the fundamental transformation of traditional political systems. One Middle East specialist who subscribes to this view is Manfred Halpern. He measures the political development of the Middle East in terms of the increasing coherence and efficacy of its militaries, bureaucracies, labor unions, parliaments, and other political institutions. With regard to political parties, for example, he writes:

> It has been customary to assume that political parties are not as important in the Middle East—or in other underdeveloped areas—as individual leaders and that few political parties matter at all. This view still had some validity during the 1940s. During the 1950s it became outdated. It is now quite apparent that individual leaders, however impressive their charismatic powers, will be unable to construct a single and enduring "political culture" unless they build effective political parties.[36]

An alternative interpretation, and one offered more frequently by Middle East specialists than by general theorists, is that traditional institutions and practices are sufficiently adaptable to cope with the increased loads imposed by modernization. By contrast, rational, secular, formal institutions, precisely because they are not rooted in Middle Eastern political cultures and traditions, will not attract or integrate large numbers of people and will never, therefore, function as they have in the West. John Peterson, who has studied political participation in the traditional Arab polities of the Gulf, asserts this:

> A prevalent assumption, based on Western historical experience, holds that these political systems must be evolutionary. According to this view, changing expectations and increasing demands for fuller participation in all aspects of political life eventually will force the transformation of these polities, either through a voluntary dispersion of power on the part of ruling families or by dissidence and revolution. This assumption, however, may display a normative bias towards conceptions of Western-style democracy as a more just form of government and therefore a desirable consequence of political development.[37]

Samir Khalaf, a Lebanese sociologist and leading advocate of the adaptive modernization school, argues that "the fact that an agency is traditional in form or structure does not imply that it must espouse traditional values, or that it must devote itself exclusively to passing on sacred values or preserving traditional lore and skills. Conversely, a seemingly modern institution . . . is no guarantee that man will undergo a drastic transformation in his spirit and that he

---

[35]See Gabriel A. Almond and G. Bingham Powell, Jr., *Comparative Politics: Systems, Process and Policy* (Boston: Little, Brown and Company, 1978).

[36]Manfred Halpern, *The Politics of Social Change*, 281.

[37]Peterson, *The Arab Gulf States*, 13.

will, after all, acquire modern life styles."[38] Khalaf has conducted research for many years on such entities as family business firms, formally organized family associations, religious and communal voluntary associations, and patrimonial political leaders in order to demonstrate how they "have been effective in meeting some of the secular and rational demands of modernization (i.e., openness, receptivity to change, the ability to cope with problems and imbalances) without diluting primordial loyalties or dehumanizing the social fabric of society."[39]

The adaptive modernization school has been influenced by the poor performance of Western-inspired institutions in the Middle East as compared with many indigenous ones. When Manfred Halpern was writing his major work on the Middle East in the late 1950s and early 1960s, Nasserism, Ba'thism, and radical Arab nationalism more generally were in their heydays. Each version was accompanied with elaborate ideological and organizational formulations. It appeared as if it would be only a matter of time before the last vestiges of traditionalism, including the tribal rulers of the Gulf shaikhdoms, would be swept away. History, however, proved these tribally based polities to be more tenacious than even Gamal Abdel Nasser could have anticipated. "Although twenty-five years ago the conventional wisdom held that such systems were curious anachronisms ready to collapse of their own weight, yielding to Nasserism and other brave new Arab ideologies, these systems have survived, while it is the latter that are endangered species."[40]

Survival of traditional institutions and practices is due to the fact that they have been favored by many ruling elites over modern, potentially radical competitors and to the fact that they have adapted to perform the new functions required in these increasingly complex sociopolitical systems. While political parties have continued to be banned in the Arab Gulf states, loose networks of friendships formed among and within "school acquaintances, cultural and sport clubs, and the mosque and, among the Shia, the funeral homes," have served as vehicles through which political demands have been formulated and pressed on governments.[41] Tribes have been particularly adaptable sociopolitical institutions. In Kuwait, for example, during the 1985 parliamentary primary elections, they proved to be much more effective organizations for selecting suitable candidates than ostensibly more modern groupings composed of merchants, Islamic fundamentalists, or the liberal/left nationalists.[42] Similarly, in the 1984 Jordanian parliamentary by-elections, tribes played a crucial role. "But there was

---

[38]Samir Khalaf, *Lebanon's Predicament* (New York: Columbia University Press, 1987), pp. 17–18.

[39]Ibid., p. 19.

[40]Malcolm C. Peck, *The United Arab Emirates: A Venture in Unity* (Boulder, Colo.: Westview Press, 1986), p. 125.

[41]Abdo I. Baaklini, "Legislatures in the Gulf Area: The Experience of Kuwait, 1961–1976," *International Journal of Middle East Studies* 14 (August 1982): 361. See also Fred H. Lawson, *Bahrain: The Modernization of Autocracy* (Boulder, Colo.: Westview Press, 1989), ch. 4.

[42]Nicolas Gavrielides, "Tribal Democracy: The Anatomy of Parliamentary Elections in Kuwait," in *Elections in the Middle East: Implications of Recent Trends*, ed. by Linda L. Layne (Boulder, Colo.: Westview Press, 1987), pp. 153–214.

no 'return to tribalism.' . . . New definitions are emerging about what it means to be a tribesman in Jordan today. . . . These new definitions of tribal identity are not contradictory with citizenship. . . ."[43]

The question does remain, however, as to whether such traditional institutions as tribes, *majlises* (councils), and informal networks can continue to cope with the increased loads imposed by modernization. If such institutions are utilized by regimes to protect their rule and to prevent the expansion of participation, they will not continue to adapt and will, therefore, ultimately be swept aside. As John Peterson states,

> The nostalgic and mythologized arguments that they [Arab Gulf states] possess a "tribal" or "social" democracy becomes increasingly specious as traditional ways disappear. . . . Such key democratic institutions as national councils are likely to be increasingly necessary as time goes on, particularly as growing populations and faster-paced lifestyles result in less personal contact between citizens, governments become more complex, access to rulers and ruling families decreases, and informal participation through traditional means, such as the *majlis*, or modern means, such as policy-influencing positions within the bureaucracy, loses relevance or possibility.[44]

Whatever ultimately occurs, for the foreseeable future the political systems of most Middle Eastern countries will continue to be heterogeneous. There will always be those composed of traditional institutions—some stagnating, others adapting to changing conditions—and composed of modern organizations, both those that become increasingly coherent, rational, and effective and those that languish: the unassimilated transplants, serving only as arenas in which traditional, ascriptive behavior continues unmodified. Modern, ostensibly rational organizations, however, have indisputably been wholly or partially incorporated into Middle Eastern political systems as essential elements of state-building. It is therefore important to examine both militaries and bureaucracies, as well as the weaker institutions of politics, the most widespread and probably most important of which are legislatures.

The Military

The Middle East is the most militarized region in the world as measured by size of military establishments in relation to population, and by military expenditures in proportion to economic output and governmental expenditures. In absolute terms, the military in the Middle East is larger and more expensive than anywhere else in the Third World. Turkey's 850,000-man army is the world's fifth-largest peacetime military establishment. The manpower of Iran's regular armed forces combined with the *pasdaran*—the Revolutionary Guard militia that was built up to some 350,000 men during the war with Iraq—is almost the size of

---

[43]Linda L. Layne, "Tribesmen as Citizens: Primordial Ties and Democracy in Rural Jordan," in Layne, *Elections in the Middle East,* p. 135.

[44]Peterson, *The Arab Gulf States,* pp. 22, 120–121.

Turkey's military. Iraq's army grew from 140,000 in 1977 to about 1 million in 1990. Israel now inducts into its military most males, who have to serve in the reserves until age fifty-five, making Israel's conscript army of over one-half million (including reserves) the world's largest as a percentage of its population.[45] The Egyptian military, which had declined to some 350,000 in 1977 from more than a half-million at the time of the 1973 October War, has since been built back up to some 450,000. Syria, with a population less than one-quarter that of Egypt's, has almost 400,000 men under arms plus 300,000 reserves.

Such massive military establishments consume a large share of these countries' resources. Of the ten developing countries identified by the International Monetary Fund (IMF) in 1991 as consistently spending more than 15 percent of their gross domestic product on the military, nine were in the Middle East.[46] Although the share of national income spent on the military by all Middle Eastern countries other than Kuwait has declined in the decade of the 1990s, that share remains high by global standards. In the Middle East as a whole, slightly less than 10 percent of GDP is spent on the military, more than twice the global average of 4.2 percent in 1996.[47] The Middle East is the largest market for the international arms trade, absorbing 43 percent of the world's total in the 1992–1994 period, and $15.3 billion of $39.9 billion of arms sold in 1996, or 40 percent of the total. The three top arms importing nations in the world since 1994 have all been in the Middle East. The world's biggest arms importer, which received deliveries worth $9.1 billion in 1996, is Saudi Arabia.[48]

Weapons at the disposal of the region's militaries are increasingly lethal. They now include the most advanced warplanes in the world, thermonuclear bombs, and short- and medium-range ballistic missiles capable of inflicting great destruction, as indicated by the devastation such missiles visited on Iranian cities during the final months of the Iran-Iraq war and on Israel and Saudi Arabia in the second Gulf war. Prior to 1991, Iraq possessed massive stockpiles of chemical weapons, which it used against Iranian troops and its own Kurdish population. Israel, one of the world's seven nuclear powers, has what is widely reputed to be

---

[45]In recent years, however, the Israeli military has begun the transition from being a conscript, or "people's army," to a "far more 'professional' force." The percentage of conscripts released from military service or granted early discharges has steadily increased, while the age ceilings and periods of service of reservists have steadily been lowered. Stuart A. Cohen, "The Peace Process and Societal-Military Relations in Israel," in *The Middle East Peace Process: Interdisciplinary Perspectives*, ed. by Ilan Peleg (Albany: State University of New York Press, 1998), pp. 107–120. The number of soldiers joining the reserves is now lower than the number of those who leave, even though the age cohorts are growing. Service for women has been reduced from twenty-four to twenty-one months. Yoram Peri, "Civilian-Military Relations in a Post-War Society," in *Israeli Society and the Challenge of Transition to Coexistence*, ed. by Tamar Hermann and Ephraim Yuchtman-Yaar (Tel Aviv: Tel Aviv University, 1997), pp. 101–112.

[46]Alex Brummer, "How Military Spending Causes Social Degradation," *Guardian Weekly* (July 14, 1991), p. 6.

[47]International Institute for Strategic Studies. *The Military Balance 1996/97* (London: Oxford University Press, 1996), pp. 306–311.

[48]F. Gregory Gause, III, "Arms Supplies and Military Spending in the Gulf," *Middle East Report* (July–September 1997): 12–14.

the fifth most powerful military in the world and has joined the exclusive list of states that have sent satellites into orbit, indicating among other things that it possesses nuclear-capable intercontinental ballistic missiles.

Given the size and costliness of virtually all Middle Eastern militaries, it appears logical that they would play vitally important political roles. This, however, does not seem to be evident by the standard indicators of military intervention into politics: coups d'etat and presence of military officers within political elites. The frequency of coups has steadily declined since the early 1970s. The percentage of officers in top-level political positions has also generally declined. In Egypt, for example, there was a progressive reduction of officers serving in cabinet positions after Nasser's death. Military presence in that body reached a peak in the wake of the 1967 June War, when it was 65.4 percent.[49] Over the entirety of the Nasser period, officers constituted about one-third of cabinet members. By comparison, those with military backgrounds constituted less than 13 percent of all Sadat's ministers, and two-thirds of these were officers who had further technical training.[50] In the final Sadat cabinet, only the portfolios of defense and foreign affairs were held by those of military background. Mubarak's cabinets typically had three or four officers in the 1980s but as few as one in the 1990s. The downward trend of officer representation in the cabinet reflects the situation in other organs of government. Sadat, for example, engineered a demilitarization of governorships; by 1980, fewer than five were held by military men, compared with twenty-two of twenty-six in 1964. Under Sadat and Mubarak, there has been a gradual but steady decline in the ratios of former officers in the bureaucracy, including the prestigious ministry of foreign affairs.[51] The last successful coup d'etat in Egypt was that which brought Gamal Abdel Nasser, General Muhammad Naguib, and the Free Officers to power in July 1952.

In the Fertile Crescent region, Arab armies have also been further distanced from government. In Lebanon, the military sought a gradual takeover of power after its commanding officer, General Fuad Shihab, was elected president in 1958. From then until 1970, "The army, with the violent opposition of some legislatures *[sic]*, came to play a major role in political decision making."[52] In the 1970 election, however, the army failed to engineer the election of its candidate, Elias Sarkis. Civilian MPs immediately set about taking their revenge. In 1972, the Chamber of Deputies established a committee to investigate corruption in

---

[49]Richard H. Dekmejian, "Egypt and Turkey: The Military in the Background," in *Soldiers, Peasants, and Bureaucrats*, p. 33.

[50]Mark N. Cooper, *The Transformation of Egypt* (Baltimore: Johns Hopkins University Press, 1982), p. 144. See also Mark N. Cooper, "The Demilitarization of the Egyptian Cabinet," *International Journal of Middle East Studies* 14:2 (May 1982): 203–225; and Raymond A. Hinnebusch, Jr., *Egyptian Politics Under Sadat: The Post-Populist Development of an Authoritarian-Modernizing State* (Cambridge: Cambridge University Press, 1985), pp. 100–105.

[51]Robert Springborg, "The President and the Field Marshal: Civil-Military Relations in Egypt Today," *Merip Middle East Report* 147 (July–August 1987): 5.

[52]Abdo I. Baaklini, *Legislative and Political Development: Lebanon, 1842–1972* (Durham: Duke University Press, 1976), p. 232.

the army. "The thoroughness of its investigation and the candidness with which it reported its findings firmly reestablished the political authority of the Chamber over the army."[53] During the 1975–1976 civil war, General Ahdab sought to impose the military's will in what became known derisively as "the TV coup," for the hapless general appeared on television announcing a takeover while the troops that were supposed to accomplish this dwindled to naught. General Michel Aoun, commander of the military at the time of the scheduled 1988 presidential election, coveted the presidency but could not mobilize sufficient support to obtain it. In late 1990, he was dispatched into exile by Syria. For the past thirty years the Lebanese political system has not managed to do much, but it has succeeded in keeping the military from coming to power.

In neighboring Syria, the military plays a key political role, but it has not imposed a military dictatorship. Civilians occupy important posts in the cabinet and the Ba'th Party. Perhaps the most accurate and recent test of strength between the incumbent, semimilitary regime of Hafez al-Assad and challengers whose strength was based almost entirely on command of various military units occurred when President Assad became ill in the fall of 1983. When it appeared he might die, several hopeful successors, including al-Assad's brother Rif'at, made their bids by mobilizing troops they commanded in and around Damascus. The president recovered sufficiently to appear in public, organize a mass demonstration in his support, and then cut the ground from under his challengers. In so doing, he brought the military back under effective control.

Even more impressive testimony to the ability of civilians to subordinate the military to their control are the changes that have taken place in Iraq. The first military coup in the Arab world was conducted there in 1936. Several more occurred subsequently until the Ba'th Party, acting through sympathetic military officers, seized power in July 1968. The civilian wing of the party then gradually asserted itself over Ba'thist officers and the military more generally. The culmination of this process was symbolized by Vice President Saddam Hussein's replacement of the president, General Ahmad Hassan al-Bakr, in June 1979. Saddam, a party stalwart, was trained as a lawyer. As Iraq fought against Iran a war that required total mobilization and resulted in hundreds of thousands of casualties, the military was kept under strict control by the president and the party. U.S. attempts to induce the military to overthrow Saddam Hussein after Iraq's invasion of Kuwait had by mid-1998 come to nothing. The war against Iraq also failed to produce a military takeover in Iran. In fact, it provided an opportunity for the Islamic government to bring the military more directly under its control.

In the other two non-Arab countries in the region, Israel and Turkey, however, trends in civil-military relations appear to be running in favor of the latter. In Israel, military officers continue to occupy a high percentage of key government positions. Turkey witnessed a coup d'etat in September 1980 that brought to an end a decade of uninterrupted parliamentary government. These developments are paradoxical, for Israel and Turkey have the longest, best-established traditions of participatory government in the region.

---

[53]Ibid., p. 233.

Israel, since its creation in 1948, has been characterized by widespread participation in politics by military officers. Service in the Haganah, the chief military organization of the Yishuv, the Jewish community in Palestine prior to the creation of the state of Israel, was a primary pathway into the cabinet. Since 1948, over one-third of senior cabinet posts, including prime minister, deputy prime minister, and defense and foreign affairs ministers, have been held by professional officers, and their percentage has been steadily increasing.[54] Whereas before 1967 there had never been more than two reserve officers in the cabinet, since then the range has been between three and five officers. In the Knesset, comparative figures are between zero and five until 1967, and between five and ten after that time. In primary elections to determine the parties' candidates for the May 1996 parliamentary elections, reserve generals who were then serving as ministers or deputy ministers won four of the top ten positions on the Labor Party's list, while three ex-generals placed among the five leading Likud candidates. Binyamin Netanyahu, elected prime minister in those elections, had served as a soldier in the *Sayeret Matkal,* Israel's elite counter-terror army unit. His commander in that unit was Ehud Barak, a general and former chief of staff, who in June 1997 was elected leader of the Labor Party.

Before 1967 the office of defense minister had never been filled by a senior army officer, but that post has now become virtually monopolized by former officers. Between 1948 and 1977, one-third of all retired generals became involved in full-time political careers.[55] The heads of the Mossad (intelligence service), Border Police, Civil Guard, Civilian Administration, and Airports Administration are now invariably senior officers, as are the directors of businesses considered essential to security, such as the electric company, oil refineries, and the national airline, El Al. Even in municipal elections, officers have since the 1970s been playing much more active roles, both as candidates and as staff of party organizations.[56] The political system at all levels, as well as senior management positions in both the public and private sectors, have become areas in which Israeli military officers play increasingly important roles.

The Turkish military, which has never been as heavily represented in the political elite as its Israeli counterpart, intervened directly in politics in 1960, 1971, and 1980, in each case returning to the barracks after altering the constitution in accordance with its own preferences. The longest interregnum of military rule followed the coup of September 12, 1980, with the return to civilian government through elections coming in November 1983. However, while the Turkish military has on these three occasions intervened and restructured the civilian political system, thereby underlining its permanent presence in the wings, it has not invariably been able to dictate its specific political preferences to the voters or the politicians. In the 1980–1981 episode, the architect of the military intervention, General Kenan Evren, attempted to pave the way for a more perma-

---

[54]Peri, *Between Battles and Ballots,* pp. 102–104.

[55]Alex Mintz, "The Military-Industrial Complex: The Israeli Case," in *Israeli Society and Its Defense Establishments,* p. 108.

[56]Peri, *Between Battles and Bullets,* p. 105.

nent, supervisory role for the military. He ran successfully for president, while an officer-dominated National Security Council (NSC) was created to oversee the civilian political process, a function that included screening candidates for office. In the 1983 elections, the NSC refused permission to virtually all formerly prominent political leaders to offer their candidacies. Nevertheless, in those elections the military-backed candidate, former four-star general Turgut Sunalp, whose Nationalist Democracy Party ran on a slogan proclaiming that it would be guided by the philosophy of the "September 12 Movement," failed to win. His party received less than one-quarter of the votes and finished third, the victor being Turgut Ozal's Motherland Party. Although Ozal had served as the NSC's deputy prime minister and minister of state for economic planning until July 1982, he won not because of his association with the military but because he was the candidate most distant from it.[57] In October 1989, Ozal succeeded Evren as president. In October 1991, freely conducted parliamentary elections brought Suleyman Demirel, who more than a decade before had been ousted by the military, back to the prime ministry.

Complete civilian control of the Turkish military, however, has not been established. Indeed, a series of clashes between the military, as represented by the NSC, and the Islamist-led coalition government that came to power in 1996 demonstrated that the military would not tolerate policy changes it considered to violate Kemalist traditions. In April 1997, it forced the Islamist prime minister, Necmettin Erbakan, to dismantle much of the Islamic educational system that he had established under state auspices. Moreover, as Erbakan was seeking to reorient Turkish foreign policy according to Islamist principles, the Turkish military intensified linkages with the Israeli military on the basis of an agreement it, rather than the civilian leadership, had signed with the government of Israel. The military then, in the summer of 1997, engineered Erbakan's replacement by another civilian politician but one directly beholden to it, and in January 1998, the Turkish Supreme Court, apparently under pressure from the military, banned Erbakan's Welfare Party. Thus with regard to domestic and foreign policy, to political participation and actual tenure in office, the Turkish military has clearly defined its resistance to transgressions by civilian politicians of the Kemalist traditions of which it claims to be the guardian.

Coups d'etat in Sudan in 1989 and in Algeria in 1992—the first bringing to power an Islamicist-influenced government and the second preventing that from happening—indicate that the growing challenge of Islamic revivalism may cause Arab militaries once again to assume direct control of government (as also appears to be the case in Turkey). If this were to occur, it would suggest that what had been an interregnum of mainly civilian rule was a period in which those civilians were a facade behind which the military had always lurked. However, whether the military returns to a more direct, active role in politics or retreats further from them, there is a widespread belief in the region—and especially in the Arab world—that armed forces, and the governments they originally

[57]John H. McFadden, "Civil-Military Relations in the Third Turkish Republic," *The Middle East Journal* 39 (Winter 1985): 69–85.

fostered, have impeded and not enhanced development. The decreasing legitimacy of military rule, for example, probably inspired the decision by the Algerian military, in the wake of its January 1992 takeover, to form a High State Council and select Muhammad Boudiaf, one of the historic leaders of the war of independence, to head it. When Boudiaf was then assassinated on June 29, 1992, the military strongman, General Khalid Nezzar, immediately nominated a successor, lest there be no screen behind which he and the military could hide.

The Failures of Military Rulers

The coups d'etat that brought military officers to power in many Arab countries in the 1950s and 1960s were generally greeted enthusiastically by their populations. Anciens regimes, dominated by royal families and by oligarchies of landowners, frequently with ethnic or religious minorities occupying key economic positions, had failed to appreciate the depth of nationalist sentiment. Nor had they rapidly expanded either their economies or political participation. They were, therefore, weak and unpopular. Young military officers, on the other hand, imbued with nationalist, populist ideologies and possessing a variety of modern skills, appeared to offer great hope for a better national future. Many Western analysts concurred in this view. Manfred Halpern, for example, interpreted Middle Eastern militaries as "the instrument of the new middle class."[58] Middle Easterners—and Halpern—expected the military and other elements of that progressive class to modernize the economy and the polity.

These expectations were frustrated in less than two decades of military rule. Military officers were committed to secular nationalisms and various interpretations of socialism. They sought to impose these Western-derived systems of political beliefs on populations that did not understand them and were prepared to accept them only as long as their governments performed adequately:

> The ideologies of Turkicization in Turkey carried out by Ataturk and his followers, Persianization in Iran adopted by Rida Shah Pahlavi and his successors, and Arab nationalism in Egypt adopted by Nasser and in Syria and Iraq by the Ba'th Party—these have not yet successfully superseded the religious folk base. In spite of many decades of elitist indoctrination in Turkey, Iran, Egypt, Syria, and Iraq, traditional religious organizations . . . plus a wide variety of community-based political alliances, still remain the basic instruments of collective action at the popular level. The gap between military elitist ideology at the top and the continuation of religious and community-based organisations at the graft is a source of tension to military regimes.[59]

As long as those military regimes were able to claim successes in domestic and foreign affairs, their ideological formulations went more or less unchallenged. When their performance lagged, however, they were immediately confronted by those religious and community-based organizations that had re-

---

[58]Manfred Halpern, *The Politics of Social Change*, p. 253.

[59]Khuri, "The Study of Civil-Military Relations," pp. 20–21.

mained impervious to the protracted ideological onslaught. The Arab failure against Israel in the June 1967 war led to regime changes in both Syria and Iraq and paved the way for the de-Nasserization of Egypt. The avant-garde ideology of opposition in the Middle East, by the mid-1970s, had become that of Islamic fundamentalism.

The political failure of the military was matched by its inability to guide national economies toward development. Overspending on itself has been one of the causes, but there are others. Too many resources have been allocated by governments dominated by officers to large, showcase projects. While civilian regimes have also suffered from the "edifice complex," "a new political language focusing on the big, the magnificent, the visible socially and politically, seems to always mark the ascendancy of the military to power."[60] A desire to maintain control over all aspects of the economy, which led to massive nationalizations, also did tremendous damage. The military and its associates in the bureaucracy lacked the skills to manage the thousands of enterprises they came to own. Corruption inevitably accompanied such control. It gradually suffused the civilian and military sectors. Egyptian officers, for example, enriched themselves during the war in Yemen (1962–1967) by loading up on duty-free goods in Aden and shipping the loot home on military aircraft. They subsequently retired into bureaucratic sinecures in the public sector, where many of them supplemented their incomes with ill-gotten gains. A sizable proportion of the real estate and movable property confiscated from the Egyptian royal family from assorted "feudalists" and from those whom the regime simply did not like ended up in the hands of officers.

The Syrian military has, if anything, exceeded the Egyptian in laying claim to the country's wealth. Officers control various aspects of the economy and demand bribes before authorizing the delivery of goods or services. The Syrian officer corps has, since the Lebanese civil war, managed a sprawling business in smuggled merchandise in Syria and Lebanon. The military economic corporations set up by President Ja'far Numairi in the Sudan in 1982 became satrapies into which Numairi could dump retiring officers, thereby buying the loyalty of his military, and where they, in turn, obtained illegal "commissions."[61] By arrogating to themselves rights and privileges denied other sectors of the population and by extorting goods and services from the public they were in theory protecting, Middle Eastern militaries undermined their very claim to rule.

The military also failed to achieve the principal goal it set for itself, which was to integrate the population into a national whole, with the military itself serving as the model for that integration. Middle Eastern societies are not substantially less divided along class, ethnic, and religious lines than they were before military officers seized power. Militaries themselves have not developed into meritocratic, classless, nonsectarian institutions. In some, such as the Syrian and Iraqi militaries, Alawis and Sunni Arabs, respectively, predominate in key command positions. Militaries there serve as instruments of control for minorities.

---

[60]Khuri, "The Study of Civil-Military Relations," p. 17.

[61]Henry Bienen and Jonathan Moore, "The Sudan: Military Economic Corporations," *Armed Forces and Society* 13 (Summer 1987): 489–516.

In the Iraqi army, Shi'i Arabs constitute 80 percent of the fighting ranks but only 20 percent of the officer corps.[62] The Sudanese military is controlled by northern Arabs who use it to subdue Christian and animist southerners. The South Yemeni military was dominated by the tribe of its former president, killed in the January 1986 civil war.

In many militaries in the region, the officer corps has become increasingly elitist as it has enriched itself. The gap in salaries and conditions between officers and enlisted men is huge. While the former are supplied with apartments, automobiles, privileged access to health care, educational and other facilities, soldiers frequently have to depend on their families for supplements to their meager incomes. This division between officers and enlisted men has contributed to growing disaffection among the latter, one manifestation of which is their increasing tendency today to join radical underground Islamic movements.

In Egypt, for example, numerous such groups have been apprehended since the assassination of Sadat in October 1981. Many of them have contained soldiers, and some have had noncommissioned officers. A few—including the al-Jihad group that killed Sadat and the so-called Video group (because it burned shops dealing in "decadent" videos)—have had commissioned officers as members. More than thirty officers and a hundred enlisted men were dismissed from the military in the wake of Sadat's assassination because of their sympathy for Islamic fundamentalism.[63] This and other evidence suggests that the Egyptian military is divided between an officer corps that is increasingly indulged by a regime anxious to placate it and enlisted men who are treated as cannon fodder; between officers who benefit disproportionately from spoils and those who resent the greed of their colleagues; and between those who are attracted by Islamic activism and those who adhere to the canons of secular nationalism. The Egyptian military, like others in the region, is neither a model for nor a vehicle of national integration. It even could, in certain conditions, become an instrument of national disintegration.

The Middle Eastern military has succeeded in a comparatively short period in discrediting itself and its claim to integrate nations socially and politically, to develop them economically, and, in the case of the Arab armies, even to discharge adequately the task of national defense. Consequently there is widespread hostility toward politicians in uniforms, a factor that has contributed to the decline of military intervention into politics. That decline also attests to the fact that most armies are much more complex organizationally, socially, and politically than they were in the 1950s and 1960s. Universal conscription has brought those from diverse religious, ethnic, and regional backgrounds into the military. While officer corps were stridently nationalistic prior to the 1970s, now they are ideologically much more heterogeneous. The tremendous increase in size and the growing technical sophistication of military establishments impede the formation of similar worldviews among officers and make plotting more difficult. Neither the composition and structure of contemporary armed forces nor

---

[62]Faleh Abd al-Jabber, "Why the Uprisings Failed," *Middle East Report* 176 (May–June 1992): 2–14.

[63]Satloff, *Army and Politics in Mubarak's Egypt,* p. 31.

the political milieu in which they operate is now conducive to their playing the overt political role they once did.

MEANS OF REGIME CONTROL

Regimes do not rely on abstract sociological phenomena when confronting matters as critical as subordinating the military. Each government develops a system of control by which it seeks to defend itself from politically ambitious officers. These methods, which differ according to level of political development, include dependence on tribes, sects, and/or mercenaries; reliance on manipulative strategies rooted in patrimonialism; and use of political institutions. Many governments employ more than one method, either simultaneously or sequentially.

Use of Tribes, Sects, and/or Mercenaries   In the most traditional political systems in the region, control over the military is asserted by rulers through their families and the tribes with which they are allied, an arrangement that occasionally is buttressed by the use of mercenaries. In Saudi Arabia, for example, a large force of Pakistani mercenaries was maintained as the ultimate guarantor of the regime for much of the 1980s. In the United Arab Emirates, most enlisted men and noncommissioned officers are Omanis or Baluchis, while Jordanians, Pakistanis, and British, as well as a few Emirate citizens, make up the officer corps. In Oman, the Sultan's Armed Forces, which along with the Iranian military put down the uprising in the Dhofar Province in the early 1970s, consisted primarily of British, Australian, South African, Jordanian, and other mercenaries. The Omani military still relies heavily on foreign troops and officers. One of the most famous military officers in the Middle East since World War II was John Glubb, or Glubb Pasha as he was known, an Englishman who commanded Jordan's Arab Legion until dismissed by King Hussein in 1956. A primarily Shi'i political protest movement in Bahrain that was launched in December 1994 encountered severe repression at the hands of Bahraini security forces directed by British expatriots.

As these states have modernized, however, they have relied less on foreigners and more on families and tribes to control the military. Saudi Arabia has developed this method of tribal control most fully. Hundreds of Saudi princes are in the Saudi army, navy, and air force. The ministry of defense and aviation is a stronghold of the powerful Sudairi clan, which includes King Fahd and his brothers through the Sudairi wife of Abdul Aziz Ibn Saud, the founder of the state. The minister of defense is Fahd's brother Sultan. Nearly all of Sultan's sons are senior air force officers, including Prince Khalid, who heads air defenses, the fourth command of the Saudi armed forces. Sultan's deputy is his brother Turki. The National Guard and ministry of interior are also headed by a half-brother and brother of the king, respectively. "In short, no ministerial post related to national security is outside the hands of the sons of Ibn Saud, and it has always been this way."[64]

---

[64]Ghassan Salameh, "Political Power and the Saudi State," *Merip Reports* 91 (October 1980): 9–10.

In Jordan, three-quarters of the officer corps is drawn from East Bank tribes closely attached to the royal family. In North Yemen, following the truce that ended the civil war of the 1960s and prior to the coup that brought the modernizing officer Ahmad Hamdi to power in 1974, the state itself was so weak that the army was controlled by the country's dominant tribes.[65] In South Yemen, the radical Marxist Yemeni Socialist Party (YSP) sought to control the military at least in part through tribal connections. This strategy backfired in January 1986 when Dhali and Awaliq tribesmen, loyal to the rebel, radical faction in the YSP, turned their guns on officers and soldiers of the Dathina tribe, which was loyal to President Ali Nasir Muhammad.

Another primordial allegiance employed in controlling Middle Eastern militaries is that of sect or ethnic group. President Hafez al-Assad of Syria, himself an Alawi, relies heavily on members of his family, clan, and the Alawi sect in staffing key units. The Iraqi officer corps, especially at the higher levels, is dominated by Sunni Arabs from the so-called triangle area of Baghdad-Anah-Mosul, where they are predominant, and at the very highest levels by President Hussein and his relatives from his hometown of Takrit. Since the early 1980s Saddam Hussein has drawn increasingly on tribal loyalties to reinforce his control of the military. He has staffed crucial Republican Guard units, for example, almost exclusively from his own Al-bu Nasir tribe and from the closely related Jubbur and 'Ubayd tribes.[66] But in Syria and Iraq, sectarian recruitment into the officer corps is neither absolutely ubiquitous nor deemed a sufficient means of control. The governments of these countries also rely on other techniques.

Patrimonial Strategies   A wide array of manipulative strategies is employed in those states where neither traditional nor modern institutions are sufficiently cohesive to insulate rulers from their organizations of coercion. One such strategy is to divide and thereby rule the officer corps. President Sadat of Egypt preferred this method. No sooner would he promote an officer into a command position or to the lofty heights of chief of staff or minister of defense than he would begin to look about for a successor. In the decade of Sadat's rule, he rotated seven officers through the post of minister of defense. Of the five generals who served as field marshal of the Egyptian military since 1952, two died under mysterious circumstances, one died of cancer shortly after his appointment, another was removed after one day in the post, and the last one, Muhammad Abu Ghazala, was removed after his reputation was destroyed in a press campaign that linked him to a belly dancer and to illegal arms dealings. The shah of Iran was also a master of the divide-and-rule strategy, so much so that the military simply fell apart when subjected to intense pressure at the time of the revolution. The commanders of the army, navy, air force, and national police force and the di-

[65]Robert Burrowes, "State-Building and Political Construction in the Yemen Arab Republic, 1962–1977," in *Ideology and Power in the Middle East: Studies in Honor of George Lenczowski*, ed. by Peter J. Chelkowski and Robert J. Pranger (Durham, N.C.: Duke University Press, 1988), pp. 210–238.

[66]Amatzia Baram, "Neo-Tribalism in Iraq: Saddam Hussein's Tribal Policies 1991–96," *International Journal of Middle East Studies*, 29, 1 (February 1997): 1–31.

rectors of the various intelligence organizations were permitted to communicate with one another only through the shah or his personal staff.

The sensitive task of gathering intelligence on the military is typically divided between several agencies, lest one become too powerful. In the shah's Iran, there were a dozen different military-security organizations, all bound in mutual competition to the person of the shah. Although the situation has become somewhat simplified in the Islamic Republic of Iran, that government for a time witnessed considerable tension between the *pasdaran* (revolutionary guards) and the regular army. In Syria, "Three military intelligence bureaus spend as much or more energy supervising the behavior of the officer corps than they do on conventional espionage."[67]

The Saudis, not content to control the military only by monopolizing key positions, have created a National Guard as an entirely separate structure from the regular military. It is "an extension of loyalist tribal groups, while the army is an outgrowth of the Hijazi troops inherited from the Sherif of Mecca."[68] The Guard is under the control of Crown Prince Abdullah, who is a half-brother and rival to Minister of Defense Sultan. While the military recruits throughout the country, the Guard draws on tribesmen in the region of its various garrisons. Its chain of command is based on tribal authority rather than on military rank order. It is, in every way, intended to be separate from and a counterbalance to the military. Similarly, in Syria, Hafez al-Assad in the 1970s carved the army into a handful of different units, each with its own commander, uniform, internal loyalties, and patronage networks. The largest of these, the Siraa al-Difaa, was under the command of Hafez's younger brother Rif'at until it was disbanded in 1984–1985. Nasser created a counterweight to the Egyptian regular army in the wake of Field Marshal Abd al-Hakim Amer's unsuccessful coup attempt in August 1967. This was the Presidential Guard that Nasser placed under General al-Laithi Nassif, who, along with his troops, provided the means by which Sadat subsequently levered his chief opponents, including Minister of War Muhammad Fawzi, out of office in May 1971.[69] Nasser also created the Central Security Force (CSF) under the minister of interior in 1968 to control domestic dissenters. Sadat expanded it after the 1977 riots to over 300,000 men, in part to serve as a check on the regular military.

Rulers have also tried to erect legal and geographical barriers between their military establishments and the political order. President Bourguiba disenfranchised the military and denied officers and enlisted men the right of political association, even in the ruling Destourian Socialist Party.[70] Sadat prohibited officers from running for elected office. Joining a political party other than the

---

[67]Yahya M. Sadowski, "Ba'thist Ethics and the Spirit of State Capitalism," in *Ideology and Power,* pp. 179–180.

[68]Salameh, "Political Power and the Saudi State," p. 9.

[69]General Nassif, whose political sympathies were on the left, was shortly thereafter found dead, having fallen from his hospital window in London. Many Egyptians believe he was pushed. See Steve Negus, "The Marshal's Ghosts," *Cairo Times* (21 August–3 September, 1997), p. 7.

[70]L. B. Ware, "The Role of the Tunisian Military in the Post-Bourguiba Era," *The Middle East Journal* 39 (Winter 1985): 27–29.

Ba'th is a capital offense for Iraqi officers. In Syria, "Fraternization between officers and civilian elites . . . [is] carefully policed by the Ba'th's Political Bureau."[71] President Mubarak has sought to insulate the Egyptian military, especially conscripts and noncommissioned officers, from political trends, such as Islamic fundamentalism, by shifting army camps away from populated areas and into the desert.

Patrimonial control mechanisms include the carrot as well as the stick. Expenditure on Middle Eastern militaries are due in part to the desire to maintain the loyalty and subservience of the officer corps. An increasing percentage of military budgets appears to be dedicated to officers' well-being. Conditions that obtain in Syria are typical in the region: "Officers are pampered: army cooperatives provide them with cost-price articles and with duty-free foreign imports not obtainable elsewhere in the country; interest-free loans allow them to buy villas and speculate in very lucrative real estate; and they receive generous salaries, free medical care, liberal travel allowances, and miscellaneous other fringe benefits."[72]

Political Institutions   In the former communist systems, the military was subordinated to political decision makers largely through the efforts of the party and other elements of the state apparatus. In democratic polities, a participatory political infrastructure insulates the civilian political system. In the Middle East, examples of both such arrangements exist. "The party commands the gun, and the gun must never command the party," is Mao's colorful statement of the Leninist approach to civil-military relations.[73] In the Arab world, the Iraqi Ba'th Party most closely resembles the communist prototype. Party supremacy over the military is sought through indoctrination of officers and men and by the dispersal throughout the armed forces of political commissars, whose job is to ensure strict adherence to the Party's line. Officers are required to attend formal classes in Ba'thist doctrine. Party membership is a virtual prerequisite for promotion. Only members of the Party gain entrance to the military academy. No other political party is allowed contact in any way with military personnel. This Iraqi version of the classic Soviet and Maoist technique of subordinating army to party, in combination with a variety of other mechanisms, ensured President Saddam Hussein's control of the military during the long war with Iran and in the wake of Iraq's catastrophic defeat in 1991.

After the revolution in 1979, the Iranian system of control over the military came to resemble that of Iraq. Immediately after Ayatollah Khomeini came to power, a purge of the military was instituted. By 1986, over 23,000 officers had been liquidated or retired, some 45 percent of the officer corps. This purge was partly intended to intimidate remaining officers so that they would obey orders.[74] As further safeguard, in October 1980, the government created the

---

[71]Sadowski, "Ba'thist Ethics and the Spirit of State Capitalism," p. 179.

[72]Drysdale, "The Syrian Armed Forces in National Politics," p. 70.

[73]Mao Tse-tung, *Selected Military Writings* (Peking: Foreign Languages Press, 1963), p. 272.

[74]Schahgaldian, *The Iranian Military Under the Islamic Republic* (Santa Monica, Calif.: Rand, 1987), p. 27.

Supreme Defense Council (SDC), the secretariat of which provides civilian political and ideological oversight of the armed forces.

The other notable example of Leninist-style party control over the military
occurred in the Yishuv and then in the early years of Israeli statehood. The
highly politicized Zionist migrants to Palestine from Russia—especially those
who came between 1904 and 1914 and who constituted the crucially important
second *aliya*—or wave of migration, had formed their attitudes and approaches
to politics in Russian revolutionary movements. They subscribed to the Leninist
principle of "building an effective political organizational structure so as to ensure the party's hegemony in society."[75] When they set about constructing a military wing in the late 1920s, which they named Haganah (Defense), they placed
it first under direct control of the Mapai Party, and then under the Histadrut, an
arm of Mapai responsible for labor organization. Subsequently the Haganah was
transferred to the representative institutions of the Zionist movement over
which Mapai, which eventually became the Labor Party, had control.

The Leninist formula of party control of the military was inappropriate once
the state of Israel was created as a parliamentary democracy. David Ben-Gurion,
first prime minister and minister of defense, recognizing that fact, transferred
control of the Hanagah to the state itself, renaming it Zahal (Israeli Defense
Forces—IDF). However, the strong links between the military and Mapai, which
had been forged over a twenty-year period, were not dissolved overnight. The
nexus between the two had been mutually beneficial. Of forty-four generals who
served in the highest posts in the General Staff from 1949 to 1977 (when Labor
was voted out of office), almost 70 percent were Mapai members and another 15
percent were nonactive Mapai supporters.[76] The Servicemen's Department of
Mapai, which was established in 1949, served as the major link between army
and party. Its primary tasks were to screen officers for promotion and to recruit
them into the party, which it did in semiclandestine, quasi-legal fashion.[77] Shimon Peres, later to become prime minister, was a key figure in the organization
from 1949 until 1965. Moshe Dayan, whose last major post was foreign minister
in the first Begin government, likewise was active in it.

The continuing increase in the number of former officers in Israeli politics
suggests that the party's control is inadequate. Israel between 1948 and 1977 was
not a single-party but a one-party-dominant state. Mapai could not dominate the
military in the same fashion as did the Soviet Communist Party or the Ba'th in
Iraq. The balance between party and military, which favored the former in 1948,
tilted gradually in the latter's favor as Mapai declined. Officers gradually became
able to dictate terms to civilian party members, rather than vice versa. In 1977,
when Likud won a plurality of seats in the Knesset and formed its first government, what was left of the Labor-military connection was rendered meaningless.
Significantly, Likud itself seized advantage of its incumbency in government to
tie itself more closely to the military. It promoted such officers as Raful Eytan,

---

[75]Yoram Peri, "Party-Military Relations," in *Israeli Society and Its Defense Establishment,* p. 47.

[76]Ibid., p. 52.

[77]Ibid., p. 55.

who became chief of staff and whom Likud leaders saw as sharing a similar conservative political outlook. Likud, however, has been no more capable of controlling officers than was Labor. Eitan himself subsequently commenced a political career, founding his own ultranationalist Tsomet Party. Similarly, Ariel Sharon, the retired general whom Menachem Begin made minister of defense following Likud's second election victory in 1981, has become a dominant figure in that party. The system of party control over the military has, in short, collapsed.

There are, however, two additional methods by which the Israeli military's influence is restrained. One is the systematic prevention of the creation of a barrier between the military and the rest of society. Universal conscription, reliance on reserves who can be rapidly mobilized, and steps to prevent the emergence of an elitist, separatist officer corps, including the absence of a military college for officer training, and early retirement of officers all serve to ensure that the military is an integral part of Israeli society.[78] A measure of the success of this method is that politically active former officers hold a wide array of opinions and are members of political parties ranging from the most dovish to the most hawkish. Widespread participation within interest groups, political parties, and parliament is the second barrier between the military and outright political control. It is this means of institutional control that will become more important as the Israeli military continues to be transformed from a civilian to a professional army. Such control is already becoming apparent as the "Judge-Advocate General and civil courts pry deeper into the army than they did in the sixties or seventies," and "the media penetrate the army and criticize it far more than they did even a decade ago."[79]

In Turkey competition between the military and institutions of political participation is intensifying. In 1960, the military, displeased by the increasingly autocratic tendencies of the Menderes government and its assault on the socioeconomic bases of Kemalism, forced the introduction of various democratizing measures, such as an electoral system based on proportional representation and guarantees of freedoms to universities, interest groups, and the media. In 1971, the military intervened once again to thwart anti-Kemalist forces and to contain growing student unrest. In 1980, after almost a decade of political immobilism and a rising tide of political violence, the military again seized power, abrogated the constitution, and imposed harsh restrictions on political behavior. On each of these occasions two factors worked to ensure that the military ultimately restored a substantial measure of autonomy to civilian politicians. The first was that the officer corps was not unanimously agreed on a course of action. The second factor is that since the elections of 1950, Turkey has had a tradition of representative democracy. While there is much cynicism about politicians and political parties, Turks are relatively committed to political institutions, especially parliament. While certain elements in the military "argued in 1960 and

---

[78]The ratio of career professionals has in recent years, however, begun to rise as the provision mandating retirement after twenty-one years of service has increasingly been waived as the Israeli military is being transformed into a smaller, "smarter" force.

[79]Peri, "Civilian-Military Relations in a Post-War Society," p. 104.

again in 1971 for the indefinite dissolution of the National Assembly . . . the certainty of public resistance" to this repressive measure ultimately caused those in control of the military to reject this proposal[80] as it did again after the 1980 coup. In 1997, the military essentially dictated the formation of a new government that is heavily dependent on it, although comprised of civilians.

Elsewhere in the region, civilians have enjoyed only episodic success in creating and sustaining political institutions that could serve as checks on the expansion of the military into general policy-making areas. In Sudan, for example, the widespread mobilization by political parties, universities, and political groupings opposed to military domination caused the army to retreat to the barracks in 1964 and again in 1985–1986. In 1989, however, the military, in league with Islamicists, staged another coup. It then instituted a reign of terror against opposition political groups. In general, civilian political institutions remain too weak in the Middle East to restrain the military; it must be checked through the traditional or patrimonial methods we've just seen.

THE MILITARY-INDUSTRIAL COMPLEX

The paradox of high military expenditures and oversize armed forces but an almost complete absence of coups and relatively few officers in political elites may be more apparent than real. The growth of military-industrial complexes in the region has changed the socioeconomic nature of military establishments and altered relations between them and the political order. Civilian and military economic enterprises are in many countries closely integrated. In the past, the military, to assert influence over policy, had to seize power. With the development of military-industrial complexes, the military's influence over policy is becoming more diffuse, broadly based, and substantive. Officers do not have to be in cabinets or parliaments or stage coups d'etat to have significant influence over important economic and political decisions.

The production of increasingly sophisticated weapons in factories under direct military control, the manufacture of civilian goods by those same factories, and the increasing dedication of civilian industry to military production result in officers assuming the roles of managers, engineers, and businessmen. This development, in combination with the officer corps' preferential access to goods and services and its recruitment of highly trained personnel, has led to the embourgeoisement of the military. Whereas in the 1950s and 1960s Middle Eastern military officers were drawn primarily from the lower middle classes, they are now being recruited from among the sons of officers who have capitalized on their fathers' positions by gaining entry to military academies. Young officers are also being recruited from the urban middle and upper middle classes, who can

---

[80]Marvin G. Weinbaum, "Classification and Change in Legislative Systems: With Particular Application to Iran, Turkey and Afghanistan," in *Legislative Systems in Developing Countries*, ed. by G. R. Boynton and Chong Lim Kim (Durham, N.C.: Duke University Press, 1975), p. 62. See also Ümit Cizre Sakallioğlu, "The Anatomy of the Turkish Military's Political Economy," *Comparative Politics*, 29, 2 (January 1997), pp. 151–166.

afford to educate their children to the level required by modern militaries. Political attitudes reflect changing class origins. Whereas the previous generation of officers tended to be radical nationalists who favored state control of the means of production, those of the present generation are much more conservative. Their nationalism is of a more moderate nature, and they are more inclined to favor the private sector than did the previous generation of officers. Even the Islamicist-influenced military government in Sudan, for example, has embarked on an ambitious privatization program.

The growth of military-industrial complexes is evident throughout the Middle East. Arms production in the region, which was minimal at the end of World War II, amounted to some $4 billion by 1987. Of the twenty-three Third World countries that produce significant quantities of arms, five are in the Middle East. Israel is the largest arms exporter in the Third World and one of the world's leading producers of weapons. Egypt, Turkey, Iran, and Pakistan are also major arms producers, and Algeria, Iraq, Jordan, Morocco, Saudi Arabia, Syria, Sudan, and Tunisia all manufacture munitions and small arms.[81]

Although Jews living in Palestine in the 1930s and 1940s created small arms and ammunition workshops, large-scale arms manufacturing in Israel really began after the 1967 war. In the following decade there was a tenfold increase in arms production. The proportion of employees in the defense sector to all Israeli employees increased two and a half times between 1967 and 1980. During that period Israeli Aircraft Industries (IAI), a government-owned firm that is at the heart of the military-industrial complex, increased its workforce almost fivefold. One-quarter of all of Israel's exports are arms, and 75 percent of its electronic and metal exports are in the form of weapons. Israel's ratio of armaments exports to total exports is the world's highest. Approximately 46 percent of all Israeli government expenditures for research and development are for arms and ammunition, compared with 2 percent in Japan, 3 percent in Holland, and 8 percent in Canada.[82]

As military industries have grown in Israel, so has integration increased between the defense and civilian sectors of the economy, and in both sectors the role of officers and retired officers has grown. It has become common practice for retired officers and reserve officers to hold senior positions in all firms involved in weapons production. IAI, Beit Shemesh (which builds engines), the large metal firms Elbit and Koor, and specific weapons projects such as the Merkava tank and the Lavi fighter (until it was canceled) have all been headed by senior reserve officers. Conversely, these officers, once they have served in defense industries, commonly assume crucial positions in the ministry of defense. Moshe Arens, for example, who served as minister of defense in the 1980s under the Likud government and who became foreign minister after the 1988 elections, previously was deputy director general of IAI. "It thus emerges that

---

[81]Joe Stork, "Arms Industries of the Middle East," *Merip Middle East Report* 144 (January–February 1987): 12.

[82]Mintz, "The Military-Industrial Complex," pp. 110–112.

there is a network of senior military officers in key positions extending over all branches of the complex," leading to "the increased influence of the complex . . . upon the formation of perceptions and policies."[83]

In Turkey, a military-industrial complex has emerged since the 1960s. The financial driving force behind the military's entry into the industrial and service economies has been military support funds. The first of these, Oyak, runs a chain of supermarkets; has large interests in Turkey's leading petrochemical, automotive, and food-processing businesses; and serves as the primary local partner in joint ventures with Renault, Goodyear, and various other multinational corporations. The other armed forces followed the lead of Oyak and the army. The air force, for example, created a support fund that in turn took up 45 percent of the shares of Tusas (Turkish Aircraft Industries), established in 1973. In a joint venture with General Dynamics and General Electric, it now produces the F-16 fighter plane.[84] Turkey's military industries by the mid-1980s employed over 40,000 people and exported almost a half-billion dollars' worth of weapons. By the 1990s Turkey had become one of the world's top twenty arms producers.[85]

Successive Turkish governments have sought not only to encourage military production but also to integrate the activities of the military support funds, the public sector, and private firms. In 1986, the government established the Defense Industry Development and Support Administration in order to determine arms manufacturing priorities and to allocate $650 million annually in "defense funds."[86] Partly as a result of this encouragement, private firms are rapidly commencing defense-related manufacturing operations, particularly in the form of joint ventures with foreign companies. These developments have served further to interconnect military officers with the private sector of the economy. "It has now become almost a tradition to offer positions on the executive boards of corporations to high officers, especially generals."[87]

In many Arab countries the pattern of increased arms production by the military and by public and private sectors and joint venture firms, accompanied by the expansion of military enterprises into the civilian economy and the deployment of military officers into technical and managerial positions, is also being followed. Egypt has gone furthest in this direction. By the early 1980s, it was the Third World's ninth leading producer of weapons, manufacturing annually approximately $1.4 billion worth of arms. Two percent of the urban labor force (85,000 Egyptians) are employed in the arms industry, which makes Egypt the Third World's fourth-largest employer for weapons production. The military under President Mubarak has come to play an increasingly important economic

---

[83]Ibid., p. 109.

[84]"The Private Sector Mounts an Attack," *South* (March 1988): 12.

[85]Omer Karasapan, "Turkey's Armaments Industries," *Merip Middle East Report* 144 (January–February 1987): 27–31.

[86]Omer Karasapan, "Turkey's Super Rich," *Merip Reports* 142 (September–October 1986): 31.

[87]Ahmed Kemal, "Military Rule and the Future of Democracy in Turkey," *Merip Reports* 122 (March–April 1984): 13.

role. It produces approximately one-fifth of all domestically produced and marketed foodstuffs; reclaims large tracts of desert land; builds more roads and installs more communication facilities than any other institution in the country; and runs hospitals, training academies, tourist resorts, shopping centers, and newly constructed desert cities. The military, in sum, operates a vast empire that extends far beyond weapons manufacturing. Thousands of officers and former officers are employed in these various operations. As a group they have become one of the very wealthiest categories of professionals in the country.[88]

In Syria, Iraq, and Sudan, as in Egypt, military officers now perform a wide variety of economic roles, many in association with local private sector firms or multinational corporations. Syria's military, although supporting a comparatively small arms industry, operates the largest construction business in the country, produces and processes large quantities of food, and manages a nationwide chain of retail outlets. The Iraqi military controls the Military Industries Commission, which produced, among other things, the modified Scud missiles used to bombard Iran and, subsequently, Israel and Saudi Arabia. Sudan's Military Economic Corporations, which operated in the final years of the Numairi era, became the largest business conglomerate in the country, concentrating particularly in importation and marketing. An estimated 80 percent of its trade was conducted with the private sector.[89] In these and other Arab countries, officers are rapidly developing into a visible and powerful economic elite.

The emergence of military-industrial complexes is associated with the development of a new political role for the armed forces. In the two decades or so after World War II, Middle Eastern militaries, fired by nationalist ideology, played basically progressive roles, overthrowing oligarchies and establishing the state as the guiding force in economies. Since that time they have become much more conservative. Increasingly allied with urban middle and upper classes and tied to indigenous and foreign private businesses, officers no longer constitute a vanguard for radical change. Indeed, Middle Eastern militaries have come to play a role similar to that played for several decades by many of their Latin American counterparts. Samuel P. Huntington proposes this reason:

> As society changes, so does the role of the military. In the world of oligarchy, the soldier is a radical; in the middle-class world he is a participant and arbiter; as the mass society looms on the horizon he becomes the conservative guardian of the existing order. Thus, paradoxically but understandably, the more backward a society is, the more progressive the role of its military; the more advanced a society becomes, the more conservative and reactionary becomes the role of its military.[90]

Armed forces in the Middle East now desire not the expansion of political participation but the containment of it. Their preferred political role is a supervisory one, standing in the wings to ensure that the politicians do not undertake

---

[88]Robert Springborg, "The President and the Field Marshal," pp. 4–16.

[89]Bienen and Moore, "The Sudan: Military Economic Corporations," p. 503.

[90]Samuel P. Huntington, *Political Order in Changing Societies* (New Haven, Conn.: Yale University Press, 1968), p. 225.

initiatives that run counter to the military's interests. L. B. Ware, commenting on the Tunisian military, sees this as a process of internal "colonization," where "senior military officers exercise a careful surveillance over important civilian posts—much in the same way the French organized a system of *contrôle civil* parallel to the beylical government during the Protectorate period."[91] The Turkish military hesitated to seize power in the late 1970s despite the rising spiral of violence.

> The officers' class interests dictated a continuation of the status quo . . . rather than the assumption of direct military rule. Indeed, it was safer for the military to stay in the background and permit the civilian politicians to carry out its wishes and be blamed for the consequences. This conservative orientation of the military elite was in sharp contrast to the reformist sentiments of the Turkish military in previous decades[92]

In sum, the military in the Middle East may be no less powerful politically than it was when officers dominated cabinets and staged repeated coups d'etat. What is new is that its influence is exerted subtly and through many channels. The outlook and political alliances of the military have also changed. Equally, Middle Eastern societies, economies, and polities have become more complex. Demands for political participation are increasing, as are criticisms of the military, its embourgeoisement, and its "colonial" political role. The military and its critics are, therefore, set on a collision course that may, in some countries of the region, result in major conflicts, as it already has done in Algeria and Sudan.

The Bureaucracy

Middle Eastern bureaucracies are in one of four possible stages of sequential development. The initial phase is characterized by the continuing supremacy of traditional political forces (rural notables, families, tribes) over bureaucracies as well as other governmental institutions. At this stage, bureaucracies, although they may be growing and staffed by increasingly well-trained personnel, lack political allies and administer only with sustained interference by powerful traditional forces. They are thoroughly penetrated by clientage networks that extend downward from traditional elites. The Saudi civil service, for example, expanded from a few hundred employees in the 1940s to about one-quarter of a million in 1980 and 624,000 in 1991.[93] Despite such rapid growth, the Saudi bureaucracy remains subordinate to royal authority. Until very recently this was exercised in a highly capricious fashion.

---

[91]Ware, "The Role of the Tunisian Military," p. 41.

[92]Dekmejian, "Egypt and Turkey," p. 46.

[93]Abdul Rahman Osama, *The Dilemma of Development in the Arabian Peninsula* (London: Croom Helm, 1987), p. 66; and John Presley and Tony Westaway, "Economic Liberalisation in Saudi Arabia." Paper presented to the Symposium on Economic Liberalisation and Its Social and Political Effects in the Middle East, Exeter University, Exeter, England (September 26–28, 1991), p. 6.

Given the centralization of authority in the hands of the king and senior officials, initiative was rare and since promotion depended on ascriptive factors rather than on ability or performance, there was hardly an incentive to perform well. Further, the importance of family ties dictated that senior bureaucrats promote family members and tribal relations regardless of their qualifications. Nepotism, far from being looked down upon, was a requisite and expected practice.[94]

The Jordanian civil service grew by 300 percent in fifteen years—from 27,000 in 1970 to 74,000 in 1985. Despite various attempts to professionalize new recruits, "The Jordanian bureaucracy remains constrained by a particularistic style of decision making at all levels. Over the years, tribal loyalties have been a more powerful focal point of identification and action than loyalties to the state.[95] While the Jordanian and Gulf states' bureaucracies have become somewhat more insulated from interventions by tribes and ruling families in recent years, they are still far from playing the leading role in modernization that their counterparts have played elsewhere in the region.

The Lebanese bureaucracy, which along with the military was intended by President Fuad Shihab, who came to power in 1958, to serve as a principal tool of development, was not equal to the task. Traditional leaders of the various confessions mobilized against Shihabism, an alliance of the bureaucracy and the military, and defeated it in the 1970 election. The Lebanese bureaucracy, which for just over a decade had held out the promise of becoming a professional organization at least partially insulated from traditional notables, reverted to its previous role of being a source of patronage for these elites.

The second phase of bureaucratic development occurs when, usually in alliance with the military and typically led by a strong, modernizing figure, the bureaucracy takes charge of a wide range of development tasks and by so doing enhances its prestige and rewards. Joining the bureaucracy becomes the preferred career choice of bright, well-trained young men and women. This pattern was established, for example, under Ataturk and into the 1950s in Turkey. In Egypt, Nasser relied heavily on the bureaucracy. Prominent bureaucrat-administrators became leading figures in the country. The bureaucracy came to overshadow not only policy-making institutions such as the parliament and single party but also the private sector of the economy. Similarly, Israel at independence in 1948 inherited a coherent, professional bureaucratic apparatus from the Yishuv. That bureaucracy continued to play important political and economic roles for the next thirty years until a reaction against it began to gain momentum in the late 1970s.

Erosion of professionalism, internal incoherence, weakening status, and decreasing rewards characterize the third phase through which bureaucracies pass. In Turkey, the transition from stage two to stage three began comparatively early. In the heyday of Kemalism, the bureaucracy "by itself jealously assumed the bur-

---

[94]Summer Scott Huyette, *Political Adaptation in Sa'udi Arabia: A Study of the Council of Ministers* (Boulder, Colo.: Westview Press, 1985), pp. 105–106.

[95]Jamil E. Jreisat, "Bureaucracy and Development in Jordan," *Journal of Asian and African Studies* 24 (1989): 99.

den of the modernization function."[96] As the Turkish polity modernized, however, new groups arose to challenge the hegemony of the bureaucracy. Politically, that challenge took the form of the Democrat Party, which recruited widely from among the emerging independent bourgeoisie. The Democrat Party won the 1950 election advocating laissez-faire policies. For the next three decades, Turkish politics centered on a struggle between the bureaucracy and new middle-class elements that supported it, most of which were loyal to the Republican People's Party (RPP) on the one hand and a coalition of opposing forces, including small-town petit bourgeoisie and urban industrialists, merchants, and independent professionals on the other. Initially the military sided with the bureaucracy. The 1960 intervention was intended to support the civil administration and its call for state control of the economy at a time when such programs were losing their appeal. Those lower in the social order resented the prestige, power, and rewards of the bureaucrats. Entrepreneurs viewed bureaucrats as obstacles to their activities and a drain on the public treasury. Consequently, the RPP could not win parliamentary majorities and maintain control of government. Simultaneously, the growth of the military-industrial complex, which resulted in an embourgeoisement of the officer corps, placed increasing strain on the military-bureaucratic alliance. In 1980, when the military intervened once again, it associated itself not with the civil administration but with its opponents and their preferred policy of supporting export-led economic growth under the auspices of the private sector.

Various manifestations of bureaucratic decay characterized this period of confrontation between the emerging bourgeoisie and the Turkish civil service, including loss of parliamentary seats by bureaucrats and their allies; growing strain in the alliance between the bureaucracy and the political party that formerly represented its interests; diminution of the status of bureaucrats; increasing conflict within the bureaucracy; and rising job dissatisfaction.[97] Civil servants, who constituted over half of the deputies in the 1927 Grand National Assembly and over a third in the 1946 Assembly, in the 1961, 1965, 1969, and 1973 Assemblies garnered about one-quarter of the seats. In 1977, civil servants won only 15 percent of the seats. Between 1950 and 1965, the purchasing power of the civil servants dropped by half.[98]

A further characteristic of the era of conflict between administrators and members of the bourgeoisie is that the latter, despite their growing influence, are still unable to establish autonomy and coherence as a collective pressure group. This is common in Third World settings, where "there develops a symbiotic relationship of 'antagonistic cooperation' between government official and

---

[96]Metin Heper, "Political Modernization as Reflected in Bureaucratic Change: The Turkish Bureaucracy and a Historical Bureaucratic Empire Tradition," *International Journal of Middle East Studies* 7 (October 1976): 510.

[97]Leslie L. Roos, Jr., and Noralou P. Roos, *Managers of Modernization: Organizations and Elites in Turkey (1950–1969)* (Cambridge, Mass.: Harvard University Press, 1971), pp. 201–206.

[98]Metin Heper, "The Recalcitrance of the Turkish Public Bureaucracy to 'Bourgeois Politics': Multi-Factor Political Stratification Analysis," *The Middle East Journal* 39 (Autumn 1976): 492.

private entrepreneur. The official supplements his inadequate official income. In exchange, the businessman is permitted to violate regulations."[99] In Turkey the parasitic character of indigenous capitalism is long-standing, where "dependence upon the state promoted an inclination to become grand manipulators of the bureaucratic mechanism. To have 'connections' and to develop close relations with the key figures in the bureaucracy have become most desirable."[100] Because businessmen seek connections to individuals in government rather than engaging in collective action to bring about structural changes, political organizations representing them remain weak and fragmented, as they did in Turkey through at least the mid-1970s.

Much of the Arab world is currently in this third stage of bureaucratic evolution. The military has from the late 1970s been deserting its former civil service allies, its officers instead seeking contacts with private entrepreneurs. Arab bureaucracies, although large, have not continued to expand rapidly in the 1990s. In Iraq, for example, in the final stages of the war with Iran, the government abolished entire administrative departments, giving bureaucrats the choice of unemployment or volunteering for military service. In Egypt, the government has not yet dared to amend the Nasserist decree that provided every graduate the right to a government job, but it has expanded to several years the delay between graduation and appointment to a bureaucratic sinecure. The Egyptian civil service grew from 1.2 million employees in 1969–1970, when it constituted some 3.8 percent of the population, to over 5 million in 1992, or some 10 percent of all Egyptians and almost one of every two persons employed in the urban work force.[101] However, the Egyptian bureaucracy has plateaued at about the 5 million level.

The tremendous growth of the Egyptian and other Middle Eastern bureaucracies was due in large measure to the desire by governments to buy the compliance of their citizens. That strategy is now being undermined because bureaucratic sinecures pay so little. Middle-ranking administrators in most Middle Eastern bureaucracies receive salaries that place them economically in the lower middle class, their incomes being below those of skilled tradesmen. Moonlighting is a ubiquitous practice among Middle Eastern civil servants. The extortion of *bakhshish* (tips) from those wanting services has become a standard expectation.

The transition from stage two to stage three in the evolution of many Arab bureaucracies occurred in the wake of the October 1973 war and the associated oil embargo that ultimately resulted in vastly increased revenues for oil producers. President Sadat declared the policy of *infitah* (opening), which entailed, among other things, encouragement of the private sector and an attack on the institutional legacies of Nasserism, including the swollen bureaucracy. Other Arab countries followed suit, but in none of them has the bureaucracy's power been so reduced and that of representative institutions and voluntary associa-

[99]Riggs, "Bureaucrats and Political Development," p. 422.

[100]Heper, "The Recalcitrance of the Turkish Public Bureaucracy," p. 496.

[101]Robert Springborg, *Mubarak's Egypt: Fragmentation of the Political Order* (Boulder, Colo.: Westview Press, 1989), pp. 137–138.

tions so increased that the bureaucracy could be said to have become a servant of the popular will.

Bureaucratic tenacity is due principally to the fact that ruling elites, much of whose power rests on the bureaucracy, are wary of abandoning this support base for the unknown of democratic, participatory politics. Social forces desirous of increased freedoms and a reduction of the power of the bureaucracy, including entrepreneurial bourgeoisies, are insufficiently powerful to force this transformation. For their part, bureaucracies operate from entrenched bases of power and are not easy to dislodge. They either control or operate in conjunction with ruling political parties. The various rewards and punishments that the bureaucracy doles out, such as issuing of licenses, discriminatory application of regulations, and so on, underpin the dominant position of ruling parties and are at the heart of systems of political control. Therefore, while Arab bureaucracies generally are on the defensive, they have yet to be brought to heel by their challengers.

The transition from stage three to stage four, at which point the bureaucracy becomes thoroughly depoliticized, professionalized, and subordinated to popularly selected political leaders, is not an easy one. No Arab country has, in fact, made it. Israel, however, is in the process of significantly reducing the power of its civil administrations and enhancing the autonomy of other economic and political actors. This change commenced when the Likud bloc won the 1977 elections. Much of the power of its chief rival, the Labor Party, had historically been based on its interconnections with first the Zionist and subsequently the Israeli governmental bureaucracies. Likud adopted the strategy of seeking to undermine the bureaucracy while trying to seize control over as much of it as possible. Since the late 1970s, bureaucratic salaries and conditions have deteriorated, the private sector's share of economic output has increased, and the nexus between the bureaucracy and the Labor Party is neither as strong nor as efficacious as it was previously. Although these developments are not yet irreversible, Israel appears to have accomplished a reduction in the power of its civil administration, although it remains a much more prominent force in the political arena than its counterpart in the United States or in most European countries. The other components of the fourth stage of bureaucratic development, which are impartiality and competence, have yet to be fully achieved—but then they frequently are not in the First World either.

The level of bureaucratic development is a good measure of political development more generally. In the most traditional Arab countries, ruling oligarchies remain suspicious of bureaucrats and fear their political ambitions, so they continue to control them through personalistic means. Bureaucrats compete with oligarchs to establish clienteles and spheres of influence. Most other Arab states have passed on to a third stage, where the shortcomings of bureaucratic- and military-led development have resulted in economic and political crises that remain unresolved. Despite much lip service to democratization and reforms that would enhance the efficiency and integrity of their bureaucracies, political elites in most of these countries have come to power through the military-bureaucratic alliance. So far they have been unwilling to take the gamble of seeking to transform the system into a much more participatory one in which the bureaucracy's power would be reduced. Until this is attempted, the bourgeoisie and other social forces will continue to predicate both their economic and political strategies on assumptions of bureaucratic hegemony. Only in Israel and to a lesser extent in Turkey—which also have traditions of bureaucratic domination but comparatively well-developed countervailing institutions of political participation—has bureaucratic hegemony been truly challenged.

Legislatures

Legislatures are typically the major governmental arena within which political forces legally contend for influence. Although in the Middle East most governments restrict access to legislatures and in various other ways prevent them from becoming representative bodies within which policies are made, legislatures are nevertheless worthy of analysis. They serve as a barometer, measuring degrees of institutionalized political participation. If legislatures are hampered by restrictions, so too will be political parties, interest groups, and other organs of the political infrastructure. Legislatures are also more widespread in the region than political parties, which are banned in all the Arab monarchies of the Gulf.

There is, both in Islam and in tribal traditions, respect for the practice of consultation, which in turn serves as cause and justification for the creation of consultative assemblies. Through the process of adaptive modernization described above, those assemblies may ultimately develop into full-blown legislatures. Indeed, it was precisely this path of development that parliaments followed in Europe. They began as assemblies of notables who advised the sovereign and served on his sufferance. Eventually they developed internal factions that, in turn, ultimately looked outside the assembly to mobilize political support. In so doing they laid the foundations of political parties and parliamentary democracy.

Parallel developments have occurred in Middle Eastern legislatures. Khedive Isma'il of Egypt, for example, created an Assembly of Notables in 1866 in order to diffuse domestic criticism of his profligate expenditures and to enhance his standing with Western creditors. That Assembly, intended by Isma'il to be a docile gathering of traditional rural notables, grew increasingly vociferous in its criticism of the khedive, becoming a focal point for mobilization against him and the European powers. In 1878, a petition was presented to Isma'il demanding that he transfer some of his powers to the Assembly. He responded by dismissing it. The following year he was forced to abdicate in favor of his son Tawfiq.

The struggle between the Ottoman sultan Abd al-Hamid and liberal reformers also centered on parliament, which the sultan prorogued in 1878. The sultan was subsequently deposed by the Young Turks, who convened in 1908 a Majlis al-Mab'uthan (Chamber of Delegates), a federal parliament for the empire. Confrontation between Muhammad Ali Shah and the combined clerical and modernist opposition in Iran at the turn of the century crystallized on the demand by the latter for a parliament, a demand finally realized as a result of the 1905–1906 constitutional revolution. In 1908, the shah repudiated the constitution and ordered his Cossack brigade to bombard the parliament. The following year he was forced to abdicate in favor of his son, and a new parliament was elected. Almost a half century later, the challenge to Muhammad Reza Shah mounted by his prime minister, Muhammad Musaddiq, was channeled through parliament. In 1976, President Sadat permitted relatively free elections to the People's Assembly, in part to impress Washington, with which he was developing an alliance. Three years later he had to terminate the legislative session before it had completed half its legal term, for some of its members seized the opportunity to register their protest against his policy of peace with Israel. In Turkey the National Assembly is the principal focus of governmental legitimacy. By so being, it has compelled the military to return to the barracks following its three interventions into politics since 1960.

WHY RULING ELITES ESTABLISH LEGISLATURES

Currently there are three different types of legislatures in the Middle East. The least well institutionalized, which generally are the newest, perform only consultative and not truly legislative functions. They serve at the behest of monarchs. A significant percentage if not all of their members are appointed by the ruler. Such bodies exist in Bahrain, Oman, the United Arab Emirates, Qatar, and Saudi Arabia. The second type are legislatures that have some involvement in lawmaking; that enjoy, at least intermittently, the possibility of openly criticizing regime policies and personnel; that are constituted primarily through elections that are subject to manipulation; and that may incorporate formal or quasi-formal oppositions. These legislatures currently are to be found in Algeria, Egypt, Iran, Iraq, Jordan, Kuwait, Lebanon, Morocco, Sudan, Tunisia, Syria, and Yemen. Finally, legislatures that have major responsibilities for lawmaking; that are constituted as a result of reasonably free and fair elections that are contested by two or more parties; that serve as the basis on which government is formed; and in which active, formal oppositions have a well-established role are to be found in Israel and Turkey. The Lebanese parliament prior to 1975 was also within this third category, although it never established the autonomy and legislative powers characteristic of both the Israeli Knesset and the Turkish National Assembly.

All legislatures now functioning in the Middle East, except those in Turkey and Israel, have been created as a result of unilateral decisions by ruling elites. As there are numerous examples of parliaments challenging rulers, it must be asked why elites take the risk of bringing into existence bodies that could ultimately turn against them.

Legitimation Eight monarchies remain in the Middle East, more than in any other region of the world. Their subjects today, in contrast with previous eras, "are profoundly aware of alternatives to dynastic rule." Such rule must, therefore, "be made to appear 'natural' and 'just.' . . . The late shah went so far as to assert that Persian kingship was based upon the will of the people. . . . Other Gulf rulers continue to make analogous claims."[102] In short, kingship no longer

---

[102]Dale F. Eickelman, "Kings and People: Oman's State Consultative Council," *The Middle East Journal* 38 (Winter 1984): 51.

legitimates itself, if indeed it ever did. Royal authority now must be buttressed at a minimum by lip service being paid to popular participation in decision making. Parliaments perform this function better than other institutions.

> By its mere existence, the legislature creates the idea that the broad public is represented. Nothing is more likely to legitimate a political system than the feeling that those who govern are representative of groups or interests in society. Because so many countries today are subdivided into political subcultures, the legislature is the critical means for creating the feeling that "one (or more) of ours is up there too!"[103]

Legitimation of regimes in the eyes of their neighbors and before the world is facilitated by the creation of legislatures or by enhancing the standing of preexisting ones. The al-Sabah rulers of Kuwait created a National Assembly immediately after attaining independence in 1961 in order to establish their country's claim to sovereignty against an Iraqi challenge. The al-Khalifa of Bahrain created an assembly in 1973 shortly after announcing their islands' independence from Great Britain. President Sadat had his eye on Washington when he upgraded the Peoples' Assembly in the wake of the 1976 elections. Saddam Hussein, in announcing shortly after he became Iraq's president in June 1979 that elections to a newly created National Assembly would be held, was declaring before the Middle East and the world that the Ba'thist regime, which had been established eleven years earlier by a coup, was now legitimate, well established, and confident of its popularity. In Oman, Sultan Qabus, who was placed on the throne in 1970 by a British-supported coup against his tyrannical father, Sultan Said bin Taimur, had several years later still done nothing to establish any form of permanent advisory council other than the cabinet. Western diplomats, mindful of the insurrection that had nearly succeeded in the Dhufar Province of Oman, urged Qabus to initiate steps to create some "form of consultative body such as had by then come into existence in neighboring states."[104] In 1981, the State Consultative Council was created, its forty-five members were appointed by the sultan, and Oman entered the ranks of the more than 130 countries that have some form of legislature. A decade later, the Council was renamed the Omani Consultative Council, and its membership was expanded to fifty-nine. Although the Sultanistic decree mandating these changes stated that its members were to be elected, in reality each member was selected by the Sultan from a list of three candidates nominated by caucuses in each of the country's fifty-nine *wilayat* (provinces). This has not deterred candidates' enthusiasm to gain entry to the Council, however, as witnessed by the fact that in the 1997 elections, over 800 candidates contested for seats.[105] In Iran, the existence of a national legislative body (the Majlis) survived the shattering revolution of 1978–1979. The Na-

---

[103]LaPalombara, *Politics Within Nations*, p. 159.

[104]Eickelman, "Kings and People," p. 54.

[105]On the Omani Consultative Council, see Abdullah Juma Al-Haz, "The Politics of Participation in the Gulf Cooperation Council States: The Omani Consultative Council," *The Middle East Journal* 50, 4 (Autumn 1996): 559–571.

tional Consultative Assembly has given way to the Islamic Consultative Assembly, an institution that is the scene of lively debate and intermittently effective executive oversight.

Communication   Creation of legislatures also facilitates communication among elite members as well as between the elite and the masses. In Oman, for example, the members of the State Consultative Council (SCC), when it was created in 1981, were drawn principally from the ranks of civil servants and from the tribal and mercantile notabilities. Oman is highly diverse, both demographically and geographically. Civil servants and traditional notables, despite their elite status, had little if any previous contact. "A major achievement of the SCC has been to provide regional delegates with a structured forum through which they can develop working relationships with participating senior officials and delegates from other regions. Conversely, it provides officials participating in the SCC with regular access to the views from the periphery."[106] When the SCC was reorganized in 1991, representation of each of the country's provinces was mandated by the sultan.

The Lebanese parliament formerly provided an arena in which communication within the elite could occur. Those contacts were absolutely vital to the functioning of the country's "consociational democracy." This is a form of democracy in deeply divided societies in which lack of contact and mutual hostility between different ethnic and religious groups at the mass level is overcome by flexible, accommodating elites.[107] The Lebanese parliament provided an important arena in which Muslim and Christian elites could fraternize. Its virtual demise contributed to the polarization that characterized confessional relations at both the mass and elite levels during and after the civil war. Resuscitated in the wake of the Ta'if Accord of 1989, the Lebanese parliament remains hobbled by Syrian influence and is unable, as it once did, to facilitate extensive communication within the elite, in part because significant members of that elite are no longer in parliament.

Communication between elites and masses may have been only marginally improved by many Middle Eastern legislatures. Since many of them are consultative assemblies of notables, or their membership is heavily dominated by government officials and those of the upper-middle and upper classes, the masses are generally not represented. There have been occasional efforts to rectify this deficiency. Nasser, for example, required after 1961 that 50 percent of members of parliament be "workers or peasants." Each constituency in the country had to elect a worker or peasant along with a candidate in the "other" category. In the 1964 parliament, 60 percent of MPs were workers or peasants. While some of them were in reality government employees in administrative positions or were medium-sized landowners who managed to pass themselves off as peasants, during the Nasser era parliament did provide an important channel of access for

---

[106]Ibid., p. 60.

[107]Arend Lijphart, "Consociational Democracy," *World Politics* 21 (January 1969): 207–225.

these elements into national politics. Conversely, the presence there of relatively humble individuals provided a network through which the elite could communicate with rural and lower-middle-class urban Egypt. Under Sadat and Mubarak, the 50 percent requirement has been retained despite pressure to abolish it. Definitions of workers and peasants are now so elastic, however, that virtually anyone can qualify under either category. As a result, the Mubarak regime has lost an important channel of communication and is increasingly isolated from Egyptian mass society.

Co-optation/Appeasement   Functions closely related to communication also performed by legislatures include co-optation and appeasement of various social forces. Were those forces to gain permanent footholds within the elite through participation in legislatures, those bodies could be said to be recruiting and assimilating new members and the groups they represent. In fact, however, regimes tend to grant access only temporarily, ejecting representatives of threatening social forces when it suits them to do so. In Bahrain's first and only election to the National Assembly, created following independence in 1971, sixteen of the thirty elected seats were won by Shi'is. The popular bloc, consisting of leftists, nationalists, and reformers, won eight seats, and the religious conservative bloc won six seats. It appeared as if the al-Khalifa ruling family was set on a course of utilizing the National Assembly to absorb these groups into the political order, rather than to exclude and repress them as it had done previously. Less than two years later, however, in August 1975, after labor riots and the Assembly's rejection of the amir's proposed legislation that would have given the ministry of the interior authority to arrest and detain for three years "anyone suspected of working against the state or even intending to act," the amir dissolved the Assembly and suspended the constitution.[108] The security law was declared to be in force, and various political activists were arrested, including three Assembly members. Since that time, no new elections have been held, and an Assembly whose members are appointed has been substituted for the previously elected one. Resentment against the ruling family persists, as indicated by an attempt by Islamicists to overthrow al-Khalifa rule in 1981 and, since December 1994, by intermittent demonstrations, strikes, and acts of violence.

The Kuwaiti National Assembly, from its creation in 1963 until it was suspended for the first time in 1976, also initially appeared to be functioning as an effective channel of political recruitment. "The old oligarchy of shaykhly families and the merchant elite, which had monopolized power in Kuwait in the past, found itself sharing power with sedentarized bedouin . . . and with the emerging middle class of businessmen, government officials, professionals, and intellectuals. Nearly a quarter of the first assembly's members were liberal nationalists."[109] Following the 1975 elections that resulted in many young, liberal reformers winning seats, and then a series of tense parliamentary sessions in the summer of

[108]Peterson, *The Arab Gulf States*, p. 76.

[109]Ibid., p. 38.

1976, the al-Sabah family became frightened of the Assembly they had created. In August 1976, Prime Minister Jabir al-Ahmad al-Sabah submitted his resignation to Amir Abdullah al-Salim al-Sabah, who immediately dissolved the Assembly, imposed press censorship, and suspended various articles of the constitution.

The al-Sabahs tried to create a pliant Assembly again in 1981, holding elections under a new electoral law that discriminated against their modernist opponents in favor of their traditional tribal allies. Encouraged by the relatively successful (i.e., quiescent) Assembly that resulted, the al-Sabahs permitted fresh elections in 1985. However, this time more critics of the government were elected, and the 1986 session was one in which the government came under increasing criticism. The amir responded by suspending the Assembly on July 3, 1986, once again imposing press censorship and unilaterally amending the constitution. Some three and a half years later, Amir Jabir sought to deflect demands for the restoration of parliament by declaring the existence of a National Council of seventy-five members, twenty-five of whom were to be appointed by him. The opposition's boycott of the June 1990 elections derailed this attempt to establish a pseudo-parliament and created a state of political crisis that prevailed when the country was invaded by Iraq in August.

While in exile during the Iraqi occupation, the al-Sabah rulers led the opposition to believe that once the country was liberated, parliament would be restored. In fact, however, on his return to Kuwait, Amir Jabir declared martial law. He subsequently consented under pressure to hold parliamentary elections in October 1992 in which independents and members of the opposition won thirty-five of fifty seats. Although that parliament enjoyed some success in its attempts to oversee the executive, by the time of the next elections in October 1996, it was apparent that it had not lived up to the voters' expectations. Half of the successful candidates were newcomers to parliament, and many well-known figures, especially among the independents and those in opposition, were defeated. Almost half of the Assembly was made up of representatives of tribal areas, who were generally supportive of the government. The al Sabah, in sum, have managed more or less successfully to utilize the legislature to co-opt and/or appease groups and individuals, although in so doing they have had to make concessions that constrain their exercise of power.

Jordan's former King Hussein pursued a similar strategy in his relations with popular assemblies. After permitting free elections in the 1950s to parliaments that became increasingly critical of governmental policies, Hussein finally struck back following an abortive coup attempt in 1957, expelling all radical members of parliament. In 1978, two years after dismissing an elected legislature, Hussein appointed members to a National Consultative Council in order to "co-opt intellectuals and businessmen, to appease traditional sectors of society, and to mobilize support for Royal policies."[110] As one of the measures taken to defuse tension in the wake of riots that shook the country in April 1989, King Hussein held elections to a new parliament in November of that year. This step proved to be

---

[110]Nabeel Khoury, "The National Consultative Council of Jordan: A Study in Legislative Development," *International Journal of Middle East Studies* 13 (November 1981): 428.

prescient, for that parliament co-opted many potential dissenters, thereby helping to absorb much of the political pressure that resulted from the Gulf crisis and war of 1990–1991. Former King Hassan of Morocco, a veritable political maestro when it came to playing off and with the opposition, responded to the 1984 food riots by holding parliamentary elections. These played a major role in defusing the crisis because they brought into parliament some opposition elements. There they were easily dealt with by the king.

In every major crisis since 1962, the rulers of Saudi Arabia promised to create an assembly but reneged on that pledge once the threat to their rule had passed. In the wake of Operation Desert Storm, however, dissatisfaction among the Islamicist and modernist-nationalist oppositions with the manner in which the ruling family had dealt with the crisis forced King Fahd to commit himself in March 1992 to creating a sixty-member appointive advisory council that then came into existence the following year.

It is not just monarchs who utilize legislatures to co-opt and appease critics. President Saddam Hussein of Iraq created an all-Kurdish parliament as part of his plan to reconcile Kurds to Iraqi sovereignty after the suppression of the Kurdish insurrection in 1975. That parliament had very limited powers over the country's predominantly Kurdish provinces, yet it did serve to co-opt various leadership elements and by so doing divided the Kurdish national movement. The Mubarak regime, in permitting a Muslim Brotherhood–dominated alliance of parties to emerge as the largest opposition force in parliament following the April 1987 elections, sought to soften the criticism of government by Islamicists, to attract some of their representatives into governmental sinecures, and to divide the Islamic movement between conservatives represented in the People's Assembly and radicals outside it.

Attempts to use legislatures to co-opt or appease demands for political participation can backfire if political mobilization is widespread. Algeria's President Chadli Benjedid responded to the violent riots of October 1988 by embarking on a rapid and dramatic political liberalization. A new constitution that authorized elections was ratified in February 1989. The Islamic Salvation Front (*al-Jabha al-Islamiyya li l-Inqadh*), known generally as the FIS, its French acronym, swept the June 1990 municipal and provincial elections. The government-backed party that had dominated the political system since independence in 1962, the FLN, could manage only 31 percent of the popular vote, compared to 55 percent for the FIS, which gave it control of thirty-two of the forty-eight provinces and over half of the municipalities. Frightened by the prospects of an FIS victory in parliamentary elections scheduled for June 1991, the government promulgated a new electoral law that replaced proportional representation with a two-round voting system that would enhance the prospects of the FLN. Islamicists associated with the FIS responded by taking to the streets, forcing the government to postpone elections for six months. When the first round of voting ultimately occurred in December, the FIS won 188 seats, compared to 16 for the FLN, thereby ensuring that in the decisive second round scheduled for January, it would win a majority of seats and thus be in position to form a government. At this point the Algerian military intervened, deposed President Benjedid, canceled the forthcoming election, imposed martial law, outlawed the FIS, imprisoned thousands of its members in remote desert camps, and sentenced its leaders to long prison terms. The strategy to co-opt and appease Algerian Islamicists by granting what was intended to be a limited role in newly created democratic structures of local and national government thus failed utterly because the FIS was too strong and the FLN too weak.

In the mid-1990s several other Arab governments found that utilization of legislatures to co-opt and/or appease competitive elites is a risky strategy, hence tended to abandon it. King Hussein of Jordan, tiring of incessant criticism from the Assembly and worried about its reaction to the peace treaty with Israel he was then contemplating, modified the electoral law prior to the 1993 parliamentary elections in order to ensure that candidates loyal to him would poll better than they had in the 1989 election, and that Islamists would see their share of seats reduced. President Mubarak, likewise irritated by the vigorous efforts of the 1987 legislature to oversee the executive, ensured through a variety of interventions that in the 1990 and 1995 elections overwhelming majorities were won by his ruling National Democratic Party. President Ali Abdullah Salih seized on the opportunity provided by the 1997 Yemeni parliamentary elections to significantly reduce the role of the Islamist *Islah* (Reform) Party within the legislature and virtually to eliminate the presence of the Yemeni Socialist Party. Strategies of co-opting and appeasing oppositional elements through their inclusion in legislatures were more suitable, hence utilized more frequently in the less tense political atmosphere of the 1980s and early 1990s, than subsequently in climates of political polarization that now prevail in many Arab countries.

Containment/Supervision Legislatures can play significant roles within rulers' strategies of supervising sprawling state apparatuses and containing opposition forces. Many Arab legislatures have come to play roles of ombudsmen, identifying irregularities that have taken place in bureaucracies and public sectors. While this serves to blow off steam, it is also a means by which rulers can supervise the performance of their administrators. Criticism by parliamentarians of programs and officials can also be used by rulers as justifications to jettison unwanted personnel, a tactic that is particularly useful to rulers seeking to deflect criticism from themselves or to undermine opposition elements that may be gathering strength. Nasser, for example, permitted parliament unusual latitude when debating the proposed annual budget of Prime Minister Zakariya Muhyi al-Din's government in 1965, in part because Nasser wanted to weaken the conservative trend that his prime minister represented. Sadat, by not signaling his displeasure, allowed parliament to criticize strongly and ultimately to reject Prime Minister Aziz Sidqi's proposed budget in 1972. Sadat had selected Sidqi to be prime minister, despite his strong personal dislike for him and his policies, because of domestic and foreign political calculations. Criticism in parliament thus served Sadat's purpose of destroying Sidqi's political career and discrediting the technocratic-socialist tendency he represented. The Syrian parliament also appears to be facilitating some liberalization of that government. In the May 1990 elections to that body, the regime ensured that private sector businessmen, selected intellectuals, and traditional leaders would win a larger proportion of seats than in any previous election under the Ba'th Party. According to Volker Perthes, this was to "be a warning to some of the regime's traditional centers of support—the party, the unions and the bureaucracy—that the regime might dispense with the critics in its own rows."[111] In Middle Eastern monarchies that have parliaments, rulers have ensured that traditional forces, especially tribes, are significantly overrepresented. This is to contain the more modern, urban-based critics of the regimes.

In sum, legislatures perform various useful services for political elites. They do, however, pose a threat to the monopoly of power enjoyed by rulers and are, therefore, closely monitored and carefully controlled. Such control focuses on the linkages between the legislature and the sociopolitical system as well as on the legislature itself.

CONTROL OVER LINKAGES BETWEEN LEGISLATURES AND SOCIOPOLITICAL SYSTEMS

Membership Selection   Control over entry into legislatures is the principal means by which the behavior of such bodies is regulated. Tightest control is maintained in Bahrain, Qatar, the United Arab Emirates, and Saudi Arabia, where all legislators are appointed by the rulers. A midpoint between appointment and election of all members is found in various countries where either the ruler appoints a set number of legislators in addition to those elected, which is the case, for example, in Egypt, or incumbents in various governmental posts have ex officio membership in the legislature. In the previous Bahrain National Assembly, for example, to which thirty members were elected in 1973, all cabinet ministers—and they were appointed by the ruler from outside the legislature—were entitled to ex officio membership. According to a Bahraini sociologist, "This voting bloc of fourteen ministers proved to be impregnable."[112] Zine al-Abidine Ben Ali, who deposed Tunisian "President for Life" Habib Bourguiba in November 1987, announced at the "Salvation Congress" of the ruling party in July 1988, as part of a short-lived package of democratic reforms, that henceforth cabinet ministers would not sit in parliament. During the Gulf crisis in the fall of 1990, Sultan Qabus, fearful of the destabilizing consequences of that crisis, made a concession to demands for democratic reforms when he announced that henceforth civil servants would not be permitted to hold seats in Oman's Consultative Council.

Except in Israel, which has had free and fair elections since the creation of the state, manipulation of elections, although less frequent in the 1990s than before, is still the norm. Such manipulation ranges from being just unfair to being completely illegal. Election districts are commonly gerrymandered, arranged in such a way as to overrepresent those individuals or social forces loyal to government. In Kuwait, the government altered the number of districts and the boundaries between them for the 1981 elections to ensure that bedouins would win a

---

[111]Volker Perthes, "Syria's Parliamentary Reform and Elections of 1990: Moving from Absolutist to Corporatist Authoritarianism?" Paper presented to the annual conference of the Middle East Studies Association of North America, Washington, D.C. (November 23–26, 1991), p. 10.

[112]Abd ul-Hadi Khalaf, "Labor Movement in Bahrain," *Merip Reports* 132 (May 1985): 25.

large number of seats and modernist reformers and Islamic fundamentalists comparatively few. In 1984, the Egyptian prime minister decreed a new election law that abolished the electoral districts that, with various minor changes, had been extant since 1923. The purpose of this change was to centralize power over nominations in the hands of the prime minister and president and to ensure the defeat of candidates not backed by them.

Resources of bureaucracies and public-sector companies are mobilized to win votes for government-backed candidates. This may take the form of the carrot—granting pay raises or extra holidays to employees just prior to elections—or the stick—refusing to grant licenses, permits, or provide other services to supporters of opposition candidates. In addition, translation of the popular vote into parliamentary seats may be unfair. In the 1984 Egyptian elections, opposition parties won 27 percent of votes but obtained only 13 percent (58) of the 448 elected seats.[113] In October 1987, Turkish Prime Minister Turgut Ozal and his ruling Motherland Party rewrote the country's electoral laws. The following month the Motherland Party and its leader won the general election, securing 292 out of 450 seats in the National Assembly, or 65 percent. The party's share of the popular vote, however, was only 36.3 percent.[114] In the April 1989 Tunisian parliamentary elections, the ruling party of President Zine al-Abidine Ben Ali won all of the seats with only 57 percent of the popular votes. The main Islamicist party, al-Nahda, despite capturing almost a quarter of the votes, did not gain a seat in parliament.[115]

A wide range of tactics designed to intimidate voters may also be employed. Ballots often are not secret; opposition candidates and their supporters may be turned away from polls or arrested on trumped-up charges; and rallies and distribution of posters and handbills are restricted or completely illegal. What are widely considered to be the freest elections held in Tunisia in over twenty years, which were by-party elections to vacant National Assembly seats in the early spring of 1988, were described as follows by a firsthand observer:

> The first thing I noticed when entering the building was that the entire entrance had been taken up by posters of the PSD (Constitutional Socialist Party) candidate—and no others. I immediately inquired but my guide—who turned out to be one of the local cell's leading members—simply said that the opposition candidates here were not very popular and had not bothered to put up posters. I entered one of the voting offices, filled to the ceiling with PSD posters in a soft pink color. I was a bit taken aback when a minute later the young woman behind the counter handed me a voting ballot: it was of the same soft pink! And later that day I was to find billboards, traffic indicators, even the cupola of a marabout shrine, swathed in pink. Inside the voting booths there were posters of the same color.[116]

---

[113]Abdel Monem Said Aly, "Democratization in Egypt," *American-Arab Affairs* 22 (Fall 1987): 18.

[114]Ken Mackenzie, "A Bizarre Affair," *Middle East International* 335 (October 7, 1988): 14.

[115]Jamal Amiar, "In Five North African States, Talk of Democracy Outpaces Action," *The Washington Report on Middle East Affairs* (July 1991): 21.

[116]Dirk Vandewalle, "Returning to Tunisia, Part II," *Institute of Current World Affairs* DJV-26 (March 1988): 3.

If such comparatively subtle techniques fail of their objective, governments are not hesitant simply to forge results. In the Syrian parliamentary election of 1990, for example, a Damascene journalist with independent views initially was announced as being among the winners. A few days later, the government overturned the result, claiming that all votes in Damascus had been recounted. In that same election Jamil al-Assad, the president's brother, won a seat in Lathaqiyyah. According to the official tally, he garnered more votes than were actually cast. Computerization of tabulation of returns has, according to a prominent Egyptian journalist noted for his satire, facilitated election fraud:

> The computer in charge of the law on election by party lists is well behaved. It speaks when we want it to speak and shuts up when we tell it to. At first it announced the election of Khaled Muhyi al-Din, leader of the NPUP, but an official glared at it, whereupon it announced the failure of Mr. Muhyi al-Din after he had won. The computer remembered that it is an official of the Ministry of Interior and announced that all candidates of the National Democratic Party had won and all opposition candidates had lost. Curses poured down on the head of the poor computer, which was only obeying orders. Then it announced that the Muslim Brotherhood and the Socialist Labor Party had won forty seats but the Wafd was finished as it had not won a single seat. Some candidate dug the computer in the ribs, whereupon the computer said forty Wafdists had been returned, then it brought down the figure to thirty-five.[117]

In general, election returns are a better indicator of the desires of the ruling elite than of the preferences of voters. If few or no critics are permitted to win an election, it signals that the elite intends to rule with an iron fist. If more opposition elements are allowed into the legislature, it means the elite is seeking through co-optation and appeasement to contain the opposition's activities at a reasonably low level. Paradoxically, it is only in the Arab monarchies of Morocco and Jordan where parliamentary and local government elections have during the 1990s become real tests of the balance of power between government and opposition and between various political parties and broader trends, such as Islamism. Elsewhere in the region, ruling elites remain too frightened of elections to allow them to proceed without extensive interference.

Control Over the Political Infrastructure   Numerous observers of Middle Eastern legislatures have been surprised by the outspoken criticism of governmental personnel and policies that frequently occurs within them. One such observer, impressed by the level of debate in the Egyptian National Assembly from 1964, assessed it as a "pioneering experiment" and a sharp departure from previous Nasserist legislatures "which were little more than rubber stamps."[118] Another commented that a visitor to one of the sessions of the Kuwaiti National As-

---

[117]al-Akhbar, April 12, 1987 (in Arabic).

[118]R. Hrair Dekmejian, *Egypt Under Nasir: A Study in Political Dynamics* (Albany: State University of New York Press, 1971), p. 155.

sembly would find it "a constant and vociferous forum for criticizing the government."[119] Following the recall of parliament by King Hussein in 1984, an expert on Jordan stated that "debates in the newly constituted Chamber of Deputies have been lively, but decorous. Quite sensitive issues, such as the way in which the government handles security measures, have been the subject of thorough debate."[120]

Ruling elites are willing to permit this surprising freedom of expression as a political safety valve to dissipate pressure building up in the system. However, while criticism of government will frequently be tolerated, attempts to establish organizational linkages are usually impeded. Legislators in the Gulf monarchies typically are allowed to form factions within their assemblies, but they are prohibited by law from joining political parties. When those legislators have appeared to be gaining popular followings, parliaments have been dissolved and the media censored. In Iraq, members of the National Assembly can in theory not be members of the ruling Ba'th Party, but in fact "candidates are screened, and only those who believe in the principles and aims of the Ba'th revolution may run for election."[121] In Egypt, where members of parliament can legally be members of opposition parties, the government, in the lead-up to the 1995 parliamentary elections, declared illegal the Muslim Brotherhood, in effect a political party and the only one with a chance of winning a significant number of seats. Even in Turkey with its long tradition of at least quasi-parliamentary government, restrictions on political organization remain. The Welfare Party, for example, which constituted government for one year after winning the largest number of seats in the 1996 election and which was deemed by the military to be posing a threat to the secular traditions of the country, as well as to its power, was banned in early 1998.

For parliamentarians to mobilize significant followings outside the legislature itself, they must be able to communicate through the media. In all countries in the region there is either outright censorship or regulated access to the media. Even the relatively free Kuwaiti press was throttled on those two occasions prior to 1990 when opposition activism in the Assembly began to threaten al-Sabah domination of the state. In many Arab countries control over the print media has been steadily relaxed but remains very tight over radio and television, which are predominantly state owned, are much more influential, and which routinely deny access to opposition candidates.

For parliamentary oppositions to become truly institutionalized and thereby restrict the powers and privileges of ruling elites, they need to be rooted in politics at lower levels, such as in villages and in quarters of major cities. In the Middle East, however, as in much of the Third World, local-level politics are not easily accessible to those in the national parliament who want to mobilize

[119]Hudson, *Arab Politics*, p. 186.

[120]Peter Gubser, "Jordan—Balancing Pluralism and Authoritarianism," *Ideology and Power*, pp. 103–104.

[121]Marr, "Iraq—Its Revolutionary Experience under the Ba'th," p. 188.

opposition to the regime. Such politics are frequently dominated by traditional elements cultivated by the regime itself. Elections at the local level are unusual. Such administrative units are typically governed by appointees. Even where elections are held, however, "they tend to be of limited significance. . . . Their function becomes primarily ceremonial. Electoral contests then determine relative prestige ratings, not program or policy issues."[122] Elections are not real choices between alternative policies because local units of government, unwilling to tax their constituents, depend on the central government for revenues. Local politicians who have access to central government patronage are the ones who dominate local government. Governments also interfere more blatantly in local elections because such interventions are less likely to invite scrutiny and condemnation. In Egypt, for example, opposition political parties have been active since 1976. They have won scores of parliamentary seats. They have yet, however, to win more than a handful of seats on local councils. As one informed observer put it, representation of the opposition "is not allowed at the level of local councils . . . where the ruling party occupies 100 percent of the seats."[123] Among the some 40,000 winners of seats on local Popular Councils in the 1997 elections, none won as a result of their association with an opposition political party.

Without linkages to viable political parties, interest groups, or local-level politics, parliamentarians are left standing more or less alone if they choose to confront government. Since independence, no Arab government has been overthrown as a result of oppositional activity originating in legislatures. In almost every Arab country, the legislature has at one time or another been dissolved. Rulers can, in short, allow their legislatures to be active "talk shops," for they know that in the crunch opposition legislators have insufficient resources to convert their words into actions.

INTERNAL CONTROLS

Constitutional/Legal Restrictions The constitutional provisions under which Middle Eastern legislatures operate are generally restrictive. Those functioning in monarchical systems in the Gulf, other than Kuwait, are in fact not true legislatures, for by law they have only consultative functions. Frequently there are explicit restrictions on the subjects that may be discussed in these legislatures. In Oman, for example, the Consultative Council is unable to "concern itself with mineral resources and the distribution of revenues derived from them."[124] Since oil accounts for more than 90 percent of government revenues and virtually 100 percent of exports, this is indeed a serious restriction. The Iraqi National Assembly may not deal with "military matters or with issues of in-

---

[122]Riggs, "Bureaucrats and Political Development," pp. 131–139.

[123]Ahmed Abdalla, "Structure of Political Participation in Egypt." Paper presented to the annual conference of the Middle East Studies Association of North America (November 23–26, 1991), p. 3. In the 1992 local council elections, opposition parties won several seats.

[124]Eickelman, "Kings and People," p. 58.

ternal security," restrictions that have rendered the Assembly virtually meaningless since 1980.[125]

In the Iraqi Assembly, as in most others, the primary legislative obligation is to review proposed legislation forwarded from a higher authority, in this case, the Revolutionary Command Council. The Iraqi Assembly, like most of those in other nonmonarchical systems, may in theory also initiate legislation. That step, however, typically requires a significant number of supporters. In Iraq's case, it is 25 percent of the membership. By comparison, the Federal National Council in the United Arab Emirates may not initiate any legislation, "but only offers recommendations on draft laws issued by the Council of Ministers, which is not, in turn, obliged to accept any of the FNC's proposals."[126]

In Arab countries, governments are formed by executives who are not responsible to legislatures and who are not obliged to choose ministers from them. There are severe restrictions on votes of no confidence. In Kuwait, for example, the Assembly can vote no confidence in a particular minister but not in the cabinet as a whole. Legislative sessions are typically commenced and terminated on the initiative of the executive or the head of the legislature, who is in every case chosen by government. The speaker of the Egyptian parliament, for example, was from 1984 until 1987 not even an elected member of that body. In 1985 and again in 1986, he terminated the legislative session ahead of schedule in order to forestall opposition criticism. In 1987–1988, President Mubarak delayed the opening of parliament for several months, finally permitting the session to commence only after the opposition threatened a boycott. Constitutional provisions favorable to legislative development are frequently ignored with impunity. The Qatar constitution calls for elections to an assembly, but they have never been held. Similarly, the Iraqi constitution of 1970 called for a representative assembly, but for nine years none was created.

Internal Administration   To operate effectively, parliaments must provide their members with staff and appropriate physical facilities, there must be a committee system, and the sessions must be of sufficient duration for reasonable deliberation to occur. These three conditions are nowhere completely satisfied. The consultative assemblies have no professional staffs. In the most highly developed Arab parliament now functioning—Egypt—the staff provided is principally for administration, not research or other policy-relevant assistance to members. Furthermore, it is available only to committee chairmen. In Oman, the council meets three times a year. The longest continual session in the region is that of Egypt's People's Assembly, which officially convenes in November and terminates in early summer. Even when in session, however, the Assembly rarely meets more than three times a week. Its committees typically convene only a few times

[125]Ahmad Yousef Ahmad, "The Dialectics of Domestic Environment and Role Performance: The Foreign Policy of Iraq," in Bahgat Korany and Ali E. Hillal Dessouki, *The Foreign Policies of Arab States* (Boulder, Colo.: Westview Press, 1984), p. 156.

[126]Peck, *The United Arab Emirates*, p. 123.

throughout the year. Arab legislative committees generally do not draft legislation but approve (or occasionally reject or amend) proposed legislation handed down from the executive.

Guarantees of Members' Freedoms   If legislatures are to perform even the comparatively unimportant task of consultation, their members must be provided reasonable guarantees against retribution for their words and actions. Parliamentary immunity is generally recognized in Middle Eastern constitutions but is frequently not absolute, and legal guarantees are occasionally violated by governments. The underlying attitude of those in authority toward the idea of complete freedom of expression for legislators is conveyed by a comment of an advisor to the late King Hussein: "Parliamentary immunity does not mean you can say whatever you think."[127] The Kuwaiti and Egyptian constitutions stipulate that the government must request the legislature to waive the immunity of a member if the government wishes to prosecute him.

In the Kuwaiti Assembly's first eleven years, the government requested waivers of immunity on nine separate occasions, six of which were for statements made to the press by deputies. In all cases but one, the Assembly refused the request if the member chose to claim immunity.[128] Subsequently, however, when the Assembly was dissolved, large numbers of journalists, including former members of the Assembly, were arrested. On two occasions in Egypt under Sadat, the immunity of members of the People's Assembly was lifted when they criticized the president. Those members were also expelled from the Assembly. In Oman and Qatar, laws governing freedom of expression restrain not the government but members of the consultative assemblies. In Oman, delegates are prohibited from discussing Assembly deliberations with nonmembers, and in Qatar, the Advisory Council's sessions are not public and proceedings may not be published.

Authoritarian But Not Totalitarian

Most Middle Eastern governments can be classified as authoritarian. The autonomy of their political institutions is limited, and there are serious constraints on personal political freedoms. These governments are, nevertheless, not totalitarian. The sharp distinction between the public and the private sphere, with strong traditions supporting the sanctity of the latter's freedom from governmental interference, combined with the weakness of Middle Eastern governments in comparison with the totalitarian archetype, means that governments dominate the formal, public political arena but largely ignore the private sphere.

Patterns of political communication in the region illustrate the difference between authoritarian and totalitarian government and public as opposed to private domains. William Rugh states the following about restrictions on the media in the Arab world.

---

[127]Day, *East Bank/West Bank,* p. 44.

[128]Baaklini, "Legislatures in the Gulf Area," pp. 368–369.

[They] are by no means comprehensive. The media have not been forced, even under one-party regimes, into the single-minded agitation and propaganda effort of the kind found in the Soviet or other totalitarian systems. The most restrictive Arab regimes have, in general, been satisfied with outward compliance by press, radio, and television, and they have not invaded the sphere of private, face-to-face communication which is still so important in the Arab societies.[129]

Governmental pressure, moreover, is typically applied not in a crude, official style but in more indirect, personal fashion. Implied threats are typically balanced with positive inducements. A Jordanian political scientist once described the late King Hussein's manner of containing the parliamentary opposition as follows:

> Often only a rumor among the "notables," the "personalities," is enough to make a prospective candidate decide not to run. It simply goes like this: "The Palace (meaning the King) or the government (meaning the Ministry of Interior) is not happy with so-and-so" . . . the candidate is in a sense "refrigerated"; he is "put on ice" for a term, or maybe two. This makes him unhappy, but not so unhappy as to conspire. Well, there is always "next time"; furthermore, his relative or friend may be elected. . . . Elements of democracy do exist; people actually vote; on occasion a veto is overridden or a government is forced to resign. Antigovernment editorials appear in newspapers, and people make speeches and criticize. There are no large-scale concentration camps and no organized system of violence by the government. In other words, freedom of action extends only to the limits decided upon by the regime.[130]

The intense personalism of Middle Eastern sociopolitical systems is a strong deterrent to ideologies and forms of government that seek to impose total submission to the state. Formal governmental authority is comprehended, deflected, and, if possible, exploited through familial, local, small-group, and other primordial ties. The gap between state and society, which is vigorously defended by informal social groupings, protects society from totalitarian rule, but it also prevents it from subordinating government to the popular will.

As social mobilization proceeds, the battleground between state and society may slowly shift to formal political organizations that constitute civil society, the "level between the family and the state (which) . . . is of crucial importance for the power of citizens to affect public life. . . ." The critical issues increasingly will become, according to Kevin Dwyer, "How and to what extent do people with similar ideas come together to form groups and associations, to publish journals, hold meetings, lobby, create public pressure, attempt in any of various ways to put their ideas into the public arena in an organized manner?"[131]

One indicator of the emergence of stronger demands for formal political participation is the growth of human rights organizations throughout the Middle East. Such organizations could be precursors of more broadly based, policy-oriented interest groups and political parties. Although their membership is

---

[129]William A. Rugh, *The Arab Press* (Syracuse N.Y.: Syracuse University Press, 1987), p. 28.

[130]Abu Jaber, "The Legislature of the Hashemite Kingdom," p. 111.

[131]Dwyer, *Arab Voices*, p. 146.

largely confined to the intelligentsia, they are perceived as irritants and sometimes as threats by governments in the region. The Arab Organization for Human Rights (AOHR), created in 1983, is the largest of its type in the region. It has branches or associated groups in Egypt, Jordan, Kuwait, Lebanon, Yemen, and the states of the Maghrib other than Libya. It has been able to focus public attention on human rights abuses and possibly to prevent their occurrence at various times and places, but it has not been able to put an absolute stop to them or to evade harassment, intimidation, and, in some cases, arrest and torture of its members. In addition, many of the successes of the AOHR have been quixotic. Egypt and Tunisia, for example, are the only two Arab countries that acceded to pressure from the AOHR and other human rights organizations to sign the Convention against Torture and Other Forms of Cruel, Inhuman or Degrading Treatment and Punishment. Yet, in June 1992, the Tunisian government dissolved the fifteen-year-old Human Rights League, the country's main human rights organization, while further intensifying its campaign of mass arrests and torture of Islamicists. Since the late 1980s, Tunisia and Egypt have repeatedly been cited by Amnesty International, the U.S. State Department, and other authoritative sources as indulging in systematic violations of human rights, including torture and other inhumane punishments. This suggests that the contraction of arbitrary state authority and concomitant expansion of civil society beyond the level of the family and small informal groups will not be brought about only by comparatively small numbers of intellectuals grouped in human rights organizations. At most they can provide openings through which larger, more broadly based movements may ultimately move to establish meaningful principles of political participation.

Evidence on the degree to which political participation has already been institutionalized is mixed. In the Arab Gulf states there are now five consultative assemblies and one legislature, whereas there were no such bodies prior to the independence of those states. Yet Kuwait and Bahrain have dissolved their legislatures a total of four times, and the consultative assemblies are constrained by a host of restrictions. The Tunisian legislature, which held out the promise of becoming a more vigorous body in the wake of the coup that brought President Ben Ali to power, has declined into irrelevance since the government decided in the wake of the 1989 elections to deal with the opposition by arrest and torture rather than through democratic means. In Turkey, the military steadily imposed more restrictions on political freedom as the challenge to Kemalism by the Kurdish insurrection and by Islamists, especially those within the Welfare Party, steadily increased in the 1990s

The Egyptian parliament under Mubarak, reinforced by comparatively outspoken opposition parties and newspapers, stands out as one of the more successful, sustained experiences of political institution-building in the 1980s. In the 1990s, however, the government has increased its control over parliament. The opposition political parties, which emerged with great hopes at the time of the 1984 election, are now languishing, for they have no arena in which peacefully to contest government policy. The democratically elected government of Sadiq al-Mahdi in the Sudan, while presiding over the return of parliamentary life after an effective seventeen-year absence, proved unable to deal with the many threatening crises and fell in a coup in 1989. Since then the Sudanese parliament has become a vehicle of Islamist mobilization rather than an arena in which different political tendencies are represented and can seek to influence public policy. The political liberalization that commenced in late 1988 in Iraq was stillborn, while that which began in Syria with the 1990 parliamentary elections has progressed glacially.

At the popular level, demands for political participation are intensifying and will continue to do so. Simultaneously, many of what are seen as prerequisites for democracy are being fulfilled. Literacy is growing, generation and dissemination of information is expanding, and economies are becoming increasingly diverse. Many Middle Easterners, having enjoyed a higher standard of living during the oil boom, are now experiencing an erosion of their economic well-being, a condition that typically stimulates political demands. Precisely how the contradiction between increasing demands for participation on the one hand and government intransigence on the other will be resolved is difficult to foretell. If repression is the only response, then political breakdown may occur. Informal participation in the private sphere and quasi-institutionalized formal political participation in the public sphere are unlikely to absorb enough citizens into politics to maintain the status quo indefinitely.

SELECTED BIBLIOGRAPHY

Baaklini, Abdo I. *Legislative and Political Development: Lebanon, 1842–1972*. Durham, N.C.: Duke University Press, 1976.

———, Guilain Denoeux, and Robert Springborg. *Legislative Politics in the Arab World: The Resurgence of Democratic Institutions*. Boulder, Colo.: Lynne Rienner Publishers, 1999.

Barnett, Michael N. *Confronting the Costs of War: Military Power, State, and Society in Egypt and Israel*. Princeton: Princeton University Press, 1992.

Be'eri, Eliezer. *Army Officers in Arab Politics and Society*. Jerusalem: Israel Universities Press, 1969.

Ben Meir, Yehuda. *Civil-Military Relations in Israel*. New York: Columbia University Press, 1995.

Birand, Mehmet Ali. *Shirts of Steel: Anatomy of the Turkish Officer Corps*. London: I. B. Tauris, 1991.

Dwyer, Kevin. *Arab Voices: The Human Rights Debate in the Middle East*. New York: Routledge, 1991.

Halpern, Manfred. *The Politics of Social Change in the Middle East and North Africa*. Princeton: Princeton University Press, 1963.

Hinnebusch, Raymond A. *Authoritarian Power and State Formation in Ba 'thist Syria: Army, Party and Peasant*. Boulder, Colo.: Westview Press, 1989.

Hurewitz, J. C. *Middle East Politics: The Military Dimension*. New York: Frederick A. Praeger, 1969.

Jreisat, Jamil E. *Politics without Process: Administering Development in the Arab World*. Boulder, Colo.: Lynne Rienner Publishers, 1997.

Landau, Jacob M., Ergun Ozbudun, and Frank Tachau. *Electoral Politics in the Middle East: Issues, Voters and Elites.* London: Croom Helm, 1980.

Lawson, Fred A. *Bahrain: The Modernization of Autocracy.* Boulder, Colo.: Westview Press, 1989.

Palmer, Monte, Leila Ali, and El Sayed Yassin. *The Egyptian Bureaucracy.* Syracuse: Syracuse University Press, 1988.

Peri, Yoram. *Between Battles and Ballots: Israeli Military in Politics.* Cambridge: Cambridge University Press, 1983.

Peterson, J. E. *The Arab Gulf States: Steps Toward Political Participation.* New York: Frederick A. Praeger, 1988.

Rugh, William A. *The Arab Press.* Second ed. Syracuse: Syracuse University Press, 1987.

Chapter 7

The Arab-Israeli Conflict: The Politics of Competitive State-Building

No other aspect of Middle Eastern politics has received the attention that has been devoted to the Arab-Israeli conflict. Paradoxically, even close observers have often failed to understand this important issue. For some, the conflict is so emotionally charged that they are unable to analyze it rationally and objectively. For all, it is extremely complex, involving actors and interactions at and between three different levels.

At the heart of the dispute is competition between two peoples, Israeli Jews and Palestinian Arabs, to control the same piece of land, known to the former as Israel and to the latter as Palestine. To Zionists—those who believe that Jews have a right to a national home in historic Palestine—the claim to this land is based on the existence of a Jewish nation there some two thousand years ago. It is further justified by perceptions of abiding anti-Semitism, by the trauma of the Holocaust, by claims that Jews have "made the desert bloom," by the relatively democratic nature of the state, and by the assertion that Palestinian claimants to the land are Arabs and thus should be accommodated by one or more of the many Arab states in the region.

Palestinian counterclaims rest on their ownership and occupation of the land for centuries, on the fact that they played no part in the Holocaust and their denial that they harbor anti-Semitic beliefs (both Arabic and Hebrew are Semitic languages), on the argument that Western powers implanted Israel in the region without the permission of its residents, and on the basis that Palestinian national and civil rights are denied by the presence of a state that accords such rights exclusively or primarily to Jews. Since the beginning of Zionist settlement in Palestine in the late nineteenth century, each side has considered the other a mortal threat to its existence, an enemy with whom compromise may be more dangerous than resolute opposition.

The Arab states constitute a second level of participants in the conflict. That these twenty-one states—which possess almost two-thirds of the world's proven oil reserves, now number 260 million people, and have several million men under arms—have not been able to gain the upper hand diplomatically or militarily against Israel, to say nothing of regaining all of the West Bank and Gaza, an area about the size of metropolitan Los Angeles, attests to the fact that the Arab states have not really united behind the Palestinians. From the moment Jewish settlement began to pose a serious threat to Palestinians, Arab leaders sought to gain advantage for themselves and their states out of the confrontation between those two peoples.

Amir Faisal, who had cooperated with the British in leading the Arab revolt and who sought European consent to the establishment of his Arab Kingdom centered on Damascus, pledged in 1919 to the Zionist leader Chaim Weizmann his support for Jewish immigration to Palestine. In exchange, Weizmann promised that Zionists would use their influence in European capitals in support of Faisal's endeavor. In 1937, when the British Peel Commission proposed the creation of a Jewish state through the partition of Palestine, leaders of surrounding Arab states "saw the British predicament in Palestine as a unique opportunity to gain influence with His Majesty's Government, as well as to assert their rival claims to Arab leadership."[1]

In 1938, Transjordan proposed incorporating that part of Palestine allotted to the Palestinians in the 1937 partition plan into a United Kingdom, a scheme that was to give King Abdullah control over the Palestinians, thereby elevating his leadership pretensions. The Egyptian, Lebanese, and Syrian military interventions in May 1948 into the civil war that had been raging since December 1947 between Jews and Palestinians "was not aimed at destroying the Jewish State. It was intended to prevent Abdullah from annexing the Arab part of Palestine as the first step in the implementation of his British-inspired Greater Syria plan. . . . Both [Abdullah and his Arab opponents] were ready to consider an alliance with Israel to further their aspirations."[2]

The Arab states have never fought a war against Israel to liberate Palestinians from Israeli control by military means. In 1956, Egypt defended itself against the Israeli, British, and French tripartite invasion. Egyptian-Syrian rivalry and attempts by each to outbid the other's radicalism, although neither had the intention of waging war, paved the way for the Israeli attack of June 1967. The War of Attrition along the Suez Canal in 1969–1970 was an attempt by Nasser to prevent Israel's occupation of Sinai from becoming a fait accompli. The October 1973 war was initiated by Egypt and Syria for the limited purpose of altering the context for diplomacy aimed at regaining the Sinai and Golan Heights and possibly the West Bank and Gaza.

---

[1]Aaron S. Klieman, "The Arab States and Palestine," in *Zionism and Arabism in Palestine and Israel,* ed. by Elie Kedourie and Sylvia G. Haim (London: Frank Cass, 1982), p. 118.

[2]Simha Flapan, *The Birth of Israel: Myths and Realities* (New York: Pantheon Books, 1987), pp. 150, 151.

Just as the Arab states have hesitated to dedicate themselves to the military objective of "liberating Palestine," so have they been unable to coordinate diplomatic strategies to that end. Since the 1930s, ruling elites in the Arab states have placed paramount emphasis on inter-Arab politics. They have subordinated their concerns for Palestinians and their conflicts with Israel to the desire of maintaining or enhancing their position within the never-ending Arab Cold War.[3] As Walid Kazziha states, "As far as the Arab regimes are concerned, the Palestinian cause is, and has been, a pawn in inter-Arab rivalry."[4]

Arab political leaders are also constrained by their obligations to seek to maximize their own states' interests—by *raison d'état*. They are aware that selfless national dedication to the Palestinian cause would lead immediately to a confrontation with Israel that no Arab state could win alone, even with support of several others. Nasser urged his people to make considerable sacrifices for the Palestinians, resentment over which ultimately helped pave the way for Sadat's action—his "Egypt-first" policy. Statehood and resulting state interests inevitably erected a barrier between stateless Palestinians and other Arabs. Ruling elites could surmount this obstacle only by calling on their populations to risk a fight to the death, as the Palestinians have done. The alternative is partial commitment and diplomatic maneuvering involving the Arab states, Israel, the Palestinians, and various outside parties. Out of this diplomatic maneuvering, leaders of the Arab states hope a favorable resolution of the Arab-Israeli conflict might emerge, but they are reluctant to take great risks to achieve that end.

A plethora of extraregional actors who are involved in the Arab-Israeli conflict constitute the third dimension of analysis. No other conflict in the Third World has for so long attracted the interests of such a broad range of states and international organizations. Zionist aspirations in Palestine could never have been fulfilled had it not been for British support during and after World War I and American support since World War II. Even the fascist governments of Germany and Italy sought to further their own interests by supporting Zionism.[5] The Soviets first became heavily involved in the conflict after World War II. They supported the Zionists at that time out of the calculation that a Jewish state would reduce British influence in the Eastern Mediterranean region. The United Nations presided over the creation of the state of Israel by virtue of the General Assembly's endorsement of the Partition Resolution on November 29, 1947. Since then the United Nations and its various organizations have served as arenas in which much of the diplomacy surrounding the conflict has been conducted.

---

[3]The term *Arab Cold War* was coined by Malcolm Kerr to apply to the struggle for power between Nasser and his opponents in the 1950s and 1960s. It remains appropriate today. See Malcolm Kerr, *The Arab Cold War, Gamal'Abd al-Nasir and His Rivals, 1958–1970,* 3d ed. (Oxford: Oxford University Press, 1971).

[4]Walid Kazziha, *Palestine in the Arab Dilemma* (London: Croom Helm, 1979), p. 17.

[5]On relations between Zionism and European fascist movements and governments between 1920 and World War II, see Lenni Brenner, *Zionism in the Age of Dictators* (London: Croom Helm, 1983); and Brenner, *The Iron Wall: Zionist Revisionism from Jabotinsky to Shamir* (London: Zed Books, 1984). See also Francis R. Nicosia, *The Third Reich and the Palestine Question* (Austin: University of Texas Press, 1985).

The Arab-Israeli conflict has received more attention than any other Third World issue in such disparate organizations as the European Community, the Organization of African States, the Non-Aligned Movement, and the International Socialist Organization. In much of the Third World, the Arab-Israeli conflict epitomizes and symbolizes the legacy of colonialism and continuing intervention by the West into formerly colonized areas. The conflict served for over forty years as a testing ground for the military equipment, ideological appeal, international leverage, and diplomatic capacities of the superpowers. The inability of the world's other major powers, including the Europeans, Chinese, and Japanese, to affect substantially the course of the conflict stands as a stark reminder of their subordinate status in global politics even after the collapse of the USSR. The world's states and political organizations have, in sum, become entangled in the Arab-Israeli conflict in differing and unique ways, thereby rendering it all the more complex and difficult to resolve.

Precisely because of the intensity, durability, and intractability of the Arab-Israeli conflict, observers and policy makers commonly seek to render it comprehensible by sharply reducing its complexity in their own minds. This is understandable and occasionally desirable, for in order to act decisively, decision makers may need to simplify reality. President Jimmy Carter, for example, interpreted the conflict in religious terms, as the title of his book on the subject, *The Blood of Abraham,* suggests.[6] President Ronald Reagan, on the other hand, viewed the conflict as one pitting pro-Soviet against pro-American forces in the region. However, there are dangers and costs in simplifying reality, as both Presidents Carter and Reagan discovered when their attempts to resolve the conflict met with failure. Their simplified perspectives impeded understanding of the motives and behavior of key actors in the dispute. For presidents and public alike, so many adages, myths, and outright fallacies have grown up around the Arab-Israeli conflict that its analysis is unusually problematical. Beliefs held by these two former American presidents reflect the broader situation.

According to Jimmy Carter: "To understand the roots of the hatred and bloodshed that still shape the relationships among the people of the region, it is useful to go back to the holy scriptures of ancient times. To a remarkable degree, the will of God is the basis for both esoteric debates and the most vicious terrorist attacks among Jews, Muslims, and Christians."[7] This perspective—that the contemporary Arab-Israeli conflict is a modern manifestation of a recurring religious conflict of ancient origins—is inaccurate and misleading. There were no "Arabs" (hence no Arab-Israeli conflict) in *Eretz Yisrael* (the biblical term for the land of Israel). The Arab invasion of Syria-Palestine occurred in the seventh century, more than a half-millennium after the Romans put down Jewish rebellions in Judea, sending some of the population into exile. A larger percentage of the Jewish population, in fact, remained in what in the later Roman Empire was called Palestine, a name the Greek historian Herodotus introduced into the

---

[6]Jimmy Carter, *The Blood of Abraham* (Boston: Houghton Mifflin, 1985).

[7]Ibid., p. 4.

written record in the fifth century B.C. The majority of Jews who remained converted to Christianity. Following the Arab invasion of Palestine, the majority of Christians converted to Islam. It is most probably the case, therefore, that a significant percentage of Muslim and Christian Palestinians are descended from Jews who converted over a thousand years ago.

The equation of ancient Hebrews with modern Jews is also questionable, for "serious study of this matter has shown that the latter have no basis to claim genuine descent from the former to any meaningful extent."[8] According to Maxime Rodinson, "It is very probable, that the so-called Arab inhabitants of Palestine . . . have much more of the ancient Hebrews' 'blood' than most of the Jews of the Diaspora, whose religious exclusiveness in no way prevented them from absorbing converts of various religions."[9] For 1,300 years Middle Eastern Jews have lived under Muslim rule. Until modern times, there were remarkably few incidents of religious conflict. Most clashes occurred after Zionism made its presence felt in the Middle East in the twentieth century. The contemporary Arab-Israeli conflict is not simply a rerun of ancient religious dramas but a product of the creation of the state system in the area after the collapse of the Ottoman Empire in 1918.

Interpretation of the conflict as nothing more than an extension of superpower rivalry was also inaccurate and misleading. Yet this was the predominant view of the Reagan administration and an outlook previously associated with President Eisenhower's secretary of state, John Foster Dulles. Communism had little popular support or organizational capacity in the region. Those states that had developed close relations with the Soviet Union did so out of *raison d'état* rather than ideological concerns. Arab states sought to draw the Soviet Union into the region to counterbalance U.S. support for Israel, but even this tactic was subject to reversal, as Sadat demonstrated by ordering Soviet military advisors out of Egypt in July 1972 and by subsequently forging an alliance with the United States. Middle Eastern decision makers are motivated by regional, not global, concerns, a fact that leaders of the United States, whose perspectives are precisely opposite, have been prone to overlook.

Those most intimately involved in the conflict reduce its complexity by creating caricaturized images that portray their enemies in unidimensionally evil terms. Many Israelis transpose images of the Nazis onto the Arabs. David Ben-Gurion, first prime minister and minister of defense and the "father" of Israel, described Arabs as "the pupils and even the teachers of Hitler, who claim that

---

[8]Ray L. Cleveland, "The Palestinians and the Diminution of Historical Legitimacy," in *Palestine: Continuing Dispossession*, ed. by Glenn E. Perry (Belmont, Mass.: Association of Arab-American University Graduates, 1986), p. 104. On this point, see also Raphael Patai and Jennifer P. Wing, *The Myth of the Jewish Race* (New York: Scribner, 1975).

[9]Maxime Rodinson, *Israel: A Colonial Settler State?* (New York: Monad Press, 1973), p. 79. A group of ultra-Orthodox rabbis and scientists in Israel are of the opinion that there are specifically Jewish genes and therefore a Jewish race. This theory, however, is generally discarded by other Israeli scientists and intellectuals as being religiously motivated, unscientific speculation. See Hila Tov, "The Theory of the Jewish Race," *Hadashot* (March 13, 1992), reprinted in *From the Hebrew Press: Monthly Translations and Commentaries from Israel* 4 (May 1992): 10–16.

there is only one way to solve the Jewish question—one way only: total annihilation."[10] Menachem Begin, who served as Israeli prime minister from 1977 until 1983, referred to members of the Palestine Liberation Organization (PLO) as "two-legged animals" and justified Israeli attempts to kill Yasser Arafat in Beirut in the summer of 1982 by comparing the mission to the Allied bombings of Berlin in World War II intended to destroy Hitler in his bunker.[11] Prime Minister Yitzhak Shamir, condemning the UN General Assembly's move to Geneva in December 1988 to enable Yasser Arafat to address it, compared him to Nazi propaganda chief Goebbels.[12]

The perception of Arabs as bent on the destruction of Israel is accompanied by a heightened concern—bordering on a fixation—with security (*bitahon* in Hebrew). It is, according to Jean-Pierre Langellier, "the sledgehammer argument."[13] Bitahon is cited to justify a range of uncompromising policies, from refusal to withdraw from the occupied territories to bulldozing Palestinian houses.

Many Arabs perceive Israelis as modern-day Crusaders, or colonial settlers, such as the Boers in South Africa, the French in Algeria, or the British or Spanish in various parts of the New World.[14] These images call for *sumud,* the Arabic term for persistence, steadfastness, perseverance. According to this perspective, sumud will ultimately reward the Arabs with the departure of the Israelis, just as the Crusaders and the French colonists were forced to depart. Thus, for each side, caricaturized images serve to justify uncompromising behavior and policies toward the other. Rooted so deeply in the political consciousnesses of the two peoples, policies of intransigence are extremely difficult to replace with those of accommodation.

Surrounding the adverse images of the enemy and the determined adherence to policies based on bitahon or sumud are partially or largely mythologized versions of the conflict itself. Over the years both sides have created their own interpretations, their own stories of the events that have made up this conflict during the course of the twentieth century. Each has sought to convince the rest of the world that its version is the correct one. Israel has enjoyed greater success in this effort for a variety of reasons, which are summed up in Rashid Khalidi's phrase, "History is written by the victors."[15] In this case the victors, largely of European origins, had the skills, contacts, and receptive audiences in the West that ensured the predominance of their arguments.

---

[10]David Ben-Gurion, *Memoirs* (Tel Aviv: United Kibbutz, 1974), vol. 4 (in Hebrew), p. 392, cited in Flapan, *The Birth of Israel,* p. 235.

[11]Ibid., p. 235.

[12]World press services, December 13, 1988.

[13]Jean-Pierre Langellier, "The New Palestinian Nationalism Changes Israeli Society," *The Guardian Weekly* 136 (June 14, 1987): 13.

[14]Rodinson, *Israel: A Colonial Settler State?* pp. 27–29; and Edward W. Said, *The Question of Palestine* (New York: Vintage Books, 1979), pp. 56–114.

[15]Rashid Khalidi, "Palestinian Peasant Resistance to Zionism Before World War I," in *Blaming the Victims: Spurious Scholarship and the Palestinian Question,* ed. by Edward Said and Christopher Hitchens (New York: Verso, 1988), p. 207.

In recent years, first steps have been taken to restore balance in the struggle over the "truth" of the conflict. Palestinians, other Arabs, Western, and, most important, Israeli scholars, have undertaken to write histories that seek to revise accepted wisdoms by bringing to light newly released information or by reinterpreting old facts.[16] Of greatest importance in this regard has been the effort to disentangle myth from reality concerning the creation of Israel. The events of 1947–1949 are of special significance because interpretation of them served to legitimate Israel's claim to statehood and its refusal to accept the return of Palestinian refugees. Thus, contemporary efforts to negotiate a peace settlement inevitably turn back to this period, such as, for instance, the PLO's proposal in November 1988 to resolve the conflict on the basis of UN Resolution 181 of 1947, known as the Partition Resolution. The Israeli victory in 1967 had an analogue in the creation of Israel in 1947–1949 because it entailed the occupation of Arab land and the dispossession of many of its inhabitants. It thereby, once again, raised questions about borders and relations with Arabs, issues that have yet to be resolved.

The Creation of Israel: Old Myths and New Truths

PARTITION PLAN

Leaders of the Yishuv (Jewish community in Palestine) accepted the November 29, 1947, Partition Resolution of the United Nations, but Palestinians rejected it. This has been commonly interpreted as indicating the moderateness of the former and the intransigence of the latter, despite the fact that by the conclusion of the armistice agreements with the Arab states in 1949 the new Jewish state occupied nearly 80 percent of the territory of Palestine, compared with some 55 percent that had been allotted it in the Partition Resolution. Palestinian rejection of partition helped deny them their state and facilitated the incorporation of their territory into Israel and Jordan.

That the Partition Resolution was unfavorable to Palestinians, both in its substance and in the procedure by which it was approved, has been part of the historical record since 1947, although it has not received wide attention. At the beginning of 1947, Palestinians numbered 1.3 million, compared with a Jewish population of 600,000. The latter owned only 6 to 7 percent of the total land area. Nevertheless, the Partition Plan awarded the Jewish state the larger portion and by so doing necessarily included within it an Arab minority of some 250,000, or about 40 percent of the population. That almost a third of Palestinians were to be denied their hope for an independent Arab state and were to live under Jewish rule; that control over a large amount of property was, in effect, to be

---

[16]For a critical review of revisionist histories of Israel and its founding, see Efraim Karsh, *Fabricating Israeli History: The "New Historians"* (London: Frank Cass, 1997). For a review of Karsh's work, see Benny Morris, "Refabricating 1948," *Journal of Palestine Studies* 27, 2 (Winter 1998): 81–95.

transferred from Arab to Jewish hands; and that the Arab state was to be relatively small, deprived of most of the fertile coastal area and cut off from Syria and
the Red Sea, were the reasons that the Palestinians rejected the Partition Plan.
Insult was added to Palestinian injury by the manner in which the resolution was
passed in the United Nations, of which, at the time, few Third World nations
were members. The United States, after an intense lobbying effort by American
Zionists directed at the White House, brought leverage to bear on several recalcitrant but vulnerable member-states to induce them to vote for partition.[17]

An important addition to the historical record, made by Israeli revisionist
and other scholars (most especially by Simha Flapan, an Israeli intellectual and
political activist who died in 1987) is information that Jewish acceptance of partition was only a tactical move designed to pave the way for a military confrontation with the Palestinians. Jewish leaders knew them to be weak, neither desirous
of nor prepared for war. David Ben-Gurion and others assumed that the Palestinians would lose further territories to the new Jewish state and that those Palestinians not under Jewish control would be denied statehood by King Abdullah of
Jordan, with whom the Jewish leadership had made a secret arrangement.[18] Ben-
Gurion is revealed by his diary and other sources to have accepted the principle
of partition from 1937 on the grounds that it would legitimate the Jewish state,
pave the way for the "transfer" of much if not all of the Arab population to surrounding Arab states, and leave open the question of borders, which he thought
would ultimately be determined in a favorable manner by force of arms. In 1937,
for example, he stated, "We shall accept a state in the boundaries fixed today—
but the boundaries of Zionist aspirations are the concerns of the Jewish people
and no external factor will be able to limit them."[19] In a letter written at this time
he asserted, "We must expel Arabs and take their places."[20] In the following year,
Ben-Gurion defended partition on the grounds that following the establishment
of the state, "We will cancel the partition of the country (between Jews and
Arabs) and we will expand throughout the land of Israel."[21] Three and a half
months after fighting commenced between Palestinians and Jews in the wake of
the UN's endorsement of the Partition Resolution, Ben-Gurion assessed the opponent as follows: "They, the decisive majority of them, do not want to fight us,
and all of them together are unable to stand up to us."[22] For the Yishuv, partition

[17]For a judicious review of these lobbying activities, see John Snetsinger, *Truman, the Jewish Vote, and the Creation of Israel* (Stanford: Hoover Institution Press, 1974), pp. 58–72.

[18]Flapan, *The Birth of Israel*, pp. 13–80. See also Avi Shlaim, *The Politics of Partition: King Abdullah, the Zionist Movement, and the Partition of Palestine, 1921–1951* (New York: Columbia University Press, 1990).

[19]Ben-Gurion, *Memoirs*, vol. 4, p. 151, cited in Flapan, *The Birth of Israel*, p. 53.

[20]Letter from David Ben-Gurion to A. Ben-Gurion, October 5, 1937, cited in Shabtai Teveth, *Ben-Gurion and the Palestine Arabs* (Oxford: Oxford University Press, 1985), p. 89.

[21]Protocol of the meeting of the Jewish Agency Executive, June 7, 1938, Central Zionist Archives, 28, cited in Benny Morris, *The Birth of the Palestinian Refugee Problem, 1947–1949* (Cambridge: Cambridge University Press, 1987), p. 24.

[22]Document no. 274, p. 460, of the Central Zionist Archives, December 1947–May 1948), cited in ibid., p. 73.

was a golden opportunity to establish a Jewish state in almost all of Palestine, while at the same time opening the door for the expulsion of the Arabs.

PALESTINIAN EXODUS

Between December 1947 and September 1949 over 700,000 Palestinians, or more than half the total population, fled their homes, while 130,000 to 160,000 remained behind in the new state of Israel. The voluntary or compulsory "transfer" of the Arab population out of the Jewish state, which was a manifest Zionist desire to outside observers as early as 1919 and which had become an integral part of Zionist thinking no later than the 1930s, had been all but accomplished.[23] But how did this "miracle," as Ben-Gurion termed it, happen?

The claim "found in all official Zionist history and propaganda and all Israeli information publications" is that Israel was not responsible for the Palestinian exodus. Indeed, it tried to stop it.[24] A key piece of evidence for this proposition is the allegation that Arab leaders broadcast radio messages urging Palestinians to flee, an assertion that continues to be found in pro-Israeli literature.[25] In 1961, Erskine Childers, an Irish journalist, later to become president of Ireland, proved beyond doubt that "there was not a single order, or appeal, or suggestion about evacuation from Palestine from any Arab radio station, inside or outside Palestine, in 1948. There is repeated monitored record of Arab appeals, even flat orders, to the civilians of Palestine to stay put." Childers did find evidence, however, that Zionist stations had been broadcasting in Arabic urging Palestinians to leave.[26]

The Palestinian claim is that the Zionists adopted a systematic campaign of terrorizing Arabs to induce them to flee and, when and if that failed, simply forced them from their homes and into exile at gunpoint. This interpretation may be closer to the truth, but it is not entirely correct. There were incidents of purposeful brutality. The massacre of more than 250 villagers at Deir Yassin, on April 9, 1948, by the Jewish underground groups known as the Irgun Zvai Leumi, led by Menachem Begin, and the Lohamei Herut Yisrael (LEHI, or Stern Gang), of which Yitzhak Shamir was a leader, was intended to strike terror into the Palestinian population and frighten the people into leaving. Following the massacre, Zionist forces drove into Arab villages with loudspeaker trucks instructing the inhabitants "to run for your lives unless you want another Deir

---

[23]For a review of the development of the notion of "transfer," see Morris, *The Birth of the Palestinian Refugee Problem*, pp. 23–28. The King-Crane Commission, sent to Palestine on a fact-finding mission in 1919, reported that "the Zionists look forward to a practically complete dispossession of the Palestinian people." Cited in Edward W. Said, et al., "A profile of the Palestinian People," in *Blaming the Victims*, ed. by Said and Hitchens, p. 238.

[24]Flapan, *The Birth of Israel*, p. 84.

[25]See, for example, Leonard J. Davis, *Myths and Facts 1985: A Concise Record of the Arab-Israeli Conflict* (Washington: Near East Report, 1984).

[26]Erskine Childers, "The Other Exodus," *The Spectator* (May 12, 1961), reprinted in *The Arab-Israeli Reader: A Documentary History of the Middle East Conflict*, ed. by Walter Laqueur and Barry Rubin (New York: Penguin, 1984), pp. 143–151.

Yassin."[27] Virtually the entire populations of two major Palestinian towns, Lydda and Ramle, which numbered some 50,000 to 70,000 inhabitants, were stampeded by the Yishuv's army, the Haganah, into a mass exodus as a result of a direct order given by Ben-Gurion to Generals Yigal Allon and Yitzhak Rabin.[28]

In mid-March 1948, Jewish military commanders put into effect Plan D, which embodied a military strategy to secure territory. The doctrinal underpinning of Plan D was that the fewer Palestinians left behind, the better.[29] Nevertheless, "Plan D was not a political blueprint for the expulsion of Palestine's Arabs."[30] The overall consequence of Israeli action, however, was to contribute overwhelmingly to the Palestinians' desire to flee. According to Israeli military estimates of the time, "84 percent left in direct response to Israeli actions."[31] The government of Israel, however, has from the outset contended that because Palestinians fled of their own accord, as well as for other reasons, they have no right to return or to repatriation, as is specified in UN General Assembly Resolution 194 of December 1948.

PEACE NEGOTIATIONS

Another myth widely accepted as fact is that whereas Israel sought peace with the Arabs from the moment of its creation, the Arabs remained intransigent, consistently refusing to negotiate. Actually, before, during, and after the first Arab-Israeli war, leaders of the Arab states made numerous peace overtures that were rebuffed by an Israeli leadership "which maintained that time was on Israel's side and that Israel could manage perfectly well without peace with the Arab states and without a solution to the Palestinian refugee problem."[32] King Abdullah of Transjordan made a secret agreement with the Israelis prior to the outbreak of hostilities in 1947 to the effect that his troops would occupy the areas awarded to the Palestinians in the partition plan but would not attack Jewish positions. While Abdullah kept his side of the agreement, the Israelis did not keep theirs, seizing by force of arms portions of the Arab territory. In September 1948, Ben-Gurion even tried to persuade his provisional government to launch an all-out attack on the West Bank, including the Old City of Jerusalem,

---

[27]Ibid., p. 148.

[28]Morris, *The Birth of the Palestinian Refugee Problem*, p. 207.

[29]Ibid., pp. 62–64, 113, 289.

[30]Ibid., p. 62. Some revisionist historians do not accept this interpretation and argue instead that Plan D was part of an overall strategy to drive Palestinians out of areas occupied by Jewish forces. For a debate over this issue, see Norman Finkelstein, Nur Masalha, and Benny Morris, "Debate on the 1948 Exodus," *Journal of Palestine Studies* 21 (Autumn 1991): 66–114; and Norman Finkelstein, "Debate on the 1948 Exodus: Rejoinder," *Journal of Palestine Studies* 21 (Winter 1992): 61–71. See also Laurence J. Silberstein, ed., *New Perspectives on Israeli History: The Early Years of the State* (New York: New York University Press, 1991); and Ilan Pappe, *The Making of the Arab-Israeli Conflict, 1947–1951* (London: I. B. Tauris, 1992).

[31]Flapan, *The Birth of Israel*, p. 89.

[32]Avi Shlaim, "Husni Za'im and the Plan to Resettle Palestinian Refugees in Syria," *Journal of Palestine Studies* 60 (Summer 1986): 79.

to incorporate it into the new state and deny Abdullah any land west of the Jordan River. That proposal was rejected for fear that it would jeopardize Israel's relations with Britain, the United States, and the UN.[33] Meanwhile, Abdullah continued to receive Israeli emissaries and make proposals for reducing the level of conflict right up until his assassination in February 1951.[34]

Other Arab leaders behaved like Abdullah, meeting with Israeli government officials and stating their conditions for terminating hostilities and recognizing Israel. Egyptian officials, including two prime ministers, had been in touch with leadership of the Yishuv prior to the outbreak of war for the purpose of trying to come to terms with the Jewish community. In September 1948, King Farouk offered to negotiate a separate peace with Israel. As these negotiations were proceeding, Ben-Gurion ordered military offensives against Egyptian positions in the Negev, thereby terminating the possibility of an Israeli-Egyptian settlement.[35] Several years later, President Nasser indicated a willingness to talk about peace with Israel, receiving an American mediator for that purpose. A massive raid on Egyptian positions in the Gaza ordered by Ben-Gurion in February 1955 caused those efforts to be stillborn.[36] In 1949, Husni Za'im, the Syrian leader, stated his desire to meet Ben-Gurion, sign a peace treaty with Israel, and settle at least 350,000 Palestinian refugees in eastern Syria. The U.S. State Department urged the Israeli prime minister to pursue the offer. His response was to set such impossible conditions that the "Americans could not believe their ears."[37]

Flapan's conclusion from the historical evidence is that "from the end of World War II to 1952, Israel turned down successive proposals made by Arab states and by neutral mediators that might have brought about an accommodation."[38] It did so because it did not want to make territorial concessions, to allow creation of a Palestinian state, or to repatriate even a token number of refugees. As a consequence, not only did it become more difficult for the Arab states in subsequent years to entertain the possibility of recognizing and negotiating a final peace with Israel, but the unresolved Palestinian issue ensured the perpetuation of hostility and violence that has as yet to abate.

Myths surrounding partition, the Palestinian exodus, and peace negotiations are only some of those that have grown up since 1947–1949, but they are those that careful historical scholarship has now most fully exposed. The prevalence of misconceptions detrimental to the Arab position is not, however, an indication that only the Israelis have taken liberties with the truth in presenting

---

[33]Tom Segev, *1949: The First Israelis* (New York: The Free Press, 1986), p. 14.

[34]Ibid., pp. 15–21. See also Avi Shlaim, *The Politics of Partition.*

[35]Flapan, *The Birth of Israel,* pp. 133–134, 205–208.

[36]Elmore Jackson, *Middle East Mission* (New York: W. W. Norton, 1983).

[37]Segev, *1949: The First Israelis,* p. 16.

[38]Flapan, *The Birth of Israel,* p. 10. For contrasting views of the proposition that Israel's intransigence was the key factor that impeded peace settlements with its Arab neighbors at this time, see Itamar Rabinovich, *The Road Not Taken: Early Arab-Israeli Negotiations* (New York: Oxford University Press, 1991); and Benny Morris, *"Israel's Border Wars, 1949–1956: Arab Infiltration, Israeli Retaliation, and the Countdown to the Suez* War (New York: Oxford University Press, 1993).

an interpretation favorable to themselves. The Arab states have sought to do the same, the difference being that they have been considerably less successful.

Nasser tried to justify the crushing defeat of his military in 1967 by claiming that planes from the U.S. Sixth Fleet had attacked Egypt. Although initially accepted as true by large numbers of Egyptians and Arabs, this claim was subsequently discarded as the fabrication it was.[39] Sadat portrayed the October 1973 war as an outright Egyptian victory despite the encirclement of his Sixth Army in the Sinai and the presence of Israeli forces west of the Suez Canal. That attempt at myth making was also unsuccessful. Palestinians, more concerned with discrediting myths created at their expense than inventing new ones, have nevertheless occasionally succumbed to the temptation to lay the blame for everything at Israel's doorstep. Israel is not responsible for all the assassinations of Palestinian political activists that have occurred, despite ritualistic accusations to that effect by the PLO. Nor is it conceivable that Israeli agent provocateurs are behind attacks on Jewish institutions in Europe or elsewhere, as has sometimes been claimed by Palestinian political figures. Israel was alleged by Yasser Arafat and his supporters in the PLO to have distorted the record of Palestinian support for the Iraqi invasion of Kuwait in 1990. It was Arafat himself, however, who in the presence of a battery of television cameras had embraced Saddam Hussein immediately after Iraqi troops had stormed into Kuwait. Finally, many Arabs have constructed an elaborate general myth in which Israel is blamed for all internal Arab bickering, their own clumsy public relations, their political instability, and other social and economic problems.

Israel's comparative success in convincing important audiences of the veracity of its claims and the justness of its position is due in part to the fact that in the critical period from the end of World War I until 1948, Zionists built far more effective political institutions than did the Palestinians. As Benny Morris observes, "The British Mandate of 1920–1948 can be seen as a nursery in which two societies competed and raced to achieve self-government. The Yishuv won the race outright. Its 'National Institutions' almost from the first were built with an eye to conversion into institutions of state."[40] By contrast, Palestinian political structures remained weak, riven with factionalism, and lacking support from the Arab states, which at the time were under the direct or indirect control of imperial powers. Thus, while Jewish state formation is virtually a textbook case of the skillful combination of ideology, organization, and external support, Palestinian attempts to formulate mobilizational ideologies, construct large-scale organizations, and successfully enlist outside assistance only began to witness a modicum of success after the June 1967 war. But by that time, less than half the Palestinian population remained in the territory that had been Mandate Palestine.

---

[39]For judicious assessments of this claim and an allegation that U.S. air force planes had provided reconnaissance assistance to the Israelis, as well as for more general accounts of the American role in the 1967 war, see Richard B. Parker's excellent recent works, including *The Politics of Miscalculation in the Middle East* (Bloomington: Indiana University Press, 1993), pp. 99–122; (as editor) *The Six Day War: A Retrospective* (Gainesville: University Press of Florida, 1996); and "USAF in the Sinai in the 1967 War: Fact or Fiction?" *Journal of Palestine Studies* 27, 1 (Autumn 1997): 67–75.

[40]Morris, *The Birth of the Palestinian Refugee Problem*. p. 16.

Israeli State Formation

The leadership of the Yishuv declared the creation of the state of Israel on May 15, 1948. The two superpowers rushed to recognize the Jewish state, both hoping to establish preeminent influence within it. In a matter of weeks, the Israeli army had absorbed the initial advance by the armies of the Arab states and thrown them back, accumulating more territory in the process. Israel's war of independence was brought to successful conclusion in 1949 with the signing of armistice agreements with Egypt, Lebanon, Syria, and Transjordan. In that year the first Knesset elections were held, and the process of absorption of the additional 700,000 Jews who had arrived by 1952 began. Since then, Israel has emerged not only as the militarily most powerful country in the region but also the one within which the participatory infrastructure—of interest groups, political parties, and a parliament—is best established. These successes owe much to the "state idea" of Israel—its legitimating ideology—that is Zionism.

Zionism is a product of the tumult of nineteenth-century Europe. The French revolution opened the door to the assimilation of French Jews, and that process rapidly spread throughout Western Europe. In Eastern Europe, on the other hand, and especially in Russia, Jews met with increasing persecution and enforced isolation from non-Jewish society. In this hostile environment, thoughts of establishing a Jewish state began to be expressed and to take organizational form. Y. L. Pinsker in 1881 published *Autoemancipation,* in which he argued that Jews must liberate themselves by becoming self-sufficient. This required their own territory somewhere, although not necessarily in Palestine. Pinsker subsequently became the leader of the Hibbat Zion (The Love of Zion) movement, which sent immigrants to Palestine, although at this stage most were inspired not by political Zionism and its commitment to a radical, agrarian-socialist nationalism but by religion.

Ultimately, Western Europe also provided critical ideological, organizational, and financial resources for the Zionist movement. The stimulus for Zionism there, as in Russia, was anti-Semitism. By the 1890s, commitment to assimilation into Western European society was being questioned by even prominent, well-established Jewish professionals, the most famous of whom was Theodor Herzl.

A Viennese journalist born in Budapest, Theodor Herzl as a young man believed that discrimination against Jews was incompatible with the secular, liberal societies he saw emerging in Western Europe and would, therefore, disappear. That belief was shattered by the incidents of anti-Semitism he observed in France while a correspondent there in the early 1890s. The Dreyfus case, in which a French Jewish officer was wrongly convicted of treason, ultimately convinced Herzl that Jews could achieve true equality only if they created their own state, a position that he defended forcefully in *Der Judenstaat (The Jewish State),* published in 1896.

Like Pinsker, Herzl was less concerned with the location of that state than with the fact that sovereign control over territory would provide Jews guarantees against discrimination. Unlike Pinsker, Herzl was an established member of the bourgeoisie who sought to enlist the support of Europe's wealthiest Jews for his plan to colonize territory. At the first conference of the World Zionist

Organization, convened in Basel by Herzl in 1897, it was agreed that Palestine should be the location for the proposed Jewish state, which was referred to officially as a "home" because it was thought unadvisable to offend the Ottomans by calling for the creation of a state on their territory.

European anti-Semitism stimulated Jewry's search for an answer to discrimination. The form that response took was an ideology that borrowed heavily from the predominant European belief systems of the day. These were strongly nationalist and colonialist as well as tinged with notions of racial supremacy. As Maxime Rodinson notes, "Colonization at the time was essentially taken to mean the spreading of progress, civilization and well-being."[41] Inhabitants of the Third World, referred to as "natives" and thought by most Europeans to be culturally if not physiologically inferior to themselves, were to be "civilized" through colonization. Resistance by "natives" or "savages" to European settlement was taken as an indication of their failure to understand and appreciate the benefits of an "advanced" civilization, another sign of the indigenes' own backwardness. Progress required subordination of the local population, by force if necessary. An alternative interpretation was to discount the very existence of such populations. Their failure to "develop" the lands they occupied virtually disqualified them as humans equal to Europeans, or at the very least disallowed their claims to that land.

Arabs, like other "natives," were described by European intellectuals of the day in terms that are today recognized as racist. R. A. Macalister intoned:

> It is no exaggeration to say that throughout these long centuries the native inhabitants of Palestine do not appear to have made a single contribution of any kind whatsoever to material civilization. It was perhaps the most unprogressive country on the face of the earth. Its entire culture was derivative.[42]

Sir Flinders Petrie, the renowned archaeologist, asserted that "the Arab has a vast balance of romance put to his credit very needlessly. He is as disgustingly incapable as most other savages, and not more worth romancing about than Red Indians or Maoris."[43]

Zionist ideology incorporated the prevailing European approach to Asia and Africa and applied it to Palestine. The Zionist slogan, "A land without a people for a people without a land," reflects the phenomenon of discounting to the point of nonexistence civilizations other than those of Europe or European origins. Herzl presented the Jewish state he advocated in his celebrated work as one that would form a defense for Europe's civilization against Asia's barbarism. Chaim Weizmann, who succeeded Herzl as the leader of the Zionist movement, argued that the land of Palestine, "one of the most neglected corners of the mis-

---

[41]Maxime Rodinson, *Israel: A Colonial-Settler State? p. 42.*

[42]Cited by Miriam Rosen, "The Last Crusade: British Archeology in Palestine, 1865–1920." Unpublished M.A. thesis, Hunter College, 1976, pp. 18–21, cited by Edward W. Said, *The Question of Palestine* (New York: Vintage Books, 1979), p. 81.

[43]Ibid., p. 80.

erably neglected Turkish Empire," needed to be "redeemed" by Jewish labor and capital.[44] Weizmann's analogy for the comparison of Arab to Jew was "the desert against civilization."[45] It mattered little that in reality most of Palestine, other than the Negev, was no desert but an intensely and successfully cultivated fertile area. Max Nordau, a close friend of Herzl's from the time both were newspaper correspondents in Paris, stated that "we are going to Palestine to extend the moral boundaries of Europe as far as the Euphrates."[46] Such attitudes reflect the fact that the Zionist enterprise was part of the broader pattern of European colonization, requiring for its success cooperation with the imperial powers and subordination of the indigenous population.

There was no question in the minds of the early Zionists, such as Herzl and Weizmann, that their desire to create a Jewish state in Palestine could succeed only were it to appeal to powerful forces within Western nations, especially Britain. The organizational infrastructure created under Herzl's tutelage, including the Jewish National Fund founded in 1901, was modeled on the great "companies" that emerged in the seventeenth century, which effected colonial settlement and imposition of imperial control, such as the British and Dutch East India Companies. Herzl sought to make the enterprise attractive to potential investors, stating that "the Jewish Company is conceived partly on the model of the great land-development companies . . . [and] will be set up as a joint-stock company, incorporated in England, under British laws and protection."[47] He successfully courted the support of the wealthy Rothschild family, to whom the first draft of *The Jewish State* was addressed. The famous Balfour Declaration of November 2, 1917, by which the British government pledged its support for "the establishment in Palestine of a national home for the Jewish people," took the form of a letter from the foreign secretary, Arthur J. Balfour, to Lord Lionel Rothschild, head of the most powerful branch of the House of Rothschild.

At the level of state interests, Zionists couched their appeal to European leaders in terms that stressed the potential utility of a Jewish state in Palestine to their imperial ambitions. Moses Hess, a nineteenth-century German socialist-Zionist, foresaw that the opening of the Suez Canal in 1869 would be accompanied by European settlement "along the road to India and China, settlements of such a character as will transform the neglected and anarchic states of the countries . . . into legal and cultivated States. This can occur only under the military protection of the European powers." Hess counseled Zionists to seize this

---

[44]Chaim Weizmann, *Trial and Error: The Autobiography of Chaim Weizmann* (New York: Harper & Row, 1959) pp. 125, 128–129.

[45]Chaim Weizmann, "The Position in Palestine," *Palestine Papers* 2 (London: Jewish Agency for Palestine, 1929–1930), p. 24, cited by Richard P. Stevens, "Smuts and Weizmann," in Richard P. Stevens and Abdelwahab M. Elmessiri, *Israel and South Africa: The Progression of a Relationship* (New Brunswick, N. J.: North American, 1977), p. 36.

[46]Cited by Kenneth Brown, "Iron and a King: The Likud and Oriental Jews," *Merip Reports* 114 (May 1983): 7.

[47]Cited in *Theodore Herzl*, ed. by Ludwig Lewisohn (Cleveland World, 1955), p. 256.

opportunity to offer their services as middlemen between Europe and Asia.[48] Herzl originally sought to interest Bismarck and the Germans in fostering the establishment of a Jewish state to protect the proposed Berlin-Baghdad railroad.[49] When that failed, he turned to the British, to whom the pointed out that a "substantial colonization of our people at the strategic point where Egyptian and Indo-Persian interests converge" would strengthen British influence.[50]

By World War I, this logic had strong appeal to the British government, which saw multiple advantages in supporting the creation of a Jewish state in Palestine. It would serve to counter French interests in the Levant, while it would also gain the support for British war aims of influential Jewish communities in the United States and Russia. The Balfour Declaration was duly issued and almost five years later, on July 24, 1922, was incorporated into the terms of the Mandate for Palestine, awarded by the League of Nations to Britain. At that time the Arabs of Palestine, of whom there were in excess of 600,000, outnumbered the Jewish population ten to one.

The three principal requirements for successful state formation—a "state-idea" or ideology, political organizations, and international support—were accomplished by the Yishuv prior to the two great waves of Jewish migration. At the end of World War I, there were only 55,000 Jews in Palestine. Although Zionist organizations actively promoted immigration following the establishment of the Mandate in 1922, prior to 1933 the annual quota established by the Mandate was not filled. The coming to power of the Nazis, however, and the threatening climate of Europe stimulated immigration, so that by the outbreak of World War II the Jewish population had reached 450,000—about 30 percent of the total.

The second immigration wave began just after the declaration of independence in May 1948. In a year and a half, Israel's population had increased by 50 percent. These migrants, who by 1952 numbered almost three-quarters of a million, differed from their predecessors in that almost half were drawn from the Arab countries of the Middle East and North Africa, whereas about 80 percent of the Jewish population at the outbreak of hostilities in 1947 was of European origin. Absorption of this huge influx of diverse peoples, a large proportion of whom were utterly destitute and who, like almost all other new arrivals, spoke no Hebrew, is a testament to the capacities of the new state.

Zionism, which had in its early formulations included various and contradictory notions of agrarian socialism, Jewish capitalism, ardent secularism, and Orthodox religious beliefs, was, however, in its essence a single idea: Jews should have a right to a state of their own, and that state was Israel. The Holocaust and the subsequent arrival of European Jewish refugees and over 200,000 Jews from

---

[48]Moses Hess, *Rome and Jerusalem* (New York: Bloch, 1945), pp. 227–229, 139, cited in Stephen Halbrook, "The Philosophy of Zionism: A Materialist Interpretation," in Ibrahim Abu-Lughod and Baha Abu-Laban, *Settler Regimes in Africa and the Arab World: The Illusion of Endurance* (Wilmette, Ill.: The Medina University Press International, 1974), p. 22.

[49]Theodore Herzl, *The Diaries of Theodore Herzl*, ed. by Marvin Lowenthal (New York: Grosset & Dunlap, 1962), pp. 120–122.

[50]Ibid., p. 371.

Arab countries by 1951 overwhelmed any other considerations and caused the new state of Israel to set about forging a collective identity "by means of education, ceremonies, festivals, urban and regional development, and the control of public discourse in the media." For this purpose "the Bible as a Jewish 'deed' to the land of Israel/Palestine has played a prominent role, prompting Zionist writers and educators to portray modern Jewish nationalism as a direct extension of biblical Hebrew kingdoms."[51]

Two levels of organization facilitated the construction of the new state and assimilation of immigrants. The first was the infrastructure of international Zionist organizations that operated globally and within Israel, chief of which were the World Zionist Organization, the Jewish National Fund, and the Jewish Agency. They were responsible for raising funds, propagating Zionism, facilitating migration, lobbying governments, and purchasing and managing land in Palestine and then Israel. The second level of organization consisted of the various political movements within Palestine, most of which became political parties contesting elections after the creation of Israel. The Yishuv was an intensely political environment, characterized by tightly knit, highly ideological groupings, most of which had been influenced by their origins in Russia and Poland. While there were disagreements between these political movements, together they served as instruments for the articulation and aggregation of political demands, for recruitment of political leadership, for absorption of new participants into the political system, and for control of the geographically far-flung Zionist administration.

The dominant grouping, Mapai (Mifleget Poalei Eretz Yisrael, or the Land of Israel Workers Party), which was formed in 1930 and which ultimately became the Labor Party, was particularly closely linked to the international Zionist organizations. This close association was in part a result of the group's control of the Histadrut, the all-embracing Jewish labor organization. The World Zionist Organization distributed its funds through the Histadrut, thereby providing Mapai with the patronage necessary to expand its organization. By the mid-1930s, Mapai so dominated the World Zionist Organization that its chief rival, the Zionist Revisionists led by Vladimir Jabotinsky, left the organization and formed the New Zionist Organization. At the time of the creation of Israel, Mapai and its leader, David Ben-Gurion, had control over the nascent state structures and predominant influence in all the international Zionist organizations. The challenges from the right by the Revisionists and from the left, mounted principally by Mapam (Mifleget Poalim Meuhedet, or United Workers Party), were easily beaten back. The one-party-dominant political system, which came into being as a result of the first Knesset elections in 1949, lasted for almost three decades. It provided for close integration between the leading political party, Mapai, and state structures. This relationship initially facilitated the tasks of state-building, but subsequently led to deterioration in the form of malaise, corruption, and lack of ideological clarity typical of one-party systems everywhere.

---

[51]Oren Yiftachel, "Israeli Society and Jewish-Palestinian Reconciliation: 'Ethnocracy' and Its Territorial Contradictions," *Middle East Journal* 51, 4 (Autumn 1997): 505–519.

Increased Political Tension Within Israel

Divisions between the major political movements in the Yishuv, which on at least one noted occasion led to Jew fighting Jew,[52] were not forgotten as a result of the creation of the Jewish state. They were put aside in the early years of statehood as the tasks of state-building were all-consuming, and Mapai was in an overwhelmingly dominant position. The contentious issues, which involved disputes over the proper place of religion in society and in the legal system, the role of the state in the economy, relations with the United States, the USSR, and European countries, and, finally, the approach to be taken toward the Palestinians and the Arab states, remained unresolved. That they reemerged with such intensity and divisiveness in the 1970s was due in part to the gradual enervation of the Labor Party.

ETHNICITY

Underlying Labor's decay was a basic demographic shift. While at independence Ashkenazim (European Jews) outnumbered Sephardim (Oriental Jews, also known as Mizrahim) four to one, by the late 1990s the latter had come to constitute at least 60 percent of the total population. Moreover, Haredi (Haredim in the plural), or ultra-Orthodox Jews, who seek to lead "pure" Jewish lives by segregating themselves from surrounding society and who in the main are Sephardim, also dramatically increased in numbers and their percentage of the Israeli population in the 1980s and 1990s, reaching 12 to 14 percent by 1998. While Sephardim are by no means a homogeneous group but come from enormously varied national, class, ethnic, and other backgrounds, a great many share in common the experience of having been discriminated against by Ashkenazim, who constituted the elite of virtually all political and state structures until recently. Not surprisingly Sephardim gave indications even as early as 1949 that their response to discrimination by the party that controlled government, Mapai, would be to vote for the opposition, especially Herut, the party led by Vladimir Jabotinsky's disciple and inheritor of the leadership of Zionist Revisionism, Menachem Begin.[53] But it was not until the 1977 election that massive defection of Sephardim to Likud, the alliance of which Herut formed the core, occurred. In that election, 66 percent of all Sephardim voted for Likud, and 71 percent of those under thirty so voted. In all elections since that time, Sephardim have accounted for more than two-thirds of votes for Likud, while Ashkenazim have provided almost the same proportion of Labor Party votes.

---

[52]The subordination of the Revisionists to Mainstream Zionists led by Mapai was ultimately accomplished when, shortly after the declaration of independence in May 1948, Ben-Gurion ordered the military to shell the *Altalena*. This ship, carrying immigrants and weapons for the main underground terrorist organization associated with the Revisionists, the Irgun Zvai Leumi, caught fire and sank with many on board.

[53]Zalman Aran of the Mapai Central Committee observed in December 1949, "The Orientals are the mainstay of Herut. . . . In the poorer quarters of Tel Aviv they voted for Herut to revenge themselves on our party, for the sins of a whole generation." Cited in Segev, *1949: The First Israelis*, p. 174.

During the spring 1992 election campaign, a pessimistic Labor Party activist observed that "each time an Ashkenazic Labor supporter and peace advocate is laid to rest in Tel Aviv, chances are that three Sephardim and potential Likud voters are born."[54] In the 1996 electoral contest for prime minister between Likud's Binyamin Netanyahu and Labor's Shimon Peres, the former received on average 73 percent of votes from the so-called "development towns," which are populated virtually exclusively by Sephardim, and over 90 percent of votes cast by Haredim.[55]

Sephardim vote for Likud and other conservative parties not just out of resentment against Labor and its alleged role as a vehicle of Ashkenazi interests, but also because of their conservatism. It is true that there are marked differences between Sephardim of Moroccan and Yemeni backgrounds on the one hand and those from Egypt, Libya, Tunisia, Syria, and Iraq on the other, the former generally being more traditional than the latter. It is also the case that polling data reveal little difference in political attitudes between Sephardim and Ashkenazim of equivalent incomes. However, because Sephardim are generally poorer and because the Moroccan and Yemeni communities are comparatively large, as a whole, Sephardim are markedly more conservative than Ashkenazim. They are more religious, adhere to stricter personal codes of behavior, tend to favor private enterprise over government control and, most important, favor much harsher treatment of Arabs. A 1984 poll, for example, revealed that although 53 percent of Ashkenazim favored returning at least some of the occupied territories, 60 percent of Sephardim, and 64 percent of young Sephardim, favored outright annexation, despite the fact that Sephardim constitute only a very small percentage of Jewish settlers in the occupied territories.[56] A previous poll found that 91 percent of Sephardim would refuse to rent a room to an Arab, as compared to 80 percent of Ashkenazim.[57] With regard to the peace process, the strongest predictor of attitudes is degree of religiosity, which is also highly correlated with Sephardi ethnicity. Only 14 percent of those asked in 1995 whether they supported that process and who identified themselves as ultra-Orthodox replied in the affirmative, compared to 20 percent of those who stated they were religious and 64 percent who identified themselves as being secular.[58] The rising percentage of Sephardim in the population, coupled with their

---

[54]Cited in Leon T. Hadar, "The Israeli Labor Party: Peacemaker or Likud II?" *Journal of Palestine Studies* 21 (Spring 1992): 83.

[55]Yiftachel, "Israeli Society," p. 517, and Don Peretz and Gideon Doron, "Israel's 1996 Elections: A Second Political Earthquake?" *Middle East Journal* 50, 4 (Autumn 1996): 529–546.

[56]Seker Dahaf (in Hebrew), May 1984, cited in Mordechai Bar-On, "Trends in the Political Psychology of Israeli Jews 1967–86," *Journal of Palestine Studies* 65 (Autumn 1987): 30–31.

[57]Yohanan Peres, "Ethnic Relations in Israel," *American Journal of Sociology* 76: 6 (1971): 1021–1047, cited by Maurice M. Roumani, "The Sephardi Factor in Israeli Politics," *The Middle East Journal* 42 (Summer 1988): 425.

[58]Tamar Hermann, "Trends in Israeli Jewish Public Opinion Concerning the Political Process and Its Implications," in Tamar Hermann and Ephraim Yuchtman-Yaar, eds., *Israeli Society and the Challenge of Transition to Co-Existence* (Tel Aviv: The Tami Steinmetz Center for Peace Research, Tel Aviv University, 1997), pp. 30–38.

increased political participation and the more conservative attitudes of younger Sephardim, thus contributed to the weakening of the Labor Party and the growing political polarization of the country.

THE ELECTORAL SYSTEM

The growing division between secular and religious Israelis, however, is not just a consequence of the demographic shift. It is also an indirect result of Israel's electoral system based on proportional representation, which awards seats in the Knesset to parties in exact proportion to their share of the total vote. Such electoral systems invariably lead to the fragmentation of party systems, as it has done in Israel, where in 1992, ten and in 1996, eleven parties won seats in the 120-member Knesset.[59] Even Mapai in its heyday could not obtain a majority of parliamentary seats and thus form a government alone.

Because Mapai rejected parties associated with right-wing Revisionist Zionism as unsuitable coalition partners, as well as those of the far left, it had no alternative but to form governments with the religious parties. The agreed tradeoff was that Mapai would be given a free hand and key portfolios in the areas of foreign affairs, defense, internal security, economics, and finance in exchange for the religious parties' being awarded portfolios with direct relevance to religious practices, including those of education and religion. This led to the reinforcement of a separate religious education system and the introduction of religion into the public school system, the exemption of Yeshiva (religious seminary) students from military service, the banning of public transportation on the Sabbath and public holidays, and the awarding of jurisdiction over all personal status questions to religious courts. As a result, large numbers of Israeli youths have been educated in religious schools, and the curricula of public schools have incorporated religious material and values. All Israelis are subjected to religious law in their personal lives, which among other things means that there is no secular marriage or divorce; hence, women cannot initiate divorces. Possibly mindful of the consequences of having in the past awarded the education portfolio to religious parties, Labor Prime Minister Yitzhak Rabin, when forming his first government after the June 1992 elections, installed Shulamit Aloni, an outspoken secular leftist as minister of education. The United Torah Party, an ultra-Orthodox grouping, refused to join the coalition government in protest, alleging that Aloni "would lead a million children to 'apostasty' and 'assimilation.'"[60]

It should be noted, however, that some analysts of Israeli politics believe that even had there been a different electoral system that gave less leverage to the re-

---

[59]In order to contain this fragmentation, the 1996 elections were conducted under a revised electoral law whereby the prime minister was elected by majority popular vote rather than chosen by the core party of the governing coalition. The intent of this change was to give the prime minister enhanced leverage so as to reduce the bargaining power of smaller parties. In reality, however, this did not occur, for Binyamin Netanyahu has, since May 1996, encountered at least as much difficulty as his predecessors in cobbling together and then maintaining a governing coalition.

[60]"Shas Finally Breaks Free of Rabbi Schach," *The Jerusalem Report* (July 30, 1992), p. 6.

ligious parties, religiosity would still have spread. Akiva Orr, for example, argues that growing religiosity is inherent in Zionism because the definition of who is a Jew ultimately has always to be decided on religious grounds. No other bond unites the highly diverse population of Israel.[61]

Whether its cause was inherent in the fact of Israel's being a multiethnic Jewish state or whether it was just a result of the electoral system, the outcome is the same; namely, Israel has become more religious, both in terms of personal beliefs and in the institutionalized power of religion. An indicator of both is the trend of support for religious parties contesting for seats in the Knesset. In the 1996 elections, those parties, consisting of Shas, the National Religious Party, and the United Torah Judaism parties, increased their number of seats from sixteen to twenty-three, surpassing their historic high of eighteen seats won in the 1988 elections. Holding the balance of power in the new Knesset, these parties banded together to make demands for "stricter interpretation of Jewish personal status laws, stricter Sabbath observance, a narrower definition of Jewish identity, and a substantial increase in government funding for their educational and other institutions."[62]

THE OCCUPATION OF ARAB LAND

The factor of greatest importance in exacerbating tension between the major political trends, however, has not been the demographic shift or the rise of religiosity. It is the effect of the seizure of Arab territory in the 1967 war. By that act the issues that had divided the Mainstream, Revisionist, and religious trends in Zionism prior to 1948 were thrust back onto center stage, paradoxically because the 1967 victory differed from that of 1948 in two important respects. First, in 1948, territory beyond the partition lines conquered by Israel was taken primarily from what was to have comprised the Palestinian state. In 1967, however, land taken in the Golan, West Bank, Gaza, and Sinai Peninsula belonged to the Arab states of Syria, Jordan, and Egypt. This added a very important territorial issue to the conflict between Israel and those states.

Of even greater importance was that in 1947–1949 the majority of Palestinians left the area that was incorporated into Israel, not more than 160,000 remaining behind. In 1967, between 200,000 and 300,000 more Palestinians had to leave their homes, but over 1 million stayed put. Palestinians were a small minority in post-1948 Israel. They posed no real security threat to the state and were easily controlled. In territories occupied in 1967, however, there were some 1.3 million Arabs and virtually no Jews. The question arose immediately as to what should be done with this land—the question that stands as a central issue facing Israel today.

Except for East Jerusalem and the Old City, which along with 18,000 acres of adjoining land were, with virtually unanimous support by the Jewish population, formally annexed to Israel on June 28, 1967, the Israeli public has remained divided over the disposition of the territories. Until well into 1968, a

---

[61]Akiva Orr, *The Unjewish State: The Politics of Jewish Identity in Israel* (London: Ithaca Press, 1983).

[62]Peretz and Doron, "Israel's 1996 Elections," p. 538.

solid majority of Israelis expressed a desire to return the conquered lands in exchange for peace with and recognition by the Arab states.[63] From then until 1991, there was a declining willingness to make the "land for peace" swap. In March 1986, only 41 percent of those polled thought that should be done, while 50 percent opposed it.[64] In September 1986, 38 percent of respondents in a *Jerusalem Post* poll agreed with the statement "I support anyone who acts to get Arabs to leave Judea and Samiria."[65] By 1987, within the eighteen- to twenty-two-year-old age group, 73 percent were opposed to making any territorial concessions.[66] In August 1988, almost one-half of a sample group polled by the Israel Institute of Applied Social Research endorsed "transfer" as a means to preserve "the democratic and Jewish nature of the state."[67]

In the wake of the second Gulf war, however, Israeli public opinion became markedly less intransigent. By 1992, about 60 percent of Israelis endorsed the land-for-peace trade, more than one-third were willing to accept an independent Palestinian state, and 90 percent supported peace negotiations with the Arabs, compared to 57 percent in 1986.[68] Since the signing of the Declaration of Principles, also known as the Oslo Accords, in September 1993 and the commencement of the peace process according to its terms, these percentages have not changed significantly. Somewhat more than one-half of Israelis continue to support the broad concept of exchange of land for peace with the Palestinians, although being much more hawkish on specific issues, such as methods of dealing with terrorism, precise amount of territory to be traded, and so forth.[69] A summer 1997 Gallup poll found that "60 percent of Israelis would accept a demilitarized Palestinian state and even some sharing of Jerusalem in order to achieve peace."[70] A Gallup poll conducted in April 1998 that asked Israelis to speculate about Palestinian-Israeli relations in the future revealed that 68 percent of Israelis believed that an independent Palestinian state would exist alongside Israel.[71]

Public opinion toward the occupied territories has closely paralleled government policy, which in turn is remarkably similar to that implemented by the Yishuv during the Mandate era (1922–1948) and by Israel in its own Galilee re-

---

[63]Bar-On, "Trends in the Political Psychology of Israeli Jews," p. 24.

[64]Ibid., pp. 24–25.

[65]*The Jerusalem Post*, October 11, 1986.

[66]Langellier, "The New Palestinian Nationalism," p. 13.

[67]Glenn Frankel, "Expulsion of Arabs Favored," *The Guardian Weekly*, November 13, 1988, p. 18.

[68]Leon T. Hadar, "The Israeli Labor Party," pp. 80–94.

[69]For a comprehensive review of Israeli public opinion in the early 1990s, see Asher Arian, *Security Threatened: Surveying Israeli Opinion on Peace and War* (Cambridge: Cambridge University Press, 1995). For an interesting contrast of Israeli Jewish and Arab views toward the peace process during this period, see Tamar S. Hermann and Ephraim Yuchtman-Yaar, "Two People Apart," in *The Middle East Peace Process: Interdisciplinary Perspectives*, ed. by Ilan Peleg (Albany: State University of New York Press, 1998), pp. 61–83.

[70]Cited in Augustus Richard Norton, "Clinton's Middle East Legacy: A Scuttled Peace?" *Current History* 615 (January 1998): 2.

[71]*Mideast Mirror*, May 1, 1998.

gion after 1948. Land acquisition by the Jewish National Fund was designed prior to 1948 to pave the way for colonization and eventual creation of the Jewish state. The strategy was to create a security belt of Jewish settlements, then to populate that area as densely as possible. After 1948, the only region within Israel that had an Arab majority was the northern district of Galilee, which was 63 percent Arab. "In a concerted effort to break up this concentration and reduce the Arab population to minority status, the Israelis confiscated as much land as possible, destroyed villages and implanted Jewish settlements."[72] That was the essence of the Israeli approach to the occupied territories between 1967 and 1993, with the exception of the Sinai, where settlements were established but that was eventually traded back to Egypt for the peace that grew out of the Camp David Accords of 1978.

One of the first steps taken by the Labor government formed by Yitzhak Rabin in July 1992 was to declare that there would be no new settlements in the occupied territories. In the following September, Prime Minister Rabin committed Israel to handing over at least some portions of those territories to the Palestinians as a result of his signing with Yasser Arafat the Oslo Accords (named after the city where they had been secretly negotiated) on the White House lawn. However, neither the Labor Party, which condoned the "thickening" of settlements already established, nor the Likud Party that took power after the May 1996 elections and recommenced the implantation of new settlements, abandoned the goal of placing more Jewish settlers in the occupied territories.

In the other two critical border areas seized in 1967, the Golan Heights and the Jordan Valley, settlement began almost as soon as the guns fell silent and was carried out under the auspices of the Labor Party. On July 15, 1967, Kibbutz Merom Hagolan, the first Jewish settlement in the occupied territories, was established adjacent to Qunaitra in the Golan. This area had essentially been cleared of its Arab inhabitants during the hostilities, when more than 90,000 of its some 100,000 residents were driven out. Similarly, in the major urban area of the Jordan Valley, which is the Jericho region, only 10,000 Palestinians of the 85,000 resident there on June 5, 1967, remained a week later. The Allon Plan, proposed in 1967 by General Yigal Allon, the mentor of Yitzhak Rabin, called for a string of over twenty settlements along the Syrian frontier in the Golan with 7,000 residents, a target that was in fact reached by the time the Golan was annexed by Israel in 1981. The Allon Plan also recommended "absorption into Israel of a security zone running the length of the Jordan rift" (i.e., the Jordan Valley), a zone that was initially described as being ten to fifteen kilometers wide but that was "thickened" over the years so that, by 1975, it stretched "to the very margins of Arab cultivation in the West Bank highlands."[73] By 1981, Israel controlled about half the cultivable land in the Jordan Valley. Jewish domination of

---

[72]Janet Abu-Lughod, "Israeli Settlements in Occupied Arab Lands: From Conquest to Colony," in *Palestinian Rights: Affirmation and Denial,* ed. by Ibrahim Abu-Lughod (Wilmette, Ill.: Medina Press, 1982), p. 122.

[73]William Wilson Harris, *Taking Root: Israeli Settlement in the West Bank, the Golan and Gaza Sinai, 1967–1980* (New York: Research Studies Press, 1980), pp. 105–106.

Jerusalem was also a top priority. It was accomplished by destroying the Maghribi Arab quarter of the Old City and replacing it with new accommodation for Jews and by establishing settlements on the surrounding hills that were incorporated into the Jerusalem municipality, thereby increasing its size by 60 percent.

The West Bank, however, other than the annexed Jerusalem area or the Jordan Valley, posed a much more intractable problem. Had it been annexed in the wake of the 1967 war, it would have added 600,000 Arabs to Israel's population, more than doubling the total number of Israeli Arabs. The Allon Plan, which subsequently informed both prime ministers Rabin's and Netanyahu's negotiating positions, and possibly embodied their ultimate goals, was designed to gain control of the land but not add the Arab population to that on the other side of the "Green Line" (the 1949 armistice line) in Israel proper. The imperative of demography in the calculations of Allon and subsequent Israeli policy makers is indicated by the fact that Arabs in Israel itself and in the occupied territories made up 38.8 percent of the population in 1991 and were forecast in 1992 to constitute 45 percent of those living under Israeli rule by the year 2000. In fact, this percentage had already been reached by 1998, at which time the Israeli Arab population was almost 900,000. In the West Bank and Jerusalem, it was about 1.5 million, and in Gaza, some 700,000, thus making the total Palestinian population over 3 million, compared to slightly less than 5 million Jews.[74] By the end of the Labor era, twelve settlements had been established on the West Bank highlands and were connected to those in the Jordan Valley by the "Allon Plan Road." With the coming to power of Likud in 1977, the pace of settlement was accelerated dramatically. By 1988, the Israeli government had confiscated 52 percent of all land on the West Bank and established 135 settlements there with over 65,000 inhabitants. By 1992, in the occupied territories as a whole, there were 212 settlements with 112,000 inhabitants, who constituted 13 percent of the West Bank and Gaza population and nearly 6 percent of the entire population of Israel. Nevertheless, the issue of what to do with the Palestinian population, exacerbated by this Jewish settlement, remained unresolved.

The Gaza Strip, which had 400,000 Palestinians in 1967, presented even greater demographic and security problems than the West Bank. The original intention, as stated by the prime minister in the summer of 1967 and as reiterated in the Allon Plan, was to annex Gaza and resettle the 1948 refugees living there in the West Bank and Sinai. In 1973, Prime Minister Rabin called for the population to be dispatched to Jordan.[75] But the Labor Government, after breaking the back of Palestinian underground resistance in Gaza in 1971, did not put into effect the provisions of the Allon Plan for this area. It did not commit the required material resources or imbue the undertaking with sufficient ideological zeal to lure Jewish settlers to move into Gaza, where there were only

---

[74]Andrew North, "Israel's Demographic Dilemma," *The Middle East* (May 1992), p. 12. Anthony H. Cordesman, *Perilous Prospects: The Peace Process and the Arab-Israeli Military Balance* (Boulder, Colo.: Westview Press, 1996), pp. 129–134.

[75]*Ma'ariv*, February 16, 1973, cited in Joan Mandell, "Gaza: Israel's Soweto," *Merip Reports* 136–137 (October–December 1985): 10.

500 in four settlements when Likud took power. Over the next ten years, however, more government support for settlement was forthcoming. Fourteen new settlements were established, and the Jewish population increased fivefold. Despite the fact that Gaza's Arab population in the early 1990s exceeded a half-million (who were crammed into an area of 140 square miles, giving this artificial entity a population density equivalent to that of Hong Kong), the Israelis by 1992 had confiscated more than a third of the total area and awarded it to Jewish settlers who constituted one-half of 1 percent of the population. Settlers on average have 2.6 acres of land in Gaza, while Palestinians have 0.006 acre each.[76]

Just as land seizures and the implantation of settlements in the occupied territories paralleled previous patterns established first in the Yishuv and then in Israel after 1948, so did other policies directed at the Palestinian population there resemble those used to contain the Arabs left in Israel at the end of hostilities in 1949. Because of the very different demographic balance that obtained in the occupied territories, however, and because of the much greater politicization of Palestinians since 1967 in comparison with 1948, Israeli policies intended to subordinate the Arab population of the occupied territories had to be much more severe than those used in Israel. Whereas demolition of houses, wanton disregard for civil rights, imprisonment without trial, torture, deportation, and political killings have seldom occurred in Israel proper, they were commonplace in the territories until 1993. Between 1967 and the beginning of the Palestinian intifada (uprising) in December 1987, there were more than a half-million detentions and arrests (an average of about one arrest/detention for every three Palestinians); there were also over 2,000 deportations and 1,500 house demolitions. From 1982 to 1987, more than 130 Palestinians lost their lives in political killings at the hands of Israeli soldiers or settlers.[77] By comparison, between 1968 and 1983, Israeli government statistics reveal that fourteen Israeli civilians and twenty-two soldiers were killed by West Bank Palestinians. From April 1986 to May 1987 alone, Israeli forces killed twenty-two Palestinians, while armed attacks on Israelis took two lives.[78]

As early as 1977, the torture of Palestinians under detention was described as being "so widespread and systematic that it cannot be dismissed as 'rogue cops' exceeding orders. It appears to be sanctioned as deliberate policy."[79] Ten years later, a special Israeli judicial commission headed by former Supreme Court president Moshe Landau was formed to investigate allegations of torture against Shin Beth (the General Security Service). The commission reported that for the period covered by its review (1971–1987), Shin Beth officers had routinely extracted confessions by applying "physical and psychological pressure" and that they had regularly perjured themselves by denying in court that they

[76]*Middle East Report* 152 (May–June 1988): 35.

[77]Meron Benvenisti, *1987 Report: Demographic, Economic, Legal, Social and Political Developments in the West Bank* (Jerusalem: West Bank Data Project, 1987).

[78]"Israel and the Palestinians, 1948–1988," *Middle East Report* 152 (May–June 1988): 35.

[79]*The Sunday Times,* June 17, 1977, cited in *Journal of Palestine Studies* 6 (Summer 1977): 190–219.

had mistreated detainees.[80] Instead of condemning these practices and prohibiting their future use, the Landau Commission recommended that Shin Beth interrogators officially be permitted to use "psychological pressure and light violence when interrogating those suspected of terrorist acts."[81] There is an abundance of evidence, including that provided by the U.S. government, to suggest that torture has continued to be employed by Israeli security forces against Palestinians.[82]

Associated with measures to facilitate Israeli control and restrict personal and collective political expression by Palestinians were policies intended to deny them physical and economic resources. Access to water was progressively limited by direct prohibition of its use by Palestinians and by diversion of it to Jewish settlements and to Israel. In 1990, the 1.1 million Palestinians in the West Bank received 119 cubic meters of water per person, compared to 354 cubic meters provided to each of the 110,000 Israeli settlers.[83] Economic resources were systematically siphoned out of the occupied territories into Israel. More than 100,000 Palestinians worked in Israel in the late 1980s, mainly in menial and poorly paid jobs. In the first twenty years of occupation, $1 billion was deducted from the wages of Palestinians employed in Israel for employment benefits for which they were ineligible.[84] From 1967 to 1987, residents of the occupied territories paid $800 million in taxes, two and a half times the total investments in the territories over that period.[85] Given this outward flow of resources, it is not surprising that Palestinian agriculture and industry stagnated. Total industrial production by 1988 was a trifling $85 million, which constituted 8 percent of West Bank gross domestic product. In 1967, industry had accounted for 9 percent of the West Bank's GDP.[86] By the early 1990s, about half of the Palestinians in the occupied territories were unemployed. Of the 26,000 Palestinian high school students who graduated in 1990, some 20,000 joined the ranks of the unemployed. Only 1,000 found steady employment. The GNP per capita in the West Bank and Gaza Strip dropped from $1,562 and $1,081, respectively, in 1987, to $1,200 and $700, respectively, in 1989. Israel's per capita GNP in 1989 was more than five times that of the West Bank and almost ten times that of the

---

[80]For a review of this report and a more general account of human rights violations in the occupied territories, see "Israel and the Occupied Territories," *Country Report for Human Rights Practices for 1987*, submitted by the Department of State to the 100th Congress (February 1988), reprinted in the *Journal of Palestine Studies* 68 (Summer 1988): 105–115.

[81]O. Nir, "Justice Under Fire," *Ha'Aretz Weekend Supplement*, March 6, 1987 (in Hebrew), cited in Raija-Leena Punamäki, "Experiences of Torture, Means of Coping, and Level of Symptoms Among Palestinian Political Prisoners," in *Journal of Palestine Studies* 68 (Summer 1988): 82–83.

[82]See, for example, The Occupied Territories *Report on Human Rights Practices for 1997* (Washington, D.C.: U.S. Department of State, 1998).

[83]Jonathan C. Randal, "Water Becomes Increasing Bitter Issue in Mid-East," *The Guardian Weekly* (May 24, 1992): 19.

[84]Raja Shehadeh, "Occupiers' Law and the Uprising," *Journal of Palestine Studies* 67 (Spring 1988): 33.

[85]"Israel and the Palestinians," p. 36.

[86]Ibid., p. 36; and Benvenisti, *1987 Report*, p. 22.

Gaza Strip.[87] In a 1986 survey of the attitudes of Palestinians living under occupation, 2.1 percent said their living conditions had improved, 11.2 percent said their conditions had not changed since 1967, and 84.5 percent said that their conditions had deteriorated.[88]

Although repression of Palestinians in the occupied territories prior to December 1987, when the intifada commenced, was harsh, it became truly draconian after that time. In the first two years of the intifada, 159 children under age sixteen, with an average age of ten, were killed by soldiers. More than half of those slain were not near a demonstration when they were killed, and less than one-fifth were involved in stone throwing. As many as 63,000 children were gassed, beaten, or wounded.[89] In 1991, Israeli forces combating the intifada deported 8 Palestinians, killed 99, wounded 13,500, and at any one time in that year, had over 11,000 Palestinians in prison. Of the 99 killed, 27 were shot by "nonuniformed security personnel," otherwise known as death squads. Palestinian attacks on Israeli soldiers and civilians in 1991 resulted in 12 deaths.[90] By July 1992, the toll of human rights violations by Israeli forces during the intifada included 1,045 deaths, 122,700 injuries, 66 expulsions, 2,100 house demolitions/sealings, and 15,200 administrative detentions.[91] The world community, including Israel's closest allies, unanimously condemned Israel's repressive measures. Within Israel, the intifada brought into even sharper focus the basic divisions that have characterized Zionism from the outset and in 1993 led one of its factions to launch a dramatic bid for peace with the Palestinians.

Divisions Within Zionism

For over a half-century, there have been three major trends within Zionism. Mainstream Zionism, made up primarily of secular social democrats, represented first by Mapai and then by the Labor Party, is similar to European social democracy in its political agenda and strategies. Antagonistic to the radical left, especially to communists, mainstream Zionists have preferred to compromise with conservatives in order to exercise power. From 1949 to 1977, that compromise took the form of a coalition with the religious parties. Between 1984 and 1989, it was manifested in a coalition with Likud, the organizational legacy of Revisionism, historically the major competitor to Mainstream Zionism.

Divided almost from the outset into those who favored territorial compromise and accommodation and those who preferred an activist military policy to

---

[87]Bernard Sabella, "The Demography of Conflict: A Palestinian Predicament," *New Outlook* 9 (April–May 1991): 9–11.

[88]Mohammed Shadid and Rick Seltzer, "Political Attitudes of Palestinians in the West Bank and Gaza Strip," *The Middle East Journal* 42 (Winter 1988): 21.

[89]These figures are provided in a study conducted by the Swedish Save the Children organization, cited in Colman McCarthy, "Exposing Israeli Violence," *Washington Post* (July 15, 1990), p. F2.

[90]*Country Report*, pp. 115–117.

[91]*The Washington Report on Middle East Affairs* (July 1992), p. 23.

impose a solution on the Arabs, Mainstream Zionism over the years became increasingly dominated by those of the activist persuasion. Labor's leadership reflected this trend. Former generals such as Shimon Peres and Yitzhak Rabin, who from the mid-1970s until the mid-1990s alternated as leader and deputy leader of Labor, came to exercise enormous influence within the party. Throughout the 1970s and 1980s, they perpetuated Mainstream Zionism's primary strategy concerning the Arabs, which evolved almost a half-century ago. The plan was to cooperate with Jordan in preventing the emergence of a Palestinian state. Thus, after 1967, the Labor Party was willing to return some part of the West Bank to Jordan, but for various reasons such a deal was never struck. With the unilateral termination of the "Jordanian option" by King Hussein in July 1988, the Labor Party was left without a coherent foreign policy to present to Israeli voters in the November 1988 elections. Unwilling to countenance the creation of a Palestinian state, Labor resorted initially to seeking to repress Palestinian nationalism and to hang on to the territories.

This repressive strategy became increasingly counterproductive because it did not differentiate Labor from its chief rival, Likud; because it failed to stop the intifada; and because it had catastrophic consequences for Israel internationally. Abandoning its junior-partner role in the coalition with Likud in the summer of 1989 in protest against Prime Minister Shamir's acceptance of his party's hardliners' conditions for proposed Palestinian elections, Labor began to distance itself from government policies, especially when it became evident in the fall of 1991 that they were seriously eroding support for Israel in the United States.

In the 1992 election campaign, Labor promised that it would trade land for peace if it were elected. Paradoxically, its policy toward the Palestinians was to offer them not a state but "autonomy"—that is, some form of self-government under Israeli sovereignty. The possibility of a Palestinian state ultimately emerging from that self-governing enclave, however, was not precluded. The proposal of autonomy for the Palestinians had first been made by the Likud government of Menachem Begin in 1977 and was embodied in the Camp David Accords negotiated between Begin and President Sadat of Egypt in 1978. Prime Minister Shamir had also proposed limited autonomy in his plan announced in early 1989, but due to opposition from the right wing within the Likud Party and his own inflexibility, that plan had become a dead letter by the summer of 1990, when Iraq invaded Kuwait and altered fundamentally the diplomatic context surrounding the Arab-Israeli conflict.

Likud's reaction to American preeminence in the region to the further weakening of the Arabs in general and the Palestinians in particular, and to the prospect of much greater Jewish migration from the former Soviet Union was to delay negotiations and "create facts" (i.e., Jewish settlements) that would render Palestinian claims irrelevant. This strategy, however, became untenable in the face of opposition from the Bush administration. An opportunity was thus created for the Labor Party to offer a compromise and thereby win the tacit support of the U.S. government, which, among other things, signaled to the Israeli electorate that if Labor were to win the elections, Washington would look more favorably on Israel's request for $10 billion in loan guarantees to finance the resettlement of Jewish immigrants. Likud's ambitions and diplomatic incompetence thus paved the way for Labor to co-opt Likud's policy of autonomy for the Palestinians, which helped to facilitate the Labor victory in the 1992 elections.

Revisionism, the second major trend within Zionism, was more or less "beyond the pale" in the eyes of many Zionists until Likud formed its first government in 1977. So named because its founder, Vladimir Jabotinsky, urged revision of the Palestine Mandate to include Transjordan and thereby make possible the creation of a Jewish state on both sides of the river Jordan, Revisionism sought to establish that state through violence directed against Arabs, the British, and even neutral mediators.[92]

The balance of power between Mainstream and Revisionist Zionism began to shift in favor of the latter after 1967, partly because of the polarizing and conservatizing effects of the occupation. In 1977, Likud, the party most closely associated with Revisionism, won forty-three seats, compared with Labor's thirty-two. Likud formed a government with two religious parties and a breakaway faction from Labor. Some 51 percent of voters under age twenty-five in 1977 had chosen Likud, whereas only 20 percent of them voted Labor. From then until 1992, Likud was always in government, even though it ran only about neck and neck with Labor at the polls, capturing forty-eight, forty-one, forty, and thirty-two seats, compared with Labor's forty-seven, forty-four, thirty-nine, and forty-five seats in the 1981, 1984, 1988, and 1992 elections, respectively. Throughout this period, Likud remained loyal to the basic tenets of Jabotinsky's Revisionism— that is, no withdrawal from the territory of Eretz Yisrael, no compromise with the Palestinians, little hesitation in using violence for political purposes, a commitment to self-reliance based on distrust of non-Jews, and support for private enterprise. While Jabotinsky was essentially a secularist, under Begin's leadership Revisionism became imbued with Jewish religious traditions and symbols.

The replacement of Labor by Likud as the dominant force in Israeli politics was not just due to the change in their respective electoral fortunes but was also a result of the shift by Zionism's third major trend—the religious one—from an alliance with Mainstream to one with Revisionist Zionism. This realignment was signaled by the defection of two religious parties from Labor to Likud in 1977. Subsequently, the strength of the religious tendency was reinforced with the emergence of a group of ultra-Orthodox and ultranationalist parties even further to the right of the existing religious parties. The National Religious Party (NRP), also known by its Hebrew acronym Mafdal, which for fifty years prior to 1977 had been allied with Mainstream Zionism, joined the coalition with Likud as a result of growing nationalism among its younger members, many of whom had close links with the activist settler organization Gush Emunim (Bloc of the Faithful). Agudat Israel (Federation of Israel), made up principally of Hasidic (ultra-Orthodox) Jews, joined the Likud government out of its desire to have implemented the *halacha* (Orthodox Jewish law).

---

[92]Count Folke Bernadotte, a UN envoy, proposed during negotiations following the 1948 war that the UN take responsibility for Jerusalem and that Israel return areas conquered beyond the partition line to the Arab state called for in the 1947 Partition Plan. He was assassinated in 1949 by members of the Stern Gang.

Various ultra-Orthodox and ultranationalist parties subsequently have emerged to the right of the NRP and Agudat Israel, of which the most successful was Shas (Sephardi Torah Guardians), comprised mainly of Sephardim who broke away from Agudat Israel. Shas won four seats in 1984, six in 1988, seven in 1992, and ten in 1996, making it the third-largest party in the Knesset. Its members are predominantly of Moroccan origin and of the Sephardi lower middle class. It runs a network of schools that educates 80,000 children and in various other ways operates more like a social movement than a political party. Shas, along with Agudat Israel and another ultra-Orthodox party, Degel Hatorah (Torah Flag Party), demanded in the wake of the 1988 elections, as their price for joining a Likud-dominated government, the banning of abortion, closing of all forms of entertainment on the Sabbath, upgrading the importance of rabbinical courts, and, most critical to Israel's foreign relations, requiring all Jewish converts to gain Orthodox rabbinical approval before becoming Israeli citizens, a demand that Shas repeated when brought into the Likud-dominated coalition that formed the government after the 1996 election. Since the overwhelming majority of American Jews are of the Conservative or Reform branches of Judaism, this measure that, in effect, defines who is a Jew and was ultimately embodied in legislation in 1997 strained relations between Israel and American Jewry.

The ultranationalist parties share a generally anti-Arab perspective with the ultra-Orthodox, but the two tendencies are sharply divided over religious matters, with the ultranationalists being strong advocates of secularism. Raful Eytan's Tzomet Party had been the most successful of the ultranationalist parties, tripling its votes between 1988 and 1992 and becoming the fourth-largest party in the Knesset before then splitting at the time of the 1996 election into at least three factions, leaving Eytan's group with four seats. Eytan, who served as the army's chief of staff under Begin and entered politics with the Likud Party, has likened Palestinians to "stoned cockroaches" and divided them into good and bad: "The bad ones should be killed, the good ones deported."[93] Moledet (Homeland) an ultranationalist party to the right of Tzomet that openly endorses "transfer" of the entire Palestinian population, including that resident in Israel, unlike Tzomet, did not improve on its 1988 performance in the 1992 elections and lost another seat in the 1996 election, reducing its presence in the Knesset to two members. In April 1998, however, Prime Minister Netanyahu, anxious to shore up his razor-thin majority after the defection of David Levy's Gesher Party from the ruling coalition earlier in the year, invited Moledet's leader, Rehavam Zeevi, into the cabinet, thereby further reinforcing the already strong position of the ultra-Orthodox and ultranationalists within the Likud government. Zeevi is among the most controversial politicians in Israel, having referred to Yasser Arafat as a "war criminal" and a "son of a bitch"; Arab members of the Knesset as "agents for Arafat"; and the U.S. undersecretary of state for the Middle East, Martin Indyk, a "kike." When members of the Palestinian Legisla-

---

[93]Peretz Kidron, "Rabin's Balancing Act Threatens His Commitment to Peace," *Middle East International* (July 10, 1992): 3–4.

tive Council visited the Knesset, he screamed "Murderers have entered this building! Will these murderers be allowed to remain here?"[94]

That such an intemperate, radical ultranationalist had become a cabinet minister in a Likud-dominated government reflects the redistribution of power that has occurred between the three major trends of Zionism—Mainstream or Labor Party Zionism, Revisionism, and the religious and ultranationalist right wing. Prior to 1977, ultranationalism and the ultra-Orthodox were politically marginal. Labor governments were based on alliances with the religious parties that had little interest in foreign affairs generally or relations with the Arabs and Palestinians specifically and were concerned primarily with Judaizing the country's legal and educational systems. The formation of the Likud government in 1977 signalled two major changes. First, the religious parties joined Likud in a coalition that, except for Shas' defection back to Labor in 1992–1996, has become a permanent feature of Israeli politics. Second, the political power, range of policy concerns, and ideological predispositions of the religious and ultranationalist political parties began the process of becoming steadily more expansive that has continued until the present, a process that is based on a fundamental demographic shift from a slim Ashkenazim majority in the early 1970s to a substantial Sephardim and Haredim (ultra-Orthodox) majority by the 1990s. This process, however, has not been fundamentally altered by the arrival of several hundred thousand Russian Jews in the 1980s and 1990s. As Sephardim and Haredim have become more numerous, so too have they become more politically assertive and less willing to accept the leadership of either Labor or Likud, both of which are led by Ashkenazim. They are also more interested in affecting policies toward the Arabs in general and the Palestinians specifically, toward which they are considerably less favorably disposed than are Ashkenazim.

The distribution of Knesset seats reflects the changing balance of power between these three forces. In the 1996 election, Labor won thirty-four seats, Likud thirty-two (of which in fact four were contributed by Raful Eytan's ultranationalist Tzomet Party and five by David Levy's Gesher Party, which draws heavily on the North African Sephardi vote), while the three religious parties (Shas, the National Religious Party, and United Torah Judasim) won twenty-three, and the ultranationalist Moledet Party 2. The secular left, which has always been allied with Labor, saw its number of seats decline from twelve in 1992 to nine in 1996. The religious right, combined with the secular far right, has thus become almost as strong as the traditional two major contenders for power—Labor and Likud. This in turn implies that for Labor to form governments in the future it is likely that it will have to forge a coalition with the Arab parties, whose number of seats increased from five in 1992 to nine in 1996, largely because Arab voters who traditionally had voted for Labor or other Jewish parties defected. For its part, Likud has no alternative but to bring the radical religious and secular right-wing parties into its governing coalitions, thereby surrendering to them a very considerable measure of influence over domestic and foreign policies. Thus, Israel now

---

[94]Cited in *Mideast Mirror* (April 27, 1998).

and for the foreseeable future will have a sharply bifurcated polity, with both sides (Labor, secular left, and Arab parties versus Likud and the ultranationalist, religious, and ultra-Orthodox parties) having an almost equal share of votes and parliamentary seats. As the balance tips from one side to the other, as it did in 1992 and again in 1996, it has profound implications for Israel's policy toward the Arab states and the Palestinians.

The United States and Israel

The third critical ingredient for successful state-building, which is external support, has been provided to Israel in abundant measure by the United States. The "special relationship" between the United States and Israel results from the perception by key American officials that Israel is a strategic asset for the United States in the Middle East and from the impact of the pro-Israeli lobby on foreign policy decision making. Prior to the collapse of the Soviet Union, Israel was generally considered by U.S. administrations to be vital to U.S. security interests in the region because it provided military assets that could be used against both the USSR and radical Arab nationalism. Ronald Reagan, for example, stated that "Israel is the [American] military offset to the Soviet Union in the Middle East."[95] Secretary of State George Shultz told participants in the annual conference of the American Israel Public Affairs Committee (AIPAC), the main organization of the pro-Israeli lobby, in April 1985: "Every year we provide more security assistance to Israel than to any other nation. We consider that aid to be one of the best investments we can make—not only for Israel's security but for ours as well."[96]

The countervailing argument, prior to the demise of the USSR, was that support for Israel provided opportunities for the Soviets in the Arab world and led to destabilization of conservative Arab regimes. The "Israel first" policy, according to Michael Hudson, "places great strains on Arab regimes like Jordan, Egypt and Saudi Arabia. . . . One of the main consequences of 'Greater Israel' and United States support for 'Greater Israel' has been the growth of radical Islamic fundamentalist movements that threaten even the personal security of Americans in the Middle East."[97] Various secretaries of defense, including the first, James Forrestal, and Frank C. Carlucci and Caspar Weinberger, both of whom served under Reagan, considered the strategic relationship with Israel to be a mixed blessing. In particular they wanted to develop closer military relations with a variety of Arab states.

The second Gulf war and the almost simultaneous self-destruction of the Soviet Union fundamentally altered strategic realities in the region. United States

---

[95] *The Middle East* (December 1980): 36.

[96] George Shultz, "The United States and Israel: Partner for Peace and Freedom," *Journal of Palestine Studies* 56 (Summer 1985): 123.

[97] Michael C. Hudson, "United States Policy in the Middle East: Opportunities and Dangers," *Current History* 85 (February 1986): 50–51.

interests were no longer threatened by either a communist or a radical Arab state, while the conservative Arab states of the Gulf lined up to sign military agreements with Washington and to purchase huge quantities of arms from American weapons manufacturers. The benefits to the United States of the strategic relationship with Israel were now very much less, while the costs had significantly increased. President Bush, therefore, could well afford to be much less responsive to Israeli requests than had his predecessors. However, the "special relationship," resting as it does on the influence Israel is able to muster in the American political system, did not dissolve as a result of the changed security environment. For one thing, supporters of Israel argued successfully that although the Cold War had ended, American interests in the Middle East continued to be threatened by Iran, Iraq, Libya, Sudan, and the radical Islamist movement more generally, hence the U.S.-Israeli relationship remained vital to the successful pursuit of American objectives in the region. As part of this overall approach, Israel's supporters crafted what became known as the "Dual Containment" policy, whereby the U.S. committed itself to seeking to isolate both Iran and Iraq and, with regard to the latter, overthrow its government. For another thing, the election of Bill Clinton in 1992 brought into office the most staunchly pro-Israeli president in American history, as indicated, among other things, by recruitment of several key policy makers on the Middle East from various organizations of the pro-Israeli lobby.

"The Lobby," as pro-Israeli forces spearheaded by the AIPAC and, since 1985, the Washington Institute for Near East Policy have come to be known, is beyond question the most powerful nongovernmental participant in Middle East foreign policy decision making in Washington.[98] Based on the support of a large proportion of America's six million Jews, reinforced by the resources of the Israeli state, and further assisted by general sympathy for Israel in the United States, especially among fundamentalist Christians, the pro-Israeli lobby had established what appears to be an unassailable power base in Congress.

Such influence is built partially on this lobby's ability to raise campaign funds for candidates. Pro-Israeli political action committees, for example, have become the second-largest source of funds for Democratic candidates for the Senate; only organized labor contributes more to their campaigns.[99] Several incumbent congressmen, including Paul Findley (Illinois), Roger Jepsen (Iowa), and Paul (Pete) McCloskey (California), as well as Senators Walter Huddelston (Kentucky) and Charles Percy (Illinois), have lost reelection campaigns primarily because the pro-Israeli lobby targeted them for defeat and contributed large sums to the campaigns of their opponents. As the pro-Israeli lobby's leverage in Congress has increased, so has its influence within the executive branch grown. Each successive administration since that of Eisenhower has provided more economic and military assistance and, with the partial exception of the Carter and Bush administrations, more diplomatic support to Israel than its predecessor.

---

[98]Edward Tivnan, *The Lobby: Jewish Political Power and American Foreign Policy* (New York: Simon & Schuster, 1987).

[99]Rex B. Wintergerter, "The Pro-Israel PACs and the 1988 Elections," *Middle East International* 336 (October 21, 1988): 16.

ECONOMIC ASSISTANCE

From 1952 to 1965, U.S. economic and military assistance to Israel averaged $60 million annually. For the next eight years, up to 1973, it rose to an average of $230 million. In the decade after the 1973 war, U.S. aid averaged $2.32 billion per year, and since that time it has not dropped below $3 billion annually. Whereas prior to 1985 most of this assistance was in the form of loans, after that time 100 percent of the funds have been grants that never have to be repaid. In 1984–1985, when Israel confronted a balance of payments and general economic crisis, the Reagan administration provided an emergency $1.5 billion supplementary grant over and above the $3 billion in economic and military assistance budgeted for the coming year. It also effectively wrote off Israel's $10 billion debt to the United States by pegging future economic assistance to the debt repayment schedule. Nongovernmental financial assistance to Israel from the United States, principally from American Jews, amounted to $17 billion between 1948 and 1993.[100]

In 1990, the United States responded to increased Jewish immigration to Israel from the Soviet Union by providing $400 million in loan guarantees. During and immediately after the second Gulf war Washington topped up its "normal" $3.7 billion annual assistance package with an additional $650 million economic assistance grant, authorized transfer of $700 million in U.S. military equipment to Israel, earmarked $300 million for prepositioning in Israel U.S. weaponry, and provided *Patriot* missile batteries and various special military and civilian programs worth an additional $40 to $50 million.[101] By the end of fiscal year 1996, Israel had received almost $78 billion in foreign aid from the United States.[102]

From 1978 to 1988, the U.S. government gave Israel $29 billion in economic and military assistance, more than double the cost of the Marshall Plan for all of Europe after World War II.[103] Between 1979 and 1991, the $40.1 billion provided to Israel by the United States amounted to 21.5 percent of all U.S. multilateral and bilateral aid.[104] Private U.S. contributions since 1948 have averaged $500 million per year. Most are tax deductible in the United States. Since the early 1970s, official public assistance to Israel has accounted annually for about 30 percent of U.S. aid to some seventy countries, with the percentage gradually rising, so that by the late 1980s it was over 37 percent. In 1978–1979, $4.81 billion of aid to Israel constituted 43 percent of all American foreign assistance. By the mid-1980s, Israel was receiving from the United States some $1,500 for each

---

[100]Joel Bainerman, "Looking the Gift Horse in the Mouth," *Washington Post* (October 29, 1995), p. C4.

[101]Donald Neff, "Israeli's Dependence on the US," *Middle East International* (May 1, 1992): 16.

[102]Clyde Mark, "Israel: U.S. Foreign Assistance," Washington: Congressional Research Service (August 30, 1995).

[103]Tivnan, *The Lobby,* p. 217. See also Mohamed El-Khawas and Samir Abed Rabbo, *American Aid to Israel: Nature and Impact* (Brattleboro, Vt.: Amana Books, 1984); and George T. Abed, "Israel in the Orbit of America: The Political Economy of a Dependency Relationship," *Journal of Palestine Studies* 61 (Autumn 1986): 38–55.

[104]Neff, "Israeli's Dependence on the US," p. 16.

man, woman, and child in the country,[105] at which time Israel's per capita income had risen to some $14,000, a standard only slightly below that of Western Europe. Israel receives more per capita assistance annually from the U.S. than the per capita GNPs of many Arab states, including Egypt, Mauritania, Morocco, Sudan, and Yemen. Unlike all other countries receiving U.S. assistance, Israel receives its funds at the beginning of each financial year, which provided it an additional $86 million in interest in 1991. What all this adds up to is "that Congress has transferred to Israel, one of the world's smallest nations, more of America's treasury than any country at any time in history has ever voluntarily donated to a foreign country."[106] In addition, as Democratic Senator Robert Byrd of West Virginia noted on the Senate floor on April 1, 1992: "We have poured foreign aid into Israel for decades at rates and terms given to no other nation. . . . Beyond the massive economic and military aid, however, is our so-called strategic relation with Israel. We have served as protector almost in the same sense as the government of the United States would protect one of our fifty states."[107]

MILITARY AND SECURITY ASSISTANCE

Of the largesse bestowed by the U.S. government on Israel, about two-thirds since 1970 has been in the form of military assistance. Prior to 1962, Israel received virtually no such assistance from the United States. In the Kennedy and Johnson administrations, Israel received $250 million in military aid. This figure reached $6.7 billion during the eight years of the Nixon and Ford presidencies, further escalated to $7.4 billion under Carter, and doubled again under the Reagan administration. Since 1979, the baseline annual military assistance grant has been almost $1.9 billion. In 1998, Israel requested of Congress, as part of an overall plan to reduce somewhat its share of U.S. foreign aid, that it reallocate to the military some half a billion dollars from its earmarked annual civilian foreign assistance.

Military assistance has also taken the form of the transfer of the United States' most sophisticated weapons technology, which has, in turn, been copied, manufactured, and then exported from Israel, providing further foreign currency. In 1986, the Reagan administration granted Israel non-NATO ally status, enabling it to bid on tenders offered by the Department of Defense for a wide range of military equipment. In 1986, the U.S. Department of Defense purchased $205 million worth of Israeli armaments. Israel is the single largest foreign recipient of "Star Wars" research funds. Its Arrow antimissile missile program alone had received $126 million by 1991 and was scheduled to be given an additional $210 million over the next four years,[108] a commitment that was in fact then

---

[105]Tivnan, *The Lobby*, pp. 217–218. Martha Wenger, "U.S. Aid to Israel: From Handshake to Embrace," *Middle East Report* (May–August 1990).

[106]Donald Neff, "The Backlash Against Israel's Washington Policy," *Middle East International* 338 (November 18, 1988): 15.

[107]Neff, "Israel's Dependence on the US," p. 17.

[108]Dennis J. Wamsted, "Congressional Arms Control Is Freeze for Arabs and Increase for Israel," *The Washington Report on Middle East Affairs* (July 1991), p. 15.

revised upward by the Clinton Administration. The intelligence organizations of the two countries have also established close working relationships, as indicated by cooperation between the CIA and Israel's equivalent, Mossad, in dispatching clandestine arms shipments to the Contra rebels in Nicaragua, to the Phalange and the Lebanese Forces in Lebanon, to the government of Ayatollah Khomeini in Iran, and to various other governments and guerrilla organizations.[109]

Besides their development of a policy to provide Israel with one of the most powerful militaries in the world, the United States has gradually provided increasingly explicit guarantees of Israel's security. The first quasi-official such pledge was made by President John F. Kennedy in a conversation with Golda Meir, then Israeli foreign minister, in December 1962. Kennedy's remarks were summarized as follows:

> The U.S. has a special relationship with Israel in the Middle East, really comparable only to that which it has with Britain over a wide range of world affairs. . . . We are in a position to make clear to the Arabs that we will maintain our friendship with Israel and our security guarantees. . . . I think it is quite clear that in the case of an invasion the United States would come to the support of Israel.[110]

By 1975, the United States had become willing to provide Israel with wide-ranging and direct security guarantees in writing. Two Memorandums of Agreement accompanying the Sinai II disengagement agreement of that year bound the United States to meet Israel's long-term military and economic needs and guaranteed that the United States would provide Israel with oil from its own stocks if Israel was confronted with a shortage. The agreements provided for contingency plans to give Israel emergency military assistance and committed the United States to uphold the "survival and security" of Israel.[111] According to Nadav Safran, "But for the fact that it bore the label of Executive Agreements, it exceeded in many ways a formal treaty signed by the United States."[112] During the Reagan administration, Secretary of State George Shultz constructed an elaborate network of undertakings, commitments, agreements, and assurances to Israel that, according to AIPAC's director, will "leave a legacy that will be important to Israel's security for decades to come."[113] Shultz is reported to have pledged to Thomas Dine, head of AIPAC, to "build institutional arrangements so that eight years from now, if there is a secretary of state who is not positive about Israel, he will not be able to overcome the bureaucratic relationship between Israel and the U.S. that we have established."[114]

---

[109]Benjamin Beit-Hallahmi, *The Israeli Connection: Who Israel Arms and Why* (New York: Pantheon Books, 1987). See also Andrew and Leslie Cockburn, *Dangerous Liaison: The Inside Story of The U.S.-Israeli Covert Relationship* (New York: HarperCollins, 1991).

[110]Kennedy Library NSC Box 117–118, December 27, 1962, quoted in Mordechai Gazit, "Israeli Military Procurement from the United States," in *Dynamics of Dependence: U.S.-Israeli Relations,* ed. by Gabriel Sheffer (Boulder, Colo.: Westview Press, 1987), p. 98.

[111]Cited in Dilip Hiro, *Inside the Middle East* (London: Routledge and Kegan Paul, 1982), p. 225.

[112]Nadav Safran, *Israel: The Embattled Ally* (Cambridge: Harvard University Press, 1978), p. 557.

[113]Neff, "The Backlash," p. 14.

[114]Ibid.

At the annual national convention of AIPAC in 1992, Director of Foreign Policy Issues Steven Rosen noted his organization's continuing success in entwining the Israeli-U.S. defense relationship. According to him, Israeli military exports had jumped from $10 million to $500 million annually in a decade, thanks to the provision of U.S. assistance in various forms. He further observed that there are now 321 U.S.-Israeli joint programs in defense research, worth $2.9 billion.[115] During the second Gulf war, the United States dispatched *Patriot* missiles and crews to defend Israel from Iraqi missile attacks—the first time the United States had intervened directly on Israel's behalf in a military conflict.

DIPLOMATIC SUPPORT

Israel and the United States vote together more frequently in the United Nations General Assembly than does the United States with almost any other country. In 1986, they voted together 91.5 percent of the time. Egypt, Jordan, and Saudi Arabia, by contrast, voted with the United States on only 15.3 percent, 14.2 percent, and 13.6 percent of occasions, respectively.[116] This coincidence of votes is due largely to the fact that the United States has become one of Israel's few supporters (in some cases its sole supporter) in that body. Israel and the United States, for example, were outvoted 151 to 2 in November 1988 on a resolution deploring the U.S. decision to refuse Yasser Arafat a visa so that he could address the UN. Between 1981 and 1986, the Reagan administration used its veto in the Security Council against resolutions critical of Israel thirteen times, almost twice the seven vetoes cast by the United States from 1948 to 1981. America's UN ambassador during the Carter administration voted in favor of a resolution condemning Israel's treatment of Palestinians in the occupied territories as being in violation of the Fourth Geneva Convention. The response by the pro-Israeli lobby was so intense that the president ordered the vote changed, explaining the original vote as the result of an error in communication. President Carter's previous UN ambassador had been forced to resign because he met with the PLO's UN representative, even though he did so in his capacity as chairman of the Security Council rather than as U.S. ambassador to the UN. By 1989, the United States had used its Security Council veto twenty-three times to block resolutions critical of Israel. In 1983, Congress passed a law that requires the United States to renounce its membership in the UN General Assembly if Israel were to be expelled from that body. In September 1991, President Bush, in an address to the UN General Assembly, called for repeal of the "Zionism is racism" resolution that the Assembly had adopted in November 1975. Before the end of the year, the U.S. delegation to the UN had successfully steered such a motion through the General Assembly. Following Israel's deportation of 417 Palestinians in December 1992, the United States blocked efforts in the Security Council to force Israel to allow them to return. Since the end of the Cold War, the United States has used its veto in the Security Council three times, all of which have been to support Israel's unilateral actions in Jerusalem.

---

[115]Ian Williams, "AIPAC 1992," *The Washington Report on Middle East Affairs* (June 1992), p. 16.

[116]"AIPAC Policy Statement, 1987," *Journal of Palestine Studies* 64 (Summer 1987): 113.

Paradoxically, for Israel itself, virtually total U.S. support, which had been essential to its state-building and then continued national security, had become an increasingly mixed blessing by the early 1990s. As the key U.S. ally in the region, Israel had shouldered military burdens that militarized the economy and the polity and contributed to the ongoing crises within both spheres. Compromises necessary for peace with the Arabs were rendered politically difficult to support within Israel as a result of the American carte blanche given to the Israeli government. Israelis opposed to continued occupation of the territories conquered in 1967 and willing to negotiate with the PLO to establish a Palestinian state were unable to argue convincingly to their countrymen that suppression of Palestinians, attacks on Arab states, and other aggressive acts would necessarily result in a reduction of U.S. support.

Indeed, while the United States was still unwilling to deal directly with the PLO, an obstacle that impeded progress in the negotiations between Israel and the Palestinians that had commenced in Madrid in October 1991 and then shifted to Washington, the Israeli government of Yitzhak Rabin determined that it would not be bound by this constraint. In 1993, Rabin instructed his closest advisers to begin back channel negotiations with the PLO through the good offices of the Norwegian Foreign Minister, an initiative that resulted in the Oslo peace accords of September of that year. Paradoxically, therefore, wholehearted American support for half a century had greatly facilitated the emergence of Israel as the most powerful state in the region, but by being so overwhelmingly forthcoming may, in fact, have made peace between Israel and her Arab neighbors more rather than less difficult to attain.

Palestinian State Formation

On November 15, 1988, in Algiers at the 19th session of the Palestine National Council (PNC), the 450-member parliament of the Palestinian national movement, the establishment of a Palestinian state was declared.[117] The acceptance of Security Council Resolutions 242 and 338, which implicitly recognize Israel, was announced for the first time. The PNC also renounced the use of terrorism, although in rather elliptical language. These measures were immediately denounced by Israeli Foreign Minister Shimon Peres as "tactical moves devoid of any importance" and by Prime Minister Yitzhak Shamir as "meaningless," as "gimmicks," and as "doubletalk." Shamir pledged not to negotiate with the PLO "because they're opposed to peace with Israel."[118] However, the proceedings of the 19th session of the PNC and subsequent, unambiguous declarations by Yasser Arafat accepting the critical UN resolution and renouncing terrorism were a milestone for the Palestinians themselves. They also made possible

---

[117]Two hundred fifty-two members voted for the resolution calling for the declaration; forty-six voted against it; and ten abstained. Israel had prevented members of the PNC from the occupied territories from attending.

[118]World wire services, November 15, 1988.

United States–sponsored Israeli-Palestinian negotiations that commenced in October 1991 and the 1993 Oslo Accords.

Almost exactly a year before the PNC's 19th session, the Arab states at their Amman summit conference had relegated the Palestinian issue to the back burner and had snubbed PLO chairman Yasser Arafat. Now all those states, primarily as a result of the intifada, were obliged to accept the Palestinian fait accompli and recognize the newly declared state, whatever their reservations and misgivings.[119] Just two weeks less than forty years had elapsed since the UN had approved the Partition Plan that had paved the way for the creation of Israel. In the intervening two generations, the Palestinians articulated the ideology, created the organizations, and generated the level of international support required to approach the goal of establishing a state in some part of the territory of the Mandate. If this were to occur, Palestinians would be the last Arab peoples subjected to European control after World War I to gain their independence.

The process of Palestinian state formation—which is not yet completed—began at zero point in 1948. Having officially been labeled as "non-Jewish communities" in the Balfour Declaration and "Arabs" under the Mandate, Palestinians were from 1948 referred to as *refugees,* the term applied to them in UN Security Council Resolution 242, which was the principal reason why they rejected that resolution for so long. They wanted to be called neither Arabs nor refugees but Palestinians or Palestinian Arabs. The use of that term implies recognition of their national existence and right to a state. It was not until the late 1960s, however, that Palestinian ideological and organizational resources were sufficient to make that demand with any forcefulness. Prior to that time, Palestinian politics, organized along traditional lines, dominated by competing notables, fragmented between different geographical centers, and lacking any meaningful organization, simply were no match for the Israelis.

Palestinian Nationalism

Like other Arabs in the Levant, Palestinians participated in the "Arab Awakening" in the twilight of the Ottoman Empire, redefining their personal and political identities as Arab rather than Ottoman or exclusively as Muslim, Christian, tribal, or familial. After the collapse of Amir Faisal's Arab Kingdom in Damascus, Palestinians, again like other Levantine Arabs, began to formulate nationalist sentiments and identities centered on the sovereign territory into which the British and French had divided the region. For the Palestinians this was, of course, Pales-

---

[119]Egypt, fearful of jeopardizing its relations with the United States and its role as mediator between Israel and the Arabs, and under intense pressure from U.S. and Israeli officials, at first sought to finesse the issue. It declared its support for the PNC resolution without actually recognizing the newly declared state. That evasive tactic proved untenable in the face of widespread criticism of Egypt's stance in the Arab press. Within a week of the declaration, Egypt announced its recognition of the new state, simultaneously blasting "some media circles that continue to raise questions about Egypt's position" (Alan Cowell, "Palestine State Is Recognized by Egypt," *New York Times,* November 21, 1988).

tine. However, for them, as for the Syrians, Lebanese, Iraqis, and many other Arabs, Pan-Arabist ideas continued to coexist with state-based nationalism.

In the wake of the devastating defeat of 1947–1949, an Arab identity temporarily displaced the Palestinian one. It did so because Israel and the Arab states both sought to reinforce Arabism at the expense of Palestinian nationalism and because the Palestinians, too weak to challenge Israel alone, sought to enlist the Arab states in their cause. In particular, Gamal Abdel Nasser, by championing Arab rights, appeared to the Palestinians as a potential savior. Even before the catastrophic defeat of June 1967, however, Palestinians had become aware of the divergence of interests between their cause and Nasserism, so they sought once again to center their nationalism not on Arabism but on their Palestinian identities. This process was given added momentum by the 1967 war.

ISRAELI RESPONSE

That Palestinian nationalism has become so intense is due in part to the severity and thoroughness with which its opponents, including Israel, the Arab states, and the United States, have sought to subdue it. Israel in particular tried to invalidate Palestinian claims to land occupied by Israel by obliterating references to Palestinians and manifestations of their separate culture. After the 1948 war, Israel bulldozed 385 of the 475 Palestinian villages that were inside the "Green Line" (i.e., the border between Israel and the West Bank from 1949 to 1967) and wiped their names from maps, in many cases replacing them with Hebrew names.[120] Officially, Palestinians in Israel are known as Israeli Arabs. Prime Minister Golda Meir declared in 1969 that there was no such thing as the Palestinian people—"they did not exist."[121] In that same year, Menachem Begin warned an Israeli audience of the consequences of allowing the term *Palestine* to be used. He said, "If this is Palestine and not the land of Israel, then you are conquerors and not tillers of the land. You are invaders. If this is Palestine, then it belongs to a people who lived here before you came."[122] Yitzhak Rabin, who as prime minister between 1974 and 1977 had refused to negotiate with "any Palestinian element" and who said "a third state between Israel and Jordan . . . will not be created," responded as minister of defense to the Palestinian intifada by pledging to "break their bones" and by authorizing the use of a range of lethal weaponry.[123] That Rabin's strong-arm methods failed to stop the intifada is one of the major reasons why he, as prime minister from 1992 to 1995, decided to negotiate with the PLO.

The invasion of Lebanon by Israel in the summer of 1982 was for the purpose of destroying the organizational infrastructure of the Palestinian national movement. The Israeli response to the intifada, a quintessential expression of nationalist commitment, was for almost six years to attempt to crush it. Intellec-

---

[120]"Israel and the Palestinians," p. 35.

[121] *The Sunday Times,* June 15, 1969.

[122] *Yediot Aharanot* (October 17, 1969), cited in Ari Bober, *The Other Israel* (New York: Doubleday, 1972), p. 77.

[123]"Israel and the Palestinians," p. 40.

tual efforts were also made to impede the formation, legitimation, and global acceptance of Palestinian nationalism. In 1984, for example, a Zionist author, Joan Peters, published *From Time Immemorial*.[124] This book purported to document that the great majority of Palestinians are in fact not that at all but are Arabs who illegally migrated to Palestine during the Mandate as a result of economic opportunities stimulated by Jewish settlement. The book was lauded by a great number of leading Israelis and supporters of Israel. It subsequently was convincingly argued that the author had flagrantly distorted, falsified, and concealed the true historical record.[125]

THE U.S. RESPONSE

The United States' approach to the Palestinians prior to the Oslo Accords was identical to Israel's inasmuch as the United States sought to prevent the emergence of a Palestinian state. In September 1970, the United States and Israel jointly reassured Jordan's King Hussein of their support for his military confrontation with Palestinian guerrilla organizations in that country. Five years later, Secretary of State Henry Kissinger, while mediating the second disengagement agreement in the Sinai between Israel and Egypt after the 1973 war, committed the United States not to recognize or negotiate with the PLO unless and until it specifically recognized Israel's right to exist under UN Resolution 242. A further precondition for contacts with the United States, that the PLO renounce the use of terrorism, was subsequently added.

The unambiguous acceptance of these conditions by Yasser Arafat in a press conference on December 14, 1988, paved the way for Secretary of State Shultz finally to open the door to a U.S.-PLO dialogue. This sudden departure from established U.S. policy was so surprising precisely because of the consistency of the anti-PLO position prior to that time. Secretary of State Alexander Haig had given tacit consent to the Israeli invasion of Lebanon in 1982, apparently out of the hope that the PLO would be eradicated. President Carter at Camp David in 1978 brokered a separate peace between Egypt and Israel. It spoke not of national or civil rights for Palestinians but of their "autonomy," which was interpreted by Begin and subsequently by Shamir (who initially rejected Camp David) to be perfectly compatible with their policies of settling Jews in the occupied territories and denying Palestinians both civil and national rights. Ronald Reagan endorsed the Israeli interpretation, when campaigning in 1980, by saying that he saw nothing illegal about Israel's settlements. After Camp David until

---

[124]Joan Peters, *From Time Immemorial* (New York: Harper & Row, 1984).

[125]For a discussion of the reaction to this book, see Edward W. Said, *"Conspiracy of Praise," Blaming the Victims*, pp. 23–31. The most informative reviews of the book are Norman G. Finkelstein, in "Disinformation and the Palestine Question: The Not-So-Strange Case of Joan Peters' *From Time Immemorial*," in *Blaming the Victims*, pp. 33–69; Bill Farrell, "Joan Peters and the Perversion of History," *Journal of Palestine Studies* 53 (Fall 1984): 126–134; and Yehoshua Porath, "Mrs. Peters' Palestine," *New York Review of Books* 32 (January 16, 1986): 36–39. For an authoritative account of Palestinian demography in this period, see Justin McCarthy, *The Population of Palestine: Population History and Statistics of the Late Ottoman Period and the Mandate* (New York: Columbia University Press, 1990).

December 1988, U.S. peace efforts concentrated on the "Jordanian option," which was an attempt to mediate a peace agreement between King Hussein and Israel, thereby excluding the Palestinian national movement from negotiations and precluding the possibility of the establishment of an independent Palestinian state.

Even the language used by American officials in the 1970s and 1980s was carefully chosen either to avoid the terms *Palestine* or *Palestinian* or to sharply qualify their usage. Harold Saunders, then a deputy assistant secretary of state, when testifying to Congress in 1975, referred to Palestinians as "the Arab people who consider themselves to be Palestinians." This was considered an extremely bold statement at the time.[126] Phillip Habib, U.S. presidential envoy to the Middle East, asked in July 1981 who had agreed to the cease-fire he had negotiated in southern Lebanon between the Palestinians and the Israelis, responded, "Israel." Then, after some hesitation, he added, "Israel and the other parties involved."[127] The term *Palestinian* finally entered the lexicon of U.S. administrations when President George Bush and Secretary of State James Baker, anxious to redeem pledges made to Arab leaders during the Gulf crisis of 1990–1991, embarked upon a campaign to induce Israel to offer "autonomy" to the Palestinians in the occupied territories.

THE ARAB RESPONSE

Although the Arab states were not as uniform or consistent as Israel and the United States in seeking to repress and deny Palestinian nationalism, the general thrust of Arab policy after 1947 was in that direction. During the cataclysmic events of 1947–1949, "both Transjordan and Israel pursued a policy of 'politicide,' seeking to liquidate any Palestinian leadership striving for an independent state."[128] The other Arab states, despite their opposition to King Abdullah's schemes, rejected pleas by the Palestinians in late 1947 and early 1948 for money, arms, and reinforcements. In December 1948, the Transjordanian parliament ratified the annexation of the West Bank, and Abdullah worked assiduously to undermine the government of All-Palestine that had been set up by the Palestinian nationalist leader Haj Amin al-Husaini, the mufti of Jerusalem. That government in exile fell under Egyptian influence and, for all intents and purposes, had ceased to function by 1950. In that same year, a Jordanian government decree prohibited the use of the term *Palestine* to refer to the land west of the Jordan River under its jurisdiction, substituting for it the term *West Bank*.

Since then, all the front-line Arab states have repressed Palestinian political activity at one time or another. Within six weeks of the newly formed guerrilla group Fatah's first raid into Israel on December 31, 1964, the Egyptian government had arrested all Fatah leaders in Gaza, the territory under direct Egyptian

---

[126]Kathleen Christison, "Blind Spots: Official U.S. Myths about the Middle East," *Journal of Palestine Studies* 66 (Winter 1988): 57.

[127]Bayan Nuwaihed Al Hout, "The Nature of the Palestine Liberation Organization," in *Palestinian Rights*, p. 11.

[128]Flapan, *The Birth of Israel*, p. 150.

administration.[129] In 1970, all the Arab states, with the exception of Syria, stood by as King Hussein undertook to liquidate the independent Palestinian national movement. In 1976, Syria intervened in the civil war in Lebanon to prevent a victory by the Palestinian-Lebanese Muslim alliance. Since 1983, Syria has used its own troops as well as militias under its influence in an attempt to subordinate the Palestinian national movement in Lebanon to Syrian interests. In the wake of the second Gulf war, most of the 400,000 Palestinians living in Kuwait were forced to flee as the Kuwaiti government meted out retribution for alleged Palestinian collaboration with the Iraqis.

Not surprisingly, Palestinians came to believe that Israel, the United States, and even the Arab states all strongly opposed their aspirations for independence. In a January 1982 survey of the attitudes of 2,700 Palestinians, only 4 percent believed that the Arab states really support the Palestinian cause, and 42 percent said those states are indifferent to them or plotting against them.[130] According to Rashid Khalidi, "Most Palestinians consider individuals like 'Isam Sartawi, Fahd al-Qawasmeh, and Sa'id Hamami (Palestinian political figures) martyrs killed by Arab regimes."[131] The 1982 survey also found that only 2 percent of respondents believed the United States was serious about resolving the Palestine-Israel conflict. One percent accepted the idea of autonomy advocated by the United States and Israel, and 1 percent viewed King Hussein as the sole representative of the Palestinians.[132] A *Time* survey of that year revealed that 0.5 percent thought the United States was helpful to the Palestinians.[133] A poll conducted among Palestinian residents of the West Bank and Gaza Strip in the summer of 1986 revealed that 95 percent of the respondents wanted a Palestinian state for all or part of Palestine, 1 percent wanted a Palestinian entity linked to Jordan, and 3.7 percent preferred that the West Bank be returned to Jordan and the Gaza Strip to Egypt.[134]

THE REASSERTION OF IDENTITY

The impact of the suppression of Palestinian nationalism after 1948 was such that the creation of a Palestinian national movement from the mid-1960s required the rekindling of a national identity among the dispirited, dispersed, and disorganized Palestinians. Ali Salamah, a PLO member who was eventually assassinated, probably by Israeli agents, when asked in 1972 about his reasons for belonging to that organization, responded:

> Before 1967 a Palestinian was regarded as an unrespected, unprotected, dishonored fugitive who sold his land. I rejected being that man. . . . I can never forget one day

---

[129]Joan Mandell, "Gaza: Israel's Soweto," p. 10.

[130]Fouad Moughrabi, "The International Consensus on the Palestine Question," *Journal of Palestine Studies* 63 (Spring 1987): 126–131.

[131]Rashid Khalidi, "The Palestinian Dilemma: PLO Policy after Lebanon," *Journal of Palestine Studies* 57 (Autumn, 1985): 100.

[132]Moughrabi, "The International Consensus," pp. 126–127.

[133]Cited in ibid., p. 128.

[134]Shadid and Seltzer, "Political Attitudes of Palestinians," pp. 20–21.

when I was a teenager, I had to deny my identity. I was afraid of saying "I am a Palestinian" to a group of vagabonds, so I said that I was a Syrian. . . . Going back to Haifa is not the problem. The restoration of my identity is the problem.[135]

The process of restoring Palestinian identity took several forms, from writing nationalist poetry to adopting terrorist tactics on a global scale to prove to the world, and to the Palestinians themselves, that they still constituted a nation in need of a state. Thus, the armed struggle came to symbolize the assertion of Palestinian identity, as indicated by the slogan *"Hawiyyati bunduqiyyati"* ("My identity is my rifle") scrawled on the walls of refugee camps in the 1960s.[136]

Accompanying the use of violence as a tool to emphasize the reemergence of Palestinian national consciousness was the assertion of maximalist political claims, as embodied, for example, in the Palestinian National Covenant. That document, originally adopted by the first meeting of the Palestine National Council in May 1964 and subsequently amended at the fourth meeting of the council in July 1968, stated in Article 19 that "the partition of Palestine in 1947 and the establishment of the state of Israel are entirely illegal." Articles 5 and 6 designated those who have a right to live in Palestine, a definition that included all Palestinian Arabs and excluded all Jews who came there after 1917, and their children.[137] In the years after 1968, as Palestinian identity reformed and its organizational manifestations grew in size and capability, so did the maximalist position of armed struggle for the liberation of all Palestine give way to the more realistic position of negotiating a compromise settlement with Israel, a step that was finally taken in 1993. Palestinian nationalism thus passed from the stage of identity formation to a more self-confident phase in which negotiations could be entered into and compromises entertained because of the security of that national identification and because of the supremacy of the main organizational embodiment of Palestinian nationalism, the PLO.

Palestinian Organizations

During the Mandate, Palestinian political organization was no match for the Zionists, the British, or the Arab states. An overwhelmingly rural society, Palestine had no truly national political leadership. What passed as such were the traditional notables of the largest cities, especially in Jerusalem, where political leadership was closely associated with the religious traditions and institutions of the city. Two families in particular, the Husainis and Nashashibis, competed throughout the Mandate for preeminence—a struggle that reached down into villages as clients of the two families struggled against one another.

Only during the revolt of 1936–1939 were the Palestinians able to overcome factionalism and, largely through the mobilization of the peasantry, mount sustained opposition to Zionist settlers and the British. The revolt, however, was ul-

---

[135]Al Hout, "The Nature of the Palestine Liberation Organization," p. 19.

[136]Ibid., pp. 20–21.

[137]See Yehoshofat Harkabi, *Palestinians and Israel* (Jerusalem: Keter Publishing, 1974), pp. 49–69.

timately crushed by an overwhelming application of force by the British, who were desperate to secure their control of this strategic area as the Second World War approached. Less than a decade later, the Palestinians were confronted with another *force majeur*, this time the creation of Israel. In their state of weakness and disorganization, Palestinians were unable to act decisively. For at least a decade after 1948, there remained an organizational vacuum as the last surviving manifestations of traditional leadership, Haj Amin al-Husaini's Arab Higher Committee and the Government of All Palestine, withered in Beirut and Cairo, respectively. Security services of the Arab states and Israel frustrated efforts by other contenders.

The roots of most contemporary Palestinian political organizations are to be found in the 1960s. By then a new generation of educated, primarily middle-class Palestinians, strongly inspired by nationalism and intent on modernizing Palestinian politics, had emerged. In Cairo, leaders of the Palestine Students Union, including Salah Khalaf (Abu Iyad), Khalil al-Wazir (Abu Jihad), and Yasser Arafat (Abu Ammar) formed the nucleus of a group that in 1964 was to found the guerrilla organization Fatah. In Beirut, the Arab National Movement, which after the 1967 war was to spawn the Popular Front for the Liberation of Palestine (PFLP) and then a breakaway faction from that guerrilla group, the Popular Democratic Front for the Liberation of Palestine (PDFLP), was formed by students, the best known of whom was Dr. George Habash, a Greek Orthodox Christian.

Young, well-educated Palestinians dispersed throughout the Arab world provided the leadership for these new groups, which recruited guerrillas from among the destitute youths of the refugee camps. These small organizations would not have prospered even with an abundance of recruits, however, had it not been for the Arab Cold War. The radicalization of the Arab world that gathered pace after 1958 and that saw various attempts to outbid Nasser from the left created a climate in which Palestinian nationalist organizations could flourish. Syria, for example, supported Fatah in the early stages to demonstrate its leftist credentials and to undermine Nasser. He, in turn, seeking to contain independent Palestinian political activities and the general drift toward confrontation with Israel, engineered the creation of the Palestine Liberation Organization, which held its first meeting in Jerusalem in May 1964. Ahmad al-Shuqairi, a lawyer noted for his bombast, who formerly had served as Saudi Arabia's representative at the United Nations, was selected by Nasser to head the PLO. Most young Palestinian political activists assessed Shuqairi and the PLO as tools of the Arab regimes, rejecting them in favor of guerrilla organizations that embodied independent Palestinian interests.

The 1967 war, which discredited the Arab states, created as many as 300,000 new Palestinian refugees, mobilized much of the population of the Arab world, made available new sanctuaries from which guerrilla war could be launched, and provided the opportunity for the Palestinians to consolidate their hold over the Palestinian national movement. This they accomplished by finally taking over the PLO at the fifth session of the Palestine National Council (PNC) in February 1969. Yasser Arafat was elected chairman of its executive committee, and Fatah took the majority of seats reserved for guerrilla organizations, an arrangement that has persisted until now. Although dominated by Arafat and Fatah, the

PLO since 1969 has in fact been an umbrella organization into and out of which the competitors of Fatah have drifted as their relations have waxed and waned.

The PLO, however, rapidly became more than just a collection of guerrilla organizations. In order to serve as the principal vehicle of Palestinian nationalism, it expanded its membership to include representatives of as many sectors of the far-flung Palestinian population as possible. The PNC, which served as the Palestinian "parliament" until 1996 when, in accordance with the Oslo Accords a Palestinian legislative council was elected, expanded from 105 members at its fifth session in 1969 to 180 in 1973 and ultimately to 490 members in 1992. The last time the PNC met was in April 1996, when it was convened in Gaza in order to change the articles in the Palestinian Charter that had been rendered irrelevant or were in contradiction with the peace process, such as those articles that called for Israel's destruction.[138]

Paralleling the expansion of the Palestinian parliament was the growth of the PLO's bureaucratic infrastructure, which employed some 8,000 Palestinians in noncombatant capacities by the 1980s. In 1982, it included a health care service with 13 hospitals and 100 clinics; a vocational training unit for industry and agriculture; and a host of departments such as information and culture, mass organizations, social affairs and welfare, education, information, and politics, which functioned as ministries do in the states of the Middle East. Most of this organizational infrastructure was located in Lebanon and was destroyed during the Israeli invasion in 1982, but some of it was subsequently reconstructed, principally in Tunis, to where the PLO relocated.

The PLO, in short, built after 1969 the political, military, and bureaucratic organizations characteristic of statehood. This institutionalization of the chief organization of the national movement led to the usual pathologies of statism in the region, including corruption, abuse of power, favoritism, and the like, pathologies that vastly increased in the wake of the Oslo Accords. However, precisely because the Palestinians do not yet have a state, most have clung to the PLO that, as a result of the Oslo Accords, became after 1993 in the Occupied Territories the Palestine Authority (PA), although for purposes of representing diaspora Palestinians has continued to exist as the PLO in Tunis. The PLO and PA symbolize their national aspirations; to abandon them is to abandon hope for an independent state.

The PLO confronted both external and internal threats to its hegemony over the Palestinian national movement. Israel and the Arab states mounted direct physical assaults against individuals and groups associated with it. King Hussein attempted to destroy it in 1970, Israel tried in 1982, and Syria has worked assiduously to that end in Lebanon since 1983. The two most important PLO leaders after Arafat, Salah Khalaf and Khalil al-Wazir, were both assassinated by the organization's enemies. In Wazir's case, Israel appears to have been responsible, while Khalaf was gunned down in Tunis on January 15, 1991, by agents of

---

[138]Note: In response the Israeli Labor Party, then led by Shimon Peres, voted to remove from its platform the plank rejecting the establishment of an independent Palestinian state. Almost exactly two years later, Shimon Peres, no longer leader of the Labor Party, explicitly called for the creation of such a state.

the Palestinian dissident Abu Nidal. The wealthy Arab oil-exporting states sought to bring the organization under their influence by subsidizing it. The manifest failure of that strategy, as evidenced by many Palestinians' favorable reaction to Iraq's invasion of Kuwait, caused those states, especially Kuwait and Saudi Arabia, to withdraw those subsidies and to seek in various ways to undermine the PLO. Egypt used its diplomatic leverage with the United States and in the Middle East in an effort to bring the PLO into its orbit. The United States backed various efforts to remove the PLO as a significant political actor, while the USSR attempted to induce it to toe a pro-Moscow line.

Internal threats to the PLO were, if anything, more difficult to counter. The social structure and geographical dispersion of Palestinians militated against organizational cohesion. Of the some six million Palestinians, about a fifth are still registered as refugees, many of them living in camps in the Occupied Territories, Lebanon, Syria, and Jordan. Before 1990–1991, about a million Palestinians lived in the Arab oil states of Kuwait, Iraq, Saudi Arabia, Libya, and the lower Gulf principalities. About half of the Palestinians residing in those countries left them immediately before, during, or after the 1990–1991 Gulf crisis. Over 300,000 fled from Kuwait alone, with a quarter of a million of them going to Jordan. Almost 900,000 Palestinians reside in Israel, and another 2 million live in the Occupied Territories, so that slightly less than half of all Palestinians are under direct Israeli control. About 7 percent of Palestinians no longer live in the Middle East, having taken up residence in Europe, North America, or elsewhere.[139] The Palestinian population has the highest level of educational achievements of any Arab peoples, but it also has a high percentage of people living in squalor and destitution. The overwhelming majority of Palestinians are Sunni Muslims, yet the Christian minority is politically influential and comparatively well off. In the absence of a single state structure to impose order on such a diverse and far-flung population, maintaining unity of purpose and preventing underlying sociogeographical divisions from becoming politically unmanageable has been a major and continuing task.

With the commencement of the intifada in December 1987, it was clear that the center of Palestinian political activity had shifted to the Occupied Territories and that even Palestinians in Israel, long marginal to the nationalist movement, were closer geographically and politically to this new epicenter than Palestinians in Beirut, Amman, or elsewhere. This marked a fundamental change, for the PLO had arisen as a diaspora organization. The relatively conservative society of the West Bank, Israel's presence there, PLO infatuation with the armed struggle, and recruitment into guerrilla organizations from refugee camps, especially those in Lebanon, all caused the PLO before 1974 to concentrate its efforts outside historic Palestine. In the wake of the 1973 war, however, as a negotiated settlement appeared to be possible and as the PLO began to moderate its stance, so did the Occupied Territories come to play an increasingly important role in overall strategy.

---

[139]Janet Abu-Lughod, "The Continuing Expulsions from Palestine: 1948–1985," in Glenn E. Perry, *Palestine: Continuing Dispossession* (Belmont, Mass.: Association of Arab-American University Graduates, 1986), pp. 17–45. See also Sabella, "The Demography of Conflict," pp. 9–11.

This tendency was reinforced by the competition the PLO faced from Jordan's King Hussein, who sought to regain control of the West Bank and preempt the creation of a Palestinian state. The other Arab states, however, not wanting Hussein to succeed in this effort, designated the PLO the "sole legitimate representative of the Palestinian people" at their Rabat summit conference in 1974. By so doing, the Arab states drew the PLO further into the diplomatic process, thereby adding momentum to its transformation from a collection of guerrilla organizations into a broadly based national movement with strong connections to the Occupied Territories.

From then until the PLO assumed control of the Palestinian Authority in the Occupied Territories as a result of the Oslo Accords, the ongoing problem for it was to reconcile its roots in the diaspora and its official exclusion from Israeli-controlled territory on the one hand with the aspirations and organizations of those in the Occupied Territories on the other. The different conditions there, the need for local leadership to take initiatives, and the constant attempts by Israel to quash organizational activity connected to the PLO all contributed to organizational autonomy within the overall framework of the PLO. The Palestinian National Front (PNF), which operated from 1973 to 1978 in the West Bank and Gaza, was, like the PLO with which it was affiliated, an umbrella organization that coordinated political activities by various groups. It backed candidates in the April 1976 municipal elections, winning control of eighteen of the twenty-four municipal councils. When the PNF was ultimately dissolved as a result of Israeli pressure in October 1978, its role was quickly filled by the National Guidance Committee, which was led by heads of unions, professional associations, and municipal officials. It succeeded in preventing the Village Leagues, which were another Israeli-backed effort to create an alternative to PLO-affiliated leadership, from becoming established. The National Guidance Committee was outlawed in May 1982. In its place a plethora of local-level groups, like Shabiba (Youth), which was tied to Fatah, sprang up.

Proliferation of Palestinian organizations in the 1980s, especially those of an Islamicist character, contributed to a rising spiral of violence. Minister of Defense Yitzhak Rabin, in an attempt to crush these activities, declared an "iron fist" policy on August 4, 1985. By October, twelve Palestinians had been deported, five were killed, scores were placed under administrative detention (imprisonment without charges), and strict censorship was imposed. By the time the intifada broke out two years later, hundreds of administrative detention orders had been issued, over one hundred homes had been demolished, more than twenty Palestinians were killed, and Palestinian schools and universities were repeatedly closed.[140]

The Rise of Islamism

The paradox of the intifada, however, is that it was brought to an end not by Israeli coercion but as a reaction to the process of Palestinian political mobilization it facilitated and the threat that mobilization posed to the continued domi-

---

[140]Mouin Rabbani, "The Twenty Years Uprising," *Middle East Report* 152 (May–June 1988): 36–37.

nance of the Palestinian national movement by the PLO. Although virtually all segments of the Palestinian population in the Occupied Territories were mobilized into political activity during the intifada, which was initiated and led not by the PLO in Tunis but by Palestinians living in the West Bank and Gaza, it was the Islamist movement whose recruitment and organizational strength was most reinforced by the violent rebellion against Israeli rule. By the early 1990s, it was clear to both the Israelis and to the leadership of the PLO that, unless the intifada were brought to an end, radical Islamist organizations would become ever stronger, thereby possibly fatally undermining the strength of the PLO and its capacity to enforce any agreement that might be negotiated with Israel. It was this perception more than any other considerations that led the leaderships of both Israel and the PLO to reach their historic agreement on a Declaration of Principles in September 1993, for the former feared the Islamists more than the PLO, and the latter did not want to be supplanted by other contenders for leadership of the Palestine national movement.

Although support for Islamism in the Occupied Territories had increased in the early 1980s, it was not until the intifada that the Islamists emerged as a challenger not only to the PLO but to indigenous secular organizations in those Territories as well. It was principally the latter that had formed the Unified Command of the intifada, which coordinated the efforts of the plethora of groups and organizations that had sprung up in refugee camps, villages, schools, universities, sports clubs, and as appendages to underground political parties. One of the two principal Islamist political organizations, Islamic Jihad, which claims to have initiated the intifada, despite engaging in terrorist acts such as knife, grenade, and shooting attacks on Israeli troops and civilians—tactics shunned by most of the secularists working under the Unified Command—did in fact cooperate with that coordinating body throughout the intifada. An offshoot of the Muslim Brotherhood and founded by Sheikh Abd al Aziz Awda and Fathi al Shaqaqi, the former of whom was expelled and the latter assassinated by the Israelis, Islamic Jihad had come by the late 1980s to be closer to Fatah and the PLO than to the Muslim Brotherhood.

This was not the case, however, with Hamas, the other major Islamist organization and the one that in the 1990s has come to be the main organizational embodiment of the Palestinian Islamist movement. Also founded by young men who broke away from the Muslim Brotherhood (but not until after the intifada had already begun), Hamas means "zeal" and is an acronym for the Islamic Resistance Movement. Its founders chose as their spiritual leader Sheikh Ahmad Yasin, a Gazan-based leader of the Muslim Brotherhood who endorsed the call for jihad, or holy war, against Israel. Yasin, a disabled and devoutly religious man, was subsequently arrested by the Israelis and held in prison by them until 1997. His immense popularity was reflected in the huge crowds that greeted him on his release, which in turn reflected the steady growth of support for Hamas and the Islamist movement generally, especially as the peace process ground to a halt after Binyamin Netanyahu was elected Israeli prime minister in May 1996. Even Arafat, locked into a political struggle against Hamas and Palestinian Islamism more generally since the early 1990s, was forced to physically and politically embrace Yassin and at least to appear to consult with him in 1998. Paradoxically, the emergence of Hamas had been due in part to support for it by the

Israeli occupying authorities in the late 1980s, a tactic intended by them to undermine the intifada by splitting the Palestinian resistance between nationalist and Islamist wings.[141]

From the outset Hamas refused to cooperate with the secular nationalists of Fatah and the PLO on the grounds that it sought an Islamic, not a secular, state and because it rejected any compromise with Israel, demanding instead the "liberation" of not just the West Bank and Gaza but of all Israel. By the fall of 1988, it was calling for general strikes on days other than those designated by the Unified Command. Following the PLO's declaration of the establishment of a Palestinian state, Hamas distributed a leaflet that declared, "This independence movement is imaginary. It is a quick move by some of the Palestinian ranks to steal the fruits of the intafada's victory."[142]

The crack between the largely secular PLO and its affiliates in the Occupied Territories on the one hand and Hamas and other Islamicists on the other was further widened by the decision reached in the fall of 1991 to participate in U.S.-sponsored peace negotiations with Israel. As the PLO was preparing to declare its willingness to sanction participation by Palestinians from the West Bank and Gaza in the U.S.-sponsored peace conference scheduled to be held in Madrid in October–November 1991, Hamas condemned the gathering as "a conference for selling land" and issued death threats to would-be participants.[143] It called for the total liberation of Palestine, an escalation of the intifada, and armed struggle against Israel. As peace negotiations proceeded in 1991 and 1992, tensions between the two opposing sides boiled over, especially in Gaza, where pitched battles occurred. In one round of fighting between armed supporters of Hamas and those of the mainstream PLO organization Fatah in July 1992, 150 Palestinians were injured and one was shot dead.

The emergence of Islamic activism in the intifada is not a sudden departure from previous political trends in the Occupied Territories. Following the Iranian revolution, there was an upsurge of recruitment into and activities by radical Islamicist organizations. By the late 1980s, Islamic Jihad, for example, may have had several thousand followers. Mosques, which doubled in numbers in the Occupied Territories between 1967 and 1988, began to take on overt political roles even prior to the intifada. Once it commenced, they became key command posts.[144] Public opinion surveys in the 1980s revealed that a quarter of the respondents wanted to live in a Palestinian state based on the sharia. Younger respondents evinced Islamicist attitudes and preferences more strongly.[145] By

---

[141]For the rise of Islamic Jihad and Hamas and details of Israeli support for the latter, see Glenn E. Robinson, *Building a Palestinian State: The Incomplete Revolution* (Bloomington: Indiana University Press, 1997), pp. 141–160.

[142]Rashid Khalidi, "The PLO and the Uprising," *Middle East Report* 154 (September–October 1988): 21–23.

[143]Daoud Kuttab, "Reaction in the Territories," *Middle East International* 406 (August 16, 1991): 9.

[144]Robin Wright, "The New Dimension of Palestinian Politics," *Middle East Insight* 5: 6 (1988): 20–29.

[145]Shadid and Seltzer, "Political Attitudes of Palestinians," pp. 223–224; and Emile Sahliyeh, *In Search of Leadership: West Bank Politics Since 1967* (Washington, D.C.: The Brookings Institution, 1988), pp. 145–147.

1992, Hamas claimed to represent one-third of the Palestinians living in the Occupied Territories.[146] During the 1990s, polls of Palestinian public opinion have consistently revealed that about one-quarter of Palestinians support Hamas. Students associated with Islamic groups have since the early 1980s vied with nationalists for control of student government bodies in the Islamic University in Gaza and in the West Bank universities, including even the Vatican-supported Bethlehem University. There have been numerous physical confrontations between nationalists and Islamic activists on campuses. Among Palestinian citizens of Israel, the Islamic Movement, a legal Islamicist political organization, has had increasing appeal. In local elections in 1989, it won 29 percent of the seats in the twelve Arab municipalities in which it ran. By 1992, it had control of seven town councils. In the 1996 Knesset elections, it succeeded for the first time in electing an Islamist Arab member, Abd al Malik Dahamshi, who headed the United Arab List, a coalition of the Democratic Arab Party and the Islamist Movement.

Islamic activists were not the only critics of the leadership of the Palestinian national movement and especially the PLO to emerge during the intifada. Dissatisfaction with the way in which Yasser Arafat responded to the Iraqi invasion of Kuwait caused many Palestinians to question his leadership and to call for greater democratization of the PLO. Khalid al-Hasan, for example, a founder of Fatah and the head of the PNC's Foreign Affairs Committee, condemned the "tyrannical line of Arafat" and called for new elections to the PNC under international supervision.[147] Even prior to the outbreak of the intifada, secular, Westernized Palestinians living in the Occupied Territories had grown increasingly critical of the "old guard," whom they saw as old-fashioned, too much in the mold of traditional Arab politicians infatuated with manipulation rather than mobilization, and not well enough equipped linguistically or intellectually to appeal to Western audiences or negotiate with Western decision makers. These younger aspiring leaders were uninterested in the interminable struggles between the "historic" guerrilla organizations and far more interested in building a political base of support as wide as possible, including Israel, where they have extensive contacts with Jewish peace activists.

The peace negotiations that commenced in October 1991 provided the opportunity for this comparatively Westernized and young Palestinian leadership from the Occupied Territories to attempt to play a more direct role in determining the fate of Palestinians living under Israeli control. The fourteen-member delegation to the Madrid conference was drawn from high-status families and from political organizations, with one-half coming from Fatah. Hanan Ashrawi, a Christian academic trained in the United States, assumed a particularly high profile as a spokesperson. However, the delegation was firmly anchored within the PLO, even though that organization remained illegal in the occupied territories and was prohibited from participating directly in the peace negotiations. The PLO Central Committee meeting of mid-October 1991 that approved Palestinian participation in the Madrid conference came up with a formula that provided the necessary latitude for the Palestinian delegation but ensured that it

---

[146]Muhammad Muslih, "The Shift in Palestinian Thinking," *Current History* (January 1992), p. 26.

[147]Ibid., p. 25.

would operate with the PLO's support and within its policy guidelines. The formula included the creation of a steering committee to advise the delegation. Members of that committee were drawn from the Palestinian diaspora and from East Jerusalem. Thus, despite the intense pressure on the PLO from the outside and fissiparous tendencies within it, the PLO nevertheless managed to maintain sufficient coherence and support to gain the acceptance of the agreement negotiated secretly between aides of Yitzhak Rabin and Yasser Arafat in 1993 in Oslo, this agreement bypassed the Madrid process and led to the establishment of limited Palestinian autonomy under Israeli rule and the possibility that the peace process it inaugurated would result ultimately in the establishment of a Palestinian state.[148]

International Support for the Palestinians

During the twenty years following the October 1973 war, the Palestinians developed sufficient international support to help convert their claim for statehood from a dream shared by few others into the core issue of a negotiating process involving Israel, the United States, various European countries and, in a sense, the whole world as at least interested onlookers. By 1993, 110 countries had granted some sort of official status to the PLO.

The Arab states, despite their discomfort with Palestinian nationalism and efforts to turn Palestinian organizations to their own purposes, nevertheless came to provide solid diplomatic backing for the PLO's efforts to obtain statehood. The Arab states, like the Palestinians, moderated their political positions toward Israel to the point that they became willing to coexist peacefully with it. At the Arab summit in Baghdad in November 1978, all participating members of the Arab League, including Syria and the PLO, agreed to pursue a negotiated settlement on the basis of Israel's withdrawing from all territories occupied in 1967 and the establishment of an independent Palestinian state. This Arab consensus was restated at the Fez summit in 1982, which declared support for "guarantees for peace for all the states of the region," meaning the acceptance of Israel. However, it took another decade, the second Gulf war, and seven rounds of shuttle diplomacy by U.S. Secretary of State James Baker actually to bring the key Arab states, the Palestinians, and Israel to the first round of negotiations at Madrid in October–November 1991. During this period, the Arab states accepted the Palestinians' prior claim to Jordan's over the West Bank and East Jerusalem and refused to countenance Damascus's attempts to subordinate the Palestinian cause to Syria's state interests.

Egypt, the most powerful Arab country, played a leading role in this process. In 1964, Egypt brought the PLO into existence. Ten years later at Rabat, Egyptian Foreign Minister Ismail Fahmy declared the PLO to be the "sole legitimate

---

[148]On these secret negotiations, see Mahmoud Abbas, *Through Secret Channels* (London: Garnet Publishing, 1995); and David Makovsky, *Making Peace with the PLO: The Rabin Government's Road to the Oslo Accord* (Boulder, Colo.: Westview Press, 1996.)

representative of the Palestinian people," thereby putting Egypt and the Arab states on record as rejecting King Hussein's bid to regain the West Bank and East Jerusalem. When Egypt left the Arab fold in 1978 as a result of negotiating a separate peace with Israel, Jordan made a comeback, which for almost the next decade placed it in constant competition with the PLO to be the rightful claimant to those territories. Egypt's return to the mainstream of Arab politics, however, which was officially recognized in November 1987, had the effect of creating a relatively coherent Arab consensus, which caused King Hussein to declare in July 1988 that Jordan was severing all legal and administrative ties to the West Bank. Jordan had neither sufficient Arab backing nor support among the Palestinians in the occupied territories to continue to press its claim.

The Arab consensus favoring negotiations with Israel, in which the Palestinians would be directly represented, was further solidified by the second Gulf war, which undermined more radical Arab positions. When those negotiations commenced in 1991, the Arab states, with Egypt playing an important role, signaled that their minimum conditions for agreeing to a permanent peace with Israel would be "autonomy" of the occupied territories from direct Israeli control. Since the "Oslo process" began in 1993, Egypt has continued as the principal Arab supporter of the Palestinians.

THE THIRD WORLD

Third World nations, which constitute a majority in the UN General Assembly, had by the early 1970s come overwhelmingly to support the creation of a Palestinian state in the occupied territories. Among African countries, for example, the UN General Assembly voting record underwent a dramatic shift from 1969 to 1973. In the former year, 34 percent of votes cast by these states were pro-Palestinian, and 28 percent were pro-Israeli. By 1973, 96 percent of votes were pro-Palestinian, and none were pro-Israeli. The African voting record remains essentially unchanged since that time.[149]

Latin American states followed the African lead. In 1969, 5 percent of their votes were pro-Palestinian; 47 percent were pro-Israeli. By 1974, the voting record was virtually reversed, 43 percent of votes being pro-Palestinian and 19 percent pro-Israeli. In 1980, 87 percent of votes cast in the UN by Latin American states were pro-Palestinian; none was pro-Israeli.[150]

Nevertheless, votes in the UN and other forms of support that were provided to the Palestinians by Third World nations had only a very marginal impact even in the 1970s and 1980s when the Third World was most active in providing such assistance. Many African and Asian states that had broken diplomatic relations with Israel in the 1960s and 1970s, in order to demonstrate their solidarity with the Palestinians and Arabs more generally (and in some cases to receive substantial payments from the oil-rich Arab countries), restored those ties as part of the

---

[149]Kemal Kirisci, *The PLO and World Politics: A Study of the Mobilization of Support for the Palestinian Cause* (New York: St. Martin's Press, 1986), p. 85.

[150]Ibid., p. 88.

general move toward a negotiated settlement that began to gather momentum after the second Gulf war and the collapse of the Soviet Union. Palestinians and the Arabs more generally did not strenuously oppose these moves, because (1) even their symbolic importance was not great; (2) the Palestinians and the Arab states had themselves entered negotiations with Israel that promised to result in mutual recognition; and (3) in the early 1990s, the Arabs and much of the Third World had come to the conclusion that Washington had successfully established a *Pax Americana* in the Middle East that rendered irrelevant actions by other external actors, including those of the Third World.

THE EUROPEAN STATES

In the 1970s and 1980s, European support for Israel eroded in favor of the Palestinians. Whereas in the General Assembly session in 1974, Western European nations had a voting record that was 43 percent pro-Palestinian and 33 percent pro-Israeli, by 1980, the comparative percentages were 39 and 8, respectively. Among Western European states, therefore, Palestinian support did not increase appreciably from 1974 to 1980, although it did after that time. Support for Israel, however, fell away markedly.[151]

European public opinion by the 1980s had come to endorse the idea that the Palestinians should be represented in Middle East peace talks and that they should have a state of their own. A 1982 British poll revealed that 55 percent of respondents found acceptable the creation of a Palestinian state on the West Bank and Gaza, and in the same year, 88 percent of Dutch citizens queried in a national poll agreed that the Palestinians are entitled to a state of their own. Sixty-one percent of the British sample thought the PLO should be included in peace talks.[152]

European diplomatic initiatives reflected growing support for Palestinians. In 1974, only three of the nine members of the European Community (EC) voted in the UN General Assembly in favor of the motion urging participation of the PLO in UN deliberations. The others abstained. Two years later, however, the nine members announced jointly that there should be a territorial basis to the pursuit of Palestinian national identity. In the Venice Declaration of 1980, the European Community recognized the right of Palestinians to self-determination and specified that the PLO should be associated with peace negotiations. In the wake of the PNC meeting of November 15, 1988, the EC labeled the PNC's resolution as "positive" and stated that the declaration of independence reflects "the will of the Palestinian people to assert their national identity." The EC states did not, however, recognize the Palestinian state.[153] As the Palestinian intifada continued in the early 1990s, the EC imposed various punitive measures on Israel and continued to urge it to respect Palestinian rights. However, Euro-

---

[151]Ibid., p. 145.

[152]Moughrabi, "The International Consensus," pp. 122–123.

[153]"EEC Welcomes 'Positive Steps' by PLO Council," *Washington Post*, November 22, 1988.

pean leverage over the conflict, like that of the Third World, has been only indirect and very secondary to that of the United States.

U.S. PUBLIC OPINION

Public opinion in the United States has generally followed the global trend of increasing support for the Palestinians. In a 1977 poll, 36 percent of respondents believed the Palestinians should have a separate nation.[154] By 1988, surveys of public opinion consistently revealed that more Americans support than oppose the establishment of an independent Palestinian state in the West Bank and Gaza. A majority of Americans continued to perceive the PLO and Yasser Arafat negatively but believed nevertheless that the PLO should be included in the peace process and that the United States should negotiate with the PLO.[155] When Arab-Israeli negotiations did commence in the fall of 1991, American public opinion became more critical of Israel and more supportive of the Arabs in general and the Palestinians specifically. A poll conducted by the *Wall Street Journal* and NBC News revealed that Americans supported, by a margin of three to one, President Bush's decision to postpone loan guarantees to Israel and that 46 percent opposed economic aid to Israel, compared to 44 percent who supported it. The poll also revealed that for the first time since 1948, more Americans considered Israel to be the principal obstacle to peace than those who blamed the Arabs (37 percent to 35 percent). Of those polled, 49 percent believed that Israel should trade the occupied territories for peace, versus 31 percent who opposed that proposition.[156] An April 1998 poll conducted by Zogby International asked a sample of Americans who was to blame for the impasse in the Middle East peace process. Of those responding, 6 percent said Israel, 9 percent said the Palestinian Authority, and 62 percent said both parties are equally to blame. When asked whom the administration should pressure to get the peace process moving again, 8 percent said Israel, 6 percent said the Palestinian Authority, and 66 percent said both sides should be equally pressured.[157]

The American public, in short, came to support the emerging international consensus on the Arab-Israeli conflict. This was that Israel should trade land conquered in 1967 for peace with the Palestinians and Arab states, along with recognition of the Palestinians' right to self-government, possibly within an independent state, and the acknowledgment of the PLO as the legitimate spokesman for that cause. The American public arrived at these positions before

---

[154]Moughrabi, "The International Consensus," p. 117.

[155]Fouad Moughrabi, "American Public Opinion Far Ahead of U.S. Policy," *The Washington Report on Middle East Affairs* 7 (January 1989): 13; see also "Nationwide Survey of U.S. Attitudes on the Middle East," *Arab Studies Quarterly* 8 (Winter 1986): 64–65; Michael W. Suleiman, "World Public Opinion and the Question of Palestine," in Perry, *Palestine*, p. 84; and Elia Zureik and Fouad Moughrabi, eds., *Public Opinion and the Palestine Question* (New York: St. Martin's Press, 1987).

[156]Cited in Leon T. Hadar, "High Noon in Washington: The Shootout Over the Loan Guarantees," *Journal of Palestine Studies* 82 (Winter 1992): 74.

[157]*Mideast Mirror,* May 1,1998.

U.S. government policy began to embrace them in the wake of the second Gulf war and before they came to serve as the foundations for the Oslo peace process. The United States government, in sum, lagged behind not only its own people, the Arab states, the Third World, and the Europeans in coming to embrace the international consensus on how to resolve the Israeli-Arab conflict, but it even lagged behind Israel itself, whose government in 1993 undertook the initiative that has, since that time, set the parameters within which the conflict has been addressed.

The Peace Process Since 1993

The secret negotiations between the PLO and the Israeli government conducted in Oslo from January 1993 resulted in an agreement known formally as the Declaration of Principles (DOP) that was signed on the White House lawn on September 13 of that year, with Yitzhak Rabin and Yasser Arafat literally being brought together by President Clinton for a historic handshake. The Oslo Accords, as they are more commonly known, included a preamble that committed both sides to "put an end to decades of confrontation and conflict, recognize their mutual legitimate and political rights, and strive to live in peaceful coexistence. . . ." These goals, which pointedly make no reference to the "national rights" of the Palestinians but which did refer to Security Council resolutions 242 and 338 (which call for Israel's withdrawal from territory captured in 1967) were to be accomplished through an "agreed political process" based on principles spelled out in the Accords that would structure the relations between the two sides over a five-year period, during which negotiations would take place for a final settlement of the conflict. Principles spelled out in that document included the establishment of a Palestinian Interim Self-Government Authority including a police force and an elected Legislative Council; a commitment that "the two sides view the West Bank and the Gaza Strip as a single territorial unit, whose integrity will be preserved during the interim period"; an understanding that "these negotiations shall cover remaining issues, including Jerusalem, refugees, settlements, security arrangements, borders, relations and cooperation with other neighbors, and other issues of common concern"; that immediately following Israeli withdrawal from the Gaza Strip and the Jericho area, authority in specified areas such as education and taxation would be transferred to the newly created Palestinian Authority; and that a redeployment of Israeli forces in the West Bank and Gaza Strip would take place "not later than the eve of elections for the Council."

In the event it took another two years for the details of this interim agreement to be hammered out, with an initial agreement in May 1994 giving Palestinians autonomy in Jericho and most of the Gaza Strip, and on September 28, 1995, a final interim agreement, Oslo II, that comprised almost 400 pages and seven annexes, was also signed at the White House. According to this agreement, the Palestinians obtained (1) direct control over about 7 percent of so-called area A on the West Bank, which included the seven major Palestinian cities, with special arrangements to be made for Hebron so that the some 450 Israeli settlers there would come under Israeli control; (2) shared control over 24 percent of the West Bank in area B, which consists of some 450 Palestinian towns and villages and 68 percent of the Palestinian West Bank population; and (3) the retention by Israel of total control over security in some 69 percent of area C, from which it was to withdraw in three stages. Area C, not coincidentally, included areas that the old Allon Plan of 1967 specified as those that should be retained by Israel, including areas of present and future Jewish settlements, roads linking those settlements, strategic high land along the ridge of the West Bank, various military facilities, and security areas along the borders and adjacent to the old "green line" that had separated Israel from Jordan until the 1967 war. In Area B, which together with area A includes some 98 percent of the Palestinian population, the PA was charged with maintaining public order under the overall security authority of Israel and for assuming civil responsibilities, such as economics, health, and education. In area C Israel will retain full control over security and public order but the PA is eventually to take responsibility for normal civil functions, as in area B.[158]

What is especially noteworthy about both Oslo I and Oslo II is that both dealt only with interim arrangements and did not address the key contentious issues, including Palestinian statehood, Jewish settlements, the status and size of Jerusalem, the fate of Palestinian refugees and their possible right of return, control over water, and the final location of borders between Palestinian- and Israeli-controlled areas. The underlying logic of this "step by step" approach was that as confidence was built through interactions between the two parties, the more difficult issues would be easier to deal with. This hopeful, even wishful, thinking was probably encouraged, at least for the PLO, by the high cost of not accepting what Israel was prepared to offer. It was fearful of being politically marginalized within the Palestinian national movement by other forces, it had lost the support of wealthy Gulf Arabs as a result of having sided with Iraq in the 1991 war, and it adjudged the U.S.-backed Madrid process, which was in deadlock at that time, as going nowhere because of lack of U.S. pressure on Israel, a reality unlikely to change with the demise of the Soviet Union. Israel, for its part, conferred legitimacy on the PLO by signing the Accords but committed itself to very little in the way of territorial or other concessions regarding the key Palestinian demands.

For both sides, however, there was great enthusiasm for the Accords and the process they initiated and structured and a considerable amount of good will

---

[158]When Prime Minister Netanyahu put forward in June 1997 his conception of a final settlement with the Palestinians, it was immediately dubbed "Allon-Plus," as it appeared to retain for Israel the territory specified in the 1967 Allon Plan, as well as the large amounts of territory settled by Israel since 1967. This included "Greater Jerusalem," which is almost two-thirds larger than Jerusalem in 1967, as it includes settlements such as Gush Etzion and Maale Adumin that lie outside the municipal borders. The original Allon Plan granted the Palestinians about 60 percent of contiguous territory in the West Bank. Under "Allon-Plus," "the most the Palestinians will get is 45 percent, segregated into separate cantons." Graham Usher, "Allon-plus, Barak minus," *Al Ahram Weekly* (12–18 June 1997): 4. Between 1967 and 1997, Israel expropriated almost 3,000 square miles of territory in the West Bank and Gaza, almost half the total land area. Ten percent of that amount was seized in the four years after Oslo I was signed. See Jan de Jong, "Fifty Years of Dispossession," *Le Monde Diplomatique*, English Edition (August 1997), www.monde-diplomatique.com.

was generated during the first two years after Oslo I. Terrorist incidents committed by Hamas slowed the negotiation process but did not cause the Israeli government to break them off or to seal off the Occupied Territories and prevent Palestinian workers from commuting to Israel. Despite the limitations of the Accords from their perspective, the vast majority of Palestinians favored them and hoped that they would pave the way not only for attainment of national rights but, at least as importantly, facilitate economic development.

With regard to the Arab states, Oslo broke the logjam that had prevented direct dealings with Israel and negotiations over peace with the front line states. In October 1994, Jordan became the second Arab state, after Egypt, to sign a peace treaty with Israel. Syria commenced bilateral negotiations with Israel that came within a hair's breadth of success before they were broken off by Prime Minister Shimon Peres in early 1996 as a result of a series of suicide bombings in Israel. Other Arab states, including Morocco, Tunisia, and Qatar, all reacted immediately to Oslo I by establishing dialogues with Israel and commencing talks on specific economic projects. The Arab League-sanctioned economic boycott of Israel was officially ended. In 1994, a program of annual regionwide economic conferences bringing together Arab and Israeli representatives of their respective governments and private sectors commenced in Casablanca. Arabs and Israelis, taking their cue from Washington but apparently believing in it, began to speak of a "new Middle East" in which peace and economic prosperity would replace conflict, war, and economic stagnation.

Alas, the "new Middle East" that beckoned in the wake of the signing of the Oslo Accords has not materialized, nor have the Accords themselves been implemented. Peace talks broken off between Israel and Syria in 1996 have not been resumed; fighting between Israeli forces and Hizbollah guerillas in South Lebanon has intensified; national economies, including that of Israel's, have, after a brief spurt, begun to stagnate; and, most importantly, the Israeli-Palestinian relationship has soured, such that what trust had been built up has evaporated.

Talks between the two parties that were supposed to be continuous were broken off in the early spring of 1997 and did not resume until October of the following year. At that time the American administration invited the Israeli and Palestinian delegations to Wye Plantation in Maryland, where, after more than a week of intense negotiations, yet another interim agreement—the Wye River Memorandum—was signed. Its stated purpose was to implement the September 1995 and January 1997 agreements, which were themselves to implement the Oslo Accords. Divided into three sections on further redeployments, security, and interim committees and economic issues, the Memorandum embodied an agreement whereby Israel would withdraw from a further 13 percent of the West Bank. In exchange, Israel would receive extensive security guarantees from the Palestinian Authority and its permission to allow the CIA to monitor compliance of its crackdown on what U.S. officials referred to as the Palestinian "terrorist infrastructure," as well as some other, less important trade-offs. The unstated purpose of the Memorandum was to pave the way for the long-delayed final status talks, in part by setting the parameters of final territorial arrangements allowing Israel to remain in occupation of some 60 percent of the West Bank. Met with positive reactions by a majority of Israelis, and rather more skeptically by Palestinians, The Memorandum immediately stimulated strong negative reactions by Israeli settlers and Palestinians opposed to the Oslo process.

The most obvious factor preventing the smoother implementation of the Oslo Accords was the victory in the May 1996 elections of Likud leader Binyamin Netanyahu and his replacement of Shimon Peres as Israel prime minister. Six months prior to that time, Yitzhak Rabin, the prime mover behind the Oslo Accords, was gunned down at an open-air political rally by Yigal Amir, a Sephardic religious fanatic. Shimon Peres, his successor, never enjoyed the support and confidence of the Israeli public in the same measure as had Rabin, and he went on to lose the election for prime minister by less than 30,000 votes, or some one-half of 1 percent. The election campaign was waged almost exclusively on the issue of the peace process, with Netanyahu charging Peres and Labor as having surrendered Israeli land and security for nothing but empty promises from Arafat and the Palestinians. A committed Revisionist Zionist, Netanyahu made it clear that he was opposed to a Palestinian state, the return of Palestinian refugees, any Palestinian claims on Jerusalem, a cessation of Jewish settlement, or the handing over of as much as half the occupied territories to Palestinian self-rule areas. His general approach to the Oslo Accords was not to reject them outright, as other Revisionists, such as former Prime Minister Yitzhak Shamir and the son of former Likud leader Menachem Begin, Beni Begin, chose to do, but to seek to interpret them in such a restrictive fashion that the Palestinians would virtually automatically be deemed to be in violation of them, hence excusing Israel from implementing its obligations under them.[159]

Thus, Israeli foot dragging, which had already commenced in reaction to Hamas's terrorist attacks in early 1996, became established policy under Netanyahu, whose ruling coalition has depended increasingly on the ultra-Orthodox and ultranationalists, as more moderate elements, such as one-time Foreign Minister David Levy and his supporters, have deserted it. Withdrawal from Hebron, which was supposed to have been completed soon after the 1995 signing of Oslo II, was delayed until after the Hebron Protocol was finally signed on January 15, 1997, and the withdrawal was much less complete than the Palestinians had originally imagined, for it left more than one-fifth of that overwhelmingly Palestinian city under Israeli control. Israeli troop redeployments, which originally were supposed to have been between March 1996 and September 1997 and completed before final status talks commenced, were subsequently renegotiated so as to commence on March 7, 1997, but in fact were delayed until after the signing of the October 1998 Wye Memorandum.

Combined with foot dragging was an increasingly belligerent approach to Palestinians. Under so-called "closures" on the West Bank and Gaza, Palestinians were prohibited from moving easily from one village, town, or city to another— and not at all into Israel or Jerusalem or from the West Bank to Gaza, or vice versa; Jewish settlement was intensified; severe restrictions on Palestinian political activities in Jerusalem were increased in order to pre-empt any Palestinian

---

[159]Ian S. Lustick, "The Oslo Agreement as an Obstacle to Peace," *Journal of Palestine Studies* 27, 2 (Autumn 1997): 61–66.

claims to that city; imprisonment of large numbers of Palestinians continued; and tax revenues owed to the Palestinian Authority were withheld. In sum, the replacement of the Labor Party by Likud, and the latter's heavy reliance on the religious and ultranationalist right wing to maintain its slim Knesset majority, fundamentally changed the nature of the Israeli approach to the Oslo process, to say nothing of bringing a new negotiating team onto the field. It is true to say, however, that the Labor Party has not provided any significant pressure on the Likud-dominated government to adhere to the agreements that it had signed. The possibility that this might occur was diminished when Shimon Peres was replaced as Labor Party leader in June 1997 by highly decorated ex-army chief Ehud Barak, who, unlike Peres, has a record of opposing Palestinian statehood and who in September 1995 abstained in a cabinet vote on the Oslo II Accords, arguing that they did not provide acceptable security guarantees for Israelis and Jewish settlers in the occupied territories.

For their part, the Palestinians have also become increasingly divided over the peace process. Most Islamists and radical secular leftists never supported it, and, as it has ground to a halt, they have been joined by an increasing number of Palestinians who at first supported Oslo but who have now given up hope in it as it has not fulfilled their expectations. Dedicated Palestinian opponents of the peace process have been able to exert tremendous leverage over it by virtue of their willingness to engage in terrorist acts against Israelis, undertakings that they know will stimulate Israeli retaliations that further slow the process and penalize Palestinians as a whole, thereby undermining support for the process itself. The security crackdown demanded by Israel and the United States and implemented in part by the police and security forces of the Palestinian Authority has itself alienated large numbers of Palestinians from the process as well, for respect for rule of law and human rights has been subordinated to the desire to apprehend and punish those responsible for, or possibly only in some way connected to, terrorist acts.

The Oslo process, whatever its shortcomings and its actual outcomes, has, however, enabled the Palestinians to begin the process of converting state-making organizations, chief of which is the PLO, into actual organizations of a state, even though that state is yet to be established. The Palestinians, in other words, are at about the same juncture in their organizational history as were the Zionists just prior to the establishment of Israel. The Oslo Accords provided for an independent self-governing authority, which since 1993 has taken institutional shape. In January 1996, an eighty-eight-member Palestinian Legislative Council (eighty-nine including the "president,") was established through free and fair elections, and Yasser Arafat elected *Ra'is*, or President, the Arabic term being demanded by Israel in order to avoid the English one that implies statehood. Since that time the Council has begun to function as a real legislature, and the executive branch has been developed through the creation of various ministries and administrative authorities. Local government elections have repeatedly been postponed, but they were scheduled to be held before the end of 1999.

Unlike the Israelis in the early years of their statehood, however, the Palestinians have yet to establish a functioning democracy, and at this stage it does not appear that even if they were to obtain a state their present political system would become democratic either immediately or in the short to medium term. The executive branch under President Arafat is overwhelmingly dominant and heavily dependent on a 40,000-man security force, which as a proportion of the Palestinian population of some 2 million is one of the largest in the world.[160] That force, as well as the executive branch more generally, is not accountable to any public or legal authorities, despite attempts by the Legislative Council to make them so. The lack of accountability inevitably has resulted in widespread corruption, which in turn undermines the legitimacy of the self-governing authority, thereby stimulating the need for yet more repressive measures by the security forces.

The Palestinians, in short, have succeeded in creating a sort of "shadow state" but one that does not enjoy sovereignty, is financially dependent on outside donors, and is not democratic, although it is constituted of reasonably well-elaborated governing institutions that could ultimately serve as the foundations for a democratic political system. The most the Palestinians can hope for at this stage is that they will indeed obtain a state but one that presides over a patchwork of noncontiguous territory divided by the homes, roads, and security installations for some 120,000 Jewish settlers whose numbers are steadily increasing. Such a state, were it to eventuate, may not be enough to satisfy Palestinian national aspirations, but even this sort of state may be too much for Israel to concede. For both the Palestinians and the Israelis, the degree of internal political conflict is intensifying, making it more difficult for both sides to adhere to agreements already negotiated, to say nothing of formulating new agreements over those vital issues that still have not been addressed within the Oslo process. The prognosis, therefore, is that the Palestinian-Israeli conflict is unlikely to be resolved when the Oslo process terminates in May 1999, so the broader Arab-Israeli conflict of which it is the core element will also continue into the indefinite future, although probably without the intensity that prevailed prior to the signing of the Oslo Accords.

SELECTED BIBLIOGRAPHY

Abu-Lughod, Ibrahim, ed. *The Transformation of Palestine.* Evanston, Ill.: Northwestern University Press, 1987.

Aruri, Naseer. *The Obstruction of Peace: The U.S., Israel and the Palestinians.* Monroe, Maine: Common Courage Press, 1995.

Avineri, Shlomo. *The Making of Modern Zionism: The Intellectual Origins of the Jewish State.* New York: Basic Books, 1981.

Ball, George W., and Douglas Ball. *The Passionate Attachment.* New York: W. W. Norton, 1992.

Brynen, Rex. *Sanctuary and Survival: The PLO in Lebanon.* Boulder, Colo.: Westview Press, 1990.

Cockburn, Andrew, and Leslie Cockburn. *Dangerous Liaison: The Inside Story of the U.S.-Israeli Covert Relationship.* New York: HarperCollins, 1991.

---

[160]Glen E. Robinson, "Authoritarianism with a Palestinian Face," *Current History* 615 (January 1998): 15.

Cohen, Mitchell. *Zion and State: Nation, Class and the Shaping of Modern Israel*. Oxford: Basil Blackwell, 1989.

Flamhaft, Ziva. *Israel on the Road to Peace: Accepting the Unacceptable*. Boulder, Colo.: Westview Press, 1996.

Flapan, Simha. *The Birth of Israel: Myths and Realities*. New York: Pantheon Books, 1987.

Khalidi, Rashid. *Palestinian Identity: The Construction of Modern National Consciousness*. New York: Columbia University Press, 1997.

Landau, Jacob. *The Arab Minority in Israel: 1967–1991, Political Aspects*. New York: Oxford University Press, 1993.

Lazin, Frederick A., and Gregory Mahler. *Israel in the Nineties; Development and Conflict*. Gainesville: University Press of Florida, 1996.

Lesch, Ann Mosely, and Mark Tessler. *Israel, Egypt, and the Palestinians: From Camp David to Intifada*. Bloomington: Indiana University Press, 1989.

Lustick, Ian. *Arabs in the Jewish State: Israel's Control of a National Minority*. Austin: University of Texas Press, 1980.

Lustick, Ian. *For the Land and the Lord: Jewish Fundamentalism in Israel*. New York: Council on Foreign Relations, 1988.

Makovsky, David. *Making Peace with the PLO: The Rabin Government's Road to the Oslo Accord*. Boulder, Colo.: Westview Press, 1996.

Morris, Benny. *The Birth of the Palestine Refugee Problem, 1947–1949*. Cambridge: Cambridge University Press, 1987.

Neff, Donald. *Fallen Pillars: U.S. Policy Toward Palestine and Israel since 1945*. Washington, D.C.: Institute for Palestine Studies, 1995.

Norton, Augustus R., and M. H. Greenberg, eds. *The International Relations of the PLO*. Carbondale: University of Southern Illinois Press, 1989.

Peleg, Ian, ed. *The Middle East Peace Process: Interdisciplinary Perspectives*. Albany: State University of New York Press, 1998.

Quandt, William B. *Peace Process: American Diplomacy and the Arab-Israeli Conflict Since 1967*. Berkeley: University of California Press, 1993.

Rabinovich, Itamar. *The Road Not Taken: Early Arab-Israeli Negotiations*. New York: Oxford University Press, 1991.

Robinson, Glenn E. *Building a Palestinian State: The Incomplete Revolution*. Bloomington: Indiana University Press, 1997.

Tessler, Mark. *A History of the Israeli-Palestinian Conflict*. Bloomington: Indiana University Press, 1994.

Usher, Graham. *Palestine in Crisis: The Struggle for Peace and Political Independence After Oslo*. Rev. ed. London: Pluto Press, 1997.

Chapter 8

The Politics of War and Revolution in the Persian Gulf

The Iranian revolution in the late 1970s, the eight-year Iran-Iraq war in the 1980s, and the internationally explosive Gulf war of the early 1990s demonstrate both the political significance and fragility of the Persian Gulf. Clustered around the Gulf are eight countries: Iraq, Iran, Oman, the United Arab Emirates, Qatar, Bahrain, Saudi Arabia, and Kuwait. Taken together, these countries account for over 60 percent of the world's proven reserves of petroleum.

It is this enormous oil wealth that magnifies the importance of every political conflict in the region, and it is this wealth also that tends to expand these conflicts into truly international issues. Therefore, when the Iraqi troops of Saddam Hussein invaded neighboring Kuwait on August 2, 1990, it was not long before a large international coalition force moved into the area to confront the aggressor.

Although the longtime U.S.-Soviet rivalry has ceased due to the dissolution of the Soviet Union, this very collapse has produced new problems and challenges for both the Persian Gulf region and the world. Inherently unstable and cut adrift from their political moorings, the Central Asian republics, from Azerbaijan on the west to Tajikistan on the east, threaten to transmit their uncertainties and difficulties down through the Persian Gulf states.

The Persian Gulf is, however, more than a "petroleum gulf" toward which international superpowers cast covetous eyes. It is a region of peoples, with all their varying hopes and aspirations, who seek to pursue what they perceive to be their political, economic, and religious interests. The drive to achieve these interests overlaps with the regional political issues of the day. Fundamental unresolved political problems exist in each of the Gulf countries. These states have yet to resolve such basic issues as national identity and political legitimacy. In a world in which the forces of democratization, participation, and liberalization gather momentum, all except one of the Arab states along the Persian Gulf remain monarchies. They continue to use their black gold to reinforce tradition, build military machines in the desert, and alternately crush and co-opt political opposition.

Of the eight political units that coexist around the Persian Gulf, only two have thus far experienced major political revolution, Iraq in 1958 and Iran in 1978–1979. The other six countries continue to be governed in the traditional patrimonial mode, with political power concentrated in the hands of ruling families. These traditional governments have large natural and financial resources at their disposal. The ruling elites of the Gulf states utilize these resources to enable them to confront the challenge of revolution that has emanated from the Iraqi and Iranian experiences. The Iranian revolution in particular intensified the challenge significantly. The fact that the traditional Gulf political systems have been able to survive in the face of such powerful challenges is worthy of analysis.

There are two main reasons why the traditional monarchies and minimonarchies of the Gulf have successfully protected their systems through the 1990s. First, petroleum reserves have been such that the ruling families have possessed the resources needed to placate their populations by meeting their growing economic demands. Since the actual size of the indigenous populations of these six countries is very small, it has been possible to upgrade the lifestyles of citizens enormously as the result of policies of distribution and redistribution of wealth. Kuwait is an important case in point.

Even with the expulsion of 350,000 Palestinians following the Gulf war, Kuwait's citizen population of 600,000 was still less than 40 percent of the overall population of the country. The huge Kuwaiti oil wealth enabled the Amir's government to shower a restless population with economic and financial gifts. Every Kuwaiti citizen family was given a valuable plot of land and an interest-free loan of approximately $175,000 to build a new house on that land. After the war ended, the government forgave these loans and other consumer loans as well. The Kuwaiti leadership increased by 50 percent grants and loans to all Kuwaiti males who marry Kuwaiti women and increased monthly child allowances from $100 to $175 per child per month. In March 1992, the government dramatically announced a 25 percent across-the-board salary increase for all Kuwaitis employed in the public sector. In accordance with the wishes of the Amir, the government decided to cancel all electric and water bills for its citizenry. Although such extravagant largesse made little economic sense, it did, in the minds of an elite seeking to placate a critical population, make eminently sound political sense. This process of "dinar politics" has until now been quite effective in enabling small family-centered elites to cling to power and privilege in the Persian Gulf.

A second factor that helps explain system preservation in the Persian Gulf concerns the element of political leadership. Over the years, the traditional Gulf states have generally been led by individuals of considerable political astuteness. The particular leaders have recognized the needs and demands of their people and have struggled to stay in touch with all strata in their societies. One of the greatest of these traditional leaders was King Faisal Ibn Abd al-Aziz, ruler of

Saudi Arabia from 1964 to 1975. Faisal boasted over half a century of political experience; at only age thirteen, he led diplomatic delegations to London. In Abu Dhabi, Shaikh Zayid has been one of the most experienced and astute leaders in the Middle East. He has led Abu Dhabi since 1966 and has demonstrated great skill as a negotiator and mediator. It was primarily due to Zayid that the United Arab Emirates was formed as a political unit in December 1971. Other underrated traditional leaders in the Gulf include the late Shaikh Rashid of Dubai and the new amir of Qatar, Shaikh Hamad.

These traditional leaders have relied very heavily on the informal institution of the *majlis* (informal assembly), where they have been regularly available to hear personally the requests and complaints of their people. Before his death in 1990, Shaikh Rashid held four majlises daily. The late Shaikh Isa of Bahrain held his majlises regularly every Friday, Sunday, and Tuesday morning, as well as one on Saturday night. In Kuwait, the *diwaniyyah,* a variant of the majlis, is the most important decisional structure. All members of the ruling Al-Sabah family have their diwaniyyahs. Such open meetings, where petitions are heard and demands presented, have been encouraged by the rulers themselves, who set the style for other members of the political elites who convene their own majlises and diwaniyyahs.

Through the continued implementation of this direct, personalistic democracy of the desert, along with the resources available to enable them to meet the demands heard in such settings, the traditional Gulf leaders have been able to hang on to power in an age of democratization and revolution. In other words, they have been able to promote rapid modernization within the traditional political context. Despite this impressive record, however, all traditional systems in the Persian Gulf possess significant weaknesses.

The traditional Gulf states face the following eight problems: (1) the shortage of indigenous manpower; (2) the existence of deep social, ethnic, and sectarian divisions; (3) the dramatic growth of a professional middle class; (4) the challenge of resurgent, populist Islam; (5) the existence of conspicuous corruption in many ruling circles; (6) the intimately close relationships between Gulf elites and Western governments; (7) the huge gap between economic modernization on the one hand and political development on the other hand; and (8) the critical issue of succession and political rulership for the future.

The manpower problem has become more serious with time as each country has elected to emphasize programs of modernization and economic growth. In Saudi Arabia and Kuwait, for example, the indigenous labor forces are far too small to carry effectively forward advanced industrialization and modernization. Yet, the labor force of expatriate workers is highly suspect socially and politically. As a result of the Gulf war of 1990–1991, for example, Saudi Arabia unceremoniously expelled nearly 1 million Yemeni workers; in Kuwait, the population of approximately 400,000 Palestinians was sharply reduced to 25,000. Besides the negative regional political fallout of such expulsions, the internal economic systems of both Saudi Arabia and Kuwait have undergone enormous stress and strain due to the absence of these skilled and unskilled workers.

The populations of the traditional Gulf states are deeply divided against themselves socially, ethnically, and religiously. Those of Persian origin (known in the region as *ajam*) compete quietly against those of Arab background. Shi'a are present in each and every Gulf country. In Bahrain, for example, the Shi'a represent nearly 70 percent of the population; in Kuwait and the United Arab Emirates, the figures are 30 and 25 percent, respectively. Even in Saudi Arabia, there is a Shi'i population of over 1 million people. Each of the six traditional Gulf states is governed by a Sunni political elite, which discriminates against the Shi'a. Shi'i-Sunni tension in the Gulf increased significantly following the Iranian revolution.

The problems of manpower and social divisiveness intersect in the situation of women in the region. Since women are largely frozen out of professional and political positions, these states seek to enter the modern world with half of their populations inactive and subdued. The place of women is particularly unfavorable in countries like Saudi Arabia, Qatar, and Oman. Even in Kuwait, however, women are not allowed to vote, and, with one notable exception, there are no female diwaniyyahs.

The dramatic growth of modern educational facilities also carries serious political implications as larger and larger numbers of young people from the Gulf acquire modern higher educations. These youths then enter the job market with high expectations and with a newly developed political consciousness. As they return from abroad in increasing numbers, they are no longer easily absorbed into the high-level political positions that they have come to expect. Lucrative private-sector positions are also increasingly scarce. Many of the professionals and technocrats who are not absorbed or absorbable into the traditional system become disgruntled and decry the personal favoritism, professional incompetence, and political repression that they allege is endemic to their countries.

Universities are the breeding grounds of this new class, and as the Gulf states build such institutions of higher learning, the ruling elites have come to understand the political risks involved. Saudi Arabia now has seven universities; the United Arab Emirates opened the new University of al-Ain in 1981; and Oman also has its own national university, Sultan Qabus University. There is a national university in Qatar, and Bahrain boasts three major institutions of higher learning. Besides these schools, the six traditional countries of the Gulf have nearly 100,000 students in Western universities. These individuals will form the questioning, challenging, professional middle classes of the future in the Persian Gulf.

Cutting across the Gulf states and transcending even Shi'i-Sunni distinctions is the gathering force of populist Islam. Those who embrace this iteration of Islam from below criticize the rapid Westernization of their societies, the personal corruption of their leaders, and the political repression that they see accompanying this moral decay. Since 1979, dedicated Islamic activists have sporadically and violently challenged their governments in countries such as Saudi Arabia, Kuwait, and Bahrain. Today, Muslim opposition movements continue to take root and grow in soil fertilized by the granules of corruption and oppression, fostered by an increasingly insensitive Persian Gulf leadership.

The huge wealth derived from oil revenues has maximized opportunities for corruption in the Gulf. The sums involved have been enormous, as individuals have used their personal and familial positions to amass huge personal fortunes from the hundreds of billions of dollars that have accrued to the Persian Gulf governments. Since wealth begets wealth and wealth follows power, many of the leading political actors are among the most avid practitioners of corruption. The ruling families usually have a handful of members who are well known for their financial greed and insatiable appetites for material wealth. This behavior has caused increasing criticism among the populations of these countries and has provided effective cause for the growing alienation of both the professional middle classes and Islamic activists.

The tight linkages forged by traditional Persian Gulf elites with the West in general and the United States in particular have also eroded the credibility of these elites in the eyes of their populations. One result of the 1991 Gulf war, for example, was the view held by Arab populations in the Middle East generally and the Gulf specifically that the Saudi and Kuwaiti ruling families had sold their souls to American mercenaries who were called in to protect the few against the many.

Also, the consistently strong support of the United States for the state of Israel has damaged both America's image and the legitimacy of those Arab political leaders who work closely with the United States. This became eminently clear in the summer and fall of 1982 with the Israeli invasion and occupation of Lebanon. In this military mismatch—which saw Israel use American-made aircraft to bomb homes, hospitals, schools, and mosques—Arabs throughout the Gulf watched in horror as other Arabs suffered and died before their very eyes on television. One less-known effect of this kind of action was that the Israeli attacks helped widen the gap of confidence between the peoples of the Gulf countries and their political leaders, whose very association with the United States indirectly implicated them in the Israeli aggression.

A major problem area, and one that has been alluded to in the discussions above, is the tension between the extraordinary economic growth on the one hand and the absence of political development on the other. In no other area of the world is the division between economic growth and political development so pronounced as it is in the Persian Gulf. In a world in which issues of democratization and political participation have become core international preoccupations, the sluggish approach of the traditional Gulf elites to political development has only increased popular discontent. This political retardation is highlighted when contrasted with the impressive efforts in the fields of military modernization, technological advancement, and economic growth.

In the face of these deep-seated and interrelated challenges, the traditional countries of the Persian Gulf require especially sensitive and prescient leadership. As time passes, even the shrewd old desert shaikhs seem overwhelmed by the problems they confront. What does the future hold in this regard?

Unfortunately, the next generation of political leaders in the Gulf appears not to be of the same quality as the present generation. In the cases of Abu Dhabi and Dubai, the sons of Zayid and Rashid are clearly inferior to their fathers in terms of both personal charisma and political acumen. In Oman, succession to Sultan Qabus will prove to be a serious difficulty, as the sultan is without any sons. In Bahrain, Shaikh Hamad is unlikely to improve upon his predecessor, Shaikh Isa. The future leadership pool in Saudi Arabia, Qatar, and Kuwait is also shallow. The members of the Al-Sabah family in Kuwait, for example, did not distinguish themselves either in anticipating the Iraqi invasion of 1990 or in developing policies to confront that invasion and its aftermath.

The social and political challenges to the traditional regimes in the Persian Gulf will surely magnify with time. The Iraqi invasion of 1990 blew the lid off the political Gulf kettle and opened the way for the massive influx of foreigners. As a result, the region will never again be the same. The ability of the Gulf political leadership to deal successfully with this new situation remains to be seen. If this ability should be lacking, there is every reason to believe that the coming years will see considerable political upheaval in the Persian Gulf.

The internal social and political problems that plague the traditional patrimonial Gulf countries do not, of course, exist in a political vacuum but fester in an explosive regional context marked by Iraqi military threats and Iranian ideological challenges. With the massive destruction of the Iraqi economic and military infrastructure by the U.S.-led coalition forces in 1991, the Iranian factor remains the most formidable regional reality. It is, therefore, essential to analyze the realities of the Iranian revolution and the circumstance of Iran today.

Iran: Superpower of the Persian Gulf

The shah's regime in Iran collapsed in 1978–1979, when the Iranian people rose en masse to overthrow the Pahlavi government. Muhammad Reza Shah Pahlavi's style of patrimonial rule had been rotting from within for years as repression and corruption became two of the defining characteristics of the regime. Meanwhile, the shah cut himself off from his people, and the channels of access to the government withered and disappeared. In the 1970s, the gap between the rich and the poor increased, and the shah sought to concentrate all power into his own hands while turning his secret police (SAVAK) loose on the people.

In the end, the Iranian revolution is best described as a multiclass uprising in which the lower-class masses and the burgeoning middle classes joined hands against the Pahlavi political elite. During the revolution, the Shi'i religious leaders became the organizing nodes of the movement; after the overthrow, it was the ulema who took control of the government of revolutionary Iran.

In 1999, Iran celebrated the twentieth anniversary of its revolution, which has now institutionalized itself. The first years of post-Pahlavi Iran were not pleasant ones for the Islamic Republic, as the new leaders found themselves entangled both with deep domestic problems and with a grim war imposed on them by neighboring Iraq. In 1981–1982 and 1988 particularly, violence and internal war stalked the cities and countryside as an inexperienced regime of religious extremists remained locked in mortal combat with a series of committed terrorist groups dominated by the Mujahedin-i Khalq, the major opponent that still actively campaigns overseas against the Islamic Republic. The turbulence that occurred in Iran after the revolutionary overthrow should not have come as a complete surprise to students of Iran.

Any successor to the Pahlavi regime would inevitably have had to confront a number of formidable problems. These included the following twelve challenges: (1) the complete lack of any political institutions designed to provide effective political participation; (2) the absence of an experienced, committed cadre of political and administrative leaders; (3) a deep class conflict that had been intensifying through time; (4) a widespread atmosphere of personal distrust and cynicism; (5) a culture of corruption; (6) a multitude of serious tribal and ethnic cleavages; (7) a fragile economic system characterized by an extremely primitive infrastructure; (8) a demoralized military in disarray; (9) the unique role of Shi'i Islam, whose leaders lacked political experience; (10) the crushing violence and disruptive costs of the revolution itself; (11) a host of regional enemies both in the Persian Gulf and in the Middle East generally; and (12) the hostility of the United States, which opposed the Iranian revolution from the very beginning.

Despite the challenging nature of these problems, the Islamic Republic has made progress in many areas. In the process, it has finally begun to move away from a state of psychological paranoia and political extremism engendered by constant external attacks and has adopted policies of political pragmatism and normalcy. The turning point occurred in 1988–1989 with the end of the Iran-Iraq war and the death of Ayatollah Khomeini, the charismatic father of the revolution. Leading the return to normalcy are competent and realistic political leaders such as President Ali Akbar Hashemi-Rafsanjani. In his speeches, Rafsanjani repeatedly asked his people to cool their ideological fervor and to dedicate themselves to the positive reconstruction of their country. The leaders of the Islamic Republic continue to struggle to institutionalize their political system while at the same time attempting to solve a series of profound problems that plague their economic system.

Politically, there has been much tangible progress. There is a constitutional system in place that includes an elected president, an elected 270-person parliament (Majlis), a cabinet appointed by the president but approved by the Majlis, a predominant *faqih* or Islamic jurisprudent, and a series of intermediate councils whose members are both appointed and elected. With the death of Ayatollah Khomeini, the role of the powerful faqih has begun to wither, and political participation and pluralism have begun to blossom as originally envisioned in the constitution.

By mid-1992, the struggle between the ideological extremists and the pragmatic reconstructionists had been won by the latter group, led by Rafsanjani. The spring 1992 Majlis elections witnessed a massive victory for the pragmatists as the system inexorably began to open up. Then, in the presidential elections of May 1997, the Iranian people voted against the establishment candidate and overwhelmingly elected Mohammad Khatami, a progressive, open-minded cleric with a modest and moderate approach to politics. Khatami immediately stressed judicial reform, freedom of speech, political participation, and called essentially for a rapprochement with the world. Although Rafsanjani remained active politically and the faqih or leader, Ali Khamenei, maintained his authority, there is little doubt that Khatami began to take his country into new directions. In so doing, he found himself challenged by the militant extremists who remained very much in evidence in the country. Khatami cleverly and quietly moved against them. As analyzed in Chapter 5, Khatami in fact represents a new man who has cut back on patrimonialism and has begun a genuine campaign of political development.

Despite these promising political events, Iran suffers from severe economic problems. In May of 1998, Khatami admitted publicly that the Iranian economy was "sick." Iran's economic problems include a high rate of population growth, a stagnant agricultural system, a lack of foreign financial reserves, high inflation and unemployment, and a bloated, inefficient, corrupt bureaucracy. The U.S.-imposed embargo only exacerbated these problems.

Iran has also confronted heavy reconstruction responsibilities resulting from the war in the 1980s. The direct costs of the war were approximately $200 billion. Furthermore, Iran carried the burden of feeding, clothing, and sheltering nearly four million refugees (Kurds, Afghans, and Shi'ites from southern Iraq). In sum, Iran, with a population of 65 million, has an infrastructure that was barely able to sustain its population of 38 million at the time of the revolution in 1978–1979.

Partially because of these crushing economic problems and partly due to Iran's return to political pragmatism, the Islamic Republic has sought to establish friendly and cooperative arrangements with its Persian Gulf neighbors. This new policy was formally announced in November 1989 at a major international conference in Tehran entitled "The Persian Gulf." The themes of this conference were solidarity (*hambastegi*), cooperation (*hamkari*), and unity (*ettehad*). Since the 1989 conference, Iran has pursued a policy of rapprochement with its Gulf neighbors.

The most significant relationship that has undergone diplomatic change is the one between the Islamic Republic of Iran and Saudi Arabia. Iran-Saudi relations warmed up considerably in 1997–1998. In December 1997, Saudi Crown Prince Abdullah visited Iran to attend the Organization of the Islamic Conference (OIC). In February 1998, former president Rafsanjani made an unprecedented ten-day visit to Riyadh. In March 1998, President Khatami's Foreign Minister, Kemal Kharrazi, traveled to Saudi Arabia. During Kharrazi's visit, King Fahd invited President Khatami to Saudi Arabia. Meanwhile, Iran and Saudi Arabia established a joint economic committee, and Saudi foreign minister Saud bin Faisal signed a wide-ranging cooperation accord while he was on an official visit to Tehran. As Iran opens up politically at home, it at the same time reaches out to its neighbors. If Iran and Saudi Arabia can cooperate seriously, the Persian Gulf will be a much more secure place.

At this point in history, one might argue that as Iran goes, so goes the Persian Gulf. Although Iran has repudiated its earlier aggressive policy of attempting to export its revolution to other Gulf states and has successfully reknit relations with these neighbors, the Iranian revolution, by its very existence, looms as a persisting threat to the vulnerable traditional regimes in the region. The revolution carries three significant points of appeal to the lower and middle classes of the traditional Gulf countries.

First, in Iran the masses of people rose successfully and overthrew a venal and repressive traditional patrimonial regime dominated by the Pahlavi family. Second, the Iranian revolution resulted in a system of government whereby the new regime managed to cut its ties of dependence on outside superpowers and to declare its national independence. The most quoted slogan of the revolution is "Neither East nor West." Third, the revolution in Iran represented a victory for Islam and a reaffirmation of the strength and relevance of that civilization in the modern world. To those who are dissatisfied and disaffected in the traditional countries of the Gulf, these three messages carry great potency.

Their appeal transcends Sunni-Shi'i divisions, tribal and ethnic distinctions, and class cleavages.

The credibility of Iran and its revolution increased dramatically as a result of the two Persian Gulf wars in the 1980s and early 1990s. In these conflicts, the other revolutionary Gulf state and Iran's major nemesis in the region, Iraq, demonstrated its ambitious and aggressive drive for hegemony in the area. At the same time, Saddam Hussein's government overextended itself and as a result found much of its economic and military infrastructure destroyed. It is Iran that has risen from the ashes of Iraq's defeat, and it is the Islamic Republic that now stands as the preeminent power in the Persian Gulf.

The other factor, besides the Iranian revolution, that has profoundly affected the future of the Gulf is the occurrence of major international warfare there. The generalized and destructive nature of this warfare has introduced psychological and political factors that promise to transform the region forever.

The Politics of War in the Persian Gulf

The 1980s and early 1990s represented an unpleasant era of violence in the Persian Gulf as the region witnessed two international wars: The first Gulf war pitted Iraq against Iran (1980–1987), and the second Gulf war saw Kuwait, supported by an international coalition dominated by the United States, in conflict with Iraq (1990–1991). In both wars, Iraq was the aggressor and Iraqi leader Saddam Hussein played a major decisional role. In the first war, the United States threw its support behind Saddam's Iraq. In the second conflict, the United States was the leading international actor opposing Saddam.

On September 22, 1980, Iraqi troops invaded neighboring Iran along a 400-mile front. At the time of the Iraqi surprise attack, the Iranian revolutionary regime was besieged and faltering. Political leaders were engaged in intense power struggles; the economy was deteriorating rapidly; the Kurds and various tribal groupings were in a state of revolt; counterrevolutionary forces were committing punishing acts of terrorism; the hostage crisis was ongoing; and the United States and its Western allies were applying severe international pressure on the Islamic Republic. Despite the fact that Iraq was clearly the aggressor state, the international community at the UN turned a blind eye to Iran's predicament, and Saddam Hussein found himself holding a blank check for aggression.

Although much has been made of Iraq-Iran tensions over control of the Shatt al-Arab waterway, religious disagreements between Sunni and Shi'i regimes, and longtime Persian-Arab ethnic differences, the principal cause of the war centered on a struggle for hegemony of the Persian Gulf. Saddam Hussein, always the ambitious political opportunist, saw the disruptive revolutionary chaos in Iran as his opportunity to take political control of the region. In the process, Iraq hoped to destroy the Iranian revolution, an appealing goal at the time to such Western powers as the United States and Great Britain and to insecure regional states such as Saudi Arabia and the Gulf shaikhdoms.

Although the sudden Iraqi attack caught Iran by surprise, the Islamic Republic responded quickly and poured reinforcements into the southwest, where badly outnumbered Iranian soldiers, police, and citizens fought a desperate war of defense. After a month of brutal hand-to-hand fighting, the city of Khurramshahr fell to the invaders. It was the only major Iranian city the Iraqis ever managed to capture. Khurramshahr was retaken by Iranian forces in May 1982. Having slowed the invasion, the Iranians counterattacked with some success in the fall of 1981 and the spring of 1982. Throughout 1983, Iran attempted to follow up its advantage and to drive into Iraqi soil, hoping for a breakthrough that would destroy Saddam's regime in Baghdad.

The decision by Ayatollah Khomeini and his advisors to continue the conflict—when Iran could have gone to the conference table and negotiated from a position of great strength—proved to be a serious strategic error. The war degenerated into a campaign of massive Iranian human-wave attacks on fixed Iraqi positions, where Saddam's forces enjoyed great technological and intelligence superiority. The casualties were horrendous. As the longest Middle East war in recent history, the Iran-Iraq conflict resulted in an estimated 400,000 deaths and 1 million wounded on the Iranian side and 300,000 deaths and 800,000 wounded on the Iraqi side. By 1987, Iran had suffered more battle deaths than the United States did in World War II, and Iran had but one-third the population that America had in 1945.

In July 1988, Iran grudgingly accepted a cease-fire, effectively ending the long, bloody Gulf war. In a rambling, poignant address to his people, Ayatollah Khomeini apologetically explained the decision to accept UN Resolution 598, which had been passed in July of 1987. Iran was simply unable to carry on any longer. In March and April of 1988, the Iraqis fired some 160 SCUD-B missiles outfitted with booster packs into Tehran, the capital city that Iranians had considered to be out of Iraqi missile range. These random attacks severely damaged the morale of the Iranian people. Even more destructive to Iran's morale was Iraq's resort to chemical warfare, first mustard gases and then deadly nerve agents such as tabun and sarin. Thousands of Iranians and Kurds died along Iran's western front as a result of Iraq's indiscriminate use of these deadly weapons. Saddam Hussein's terrifying threat to outfit his missiles with chemical warheads and to fire them into Iran's major cities was another factor that forced Iran to accept a cease-fire.

Besides Iraqi pressure, the United States and the Soviet Union took pro-Saddam positions that ultimately led to Iran's decision to terminate the fighting. Beginning in the spring of 1986, the Soviet Union, for example, dramatically began increasing its aid to Iraq, at the time its only client state in the Persian Gulf. From 1986 until the end of the conflict in 1988, the Soviets poured money and machines into Iraq. They provided Saddam's regime with an estimated $7 billion of military aid and greatly increased the number of their military advisors in Iraq.

The administration of Ronald Reagan adopted a position of neutrality during the first two years of the war. However, beginning in 1982, and especially in 1983, American policy makers began to tilt sharply to the Iraqi side. Leading State Department officials such as Secretary of State George Shultz and Secretary of Defense Caspar Weinberger deeply feared a perceived Iranian threat to Saudi Arabia.

In 1982, the United States removed Iraq from its list of countries considered supportive of international terrorism. High-level American officials began to visit Baghdad in late 1983, and the United States subsequently extended to Baghdad over $2 billion in commodity credits. In 1984, it became widely known that Iraq was benefiting from intelligence supplied through American sources. Saddam Hussein himself flatly stated in May 1984 that Iraq had the use of important intelligence provided by AWACS planes flown by American pilots based in Saudi Arabia. On November 26, 1984, the United States restored diplomatic relations with Iraq. When Iraqi-fired Exocet missiles struck the American frigate U.S.S. *Stark* on May 17, 1987, killing thirty-seven U.S. sailors, the Reagan administration quickly accepted the official Iraqi claim that the attack was inadvertent. President Reagan then curiously stated that "Iran is the real villain in the piece," and his administration issued a series of sharp warnings to Iran.

Finally, in 1987 and 1988, as Saddam's Iraq intensified its military pressure on Iran, the United States increased its naval presence in the Persian Gulf and carried out a number of attacks against Iranian ships and oil platforms. On July 3, 1988, in a tragic and infamous incident, the sophisticated Aegis-class cruiser, the U.S.S. *Vincennes*, shot down an Iranian civilian Airbus on a routine passenger flight over the Persian Gulf, killing all 290 persons aboard—a purposeful act in the minds of many Iranians. Exactly two weeks later, badly battered and bloodied, Iran accepted a cease-fire.

The strong American (and Soviet) support for Saddam Hussein and Iraq during the first Gulf war set the stage for the second Gulf war. Although President George Bush adopted a relatively more conciliatory position toward the Islamic Republic of Iran, his administration actively supported Saddam's Iraq. The heavy pro-Iraqi tilt was evident from the very beginning.

In a document titled "Guidelines for U.S.-Iraq Policy," which was prepared in January 1989 by the Bush transition team, the new administration outlined its intention to develop close relations with Saddam's Iraq. "It is up to the new Administration to decide whether to treat Iraq as a distasteful dictatorship to be shunned where possible, or to recognize Iraq's present and potential power in the region and accord it relatively high priority. We strongly urge the latter view." Bush's foreign policy analysts described Iraq's human rights record as "abysmal" but concluded that "in no way should we associate ourselves with the sixty-year Kurdish rebellion in Iraq or oppose Iraq's legitimate attempts to suppress it." The "Guidelines" deemphasized the issue of human rights and emphasized the desire to strengthen and expand U.S. commercial relations with Iraq.[1]

The Bush administration approved an additional $1 billion in agricultural trade credits, expanded American exports of high-technology goods, and protected Saddam's regime from congressional queries into Iraq's human rights violations and its use of chemical weapons against its own population. On October 26, 1989, President Bush issued a secret National Security Directive (NSD) calling for the establishment of strengthened military ties with Iraq. Although the plan was never implemented, it is instructive to note that the Pentagon was considering this proposal only three months before Saddam invaded Kuwait in

---

[1]This remarkable document was declassified by the State Department on June 1, 1992, at the urging of the House Foreign Affairs Committee. It was called to the attention of the authors by Thomas Blanton, Executive Director of The National Security Archive in Washington, D.C.

August 1990. By protecting and strengthening Saddam and by excusing and apologizing for the excesses of his regime, the United States puffed him up and inadvertently encouraged him to pursue further aggression in the region.

Iraq had long maintained that Kuwait had been artificially created in 1922, when Western colonial powers had arbitrarily drawn lines on a map that determined the boundaries of Iraq, Kuwait, and Saudi Arabia. To the overwhelming majority of Iraqis (including those in opposition to Saddam), Iraq has had a legitimate claim to Kuwait. Furthermore, following the first Gulf war, Iraq saw its financial position move from $35 billion in the black to $75 billion in the red. Much of this debt was owed to countries such as Kuwait and Saudi Arabia. Having borne the brunt of the war against revolutionary Iran, the Iraqi government felt that these debts should be forgiven. Saddam became especially irate with the Kuwaitis, whose overproduction of oil helped depress the price of petroleum, seriously threatening Iraq's economic well-being. This policy by Kuwait was, in Iraq's view, nothing less than a direct threat to Iraqi national security.

In a controversial meeting on July 25, 1990, Saddam Hussein and Tariq Aziz, his foreign minister, met with April Glaspie, U.S. ambassador to Iraq. During this meeting the two Iraqi leaders complained bitterly to Glaspie about Iraq's tenuous economic situation. In one exchange, Saddam Hussein complained that the drop in the price of oil had cost Iraq $6 billion to $7 billion, which was, in his words, a "disaster." In direct response, Ambassador Glaspie said, "I think I understand this. I have lived here for years. I admire your extraordinary efforts to rebuild your country. I know you need funds. We understand that and our opinion is that you should have the opportunity to rebuild your country. But we have no opinion on the Arab-Arab conflicts, like your border disagreement with Kuwait."[2] On August 2, 1990, the troops of Saddam Hussein's Iraq attacked Kuwait, effectively initiating the second Gulf war.

The Gulf crisis lasted from August 2, 1990, until February 28, 1991, when President George Bush declared a cease-fire. The seven-month conflict can be divided into two phases: (1) the diplomatic/economic sanction phase (August 2, 1990 to January 17, 1991) and the war/military campaign phase (January 17, 1991 to February 28, 1991). The diplomatic phase involved intensive political activities by the Bush administration as it sought to gather both domestic and international support to reverse the Iraqi occupation. Within the administration and within the country at large, there was strong support for a diplomatic and economic campaign against Saddam. There was considerably less support for military action. Internationally, the administration successfully cobbled together a large coalition of countries in opposition to the Iraqi action and skillfully used the UN to legitimize this position.

During the diplomatic maneuvering, the United States poured military troops into Saudi Arabia. President Bush first announced his intention to do so on August 6, 1990. On November 8, he stated that he was substantially reinforc-

---

[2]As quoted from an Iraqi transcript and published in Congressional Quarterly, *The Middle East*, Seventh ed. (Washington, D.C.: Congressional Quarterly Press, 1991), pp. 375–77. The transcript was translated by ABC News.

ing the 230,000 American troops already in Saudi Arabia. Ultimately, the United States moved over half a million military men and women into the region. As part of his strategy to present an image of the world against Saddam Hussein, the Bush administration was able to point to 35,000 British troops, 17,000 French troops, and, most important, 30,000 Egyptian and 19,000 Syrian troops who also joined the coalition.

The Iraqi government resisted political pressures, economic sanctions, and military threats designed to force its withdrawal from Kuwait. At an early stage in the process, George Bush decided to resort to the military option. Although he had admittedly been influenced in his decision by Britain's Margaret Thatcher, the president had become embroiled in a highly personal feud with Iraq's Saddam Hussein. Bush made the military decision despite the misgivings of several members of his own administration, a significant block of opinion in the U.S. Congress, and the overwhelming majority of Middle East experts in the scholarly community. Those who represented this position argued that economic and political pressure be continued; that a military invasion would cause the Iraqi people to rally around Saddam Hussein, converting a hated despot into a lonely hero; that such a military mismatch would harm the American image in much of the Arab and Third World; that a heavy military defeat of Iraq would transform Iran into the Persian Gulf superpower; and that the long-term consequences of such dramatic action were dangerously unpredictable. Those who preferred the continuation of sanctions also stressed the human, economic, and environmental costs that war would entail.

Those who supported military action argued that Iraqi aggression must be defeated for both political and economic (oil) reasons. They believed that Iraq, with its large military establishment, its possession of chemical weapons, and its nuclear development program had to be brought under control. Finally, those in support of war stressed the fact that diplomatic measures and economic sanctions had clearly failed to change Iraqi behavior. Iraq had, in fact, announced its annexation of Kuwait. The longer the situation prevailed, the greater the chances that the Iraqi occupation would become a fait accompli. Meanwhile, every day that the Iraqis spent in Kuwait was one more day of suffering and terror for the Kuwaiti people. Also, once in control of Kuwait, where would Saddam turn next? Neighboring oil-rich Saudi Arabia seemed a likely target.

On January 12, 1991, after three days of difficult debate, the U.S. Congress voted (52 to 47 in the Senate and 250 to 183 in the House) to give President Bush the authority to wage war against Iraq. The UN Security Council had already, on November 29, 1990, authorized the use of force. Just before primetime U.S. television news at 4:50 P.M. on January 16, 1991, allied warplanes took off from airfields in Saudi Arabia and attacked targets in Kuwait and Iraq. The second Gulf war was under way.

The military phase of the war against Iraq lasted only forty-two days as the U.S.-led coalition forces obliterated Iraqi resistance through the most intensive bombing campaign since World War II. For thirty-eight days, coalition aircraft pounded Iraq, flying an average of 2,000 sorties a day. An estimated 700,000 tons of bombs were dropped on Iraq as the world watched the onslaught on television, which, courtesy of the U.S. military, emphasized its high-tech component.

On the very first day of the bombing, the allied forces knocked out the power and water supplies in Baghdad, causing enormous hardship and suffering for the civilian population of this capital city. Despite the ferocity of the offensive, Iraq refused to capitulate. As a result, the coalition forces were compelled to initiate a ground assault.

The ground offensive that resulted in the liberation of Kuwait began on February 23 and lasted exactly 100 hours. Utilizing a cleverly conceived battle plan that focused on diversionary movements and end runs, the coalition forces easily overwhelmed the demoralized, undersupplied, war-weary Iraqi army, a force that lacked air cover and that had been softened up by coalition saturation bombing. On February 17, 1991, President Bush declared that "Kuwait is liberated. Iraq's army is defeated. Our military objectives are met." Despite the fact that Saddam Hussein and his regime survived, much of Iraq lay in smoldering ruins, and the Iraqi military had been seriously crippled. Given the risks and costs associated with carrying the war on to Baghdad, including the possible dismemberment of Iraq, the Bush administration chose to cease the military phase of the war and not to support Kurdish and Shi'i insurrections that commenced at the time. From then on, the conflict between Iraq and the United States would continue in the political and economic arenas.

Although the Gulf war was widely hailed in America and in much of the West as a glorious victory against the forces of aggression in the Persian Gulf, with the perspective of time the results are not so clear-cut. On the positive side, the coalition action preserved Kuwait's existence as an independent nation-state, which ensured that its enormous oil reserves would remain accessible to the West. The coalition campaign successfully dismantled much of Saddam Hussein's military and nuclear infrastructure. The action also demonstrated a new pattern of international cooperation within the framework of the UN in the post–Cold War world, and it paved the way for a U.S.-led effort to negotiate a settlement of the Arab-Israeli conflict. Finally, the United States proved its ability to project force across the world through the mastery of technology.

On the other hand, Saddam Hussein and his regime survived the war and used the coalition retreat as an opportunity to search, identify, and destroy all pockets of potential opposition in the country. The brutal 1991–1992 Iraqi campaigns against the Kurds in the north and the Shi'a in the south are especially noteworthy in this respect. Other human costs of the war include an estimated 200,000 Iraqi deaths (both military and civilian),[3] several hundred casualties on

---

[3]Although no one will ever know the number of Iraqi deaths caused by the Gulf war, the Pentagon has estimated that 100,000 Iraqi soldiers (with a 50 percent margin of error) were killed. Few informed estimates exist concerning civilian casualties. There is also the question of related and delayed deaths. One might argue that the slaughter of Kurds and Shi'a was directly related to the war. In May 1991, a Harvard University public health team projected that "at least 170,000 children under five years of age will die in the coming year from the delayed effects of the bombing." See the excellently researched article by Caryle Murphy in the *Washington Post* of June 23, 1991. Census Bureau demographer Beth Osborne Daponte estimated in January 1992 that 158,000 Iraqis died as a direct or indirect result of the war. Ms. Dapone was subsequently dismissed from her government job (*Washington Post*, March 6, 1992, p. A6). Both the regime of Saddam Hussein and the administration of George Bush were clearly reluctant to emphasize the issue of Iraqi casualties.

the coalition side, subsequent suffering and death in Iraq caused by disease and malnutrition, and the creation of hundreds of thousands of refugees from the Gulf region. Environmental and economic costs were also very high. Politically, although Kuwait remains independent, the continuation of the patrimonial mode of governance by the Al-Sabah family defies world trends of democratization. The conflict also divided the Arab world against itself and seriously damaged the Palestinian cause when the PLO chose to side with Saddam.

Finally, although the United States scored an impressive military/technological victory, it also demonstrated to the world its primitive understanding of the social and political realities in the Middle East. The very fact that the United States went to war against a country and a regime it had spent a decade supporting stands as an embarrassing reminder of this ignorance. This position was bluntly summarized by U.S. presidential aspirant Ross Perot:

> My position is if you don't like guys like Saddam Hussein—and obviously the president didn't at the end—don't spend ten years and billions of dollars of American taxpayers' money creating him, which Vice President George Bush did. There's a long clear record. . . . putting 500,000 people's lives at risk against nuclear, chemical and bacteriological . . . did not make a lot of sense when you had the alternative of the embargo. You had a lot of options other than open warfare.[4]

Furthermore, the United States had failed to convert military victory into a lasting peace in the region.

In 1999, nearly 30,000 American military men and women remained in the Gulf region. In September 1992, U.S. warplanes were once again in action over southern Iraq. In January 1993, just before he left office, President George Bush ordered further attacks on Iraq. These included an intensive strike of forty Tomahawk cruise missiles against a warehouse suspected of being a nuclear weapons-related facility. Such continuing attacks increasingly alienated Arabs and Muslims everywhere. Renowned novelist Jabra A. Jabra vividly describes the views of many educated Middle Easterners when he describes his reactions to the U.S. bombings. Sitting in his Baghdad study listening to a fugue by Bach, he was enjoying "complete faith in the kind of civilization that gave me such great joy. Suddenly everything began to shake. I thought, 'My God, the mongrels have taken over the West.'"[5]

In 1998–1999, Iraqis such as Jabra had cause for more concern. Upset about Iraq's possession of weapons of mass destruction and angry about Saddam's refusal to abide by UN rules concerning international inspections, the Clinton administration unleashed another bombardment against Iraq. For four nights in December 1998, the United States, with token British participation, struck Iraq with waves of cruise missiles and hundreds of other bombs. Since that time, the

---

[4]C-SPAN statement as reported in the *Washington Post*, May 24, 1992, p. C3. On another occasion, Perot made his point more graphically: "I believe we've had a pattern of covering up our past mistakes. We rescued the Emir of Kuwait. Now, if I go knock on your door and say I'd like to borrow your son to go to the Middle East so that this dude with 70 wives . . . can have his throne back, you'd probably hit me in the mouth." *Milwaukee Journal*, July 12, 1992, p. J3.

[5]*Wall Street Journal*, February 24, 1993, p. A11.

United States has intermittently carried out airstrikes against Iraqi targets in retaliation for alleged Iraqi violations of the peace agreement reached in 1991. Unlike 1990–1991, the United States found little support from its allies in Europe and the Gulf for its 1998–1999 attacks. Saddam Hussein continued to survive while his people felt the punishing effects of the onslaught. Meanwhile, the U.S. remains mired in the political quicksands of the Persian Gulf.

The Gulf wars and the continuing heavy presence of U.S. military forces in the Gulf represent a watershed in the political history of the region. The credibility of traditional rulers such as the leaders in Kuwait and Saudi Arabia suffered severely as a result of their need to call upon Western, Christian countries to preserve their power and privilege. The fact that many members of the political opposition in Kuwait, for example, chose to remain behind and fight the invaders while the ruling family fled to neighboring Saudi Arabia sharpened expectations that such loyalty presumed an enhanced future political role for all Kuwaitis.

The presence of huge numbers of foreign military men and women in the region brought to the Gulf an unprecedented firsthand experience with outside manners and mores. In Saudi Arabia, for example, the mere presence of Western women performing numerous military functions led directly to a dramatic incident in November 1990 in which Saudi women conducted a "drive-in" as an attempt to break through restrictions denying them the right to drive automobiles.

Despite their profound differences, both Ayatollah Khomeini in Iran and Saddam Hussein in Iraq astutely recognized the fact that their most important political card was their appeal to the disaffected, the dispossessed, and the disenfranchised in their countries and in the region at large. It is not often realized that the majority of citizens in several Arab countries—including Jordan, Yemen, and those of Northwest Africa—identified with many of Saddam's arguments and criticized the international coalition that rushed to the aid of Kuwait. Saddam appealed quite effectively to the "poor Arabs," who lacked both financial resources and power, and to Moroccans, Algerians, and Tunisians, whose countries had experienced brutal treatment at the hands of French colonialism.

The six traditional Gulf states are today confronted by two interrelated crises: the crisis of identity and the crisis of legitimacy. The crisis of identity involves a fundamental problem of identification and authenticity. The Gulf states exist as mobile patchwork quilts whose individual patches and colors continually run into and through one another. Composed of Persians and Arabs and Shi'ites and Sunnis, deluged by waves of expatriate workers from dozens of different countries, torn by struggles between different social classes, confused by competing cultural models emanating from East and West, frustrated by the absence of an institutionalized democratic tradition, and ruled personalistically by shaikhly families, the "traditional Gulf six" have yet to determine who they are and where they are going.

Thorny problems of legitimacy often accompany confusions about identity. In the Persian Gulf, where certain tribal families possess a near monopoly over political power and national decision making, the issue of legitimacy is particularly crucial. The Iranian revolution and the second Gulf war have forced the traditional rulers of the region to seek genuine legitimacy in the eyes of their populations. Issues such as personal freedoms and human rights, the emphasis of rule by law, and genuine political participation must be addressed. The people must have a stake in the system; they must feel part of their government. Such participation will promote a kind of shared solidarity that will strengthen the state against internal disaffection and upheaval and against external threats such as those posed by Saddam Hussein. Increasingly, the ruling families must either share power or risk losing all power. They must open up their systems in order to gain the legitimacy necessary to political survival. Many of the traditional ruling families in the Gulf, who are oftentimes corrupt and arrogant, are severely lacking in legitimacy.

The crises of identity and legitimacy have been highlighted by events such as the Iranian revolution and then widened and deepened by the two Gulf wars. Political elites in the traditional Gulf states must develop prudent and effective policies in response. Furthermore, these regional challenges have taken place in the context of a world of increasing democratization and expanding calls for effective political participation. What are the various strategies available to the besieged Gulf regimes? What policies and programs have they in fact adopted? In brief, what are the chances that such political systems can survive as humankind approaches the year 2000?

Political Strategies and Political Development in the Gulf

The leaders of the traditional patrimonial countries of the Gulf can respond to their developmental challenges by pursuing one of three political strategies: *repression, revision,* or *reform.* The reactive policy of *repression* involves battening down the political hatches and tightening the regime's control over the population. The opportunities for dissent and political participation are choked off, and the role of the police and security forces is enlarged considerably.

In a program of *revision,* the political leaders continue to tinker and revise their strategy of control. Sometimes, they take repressive measures; at other times, they loosen central control and allow more freedom of expression and temporarily open up new channels of political participation. The elite is constantly revising and modifying and shifting back and forth between policies of coercion and co-optation.

Response by *reform* is an enlightened attempt to address the challenges of identity and legitimacy by opening up the system and providing clear opportunities for individual expression, social mobility, and political participation. Reform strategies are based on a recognition of the need to address directly the issue of political development. In particular, such strategies involve elite willingness to expand channels of participation beyond the traditional networks of majlises and to introduce effective institutions of local self-government and national consultative assemblies. In traditional Middle East patrimonial systems in particular, reform strategies include a special sensitivity to the need to spread major decision-making power beyond a small group of individuals in the ruling family.

From the perspective of ruling elites, all three strategies carry risks and consequences. Policy based on repression tends to bottle up grievances in the short run but often leads to explosive upheaval in the longer run. The violent revolutions in Iraq in 1958 and in Iran in 1978–1979 are excellent examples of this proposition.[6] Repression builds social and political pressure; it does not dissipate such pressure. Programs of revision help to buy time, but they tend to be reactive and inconsistent; therefore, those who adopt them are often overwhelmed by new and unpredictable events. Also, revisionary tactics fail to address the root causes of problems. Finally, the strategy of reform requires that leaders be willing to make radical changes when necessary. Reform programs require prudent administration. Often political elites decide to introduce reform as a last resort. By then it is too little, too late. Increasingly, the reform alternative in the Middle East in general and in the Gulf in particular must take the form of nothing less than revolution from above. Otherwise, it may very well be bloody revolution from below.

With the exception of Iraq (and Iran in the years immediately following the revolution), the leaders of the Gulf states have all adopted policies of revision that are actually blendings of repression and reform, coercion and co-optation. The mixture is quite different from one country to another. In Saudi Arabia in particular, but also in Bahrain, the emphasis is away from reform and toward control. In the United Arab Emirates and Kuwait, there has been relatively greater sensitivity to the need for some broader modes of political participation. This attention to opening the system became especially acute following the Gulf war of 1991, and the early 1990s have witnessed a noticeable tilt in the direction of reform.

After thirty years of promises, the Al-Saud ruling family in Saudi Arabia announced a plan to establish a national consultative assembly. In late February 1992, King Fahd publicly described plans to establish a sixty-one-member appointive *Majlis al-Shura* with substantial advisory powers. The announcement also called for the establishment of provincial majlises and sharply changed the rules for determining succession to the throne. From now on, succession is to be decided by an electoral college of the sons and grandsons of King Abd al-Aziz Ibn Saud. Although the Saudi initiative keeps power firmly in the hands of the ruling family, it represented a response to the new conditions in the Gulf. King Fahd admitted that this decision was a direct result of the second Gulf war. In his words, "Momentous events in the recent past . . . have made it necessary to develop the country's administrative structure."[7]

The Saudi action is only part of a more general drive to limited democratization in the Persian Gulf. In Kuwait, where the Amir had twice before dissolved the national assembly, new demands for meaningful elections followed the Iraqi occupation. After a clumsy delay, the Amir finally announced that elections were to be held in October 1992. In the months preceding the elections, political dis-

---

[6]Saddam Hussein's long tenure in power in Iraq stands as an interesting exception to this principle. Saddam has, however, narrowly survived a number of assassination attempts.

[7]*Washington Post*, March 2, 1991, p. 1.

cussion and debate in Kuwait were vigorous and hard-hitting. When the election smoke cleared, the opposition had won a clear majority of the seats, and a new era of serious parliamentary politics began in the country.

Although these sporadic policies of reform are increasingly visible in the traditional countries of the Gulf, the underlying reality is one of strong central control. Policies of revision still dominate policies of reform. Police and security forces (often buttressed by powerful outside advisors) are heavily relied on to protect the status quo. With the partial exception of Kuwait, censorship is severe. Control is tightest in Saudi Arabia, which, although not a police state in the style of Saddam's Iraq, nonetheless leans heavily in the direction of repression. The financial and international power of Saudi Arabia gives it special influence in the region, and its counsel on these important developmental matters carries great weight in the decision-making processes of the other Gulf rulers. Because of Saudi pressures, Bahrain, for example, has jettisoned its traditional policy of revision and compromise and has become increasingly repressive. As a result, Bahrain has become the scene of great political unrest and popular disaffection.

The instrument through which Saudi Arabia exerts much of its political influence is the Gulf Cooperation Council (GCC), established in May 1981. Formed initially in response to the perceived threats emanating from the Iranian revolution, the GCC is composed of the six traditional Gulf states. In its first years of existence, the GCC emphasized issues of mutual defense and security. The 1990 Iraqi invasion of Kuwait demonstrated the actual weakness of this loosely knit alliance. It is questionable whether the GCC can ever succeed as long as it withholds membership from the two most populous and powerful countries in the Gulf, Iran and Iraq. Nonetheless, the GCC provides a forum where the besieged traditional Gulf countries can discuss political and developmental strategy.

Despite a growing sensitivity (often born out of necessity) to the need to respond creatively and fundamentally to the demands of their growing middle classes and deeply religious lower classes, the ruling elites of most Gulf countries have yet to implement the basic reform programs necessary to guarantee the survival of their systems in the long run. Economic inducements and announcements of promised consultative assemblies are not enough. The steady growth of an activist, political, populist Islam throughout the Gulf states provides an alternative movement whose members are not easily bought or coopted. Only genuine reform programs that frontally address the deepening crises of identity and legitimacy can stave off political upheaval.

The internal contradictions present in the traditional countries of the Persian Gulf have not yet exploded into revolutionary violence because the benefits of the processes of modernization fueled by great wealth have been shared by the relatively small populations of citizens resident there. Beginning in 1979 with the Iranian revolution, however, and continuing a decade later with the second Gulf war, the tensions have increased profoundly. Internal developments and the introduction of external forces and ideas directly into the region have combined to place an unprecedented strain on the social and political systems of the Gulf countries. The response of the ruling families to these gathering and deepening challenges will determine the future of the region.

SELECTED BIBLIOGRAPHY

Amirahmadi, Hooshang. *Revolution and Economic Transition: The Iranian Experience.* Albany: State University of New York Press, 1990.

Amirahmadi, Hooshang, and Manoucher Parvin, eds. *Post-Revolutionary Iran.* Boulder, Colo.: Westview Press, 1988.

Bill, James A. *The Eagle and the Lion: The Tragedy of American-Iranian Relations.* New Haven: Yale University Press, 1988.

Cooley, John K. *Payback: America's Long War in the Middle East.* Washington, D.C.: Brassey's, 1991.

Cordesman, Anthony, and Ahmed S. Hashem. *Iran: Dilemmas of Dual Containment.* Boulder, Colo: Westview Press, 1997.

Crystal, Jill. *Kuwait: The Transformation of an Oil State.* Boulder, Colo.: Westview Press, 1992.

Farouk-Sluggett, Marion, and Peter Sluggett. *Iraq Since 1958: From Revolution to Dictatorship.* London: I. B. Tauris, 1990.

Freedman, Lawrence, and Efraim Karsh. *The Gulf Conflict, 1990–1991* (Princeton, N.J.: Princeton University Press, 1993.

Gause, F. Gregory. *Oil Monarchies.* New York: Council on Foreign Relations Press, 1994.

Heard-Bey, Frauke. *From Trucial States to United Arab Emirates.* New York: Longman, 1982.

Holden, David, and Richard Johns. *The House of Saud.* New York: Holt and Rinehart, 1981.

Hunter, Shireen T. *Iran and the World.* Bloomington: Indiana University Press, 1990.

Keddie, Nikki R., and Mark J. Gasiorowski, eds. *Neither East nor West: Iran, the Soviet Union, and the United States.* New Haven: Yale University Press, 1980.

Khuri, Fuad. *Tribe and State in Bahrain.* Chicago: University of Chicago Press, 1981.

Long, David. *The Kingdom of Saudi Arabia.* Gainesville: University of Florida Press, 1997.

Marr, Phebe. *The Modern History of Iraq.* Boulder, Colo.: Westview Press, 1983.

Milani, Mohsen M. *The Making of Iran's Islamic Revolution.* Boulder, Colo.: Westview Press, 1988.

Palmer, Michael A. *Guardians of the Gulf.* New York: The Free Press, 1992.

Peck, Malcolm C. *The United Arab Emirates: A Venture in Unity.* Boulder, Colo.: Westview Press, 1986.

Peterson, J. E. *The Arab Gulf States: Steps Toward Political Participation.* Washington, D.C.: Center for Strategic and International Studies, 1988.

Piscatori, James, ed. *Islamic Fundamentalisms and the Gulf Crisis.* Chicago: University of Chicago Press, 1992.

Rajaee, Farhang, ed. *The Iran-Iraq War: The Politics of Aggression.* Gainesville: University of Florida Press, 1993.

Ramazani, R. K. *Revolutionary Iran.* Baltimore: The Johns Hopkins University Press, 1986.

Schraeder, Peter, ed. *Intervention into the 1990s.* Boulder, Colo.: Lynne Rienner, 1992.

Sick, Gary G., and Lawrence G. Potter, eds. *The Persian Gulf at the Millennium.* New York: St. Martin's Press, 1997.

Sifry, Mica L., and Christopher Cerf, eds. *The Gulf War Reader: History, Documents, Opinions.* New York: Random House, 1991.

U.S. Department of Defense. *Conduct of the Persian Gulf War: Final Report to Congress.* Washington, D.C.: Government Printing Office, 1992.

Chapter 9

Petroleum, Politics, and Development

The historical precedent set by the West, wherein state formation was linked to economic development, suggests that the process of state-building in the Middle East should have been facilitated and hastened by the great oil boom that began in 1973 and ended in 1985. And what a boom it was. The price of a barrel of crude oil, which was $1.20 in 1900 and still only $1.69 in 1970, shot up from $2.90 in June 1973 to over $11 per barrel by the end of that year, as a result of the oil embargo associated with the October 1973 Arab-Israeli War. The second oil shock, which accompanied the Iranian revolution, sent prices soaring from $13 in January 1979 to as high as $45 per barrel on the spot market later that year, the official posted price reaching an all-time high of $34 per barrel in March 1982. Middle Eastern oil revenues went from $6 billion in 1970 to over $270 billion a decade later. The revenues of Saudi Arabia alone in 1980 were over 15 times those received by all Middle Eastern countries in 1970.

While the major oil-producing states benefited directly from the price rise and growth of oil exports, countries that export little or no oil received substantial secondary benefits in the form of worker remittances, fees for the transport of oil across their territory, and public and private cash transfers and investments by the oil-rich states. The gross domestic products (GDP) of Jordan, Egypt, and what were then North and South Yemen grew during the seven "fat" years of 1974 to 1981 by an average annual rate of almost 20 percent. Per capita income in those countries more than tripled in the decade after 1972.[1] While

---

[1] George T. Abed, "The Lean Years: The Political Economy of Arab Oil in the Coming Decade," in Hisham Sharabi, *The Next Arab Decade: Alternative Futures* (Boulder, Colo.: Westview Press, 1988), p. 93.

much of the rest of the world's economy languished from the first oil shock until at least the early 1980s, during that period virtually all Middle Eastern countries recorded higher real annual economic growth rates than ever before in their histories.

The impact of petrodollars on living standards was profound. In 1970, between 15 and 22 percent of Middle Easterners suffered from some form of malnutrition. A decade later, the incidence of malnutrition was reduced by half.[2] Between 1965 and 1989, daily per capita calorie intake in the low- and middle-income countries of the Middle East and North Africa (hereafter MENA) rose from 2,153 to 3,011, the fastest growth rate in the world.[3] In that same period, the ratio of doctors to population in those countries registered the world's greatest improvement, from 1:7,740 to 1:2,410.[4] Death rates declined dramatically as a consequence of improved nutrition and health care, so the rate of population increase soared. It rose from 2.6 percent in 1972, when the world's average was 1.9 percent, to 3.1 percent in 1990, then the world's highest.[5]

The oil boom also contributed to the rapid expansion of educational facilities. Illiteracy in the Arab world dropped from 70 to 40 percent in the ten years after 1972.[6] By 1990, only in Egypt, Sudan, Oman, and Yemen was more than half the population illiterate.[7] The percentage of the age group enrolled in primary and secondary schools in the low- and middle-income MENA countries rose in the quarter century after 1964 from 61 to 90 percent and from 17 to 53 percent, respectively. In that period there was a fourfold increase in the percentage of those in the relevant age group enrolled in higher education.[8] Nevertheless, in comparative terms the MENA region failed to keep pace with growth in educational attainments in other areas. The average years of schooling per person were, in the late 1990s, comparable to Africa's and far below those of East Asia. Indonesia, the East Asian country with the poorest educational achievements, "has an educational attainment level higher than any Middle Eastern country, despite their higher relative incomes."[9]

Living conditions for most Middle Easterners improved significantly as a result of the oil boom. A panel study of poor families in Cairo, which began in 1969, revealed that by the mid-1980s, this sample of the urban poor believed "that matters have improved greatly over the last fifteen years." Indeed, many in the sample resented still being referred to as poor and by most objective mea-

---

[2]Joe Stork and Karen Pfeifer, "Bullets, Banks and Bushels: The Struggle for Food in the Middle East," *Middle East Report* 145 (March-April 1987): 6.

[3]The World Bank, *World Development Report,* 1992 (Oxford: Oxford University Press, 1992), p. 273.

[4]Ibid., p. 273.

[5]Ibid., p. 269.

[6]Abed, "The Lean Years," p. 95.

[7]*World Development Report,* 1992, pp. 218–219.

[8]Ibid., p. 275.

[9]John M. Page, Jr. "A Middle Eastern Miracle?" (Cairo: The Egyptian Center for Economic Studies, Distinguished Lecture No. 4, 1996), p. 7.

sures were no longer so.[10] Of the forty-three countries classified in 1992 as "low income" by the World Bank, only four—Egypt, Mauritania, Afghanistan, and Sudan—were in the MENA region.[11] All other countries in the region were categorized as middle- or high-income developing countries. The average per capita gross national product (GNP) of the low- and middle-income MENA countries in 1990 was $1,790, almost equivalent to that of the Latin American/Caribbean countries, almost three times higher than that of countries in East Asia, and some five times more than that of countries in South Asia or Sub-Saharan Africa.[12] Personal incomes, diets, access to health and educational facilities, and the living conditions in general of most Middle Easterners during the oil boom improved at a substantially faster pace than those of populations elsewhere in the Third World.

Providing better living conditions for important sectors of the population may be a necessary requisite, but it is not a sufficient condition for the creation of effective and legitimate states. Rapid economic growth carries with it dislocations that may destabilize governments. The pattern of growth may itself facilitate or impede the expansion of state power. Economic growth spurred principally by industrialization provided the basis for incorporating new recruits into both the economic and political systems of most Western countries. In the Middle East, however, economic development, especially since the early 1970s, has been influenced disproportionately by one commodity—oil, which constitutes 80 percent of the region's total exports. The consequences of the region having become so heavily dependent on the extraction and exportation of that single natural resource are profound for both economies and polities. Uneven growth within and between the three major sectors of national economies—industry, agriculture, and services—is one generally negative result of oil dependence.

Industry

The industrial sector in most Middle Eastern countries exhibits sharp bimodalism, the oil-associated subsector performing well while virtually all other subsectors of industry are struggling to maintain adequate growth rates. Middle Eastern oil producers, whose deposits of that mineral are truly prodigious, have come to play an extremely powerful role in the world petroleum trade. The Middle East has over two-thirds of the world's proven oil reserves. The commanding position of the Middle East, and within it of the five countries with the largest reserves—Iran, Iraq, Kuwait, Saudi Arabia, and the UAE—is, if anything, increasing. Saudi Arabia alone has 300 billion barrels of oil, more than one-quarter of the world's proven reserves. Proven oil reserves in the Arab world rose from

---

[10]Unni Wikan, "Living Conditions Among Cairo's Poor—A View from Below," *The Middle East Journal* 39 (Winter 1985): 7.

[11]*World Development Report,* 1992, p. 218.

[12]Ibid., p. 219.

57 percent of global reserves in 1986 to 63 percent a decade later.[13] It is estimated that Persian Gulf oil suppliers will be providing about half the world's requirements, between forty and forty-five million barrels per day (mb/d) of oil in 2010, compared to just over 20 percent in the mid-1990s.[14]

In addition to being plentiful, Middle Eastern oil is also cheap to produce. Depreciation, interest, and operating expenses together amount to less than $5 per barrel of oil produced in the Middle East. Elsewhere these expenses are very much higher. Additions to non-OPEC sources from 1973 to 1982 cost on average $60,000 per barrel/day, thus making oil from the three major new areas developed in the 1970s—the North Sea, North Slope, and Mexico—several times more expensive to extract and deliver to market than Middle East oil.[15] The costs of bringing upstream new oil fields in the Caspian Basin will be still higher. Whereas most Middle Eastern producers can still make profits if prices drop to even $10 per barrel, most others cannot. This is due primarily to the high rate of flow in Gulf wells, with the "Big Four" of the Gulf averaging 4,000 b/d from their wells, which is 100 times more than the average U.S. well and substantially more than other OPEC (Organization of Petroleum Exporting Countries) producers such as Venezuela and Indonesia, whose flow rate is less than 200 b/d.[16] In the four major oil producing states in the Gulf—Iran, Iraq, Kuwait, and Saudi Arabia—production costs in the late 1990s were still less than $2 a barrel.

Since the oil price increases of the 1970s, the large oil producers in the Gulf have followed a systematic policy of "moving downstream." They have assumed greater roles in the refining, transport, and marketing of petroleum and constructed modern plants for adding value to crude oil and natural gas by converting them into other products, especially petrochemicals. By 1989, 27 percent of oil exports from the Middle East OPEC countries were in the form of refined products.[17] In 1988, Saudi Arabia purchased half of the Texaco oil company's U.S. refining operations and formed a joint venture with it to supply petroleum products to some 12,000 service stations in twenty-three states. In the previous year, Kuwait had purchased over 20 percent of the shares of British Petroleum (BP), which, in addition to its string of 5,000 wholly-owned Q8 service stations in seven European countries, gave Kuwait a significant role in the world's retail petroleum market. By 1988, Kuwait was selling directly to consumers more than half of its total oil output.[18] In June 1988, Abu Dhabi, one of the seven emirates in the UAE, made a move downstream by purchasing 8.4 percent of the stock of

---

[13]Rami G. Khouri, "The Rise, or Retreat, of the Modern Arab State," *Jordan Times* (March 10, 1998).

[14]Geoffrey Kemp and Robert E. Harkavy, *Strategic Geography and the Changing Middle East* (Washington, D.C.: The Brookings Institution Press, 1997), p. 110; and Julia Devin, "Market Fundamentals and Gulf Oil Policies in the 21st Century," in *Gulf Economies: Strategies for Growth in the 21st Century,* ed. by Julia Devlin (Washington, D.C.: Georgetown University, 1997), pp. 11–19.

[15]Thomas Stauffer, "Income Measurement in Arab States," in *The Rentier State*, pp. 29–30; and Abed, "The Lean Years," pp. 98–99.

[16]Kemp and Harkavy, *Strategic Geography*, pp. 125–126.

[17]*Middle East Times* (July 9–15, 1988): 9.

[18]*MEED* (July 8, 1988): 2–3.

the French oil company Total, making it the largest investor in that company after the French government.[19] The vast expansion of petrochemical plants has made the Gulf states, and Saudi Arabia in particular, major competitors in this market. By 1992, Saudi Arabia had captured some 10 percent of the world's market for petrochemicals. Sabic (Saudi Basic Industries Corporation), which employs almost 10,000 people, was in 1992 the world's sixth most profitable petrochemical company. Saudi Arabia alone accounts for about half the region's exports of chemicals, which grew from less than $100 million in the early 1970s to almost $5 billion in the early 1990s. Excluding oil, chemicals are the region's largest export, constituting slightly more than a quarter of total exports in the mid-1990s.[20] Sabic, 70 percent owned by the government, is the only Middle Eastern company to be among the world's largest 500 corporations, ranking 313th in 1997.[21]

There is a gray area between oil and non-oil industries in which considerable development has also occurred. The Gulf oil producers have established various industries that especially benefit from cheap energy, such as aluminum smelting and steel production. Qatar and Bahrain have added some 10 percent to their GDPs with such installations, and Saudi Arabia has undertaken an even more extensive industrialization program. However, the success of these undertakings is directly proportional to the degree to which they are linked to hydrocarbon extraction, processing, and consumption and hence able to benefit from comparative advantage and outright subsidization. It remains an open question as to whether they would be competitive in the absence of access to oil and gas at less than world market prices.

In countries of the region that do not export large quantities of oil, industrial production remains concentrated in the usual areas of Third World manufacturing, which are food processing, textiles, and construction materials. Clothing and textiles together, for example, accounted for 30 percent of the region's non-oil exports in the mid-1990s.[22] Some progress has been made in establishing more sophisticated industries, such as vehicle production and electronics, but those activities generally remain limited to assembly of imported components. There is virtually no manufacturing of machine tools in the region, so almost all capital equipment involved in production must be imported.

Rates of growth in manufacturing in some key Middle Eastern countries, including Egypt, which is the most industrialized of the Arab states, were higher in the 1960s and 1970s than they have been subsequently. The average annual growth rate of industry in the low- and middle-income MENA countries was 6.3 percent from 1965 to 1980, but only 1.1 percent in the following decade, the lowest growth rate of any region in the world and less than a third of the average

---

[19]"Penetrating the Market Place," *MEED* (July 8, 1988): 2.

[20]*Claiming the Future: Choosing Prosperity in the Middle East and North Africa* (Washington, D.C.: The World Bank, 1995), p. 67.

[21]Thomas Cromwell, "No Cheer in the Region," *Middle East Times* (February 20–26, 1998): 13.

[22]*Claiming the Future,* p. 67.

of 3.9 percent for low- and middle-income countries.[23] For the region as a whole, manufacturing still accounts for less than 10 percent of GDP.[24] Industrial goods constituted only between 1 and 2 percent of exports from the MENA countries through the 1990s, which—along with Sub-Saharan Africa—is the lowest proportion in the world. Oil exports accounted for 64 percent of Arab export income in 1987, 67 percent in 1994, and 72 percent in 1996.[25] In various countries of the region, the share of manufactures in GDP and exports dropped steadily for more than two decades. In Egypt, for example, manufactured goods, including textiles, accounted for about one-third of exports in 1965 but only 18 percent by 1985. Manufacturing's share of GDP fell in Egypt from 17.4 percent in 1975 to 14.7 percent in 1994.[26] For middle-income developing countries as a whole, total manufactures constituted on average 24 percent of exports in 1965 and 50 percent in 1985.[27] The 260 million people of the MENA region export fewer non-oil goods than Finland, which has a population of five million.[28] Outside the oil sector and industries closely allied to it, industrial expansion in the region has failed to keep pace with rates of growth elsewhere in the developing world.

Agriculture

As a result of production growth rates falling behind rapidly increasing demand, the "food gap" in the Middle East widened at an alarming rate during the oil boom, and while it has not continued to grow rapidly in recent years, it remains large and threatens to widen further. The Middle East has become the world's largest food-importing region. Whereas in 1972 the Middle East was nearly self-sufficient in agricultural production, by 1986 farm output had fallen to 81 percent of needs, and imports reached a staggering $25 billion, ten times more than a decade earlier.[29] Between 1974 and 1990, low- and middle-income MENA countries increased their importation of cereals more rapidly than countries of any other region, causing them to become the most cereal-dependent region on earth.[30] Agricultural imports by Arab League states in 1990 accounted for almost one-third of all such imports by Third World countries, despite the fact that Arabs do not exceed 5 percent of the Third World's population. Idriss Jazairy, president of the International Fund for Agricultural Development, predicted in 1992 that before the end of the century the Arab food import bill could reach

---

[23]*World Development Report,* 1992, p. 221; *World Development Report,* 1997. p. 235.

[24]Chatelus, "Policies for Development: Attitudes Toward Industry and Services," p. 127.

[25]Khouri, "The Rise, or Retreat of the Modern Arab State," *Jordan Times* (March 10, 1998).

[26]*Claiming the Future,* p. 92.

[27]*World Development Report,* 1987, p. 222.

[28]*Claiming the Future* p. 4.

[29]"Bridging the Food Gap," p. 2.

[30]*World Development Report,* 1992, p. 225.

$100 billion annually.[31] Ultimately, Jazairy was wrong, but that was due less to expanding production than to demand stagnating in tandem with the region's economic decline since 1985.[32] The Arab food import bill increased by $2 billion from 1995 to 1996, taking it to a level almost twice that of 1980.[33]

Food imports, as a percentage of export earnings and GDP, illustrate how dependent the Middle East has become on the rest of the world for its "daily bread." Egypt, which was one of the Third World's major agricultural exporting nations from the 1820s through the first two-thirds of this century, and which was still self-sufficient in food when Anwar al-Sadat came to power, had by 1990 become the world's third-largest importer of grain and produced only 40 percent of its own food.[34] Nearly half of Egypt's wheat is imported from the U.S.[35] Other former major agricultural exporters in the Middle East and North Africa, including Morocco, Tunisia, Sudan, and Syria, all spend more than 25 percent of their export earnings to import foodstuffs.[36]

During the oil boom and even into the mid-1980s, many Middle Eastern governments did little to try to reduce the food gap. A policy of cheap food for urban populations was instituted in most countries to reduce the possibilities of political unrest. Changes in the international terms of trade facilitated that policy. In 1970, a barrel of oil bought about one bushel of wheat, but a decade later, the same barrel could purchase six bushels.[37] It became easier to import food than to stimulate local production and establish market linkages between rural and urban areas.

The policy of cheap, plentiful food caused consumption to skyrocket, a trend further accelerated by population growth rates that have exceeded 2 percent in all countries in the region except Israel and in some countries—including Iran, Iraq, and Algeria—have reached almost 4 percent.[38] As personal incomes rose faster than food prices during the oil boom, Middle Easterners vastly increased their per capita food consumption. In Saudi Arabia, for example, annual per capita consumption of food rose from 323 kilos in 1974 to 515 kilos in 1984.[39]

During the oil boom, Middle Easterners also changed their diets. They moved up the "food chain," substituting red and white meat and animal products for vegetable proteins and eating a higher proportion of prepackaged,

[31]Parker, "Food Gap Widens," p. 29.

[32]Alan Richards and John Waterbury, *A Political Economy of the Middle East*, second ed. (Boulder, Colo.: Westview Press, 1996), pp. 146–153.

[33]Rami G. Khouri, "The Rise, or Retreat of the Modern Arab State."

[34]Ray Bush, "Agriculture in Jeopardy," *The Middle East* (May 1992), p. 22.

[35]Richards and Natenbury, *A Political Economy*, p. 147.

[36]Stork and Pfeifer, "Bullets, Banks and Bushels," p. 5.

[37]Alan Richards, "Arab Agriculture in 1995: Apocalypse Now or Muddling Through?" in *The Next Arab Decade*, p. 116.

[38]Tarbush, "Food," p. 13.

[39]"Bridging the Food Gap," p. 6.

processed foodstuffs. Each Arab consumed annually an average of 4 kilograms of eggs in 1981–1983, about double the figure for 1970–1972. Consumption of poultry more than trebled, and red meat consumption doubled over that decade.[40] In sum, personal preferences, reinforced by local government policies and global terms of trade, led to a vastly higher demand for increasingly expensive imported food after the 1973 oil price rise.

Caught between the downturn in oil prices after 1982 and the rising demand for food, governments have struggled to stimulate domestic agricultural production while trying to restrict the growth of consumption and importation. Efforts to expand supply have met with some success, as "most countries' agricultural sectors managed at least to keep up with population growth during the 1980s."[41] But prospects for narrowing the food gap are bleak. In the wake of the Uruguay Round of negotiations on world tariffs and trade, subsidies provided to agriculture by industrial countries are being reduced. The resultant international surge in prices for food will increase the annual cost of the region's food imports by $4 billion to $5 billion.[42] The chief physical constraint to expanding food production in the region is the lack of adequate water, a constraint that can only be partially mitigated by greater adoption of more modern irrigation techniques. Although governments in the region have begun to address various policy constraints, such as by raising prices paid to producers and by reducing counterproductive governmental controls over them, the supply response has been disappointing. The average annual growth rate of agricultural output in the MENA region was about 1 percent less in 1990–1995 than it had been in the decade of the 1980s.[43]

As regards the demand side, efforts to suppress its growth have met with mixed success. Cheap, plentiful food, became a vital component of the informal "social contracts" that emerged between governments and populations in the 1970s—"contracts" that required governments to make available consumer goods at relatively low prices in return for the population's acquiescence in their rule. Constriction of food supplies is therefore a politically risky step. Since the late 1970s, food riots have occurred in Algeria, Egypt, Iran, Jordan, Lebanon, Morocco, Sudan, Tunisia, and Turkey.[44] For all governments other than those of the oil-exporting countries of the Gulf, however, there has been no alternative to reducing subsidies for food, thus causing prices to rise. Given the high population growth rates that prevail in the region, overall consumption will continue to rise in tandem with production if not outpace it, thereby causing the food gap to widen as the price of imported food rises.

---

[40]"Arab World Must Quickly Learn to Feed Itself," p. 20.

[41]Richards and Waterbury, *A Political Economy of the Middle East,* p. 148.

[42]*Claiming the Future,* p. 18.

[43]*World Development Report,* 1997, p. 235.

[44]David Seddon, "Austerity Protest: Popular Responses to Economic Liberalization in the Middle East and North Africa," in *Economic and Political Liberalization in the Middle East,* ed. by Tim Niblock and Emma Murphy (London: British Academic Press, 1993), pp. 88–89.

Services and Unemployment

Services include income-generating activities such as transportation, tourism, financial services, research-development, and engineering, as well as income-utilizing endeavors, such as the provision of health, educational, and social services.[45] Unlike industrial and agricultural sectors, service sectors of virtually all Middle Eastern countries have grown rapidly since the onset of the oil boom. In the mid-1960s, services accounted for 27 percent of the labor force in Arab countries, whereas by 1990, they accounted for some 45 percent.[46] Since 1970, expenditure on services has grown at a higher annual rate than GDP in almost all countries in the region. In states that export little or no oil, services typically account for about half of GDP; in the oil-exporting countries, the ratio of services to the non-oil GDP normally ranges between 70 and 80 percent.[47] In Saudi Arabia, for example, employment in productive sectors fell by 530,000 but increased in the service sector by 900,000 between 1985 and 1990.[48] In Kuwait, three-quarters of the labor force is employed in services.[49]

The bulk of services in Middle Eastern countries is performed by government; hence, as the service sector has expanded, so the percentage of the labor force employed by government has grown.[50] This is true regardless of the nominal categorization of a country's political economy as socialist or market-oriented. In Iran, for example, the trend of growing government employment that began under the shah continued under the Islamic Republic. In 1966, public sector employees constituted less than 10 percent of Iran's employed population. A decade later, they made up almost 20 percent of the labor force and about one-third of the urban work force. By 1986, 31 percent of the labor force was in the public sector, the ratio being 43 percent in urban areas. The average annual growth rate in public employment in Iran from the mid-1970s to the mid-1980s was 7 percent, although total employment grew at only 2.5 percent per annum.[51] In Egypt, the public sector's share of employment actually increased at a faster pace under Sadat than under Nasser, despite the fact that the former advocated liberal economic policies and the latter was a champion of

---

[45]This distinction is made by Michel Chatelus, "Policies for Development: Attitudes Toward Industry and Services," in *The Rentier State,* p. 133.

[46]*Will Arab Workers Prosper or Be Left Out of the Twenty-first Century?* (Washington, D.C.: The World Bank, 1995), p. 9.

[47]Ibid., p. 134.

[48]Presley and Westaway, "Economic Liberalisation in Saudi Arabia," p. 15.

[49]*Arab Workers,* p. 8.

[50]It is important to note, however, that banking and financial services, much of which are in the private sector, have also expanded. Of the fifty largest Middle Eastern companies, for example, twenty-five are banks. Thomas Cromwell "No Cheer in the Region," *Middle East Times* (February 20–26, 1998): 13.

[51]Paul Johnson, "The Impact of the Islamic Revolution on the State/Private Sector Symbiosis." Paper delivered to the Social Science Research Council's Conference on Expanding States and Retreating Societies, Aix-en-Provence (March 25–27, 1988), pp. 1, 9.

Arab socialism. By 1992, the Egyptian state employed 5.3 million out of a total work force of 13.9 million people, some 38 percent.[52] In Kuwait 92 percent of the indigenous labor force is on the public payroll, whereas in the countries of the region that export little or no oil, the state typically employs between 30 and 45 percent of the labor force. By comparison, in OECD countries governments on average employ 18 percent of the national labor force.[53]

Both governments and private sectors have failed to provide adequate jobs in industry and agriculture. Until recently most governments of the region acted as employers of last resort, hiring those graduates who otherwise would be unemployed, then consigning them to unrewarding, unproductive labor in sprawling bureaucracies. However, as governmental revenues have fallen and the number of such graduates has continued to expand at an ever accelerating pace, the inevitable result has been increasing unemployment. The region now has the highest unemployment rate in the world, which is on average almost 15 percent of the labor force, compared to 5 percent or less in Latin America, East and South Asia, and slightly less than 10 percent in OECD countries.[54] More than one-fifth of the labor forces of Algeria, Jordan, the West Bank and Gaza, Yemen, and possibly Lebanon are unemployed. In 1996, 1 million young people entered the MENA labor markets, of which some 200,000 were estimated to have found jobs.[55] Real wages in the region declined sharply (by about 30 percent) in the mid- to late 1980s and have failed to recover since then.[56] The average worker's wages in the region are the same now as they were in the early 1970s before the oil boom began.[57] However, largely as a result of their concentration in the services sector, especially its governmental and public sector components, those workers, despite their comparatively low wages, are not good investments as viewed from the perspective of national economic growth. Since the mid-1980s, labor productivity in the non-oil-producing counties has failed to increase and has actually fallen in the oil-producing ones by more than 4 percent each year. Annual GDP growth per worker is lower in the MENA region than any other part of the world, as is total factor productivity.[58]

The service sector, especially its governmental component, acted as a sponge that soaked up much potential unemployment until the late 1980s. It is now saturated. Although ultimately this could be a good thing were productive employment opportunities to be generated in industry and agriculture, it is scant comfort for today's unemployed youths. Moreover, as the World Bank notes, it will be "a herculean task" to reduce unemployment even gradually in the region. The population growth rate of 2.7 percent is, along with Sub-

---

[52] *MEED* (May 22, 1992): 20.

[53] *Will Arab Workers,* p. 20.

[54] *Claiming the Future,* p. 28.

[55] J. Page, "A Middle Eastern Miracle?" p. 18.

[56] *Will Arab Workers,* p. 2.

[57] *Claiming the Future,* p. 28.

[58] *Will Arab Workers,* pp. 2–3; and *Claiming the Future,* p. 28.

Saharan Africa's, the highest in the world, resulting in the regional labor force growing at about 3.5 percent per year as participation in the labor force rises from the lowest in the world for women and very low rates overall. No other region has such a rapidly expanding labor force. Jobs need to be found for 47 million new entrants to the labor force by 2010. For job creation to reduce the present number of unemployed of 9 million, the efficiency of investment would have to double as the overall amount of investment increased by a full 5 percent of GDP, outcomes that are highly unlikely in the foreseeable future.[59]

The oil boom and the oil "bust" have had major impacts on the region's political systems. In particular, the oil-price roller coaster since the early 1970s has led to two paradoxes that characterize the political economies of Middle Eastern countries. The first is that in the years of fat, between 1974 and 1983, most governments were stable, but the states themselves were not becoming stronger and more institutionalized. Sudden wealth did not facilitate the state-formation process. The second paradox is that over the lean years that began in the mid-1980s many governments have faced greater threats to their stability and even their continued existence. However, they have begun to initiate political and economic changes that may ultimately lead to the establishment of stronger states. These apparent anomalies require explanation.

Paradox One: Economic Growth and Political Decay

RENTIER STATES

European state formation occurred during a protracted period of broadly based economic growth, typically under the auspices of private sectors. In the Middle East, on the other hand, the oil boom was short lived. It was associated with rapid expansion of the service sector but not with adequate growth rates of manufacturing industry or agriculture, and the source of greatest wealth—the oil industry—was in all cases under direct governmental control. Revenues accrued to governments essentially as "rents." These included profits from the oil industry as well as other sources external to the productive economy itself and immediately available to government, such as foreign aid, borrowings, and fees imposed on the transport of oil. The "rentier state" is thus one in which the government does not have to extract much revenue from its own citizens through taxation.

Indeed, in the Middle East direct taxes on incomes, profits, and capital gains are among the lowest in the world. While in 1988, in the United States, Japan, and Canada, such taxes amounted to 50 percent, 68.8 percent, and 48.5 percent of total current revenues, respectively, in Egypt these taxes accounted for 15.2 percent, in Tunisia for 12.2 percent, and in Yemen for 13.3 percent of revenues.

---

[59] *Will Arab Workers,* pp. 7–9; and *Claiming the Future,* pp. 10–11.

In Third World middle-income countries as a whole, such taxes provide on average about one-quarter of government revenues.[60] In most of the oil-exporting states in the Gulf, such taxes are nominal or entirely nonexistent. In Kuwait, for example, direct taxes amounted to a minuscule 0.9 percent of revenues in 1985.[61] Over 60 percent of Arab governments' income in 1996 was derived directly from oil, up from 56 percent in the 1993–1995 period. Over the decade 1986–1996, tax revenues as a percentage of overall revenues stagnated, accounting for one-quarter of Arab government revenues. Of this one-quarter, only some 8 to 9 percent was collected from taxes on income and profits, most of the remainder coming from customs and excise taxes.[62]

Egypt, which has one of the most highly developed systems of direct personal taxation in the Arab world, managed to collect from that source in 1983 only £E127.3 million (£E1 = approximately U.S. $1.25 in 1983), or about £E12 for each person in the labor force, for an overall taxation rate of about 1 percent of personal income.[63] The Egyptian-born director of the International Monetary Fund's (IMF) Middle East department, Abd al-Shakur Sha'lan, used the expression "mish ma'ul" ("unbelievable," "crazy") to describe Egypt's system of taxation, which applies essentially only to government employees.[64] However, while Egypt's taxation policy may be crazy, it was understandable in the "fat" years. As a result of the oil boom, from which Egypt collected rents in various forms, the government had comparatively little need to raise revenues through taxes on individuals. In 1974, before the boom commenced, no more than 6 percent of all resources available to the government were from "exogenous" sources, such as foreign assistance, loans, and Suez Canal tolls. By 1983, the proportion had reached 45 percent, and the gross amount was many times higher.[65]

Having access to rents provided directly or indirectly from the exportation of oil, Middle Eastern governments were in the 1970s and early 1980s in what seemed to be the enviable position of being able to allocate resources to their populations rather than extract taxes from them. The emphasis on allocation, however, had negative economic and political consequences. In regard to the economy, it led to a consumption binge, facilitated by a package of economic measures known collectively as the policy of *infitah,* or opening. This policy included overvaluation of local currencies, which favored imports at the expense of exports; a general reduction of barriers to the movement of goods and services across national borders; and some preliminary, tentative steps to stimulate the private sector, which in the end worked more to the benefit of importers and

---

[60]Hazem Beblawi and Giacomo Luciani, "Introduction," *The Rentier State,* p. 9; and *World Development Report,* 1987, pp. 248–249.

[61]Ibid., p. 249.

[62]Khouri, "The Rise, or Retreat, of the Modern Arab State."

[63]Hesham Garaibeh, "Government Income Sources and the Development of the Taxation System—the Case of Jordan, Egypt and Kuwait," in *The Rentier State,* p. 206.

[64]"Shaalan Says No IMF Deal Before Six Months," *MEED* (November 1988): 6.

[65]John Waterbury, "The 'Soft State' and the Open Door: Egypt's Experience with Economic Liberalization, 1974–1984," *Comparative Politics* (October 1985): 68.

others in the service sector than to those in industry or agriculture. Infitah policies, which stimulated consumption at the expense of production, were associated with high inflation rates, stagnating rates of investment in industry and agriculture, bias toward urban consumers rather than rural producers, and ultimately, with rapidly increasing rates of indebtedness.

The apparent inability of Middle Eastern governments to seize the opportunity provided by the oil boom to convert a high proportion of rents into permanently productive assets has as its root cause the political weakness of those states. In this regard, Arab economist George T. Abed stated:

> Much of the reason why Arab development strategies have in part failed has been the prevailing illusion that economic and financial development can be accelerated in the absence of clear movement toward political modernization. Thus the absence of fully developed political institutions deprived broad sectors of the population of participation in (as distinct from benefit from) the development process and preempted the emergence of the minimal norms of public discourse and accountability essential to the prevention of waste and corruption.[66]

Middle Eastern states have not fully penetrated their respective societies, nor have those societies become permanently and actively engaged in the policymaking process. Low rates of taxation and the absence of effective formal institutions of political participation both testify to the wide gap between state and society. The social contract, by which governments dole out resources in exchange for submission to their rule, was substituted for closer integration of state and society, each of which wanted to be left alone by the other. "Rather than undertake painful and risky measures toward bridging the gap between state and society," according to Yahya Sadowski, the government of a rentier state "accepts the fact of divorce. . . . Like a veiled woman walking through the noise and dust of a *suq* [bazaar], these partioned spheres [e.g., rural life, the private sector, Islamicists, the family] are not totally isolated or invulnerable; but they are highly resistant to state control."[67] Governments remained in power, but their ability to raise taxes and compel general obedience to authority declined as oil revenues mounted.

The oil boom added further momentum to the "retreat" of the states of the Middle East and North Africa that had already begun as a result of the June 1967 war. This retreat included both the loss of legitimacy and the diminution of capacity to regulate the economy.[68] Faced with the choice of imposing some austerity in exchange for greater political freedoms or buying off the public while continuing to restrict widespread political participation, political elites opted for

---

[66]Abed, "The Lean Years," p. 102.

[67]Yahya Sadowski, "Is This Society Civil? Rethinking the Logic of State Formation in Egypt." Paper delivered to the Social Science Research Council's Conference on Retreating States and Expanding Societies, Aix-en-Provence (March 25–27, 1988), pp. 44, 56.

[68]Clement Henry Moore, "Arab Financial Reforms: Bankers as Midwives of Civil Societies?" Paper delivered to the Social Science Research Council's Conference on Retreating States and Expanding Societies, Aix-en-Provence (March 25–27, 1988), p. 1.

the second alternative. By doing so they precluded a true economic liberalization. States had to continue to dominate economies in order to obtain the resources required to fulfill their obligations for allocations required by the social contact and for patronage bestowed upon strategic elites. The partial opening, insufficient to stimulate productive entrepreneurial activities as opposed to exploitative, parasitical ones, nevertheless further eroded governmental capability to manage the economy effectively. Testament to this poor economic management is the fact that more than ten years after the greatest mineral boom in modern history, the combined GDP of all the MENA states was much less than half of the GDP of France.[69]

REGIONAL INTEGRATION

The oil boom tended to prolong the life of incumbent regimes while paradoxically undermining the power and effectiveness of the state. It also had contradictory consequences for the political economy of the region as a whole. Increasing regional integration "has been taking place simultaneously with the process of greater consolidation of individual . . . *national* economies.[70] The Muslim states in the region, especially the Arab states, being drawn by economic forces into a regional oil economy, have steadfastly resisted encroachments on their economic autonomy and political sovereignty.

Economic logic demands coordination and unification within the region, if only because disproportions between the sizes and economic resources of the countries are so very marked. Qatar, for example, in 1995 had fewer than 700,000 native inhabitants, and Kuwait, Oman, and the UAE had less than 2 million citizens each. Egypt, on the other hand, had in 1995 a population of some 60 million. Kuwait and the UAE, as a result of their vast oil deposits, have GNPs per capita in excess of $16,000, and QATAR's in 1995 was $11,000.[71] Egypt, with comparatively little oil to export, has had an annual GNP per capita of some $600–$700 since the early 1980s. Sudan's population and GNP per capita are about half of Egypt's. Yet Egypt and Sudan jointly dispose of significant industrial and agricultural resources, which are not fully developed because of a lack of capital. Economic integration of the oil-rich but otherwise resource-poor and sparsely populated oil-exporting states with the much larger but poorer states in the region appears eminently sensible. No country in the region has a sufficiently large market to support economies of scale in manufacturing, despite the fact that the region as a whole had a population of 314 million in 1989 and by the year 2000 will have increased 35 percent to 423 million.[72] A semiprotected Arab market, equivalent to that of the European Common Market, is virtually a

---

[69]Gary G. Sick, "The Coming Crisis in the Persian Gulf," in Gary G. Sick and Lawrence G. Potter, *The Persian Gulf at the Millennium.* (New York: St. Martin's Press, 1997), p. 16.

[70]Samih K. Farsoun, "Class Structure and Social Change in the Arab World: 1995," in *The Next Arab Decade,* p. 222.

[71]*World Development Report,* 1997, p. 248.

[72]Parker, "Food Gap Widens," p. 29.

prerequisite for significant growth of manufacturing industry. Equally, "It is simply an exercise in self-delusion to pretend that individual Arab oil-producing countries can achieve self-sustained economic development either in isolation or in small exclusive 'rich man's clubs.'"[73]

The oil boom did stimulate very large movements of labor and capital between Arab countries. At any one time from the mid-1970s to the end of the 1980s, over 3 million Egyptians, Syrians, Jordanians, Palestinians, Yemenis, Sudanese, Lebanese, and North Africans were working in the oil-rich states of the Gulf and in Libya. They remitted at least $7 billion annually to their home economies.[74] As a result of the oil slump and the second Gulf war, the Arab migrant labor force was reduced but not by much. Egyptian worker remittances, for example, have remained relatively stable since the early 1980s, even rising somewhat after the Gulf war.

The exchange of labor for capital has been of profound proportions for both sides. Worker remittances as a percentage of total exports at the height of the boom were in Egypt almost 30 percent, in Morocco over 40 percent, just under 200 percent in Jordan, and almost 6,000 percent in North Yemen.[75] In 1993, remittances to Egypt, Jordan, and Yemen amounted to 10 percent of their GDPs and 40 percent of their exports.[76] Between 1973 and 1989, net workers' remittances of $87 billion flowed into Arab countries.[77] In three of the labor-importing countries, immigrants make up over half the total population. In five others, they have constituted between 40 percent and 75 percent of the labor force since the 1980s.[78]

A tremendous amount of capital other than worker remittances also crossed Arab borders during the boom. Official bilateral and multilateral aid provided by the Arab oil-exporting states to other Arab countries totaled $55 billion between 1973 and 1989. However, this financial assistance peaked in 1981 when it reached $5 billion per year, and it has declined steadily since then, averaging some $500 million annually in the 1990s.[79] By far the largest transfers of funds have been for political reasons, such as supporting the Arab "front-line states" against Israel, or Iraq against Iran. In the 1970s, Egypt alone received from the Gulf states over $20 billion; during Iraq's eight-year war with Iran, it obtained probably half again as much from those same sources.[80] For opposing Iraq during the second Gulf war, Egypt and Syria were paid some $7 billion and $2 billion, respectively, by Kuwait and Saudi Arabia. Much of this capital has been

---

[73]Abed, "The Lean Years," p. 103.

[74]Ibid., p. 93.

[75]Farsoun, "Class Structure and Social Change," p. 222.

[76]*Claiming the Future,* p. 15

[77]"IMF Plots Arab Aid Trends," *MEED* (March 6, 1992): 6.

[78]Fred Halliday, "Labor Migration in the Arab World," *Merip Reports* 123 (May 1984): 4.

[79]*Claiming the Future,* p. 16.

[80]Roger Owen, "The Arab Oil Economy: Present Structure and Future Prospects," in *Arab Society: Continuity and Change,* ed. by Samih K. Farsoun (London: Croom Helm, 1985), pp. 17–18.

transferred in a manner that did little if anything to stimulate the growth of a network of financial institutions linking the various national economies; however, intra-Arab banks, development agencies, and private investment companies nevertheless have emerged.

According to Roger Owen, it is movement of labor and capital and the institutions underpinning such transfers "which allows one to speak, very generally, of an Arab 'oil economy' embracing all twenty-one of the Arab states."[81] Owen, however, is quick to add two qualifications. The first is that individual regimes have refused to surrender any measure of sovereignty or economic control. Instead, they have sought to bolster themselves against their own populations.

> Indeed, it could easily be argued that one of the major political effects of oil wealth has been to increase, not the power of Pan-Arabism, but that of the separate states, giving them new resources with which to buy off potential popular opposition with cheap food and other subsidies or, in some cases, to finance much larger and more efficient security forces.[82]

Owen's second qualification is that individual economies were integrated more tightly into the world economy than into the regional one. Echoing these reservations, Michel Chatelus states flatly, "We do not believe in the existence of such an entity as 'the Arab economy'; for only political arguments can be called upon to support this concept."[83]

Economic evidence indicates that skepticism about the existence of a discrete Middle Eastern oil economy is justified. Inter-Arab capital movements are in fact minor compared to Arab capital flows to the Western industrialized countries. Between 1974 and 1981, only about 15 percent of the current account surpluses of the Arab oil exporters were officially transferred to other Arab countries. A far higher percentage of petrodollars was invested in the West.[84] The Gulf Cooperation Council (GCC), which links six oil-exporting states in the Gulf, and the Arab Cooperation Council (ACC), which grouped Egypt, Jordan, North Yemen, and Iraq, were created in the 1980s. The former functions primarily to coordinate internal security activities of member countries. Two years after its founding in 1981, the member states of the GCC signed a free trade agreement that has yet to be implemented because they could not agree on a single tariff, a precondition for a common market. The ACC was destroyed by the second Gulf war, which further weakened and divided the Arab League. The Arab Common Market exists in name only, as a comparison to the European Economic Community (EEC) suggests. The share of intra-Arab Common Market trade in 1978 between the four founding members of that organization— Egypt, Iraq, Jordan, Syria—was just over 2 percent of both imports and exports.

---

[81]Ibid., p. 18.

[82]Ibid., pp. 18–19.

[83]Chatelus, "Policies for Development," p. 108.

[84]Samir Makdisi, "Economic Interdependence and National Sovereignty," in *The Politics of Arab Integration*, ed. by Giacomo Luciani and Ghassan Salame (London: Croom Helm, 1987), p. 126.

By comparison, member states of the EEC increased their mutual trade from 35 percent to 50 percent in the first five years of that organization's existence.[85]

Intra-Arab trade as a whole has yet to reach 10 percent of the Arab States' total trade.[86] Concessions on customs and tariffs within the Arab world have been negligible in amount and impact despite the fact that several Arab states have already or are about to sign agreements with the European Union that will, over a ten-year period, abolish tariffs on goods and services. In 1997, the twenty-two member states of the Arab League pledged to remove customs tariffs on each other's goods by an average of 10 percent every year over a ten-year period, the first time those states have included a definite timetable for tariff reduction. By mid-1998, however, the first step of the agreement had yet to be implemented in most Arab states.[87] The comparatively slow economic integration of the region is also a side effect of the stronger attraction of the center of the world's economic system, which is to be found in the advanced industrialized countries. The great bulk of the region's trade is conducted with the twenty countries of the Organization for Economic Cooperation and Development (OECD). Between two-thirds and three-quarters of all imports and exports in the Arab world come from or go to such countries.[88]

Types of imports, balance of trade, and growth of debt also suggest that the oil boom increased the Middle East's economic dependence on the West. By the early 1980s, some two-thirds of imports were industrial goods, confirming the Middle East's role as a consumer rather than producer of new technologies, a role further illustrated by commitment to research and development.[89] Whereas in 1970 the Arab countries spent 0.31 percent of their combined GNPs on research and development, in 1980 that ratio had dropped to 0.27 percent. By comparison, developing countries as a whole raised the percentage of their GNP spent for this purpose from 0.32 percent to 0.45 percent.[90] Growing economic dependence is also suggested by the changing balance of trade and the increase in external debt. In 1974, Arab oil-producing countries exported $68 billion and imported $14 billion worth of goods and services. In 1982, after eight years of the oil boom, their exports had reached $162 billion, but their imports had climbed, at a much faster rate, to $189 billion.[91] The total of Arab countries' external debt reached almost $100 billion in 1983, more than twenty times the level four years earlier. By 1988, three Arab countries alone—Iraq, Algeria, and Egypt—owed in total more than $120 billion.

---

[85]R. Paul Shaw, "The Political Economy of Inequality in the Arab World," *Arab Studies Quarterly* 6 (Winter/Spring 1984): 150.

[86]Owen, "The Arab Oil Economy," p. 19.

[87]Nadim Kawash, "Free Trade Zone Seen as Test for Arab Credibility," Agence France-Press, as cited in Gulf2000, lk 180@jambo.cc.columbia.edu (April 12, 1998).

[88]Makdisi, "Economic Interdependence and National Sovereignty," pp. 118–122.

[89]Ibid. pp. 118–122.

[90]*UN Statistical Yearbook, 1987*, pp. 5–19.

[91]Abbas Alnasrawi, "The Rise and Fall of Arab Oil Power," *Arab Studies Quarterly* 6 (Winter/Spring 1984): 8.

The petrodollars that flowed into the Middle East between 1974 and 1981 did not facilitate the development of national or regional political institutions capable of effectively managing the processes of political and economic development and integration. Governments simply opened the taps so that a deluge of consumer goods and services flowed out to their populations that were for the most part excluded from playing any significant role in national decision making. The strategy of the "social contract" depended on a continual accumulation of rents in government accounts. This income began to drop rapidly from 1982 as oil prices sagged and the share of Middle Eastern oil in world trade also fell. The first response by most governments was to borrow more money in the hope that the petrodollar bonanza would somehow return before the debts fell due. By 1986–1987, however, not even the most optimistic of political elites still clung to that hope.

Just as the response to the oil boom had been more or less uniform in the countries of the region, so too was the response to the downturn similar. Political elites began virtually in unison in the late 1980s to tighten up on government spending, accompanying austerity measures in many instances with cautious political liberalization in the hope that new political freedoms would permit steam to escape from societies smoldering with the discontent caused by unaccustomed economic hardship. State and society, in short, were forced more closely together as a result of economic recession. Governments had to augment rents with resources extracted from populations, which in turn began to demand "no taxation without representation." Conditions of scarcity were thus more conducive to political development than were those of plenty.

Paradox Two: Economic Decay and Political Growth

THE LEAN YEARS

From 1965 to 1985, the MENA region's growth of per capita income was second only to that of the high-performing East Asian economies, whereas "from 1985 to the present, the region's economic contraction has been larger than that of any other area except Africa."[92] As a result of declining oil prices and a decreasing share of a smaller world market for oil, Middle East oil exporters' revenues began to drop in 1982. By 1983, worldwide recession and increased energy savings had driven oil consumption down to the level it had been ten years earlier, just prior to the onset of the boom.[93] Between 1979 and 1983, Arab oil output fell by more than one-half.[94] Arab states, which earned a total of $213.6 billion from oil exports in 1980, received only $147.4 billion two years later. OPEC sold half as much oil in 1985 as it had in 1980, at very much lower prices.[95]

---

[92]Page, "A Middle Eastern Miracle?" p. 1.

[93]Owen, "The Arab Oil Economy," p. 22.

[94]Alnasrawi, "The Rise and Fall of Arab Oil Power," p. 7.

[95]Paul Jabber, "Forces of Change in the Middle East," *The Middle East Journal* 42: 1 (Winter 1988): 9.

By 1985, the current accounts of the three largest producers on the Arabian peninsula—Saudi Arabia, Kuwait, and the UAE—had moved into deficit in the amount of $10.6 billion, compared with a combined surplus of $78 billion in 1980. The year 1986 was even worse for oil exporters, as prices dropped from an average of $26 per barrel in 1985 to $13 per barrel. In 1988, the six Gulf countries that are members of OPEC obtained $49.6 billion from oil exports, about $4 billion less than in 1987 and less than a third of export revenues in 1980.

Oil prices and demand did begin to move up in early 1989 and were further accelerated by the Gulf crisis that commenced in August 1990. The earnings of member states of OPEC reached their highest level in a decade in 1990. Nevertheless, even Saudi Arabia, which increased its production after the Iraqi invasion of Kuwait from 5.4 million to 8.5 million barrels per day, was still operating with a budget deficit in 1992, its tenth in a row. Saudi foreign assets, which had peaked in 1982 at $141 billion, slid well below $90 billion in 1990 and continued to fall, necessitating borrowing $7 billion in early 1991 to pay expenses associated with the war.[96] Saudi Arabia's cumulative budgetary deficits between 1983 and 1994 were $165 billion, which exceeded the cumulative budgetary surpluses between 1971 and 1982 by about $100 billion. Since 1982, except for the years 1989–1991, the population of Saudi Arabia has grown faster than its economy, meaning that the per capita income of Saudis has, with the exception of those three years, been declining for more than a decade and a half. Since 1987, Saudi Arabia has been financing its deficits by borrowing heavily, principally domestically.[97]

The 1991 Gulf war provided only a temporary respite in the steady drop of both oil prices and MENA states' share of global oil production. By 1997, the real price of oil in U.S. dollars was about one-quarter of what it had been in 1980, and the share of global oil production contributed by Arab states and Iran had slid to 35 percent from a high of around 40 percent two decades previously. Per capita oil income of the member states of the Organization of Petroleum Exporting Countries (OPEC), which includes all of the major Middle East producers, declined from $1,300 (in 1994 dollars) in 1981 to $290 in 1994.[98] In the Arab world as a whole, per capita income did not rise in the ten years after 1985, a decade that saw developing countries as a whole increase per capita incomes by 40 percent and East Asian countries by 80 percent.[99] As oil income has declined, so have the major MENA producers drawn on the foreign assets they accumulated during the boom years, such that of the $270 billion of such assets held by Saudi Arabia, Kuwait, and the UAE as late as 1988, probably only one-third remained a decade later. In sum, the collapse of the great oil boom combined with the effects of the Gulf wars have substantially reduced financial

[96]Andrew Cunningham, "Why the Kingdom Has to Borrow," *The Middle East* (January 1992): 35.

[97]Eliyahu Kanovsky, "The Middle East Economies: The Impact of Domestic and International Politics," *MERIA Journal* 2 (June 1997): 12–13.

[98]Hooshang Amirahmadi, "Oil at the Turn of the Twenty-First Century," *The Emirates Occasional Papers*, no. 5, p. 26.

[99]Mohamed A. El-Erian, "Globalization and the Arab Economies" (Cairo: The Egyptian Center for Economic Studies, Working Paper no. 14, July 1997), p. 8.

surpluses of the richest Arab Gulf states and left Iran and Iraq in parlous economic circumstances. By the standards of the region's poor states, however, the Gulf oil exporters are comparatively well off.

Virtually all other MENA countries, including even the significant oil producer Algeria, which had increased its debt ten times between 1970 and 1980, borrowed more heavily as their direct or indirect earnings from oil began to fall.[100] Budget deficits, covered principally by foreign loans, grew as governments hesitated to impose economic austerity in lockstep with the precipitous fall in national incomes. By about 1986–1987, foreign indebtedness plateaued, in part because governments finally began to cut back significantly on expenditures and in part because foreign creditors, public and private, were no longer willing to lend large amounts to Middle Eastern or other Third World countries. That plateau, however, is at a disturbingly high level. Interest payments on foreign debt relative to GDP were in the late 1990s as high in the MENA region as they had been in Sub-Saharan Africa in the early 1990s or in Latin America in the 1980s, when those two regions were heavily indebted. The debt to GDP ratio in the Eastern Arab world in the mid-1990s was 114 percent, compared to a Sub-Saharan ratio of 70 percent in the same period.[101] Published Arab foreign debt, which understates the real debt because it disguises many borrowings for military purposes, averaged $141 billion in 1989–1993, and it rose to $158 billion in 1995, meaning that the Arab foreign debt remained well above 100 percent of the Arab world's total annual exports.[102]

The problem of access to capital, as manifested by high levels of indebtedness, is due increasingly to the MENA region's comparative unattractiveness to foreign private capital flows. Indeed, in the mid-1990s, it was attracting less than 1 percent of such flows to developing countries.[103] In 1995, total direct foreign investment in the MENA region was $4 billion, compared to $65 billion in South and Southeast Asia and $27 billion in Latin America.[104] Paradoxically, private Middle Eastern citizens export more capital than citizens of any other part of the developing world, holding some $350 billion abroad in the late 1990s.[105]

The combination of a downturn in oil revenues and inadequate inflows of private funds and public foreign assistance, which resulted in an increase in governmental debt, had led, by the early 1990s, to widespread recognition in the region that economic reform was essential. One by one the MENA countries turned to the IMF and World Bank for advice and assistance in stabilizing their economies and then attempting the structural adjustments necessary to bring about long-term growth. By 1996, for example, Arab governmental expenditures

---

[100]Shaw, "The Political Economy of Inequality," p. 141.

[101]*Claiming the Future,* p. 19.

[102]Khouri, "The Rise, or Retreat, of the Modern Arab State."

[103]Mohamed A. El Erian and Manmohan Kumar, "Equity Markets in Middle Eastern Countries." Washington: IMF *Staff Papers* 42, 2 (1995).

[104]John Lancaster, "Decades of Political Stagnation Hobble Economies of Arab World, *International Herald Tribune* (August 5, 1997).

[105]Page, "A Middle Eastern Miracle?" p. 15.

had fallen to 34 percent of GDP, compared to 42 percent a decade earlier.[106] The poorer countries, having the greatest need to rewrite social contracts with their populations in order to reduce their governmental expenditures, therefore also had to facilitate the greatest increases in popular political participation, as the case of Egypt demonstrates.

INFITAH INTAJI

The end of the oil boom was in Egypt conterminous with Husni Mubarak's consolidation of presidential power following Sadat's assassination in October 1981. Three factors coincided to bring pressure for change to the economic policy of infitah (opening) that Sadat had initiated in 1974. One was that it had not worked well, stimulating imports and consumption rather than exports and production. Another was that from 1983 there were insufficient resources to sustain a Sadat-style infitah. The third factor was that the infitah was unpopular, for it had exacerbated inequalities in the country, enabled numerous speculators to "get rich quick," and was associated in the public's mind with increasing dependence on the West and the United States in particular. Mubarak, in an effort to disassociate his new regime from excesses of the infitah while retaining the essence of its message of economic liberalization, declared "war on profiteers and fat cats" and announced the end of the infitah *istihlaki* (infitah of consumption) and the commencement of an infitah *intaji* (infitah of production).[107]

At the core of the infitah intaji as it developed in the mid- to late 1980s in Egypt, and then throughout the region, was an attempt by government to impose austerity, stimulate investment and production by the private sector, lift the level of exports while keeping the lid on imports, and extract an increasing proportion of revenues directly from the population rather than from exogenous sources—or rents, as they have been called. Reforms associated with these objectives varied from country to country. Generally included were some combination of currency devaluations to stimulate exports, provision of incentives for exporters, reduction of subsidies on consumer goods, increases in prices of agricultural commodities in order to stimulate production, lifting of restrictions on markets for goods and services, attempts to establish more efficient and regularized taxation systems, and preliminary moves to expand the role of capital markets in providing funds for investment. In Egypt, as in most other countries, privatization of state-owned enterprises combined with significant reductions of barriers to trade, probably the most crucial features of structural adjustment, did not receive much emphasis until the early to mid-1990s. Indeed, from 1970 to 1990, the MENA region as a whole had the highest level of public investment and the lowest rate of private investment in the developing world. Even by the late 1990s, Egypt and Algeria had levels of public ownership equivalent to those in the former socialist states of Eastern Europe, whereas in most other Arab

---

[106]Khouri, "The Rise, or Retreat, of the Modern Arab State."

[107]Waterbury, "The 'Soft State' and the Open Door," pp. 72–73.

states public sectors were smaller but still large compared to Latin America or East Asia. Financial returns to government from privatizations have been lower in the MENA region than in any other area of the globe.[108]

Throughout the region, economic reform—at least in its early stages—was closely associated with political liberalization. Beginning in the mid-1980s, a small wave of political liberalization began to wash through the poorer states of the region, such that by the end of the decade, comparatively free and fair elections to parliaments had been held in Morocco, Tunisia, Egypt, Sudan, and Jordan, and, in Yemen, in 1993. Stimulated by the need to gain political support for economic austerity, as well as by the dramatic democratizations that were then taking place in Eastern Europe and the former Soviet Union, these reforms also included the easing of restrictions on political expression and behavior more generally.

Except in Morocco, however, the momentum of political liberalization was not sustained into the late 1990s, probably for two reasons. First, the economic reforms did not succeed in stimulating sufficient economic growth to reduce unemployment or substantially increase per capita incomes in any of the poorer countries in the region, but they did tend to lead to a further concentration of wealth. As the unequal burden of economic hardship began to stimulate greater discontent in the 1990s, so did these governments begin to backtrack on the political concessions they had just made. Moreover, these governments also felt the need to deepen the structural adjustments of their economies, largely by privatizing state-owned enterprises and commencing the process of removing barriers to trade, measures that give rise to much political opposition. Instead of seeking support for intensifying the economic reform process through further political openings and dialogue, these poorer Arab governments have tended in recent years to seek to impose economic reforms while placing new restrictions on political participation.

The second reason why political liberalization has not been sustained in the mid- and late 1990s is that regional tensions, centered on the Arab-Israeli conflict, began to increase as the peace process faltered after 1994 and came to almost a dead stop following the election of Binyamin Netanyahu as prime minister of Israel in May 1996. Only Morocco, the Arab country most distant from that conflict geographically and politically, seems to have been unaffected by it and thus able to continue with its political liberalization that led, in March 1998, to the formation of a new government by a coalition of opposition political parties.

GCC States

Reforms implemented in the late 1980s and early 1990s by the wealthy oil-exporting states were less thoroughgoing than those effected elsewhere, for

---

[108]Page, "A Middle Eastern Miracle?" pp. 8, 14, 16.

these governments did not have to ask their citizens to make as many economic sacrifices. They did not feel compelled, therefore, to concede as much political participation. Economic policy changes made in Saudi Arabia, where oil revenues fell by about half between 1983 and 1988, illustrate the erratic approach to coping with the lean years among the oil-rich states of the Gulf Cooperation Council (GCC), which includes Saudi Arabia, Kuwait, Qatar, Bahrain, Oman, and the UAE. Saudi Arabia reduced imports by more than 50 percent and lowered subsidies on gasoline, electricity, water, some foodstuffs, and various other commodities in the first few years after the end of the oil boom. It attempted to make up for reductions in governmental revenues and expenditures by encouraging the private sector to invest more and become active across a broader front. Saudi Arabia and its wealthy neighbors enjoyed some success in this area, for within the GCC states, the private sector's share in the GDP almost doubled from 1976 to 1986.[109] The bulk of private-sector activity, however, remained limited to commerce and construction, which together accounted for 54 percent of commercial bank loans in 1970 and 57 percent in 1985. Commercial bank loans to private clients for purposes of investment in manufacturing accounted for 15.3 percent of their portfolios of loans in 1975; by the mid-1980s, that rate had dropped to 9 or 10 percent.[110] The associate secretary-general for economic affairs of the GCC, Abdullah Ibrahim El-Kuwaiz, commenting on the private sector, observed that "its role in the industrialization process is still below what it should be."[111]

In the wake of the second Gulf war, the government of Saudi Arabia suddenly abandoned its austerity policies, both because it had more revenue to dispense and because it hoped to divert new demands for political participation that had been stimulated by the events surrounding that war. In March 1992, the cabinet announced a surprise package of price reductions for gasoline; telephone, electricity, and water services; exit fees; port charges; and commercial registration fees. The price for gasoline was dropped 38 percent, from 64 to less than 40 cents a gallon. The government of Kuwait, also anxious to buy political support from elements disaffected by the al-Sabah's handling of the Iraqi invasion and its aftermath, began to dole out funds in the period leading up to the October 1992 elections. Government employees were paid in full for the period of the invasion, whether they were there or not. Families that had in fact stayed in Kuwait were given a bonus of $1,750. All consumer debts were forgiven, and the bad debts of all Kuwaiti banks, which totaled more than $20 billion, were written off. These measures suggest that the rulers of the oil-rich Arab states had adjudged as politically risky the austerity measures they had introduced in the mid- to late 1980s.

---

[109]Abdullah Ibrahim El-Kuwaiz, "Economic Integration of the GCC: Challenges, Achievements and Future Outlook," *American-Arab Affairs* 19 (Winter 1986–1987): 32.

[110]Robert E. Looney, "Growth Prospects of the Saudi Arabia Private Sector," *American-Arab Affairs* 23 (Winter 1987–1988): 67.

[111]El-Kuwaiz, "Economic Integration of the GCC," p. 32.

But the Gulf war–induced backtracking to the use of allocations of rent derived income to buy quiescence from populations could not be sustained because the rents themselves did not remain at sufficiently high levels. The blip in prices, caused by the removal of Iraqi and Kuwait exports from world markets, which took the price of crude oil to over $21 per barrel in 1991, did not last. Indeed, a slow but more or less steady slide in prices commenced the following year, primarily as a result of production increases by non-OPEC sources. By 1998, crude oil prices had dropped to some $12 per barrel, their lowest level in current dollars in more than a decade and, in constant dollars, less than the price of oil at the beginning of the twentieth century. Even more consequential was the prognosis that "oil prices are projected to remain flat, with growth in MENA's real oil export earnings increasing by only 2 to 3 percent a year through 2010."[112] With all GCC states having annual population growth rates in excess of 3 percent and all of them running budget deficits in the late 1990s, the prospects for enhancing and maybe even maintaining existing levels of allocations to individual citizens, while retaining a semblance of sound national financial management, were virtually nil.

Apparently in recognition of this gloomy outlook, rulers of the GCC states tended to become more diligent in the mid-1990s about pursuing economic reform, while also hesitatingly expanding political participation, as if they were testing the response before proceeding further or backtracking as most of the poorer states have done. Probably not by coincidence, the two GCC states that have the highest levels of institutionalized political participation, Kuwait and Oman, have also undertaken the most significant economic reforms, including in the former serious consideration of introduction of an income tax.[113] Elsewhere economic reform measures were more timid, typically including increases in user fees on electricity, communications, domestic air fares, water and gasoline, freezes on public sector wages, reduction of subsidies (such as those on wheat in Saudi Arabia), and imposition of higher excise taxes on luxury goods. In all GCC countries, however, the problem of reconciling family rule with thoroughgoing economic and political liberalization remains, so reforms in both areas tend to be limited, lest they impinge on family prerogatives.

Non-GCC Oil-Exporting States Economically, there are two categories of Muslim Middle Eastern countries outside the GCC—those that export significant quantities of oil and those that do not. There is, however, remarkably little difference between the political economies of these oil and non-oil states in the wake of the oil downturn. All have sought in some measure to privatize their economies and attract investments by multinational corporations, which for many constitute radical reversals of policies associated with Arab socialism in

---

[112]*Claiming the Future*, p. 17.

[113]Julia Devlin, "Market Fundamentals and Gulf Oil Policies in the 21st Century," in *Gulf Economies: Strategies for Growth in the 21st Century*, ed. by Julia Devlin (Washington: Center for Contemporary Arab Studies, Georgetown University, 1997), pp. 11–19.

one of its many forms. They have also sought to direct investments away from the service sector and into industry and agriculture. Possibly of greatest political significance is the fact that many have also sought to lower real wages, impose greater discipline on the labor force, and reduce consumption by lowering or removing subsidies and raising prices. All have also intermittently sought to at least give the appearance of granting greater political freedoms.

The MENA countries that export significant quantities of oil but are not in the GCC are Algeria, Iraq, Iran, and Libya. All accumulated significant foreign debts in the 1980s and early 1990s. By 1992, Algeria owed over $25 billion to foreign creditors. Servicing that debt, which absorbed $8.7 billion of Algeria's scarce foreign currency earnings and reserves in 1991, crippled the economy, rendering it incapable of generating jobs to alleviate massive unemployment. Iraq's debt, which exceeded $60 billion when it invaded Kuwait, was no doubt a key factor in Saddam Hussein's decision to embark on such a desperate course of action. Iran under Ayatollah Khomeini steadfastly refused to borrow abroad. With his death in June 1989 and consolidation of power by Ali Akbar Hashemi Rafsanjani, who was anxious to rebuild the economy, Iran rapidly amassed a foreign debt of $10 billion.

Until the mid- to late 1980s, the economies of these four oil-exporting countries were heavily state-dominated. Since then, all have undertaken economic liberalization programs. The Iraqi infitah, which began in hesitant form shortly after Saddam Hussein assumed the presidency in 1979, moved into high gear toward the end of the first Gulf war. Among the economic reform measures announced in 1988 were the ending of the public-sector Rafidain Bank's twenty-two-year monopoly on all banking in the country. It was also announced that the government was preparing to establish a stock market to accommodate the growing number of share transactions.[114] In the previous year, the last of the country's remaining state farms had been sold to the private sector. In the summer of 1988, it was announced that forty-seven public-sector firms would be privatized and that the private sector would be able to buy or lease government-owned tourist hotels. In 1987, privatization of the national air carrier, Iraqi Airways, was decreed. In October 1988, it was announced that public-sector companies forming joint ventures with private ones would be exempted from the requirement to pay workers a quarter share of profits. It was also revealed at the end of 1988 that the government had been holding confidential talks with General Motors to establish an automobile industry in Iraq.[115] Most of these measures were stillborn, however, for Iraq's economy was virtually destroyed by the 1991 Gulf war and then by its almost total isolation as a result of the UN sanctioned embargo.

Algeria's and Libya's infitahs in the late 1980s were stimulated by intense domestic dissatisfaction with economic austerity and political repression. In Algeria, the riots that swept through the country in October 1988 not only led to a host of political reforms but also stimulated the pace of economic change that

---

[114]*MEED* (December 9, 1988): 21.

[115]"Local Car Production Plans," *MEED* (December 2, 1988): 8.

had been under way for about a year. As the shops that had been virtually bare of goods for months were rapidly filled in the wake of the riots, hard liners in the ruling party, the FLN (National Liberation Front), who were known to oppose economic and political liberalizations, were forced out of their positions. Simultaneously it was announced that seventy state companies had been made financially autonomous and that all others would soon follow suit. Reforms that had been presaged in 1987, such as increased privatization of retail trade, improved conditions for foreign firms, introduction of credit cards, and greater managerial autonomy in the public sector, were implemented.[116] Still further reforms—including privatization of a portion of the import trade and granting citizens the right to purchase small amounts of foreign currency at the official rate—were enacted in the early 1990s.

Following the military takeover in early 1992, economic reform was put on the back burner as the military struggled to establish its political control. After a brief period, however, the new military rulers of Algeria, despite being locked into a life-and-death struggle against their Islamist opponents, had recommenced the liberalization of the economy, as signalled by the creation of a stock market, by an application to join the new World Trade Organization, and by opening up the heretofore nationalized oil industry to foreign investment. Economic liberalization was not coupled with dialogue with the regime's opponents, however, and the continued insurrection, coupled with political uncertainties more broadly, deterred private foreign investment outside the oil sector.

Even Libya's mercurial Mu'ammar Qaddafi began in the late 1980s to retreat from his previous commitment to a socialist economy. Grumbling about the lack of goods in Libya's shops paralleled the sharp drop in oil earnings from $22 billion in 1980 to $5.5 billion in 1987. By 1988, there were reports of demonstrations on university campuses in Tripoli and Benghazi by student Islamic activists.[117] The government—which had over the past twenty years nationalized all businesses, banned foreign ownership, and turned factories and most other installations over to people's committees—took fright. In mid-1988, it not only increased the flow of consumer goods that had been cut to a trickle since 1986 but also undertook numerous reforms that were dubbed by Western observers the "green perestroika," the reference being to Qaddafi's *Green Book* and Gorbachev's initiatives in the Soviet Union. The black market was legalized by Qaddafi, who referred to it as the "people's market," and investors were invited to commence activities in virtually all sectors of the economy. Much rhetoric accompanied these initiatives. Qaddafi exhorted Libyans to "produce and become a bourgeois. Create a farm, breed sheep and be their shepherd. Set up a cooperative. Become rich. That is all right."[118] In January 1989, Qaddafi pledged to reduce the size of the bureaucracy by abolishing several ministries and agen-

---

[116]"Algeria's Struggle for the Future," *MEED* (November 4, 1988): 2–3.

[117]Anthony Walker, "Gaddafi: On the Road to Damascus?" *Sydney Morning Herald*, January 19, 1989, p. 11; and Charles Wallace "Gaddafinomics Is Here," *Sydney Morning Herald*, December 3, 1988, p. 35.

[118]Wallace, "Gaddafinomics Is Here."

cies. In the early 1990s, most restrictions on the movement of goods in and out of the country were lifted. The green perestroika, however, like its equivalent in Iraq, did not bring about a full-blown liberal, neoclassical economic order and for the same two reasons. First, the leaders of both regimes clearly feared that further economic liberalization could undermine their control of the political system, and second, Libya, like Iraq, was placed under an embargo (as a result of its alleged involvement in the blowing up of a U.S. airliner over Lockerbie, Scotland, on December 21, 1988) that has essentially frozen its economy.

The revolution in Iran, combined with mobilization for the war with Iraq, resulted in the state's assuming a greater role in the economy than it had under the shah. The end of the war and the lessening of revolutionary ardor led to a reassessment by the political elite of Iran's economic and political future. A consultative body—created at Ayatollah Khomeini's request in late 1988 to draw up a reconstruction policy and composed of the president, speaker of the majlis, and chief justice, who are the three heads of government, as well as the prime minister and some twenty additional members—gave its support to opening foreign trade to the private sector. It coupled this move with de facto legalization of the foreign currency black market.[119] Other leading officials endorsed the principle that Iranians in exile, particularly those with needed skills and capital, should be induced to return to their country by being granted the appropriate freedoms, economic and political. The budget for 1989–1990 called for tax revenues to rise by 11 percent. On the tenth anniversary of the revolution in February 1989, the government announced that it would borrow from abroad to finance development projects.

After Ayatollah Khomeini's death in June 1989, the pace of economic reform quickened. Import and export regulations were further relaxed, and the stock market, which was revived in late 1990, went through a boom in the following year. In May 1992, the government abandoned the state monopoly on banking that it had established in the wake of the revolution and lifted all restrictions on foreign investors. However, like in Algeria, Libya, and Iraq, both internal political obstacles and externally imposed conditions ultimately slowed the pace of economic liberalization in Iran so that it was unable to sustain the momentum of the late 1980s and early 1990s. In this instance the primary obstacles were factional infighting within the political elite between those who favored yet more economic liberalization and those who opposed it and, on the external front, the partially successful attempt by the United States to economically isolate Iran for its alleged support for terrorism.

Political liberalization was in these countries, with the partial exception of Iran, also in a state of suspended animation at best in the late 1990s. The rulers of Libya and Iraq, locked into a struggle against the United States, and those of Algeria, pitted in deadly combat against their Islamist opponents, abandoned the partial political openings of the late 1980s or early 1990s and sought to crush their opponents. In Iran, on the other hand, the surprisingly free presidential

---

[119]"Iran Loosens the Reins," *MEED* (November 11, 1988): 2–3.

elections of May 1997 brought to power Muhammed Khatami, an open-minded cleric who enjoyed broad support among the population precisely because he stood for a more liberal political order. His election signalled the intensification of conflict between those factions of the elite gathered around Ayatollah Khomeini's successor as Faqih, Ali Khamenei, who opposed further economic and political liberalization, and those gathered around Khatami and his predecessor, Ali Hashemi Rafsanjani.

Prospects for Further Liberalization

Virtually without exception, efforts to undo the economic legacy of governmental expansion into the economy over preceding decades and to renege on at least some part of the "social contract" were accompanied in the 1980s with concessions to demands for political freedoms. Tunisian President Zine al-Abidine Ben Ali's economic reforms, for example, were pushed through during the "springtime of freedom" that followed President Habib Bourguiba's removal from office. Former King Hassan of Morocco indulged the parliamentary opposition while he oversaw Morocco's economic liberalization. Yemeni President Ali Abdullah Salih, who permitted remarkably free elections to the then North Yemeni consultative council in February 1988, as attested by the fact that 25 percent of the 128 elected seats were won by Muslim Brothers, may have taken this step to forestall an anticipated negative political reaction to planned austerity measures. In Egypt, Sadat's infitah, initiated in the mid-1970s, originally proceeded in tandem with steps to liberalize politics—a linkage that his successor maintained during the first decade of his rule.

In all cases, however, when these political liberalizations have allowed the emergence of opposition movements or parties that have challenged the government's authority, they have been vigorously suppressed, and the liberalizations themselves have been rolled back. In Tunisia, President Ben Ali, frightened of the growing power of al-Nahda (The Renaissance), an Islamicist political party, began from 1989 to restrict political freedoms. By 1992, the Tunisian government was involved in a draconian crackdown on all manifestations of political dissent. In Algeria, the military government that seized power in January 1992 suspended the political reforms that former President Chadli Benjedid had granted as part of his strategy to facilitate economic liberalization. As it moved to destroy the Islamicist Islamic Salvation Front (FIS), it was confronted with a violent backlash that included the assassination in June 1992 of Muhammad Boudiaf, the new president. In Egypt's parliamentary elections of 1987, almost one-third of the successful candidates were independents or members of opposition parties, a result that threatened the ruling National Democratic Party and indirectly the political dominance of President Mubarak. That election signalled the high tide of political liberalization in the country. Since that time, steadily greater restrictions have been placed on political participation, such that by the November 1995 parliamentary elections, the opposition was unable to win more than a dozen of the 454 seats, and in the April 1997 local council elections, virtually none of the more than 40,000 positions were contested. In the Gulf the political liberalizations promised in Kuwait and Saudi Arabia in the wake of the Gulf war have not materialized, while in Bahrain, the government, confronted since December 1994 with a strong opposition movement, has resorted to fierce political repression in order to contain it.

Political liberalization in the Muslim countries of the MENA region was originally intended as a shock absorber to accompany economic austerity measures. Such reforms, however, were quickly supplanted by other tactics when the interests of ruling elites were challenged by emerging oppositions. Most Middle Eastern countries are only in the early stages of a dialogue between state and society, between ruler and ruled. There remains a mutual lack of trust, an abiding suspicion among political elites that all political opposition is intent on subversion, and a belief by those critical of government that their rulers are just playing for time, waiting until they are once again able to impose their unquestioned domination of the polity. For the dialogue to develop into one based on trust and to lead eventually to firm guarantees of political and human rights for citizens—as well as to legitimacy and effectiveness for governments—compromise has to occur. Political elites have to surrender a part of their absolute control over decision making, while citizens have to be willing to adhere to public policies arrived at through some form of consultative process.

For these fundamental changes to occur, political systems must be insulated against the destabilizing effects of chronic economic malaise. Although some belt-tightening facilitated political liberalization, a continual increase in unemployment, deterioration of infrastructure, spreading impoverishment, and growing disparity between rich and poor individuals and states in the region—all of which have been occurring since the mid-1980s—have intensified the level of political conflicts and caused ruling elites to terminate experiments with political liberalization. Most Muslim countries of the region are thus caught in a dilemma for which none has yet devised a satisfactory answer. The dilemma is that improved economic performance requires further economic reform, including more privatization, further reduction in trade protectionism, and the creation of more favorable climates for investment and business. However, those reforms are likely—in the short term, at least—to further exacerbate inequalities and even poverty and hence to lead to political backlashes. Having first sought to couple economic reform with political liberalization, ruling elites began to back away from this strategy as the political opposition gathered strength. As a result, political liberalization has slowed in most countries of the region to almost a halt, while economic reform has not proceeded far enough to generate the investments required to raise levels of productivity and cause economies to grow faster than the rate of population expansion. Since few, if any, governments of the region are strong enough to impose thoroughgoing economic reforms on their reluctant populations, they seem condemned to economic reform in dilatory fashion, thus causing their countries to fall further behind in the global race to improve their competitive positions.

The only way out of the dilemma is for government to be strengthened to the point that it is able to pursue economic reform in a sound, consistent, and expeditious manner. Such strengthening could only be based on one of two approaches. One would be to expand and institutionalize political participation within a democratic context, so that broad-based support could be mobilized for the making of public policy through the mechanism of participation within that decision making. The other is for political participation to be mobilized through ideological means, such as Islamism, so that a populist, or at least popular, government would be able to impose its will on a receptive population. Neither solution appears to be at hand in any country of the region, suggesting that both economic and political reform will continue to be pursued in opportunistic and intermittent, rather than in systematic and dedicated, fashion.

SELECTED BIBLIOGRAPHY

Alnasrawi, Abbas. *Arab Nationalism, Oil and the Political Economy of Dependency.* Westport, Conn.: Greenwood Press, 1991.

Barkey, Henri, ed. *The Politics of Economic Reform in the Middle East.* New York: St. Martin's Press, 1992.

Beblawi, Hazem, and Giacomo Luciani. *The Rentier State.* London: Croom Helm, 1987.

Brynen, Rex, Bahgat Korany, and Paul Noble. *Political Liberalization and Democratization in the Arab World.* Vol. 1. Boulder, Colo.: Lynne Rienner Publishers, 1995.

Chaudhry, Kiren Aziz. *The Price of Wealth: Economies and Institutions in the Middle East.* Ithaca, N.Y.: Cornell University Press, 1997.

Doran, Charles F., and Stephen W. Buck. *The Gulf, Energy, and Global Security.* Boulder, Colo.: Lynne Rienner Publishers, 1991.

El-Naggar, Said, ed. *Investment Policies in the Arab Countries.* Washington, D.C.: International Monetary Fund, 1990.

Guazzone, Laura, ed. *The Middle East in Global Change: The Politics and Economics of Interdependence versus Fragmentation.* New York: St. Martin's Press, 1997.

Hansen, Bent. *Political Economy of Poverty, Equity and Growth: Egypt and Turkey.* New York: Oxford University Press, 1991.

Harik, Iliya, and Denis Sullivan. *Privatization and Liberalization in the Middle East.* Bloomington: Indiana University Press, 1992.

Henry, Clement M. *The Mediterranean Debt Crescent: Money and Power in Algeria, Egypt, Morocco, Tunisia and Turkey.* Gainesville: University of Florida Press, 1996.

Ibrahim, Ibrahim. *Arab Resources: The Transformation of a Society.* London: Croom Helm, 1983.

Ibrahim, Saad Eddin. *The New Arab Social Order: A Study of the Social Impact of Oil Wealth.* Boulder, Colo.: Westview Press, 1982.

Kerr, Malcolm H., and El Sayed Yassin. *Rich and Poor States in the Middle East: Egypt and the New Arab Order.* Boulder, Colo.: Westview Press, 1982.

Kubursi, Atif A. *Oil, Industrialization and Development in the Arab Gulf States.* London: Croom Helm, 1988.

Luciani, Giacomo, and Ghassan Salame. *The Politics of Arab Integration.* London: Croom Helm, 1988.

Niblock, Tim, and Emma Murphy, eds. *Economic and Political Liberalization in the Middle East.* London: British Academic Press, 1993.

Richards, Alan. *Food, States and Peasants.* Boulder, Colo.: Westview Press, 1986.

Richards, Alan, and John Waterbury. *A Political Economy of the Middle East.* 2d ed. New York: Westview Press, 1996.

Sadowski, Yahya M. *Political Vegetables: Businessman and Bureaucrat in the Development of Egyptian Agriculture.* Washington, D.C.: The Brookings Institution, 1981.

Salame, Ghassan. *Democracy Without Democrats: The Renewal of Politics in the Muslim World.* London: I. B. Tauris, 1994.

Tuma, Elias. *Economic and Political Change in the Middle East.* Palo Alto, Cal.: Pacific Books, 1987.

Weinbaum, Marvin G. *Food, Development and Politics in the Middle East.* Boulder, Colo.: Westview Press, 1982.

Index